Perfect Plant

Perfect Place

Perfect Plant Perfect Place

ROY LANCASTER

DK

DORLING KINDERSLEY

London • New York • Sydney • Moscow

DK

DK PUBLISHING, INC.
LONDON, NEW YORK, MUNICH, MELBOURNE, AND DELHI

EDITORS Anna Cheifetz, Clare Double, Lesley Malkin, Simon Maughan
US EDITOR Ray Rogers
ART EDITORS Martin Hendry, Stuart Perry, Helen Robson, Colin Walton
MANAGING EDITORS Mary-Clare Jerram, Anna Kruger, Jonathan Metcalf
MANAGING ART EDITORS Peter Cross, Lee Griffiths, Steve Knowlden, Amanda Lunn
PRODUCTION MANAGERS Meryl Silbert, Michelle Thomas
DTP DESIGNERS Mark Bracey, Robert Campbell, Louise Waller

Published in the United States by
DK Publishing Inc., 375 Hudson Street, New York NY 10014
A Penguin Company

DK Publishing, Inc. offers special discounts for bulk purchases for sales promotions or premiums. Specific, large-quantity
needs can be met with special editions, including personalized covers, excerpts of existing guides, and corporate imprints. For
more information, contact Special Markets Department, DK Publishing, Inc., 95 Madison Avenue, New York, NY 10016.

A Cataloging in Publication record for this book is available from the Library of Congress
ISBN 0–7894–8385–8
ISBN 0–7894–8755–1

Color reproduction by Colourscan, Singapore; GRB Editrice, Italy; and Scanner Services, Italy
Printed and bound by Star Standard Industries, Singapore

See our complete catalog at
www.dk.com

CONTENTS

INTRODUCTION

THE DIVERSITY OF PLANTS available to gardeners today is such that we need never again suffer the disappointment of watching a recently acquired plant struggling and even dying because it was planted in the wrong place, or it was not a good plant for the job.

△ GARDEN-CENTER TEMPTATIONS
It is tempting to buy a plant for the initial impact of its flowers, fruit, or foliage, instead of its suitability for your garden.

A great many people acquire plants for their garden on impulse. You see a plant that takes your fancy, or a fellow gardener offers you an offset or cutting. With little regard for its suitability you take it home and lose no time in planting it, usually wherever a space beckons.

Sometimes the site proves just right and your plant thrives. More often than not, though, the site is vacant for a very good reason; too wet or too dry perhaps, too shady, too shallow, or filled with the roots of other plants. When a plant fails for one of these reasons, you may shrug it off and keep trying or, your confidence shaken, give up and switch your attentions elsewhere.

Don't you ever ask yourself how the lovely gardens you see down your street, on television, and in magazines are achieved? Of course you do, and although it is easy to dismiss them as the gardens of experts, you suspect that if you had the time and means to check out plants before acquiring them, you too could enjoy the same success.

GARDENERS' QUESTIONS

I worked for a major British nursery for many years, advising customers on the choice of plants for their gardens. I dealt with a variety of people; some were professionals or gardening enthusiasts, who already had a good idea of the plants likely to grow in their gardens but who were seeking something new or special. Most people, however, were first-time gardeners, with little knowledge or experience of plants and their uses, but who were eager to learn and anxious to make the best choice for their money.

On the whole, my enquirers belonged to one of two categories: those who had seen a plant they liked and wanted to know if it would grow in their garden, or those who had no specific idea of what they wanted but knew what purpose they wanted it for. This confirmed my belief that most

△ AUTHOR'S GARDEN Hosta *'Halcyon'* *at the base of an armillary sundial is just one example in my garden of the use of foliage to provide a striking feature. The bloomy blue leaves match the sundial.*

◁ ORIGIN OF A SPECIAL PLANT
I grow a wide variety of plants from seed collected in the wild, such as this Callistemon viridiflorus (*bottlebrush*) *from Tasmania.*

people seeking help simply want to know either what plants will grow in a given situation, taking factors such as soil and exposure into account, or which plants will create a desired effect, such as seasonal features, color, fragrance, and ultimate size or shape.

GARDENERS' ANSWERS

Many years of visiting gardens and interviewing people for television programs about gardening have convinced me that poor or adverse conditions can often be improved. If this is not practical, some choice usually exists for most sites and situations as they stand, thanks to the wealth of garden plants that is currently available.

Perfect Plant, Perfect Place is a guide to selecting the best plants for given conditions and ornamental effects. It will assist beginners in finding the best plants for their gardens and will remind more seasoned gardeners of excellent contenders they may have over-looked. Never before have so many ornamental plants been available to gardeners. Among those in this book are a host of tried-and-tested representatives. Success with these should inspire you to try more challenging plants. Let *Perfect Plant, Perfect Place* be your guide.

For many people, choosing the best plants for indoors is almost as important as selecting those for outdoors. It is a curious fact that growing plants successfully in the relatively protected, if not cosseted, environment of your own home can provide a greater challenge than growing hardy plants in your garden. The principal reasons for this deal with climatic conditions and light levels – not surprising, considering that many of our houseplants come from warm or tropical regions of the world. Yet, despite the difficulties, we rightly accept houseplants as an essential ingredient in our lives to the extent that no home seems complete without them. Apart from their ornamental qualities, houseplants can improve the air we breathe indoors, helping to create conditions conducive to healthy living. The indoor plants section of this book sets out to familiarize you with the rich variety of plants available as well as the growing conditions needed to help them flourish.

△ SPECIAL EFFECTS IN SUMMER
This is an excellent example of what can be achieved with perennials of varied height, plus foliage and flower effect, to create an appealing summer border.

▽ A VITAL COMPONENT
Container plants are a valuable addition to the garden if carefully placed. They can provide a welcome feature or be used to fill gaps where earlier displays have finished.

How This Book Works

I N THIS BOOK, my aim is to help you choose the most suitable plants for a given garden or indoor situation, taking account of the growing conditions, plant characteristics, and any special ornamental effects. The outdoor plants chapter is divided into five sections by plant type: Perennials, Climbers, Shrubs,

Conifers, and Trees. All woody plants listed, with the exception of conifers, are deciduous unless specified evergreen. Perennials are herbaceous unless described as evergreen. The indoor plants chapter is also divided into five sections: Floral Effect, Foliage Effect, Locations, Specific Uses, and Specialist Plants.

PLANT NAMES

Currently accepted botanical names are used throughout. Well-known synonyms appear in the index and are cross-referenced. Common names in general use are given; where none exists, the generic name is repeated, or else an English name common to the whole genus is given. In the case of specialized groups such as roses, the category is specified.

KEY TO pH ACIDITY SYMBOL

The majority of plants will grow in most soils. Those that require acidic soil are highlighted with this symbol *(see p.12)*.

PH   *Requires acidic soil*

UNDERSTANDING HARDINESS

Hardiness is a measure of a plant's ability to survive and grow under local environmental conditions, especially winter cold. The United States Department of Agriculture has produced a map of 11 hardiness zones based on average annual minimum temperatures recorded from 1974 to 1986; this hardiness map appears on the endpapers of this book. Knowing your region's hardiness zone can help you determine if a plant will grow in your garden. However, many other factors, such as summer heat and humidity, soil fertility and drainage, and protection from strong winds, also influence plant hardiness. Frequently, plants will grow beyond their published hardiness zones if they are provided with extra winter protection or if other care is taken to modify its environment.

BOTANICAL AND
COMMON PLANT
NAMES •
Below each plant's botanical name is the common name or, if none exists, the generic name.

SYMBOLS FOR •
LIGHT LEVEL,
HARDINESS, AND
ACIDITY
Light level and hardiness are given for all plants. The pH symbol appears only if a plant requires acidic soil (see boxes).

Shrubs Tolerant of Shade

Y OU MAY BE SURPRISED at the range of shrubs suitable for growing in shade. Many are woodlanders in the wild, preferring to grow where they are not directly exposed to the sun's rays. This does not mean they can survive without any light – all green-leaved plants need light to photosynthesize. Some, however, are more tolerant of lower light levels than others, and it is these that are most successful when planted in the shade of deciduous trees, or that cast by buildings.

Euonymus fortunei 'Sunshine'
EVERGREEN EUONYMUS
☼ ☀ 5   ‡ 24in (60cm) ↔ 5ft (1.5m)

A low-growing, dense, evergreen shrub crowded with leathery, gold-margined leaves, looking bright gold from afar. Ideal as a groundcover or as a specimen shrub.

Euonymus fortunei var. *vegetus*
EVERGREEN EUONYMUS
☼ ☀ 5   ‡ 12in (30cm) ↔ 6ft (2m)

The presence of both creeping and erect stems enable this tough, bushy evergreen to form extensive patches. Its green leaves and pinkish seed capsules are numerous.

Crinodendron hookerianum
LANTERN TREE
☼ ☀ ☀ ❦   ‡ 10ft (3m) ↔ 6ft (2m)

From late spring through to early summer, the branches of this handsome evergreen are strung with beautiful red flowers that resemble lanterns. Dislikes dry soils.

OTHER DECIDUOUS SHRUBS TOLERANT OF SHADE

Berberis thunbergii, see p.226
Cornus canadensis, see p.184
Euonymus alatus, see p.227
Euonymus obovatus
Hydrangea macrophylla
Hypericum androsaemum
Kerria japonica
Rhodotypos scandens, see p.203
Rubus odoratus
Symphoricarpos x chenaultii 'Hancock'

200

Daphne laureola subsp. *philippi*
SPURGE LAUREL
☼ ☀ ☀ 7   ‡ 12in (30cm) ↔ 2ft (60cm)

A dwarf variety of a woodland evergreen, this is just as effective when grown in full sun. Crowded light green flower clusters emerge in late winter and early spring.

Hydrangea macrophylla 'Veitchii'
LACECAP HYDRANGEA
☼ ☀ 6   ‡ 5ft (1.5m) ↔ 8ft (2.5m)

Broader than it is high, this bold-foliaged bush carries heads of tiny flowers, each surrounded by a ring of larger florets, from mid- to late summer. Dislikes dry soils.

KEY TO LIGHT LEVEL SYMBOLS

Light preferences are given with symbols. More than one symbol indicates plant's preferred range.

☼   *Full sun – prefers, or even requires, as much sun as is available.*

☼   *Partial shade – tolerant of (some even prefer) limited or indirect sunlight.*

☀   *Shade – will grow in a site receiving low light, such as under a tree canopy.*

• PLANT
DESCRIPTION
Gives features of interest such as flowering time(s), distinctive traits, preferred site(s) or condition(s), and specifies when plant is evergreen.

PLANT DIMENSIONS

Plant dimensions vary depending on growing conditions. Sizes are a guide to mature size in average conditions. The height includes flowering stems in perennials.

↕	*Average height*
↔	*Average spread*
↕↔	*Average height and spread*

NOTE ON ANNUALS

Hardiness zones are not given for annuals, because most are grown for one season and then die. Many, however, produce seeds that overwinter and germinate the following spring, or germinate in autumn and overwinter as small plants. Others are tender perennials that may be overwintered and planted out again in spring, or started from cuttings.

THE THUMB MARKERS

The different sections of this book are identified by color thumb markers on the left- and right-hand sides of each page. Perennials are split into five subsections, each identified by their individual thumb markers: Soil and Exposure, Specific Uses, Floral Effect, Foliage Effect, and Specialist Plants.

SHRUBS TOLERANT OF SHADE

Hydrangea serrata 'Bluebird'
LACECAP HYDRANGEA
☀ ☀ 6   ↕ 4ft (1.2m) ↔ 5ft (1.5m)

The pointed leaves of this dense, bushy shrub often color well in autumn. Violet-blue, lacecap flowers in summer have pale marginal florets. Dislikes dry soils.

Pachysandra terminalis
JAPANESE SPURGE
☀ ☀ 4   ↕ 4in (10cm) ↔ 8in (20cm)

This evergreen, suckering shrublet likes moist soils and makes a superb groundcover for shade. Its dark green leaves back little white flower spikes in spring.

Skimmia japonica 'Wakehurst White'
SKIMMIA
☀ ☀ 7   ↕ 30in (75cm) ↔ 30in (75cm)

This spring-flowering cultivar will produce an abundance of white berries if you plant a male variety of this dense, low evergreen nearby to effect pollination.

Lonicera pileata
SHRUBBY HONEYSUCKLE
☀ ☀ 6   ↕ 24in (60cm) ↔ 6ft (2m)

Its low and wide-spreading habit makes this an excellent evergreen groundcover. Tiny, inconspicuous, late spring flowers are occasionally followed by violet berries.

Prunus laurocerasus 'Otto Luyken'
CHERRY LAUREL
☀ ☀ 6   ↕ 3ft (1m) ↔ 6ft (2m)

The branches of this low evergreen shrub are clothed with narrow, glossy, leathery leaves. Erect spikes of white flowers in late spring are followed by black fruits.

OTHER EVERGREEN SHRUBS TOLERANT OF SHADE

Aucuba japonica
× *Fatshedera lizei*, see p.212
Fatsia japonica, see p.216
Ilex crenata
Osmanthus heterophyllus
Rhododendron catawbiense
Rubus tricolor
Ruscus hypoglossum
Sarcococca hookeriana var. *humilis*
Viburnum davidii, see p.185

Mahonia nervosa
CASCADES MAHONIA
☀ ☀ 6 ⚘   ↕ 24in (60cm) ↔ 3ft (1m)

This evergreen, suckering shrub produces short, erect stems with handsome leaves that turn red or purplish in winter. Spikes of yellow flowers appear in early summer.

Vinca major 'Variegata'
VARIEGATED LARGE PERIWINKLE
☀ ☀ 7   ↕ 12in (30cm) ↔ 5ft (1.5m)

Striking, variegated leaves are margined creamy white and form a superb groundcover that is rampant if unchecked. Blue flowers last from spring to autumn.

201

SHRUBS

• **HEIGHT AND SPREAD**
Gives the average ultimate size of the plant, in imperial and metric.

• **THUMB MARKER**
Identifies each of the different sections in the book (see above).

OTHER PLANTS •
Lists more plants suitable for the site or effect, with page references given for those illustrated in other parts of the book.

HOW THE TREES CHAPTER WORKS

Prunus serotina
BLACK CHERRY
☀ ☀ 3   Moderate growth   ↕ 50ft (15m) ↔ 43ft (13m)

This free-growing tree has an oval crown of pendulous or arching branches. Its deep green, glossy leaves are deciduous, becoming yellow or red in autumn. Small white spring flowers are carried in drooping tassels, and give way to shining black fruits.

281

• **TREE ARTWORK**
Shows typical shape of mature tree; bare branches indicate tree is deciduous, full leaf that it is evergreen.

• **GROWTH RATE**
This is given as either vigorous, moderate, or slow.

INDOOR PLANTS – USING THE CULTIVATION NOTES

△ *Lytocaryum weddellianum*
DWARF COCONUT PALM
↕ 6ft (2m) ↔ 3ft (1m)

One of the most beautiful palms for the home and tolerant of low light. Handle the fragile roots with care when repotting. Formerly sold as *Microcoelum* or *Cocos*.

☀ Moderate to shady ❋ Warm. Moderate to high humidity ◐ Every three weeks ◌ When soil surface dry. Water sparingly in winter. Avoid waterlogging 🌱 Seed

△ *Schefflera elegantissima* 'Castor'
FALSE ARALIA, FINGER ARALIA
↕ 6ft (2m) ↔ 3ft (90cm)

This plant produces an elegant, lacy outline. The dark coppery green leaves have long, narrow leaflets that widen with age. Also known as *Aralia* or *Dizygotheca*.

☀ Bright, avoiding direct sun ❋ Warm, avoiding fluctuation. Moderate humidity ◐ Biweekly. Monthly at low winter temperatures ◌ Water when dry. Avoid overwatering 🌱 Tip cuttings, seed

395

• **CULTIVATION NOTES**

Concise notes on the most important care factors are introduced by the following five symbols. See also pages 14–21.

☀ *Light*
Light needs are divided into three categories – Bright, Moderate, and Shady. "Shady" does not mean devoid of light. "Summer sun" means scorching midday sun.

❋ *Temperature and humidity*
Temperatures are given as Low (39–48°F/4–9°C), Moderate (50–59°F/10–15°C), or Warm (61–70°F/16–21°C). Humidity is Low, Moderate, or High.

◐ *Fertilizing*
Fertilize at the specified intervals when a plant is in active growth (usually spring to autumn). Unless stated in the entry, fertilize with any general houseplant fertilizer.

◌ *Watering*
References such as "when dry" relate to the soil surface. Water when the stated conditions apply. "Sparingly" means just enough to avoid desiccation.

🌱 *Propagation*
The most common and reliable ways of increasing your plants are given in each individual entry. See pages 20–21 for a more detailed explanation of each method.

9

OUTDOOR PLANTS

A greater number and variety of plants are available to gardeners than ever before. The following is a selection of the very best. Whether your garden is large or miniscule, there is something here to give it that magic touch.

△ AUTUMN JEWEL Anemone x hydrida *'September Charm'* *is a reliable and free-flowering perennial for autumn effect.*

◁ MIDSUMMER MORNING *Bold plantings of ornamental alliums front this summer border of hardy perennials.*

Plant Finder

I F YOU HAVE a specific site, condition, or decorative effect in mind, refer to the condensed index below. The page numbers alongside each entry take you to visual lists of plants that thrive there, or to what the author recommends to achieve the desired effect. The color-coded bands match the section markers.

	PERENNIALS	CLIMBERS	SHRUBS	CONIFERS	TREES
SIZE AND SHAPE					
Bold form, foliage			216		266, 285
Columnar or tall				248	304
Large-sized			178, 188	244	266
Medium-sized			180	250	268
Small-sized			182, 186	258	270
Weeping or wide-spreading				246	288
SEASONAL FEATURES					
Spring interest	96				
Summer interest	98				
Autumn interest	102, 140		226		296, 298
Winter interest	76, 104		236		298
continued	141		238		300
Evergreen	120	170	214		286
Long flowering season	106				
COLOUR					
Blue-gray or silver leaves	136		222	263	294
Cool or pale flowers	112, 114				
Golden or yellow leaves	134		220	262	292
Hot flowers	110				
Purple, red or bronze leaves	138		224		295
Variegated leaves	130, 132		218	261	290
OTHER PLANT FEATURES					
Berries for birds			232		298
Butterflies, flowers attractive to	78		234		
Cut flowers and foliage	73, 74				
Fragrance	116, 127	172	228, 230		
Hedging and screening			208	256	281
Herbs	54				
Multipurpose trees					302
Ornamental fruits			231		298
Pest-proof	88–93		240		
Specimen plants			178, 188		266
Thorny shrubs			239		
Low allergen perennials	86				

Soil Guide

THE SIZE and proportion of clay, sand, or silt particles present in your garden soil influence its chemical and physical nature. They make it either heavy (wet and poorly drained), or light (dry and free-draining), and thus determine what plants will thrive on it. Its pH value, a measure of acidity or alkalinity, is measured on a scale of 1 to 14. Below neutral (7), soils are progressively acid; above neutral, they are progressively alkaline (limy). You can determine what type of soil you have by looking at the color, feeling the texture, and observing what kind of plants will grow on it or, if you prefer, by doing a soil test.

AVERAGE ideal for *Forsythia*
Different cultivation requirements and variable local conditions make average soil hard to define. Usually, it is moist but well-drained, with a reasonable humus content, neutral to slightly acid pH, and suits the widest range of plants.

HEAVY CLAY ideal for *Berberis*
Minute clay particles stick together, making clay soils slow-draining after rain, sticky, and likely to bake hard in hot sun. Often highly fertile, they can be improved by draining or by adding grit or coarse organic matter.

SANDY ideal for *Potentilla*
Sand particles are much larger than clay particles, making sandy soils light, free-draining, and quick to warm up in spring. Some plants may need frequent irrigation and feeding, though fertility can be improved by adding organic matter.

ACID ideal for *Rhododendron*
Peaty or acid soils are generally dark, and rich in organic matter. Acid in nature and moisture-retentive, they are favored by plants not tolerant of alkaline soil and can be made more free-draining by adding coarse sand.

ALKALINE ideal for *Kolkwitzia*
Limy or alkaline soils are usually pale, shallow, and stony. Free-draining, they warm up quickly in spring and are moderately fertile. Like sandy soils, they benefit from the addition of organic matter.

Sunlight Guide

Plants need sunlight to photosynthesize, so receiving the proper light level is crucial to plant growth and health. Many plants are flexible in their light needs, preferring one situation but tolerating another. Most thrive when open to the sky.

• *THE SUN'S POSITION*
The position of the sun varies during the year. In midwinter, the sun is lower and the shadows much longer. In the height of summer, the sun is high and the shadows are short.

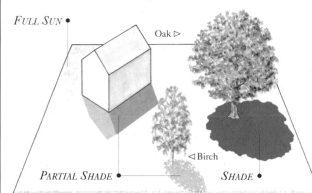

FULL SUN •

Oak ▷

◁ Birch

PARTIAL SHADE •

SHADE •

☼ FULL SUN
Open to the sun for the greater part of the day, fully sunny sites are not subject to shade cast by trees or buildings. Numerous garden plants grown for their flowering display, including many perennials, annuals, and shrubs (*see above*), prefer sunny sites. Sun and warmth ripen woody growth, encouraging flowering and fruiting. Many plants at their best in full sun will also tolerate a degree of shade, such as that found near buildings and on the edge of woodland.

☀ PARTIAL SHADE
Sites in partial shade are subject to reduced light. They are found near buildings that block direct sunlight, but do not hide the sky above. Partial shade is also found in the lee of, if not directly beneath, trees such as birch (*Betula*), which cast a light, dappled shade. If the soil is moist, these conditions suit many plants, some of which may also be tolerant of full sun or even heavier shade. Numerous foliage perennials, and those found naturally in woodland sites (*see above*) thrive best here.

☀ SHADE
This defines sites subject to permanent shade or shade during the main growing season (summer). Such sites may be closely surrounded by tall buildings or, more usually, beneath or in the lee of dense-canopied trees. Even here, the degree of shade varies. If combined with dry or compacted soil, such as that often found beneath large conifers or similar evergreen trees, the choice of suitable underplanting is limited to the few shade-tolerant plants growing in such sites in the wild.

PERENNIALS

IF TREES AND SHRUBS form the bones of a garden, then perennials provide its flesh, forming the bulk of border plants and groundcover. No other plant group offers such great variety of form, flower, and foliage, from tiny rock plants to large bamboos. This section includes bulbs (with tubers and corms), and annual or biennial plants.

△ *Oenothera speciosa* 'Rosea'

△ SUN LOVING *The bold flowerheads of a superb spurge,* Euphorbia characias *subsp.* wulfenii, *enjoy a place in the sun.*

THE BEAUTY OF PERENNIALS

- Provide massed effects in borders.
- Bold single specimens or groups can create special effects in lawns.
- Ideal for carpeting rock gardens and screes, or draping retaining walls.
- Provide mass impact as spring bulbs.
- Ideal as groundcover beneath trees.
- Perfect for planting in containers for terraces, patios, or courtyards.
- Annuals or biennials give fast results.
- Offer striking waterside or bog plants.

Some perennials have evergreen foliage, which gives year-round interest, but most are herbaceous, dying to below ground level, usually in winter. Unless otherwise stated, all plants in this section are herbaceous. The pleasurable anticipation associated with their annual re-emergence is something of which we never tire, and makes them all the more exciting and valuable in the garden.

PLANTS FOR EFFECT
For many gardeners, no finer sight exists than that of a perennial bed at its best in summer. Whether we are inspired by Gertrude Jekyll's plant associations, or prefer a more haphazard mix of color, perennials abound to suit every taste. When planting borders, foliage impact is just as important as floral display, and it is worth remembering the beautiful, nostalgic pictures that are possible in winter when certain dead seedheads are spared.

PLANTS FOR ALL PLACES
Warm, sunny sites in the garden are ideal for growing those perennials that enjoy hot, dry conditions in the wild. The abundance of plants thriving in such situations are best planted in raised beds or beneath sunny walls in cooler areas. To take advantage of shady places, consider plants native to woodland. Ferns, spring-flowering perennials, and bulbous plants such as trilliums and miniature cyclamen tolerate shade and form attractive groundcover.

△ SHADE CARPET *Miniature cyclamen* (Cyclamen repandum) *form a lovely spring carpet in a beech tree's shade.*

◁ WINTER BEAUTY *The elegance of dead seedheads and leaves in winter is further enhanced when they are coated with frost.*

▷ EARLY SUMMER SPECTACLE *This cottage garden border boasts a glorious mix of perennials, annuals, and biennials.*

Perennials through the Seasons

E ACH SEASON brings new features and its own particular character to the garden landscape. Perennials mirror this seasonal passage by offering continual changes in growth, foliage, and flowers. While spring and summer are often considered to be the high points of the gardening calendar, with careful planning, even in cold climates perennials can provide nearly year-round interest and colorful or dramatic effects, with one plant taking over as another starts to fade.

Seasonal changes in the garden are reflected most clearly in flowering and foliage displays. While some perennials flower for a relatively brief period, their spectacular blooms may be long remembered and eagerly looked forward to in subsequent years. Perennials with extended flowering periods (often spanning several months) provide strong links between the seasons, and their contribution can be relied upon year after year. This is particularly important in smaller gardens, where each plant must contribute the maximum amount of color and interest. Perennials with attractive foliage will provide an even longer season of interest, and can be invaluable where space is limited. While herbaceous plants often have richly tinted leaves in autumn, it is worth growing some of the many perennials that have evergreen or semievergreen foliage. Those with variegated or brightly colored leaves are also useful.

SPRING

The re-emergence of herbaceous perennials in spring is, for many gardeners, one of the most exciting events in the year. Rootstocks that have lain below ground all through winter now send out strong, and sometimes brightly colored, new shoots. Since many trees and shrubs begin growing in late spring, perennials provide much of the first garden color of the new year. Bulbs will bring welcome early blooms and are excellent for planting in groups, naturalizing in large drifts, or underplanting beneath trees or shrubs. Tulips, daffodils, and many

△ SPRING CONTAINER *Bulbs, like these daffodils, are ideal for naturalizing or for tubs. They are a useful source of early color in the garden, providing a rich variety of spring flower effects.*

▷ SUMMER BORDER *Perennials can bring a blaze of color to the garden during the summer months. In this border, the bright blooms of delphiniums, lupines,* Anthemis, Oenothera, *and* Geranium psilostemon *compete with a multitude of other plants for attention.*

△ EARLY WINTER *After flowering, many perennials produce decorative seedheads. These can provide enchanting effects when touched with frost or snow, a bonus that tidy-minded gardeners often forfeit.*

◁ AUTUMN COLOR *The richly tinted foliage of* Geranium macrorrhizum *is a striking backdrop for colchicums in autumn. The leaf color will continue to develop after these flowers have faded.*

other bulbs can also provide some of the first cut flowers of the year, and will thrive in containers in a patio or backyard.

SUMMER

After the initial rush of spring flowers, the garden settles down to a more leisurely pace. Many of the most popular perennials, such as yarrow (*Achillea*), shasta daisies, and other members of the huge daisy family are at their best now. Long-flowering perennials, like sundrops (*Oenothera*), bloom through summer and even into autumn. Summer is also the time when perennials with a stately habit or bold foliage attain their ultimate size, stamping their presence on the garden scene. In regions where summers are dry, it is worth growing perennials such as sea hollies (*Eryngium*) and yuccas, which tolerate sun and little water.

AUTUMN

Perennials with late flowers, fruits, or richly tinted foliage can make autumn one of the most colorful seasons, despite its place at the end of the growing year. Autumn bulbs, such as colchicums and dwarf cyclamen, flower alongside golden rod (*Solidago*) and asters. Foliage can also make an important contribution – the dying leaves of herbaceous perennials such as many hardy geraniums providing brilliant tints of purple, yellow, and red. Showy seedheads, often good for cutting, add to the display. Wise gardeners will also use ornamental grasses, like the fountain grass (*Pennisetum alopecuroides*), to add interest to borders or containers. In addition to their bold form and foliage, many of these grasses have striking flowers or long-lasting seedheads.

WINTER

The winter months are often least liked by gardeners, but this does not have to be a featureless time when the garden is either ignored or avoided. Gardeners in warmer zones can choose from the many perennials that have attractive semi-evergreen or evergreen foliage, some of it brightly colored. These foliage plants, invaluable in their own right, will also provide an attractive setting for late-winter to early spring-flowering hellebores, as well as for snowdrops and other similar miniature bulbs that signal the oncoming spring. Perennials whose dried seedheads or super-structures survive through autumn and into winter will provide further dramatic interest in the garden.

▷ LATE WINTER *Use perennials to bring warmth and color to the garden from late winter to early spring. Here, snowdrops grow with* Bergenia *'Bressingham Ruby'.*

SOIL & EXPOSURE

THE TYPE OF SOIL found on your property and how much sun or shade you have are two of the most critical factors to consider when selecting plants. While many perennials are flexible in their needs, tolerating a range of garden situations, they can be used to better effect if you are aware of their preferences.

Anemonopsis macrophylla
for moist soil in shade

Soils vary considerably in their physical and chemical nature. While most perennials thrive in what is commonly called "average" or "moist but well-drained" soil, which retains enough moisture to satisfy a plant's needs without becoming water-logged, some have much more specific requirements. Look at the color and texture of your soil and then check the soil guide on p.14 to learn which type of soil you have.

All plants require some sunlight to survive, but while some demand full sun for top performance, others tolerate, or even prefer, varying degrees of shade. Many perennials thrive in the partial shade cast by buildings, walls, or light-canopied deciduous trees, like birch, or under deeply rooted trees like oaks. A more careful choice is needed for sites in the heavy shade that occurs beneath dense tree canopies.

Perennials in this section are grouped according to their soil and lighting needs to provide planting solutions for a range of garden sites.

△ REACHING FOR THE SUN *Verbascum bombyciferum is a biennial that makes a striking, white-woolly feature in a sunny summer border. It also has a handsome rosette of overwintering leaves.*

△ SHADY BORDER *Many perennials, like these hostas and irises, enjoy a partially shady site, especially if the soil is moist.*

◁ SUNNY CORNER *Make use of warm, sheltered sites and corners to grow sun-lovers or exotic tender perennials.*

▷ DRY GARDEN *These striking sedums, sea hollies, and ornamental grasses will thrive in full sun and well-drained soil.*

Low to Medium Perennials for Heavy Clay Soil

HEAVY CLAY SOILS are often wet and sticky in winter, but hard and lumpy in dry summers. When amended with organic matter and mulched, they can also be very fertile and amenable for a wide range of perennials. None of the following will grow much above 36in (90cm) and are suited to small gardens or the front of larger borders and beds.

OTHER LOW TO MEDIUM GROWERS FOR HEAVY CLAY SOIL

Anemone × *hybrida* and cvs.
Aster novi-belgii and cvs.
Astilbe spp. and cvs.
Astrantia major
Brunnera macrophylla, see p.84
Polemonium caeruleum
Pulmonaria 'Mawson's Blue'
Solidago 'Golden Fleece'
Stachys macrantha, see p.99
Veronica gentianoides

Ajuga reptans 'Multicolor'
BUGLEWEED
☀ 3-9 ↕ 6in (15cm) ↔ 36in (90cm)

This bugleweed forms a mat of creeping stems and bronze-green leaves splashed pink and cream. Short spikes of deep blue flowers are produced in early summer.

Aster × *frikartii* 'Mönch'
FRIKART'S ASTER
☀ 5-8 ↕ 28in (70cm) ↔ 16in (40cm)

Reliable displays of large, long-lasting, lavender-blue daisies top strong stems in late summer and autumn. Well worth growing although it may require support.

Campanula takesimana
BELLFLOWER
☀◐ 5-8 ↕ 20in (50cm) ↔ 3ft (1m)

Reliable on clay soils, this suckering plant has erect stems and heart-shaped leaves. Nodding white bells, pink-flushed and spotted inside, are borne during summer.

Aquilegia vulgaris 'Nora Barlow'
EUROPEAN COLUMBINE
☀◐ 3-9 ↕ 36in (90cm) ↔ 18in (45cm)

In spring and early summer, tall, upright stems bear showers of nodding, double red pompon flowers with pale green tips above a mound of divided, grayish leaves.

Bergenia crassifolia
BERGENIA
☀◐ 3-8 ↕↔ 18in (45cm)

A tough perennial developing a mound of bold, leathery, semievergreen leaves. In late winter and early spring, reddish stems carry dark pink flowers above the foliage.

Hemerocallis 'Stella de Oro'
DAYLILY
☀ 3-9 ↕ 24in (60cm) ↔ 18in (45cm)

Clusters of bright golden yellow flowers open in succession from early summer to fall above dense clumps of strap-shaped leaves. Long-blooming and very reliable.

Hosta 'June'
HOSTA
☼ ☼ **3-9**   ↕ 16in (40cm) ↔ 28in (70cm)

This beautiful foliage plant is a sport of
the lovely *H.* 'Halcyon'. It has fleshy,
long-pointed, yellow-splashed leaves and
bears lavender flowers during summer.

Lamium orvala
LAMIUM
☼ ☼ **4-8**   ↕ ↔ 20in (50cm)

The nettle-shaped, softly-hairy leaves
form a bold, non-invasive clump. Whorls
of two-lipped, pinkish purple flowers are
produced from late spring into summer.

Paeonia lactiflora 'Laura Dessert'
PEONY
☼ **2-8**   ↕ 30in (75cm) ↔ 24in (60cm)

During late spring, large, fragrant, double
blooms with white, pink-flushed outer
petals and creamy yellow centers emerge
above a clump of deeply divided leaves.

Ranunculus aconitifolius 'Flore Pleno'
DOUBLE BUTTERCUP
☼ ☼ **5-9**   ↕ 24in (60cm) ↔ 18in (45cm)

This clump-forming perennial produces
beautiful, deeply lobed leaves and bears
branched stems of double white buttonlike flowers in spring and early summer.

Prunella grandiflora 'Loveliness'
SELF-HEAL
☼ **5-8**   ↕ 6in (15cm) ↔ 12in (30cm)

A mat-forming, semievergreen perennial
with erect stems bearing whorled heads of
two-lipped, soft pink flowers in summer.
It makes an excellent groundcover.

Rudbeckia fulgida var. *sullivantii*
'Goldsturm'
☼ ☼ **3-9**   ↕ 24in (60cm) ↔ 18in (45cm)

This colorful perennial has golden yellow
daisy flowers with dark centers from late
summer into autumn. It performs best
with moist but well-drained conditions.

Medium to Tall Perennials for Heavy Clay Soil

MANY OF THE MORE ROBUST perennials are tolerant of heavy clay soils. Some have densely fibrous rootstocks, others are deep-rooted, allowing them to survive as long as their site is not waterlogged. The following perennials, all 3–6ft (1–2m) tall, will do even better if drainage can be improved by adding organic matter, like compost, to the soil.

Delphinium 'Emily Hawkins'
DELPHINIUM
☼ 3-7 ↕ 5½ft (1.7m) ↔ 24in (60cm)

No perennial border on clay soil should be without a delphinium. This one bears neat spikes of semidouble, light violet flowers during summer with fawn-colored eyes.

Aconitum x *cammarum* 'Bicolor'
MONKSHOOD
☼ ☼ 3-7 ↕ 4ft (1.2m) ↔ 24in (60cm)

This stout perennial has deeply divided, sharply toothed, dark green leaves and bears branched heads of helmet-shaped, blue and white flowers during summer.

Centaurea macrocephala
GLOBE CENTAUREA
☼ 2-8 ↕ 4ft (1.2m) ↔ 36in (90cm)

Throughout summer, this striking, clump-forming perennial produces large, chunky heads of golden yellow flowers with shiny brown bracts atop erect, leafy stems.

Aruncus dioicus
GOAT'S BEARD
☼ ☼ 3-7 ↕ 6ft (2m) ↔ 4ft (1.2m)

An impressive perennial that forms a bold clump of large, much-divided, fernlike leaves with equally attractive plumes of frothy, creamy white flowers in summer.

Actaea simplex 'Scimitar'
KAMCHATKA BUGBANE
☼ ☼ 3-8 ↕ 6ft (2m) ↔ 24in (60cm)

A handsome perennial with tall, branched spikes of tiny white flowers that rise over the large, bold clumps of deeply divided, fernlike leaves during autumn.

Eupatorium purpureum
'Atropurpureum'
☼ 3-8 ↕ 7ft (2.2m) ↔ 4ft (1.2m)

A clump-forming native plant with tall, purplish, leafy stems bearing domed heads of pink-purple flowers, loved by bees and butterflies, during summer and autumn.

Helianthus 'Capenoch Star'
PERENNIAL SUNFLOWER
☼ ☼ **5-9** ↕ 5ft (1.5m) ↔ 36in (90cm)

The sharply toothed leaves of this bold,
clump-forming plant are joined in summer
and autumn by branched heads of large,
lemon yellow, dark-centered daisies.

Heliopsis helianthoides var. *scabra*
'Light of Loddon'
☼ ☼ **3-9** ↕ 3½ft (1.1m) ↔ 36in (90cm)

Erect, stout, stiff-branching, leafy stems
produce a regular display of semidouble,
bright yellow flowerheads with domed
centers throughout summer and autumn.

**OTHER MEDIUM TO TALL
PERENNIALS FOR CLAY SOIL**

Anemone x *hybrida*
Aster novae-angliae
Campanula lactiflora 'Loddon Anna',
  see p.34
Helenium autumnale
Helianthus salicifolius
Macleaya x *kewensis*
Rheum palmatum
Sanguisorba canadensis
Solidago spp. and cvs.

Persicaria amplexicaulis 'Firetail'
PERSICARIA
☼ ☼ **5-9** ↕ 4ft (1.2m) ↔ 36in (90cm)

A striking and reliable border perennial
with dense clumps of leafy stems bearing
long, arching, slender spikes of bright red
flowers from summer into autumn.

Rodgersia aesculifolia
RODGERSIA
☼ ☼ **4-7** ↕ 5½ft (1.7m) ↔ 36in (90cm)

This lovely rodgersia produces a clump
of long-stalked, toothed, coppery-colored
leaves topped by eye-catching plumes
of creamy white flowers during summer.

Silphium terebinthinaceum
CUP PLANT, PRAIRIE DOCK
☼ ☼ **3-8** ↕ 8ft (2.5m) ↔ 3ft (1m)

Branched heads of yellow daisies adorn
this statuesque native plant from summer
to autumn. The coarsely toothed upper
leaves have fused stalks that form cups.

Low to Medium Perennials for Sandy/Well-drained Soil

THERE ARE NUMEROUS PERENNIALS less than 3ft (1m) in height that are suitable for well-drained soils, especially for sites in full sun. These small to medium-size plants have a multitude of uses, particularly at the front of borders, in raised beds, or along the tops of walls. Some are also ideal for growing in containers on patios or paved areas.

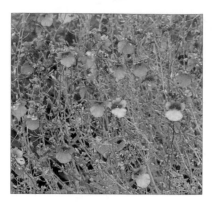

Diascia 'Joyce's Choice'
DIASCIA
☼ 7-9 ↕ 10in (25cm) ↔ 20in (50cm)

A free-flowering diascia forming a mat or carpet of trailing stems and small leaves topped throughout summer and autumn by loose sprays of apricot flowers.

Acanthus hirsutus
BEAR'S-BREECH
☼ ☼ 8-10 ↕ ↔ 12in (30cm)

This low, suckering perennial forms a clump of deeply cut, weakly spiny leaves. During summer, upright, greenish white flower spikes emerge from prickly bracts.

Artemisia 'Powis Castle'
ARTEMISIA
☼ 5-8 ↕ 24in (60cm) ↔ 36in (90cm)

The handsome, filigree, silver-gray foliage of this plant is hard to beat. It forms a low, neat mound, eventually becoming woody and untidy, when it should be replaced.

Eriophyllum lanatum
WOOLLY SUNFLOWER
☼ 5-8 ↕ ↔ 20in (50cm)

This vigorous clump-former has woolly, silver-gray leaves and bears a succession of bright yellow daisy flowers from late spring into summer. It is drought tolerant.

Agapanthus 'Midnight Blue'
AFRICAN LILY
☼ 8-10 ↕ 18in (45cm) ↔ 12in (30cm)

In summer, fleshy stems carry loose heads of dark blue, trumpet-shaped flowers over clumps of strap-shaped, dark green leaves. Grow in containers in northern gardens.

Borago pygmaea
BORAGO
☼ 5-9 ↕ ↔ 24in (60cm)

Loosely branched stems rise from rosettes of leaves to bear nodding, pale blue, bell-shaped flowers over a long period from late spring to autumn. A short-lived plant.

Eryngium bourgatii
MEDITERRANEAN SEA HOLLY
☼ 5-8 ↕ 18in (45cm) ↔ 12in (30cm)

Small blue flowerheads with collars of spine-tipped bracts emerge in summer on branching stems. The spiny, silver-veined, deeply divided leaves form rosettes.

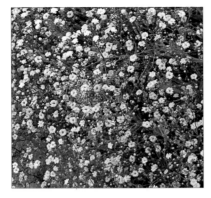

Gypsophila 'Rosenschleier'
BABY'S-BREATH
☼ 3-9 ↕ 16in (40cm) ↔ 3ft (1m)

The pretty carpet of bluish green leaves is peppered in summer with tiny, double white flowers that later turn pale pink. It is also known as *G.* 'Rosy Veil'.

Limonium platyphyllum 'Violetta'
SEA LAVENDER
☼ 3-9 ↕ 24in (60cm) ↔ 18in (45cm)

This sea lavender forms a bold rosette of large, dark green leaves. Branched heads of tiny, deep blue-violet late-summer flowers are good for cutting and drying.

Linum narbonense
NARBONNE FLAX
☼ 5-9 ↕ 20in (50cm) ↔ 18in (45cm)

During summer, the clump of slender, wiry stems, clothed in narrow, blue-green leaves, is covered by a mass of short-lived, small, deep blue flowers with white eyes.

Oenothera speciosa 'Rosea'
SHOWY EVENING PRIMROSE
☼ 5-8 ↕ ↔ 12in (30cm)

The mound of narrow leaves is decorated by saucer-shaped, pale pink blooms with yellow and white centers from summer to autumn. Free-flowering but invasive.

OTHER LOW TO MEDIUM GROWERS FOR SANDY/WELL-DRAINED SOIL

Acanthus dioscoridis, see p.32
Achillea tomentosa
Anagallis monellii
Calamintha nepeta
Centranthus ruber, see p.92
Dianthus deltoides, see p.106
Dictamnus albus, see p.114
Euphorbia nicaeensis, see p.82
Gaillardia × *grandiflora*
Geranium malviflorum
Iris innominata
Lavandula angustifolia
Lychnis coronaria
Opuntia humifusa
Sedum spp. and cvs.
Silene polypetala
Solidago sempervirens
Yucca spp. and cvs.

Origanum laevigatum 'Herrenhausen'
OREGANO
☼ 5-9 ↕ 20in (50cm) ↔ 18in (45cm)

Bees and butterflies love this plant. The stiffly erect stems, crowded with aromatic leaves, are topped by dense heads of rich pink flowers in summer and autumn.

27

Medium to Tall Perennials for Sandy/Well-drained Soil

GARDENERS WHO HAVE ADMIRED the lavender-blue spires of a *Perovskia* or a mound of *Crambe cordifolia* in bloom may already know how well these two, and other similar perennials, thrive in well-drained soil, especially in sunny sites. The following, mostly 3–6ft (1–2m) tall, also enjoy such conditions, and will bring presence to a border or bed.

OTHER MEDIUM TO TALL
GROWERS FOR SANDY SOIL

Acanthus mollis Latifolius Group
Cortaderia selloana
  'Sunningdale Silver', see p.146
Eryngium pandanifolium
Euphorbia characias subsp. *wulfenii*
Liatris aspera
Salvia interrupta
Silene regia
Silene virginica
Solidago odora

Asphodeline lutea
KING'S SPEAR
☼ 6-9   ↕ 5ft (1.5m) ↔ 12in (30cm)

Tall, slender spikes of star-shaped, bright yellow, fragrant flowers are carried from late spring into early summer above the clumps of slender, grassy, blue-gray leaves.

Crambe cordifolia
HEARTLEAF CRAMBE
☼ ◐ 4-7   ↕ 8ft (2.5m) ↔ 5ft (1.5m)

Tiny, pure white flowers are produced in huge, branching heads above mounds of bold, cabbagelike foliage in early summer. Truly imposing when in full bloom.

Echinops bannaticus 'Taplow Blue'
GLOBE THISTLE
☼ ◐ 3-8   ↕ 4ft (1.2m) ↔ 24in (60cm)

The prickly balls of bright blue flowers in mid- to late summer make this a favorite with both children and butterflies. It has handsome, deeply cut, spiny leaves.

Cortaderia selloana 'Rendatleri'
PINK PAMPAS GRASS
☼ 8-11   ↕ 8ft (2.5m) ↔ 2m (6ft)

A striking ornamental grass with a huge mound of narrow, saw-toothed, evergreen leaves. Tall stems flaunt bold plumes of rosy lilac spikelets during late summer.

Dierama pulcherrimum
WANDFLOWER
☼ 8-9   ↕ 5ft (1.5m) ↔ 4ft (1.2m)

The graceful, arching stems are hung with bell-shaped, dark pink or purple flowers in summer. Its seedheads are attractive too. It is also known as angel's fishing rod.

Eryngium eburneum
SEA HOLLY
☼ 7-10   ↕ 12ft (4m) ↔ 6ft (2m)

This statuesque plant bears tall-stemmed, branching heads of white-green flowers in summer above bold clumps of rapier-like, spine-toothed, evergreen leaves.

Linaria genistifolia subsp. *dalmatica*
TOADFLAX
☼ 5-8   ↕ ↔ 36in (90cm)

Bushy with a creeping rootstock, this toad-flax has erect stems crowded with bloomy, blue-green leaves. Spikes of snapdragon-like yellow flowers are borne in summer.

Romneya coulteri
MATILIJA
☼ 8-11   ↕ ↔ 6ft (2m)

A suckering, woody-based perennial or subshrub that forms patches of sea-green, bloomy, leafy stems. During summer, it bears large white poppy flowers.

**OTHER MEDIUM TO TALL
GROWERS FOR SANDY SOIL**

Achillea filipendulina, see p.76
Echinops ritro 'Veitch's Blue',
   see p.79
Eremurus stenophyllus, see p.39
Lilium regale, see p.116
Malva alcea var. *fastigiata*, see p.99
Salvia spp. and cvs.
Strobilanthes atropurpurea, see p.103
Verbascum chaixii 'Album', see p.109
Verbena hastata

Kniphofia 'Prince Igor'
TORCH LILY
☼ ☼ 5-9   ↕ 6ft (1.8m) ↔ 36in (90cm)

This outstanding torch lily bears narrow, rich green leaves and many sturdy stems with large, dense pokers of deep orange-red flowers from summer to autumn.

Salvia cacaliifolia
ORNAMENTAL SAGE
☼ 8-11   ↕ 4ft (1.2m) ↔ 36in (90cm)

A robust, branching, tender perennial with triangular leaves and slender sprays of deep blue flowers from midsummer to autumn. It needs a warm, sunny site.

Lavatera × *clementii* 'Kew Rose'
TREE MALLOW
☼ 6-10   ↕ ↔ 6ft (2m)

This handsome perennial has branching, woody-based stems bearing gray-green leaves and a succession of pink flowers in summer. It prefers a sheltered spot.

Perovskia 'Blue Spire'
RUSSIAN SAGE
☼ 4-9   ↕ 4ft (1.2m) ↔ 36in (90cm)

This drought-tolerant, woody-based sage has deeply toothed, aromatic, gray-green leaves. Branched spires of tiny, lavender-blue flowers open in summer and autumn.

Verbascum 'Gainsborough'
MULLEIN
☼ 5-9   ↕ 4ft (1.2m) ↔ 12in (30cm)

Beautiful but short-lived, this mullein has downy, wrinkled leaves in attractive, over-wintering rosettes. Branched spires of soft yellow flowers appear in summer.

Low-growing Perennials for Acid Soil

WHILE MOST PERENNIALS thrive in soil that is slightly acid to neutral, a few – including many beloved woodland wildflowers – prefer a site in acid soil that is rich in humus. The perennials below will not grow much above 12in (30cm) tall, making them suitable for lightly shaded woodland edges, rock gardens, or for small peat gardens and beds.

OTHER LOW-GROWING PERENNIALS FOR ACID SOIL
Blechnum penna-marina
Cornus canadensis
Gentiana sino-ornata, see p.61
Phlox stolonifera
Shortia galacifolia
Trillium spp.
Uvularia grandiflora, see p.43
Uvularia perfoliata
Vancouveria hexandra
Viola pedata

Celmisia walkeri
NEW ZEALAND DAISY
☼ ◐ **9-11**   ↕ ↔ 12in (30cm)

This mat-forming, evergreen perennial has rosettes of leathery, grayish leaves. White, yellow-centered daisies are borne on slender, sticky stems in early summer.

Gentiana × macaulayi 'Kingfisher'
GENTIAN
☼ ◐ **6-8**   ↕ 2in (5cm) ↔ 12in (30cm)

Beautiful trumpet-shaped blue flowers with white and darker blue stripes on the outside open in autumn among the semi-evergreen mats of rosetted, narrow leaves.

Dodecatheon meadia f. *album*
SHOOTING STAR
☼ ◐ **4-8**   ↕ 16in (40cm) ↔ 10in (25cm)

In spring, loose umbels of nodding white flowers with yellow beaks of stamens are borne on slender stems above a basal rosette of leaves. Prefers humus-rich soil.

Iris 'Arnold Sunrise'
PACIFIC COAST HYBRID IRIS
☼ ◐ **7-9**   ↕ 10in (25cm) ↔ 12in (30cm)

A tough, clump-forming plant producing long, narrow, semievergreen to evergreen leaves. White, yellow-stained flowers are borne in spring. Will tolerate dry soil.

Lithodora diffusa 'Grace Ward'
LITHODORA
☼ **6-8**   ↕ 6in (15cm) ↔ 36in (90cm)

Deep azure-blue flowers top the prostrate, leafy stems of this dense, carpeting, ever-green perennial or subshrub in late spring and summer. Ideal for rock gardens.

Medium to Tall Perennials for Acid Soil

THE FOLLOWING PERENNIALS all perform best in neutral to acid soil conditions. Many are natives of woodland and mountain sites and require moisture in spring and summer (but not waterlogged soil) in order to thrive. They will grow to around 3ft (1m) or more, and provide superb displays of foliage and flowers for a bed or garden with humus-rich soil.

Meconopsis chelidoniifolia
MECONOPSIS
☀ **6-9**   ↕ 3ft (1m) ↔ 24in (60cm)

Elegant yet informal, this plant develops clumps of leafy, slender, semiscandent branching stems. Nodding, saucer-shaped, pale yellow flowers are borne in summer.

Blechnum chilense
BLECHNUM
☀ ☀ **10-11**   ↕ 3ft (1m) ↔ 4ft (1.2m)

This large, semievergreen to evergreen fern forms a bold clump of leathery sterile fronds. Stiff, fertile fronds crowded with brown spore clusters rise from the center.

Thalictrum rochebruneanum
MEADOW RUE
☀ ☀ **4-7**   ↕ 4ft (1.2m) ↔ 12in (30cm)

A stately perennial with clumps of large, fernlike leaves and tall stems. Fluffy, lavender-pink flower clusters are borne in summer. Requires moist, humus-rich soil.

Iris ensata 'Variegata'
JAPANESE IRIS
☀ **4-9**   ↕ 3ft (1m) ↔ 18in (45cm)

This clump-forming iris bears red-purple flowers on upright stems in summer above the clumps of sword-shaped, gray-green, white-striped leaves. Enjoys moist soils.

Lilium auratum
GOLDBAND LILY
☀ ☀ **4-9**   ↕ 5ft (1.5m) ↔ 12in (30cm)

The tall stems crowded with lance-shaped leaves each bear up to 12 fragrant white flowers, speckled crimson and striped gold, in late summer and early autumn.

OTHER MEDIUM TO TALL PERENNIALS FOR ACID SOIL

Aruncus dioicus, see p.24
Asclepias incarnata
Chelone lyonii
Cimicifuga racemosa
Digitalis purpurea
Dryopteris dilatata
Iris versicolor
Lilium speciosum
Osmunda regalis, see p.67
Smilacina racemosa

Low to Medium Perennials for Alkaline Soil

CONTRARY TO THE popular belief that many of the choicest garden plants demand acid conditions, a wide variety of perennials thrive in, rather than dislike, neutral to alkaline soils. None of the following will grow to more than 3ft (1m) high and are therefore suitable for growing at the front of a border, as well as in raised beds and rock gardens.

Bergenia 'Beethoven'
BERGENIA
☼ ☀ 3-9   ↕ 18in (45cm) ↔ 24in (60cm)

This superb German hybrid forms a low clump of bold, leathery leaves. In spring, loose heads of white flowers with reddish calyces are borne above the foliage.

Campanula punctata
BELLFLOWER
☼ ☀ 5-8   ↕ ↔ 16in (40cm)

In early summer, this reliable perennial's erect stems are hung with large, tubular, bell-shaped flowers. Blooms are white to dusky pink and heavily spotted within.

Acanthus dioscoridis
BEAR'S-BREECH
☼ 8-10   ↕ 16in (40cm) ↔ 24in (60cm)

A striking perennial forming clumps of lance-shaped, hairy leaves. Dense spikes of rich pink flowers with green bracts are borne during spring and summer.

OTHER LOW TO MEDIUM
PERENNIALS FOR ALKALINE SOIL

Anacyclus pyrethrum var. *depressus*
Campanula glomerata
Centranthus ruber, see p.92
Coreopsis grandiflora
Euphorbia rigida
Geranium sanguineum
Gypsophila paniculata
Iris Bearded Hybrids
Platycodon grandiflorus, see p.83
Scabiosa caucasica

Allium cristophii
STAR OF PERSIA
☼ 5-8   ↕ 24in (60cm) ↔ 6in (15cm)

Large, globular heads of starry, purple-pink flowers in early summer are followed by decorative seedheads. A spectacular and also very reliable ornamental onion.

Delphinium tatsienense
DELPHINIUM
☼ 7-9   ↕ 24in (60cm) ↔ 12in (30cm)

A refreshing change from the tall, spiked hybrids, this delightful species produces slender, branching stems of long-spurred, cornflower blue flowers during summer.

Geranium 'Brookside'
CRANESBILL
☼ ◐ 5-9   ↕ 20in (50cm) ↔ 30in (75cm)

The finely cut leaves of this vigorous
plant form a low mound that is covered in
summer with showers of saucer-shaped,
deep clear blue, white-eyed flowers.

Milium effusum 'Aureum'
GOLDEN WOOD MILLET
☼ 6-9   ↕ ↔ 24in (60cm)

Handsome clumps of yellow leaves, fading
to yellow-green in summer, are topped by
golden seedheads in early summer. It will
seed freely and also comes true from seed.

Dianthus 'Mrs. Sinkins'
OLD-FASHIONED PINK
☼ 3-9   ↕ 16in (40cm) ↔ 12in (30cm)

Richly fragrant of cloves, this old cottage-
garden perennial bears abundant double,
fringed, white blossoms in early summer,
above evergreen, grayish green leaves.

Helleborus × *ericsmithii*
HELLEBORE
☼ ◐ 6-9   ↕ 12in (30cm) ↔ 18in (45cm)

This bold hybrid has attractively marbled,
bristle-toothed leaves. It bears large, white
or pink-tinted, saucer-shaped flowers in
winter. Formerly known as *H.* × *nigristern*.

Pulsatilla vulgaris 'Alba'
PASQUE FLOWER
☼ 5-7   ↕ ↔ 8in (20cm)

A beautiful white form of a popular plant
forming a clump of finely divided, silky-
hairy leaves. Silky seedheads follow the
white spring flowers.

Francoa sonchifolia
BRIDAL WREATH
☼ ◐ 7-9   ↕ 36in (90cm) ↔ 24in (60cm)

Clumps of evergreen, deeply lobed, hairy
leaves are topped in summer by slender
pink flower sprays, marked in darker pink.
The flowers are excellent for cutting.

Lathyrus vernus
SPRING VETCHLING
☼ ◐ 5-9   ↕ 12in (30cm) ↔ 18in (45cm)

The loose racemes of pealike, purplish
flowers in spring make this an appealing
perennial. Easily grown, its glossy green,
deeply divided leaves are attractive too.

Viola cornuta
Alba Group
HORNED VIOLET
☼ ◐ 6-9   ↕ 6in (15cm) ↔ 12in (30cm)

This violet's long flowering time makes it
invaluable. A continuous supply of white
flowers tops the mat of toothy, evergreen
leaves during spring and summer.

Medium to Tall Perennials for Alkaline Soil

NOT ALL THE PERENNIALS recommended for alkaline soil actually prefer it to acid or neutral soils, but they have proved themselves amenable to these conditions and can be relied upon to do well. The following selection, around 3–10ft (1–3m) high, are some of the most impressive tall perennials suitable for alkaline conditions.

Euphorbia sikkimensis
SPURGE
☼ ◐ 6-8   ↕ 4ft (1.2m) ↔ 24in (60cm)

The upright stems of this tough, reliable spurge produce narrow, willowlike leaves and yellow flower clusters during summer. Bright pink new shoots appear in spring.

Cortaderia selloana 'Pumila'
PAMPAS GRASS
☼ 8-11   ↕ 5ft (1.5m) ↔ 4ft (1.2m)

This compact cultivar of pampas grass is still large enough to make an impressive specimen for a lawn. Crowded plumes of silvery cream spikelets appear in summer.

Artemisia lactiflora
WHITE MUGWORT
☼ 4-9   ↕ 5ft (1.5m) ↔ 36in (90cm)

This vigorous plant has dense clumps of erect stems clothed in divided, jaggedly cut leaves. Branched heads of tiny cream flowers open in summer and autumn.

Campanula lactiflora 'Loddon Anna'
GREAT BELLFLOWER
☼ ◐ 3-7   ↕ 5ft (1.5m) ↔ 36in (90cm)

A reliable, easily grown bellflower with conical, branched heads of soft lilac-pink blooms that top the clumps of downy, leafy stems in summer. May need support.

Eremurus robustus
DESERT CANDLE, FOXTAIL LILY
☼ 5-8   ↕ 10ft (3m) ↔ 4ft (1.2m)

In summer, magnificent, long-stemmed racemes of star-shaped, pale pink flowers rise above clumps of strap-shaped, blue-green leaves, which wither after flowering.

Lavatera × clementii 'Barnsley'
TREE MALLOW
☼ 6-9   ↕ ↔ 6ft (2m)

A succession of white, red-eyed flowers over a long period from spring to autumn and grayish green leaves make this one of the most satisfying of all large perennials.

Thalictrum flavum subsp. *glaucum*
YELLOW MEADOW RUE
☼ 4-8   ↕ 5ft (1.5m) ↔ 24in (60cm)

The deeply divided, blue-green, bloomy
leaves of this stately plant are invaluable
for contrast with greens or purples. Fluffy
yellow flowerheads appear in summer.

Oenothera stricta 'Sulphurea'
EVENING PRIMROSE
☼ 5-8   ↕ 36in (90cm) ↔ 6in (15cm)

Over many weeks in summer, this choice
perennial bears big, fragrant, pale yellow
flowers, which open in the evening on
slender, upright stems. It will self-seed.

Veronicastrum virginicum f. *album*
VERONICASTRUM
☼ ☼ 3-8   ↕ 6ft (2m) ↔ 24in (60cm)

Distinctive clumps of slender, stiff, erect
stems clothed in whorls of narrow, toothy
leaves carry dense, tapering spikes of
white flowers from summer to autumn.

Phytolacca polyandra
POKEWEED
☼ ☼ 6-9   ↕ 4ft (1.2m) ↔ 24in (60cm)

In autumn, the fleshy stems of this bold
perennial turn crimson, the leaves yellow,
and dense, erect spikes of striking but
poisonous, glistening black fruits appear.

Polygonatum verticillatum
WHORLED SOLOMON'S SEAL
☼ ☼ 4-9   ↕ 36in (90cm) ↔ 12in (30cm)

In early summer, loose clusters of tubular,
greenish white flowers, followed by red
berries, hang from the slender stems. The
leaves are long, slender, and willowlike.

**OTHER MEDIUM TO TALL
PERENNIALS FOR ALKALINE SOIL**

Anchusa azurea
Anemone × *hybrida* and cvs.
Buddleja davidii
Campanula latifolia, see p.56
Centaurea macrocephala, see p.24
Echinops ritro, see p.76
Kniphofia spp. and cvs.
Perovskia atriplicifolia
Sidalcea malviflora
Verbascum spp. and cvs.

Perennials for Dry Soil in Sun

WITH THE INCREASING occurrence of water shortages in many regions, perennials that will tolerate dry, sunny conditions are at a premium. Fortunately, a number of plants can survive without rain or watering for long periods. Many of these have long taproots, but densely hairy or waxy leaf-surfaces also help to reduce water loss.

OTHER HERBACEOUS PERENNIALS FOR DRY SOIL IN SUN

Acanthus hirsutus, see p.26
Achillea spp. and cvs.
Cynara cardunculus, see p.136
Echinops ritro 'Veitch's Blue', see p.79
Linum narbonense, see p.27
Pennisetum setaceum
Sedum spp. and cvs.
Sempervivum spp. and cvs.
Stachys byzantina, see p.51
Verbascum chaixii

Anthericum liliago
ST. BERNARD'S LILY
☼ 5-9 ↕ 36in (90cm) ↔ 24in (60cm)

This lovely perennial bears tall, elegant racemes of small, lilylike white flowers above its clumps of grassy, grayish green leaves from late spring to early summer.

Asteriscus maritimus
ASTERISCUS
☼ 6-9 ↕ 10in (25cm) ↔ 36in (90cm)

A woody-based perennial forming a dense carpet or mound studded with daisylike yellow flowerheads during late spring and summer. Its small leaves are roughly-hairy.

Artemisia alba
ARTEMISIA
☼ 5-9 ↕ 18in (45cm) ↔ 12in (30cm)

The slender, upright, gray-white stems of this dense, woody-based plant are clothed in aromatic, finely cut, silvery gray foliage, creating an attractive, feathery effect.

Catananche caerulea 'Bicolor'
CUPID'S DART
☼ 4-9 ↕ 20in (50cm) ↔ 12in (30cm)

This short-lived perennial forms clumps of grassy leaves. White, purple-centered flowers are produced from midsummer to autumn, each on a single, erect stem.

Crepis incana
PINK DANDELION
☼ 5-7 ↕ ↔ 12in (30cm)

During late summer, beautiful, dandelion-like, clear pink flowerheads are borne on slender-branched stems above rosettes of densely hairy, grayish green leaves.

Eryngium x *tripartitum*
ERYNGIUM
☼ **5-8**　　‡ 24in (60cm) ↔ 20in (50cm)

Stiff, wiry, many-branched stems produce long-stalked leaves and small heads of violet-blue flowers with prickly gray-blue bracts from summer to autumn.

Phlomis purpurea
PHLOMIS
☼ **7-9**　　‡ ↔ 24in (60cm)

This woody-based perennial or subshrub has woolly shoots and softly-hairy, gray-green leaves. Clusters of pink to purple, two-lipped flowers are borne in summer.

Yucca gloriosa
SPANISH DAGGER
☼ **7-10**　　‡ 6ft (2m) ↔ 3ft (1m)

Evergreen, sword-shaped, spine-toothed, blue-green leaves crown the short, stout, woody stem. In late summer or autumn, a huge panicle of ivory flowers emerges.

> **OTHER NATIVE PERENNIALS FOR DRY SOIL IN SUN**
>
> *Asclepias tuberosa*, see p.110
> *Baptisia australis*, see p,98
> *Echinacea purpurea*
> *Gaillardia aristata*
> *Gaura lindheimeri*, see p.114
> *Liatris punctata*
> *Opuntia humifusa*
> *Rudbeckia maxima*
> *Silphium laciniatum*
> *Yucca filamentosa*

Papaver orientale 'Perry's White'
ORIENTAL POPPY
☼ **2-7**　　‡ ↔ 36in (90cm)

Deep-rooted clumps of stout, bristly-hairy stems carry large, solitary white flowers with maroon-purple centers in summer over the deeply cut, roughly-hairy leaves.

Tropaeolum polyphyllum
TROPAEOLUM
☼ **7-9**　　‡ 4in (10cm) ↔ 3ft (1m)

Long-spurred, orange- or deep yellow blooms crowd the shoots of this vigorous, trailing plant in summer. Its lobed leaves and fleshy stems are bloomy, blue-green.

Zauschneria californica subsp. *cana* 'Dublin'
☼ **8-10**　　‡ 12in (30cm) ↔ 20in (50cm)

An excellent native perennial for southern gardens with a bushy habit and narrow, downy, gray-green foliage. Tubular red flowers open in late summer and autumn.

37

Bulbs for Dry Soil in Sun

A GREAT NUMBER OF garden bulbs, including many tulip species, foxtail lilies, and ornamental onions, come from the Mediterranean region and similar warm, sunny, dry-summer areas of the world, including western and central Asia. All of the following bulbs prefer the warmth and brightness of full sun and a site in well-drained soil. The marginally hardy bulbs featured below can be grown outdoors in containers and overwintered in a frost-free place.

Arum creticum
ARUM
☼ **8-11** ↕ 20in (50cm) ↔ 12in (30cm)

This showy perennial develops clumps of broadly arrow-shaped, rich green leaves in autumn. A white or yellow spathe with a projecting tongue emerges during spring.

Amaryllis belladonna 'Hathor'
BELLADONNA LILY
☼ **8-11** ↕ 24in (60cm) ↔ 4in (10cm)

In time, this plant forms patches of erect, fleshy stems topped by umbels of pure white, trumpet-shaped flowers in autumn. Strap-shaped leaves emerge during spring.

Anomatheca laxa
ANOMATHECA
☼ **8-11** ↕ 8in (20cm) ↔ 3in (8cm)

A charming little plant producing small, irislike leaves and sprays of red flowers in summer. Free-seeding when established, especially in light or sandy soils.

Anemone x *fulgens*
SCARLET WINDFLOWER
☼ **6-9** ↕ 10in (25cm) ↔ 6in (15cm)

Brilliant red flowers with darker eyes are borne in spring above deeply cut, bright green leaves. This tuberous perennial is excellent for planting in groups or drifts.

OTHER BULBS FOR DRY SOIL IN SUN

Allium cristophii, see p.32
Allium schubertii
Anemone pavonina, see p.58
Calochortus spp.
Colchicum autumnale
Crocus spp. and cvs.
Eucomis zambesiaca
Ipheion uniflorum
Iris bucharica
Ixiolirion tataricum
Lilium candidum
Lilium regale, see p.116
Lilium x *testaceum*
Oxalis adenophylla, see p.61
Pancratium illyricum
Sternbergia lutea
Triteleia laxa
Tulipa kaufmanniana

Dracunculus vulgaris
DRAGON ARUM
☼ **5-11** ↕ 36in (90cm) ↔ 24in (60cm)

The darkly mottled stems of this strange and striking perennial produce deeply divided, long-stalked leaves and velvety, deep maroon-purple flowers in summer.

Hermodactylus tuberosus
WIDOW IRIS
☼ **5-8** ↕12in (30cm) ↔4in (10cm)

This curious iris relative has a somber charm. In spring, green or greenish yellow flowers join the narrow, grassy leaves. The outer petals have blackish brown tips.

Tulipa clusiana
LADY TULIP
☼ **4-8** ↕12in (30cm) ↔4in (10cm)

A beautiful tulip producing narrow grayish leaves and white spring flowers with dark crimson eyes. Crimson backs to the outer petals give blooms a striped appearance.

Eremurus stenophyllus
FOXTAIL LILY
☼ **5-9** ↕3ft (1m) ↔24in (60cm)

This perennial has a divided, fleshy crown that produces a cluster of strap-shaped grayish leaves. Tall spires of starry yellow, pink, or white flowers appear in summer.

Scilla peruviana
CUBAN LILY
☼ **8-11** ↕12in (30cm) ↔6in (15cm)

The clumps of broad, strap-shaped, fleshy green leaves are topped during late spring by striking, large, conical heads of small, star-shaped, blue to blue-violet flowers.

Gladiolus communis subsp. *byzantinus*
HARDY GLADIOLUS
☼ **6-10** ↕3ft (1m) ↔10in (25cm)

Reliable and also easy to grow, this robust perennial forms clumps of narrow, sword-like leaves that sport bold spikes of vivid magenta flowers during summer.

Triteleia hyacinthina
WILD HYACINTH
☼ **6-11** ↕28in (70cm) ↔2in (5cm)

Like a white-flowered ornamental onion without the smell, this very attractive and reliable bulb bears umbels of star-shaped flowers on slender stems in early summer.

Tulipa tarda
TULIP
☼ **4-8** ↕6in (15cm) ↔4in (10cm)

This reliable and lovely small tulip species produces a rosette of glossy, narrow leaves and bears star-shaped yellow flowers with white tips above the foliage during spring.

Perennials for Dry Soil in Shade

DRY, SHADY SITES are one of the most difficult garden situations to deal with successfully. One easy solution is to plant these areas with the perennials listed here. Avoid planting in the soil under shallow-rooted trees, like maples; simply mulch these sites instead. Under deep-rooted trees, such as oaks, dig "planting pockets" between the roots.

OTHER PERENNIAL GROUND-COVERS FOR DRY SOIL IN SHADE

Convallaria majalis
Epimedium spp. and cvs.
Helleborus hybridus, see p.90
Lamium maculatum 'Beacon Silver', see p.91
Liriope muscari, see p.71
Ophiopogon japonicus
Pachysandra terminalis
Vinca major
Waldsteinia ternata

Buglossoides purpurocaerulea
PURPLE GROMWELL
☼ ☼ 6-8   ↕ 24in (60cm) ↔ 36in (90cm)

This handsome, low-growing perennial sends out long shoots that root at the tips. From late spring to summer, erect stems bear purple flowers that turn deep blue.

Epimedium perralderianum
EPIMEDIUM
☼ ☼ 5-8   ↕ 12in (30cm) ↔ 24in (60cm)

A semievergreen or evergreen perennial with bright yellow spring flowers. The glossy, dark green leaves, each with three leaflets, are bronze-red when young.

OTHER PERENNIALS FOR DRY SOIL IN SHADE

Cyclamen hederifolium, see p.102
Dicentra eximia
Dryopteris filix-mas
Geranium macrorrhizum, see p.89
Helleborus foetidus
Hyacinthoides non-scripta
Polygonatum odoratum
Polypodium vulgare
Polystichum acrostichoides
Pulmonaria saccharata

Claytonia sibirica
SIBERIAN PURSLANE
☼ ☼ 5-9   ↕ 8in (20cm) ↔ 6in (15cm)

Short-lived but free-seeding, this plant develops tufts of fleshy green leaves and freely bears loose heads of small pink or white flowers from late spring to summer.

Euphorbia amygdaloides var. *robbiae*
WOOD SPURGE
☼ ☼ 6-8   ↕ 30in (75cm) ↔ 24in (60cm)

A vigorous, creeping perennial with erect stems bearing leathery, dark green leaves. Crowded racemes of greenish yellow flowers appear in spring and early summer.

Geranium phaeum 'Album'
HARDY GERANIUM
☼ ☼ 5-8　↕ 32in (80cm) ↔ 18in (45cm)

A lovely geranium bearing showers of
pendent white, yellow-beaked flowers
above semievergreen clumps of shallowly
lobed, soft green leaves in mid spring.

Iris foetidissima var. *citrina*
STINKING IRIS
☼ ☼ 6-9　↕ 30in (75cm) ↔ 24in (60cm)

A useful and adaptable evergreen with
clumps of strong-smelling, strap-shaped,
shiny leaves and yellow summer flowers.
It bears pods of orange seeds in autumn.

Lamium galeobdolon
'Hermann's Pride'
☼ ☼ 4-9　↕ 24in (60cm) ↔ 4ft (1.2m)

A tough groundcover producing spreading
mounds of handsome, silver-marbled
leaves. It produces clusters of two-lipped
yellow flowers in the leaf axils in summer.

Saxifraga stolonifera
STRAWBERRY GERANIUM
☼ ☼ 3-9　↕ 12in (30cm) ↔ 8in (20cm)

Red runners, forming new plantlets at
their tips, grow from the rosettes of long-
stalked, pale-veined leaves. Erect stems
bear tiny white flowers in summer.

Symphytum 'Hidcote Pink'
COMFREY
☼ ☼ 5-9　↕ ↔ 18in (45cm)

An excellent, creeping perennial groundcover forming low patches of erect, leafy
stems. Pendent clusters of funnel-shaped,
pink and white flowers emerge in spring.

Tolmiea menziesii
PIGGY-BACK PLANT
☼ ☼ 6-9　↕ ↔ 24in (60cm)

A creeping perennial with loose clumps of
hairy leaves that bear new plants at their
bases. In spring and summer, airy panicles
of tiny, brownish green flowers appear.

Trachystemon orientalis
TRACHYSTEMON
☼ ☼ 5-9　↕ 12in (30cm) ↔ indefinite

A creeping plant eventually forming large,
dense patches of long-stalked, roughly-
hairy leaves. The bristly stems bear blue
flowers with "beaks" of stamens in spring.

Perennials for Moist Soil in Shade

SOME OF THE MOST EXQUISITE perennials are native to deciduous woodlands where they receive protection from the harsh summer sun. These woodland plants are obvious choices for a wildflower garden, but are also ideal for beds on the shady side of the house, under trees, and other cool sites where moisture is guaranteed during the growing season.

Actaea rubra
RED BANEBERRY
☼ 4-8 ↕ 18in (45cm) ↔ 12in (30cm)

A poisonous plant but well worth growing for its clump of deeply divided leaves and dense, terminal clusters of shining red berries borne in late summer and autumn.

Convallaria majalis var. *rosea*
LILY-OF-THE-VALLEY
☼ ☼ 4-9 ↕ 8in (20cm) ↔ 12in (30cm)

This very pretty variant of a much-loved perennial forms a carpet of paired leaves. It bears loose racemes of nodding, mauve-pink, bell-shaped flowers during spring.

Dactylorhiza foliosa
MADERIAN ORCHID
☼ 7-8 ↕ 24in (60cm) ↔ 6in (15cm)

In time, this terrestrial orchid develops a clump of stout, lush, leafy stems. These sport bold, dense spikes of bright purple flowers in late spring or early summer.

Anemonopsis macrophylla
FALSE ANEMONE
☼ 5-8 PH ↕ 30in (75cm) ↔ 18in (45cm)

This handsome woodland plant produces a clump of ferny leaves and bears delicate sprays of cup-shaped, nodding, waxy, lilac and violet flowers during late summer.

Corydalis flexuosa
BLUE FALSE BLEEDING HEART
☼ 5-8 ↕ ↔ 12in (30cm)

During spring and early summer, showers of blue flowers are carried above the ferny, blue-green foliage. The leaves emerge in autumn and die down in summer.

Deinanthe caerulea
DEINANTHE
☼ 5-9 ↕ ↔ 12in (30cm)

The attractive, crinkly green leaves of this choice, creeping perennial will eventually form a clump. Loose panicles of nodding, fleshy blue flowers open during summer.

Trillium cernuum
NODDING TRILLIUM
☼ ☼ 5-9 PH ↕ 20in (50cm) ↔ 12in (30cm)

Impressive when planted in groups, this charming perennial has clumps of broad, wavy-edged leaves and small, nodding, white to pale pink or red flowers in spring.

Glaucidium palmatum
GLAUCIDIUM
☼ ☼ 6-9 ↕ ↔ 18in (45cm)

This lovely woodlander produces a clump of large, attractively lobed and toothed leaves. In late spring and early summer, it bears poppylike mauve or lilac flowers.

Trillium sessile
TOADSHADE
☼ ☼ 5-9 PH ↕ ↔ 12in (30cm)

This native woodland plant has broad, often beautifully marbled, three-parted leaves. The stemless, erect, red or maroon flowers are produced during spring.

Hacquetia epipactis
HACQUETIA
☼ 5-7 ↕ 6in (15cm) ↔ 12in (30cm)

One of the earliest woodlanders to appear in spring, bearing curious, collared, yellow-green flowerheads followed by emerald-green leaves. Both useful and reliable.

Sanguinaria canadensis 'Plena'
DOUBLE BLOODROOT
☼ ☼ 3-9 ↕ 6in (15cm) ↔ 12in (30cm)

Lovely white blooms open in early spring as leaves appear. The lobed, gray-green leaves are loosely rolled around the stem upon emergence. Dies down by summer.

Uvularia grandiflora
GREAT MERRYBELLS
☼ ☼ 3-9 ↕ 30in (75cm) ↔ 12in (30cm)

This favorite native woodland plant forms a clump of erect, slender, leafy shoots with nodding tips. During spring, the shoots carry pendent, bell-shaped yellow flowers.

Bulbs for Moist Soil in Shade

MANY OF THE MOST POPULAR and best-loved bulbs thrive in the cool, moist soils and partial shade of deciduous woodlands. There they receive sun in early spring and shade in summer when trees are leafy. Most are easy to grow and will thrive in a shady site with minimum care. Some will form large colonies where space and conditions permit.

Cardiocrinum giganteum var. *yunnanense*
GIANT LILY
☼ 7-10   ↕ 8ft (2.5m) ↔ 18in (45cm)

Tall, erect, dark stems have heart-shaped leaves and bear long heads of pendent, fragrant, creamy white flowers in summer. The parent plant dies after flowering.

Allium moly
LILY LEEK
☼ ☼ 4-8   ↕ 10in (25cm) ↔ 4in (10cm)

This bulb soon forms substantial clumps of broad, strap-shaped gray leaves. It bears umbels of star-shaped yellow flowers in early summer. Also ideal for a site in sun.

Arisaema triphyllum
JACK-IN-THE-PULPIT
☼ ☼ 3-9   ↕ 24in (60cm) ↔ 6in (15cm)

A woodland plant with long-stalked green leaves divided into threes and hooded green, sometimes dark-striped, flowers in spring. Red berries are borne in autumn.

Arisaema sikokianum
JACK-IN-THE-PULPIT
☼ 5-8   ↕ 16in (40cm) ↔ 6in (15cm)

A striking perennial with often beautifully marked leaves divided into threes. The dark flowers borne in spring have striped spathes and a contrasting white spadix.

Brimeura amethystina
BRIMEURA
☼ ☼ 5-8   ↕ 8in (20cm) ↔ 3in (8cm)

Resembling a small, slender hyacinth, this bulb bears one-sided racemes of tubular, bright blue flowers in late spring or early summer. Will spread freely in a good site.

Erythronium 'Pagoda'
TROUT LILY
☼ 5-8   ↕ 14in (35cm) ↔ 4in (10cm)

In spring, dark stems bear pendent yellow flowers with upswept petals above lush rosettes of mottled green leaves. This is a vigorous bulb that self-seeds when happy.

OTHER BULBS AND TUBEROUS
PLANTS FOR MOIST SOIL IN SHADE

Anemone blanda
Anemone nemorosa
Arisaema ringens
Arisarum proboscideum
Arum italicum 'Marmoratum', see p.141
Begonia grandis
Camassia leichtlinii subsp. *leichtlinii*,
    see p.58
Corydalis flexuosa 'China Blue', see p.71
Corydalis solida
Cyclamen coum
Eranthis hyemalis, see p.104
Galanthus ikariae
Hyacinthoides hispanica, see p.59
Hyacinthoides non-scripta
Ipheion uniflorum
Leucojum vernum
Ornithogalum nutans

Erythronium revolutum
TROUT LILY

☀ 5-8   ↕ 12in (30cm) ↔ 4in (10cm)

Rosettes of beautifully mottled leaves are
topped by elegant pink, yellow-centered
flowers in spring. This is one of the best
trout lilies for cultivation. May seed freely.

Leucojum aestivum 'Gravetye Giant'
SUMMER SNOWFLAKE

☀ ☀ 4-9   ↕ 36in (90cm) ↔ 4in (10cm)

This robust and easily grown bulb quickly
forms erect clumps of green leaves. The
pretty umbels of nodding white, green-
tipped flowers are produced in late spring.

Galanthus elwesii
GIANT SNOWDROP

☀ 3-9   ↕ 9in (22cm) ↔ 3in (8cm)

Easy to grow and reliable, this variable
bulb usually has narrow, gray-green leaves
and white flowers in late winter with inner
segments marked green at both ends.

Galanthus plicatus
SNOWDROP

☀ 3-9   ↕ 8in (20cm) ↔ 3in (8cm)

This vigorous snowdrop has narrow, dark
green leaves with folded-under edges. Its
late winter flowers have green-tipped
inner segments. In time it forms colonies.

Narcissus pseudonarcissus
DAFFODIL

☀ ☀ 5-8   ↕ 14in (35cm) ↔ 4in (10cm)

A charming, spring-flowering woodland
species bearing pale yellow flowers with
deep yellow trumpets that are flared at
the mouths. Excellent for naturalizing.

Perennials for Warm, Sheltered Sites

FOR THOSE FORTUNATE ENOUGH to garden in mild regions, there are many exciting, often exotic-looking, perennials that are easy to grow. Some of these will also survive in colder areas if they are given a warm, sheltered site. Gardeners in northern regions can enjoy these perennials by growing them in containers and moving them indoors for winter.

Erythrina crista-galli
COCKSPUR CORAL-TREE
☼ **9-11**　　　　　‡6ft (2m) ↔ 4ft (1.2m)

Herbaceous or woody-based in cold areas, this plant forms a shrub or small tree in frost-free regions. In late summer, strong, thorny stems bear red pea-shaped flowers.

Begonia sutherlandii
BEGONIA
☼ **8-10**　　　　　‡ ↔ 18in (45cm)

In summer, drooping clusters of orange, red-stalked flowers are borne freely above the low mounds of fleshy red stems and pointed, toothed leaves.

Bletilla striata 'Albostriata'
BLETILLA
☼ ☼ **6-9**　　　　　‡ ↔ 24in (60cm)

A beautiful terrestrial orchid eventually forming patches of strongly veined, white-margined, bamboolike leaves. Magenta flowers open in spring and early summer.

Crinum x *powellii*
CRINUM
☼ **7-10**　　　‡4ft (1.2m) ↔ 24in (60cm)

In late summer and autumn, stout, fleshy stems carry loose umbels of fragrant, lily-like pink blooms above the bold clumps of long, arching, strap-shaped leaves.

Eucomis comosa
PINEAPPLE FLOWER
☼ **8-10**　　‡24in (60cm) ↔ 12in (30cm)

Dense racemes of greenish white flowers with leafy tufts at the top rise on fleshy stems in late summer above bold rosettes of strap-shaped, shiny green leaves.

Fascicularia bicolor
FASCICULARIA
☼ **10-11**   ↕ ↔ 24in (60cm)

A striking relative of the pineapple with narrow, spine-toothed, evergreen leaves in bold rosettes. In summer, the inner leaves turn red when powdery blue flowers open.

OTHER PERENNIALS FOR WARM, SHELTERED SITES

Convolvulus sabatius, see p.64
Cortaderia selloana 'Pumila', see p.34
Eucomis bicolor, see p.70
Euphorbia characias
Fuschia magellanica
Gladiolus communis
Kniphofia spp. and cvs.
Lavandula stoechas, see p.79
Lavatera cachemiriana
Lespedeza juncea

Hedychium gardnerianum
KAHILI GINGER
☼ **8-11**   ↕ 6ft (2m) ↔ 3ft (1m)

This vigorous perennial forms a clump of erect, leafy stems. These bear large heads of fragrant, pale yellow flowers with long, red stamens during late summer.

Lobelia laxiflora var. *angustifolia*
LOBELIA
☼ **8-10**   ↕ 24in (60cm) ↔ 3ft (1m)

The erect, woody-based stems of this fast-spreading lobelia bear narrow, willowlike leaves and lax, tubular, red-and-yellow flowers in late spring and early summer.

Melianthus major
HONEY BUSH
☼ **9-11**   ↕ 6ft (2m) ↔ 3ft (1m)

A spectacular foliage plant with a clump of large, lush, sharply toothed and deeply divided, bluish gray leaves. Spikes of brownish red flowers emerge in summer.

Ostrowskia magnifica
GIANT BELLFLOWER
☼ **8-11**   ↕ 4–5ft (1.2–1.5m) ↔ 18in (45cm)

The erect stems bear whorls of blue-green leaves and masses of big, outward-facing, white to pale blue bellflowers in summer. Requires a warm, well-drained site.

Puya alpestris
PUYA
☼ **10-11**   ↕ 5ft (1.5m) ↔ 4½ft (1.4m)

After several years, the evergreen rosette of narrow, spine-toothed leaves produces an erect stem topped by a striking, dense spike of waxy, blue-green summer blooms.

OTHER TENDER PERENNIALS FOR WARM, SHELTERED SITES

Abutilon × *hybridum*
Agapanthus spp. and cvs.
Beschorneria yuccoides
Brugmansia spp. and cvs.
Helichrysum petiolare
Geranium maderense
Nierembergia 'Mount Blanc'
Pelargonium spp. and cvs.
Plectranthus argentatus
Watsonia beatricis

Senecio pulcher
SENECIO
☼ **8-11**   ↕ 24in (60cm) ↔ 20in (50cm)

The basal clumps of semievergreen, long, scalloped leaves are woolly when young. Attractive, large, carmine-purple, yellow-centered flowerheads emerge in summer.

SPECIFIC USES

WHETHER YOU WANT plants to fill a difficult site, to provide cut flowers or foliage, or to attract bees and butterflies to your garden, perennials have the variety and versatility to answer your needs. A good choice of plants is usually available to solve even the most specific garden problems.

Houttuynia cordata 'Chameleon' for water gardens

△ LOVED BY BUTTERFLIES *The flowers of perennials like* Inula hookeri *attract bees, butterflies, and other welcome insects.*

The plants in this section have been selected to help you find the right perennials for specific garden features (such as rock or water gardens), conditions (including dry, exposed, or waterlogged sites), and garden problems (like pollution or pests). When choosing plants for a particular garden feature or site, the most suitable are usually those that grow in similar situations in the wild. Water and bog gardens, for instance, require plants that are naturally tolerant of wet soils. At the other extreme, rock gardens are suited to perennials that thrive, if not depend, on sharp drainage. Similarly, coastal gardens in exposed sites require robust plants like sea holly (*Eryngium*) that are adapted to the harsh conditions. Toughness and persistence are also needed by perennials naturalized in grass, along hedges, or other wild areas, where the ability to withstand competition is vital for survival.

PROBLEM SOLVERS
Perennials offer more than just a wide range of options for specific sites; they can also help us address some of the problems that often plague our gardens. Pests, such as slugs, deer, and rabbits, may be thwarted by a surprising number of unpalatable plants. The garden can also be stocked with many low-allergen (mostly insect-pollinated) perennials, useful for gardeners who suffer from allergies that are aggravated or induced by plants.

DECORATIVE VALUE
The wide-ranging ornamental uses of perennials are not always fully appreciated. Many are excellent for containers on shady or sunny patios or paved areas, or for specimen plants. Others produce foliage and flowers good for cutting, extending their garden value into the home. During quiet periods in the garden, dried seedheads can provide the material for arrangements.

△ NATURAL EFFECT *Many perennials, especially bulbs like these fritillarias, are excellent for naturalizing in grassy sites.*

◁ ROCK GARDEN *Perennials from well-drained, rocky habitats in the wild will thrive in a rock garden or wall.*

▷ WATERSIDE *A pond planted with lush marginal and aquatic perennials makes a bold feature and a good wildlife habitat.*

Perennial Groundcovers for Sun

IN ADDITION TO BEING ORNAMENTAL, groundcovers perform one of the most useful and valuable jobs in the garden by clothing bare ground. The best perennials for this purpose are usually fast-growing. Given a sunny site, the following will repay you by providing a superb display of foliage and flowers. For faster results, plant these perennials in groups.

Helianthemum lunulatum
ROCKROSE, SUNROSE
☼ 6-9   ↕ 6in (15cm) ↔ 12in (30cm)

A carpeting, woody-based perennial with grayish green, evergreen leaves. Clusters of yellow flowers with orange-yellow stamens open in late spring and summer.

OTHER EVERGREEN PERENNIAL GROUNDCOVERS FOR SUN

Arabis caucasica
Aubrieta deltoidea
Dianthus spp. and cvs.
Erigeron glaucus
Festuca glauca 'Elijah Blue'
Iberis sempervirens
Liriope muscari, see p.71
Potentilla neumanniana
Sasa veitchii, see p.141
Sedum kamtschaticum

Ceratostigma plumbaginoides
PLUMBAGO LEADWORT
☼ 5-9   ↕ 12in (30cm) ↔ 18in (45cm)

This vigorous perennial develops a dense patch of bright green leaves that turn red-orange in autumn. The clusters of rich blue flowers emerge during late summer.

Diascia 'Salmon Supreme'
DIASCIA
☼ 7-9   ↕ 6in (15cm) ↔ 20in (50cm)

This free-flowering plant bears abundant slender racemes of pale flowers during summer and autumn above mats of small, heart-shaped, semievergreen leaves.

Geranium 'Ann Folkard'
CRANESBILL
☼ ☼ 5-8   ↕ 24in (60cm) ↔ 5ft (1.5m)

Few cranesbills will flower or scramble as freely as this one, which has black-eyed magenta flowers in summer and autumn above deeply lobed, yellow-green leaves.

Persicaria vacciniifolia
PERSICARIA
☼ ☼ 4-8   ↕ 6in (15cm) ↔ 12in (30cm)

This fast-creeping plant forms a carpet of small, glossy green leaves that color richly in autumn. Erect, deep pink flower spikes open from late summer into autumn.

OTHER HERBACEOUS PERENNIAL
GROUNDCOVERS FOR SUN

Antennaria dioica
Artemisia stelleriana
Campanula carpatica
Cerastium tomentosum, see p.136
Geranium sanguineum var. *striatum*
Oenothera tetragona
Potentilla aurea
Potentilla tridentata
Saponaria ocymoides
Thymus serpyllum

Rhodanthemum hosmariense
RHODANTHEMUM
☼ 8-10   ↕↔ 12in (30cm)

A low and spreading, woody-based plant
with dense, finely divided, silvery downy
leaves. The large daisy flowers are borne
freely from early spring to autumn.

Phyla nodiflora
CAPEWEED, MATGRASS
☼ 10-11   ↕ 2in (5cm) ↔ indefinite

Sometimes sold as *Lippia*, this perennial
soon forms carpets of slender stems and
small leaves. Long-stalked clusters of tiny
flowers are borne in summer and autumn.

Sedum spurium 'Schorbuser Blut'
STONECROP
☼ 3-8   ↕ 4in (10cm) ↔ 24in (60cm)

Popular as a vigorous carpeter, this stonecrop has glossy, evergreen leaves that are
purple-tinted when mature. Star-shaped,
deep pink flowers open in late summer.

Silene schafta
CAMPION
☼ ◐ 4-8   ↕ 10in (25cm) ↔ 12in (30cm)

Slender stems and semievergreen, bright
green leaves form a low mound, good for
edging. Long-tubed, red-pink flowers are
borne freely from summer to autumn.

Stachys byzantina
LAMB'S EARS
☼ 4-8   ↕ 15in (38cm) ↔ 24in (60cm)

A very effective groundcover producing
rosettes of white-woolly, semievergreen
leaves. White-woolly, pink-purple flower
spikes rise above the foliage in summer.

Perennial Groundcovers for Shade

SHADY AREAS CAN SUPPORT a wealth of plants as long as the soil remains sufficiently moist. Shade-loving perennials with creeping or otherwise spreading and low-growing habits are useful and attractive when used as groundcovers under shrubs or trees. Many are also evergreen, and will brighten shady spots with their year-round carpets of foliage.

Cyclamen repandum subsp. *peloponnesiacum*

☀ ☀ **7-9**   ↕ 4in (10cm) ↔ 6in (15cm)

A tuberous perennial that forms patches of heart-shaped, scalloped, silver-speckled leaves. Fragrant, pale pink flowers with darker pink mouths are borne in spring.

Duchesnea indica
MOCK STRAWBERRY

☀ ☀ ☀ **4-9**   ↕ 4in (10cm) ↔ 4ft (1.2m)

The dense, fast-growing carpet of semi-evergreen, strawberrylike leaves is dotted with yellow flowers in summer. The fruits resemble strawberries but are unpalatable.

Ajuga reptans 'Jungle Beauty'
BUGLEWEED

☀ ☀ ☀ **3-9**   ↕ 6in (15cm) ↔ 3ft (1m)

Grown here with *Lysimachia nummularia* 'Aurea', this semievergreen, far-creeping carpeter has shiny, bronze-green leaves and rich blue flower spikes in late spring.

OTHER EVERGREEN PERENNIAL GROUNDCOVERS FOR SHADE

Asarum europaeum, see p.120
Blechnum penna-marina
Euphorbia amygdaloides var. *robbiae*, see p.40
Helleborus orientalis
Heuchera americana and cvs.
Liriope spp. and cvs.
Mitchella repens
Pachysandra terminalis 'Variegata'
Saxifraga stolonifera, see p.41

Chrysogonum virginianum
GREEN-AND-GOLD, GOLDEN STAR

☀ ☀ ☀ **5-8**   ↕ 10in (25cm) ↔ 24in (60cm)

This fast-growing woodland plant forms dense carpets of small, semievergreen leaves. Bright and cheerful yellow flowers are produced during spring and summer.

Epimedium pinnatum subsp. *colchicum*
EPIMEDIUM

☀ ☀ ☀ **4-10**   ↕ ↔ 16in (40cm)

One of the most reliable epimediums, this forms clumps of slightly spiny-margined, semievergreen leaves topped in spring by loose spires of small yellow flowers.

Tiarella cordifolia
ALLEGHENY FOAMFLOWER
☼ ☀ 3-8   ↕ 10in (25cm) ↔ 12in (30cm)

A reliable old favorite especially pretty in late spring when foamy spires of white flowers rise above the foliage. The leaves are often tinted bronze-red in autumn.

Geranium macrorrhizum 'Czakor'
WILD CRANESBILL
☼ ☀ 3-8   ↕ 12in (30cm) ↔ 24in (60cm)

A first-rate carpeter with lobed, aromatic, semievergreen leaves that become purple-tinted in autumn. It bears profuse, small magenta flowers during early summer.

OTHER HERBACEOUS PERENNIAL GROUNDCOVERS FOR SHADE

Aegopodium podagraria 'Variegatum'
Asarum canadense
Convallaria majalis 'Fortin's Giant'
Cyclamen hederifolium, see p.102
Galium odoratum
Hosta spp. and cvs.
Maianthemum bifolium
Pachysandra procumbens
Pulmonaria angustifolia
Vancouveria hexandra

Lamium galeobdolon 'Florentinum'
YELLOW ARCHANGEL
☼ ☀ 4-9   ↕ 24in (60cm) ↔ 6ft (2m)

One of the most striking, but invasive, groundcovers. It produces semievergreen, silver-zoned leaves and spires of two-lipped yellow flowers in summer. Keep it confined.

Gymnocarpium dryopteris
OAK FERN
☼ ☀ 2-5 PH   ↕ 8in (20cm) ↔ 12in (30cm)

Delicate looking but hardy, this little fern forms a low patch of triangular, prettily divided fronds on slender, wiry stems. It requires cool, moist conditions to thrive.

Meehania urticifolia
MEEHAN'S MINT
☼ ☀ 6-9   ↕ 12in (30cm) ↔ 6ft (2m)

In time, this vigorous perennial forms clumps of heart-shaped leaves. One-sided spikes of two-lipped, deep violet flowers are borne in late spring and early summer.

Vinca minor 'Gertrude Jekyll'
COMMON PERIWINKLE
☼ ☀ 4-9   ↕ 6in (15cm) ↔ indefinite

Technically a creeping shrub, but a good groundcover for use with perennials. The white flowers in spring and early summer contrast with the dark green leaves.

Perennial Herbs for Borders

PERENNIALS VALUED FOR their culinary uses or medicinal attributes are frequently cultivated in separate herb gardens or combined with vegetables in kitchen gardens. This certainly makes it much more convenient for picking or harvesting, but does not always make the best use of these plants' varied growth habits, or their often ornamental foliage and flowers. In fact, herbs can be grown just as easily, and more effectively, with other perennials in beds and borders.

Achillea ptarmica 'Boule de Neige'
SNEEZEWORT
☼ 2-9   ↕ 24in (60cm) ↔ 18in (45cm)

The clumps of erect stems and narrow, toothed, dark green leaves are smothered during summer with small, double white flowerheads. All parts have medicinal uses.

Allium schoenoprasum 'Forescate'
CHIVES
☼ 3-9   ↕ 24in (60cm) ↔ 5in (12.5cm)

An attractive, vigorous form of a kitchen-garden favorite with clumps of hollow, edible leaves. The dense heads of bright purplish pink flowers open in summer.

Aristolochia clematitis
BIRTHWORT
☼ ☼ 5-9   ↕ 36in (90cm) ↔ 24in (60cm)

Curious, slender-tubed yellow flowers emerge from the axils of the heart-shaped leaves in summer. The creeping rootstock forms spreading clumps of erect stems.

Agastache foeniculum
ANISE HYSSOP
☼ 6-9   ↕ 36in (90cm) ↔ 18in (45cm)

Spikes of blue flowers with violet bracts top the four-angled stems during summer. The softly-downy, anise-scented leaves are used as a fragrant tea and in potpourri.

Althaea officinalis
MARSH MALLOW
☼ ☼ 3-9   ↕ 6ft (2m) ↔ 5ft (1.5m)

Loose clumps of erect, downy stems bear velvety, grayish, three-lobed leaves and pink late-summer flowers. Its root sugars were once used to make marshmallows.

OTHER PERENNIAL HERBS FOR BORDERS

Armoracia rusticana 'Variegata', see p.132
Cichorium intybus 'Roseum', see p.82
Foeniculum vulgare 'Purpureum', see p.125
Lavandula angustifolia
Mentha suaveolens 'Variegata'
Monarda fistulosa
Origanum vulgare 'Gold Tip'
Pulmonaria officinalis
Ruta graveolens
Salvia officinalis 'Icterina', see p.127
Saponaria officinalis 'Rosea Plena'
Scutellaria baicalensis
Symphytum peregrinum 'Rubrum'
Tanacetum balsamita subsp. balsamitoides
Tanacetum parthenium

Melissa officinalis 'Aurea'
LEMON BALM
☼ 4-9   ↕ 24in (60cm) ↔ 18in (45cm)

The hairy green, yellow-splashed leaves
of this vigorous, bushy plant are lemon-
scented when bruised. Tiny flowers, loved
by bees, are produced during summer.

Myrrhis odorata
SWEET CICELY
☼ ☼ 3-7   ↕ 36in (90cm) ↔ 5ft (1.5m)

All parts of this plant are anise-scented.
It produces bold clumps of hollow stems,
ferny leaves, and flattened heads of white
summer flowers followed by brown fruits.

Rumex scutatus 'Silver Shield'
FRENCH SORREL
☼ 4-8   ↕ 20in (50cm) ↔ 12in (30cm)

This small, woody-based perennial has
prostrate and upright stems with broadly
arrow-shaped, silver-green-topped leaves.
Spires of green flowers open in summer.

Salvia officinalis 'Tricolor'
COMMON SAGE
☼ 5-8   ↕ 32in (80cm) ↔ 3ft (1m)

A woody-based semievergreen plant or
bushy subshrub bearing aromatic, woolly,
gray-green leaves with cream, purple, and
pink zones. It has blue flowers in summer.

Levisticum officinale
LOVAGE
☼ 5-8   ↕ 6ft (2m) ↔ 3ft (1m)

Much-divided, dark green leaves clothe
the erect clumps of smooth, hollow stems.
During summer, the stems are topped by
umbels of pretty, greenish yellow flowers.

Origanum vulgare 'Aureum'
GOLDEN WILD MARJORAM
☼ 5-9   ↕ 18in (45cm) ↔ 12in (30cm)

Spreading clumps of four-angled stems
are crowded with rounded, aromatic
golden leaves. Plants bear dense clusters
of pink flowers from summer to autumn.

Perennials for Wild Margins and along Hedges

MANY OF THE LOVELIEST WILDFLOWERS are frequently found thriving beside roads or at the bases of hedges. These bold perennials, which can tolerate competition from grasses, shrubs, and other plants, will make fine additions to gardens in the right site. Use them along uncultivated garden edges or to add a colorful display to a hedge base.

Heliopsis helianthoides var. *scabra* 'Sommersonne'
☀ 3-9 ↕ 36in (90cm) ↔ 24in (60cm)

The bold clumps of leafy, branched stems carry large, single to semidouble, golden yellow daisy flowers with brown-yellow centers during late summer and autumn.

Anemone x *hybrida* 'Königin Charlotte'
JAPANESE ANEMONE
☀ ☀ 5-8 ↕ 5ft (1.5m) ↔ indefinite

A vigorous perennial forming colonies of branched stems with handsome, downy, gray-green leaves. Big, semidouble pink flowers open in late summer and autumn.

Carex pendula
DROOPING SEDGE
☀ ☀ 5-9 ↕ 4ft (1.2m) ↔ 5ft (1.5m)

Arching, three-cornered stems and dark green leaves form large clumps topped in late spring and summer by long, pendent green flower spikes. Prefers moist shade.

Lathyrus latifolius
PERENNIAL PEA
☀ 5-9 ↕ ↔ 6ft (2m)

This vigorous, herbaceous climbing plant produces long-stalked racemes of pink or purple, pea-shaped flowers from summer to autumn on scrambling, winged stems.

Campanula latifolia
GREAT BELLFLOWER
☀ ☀ 3-7 ↕ 5ft (1.5m) ↔ 24in (60cm)

In summer, the stout clumps of erect leafy stems produce large, bell-shaped, pale to deep violet or white flowers from the axils of the uppermost leaves.

Helianthus x *multiflorus*
PERENNIAL SUNFLOWER
☀ 4-8 ↕ 6ft (2m) ↔ 36in (90cm)

Dark green leaves clothe the tall clumps of branching stems, which produce yellow, dark-centered daisy flowers during late summer and autumn. Prefers a moist site.

OTHER LOW-GROWING PERENNIALS FOR WILD AREAS

Convallaria majalis
Epimedium spp. and cvs.
Euphorbia amygdaloides var. *robbiae*, see p.40
Geranium macrorrhizum, see p.89
Iris foetidissima var. *citrina*, see p.41
Narcissus spp. and cvs.
Oenothera speciosa 'Rosea', see p.27
Vinca major
Vinca major 'Variegata', see p.133

Lysimachia punctata
LOOSESTRIFE

☼ ☼ [4-8]   ↕ 3ft (1m) ↔ 24in (60cm)

A reliable, robust perennial with clumps of leafy, erect stems. In summer, the leaf axils are crowded with cup-shaped yellow flowers. Too invasive for beds or borders.

OTHER MEDIUM TO TALL PERENNIALS FOR WILD AREAS

Aster novae-angliae
Baptisia spp. and cvs.
Campanula rapunculoides
Campanula trachelium
Coreopsis tripteris
Dryopteris filix-mas
Echinacea purpurea
Hemerocallis spp. and cvs.
Leucanthemum x *superbum*
Myrrhis odorata, see p.55

Saponaria officinalis 'Rubra Plena'
SOAPWORT

☼ [2-8]   ↕ ↔ 36in (90cm)

The creeping rootstock of this reliable and easily grown plant forms patches of leafy stems, crowned in summer with fragrant, double, rose-pink flower clusters.

Rumex sanguineus
BLOODY DOCK

☼ [6-8]   ↕ 36in (90cm) ↔ 12in (30cm)

This tap-rooted dock is valued mainly for its rosetted, red- or purple-veined leaves. In autumn, erect stems first bear clusters of tiny green flowers, then brown fruits.

Symphytum orientale
WHITE COMFREY

☼ ☼ ☼ [4-7]   ↕ 28in (70cm) ↔ 18in (45cm)

Nodding clusters of funnel-shaped white flowers open on the erect, little-branched stems of this hairy plant in late spring and early summer. It tolerates dry shade.

Vinca major subsp. *hirsuta*
GREATER PERIWINKLE

☼ ☼ [7-9]   ↕ 18in (45cm) ↔ indefinite

This vigorous, scrambling or creeping, evergreen perennial or subshrub produces narrow-lobed violet flowers as new shoots emerge in spring, and into summer.

Bulbs for Naturalizing

THERE ARE FEW SIGHTS more inspiring than a meadow or woodland floor studded with wildflowers, creating a carpet of color as far as the eye can see. In the garden, bulbs especially lend themselves to such displays, and there is a multitude of species and cultivars available for this purpose. For a natural effect, plant bulbs in scattered groups, arranged in a free-form pattern. When planting, allow enough space between the bulbs for spreading clumps or self-seeding.

Anemone pavonina
ANEMONE
☀ 8-10 ↕10in (25cm) ↔6in (15cm)

This feathery-leaved anemone produces glowing red flowers with a white ring and dark eye in spring. Plant in sunny, well-drained sites in short grass or in a border.

Crocus vernus 'Jeanne d'Arc'
DUTCH CROCUS
☀ 3-9 ↕5in (12cm) ↔2in (5cm)

Attractive and reliable, this large-flowered crocus forms clumps of grassy leaves in borders or short grass. White flowers with orange stigmas are produced in spring.

Erythronium dens-canis
DOGTOOTH VIOLET
☀ ☼ 2-7 ↕6in (15cm) ↔4in (10cm)

The exquisite, pinkish purple flowers are poised above rosettes of fleshy, beautifully mottled leaves in spring. Excellent for use in short grass and in woodlands.

Fritillaria meleagris
CHECKERED LILY
☀ ☼ 4-8 ↕12in (30cm) ↔3in (8cm)

A charming bulb with narrow leaves and nodding, bell-shaped, checked flowers on slender stems in spring. It thrives in moist grass or planted beneath shrubs.

OTHER BULBS OR TUBERS FOR NATURALIZING IN SHADE

Anemone blanda
Arisarum proboscideum
Arum italicum 'Marmoratum', see p.141
Colchicum speciosum
Crocus kotschyanus
Crocus tommasinianus, see p.104
Cyclamen coum
Cyclamen hederifolium, see p.102
Eranthis hyemalis, see p.104
Erythronium oregonum
Galanthus elwesii, see p.45
Hyacinthoides non-scripta
Leucojum aestivum
Lilium pyrenaicum
Narcissus spp. and cvs.
Ornithogalum nutans
Puschkinia scilloides, see p.63
Scilla spp. and cvs.

Camassia leichtlinii
CAMASSIA
☀ ☼ 3-8 ↕4½ft (1.3m) ↔4in (10cm)

Long spires of star-shaped, blue or cream flowers rise in summer above the slender leaves. This is an easily grown bulb ideal for moist meadows or grassy sites.

Galanthus nivalis
COMMON SNOWDROP
☀ 3-9 ↕↔4in (10cm)

Drifts of this familiar woodland snowdrop are a spectacular sight during early spring. It naturalizes readily by seed and division, and will tolerate sun if the soil is moist.

Nectaroscordum siculum
NECTAROSCORDUM
☼ ☼ **6-10**   ↕ 4ft (1.2m) ↔ 4in (10cm)

In summer, tall, strong stems carry loose
umbels of drooping, bell-shaped green
flowers flushed with purple. The straw-
colored seed capsules are also ornamental.

Hyacinthoides hispanica
SPANISH BLUEBELL
☼ ☼ **4-9**   ↕ 16in (40cm) ↔ 4in (10cm)

This robust bulb forms large patches of
shiny leaves with nodding blue, white, or
pink flowers on strong stems in spring. It
may be too vigorous for a small garden.

Tulipa sylvestris
TULIP
☼ **4-10**   ↕ 18in (45cm) ↔ 4in (10cm)

This tulip is easily established in grass-
land or in open woodland, where it forms
patches. Star-shaped yellow flowers open
in spring, but are not always freely borne.

Lilium martagon
MARTAGON LILY
☼ ☼ **3-8**   ↕ 6ft (2m) ↔ 10in (25cm)

An old and reliable lily for naturalizing in
grass or in a border. The tall stems bear
whorled leaves and panicles of nodding
flowers in a variety of colors in summer.

Narcissus bulbocodium
HOOP-PETTICOAT DAFFODIL
☼ **6-9**   ↕ 6in (15cm) ↔ 3in (8cm)

A real charmer with narrow, threadlike
leaves and striking, funnel-shaped, pale
yellow flowers in spring. It will thrive and
seed itself on a moist, grassy, sloping site.

**OTHER BULBS OR TUBERS FOR
NATURALIZING IN SUN**

Allium flavum
Allium unifolium
Anemone canadensis
Camassia quamash
Chionodoxa gigantea
Chionodoxa luciliae, see p.96
Colchicum autumnale
Crocus spp. and cvs.
Gladiolus communis subsp. *byzantinus*,
  see p.39
Lilium canadense
Lilium lancifolium
Lilium superbum
Muscari spp. and cvs.
Narcissus spp. and cvs.
Sternbergia lutea
Tulipa fosteriana
Tulipa kaufmanniana

Perennials for Rock Gardens

SOME OF THE LOVELIEST and most satisfying flowering perennials are those suited to the well-drained conditions of a rock garden. Many of these plants have a carpeting habit and are excellent groundcovers. Others form small clumps or mounds and associate well with miniature bulbs, such as crocuses, scillas, and glory-of-the-snow (*Chionodoxa*).

Dianthus 'Pike's Pink'
ALPINE PINK

☼ 5-8 ↕ 6in (15cm) ↔ 8in (20cm)

The low, evergreen cushion of narrow, blue-gray leaves is topped in summer by double pale pink flowers with darker pink centers. Flowers have a lovely clove scent.

OTHER PERENNIALS FOR ROCK GARDENS

Anthemis biebersteiniana
Armeria cespitosa
Armeria maritima
Eriogonum umbellatum
Euphorbia myrsinites
Hypericum kamtschaticum
Iris pumila
Linaria alpina
Phlox subulata and cvs.
Potentilla nitida

Aethionema 'Warley Rose'
PERSIAN STONECRESS

☼ 4-9 ↕ ↔ 8in (20cm)

A handsome, shrubby perennial forming an evergreen mound of slender stems with narrow, blue-gray leaves. Its pink flowers are borne in late spring and early summer.

Anthyllis montana
ALPS ANTHYLLIS

☼ 6-9 ↕ 12in (30cm) ↔ 24in (60cm)

Small, rounded, cloverlike heads of pink to purple, white-tipped flowers cover the dense carpet of deeply divided, silky, gray-green leaves from spring to summer.

Anemone sylvestris
SNOWDROP ANEMONE

☼ ☼ 3-8 ↕ ↔ 12in (30cm)

This low-grower forms patches of deeply cut, ferny leaves. Pure white flowers with gold stamens are borne in spring and early summer followed by silky seedheads.

Campanula carpatica 'Chewton Joy'
CARPATHIAN BELLFLOWER

☼ ☼ 3-8 ↕ 12in (30cm) ↔ 20in (50cm)

Low, trailing stems clothed with toothed, heart-shaped leaves bear upturned, bell-shaped blue flowers with paler centers for several months during summer.

Diascia barberae 'Blackthorn Apricot'
DIASCIA

☼ 8-10 ↕ 10in (25cm) ↔ 20in (50cm)

This handsome diascia cultivar bears abundant, slender racemes of attractive apricot flowers in summer above the mat or carpet of trailing green stems.

OTHER PERENNIALS FOR
ROCK GARDENS

Aubrieta deltoidea
Helianthemum nummularium and cvs.
Houstonia caerulea
Lewisia cotyledon hybrids, see p.65
Lewisia rediviva
Lithodora diffusa 'Heavenly Blue'
Oxalis enneaphylla
Potentilla aurea
Saxifraga spp. and cvs.
Tanakaea radicans

Gentiana sino-ornata
AUTUMN GENTIAN
☼ ☀ [5-7] PH ↕ 3in (7cm) ↔ 12in (30cm)

This is one of the most striking autumn-
flowering gentians. It produces an overwintering mat of trailing, leafy stems and
upturned, deep blue trumpet flowers.

Gypsophila repens 'Rosa Schönheit'
CREEPING BABY'S-BREATH
☼ [3-8] ↕ 8in (20cm) ↔ 20in (50cm)

The semievergreen mat of slender, bluish
green stems and leaves is smothered for
many weeks during summer by tiny pink
flowers. Also known as 'Pink Beauty'.

Geranium cinereum 'Ballerina'
GRAYLEAF CRANESBILL
☼ ☀ [4-10] ↕ 6in (15cm) ↔ 12in (30cm)

A neat little perennial producing a loose
mound of small, gray-green leaves. Pale
purplish red flowers with dark veins and
eyes appear over a long period in summer.

Oxalis adenophylla
ALPINE OXALIS
☼ [7-11] ↕ 4in (10cm) ↔ 6in (15cm)

The tuft of deeply divided, grayish green
leaves is accompanied during spring by
funnel-shaped, purplish pink flowers with
pale centers and dark throats.

Roscoea cautleoides 'Kew Beauty'
ROSCOEA
☼ ☀ [7-9] ↕ 16in (40cm) ↔ 6in (15cm)

Appearing in late spring, this gorgeous
perennial produces a small clump of erect,
leafy stems that carry loose spikes of large,
pale yellow, orchidlike flowers.

61

Bulbs for Rock Gardens

ROCK GARDENS AND RAISED BEDS are excellent sites for growing the many miniature bulbs available. They are also ideal for larger bulbous plants that like well-drained, gritty soil and full sun. Most of the following are hardy and should be planted in groups or drifts for best effect. All will also thrive in containers, or in a scree garden – a well-drained bed with soil heavily amended with grit or fine gravel and mulched with additional gravel.

Eucomis autumnalis
PINEAPPLE LILY
☼ **8-10**   ↕12in (30cm) ↔8in (20cm)

Fleshy stems bear crowded, green-white flower spikes from late summer to autumn above bold clumps of broad, strap-shaped, wavy-edged leaves. Likes a sheltered site.

Allium insubricum
ORNAMENTAL ONION
☼ **4-9**   ↕12in (30cm) ↔ 2in (5cm)

Clusters of nodding, bell-shaped, red-purple or pale pink flowers are borne on upright stems in summer. The grasslike, grayish green leaves form a small clump.

Colchicum agrippinum
AUTUMN CROCUS
☼ **4-9**   ↕5in (12cm) ↔4in (10cm)

A vigorous and unusual plant producing its strap-shaped, glossy green leaves in spring. The deep purple-pink, heavily tessellated flowers appear in autumn.

Fritillaria pallidiflora
FRITILLARIA
☼ **5-8**   ↕16in (40cm) ↔3in (7.5cm)

During late spring and early summer, this handsome bulb bears nodding, creamy yellow bell-shaped flowers from the axils of long, narrow, bloomy, gray-green leaves.

Chionodoxa forbesii
GLORY-OF-THE-SNOW
☼ **3-9**   ↕8in (20cm) ↔4in (10cm)

A free-flowering, reliable bulb forming small tufts of narrow green leaves. In early spring, it produces loose clusters of lovely star-shaped blue flowers with white eyes.

Crocus cartwrightianus 'E.A. Bowles'
CROCUS
☼ **3-8**   ↕3in (7cm) ↔2in (5cm)

This popular, spring-flowering crocus produces slender green leaves and lemon-yellow flowers, each with a bronze-green base and purple feathering on the outside.

OTHER BULBS FOR ROCK GARDENS

Allium beesianum
Allium moly, see p.44
Colchicum autumnale
Fritillaria meleagris, see p.58
Iris bucharica
Iris magnifica
Ixiolirion tataricum
Narcissus biflorus
Tulipa kaufmanniana
Tulipa humilis Violacea Group

OTHER MINIATURE BULBS FOR ROCK GARDENS

Allium mairei
Allium oreophilum
Crocus biflorus
Crocus chrysanthus
Iris reticulata
Muscari comosum
Narcissus bulbocodium var. *conspicuus*
Narcissus triandrus
Ornithogalum collinum
Tulipa batalinii

Iris danfordiae
DANFORD IRIS
☼ 5-9   ↕ 4in (10cm) ↔ 2in (5cm)

One of the most beautiful early bulbs, this miniature iris produces slim, four-angled leaves and yellow flowers with greenish yellow markings in late winter and spring.

Scilla bifolia
SCILLA
☼ 3-8   ↕ 6in (15cm) ↔ 2in (5cm)

An easily grown bulb that increases very rapidly. It bears two narrow green leaves and loose sprays of star-shaped, blue to purple-blue flowers during early spring.

Narcissus minor
MINIATURE DAFFODIL
☼ 5-9   ↕ 5in (12.5cm) ↔ 3in (7.5cm)

This little daffodil forms tufts or patches of narrow, gray-green leaves. The inclined, small, trumpet-shaped yellow flowers are carried above the foliage in early spring.

Puschkinia scilloides
PUSCHKINIA
☼ 3-9   ↕ 6in (15cm) ↔ 3in (7.5cm)

Cheerful and reliable, this perennial soon forms a small clump of slender leaves accompanied in spring by clusters of very pale blue flowers with darker blue stripes.

Tulipa aucheriana
TULIP
☼ 4-7   ↕ 10in (25cm) ↔ 6in (15cm)

Starry pink flowers with yellow centers and stamens are borne singly or in twos or threes during spring. The narrow, bloomy green leaves are also attractive.

Perennials for Wall or Rock Crevices and Paving

Rock crevices are the favored habitat of a wide range of attractive perennials, many of which have carpeting or trailing stems or form small rosettes or mounds. In the garden, these plants, which require well-drained soil, can be grown in the cracks of a dry stone wall or between paving slabs, where they will get the good drainage they need.

SPECIFIC USES

Asarina procumbens
ASARINA

☼ ☼ **6-8**   ↕ 2in (5cm) ↔ 24in (60cm)

This semievergreen trailer has hairy stems and produces pale yellow, snapdragon-like flowers from the axils of its grayish green, kidney-shaped leaves during summer.

Aurinia saxatilis 'Dudley Nevill'
BASKET-OF-GOLD

☼ **3-7**   ↕ 8in (20cm) ↔ 12in (30cm)

A popular, clump-forming, woody-based plant with evergreen, gray-green leaves and clusters of tiny, soft yellow-buff flowers from late spring to early summer.

Convolvulus sabatius
CONVOLVULUS

☼ **7-9**   ↕ 6in (15cm) ↔ 24in (60cm)

The trailing, leafy stems of this carpeting, fast-growing perennial are studded with pale to deep lavender-blue flowers over many weeks during summer and autumn.

Aubrieta 'J.S. Baker'
AUBRETIA

☼ **4-8**   ↕ 2in (5cm) ↔ 24in (60cm)

Aubretias are among the most colorful and reliable evergreen perennials for walls or rock-work. This one is smothered with purple, white-eyed flowers during spring.

Campanula carpatica 'Jewel'
CARPATHIAN BELLFLOWER

☼ ☼ **3-8**   ↕ 4in (10cm) ↔ 18in (45cm)

The small, dense, heart-shaped leaves of this popular and attractive compact bell-flower are almost hidden by its upturned, bright purple-blue blooms in summer.

Erigeron karvinskianus
MEXICAN FLEABANE

☼ **5-7**   ↕ 12in (30cm) ↔ 3ft (1m)

In summer, a succession of little white daisies, which fade to pink then to purple, smother this charming perennial's loose clump of slender, branching, leafy stems.

HERBACEOUS PERENNIALS FOR WALLS OR PAVING

Aethionema iberideum
Anthemis biebersteiniana
Campanula 'Birch Hybrid'
Erinus alpinus
Eriogonum umbellatum
Erodium chrysanthum
Hypericum kamtschaticum
Mazus reptans
Saponaria ocymoides 'Rubra Compacta'
Viola tricolor

Gypsophila repens 'Dorothy Teacher'
CREEPING BABY'S-BREATH
☼ 3-8 ‡ 2in (5cm) ↔ 16in (40cm)

Slender, crowded stems carpet the ground with small, narrow, blue-green leaves. The mass of beautiful, tiny, pale pink flowers borne in summer darkens with age.

Helianthemum 'Wisley White'
ROCKROSE, SUNROSE
☼ 5-10 ‡ 10in (25cm) ↔ 18in (45cm)

This woody-based evergreen perennial bears gray-green leaves and creamy white, yellow-centered flowers over a long period from late spring into midsummer.

Saxifraga 'Southside Seedling'
SAXIFRAGE
☼ ☼ 4-6 ‡ 12in (30cm) ↔ 8in (20cm)

The bold, arching sprays of red-spotted white flowers appear during late spring and early summer above the basal rosette of evergreen leaves. Also good in a trough.

EVERGREEN AND SEMIEVERGREEN
PERENNIALS FOR WALLS OR PAVING

Antennaria dioica
Armeria maritima
Corydalis lutea, see p.88
Dianthus gratianopolitanus
Erigeron glaucus
Euphorbia myrsinites
Lithodora diffusa 'Heavenly Blue'
Phlox subulata
Sempervivum spp. and cvs.
Thymus pseudolanuginosus

Haberlea rhodopensis 'Virginalis'
HABERLEA
☼ ☼ 5-7 PH ‡ 6in (15cm) ↔ 10in (25cm)

Loose umbels of funnel-shaped white flowers top the dense, evergreen clump of hairy, coarse-toothed leaves in late spring and summer. Charming for a shady wall.

Lewisia cotyledon hybrids
LEWISIA
☼ ☼ 5-9 PH ‡ 10in (25cm) ↔ 12in (30cm)

From late spring to early summer, loose heads of attractive, magenta-pink, yellow, or orange flowers rise above the rosette of thick, wavy-margined, evergreen leaves.

Verbascum dumulosum
MULLEIN
☼ 6-10 ‡ 10in (25cm) ↔ 16in (40cm)

An evergreen, woody-based perennial that produces downy, gray-green stems and leaves. A succession of rich yellow flowers is borne during late spring and summer.

Perennials for Bog Gardens and Waterside Areas

A WEALTH OF ORNAMENTAL PERENNIALS are available for those fortunate enough to have water in their garden, even if it is only a wet, muddy depression. These plants rely on a constant supply of moisture for top performance. They include perennials that bear large or colorful flowers as well as those with bold or even variegated foliage.

Iris laevigata
RABBIT-EAR IRIS
☼ ◐ **5-9**   ↕ 32in (80cm) ↔ 8in (20cm)

A handsome iris from Japan with erect, gray-green leaves and single lavender-blue, purple, or white flowers produced in summer. It will grow in

---

OTHER FOLIAGE PERENNIALS FOR BOG & WATERSIDE GARDENS

Acorus calamus 'Variegatus'
Ajuga reptans 'Multicolor, see p.22
Carex elata 'Aurea', see p.134
Gunnera manicata
Hosta spp. and cvs.
Iris pseudacorus 'Variegata', see p.122
Lysimachia nummularia 'Aurea', see p.134
Matteuccia struthiopteris, see p.71
Petasites japonicus var. *giganteus*

Astilbe chinensis 'Purpurlanze'
ASTILBE
☼ ◐ **3-8**   ↕ 4ft (1.2m) ↔ 36in (90cm)

The English name 'Purple Lance' aptly describes the stiff, purple-pink flower panicles of this late-flowering astilbe. Its deeply divided leaves form bold clumps.

Filipendula palmata 'Rubra'
SIBERIAN MEADOWSWEET
☼ **3-8**   ↕ 4ft (1.2m) ↔ 24in (60cm)

Sometimes confused with *F. rubra*, this stately, clump-forming perennial produces boldly lobed or divided leaves and dense plumes of tiny, rose-red summer flowers.

Darmera peltata
UMBRELLA PLANT
☼ ◐ **5-7**   ↕ 3½ft (1.1m) ↔ 30in (75cm)

This handsome perennial has creeping rhizomes that form a large patch of long-stalked leaves, coloring richly in autumn. Pink flowerheads are produced in spring.

Hosta 'Zounds'
HOSTA
☼ ◐ **3-9**   ↕ 22in (55cm) ↔ 3ft (1m)

Striking and also relatively slug-proof, this hosta develops a bold clump of corrugated leaves. White flowers appear in summer and the yellow-green foliage ages to gold.

Lysichiton americanus
YELLOW SKUNK CABBAGE
☼ ◐ **4-8**   ↕ 3ft (1m) ↔ 4ft (1.2m)

A spectacular, easily recognized perennial that bears large yellow flowers in spring followed by huge paddle-shaped leaves. It will grow in moist soil or standing water.

Oenanthe javanica 'Flamingo'
WATER DROPWORT
☼ ☀ 9-11   ↕ 16in (40cm) ↔ 36in (90cm)

The deeply cut, green-and-white leaves of this creeping, fleshy-stemmed plant are flushed with pink in autumn. Small white flowerheads emerge in late summer.

Osmunda regalis
ROYAL FERN
☼ ☀ 3-9   ↕ 5ft (1.5m) ↔ 4ft (1.2m)

An impressive fern forming a bold clump of deeply divided fronds that often color richly in autumn before dying. It produces spikes of red-brown spores in summer.

Primula prolifera
CANDELABRA PRIMROSE
☼ ☀ 6-8   ↕ 24in (60cm) ↔ 6in (15cm)

In early summer, slender, erect stems with many whorls of yellow flowers rise above the basal rosettes of deep green leaves. It is excellent for planting in large drifts.

Rheum palmatum 'Bowles' Crimson'
ORNAMENTAL RHUBARB
☼ ☀ 5-9   ↕ 8ft (2.5m) ↔ 6ft (1.8m)

The big, jaggedly lobed leaves of this spectacular perennial emerge crimson and form a giant clump. Statuesque panicles of red flowers are produced in early summer.

Rodgersia pinnata
RODGERSIA
☼ ☀ 5-8   ↕ 4ft (1.2m) ↔ 30in (75cm)

Superb for both foliage and flowers, with deeply divided, veined leaves, tinted red in autumn and spring. The frothy white flower plumes appear during summer.

OTHER FLOWERING PERENNIALS FOR BOG & WATERSIDE GARDENS

Eupatorium purpureum 'Atropurpureum', see p.24
Euphorbia palustris
Filipendula purpurea, see p.128
Iris ensata and cvs.
Kirengeshoma palmata, see p.115
Ligularia spp. and cvs.
Lobelia cardinalis and cvs.
Lysichiton camtschatcensis
Primula japonica

Zantedeschia aethiopica 'Crowborough'
CALLA LILY
☼ ☀ 7-11   ↕ 36in (90cm) ↔ 24in (60cm)

This handsome perennial has large, arrow-shaped leaves and beautiful, long-stalked white flowers in summer. It will grow in either moist soil or shallow water.

THERE ARE VERY FEW RICHER, or more ornamental, wildlife habitats in the garden than in and around a well-planted pond. Marginal perennials, as well as those that prefer deeper water, will attract a range of birds, insects, and other wildlife. Large ponds offer the most scope for planting, but water can be introduced into even a small backyard. Planting advice below gives optimum water depth; plant heights are from water level.

Nymphaea 'Fire Crest'
WATER LILY
☼ 3-11   ↕ 3in (7.5cm) ↔ 4ft (1.2m)

This water lily's rounded, floating leaves are purple when young. Its fragrant pink flowers open in summer. Ideal for a small pond. Plant 6–18in (15–45cm) deep.

Aponogeton distachyos
WATER HAWTHORN
☼ ☀ 9-10   ↕ 3in (7.5cm) ↔ 4ft (1.2m)

In spring and autumn, curious spikes of vanilla-scented white flowers rise above the floating, semievergreen, oblong leaves. Plant in water 12–24in (30–60cm) deep.

Houttuynia cordata 'Chameleon'
HOUTTUYNIA
☼ ☀ 5-8   ↕ 12in (30cm) ↔ indefinite

Handsome leaves are variegated with pale yellow, green, and red. A fast-spreading marginal aquatic, ideal for water to 4in (10cm) deep. Quite invasive in moist soil.

Nymphaea 'Gladstoneana'
WATER LILY
☼ 3-11   ↕ 3in (7.5cm) ↔ 8ft (2.4m)

This popular, vigorous water lily has starry white summer flowers. The wavy-edged, rounded, floating leaves are bronze when young. Plant 45–90cm (18–36in) deep.

Butomus umbellatus
FLOWERING RUSH
☼ 5-7   ↕ 4ft (1.2m) ↔ 18in (45cm)

A robust plant for pond margins forming a patch of grassy, three-cornered leaves. Tall stems bear umbels of rose-pink flowers in summer. Plant 3–5in (7–13cm) deep.

Nymphaea 'Marliacea Chromatella'
WATER LILY
☼ 3-11   ↕ 3in (7.5cm) ↔ 5ft (1.5m)

Free-flowering and vigorous, this reliable plant has beautiful, canary yellow flowers in summer and bronze-splashed floating leaves. Plant 18–36in (45–90cm) deep.

Nymphoides peltata
FLOATING HEART
☼ 6-10   ↕ 3in (7.5cm) ↔ indefinite

Ideal for a large pond, this fast-spreader has rounded, floating leaves and golden, funnel-shaped, fringe-petaled flowers in summer. Plant 12–24in (30–60cm) deep.

Orontium aquaticum
GOLDEN CLUB
☀ 6-11   ↕ 12in (30cm) ↔ 24in (60cm)

A vigorous, native marginal aquatic with
oblong, blue-green leaves. Curved white
stalks bear yellow flower spikes in spring.
Plant 12–16in (30–40cm) deep.

Pontederia cordata
PICKEREL WEED
☀ 3-11   ↕ 30in (75cm) ↔ 24in (60cm)

From summer to early fall, spikes of blue
flowers poke through the clumps of erect,
glossy leaves. Plant this vigorous marginal
3–5in (7–13cm) deep, or in very moist soil.

Sagittaria latifolia
ARROWHEAD, DUCK POTATO
☀ 4-11   ↕ ↔ 36in (90cm)

A tuberous marginal aquatic with slender,
triangular stems and arrow-shaped, long-
stalked leaves. In summer, whorls of white
flowers open. Plant 3–5in (7–13cm) deep.

Stratiotes aloides
WATER SOLDIER
☀ 6-9   ↕ 6in (15cm) ↔ 8in (20cm)

Pineapple-like rosettes of saw-toothed
leaves rise to the water surface in summer
as the erect, three-petaled white flowers
are borne. Plant 12–36in (30–90cm) deep.

OTHER AQUATIC PERENNIALS

Acorus calamus
Acorus gramineus
Alisma plantago-aquatica
Calla palustris
Hydrocotyle verticillata
Iris laevigata, see p.66
Iris pseudacorus
Iris versicolor
Lysichiton spp.
Marsilea mutica
Menyanthes trifoliata
Myriophyllum verticillatum
Nelumbo nucifera
Nymphaea spp. and cvs.
Peltandra virginica
Sagittaria sagittifolia
Saururus cernuus
Thalia dealbata
Typha laxmannii

Typha minima
MINIATURE CATTAIL
☀ 3-11   ↕ 30in (75cm) ↔ 18in (45cm)

A rushlike marginal aquatic with slender
leaves. The stems of brown flowerheads
in summer turn into fluffy seedheads in
winter. Plant 2–4in (5–10cm) deep.

Perennials for Containers in Sun

ONE OF THE MAIN ADVANTAGES of growing perennials in containers is that they can easily be moved around the garden or patio, just like furniture inside the house. Containers also allow less hardy plants, like some of the sun-lovers below, to be grown outdoors for summer effect, then moved under cover for protection in winter.

Agapanthus 'Loch Hope'
AFRICAN LILY
☼ 7-10   ↕ 4ft (1.2m) ↔ 24in (60cm)

This bold, clump-forming perennial has slender, grayish green leaves. Deep blue trumpet-shaped flowers are borne in loose heads from late summer into autumn.

Argyranthemum 'Jamaica Primrose'
MARGUERITE
☼ 9-11   ↕ ↔ 3ft (1m)

A bushy evergreen, grown as an annual, with fernlike, gray-green leaves. Its long-stalked, primrose yellow daisies are borne over a long period from spring to autumn.

Canna 'Assaut'
INDIAN SHOT
☼ 7-11   ↕ 5ft (1.5m) ↔ 20in (50cm)

A striking tender perennial with purple-brown leaves and erect, leafy stems that bear heads of gladiolus-like, orange-scarlet flowers in summer and autumn.

Eucomis bicolor
PINEAPPLE FLOWER
☼ 8-11   ↕ 18in (45cm) ↔ 12in (30cm)

Dense, erect spikes of pale green, purple-edged flowers with pineapple-like crowns rise above the broad, strap-shaped, fleshy leaves during late summer.

Osteospermum 'Silver Sparkler'
OSTEOSPERMUM
☼ 9-11   ↕ 24in (60cm) ↔ 18in (45cm)

This vigorous, bushy plant has creamy white-margined leaves. Dark shoots bear long-stalked white daisy flowers, darker on the reverse, from summer into autumn.

TENDER PERENNIALS FOR CONTAINERS IN SUN

Agapanthus spp. and cvs.
Anisodontea × *hypomadarum*
Brugmansia × *candida*
Cortaderia selloana 'Pumila', see p.34
Cosmos atrosanguineus
Helichrysum petiolare
Heliotropium arborescens
Lavandula stoechas, see p.79
Lotus berthelotii
Pelargonium spp. and cvs.

Verbena 'Peaches and Cream'
VERBENA
☼ 8-10   ↕ 18in (45cm) ↔ 20in (50cm)

Domed heads of pale orange-pink flowers, which age to apricot then creamy yellow, cover the mound of toothed, dark green, roughly-hairy leaves from summer to fall.

Perennials for Containers in Shade

OTHER PERENNIALS FOR
CONTAINERS IN SHADE

Bergenia cordifolia 'Purpurea', see p.120
Dryopteris erythrosora, see p.148
Hakonechloa macra 'Aureola', see p.130
Helleborus argutifolius, see p.120
Heuchera spp. and cvs.
Hosta spp. and cvs.
Lilium longiflorum
Saxifraga stolonifera, see p.41
Tolmiea menziesii 'Taff's Gold',
    see p.131

S HADY PATIOS, BACKYARDS, and similar sunless situations, particularly when paved or close to the house, are not always the easiest places to accommodate plants unless they are grown in containers. Foliage perennials are especially useful in shade and are striking in containers either used as specimens or arranged in groups.

Aspidistra elatior
ASPIDISTRA, CAST-IRON PLANT
☼ ☼ 7-11   ↕ ↔ 24in (60cm)

A houseplant in northern zones, this easy-to-grow plant forms handsome, evergreen clumps of broad, strap-shaped, beautifully veined and glossy foliage.

Hosta 'Sum and Substance'
HOSTA
☼ ☼ 3-9   ↕ 30in (75cm) ↔ 36in (90cm)

One of the best hostas for brightening a shady corner with bold clumps of heart-shaped, yellow-green to yellow leaves. It bears pale lilac flowers in summer.

Matteucia struthiopteris
OSTRICH FERN
☼ 2-6   ↕ 4ft (1.2m) ↔ 20in (50cm)

The bold, elegant clumps of featherlike fronds surround a central cluster of dark brown, spore-bearing fronds from late summer onward. It needs moist, rich soil.

Corydalis flexuosa
'China Blue'
☼ 5-8   ↕ 10in (25cm) ↔ 8in (20cm)

Worth growing just for its attractive, ferny, mounds of bright green foliage, which die down in early summer as the racemes of tubular, striking blue flowers fade.

Liriope muscari
LILYTURF
☼ ☼ 6-8   ↕ 12in (30cm) ↔ 18in (45cm)

Dense tufts of evergreen, strap-shaped, dark green leaves are joined in autumn by stiff, crowded spikes of small violet-mauve flowers. An excellent groundcover too.

Rodgersia pinnata 'Superba'
RODGERSIA
☼ ☼ ☼ 5-8   ↕ 4ft (1.2m) ↔ 30in (75cm)

This vigorous clump-former has the dual attractions of bold, fingered, veiny leaves, bronze-purple when young, and conical, rich pink flower plumes in summer.

Climbing Perennials

OTHER CLIMBING PERENNIALS

Aconitum hemsleyanum
Apios americana
Aster carolinianus
Calystegia hederacea 'Flore Pleno'
Clematis × eriostemon
Codonopsis clematidea
Dioscorea batatus
Lathyrus latifolius, see p.56
Lathyrus rotundifolius
Passiflora caerulea
Tropaeolum tuberosum

SPECIFIC USES

Clematis × durandii
CLEMATIS
☼ 6-9　　　　↕ 6ft (2m) ↔ 3ft (1m)

Excellent as a groundcover or for training over a small bush, the slender stems bear summer flowers with creamy stamens and wide-spaced, indigo blue tepals.

Lathyrus grandiflorus
PERENNIAL PEA
☼ ☼ 6-9　　　　↕ ↔ 5ft (1.5m)

An old cottage-garden favorite providing dense cover with its rampant, slender stems. Long-stalked clusters of pink, red, and purple flowers are borne in summer.

Humulus lupulus 'Aureus'
GOLDEN HOP
☼ ☼ 6-9　　　　↕ ↔ 20ft (6m)

The twining stems of this fast-growing, vigorous climber blanket its support with golden yellow leaves. Bunches of greenish yellow seedheads are produced in autumn.

Lathyrus latifolius 'Albus'
PERENNIAL PEA
☼ ☼ 6-9　　　　↕ ↔ 6ft (2m)

Easy and reliable, this scrambler is ideal for a wall or hedge, or for covering a steep bank. In summer and autumn, it produces pea-shaped, pure white flowers.

Tropaeolum speciosum
VERMILION NASTURTIUM
☼ ☼ 7-9 PH　　　↕ ↔ 10ft (3m)

Spectacular when in flower in summer and autumn, the long-spurred, flame red blooms are followed by small blue fruits with red collars. It needs cool, moist soil.

Perennials with Leaves for Cutting

IN THE HOME, AS IN THE GARDEN, foliage is as important and decorative as flowers. Many perennials can provide a regular and reliable supply of attractive leaves for cutting whenever required. Useful for adding a green, gray, or golden foil to flower arrangements, cut leaves will also make an effective display by themselves.

Paeonia lactiflora 'Edulis Superba'
PEONY
☀ ☀ **2-8**   ↕ ↔ 36in (90cm)

Most herbaceous peonies have attractive, dark green foliage with contrasting red or purplish stalks. This one also has double pink flowers that are excellent for cutting.

OTHER PERENNIALS WITH LEAVES FOR CUTTING

Artemisia ludoviciana
Arum italicum 'Marmoratum', see p.141
Astilbe spp. and cvs.
Bergenia cordifolia 'Purpurea', see p.120
Hakonechloa macra 'Aureola', see p.130
Heuchera americana and cvs.
Lavandula angustifolia
Polystichum spp. and cvs.
Rodgersia pinnata, see p.67
Vinca minor 'Gertrude Jekyll', see p.53

Hosta 'Hadspen Blue'
HOSTA
☀ ☀ **3-9**   ↕ 10in (25cm) ↔ 24in (60cm)

Hostas are invaluable for cut foliage and those with blue-gray leaves are especially useful. This exceptional example provides handsome, bold, heart-shaped leaves.

Hosta 'Green Fountain'
HOSTA
☀ ☀ **3-9**   ↕ 18in (45cm) ↔ 3ft (1m)

This hosta's arching, lance-shaped leaves are glossy and wavy-margined. Ideal for picking, they form a bold clump. Arching stems bear pale mauve flowers in summer.

Iris pallida 'Argentea Variegata'
VARIEGATED SWEET IRIS
☀ ☀ **4-8**   ↕ 32in (80cm) ↔ 24in (60cm)

One of the most spectacular variegated perennials with sword-shaped, boldly margined leaves lasting long into autumn. Fragrant flowers appear in early summer.

Polygonatum odoratum 'Variegatum'
SOLOMON'S SEAL
☀ ☀ **5-8**   ↕ 24in (60cm) ↔ 12in (30cm)

This charming perennial forms a clump of arching reddish shoots with rich green, cream-margined leaves. In spring, it bears clusters of pendent, bell-shaped flowers.

Perennials for Cut Flowers

HAVING FLOWERS AVAILABLE for cutting is one of the most enjoyable bonuses of growing perennials in the garden. Cut selectively, preferably from well-established perennials, to ensure that the plants remain well-shaped, attractive, and vigorous. Although some perennials, like chrysanthemums, have long been popular among florists, many more produce flowers suitable for cutting. Once cut, stand the flowers in a deep container filled with luke warm water overnight before use.

Astilbe 'Professor van der Wielen'
ASTILBE
☼ ☼ **3-9**   ↕ 4ft (1.2m) ↔ 3ft (1m)

In summer, tall, arching plumes of tiny white flowers rise over mounds of much-divided leaves. One of the boldest and most satisfying astilbes for cool, moist soil.

Catananche caerulea
CUPID'S DART
☼ **4-9**   ↕ 32in (80cm) ↔ 12in (30cm)

The slender clusters of erect, wiry stems are tipped in summer with papery, pearly white buds, opening to blue flowers. The flowers are also attractive when dried.

Aquilegia McKana Group
COLUMBINE
☼ ☼ **3-9**   ↕ 30in (75cm) ↔ 24in (60cm)

This striking but short-lived perennial produces its attractive, large, long-spurred flowers in shades of blue, yellow, and red from late spring through to midsummer.

**OTHER SPRING AND EARLY
SUMMER FLOWERS FOR CUTTING**

Baptisia australis, see p.98
Convallaria majalis
Hyacinthoides hispanica, see p.59
Iris sibirica and cvs.
Leucojum aestivum 'Gravetye Giant', see p.45
Narcissus spp. and cvs.
Thermopsis caroliniana
Tulipa spp. and cvs.
Viola odorata and cvs.

Aster x *frikartii* 'Wunder von Stäfa'
FRIKART'S ASTER
☼ **5-8**   ↕ 28in (70cm) ↔ 16in (40cm)

A reliable perennial for a late summer or early autumn border with a multitude of long-lasting blue, orange-centered daisies. Its stems may flop if not given support.

Gaillardia x *grandiflora* 'Kobold'
BLANKET FLOWER
☼ **4-9**   ↕ 12in (30cm) ↔ 18in (45cm)

This showy but short-lived, bushy plant bears an abundance of large, brilliant red, yellow-tipped daisy flowers on leafy stems during summer and early autumn.

Iris unguicularis 'Mary Barnard'
WINTER IRIS
☼ 7-9   ↕ 12in (30cm) ↔ 24in (60cm)

The fragrant, solitary flowers of this sun-loving iris appear from late winter to early spring and are best picked when in bud. Its evergreen leaves form a grassy clump.

Leucanthemum × *superbum*
'Cobham Gold'
☼ ☼ 4-8   ↕ 24in (60cm) ↔ 8in (20cm)

This lovely selection is one of the Shasta daisies, which are all excellent for cutting. It forms robust clumps with double white flowers during summer and early autumn.

Liatris spicata 'Kobold'
SPIKE GAYFEATHER
☼ 3-9   ↕ 20in (50cm) ↔ 18in (45cm)

Erect, dense spikes of purple flowers open in late summer and autumn above clumps of slender leaves. A striking and reliable perennial for moist but well-drained soils.

Lilium African Queen Group
TRUMPET LILY
☼ ☼ 4-8   ↕ 5ft (1.5m) ↔ 12in (30cm)

Most lilies are good for cutting, and this is no exception. Its tall stems bear narrow, crowded leaves and terminal umbels of fragrant, nodding flowers in summer.

OTHER SUMMER FLOWERS FOR CUTTING

Achillea spp. and cvs.
Campanula persicifolia and cvs.
Crocosmia masoniorum, see p.110
Delphinium spp. and cvs.
Echinacea purpurea and cvs.
Galtonia candicans
Gypsophila paniculata 'Bristol Fairy', see p.99
Phlox paniculata and cvs.
Platycodon grandiflorus, see p.83

Paeonia officinalis
PEONY
☼ 3-8   ↕ ↔ 28in (70cm)

This bold, clump-forming peony produces handsome, divided, deep green foliage. It bears large, garnet red blooms with golden stamens in late spring or early summer.

Schizostylis coccinea 'Viscountess Byng'
KAFFIR LILY
☼ 7-9   ↕ 24in (60cm) ↔ 12in (30cm)

A very useful autumn-flowering perennial forming dense clumps of narrow, irislike leaves and bearing graceful, loose spikes of star-shaped, pale pink flowers.

Solidago 'Laurin'
GOLDENROD
☼ 4-9   ↕ 30in (75cm) ↔ 18in (45cm)

This compact version of an old-fashioned, cottage-garden stalwart carries branched, spreading heads of deep yellow flowers on clumps of leafy stems during late summer.

SPECIFIC USES

Perennials with Decorative Winter Seedheads

M OST GARDENERS NOW RECOGNIZE that taking too tidy an approach to the garden at the end of the growing season can rob them of some striking winter effects. Any perennial that ends the growing season with attractive seedheads can provide winter interest. Their architectural beauty will be further enhanced by a covering of snow or frost.

SPECIFIC USES

Miscanthus sinensis 'Kleine Fontäne'
MISCANTHUS
☼ 5-9 ↕ 5ft (1.5m) ↔ 4ft (1.2m)

In autumn, handsome clumps of tall, erect stems with narrow leaves bear fingerlike spikelets that turn fluffy and from buff to white in winter. Ideal for small gardens.

Achillea filipendulina
FERNLEAF YARROW
☼ 3-9 ↕ 4ft (1.2m) ↔ 18in (45cm)

The flattened seedheads of this clump-forming, stiff-stemmed perennial provide a ready platform for snow or frost. Its yellow flowers are produced in summer.

Echinops ritro
GLOBE THISTLE
☼ ☼ 3-8 ↕ 24in (60cm) ↔ 18in (45cm)

When covered in frost, the globular, spiky seedheads of this easy-to-grow perennial look like decorative baubles. The flowers emerge steely blue in early summer.

OTHER PERENNIALS WITH DECORATIVE WINTER SEEDHEADS

Actaea simplex
Astilbe spp. and cvs.
Baptisia australis, see p.98
Echinacea purpurea
Eupatorium purpureum
Pennisetum alopecuroides
Rudbeckia spp. and cvs.
Sedum spectabile, see p.108
Thermopsis caroliniana

Chasmanthium latifolium
NORTHERN SEA OATS
☼ ☼ 5-9 ↕ 3ft (1m) ↔ 24in (60cm)

This gorgeous grass forms loose clumps of leafy stems. These bear drooping clusters of flattened, green or pink-tinted spikelets that turn pale brown during winter.

Gypsophila paniculata
'Compacta Plena'
☼ 3-9 ↕ 12in (30cm) ↔ 24in (60cm)

This dwarf, double-flowered baby's-breath produces small, soft pink to white flowers in summer. Its dried branches are attractive in winter when covered by frost.

Monarda 'Beauty of Cobham'
BEE BALM
☼ ☼ 3-9 ↕ 36in (90cm) ↔ 18in (45cm)

Flowering during late summer and early autumn, this lovely plant bears crowded heads of pink flowers, with purple bracts that turn a warm brown in winter.

Nassella tenuissima
FEATHER GRASS
☼ 6-10   ↕ ↔ 24in (60cm)

A densely tufted grass with ever-moving, erect then arching stems. These bear long, feathery heads of green-white spikelets that turn a warm buff color during winter.

Phlomis tuberosa
PHLOMIS
☼ 5-8   ↕ 5ft (1.5m) ↔ 36in (90cm)

Two-lipped, rose-lilac flowers with reddish calyces are produced in summer. During winter, the striking clumps of tall, leafless stems carry dense brown seedheads.

Phlox paniculata 'Lichtspel'
BORDER PHLOX
☼ 4-8   ↕ 4ft (1.2m) ↔ 24in (60cm)

During summer, the clumps of erect, leafy stems carry panicles of lilac-rose flowers. The stems and remaining flowerheads fade to a warm pale brown during winter.

Phormium tenax Purpureum Group
NEW ZEALAND FLAX
☼ ◐ 9-10   ↕ 6–8ft (2–2.8m) ↔ 6ft (2m)

All the phormiums have decorative seed capsules in winter, but this group is more reliable than most. The high-branching stems lift the capsules like trophies.

Veronicastrum virginicum
CULVER'S ROOT
☼ ◐ 3-9   ↕ 6ft (2m) ↔ 18in (45cm)

Tapered spikes of blue-purple flowers top dense clumps of erect stems with whorled leaves in summer and autumn. In winter, the spikes lengthen and turn brown.

Perennials Attractive to Bees, Butterflies, and Other Insects

BUTTERFLIES ARE ALWAYS WELCOME garden visitors, but many other less decorative insects have more important roles to play. These include bees, which are essential garden pollinators, and also hoverflies, whose larvae feed on aphids and other similar insects, acting as a natural method of pest control. They will all be attracted by the following perennials.

OTHER PERENNIALS ATTRACTIVE TO BEES AND BUTTERFLIES
Achillea spp. and cvs.
Asclepias tuberosa, see p.110
Aster novae-angliae and cvs.
Centranthus ruber, see p.92
Coreopsis lanceolata
Echinacea purpurea
Linaria purpurea 'Canon Went'
Mentha spp. and cvs.
Monarda didyma
Nepeta spp. and cvs.

Allium hollandicum 'Purple Sensation'
ORNAMENTAL ONION
☼ 3-8 ↕ 36in (90cm) ↔ 4in (10cm)

All the alliums are attractive to insects, but this one is particularly impressive. The tall stems carry spangled globes of starry, deep violet flowers during summer.

Leuzea centauroides
LEUZEA
☼ 3-8 ↕ 4ft (1.2m) ↔ 24in (60cm)

This bold clump-former has handsome, silver-gray foliage. During summer, erect, branching stems carry striking, rose-pink flowerheads with scaly, silvery bracts.

Calamintha nepeta 'White Cloud'
CALAMINT
☼ ☼ 5-9 ↕ 18in (45cm) ↔ 30in (75cm)

Bees especially love this small-flowered perennial. Throughout summer, the low mound of crowded, aromatic leaves is peppered with tiny, pure white blooms.

Cephalaria gigantea
GIANT SCABIOUS
☼ ☼ 3-8 ↕ 8ft (2.5m) ↔ 36in (90cm)

A special favorite with bees, this large perennial forms clumps of deeply lobed leaves and bears primrose yellow flower-heads on tall, branched stems in summer.

Doronicum pardalianches
LEOPARD'S BANE
☼ 4-8 ↕ 36in (90cm) ↔ 4ft (1.2m)

In time, this creeping perennial will form a substantial patch of heart-shaped, softly-hairy leaves. Yellow daisies are borne over a long period in spring and summer.

Salvia pratensis Haematodes Group
MEADOW SAGE
☼ ☼ 3-9   ↕ 36in (90cm) ↔ 12in (30cm)

Short-lived but free-seeding, this lovely sage produces large, branching heads of blue-violet flowers during summer above rosettes of large, aromatic green leaves.

Echinops ritro 'Veitch's Blue'
GLOBE THISTLE
☼ ☼ 3-8   ↕ 4ft (1.2m) ↔ 30in (75cm)

During summer, the spherical, spiky blue flowerheads make this a favorite with both children and bees. Its spine-toothed, deep-cut leaves are white downy beneath.

Lavandula stoechas
FRENCH LAVENDER
☼ 7-9   ↕↔ 24in (60cm)

Bushy, with a dense, compact habit, this aromatic evergreen has narrow, gray-green leaves. Long-stalked spikes of purple flowers appear in late spring and summer.

Sedum 'Herbstfreude'
SHOWY STONECROP
☼ 3-9   ↕↔ 24in (60cm)

Butterflies and bees cover the deep pink autumn flowers, which mature to copper-red. The fleshy leaves are grayish green. Commonly known as *S.* 'Autumn Joy'.

Inula hookeri
INULA
☼ 4-8   ↕↔ 36in (90cm)

In summer and autumn, the bold clumps of downy, leafy stems bear golden daisy flowers with threadlike petals from woolly buds. A striking plant, popular with bees.

Melittis melissophyllum
BASTARD BALM
☼ ☼ 6-9   ↕↔ 12in (30cm)

This softly-downy plant has four-angled stems and honey-scented foliage. Loved by bees, the purple-lipped, white to pink flowers open in spring and early summer.

Solidago 'Goldenmosa'
GOLDENROD
☼ 3-9   ↕ 3ft (1m) ↔ 24in (60cm)

A compact, bushy perennial with upright, leafy stems bearing conical heads of bright yellow flowers from late summer to fall. It is excellent for smaller gardens.

Perennials Tolerant of Air Pollution

CAR EXHAUST AND OTHER AIR POLLUTANTS can have a detrimental effect on all plants, and prolonged exposure may ultimately kill them. Fortunately, such cases are the exception rather than the rule. The following perennials can generally be relied upon to tolerate all but the most extreme conditions along roadsides, driveways, or industrial areas.

SPECIFIC USES

Leucanthemum × superbum 'T.E. Killin'
SHASTA DAISY
☼ 4-8   ↕ ↔ 24in (60cm)

The large, double white flowerheads of this reliable, summer-blooming Shasta daisy have yellow anemone centres. They are excellent for cutting.

Geranium pratense 'Plenum Caeruleum'
☼ ☼ 3-8   ↕ 36in (90cm) ↔ 24in (60cm)

All forms of this popular hardy geranium are reliable. This strong-growing selection produces attractive, small, loosely double, lavender-blue flowers during summer.

Achillea ptarmica The Pearl Group
SNEEZEWORT
☼ 2-9   ↕ 30in (75cm) ↔ 24in (60cm)

This tough favorite develops clumps of aromatic, narrow, toothy leaves. The dense heads of buttonlike white flowers are produced in summer. It reseeds freely.

Lupinus 'My Castle'
LUPINE
☼ 3-6   ↕ 36in (90cm) ↔ 30in (75cm)

Spikes of pealike, rose-pink flowers top bold clumps of erect stems and finger-like leaves in summer. Lupines do not thrive in areas with hot, humid summers.

Aster novae-angliae 'Andenken an Alma Pötschke'
☼ ☼ 3-8   ↕ 4ft (1.2m) ↔ 24in (60cm)

Often known simply as 'Alma Pötschke', this clump-forming New England aster lights up the early autumn days with its brilliant salmon-pink daisy flowers.

Geum 'Lady Stratheden'
AVENS
☼ ☼ 4-7   ↕ ↔ 24in (60cm)

An old favorite and a contrast to scarlet *G.* 'Mrs. Bradshaw' bearing loose sprays of semidouble, rich yellow summer flowers and deeply divided, fresh green leaves.

OTHER FLOWERING PERENNIALS TOLERANT OF AIR POLLUTION

Anaphalis margaritacea, see p.84
Anemone × hybrida
Dicentra eximia and cvs.
Geranium × magnificum
Hemerocallis spp. and cvs.
Liatris spicata
Lychnis chalcedonica
Rudbeckia spp. and cvs.
Sidalcea candida
Solidago spp. and cvs.

OTHER FOLIAGE PERENNIALS
TOLERANT OF AIR POLLUTION

Artemisia ludoviciana 'Silver Queen',
  see p.92
Festuca glauca
Miscanthus spp. and cvs.
Pennisetum alopecuroides
Sedum spp. and cvs.
Sempervivum spp. and cvs.
Stachys byzantina, see p.51
Telekia speciosa, see p.129
Yucca spp. and cvs.

Solidago 'Golden Wings'
GOLDENROD
☼ 3-9   ↕ 6ft (1.8m) ↔ 36in (90cm)

During late summer and autumn, the
erect, leafy stems of this robust perennial
are crowned with spreading, branched
clusters of small, golden yellow flowers.

Lupinus 'Noble Maiden'
LUPINE
☼ 3-6   ↕ 36in (90cm) ↔ 30in (75cm)

A lovely lupine with tapered racemes of
creamy white, pealike flowers that rise in
summer above clumps of divided foliage.
Like most lupines, it is attractive to slugs.

Pentaglottis sempervirens
GREEN ALKANET
☼ ☀ 7-9   ↕ 36in (90cm) ↔ 24in (60cm)

The robust clump of overwintering, hairy
leaves is topped in spring by erect, leafy
stems bearing rich blue flowers. Excellent
for planting along hedges or in woodlands.

Malva moschata
MUSK MALLOW
☼ 3-7   ↕ 36in (90cm) ↔ 24in (60cm)

Attractive and easily grown, this perennial
forms clumps of finely divided, aromatic
leaves. It bears racemes of pink hibiscus-
like flowers from midsummer onward.

Potentilla 'Gibson's Scarlet'
POTENTILLA
☼ 4-8   ↕ 18in (45cm) ↔ 24in (60cm)

This potentilla produces its bright scarlet
blooms in summer above clumps of long-
stalked, deeply divided leaves. Striking in
flower and popular for use in borders.

Veronica spicata 'Rotfuchs'
SPIKE SPEEDWELL
☼ 3-8   ↕ ↔ 12in (30cm)

During summer, erect, tapering spikes
of eye-catching, deep pink flowers rise
above the low clump of willowlike leaves.
In English, its name means 'Red Fox'.

Perennials Tolerant of Coastal Exposure

EXPOSURE TO STRONG WINDS, SALT SPRAY, AND SUN are the three main features of life by the seaside. As the soil here is also often sandy and fast-draining, to survive plants must be robust and adaptable. A surprising number of perennials can cope successfully and even thrive in these conditions and are ideal for a coastal garden.

Euphorbia nicaeensis
SPURGE
☼ 5-8   ↕ 32in (80cm) ↔ 18in (45cm)

This superb, woody-based plant is valued for its reddish green stems and narrow, blue-bloomy leaves. Green-yellow flowerheads appear in late spring and summer.

Allium giganteum
GIANT ONION
☼ 4-8   ↕ 5ft (1.5m) ↔ 6in (15cm)

Round heads of starry, lilac-pink flowers top the tall stems of this striking plant in summer. Its two strap-shaped, gray-green basal leaves wither before flowering.

Cichorium intybus 'Roseum'
CHICORY
☼ 3-10   ↕ 4ft (1.2m) ↔ 24in (60cm)

A tap-rooted perennial producing a clump of jaggedly lobed and toothed leaves. Spikes of dandelion-like pink flowerheads are carried on branched stems in summer.

Geranium sanguineum 'Max Frei'
BLOODY CRANESBILL
☼ 3-8   ↕ 8in (20cm) ↔ 12in (30cm)

The neat, rounded mounds of deeply cut leaves often become richly red-tinted in autumn. A mass of deep magenta flowers appears atop the foliage in summer.

Centaurea hypoleuca 'John Coutts'
KNAPWEED
☼ 3-7   ↕ 24in (60cm) ↔ 18in (45cm)

In summer, erect stems bear long-lasting, fragrant, deep rose-pink flowerheads above bold clumps of deeply lobed, wavy-edged leaves that are gray-white beneath.

Erigeron 'Charity'
FLEABANE
☼ ☼ 5-9   ↕ 24in (60cm) ↔ 18in (45cm)

Leafy clumps of stems produce cheerful, lilac-pink, yellow-centered daisies, singly or in clusters, throughout summer. The flowers are especially popular with bees.

Glaucium flavum
YELLOW HORNED POPPY
☼ 6-9   ↕ 24in (60cm) ↔ 18in (45cm)

Mostly found on sand or gravely soil in the wild, this poppy bears bloomy blue-green leaves and stems. Yellow summer flowers are followed by narrow, curved fruits.

Kniphofia 'Atlanta'
RED HOT POKER
☼ ☼ 5-9 ↕4ft (1.2m) ↔30in (75cm)

A magnificent evergreen forming bold clumps of strap-shaped, gray-green leaves. Stout-stemmed orange-red pokers open to yellow flowers in late spring and summer.

OTHER PERENNIALS TOLERANT OF COASTAL EXPOSURE

Achillea tomentosa
Armeria maritima
Artemisia stelleriana
Centranthus ruber, see p.92
Crambe cordifolia, see p.28
Erigeron glaucus
Eryngium spp. and cvs.
Hemerocallis spp. and cvs.
Limonium spp. and cvs.
Yucca filamentosa

Pennisetum alopecuroides 'Hameln'
FOUNTAIN GRASS
☼ 6-9 ↕3ft (1m) ↔4½ft (1.4m)

Bottlebrush-like, greenish white heads of spikelets, borne in summer, age to gray-then golden brown above arching, elegant mounds of grassy leaves.

Papaver orientale 'Cedric Morris'
ORIENTAL POPPY
☼ 2-7 ↕↔36in (90cm)

An exquisite form of a cottage-garden staple forming bold clumps of hairy gray leaves. Its large, frilly-margined, soft pink blooms open from late spring to summer.

Platycodon grandiflorus
BALLOON FLOWER
☼ ☼ 3-8 ↕24in (60cm) ↔12in (30cm)

Large, bell-shaped, purple-blue flowers open from balloonlike, inflated buds in late summer. Blue-green leaves clothe the clumps of erect, branching stems.

Senecio cineraria 'Silver Dust'
SENECIO
☼ 7-9 ↕↔12in (30cm)

Silver-gray felt covers the deeply divided leaves and stems of this striking plant, often grown as an annual. Loose heads of mustard yellow flowers open in summer.

Perennials Tolerant of Exposed, Windy Sites

EXPOSURE TO PERSISTENT or strong winds and heavy rain, particularly in cold areas, can severely damage or stunt the growth of garden plants. Fortunately, a surprisingly large number of hardy perennials will grow and even thrive in such conditions. For best results, protect these perennials with a hedge, shrub border, or other barrier on the windward side.

OTHER PERENNIALS TOLERANT OF EXPOSED, WINDY SITES
Achillea ptarmica
Anchusa azurea
Asclepias tuberosa, see p.110
Astilbe chinensis var. *pumila*
Echinops spp. and cvs.
Eryngium maritimum, see p.126
Limonium spp. and cvs.
Physostegia virginiana
Solidago spp. and cvs.
Viola cornuta, see p.87

Alchemilla conjuncta
LADY'S MANTLE
☼ ☼ 4-8   ↕ 4in (10cm) ↔ 20in (50cm)

A tough, creeping perennial providing excellent ground cover with its carpet of attractively fingered leaves, silvery-silky beneath. Green flowers open in summer.

Astrantia 'Hadspen Blood'
MASTERWORT
☼ ☼ 5-8   ↕ 18in (45cm) ↔ 24in (60cm)

Attractive enough with its clumps of long-stalked, deeply lobed and toothed leaves, this masterwort has the added bonus of loose heads of dark red flowers in summer.

Brunnera macrophylla
SIBERIAN BUGLOSS
☼ 3-8   ↕ 18in (45cm) ↔ 24in (60cm)

This tough, reliable perennial produces branched heads of bright blue, forget-me-not flowers in spring above bold clumps of heart-shaped, softly-hairy leaves.

Anaphalis margaritacea
PEARLY EVERLASTING
☼ 4-8   ↕ ↔ 24in (60cm)

The upright clumps of woolly gray stems bear narrow leaves, white-woolly beneath. Clusters of "everlasting", papery flowers are produced from summer to autumn.

Bergenia x *schmidtii*
BERGENIA
☼ ☼ 4-8   ↕ 12in (30cm) ↔ 24in (60cm)

A dependable perennial that bears large clusters of rose-pink flowers in late winter and spring above its handsome mounds of rounded, leathery, evergreen leaves.

Centaurea montana 'Alba'
PERENNIAL CORNFLOWER
☼ 3-8   ↕ 18in (45cm) ↔ 24in (60cm)

This handsome form of the popular, blue-flowered perennial bears bold, pure white, lacy flowers above clumps of gray-green, leafy stems from late spring into summer.

Euphorbia polychroma
CUSHION SPURGE
☼ ☀ 3-8   ↕ 16in (40cm) ↔ 12in (30cm)

An invaluable and utterly reliable plant forming a rounded clump of erect, densely leafy stems that bear long-lasting, greenish yellow flowers from spring into summer.

Leucanthemum × superbum
'Wirral Pride'
☼ ☀ 4-8   ↕ 30in (75cm) ↔ 24in (60cm)

In summer, this clump-forming perennial bears solitary, large, double white daisy flowers with yellow anemone-type centers on erect stems with dark green leaves.

Polemonium 'Lambrook Mauve'
JACOB'S LADDER
☼ ☀ 3-7   ↕↔ 18in (45cm)

Erect, branching stems bear loose clusters of bell-shaped, lilac-blue flowers during late spring and early summer above the rounded clumps of deeply divided leaves.

Primula 'Wanda'
PRIMROSE
☼ ☀ 4-8   ↕ 6in (15cm) ↔ 8in (20cm)

This vigorous, reliable garden primrose produces its dark, claret red flowers over a long period in spring above compact, low clumps of toothy, purplish green leaves.

Rhodiola rosea
ROSEROOT
☼ 2-8   ↕↔ 8in (20cm)

Dense heads of tiny, bright yellow flowers top the low clump of fleshy, leafy, blue-green bloomy stems in summer. It is ideal for a rock garden, dry wall, or as edging.

Thermopsis rhombifolia
THERMOPSIS
☼ ☀ 3-8   ↕↔ 36in (90cm)

In early summer, this creeping perennial bears spires of lupine-like yellow flowers above leaves divided into threes. It forms extensive patches and can be invasive.

SPECIFIC USES

Low-allergen Perennials

FOR PEOPLE WHO SUFFER FROM ASTHMA, hayfever, or other allergies aggravated by air-borne pollen, gardening and gardens often have to be avoided at certain times of the year, especially during summer. Brushing or touching the foliage or flowers of certain plants can also cause or exacerbate some skin allergies. The following insect-pollinated perennials, however, can usually be relied upon to be non-allergenic, and will allow everyone to enjoy the garden all year round.

Campanula trachelium 'Bernice'
NETTLE-LEAVED BELLFLOWER
☼ ☼ 5-8   ↕ 30in (75cm) ↔ 12in (30cm)

A beautiful perennial with clumps of erect stems clothed in sharply toothed leaves. It bears axillary, double, bell-shaped, violet-blue summer flowers. May need support.

Ajuga reptans 'Catlin's Giant'
BUGLEWEED
☼ ☼ 3-9   ↕ 6in (15cm) ↔ indefinite

This excellent groundcover produces large, brown-green, semievergreen leaves that age to green. Dark blue flower spikes are borne during late spring and summer.

Astilbe × *arendsii* 'Irrlicht'
ASTILBE
☼ ☼ 3-9   ↕ ↔ 20in (50cm)

In late spring and early summer, striking, erect plumes of tiny white flowers top this astilbe's bold clumps of much-divided, dark green leaves. It thrives in moist soil.

Aquilegia chrysantha 'Yellow Queen'
GOLDEN COLUMBINE
☼ ☼ 3-9   ↕ 36in (90cm) ↔ 24in (60cm)

The branched stems of this vigorous, erect perennial bear attractive, divided, ferny leaves and slender-spurred, golden yellow flowers during late spring and summer.

Bergenia 'Bressingham White'
BERGENIA
☼ ☼ 3-9   ↕ 18in (45cm) ↔ 24in (60cm)

During spring, fleshy, upright stems freely bear loose clusters of bell-shaped, pure white flowers. The robust clumps of large, leathery leaves are usually evergreen.

Digitalis 'Glory of Roundway'
FOXGLOVE
☼ ☼ 4-8   ↕ 36in (90cm) ↔ 12in (30cm)

This choice hybrid of *D. purpurea* and *D. lutea* has branched, narrow-leaved stems and long racemes of funnel-shaped, pale yellow, pink-tinted flowers in summer.

Geranium psilostemon
ARMENIAN CRANESBILL
☼ ☀ 5-8 ↕ 4ft (1.2m) ↔ 36in (90cm)

Fantastic in flower, this striking cranesbill sends up a mound of dense, leafy stems that are covered throughout summer with bright magenta, black-eyed blooms.

Hosta 'Blue Blush'
HOSTA
☼ ☀ 3-9 ↕ 8in (20cm) ↔ 16in (40cm)

This striking hostas has clumps of lance-shaped, strongly veined, dark blue-green leaves. It produces stalks of bell-shaped, lavender-blue flowers during summer.

Paeonia lactiflora 'Duchesse de Nemours'
☼ ☀ 3-8 ↕ ↔ 32in (80cm)

The large, fragrant, double white flowers of this strong-growing peony have yellow-based inner petals. Flushed green in bud, the blooms open in early summer.

Penstemon 'Andenken an Friedrich Hahn'
☼ ☀ 6-9 ↕ 30in (75cm) ↔ 24in (60cm)

Also known as *P.* 'Garnet', this is probably the most reliable perennial penstemon. Its deep red flowers are produced on strong, leafy stems from midsummer onward.

Sidalcea 'Oberon'
CHECKERBLOOM
☼ 5-8 ↕ 4ft (1.2m) ↔ 18in (45cm)

During summer, loose racemes of clear rose-pink, hollyhock-like flowers appear on erect, leafy stems. The stem leaves are deeply lobed, the basal ones less so.

Veronica spicata subsp. *incana*
SPIKE SPEEDWELL
☼ 3-8 ↕ 24in (60cm) ↔ 18in (45cm)

Showy, dense spikes of tiny purple-blue flowers, borne during summer, provide striking contrast with the densely silver-hairy stems and mat of silvery foliage.

OTHER LOW-ALLERGEN PERENNIALS

Allium spp. and cvs.
Aruncus dioicus, see p.24
Astilbe spp. and cvs.
Dicentra spp. and cvs.
Epimedium spp. and cvs.
Hemerocallis spp. and cvs.
Hosta spp. and cvs.
Iris sibirica and cvs.
Polemonium spp. and cvs.
Solidago spp. and cvs.

Viola cornuta
HORNED VIOLET
☼ ☀ 6-9 ↕ 6in (15cm) ↔ 16in (40cm)

An excellent and reliable small perennial with a low-spreading, slightly bushy habit. Lightly scented, lilac-blue to violet flowers appear in late spring and summer.

SPECIFIC USES

Slug-proof Perennials

SLUGS AND SNAILS have a voracious appetite when they
discover a tasty plant, but what they devour in one garden
they may only nibble at in another. Some plants, including
many hostas, are always a gourmet treat for slugs and snails
and are readily consumed. Others, especially those that have
hard-textured, hairy, or poisonous leaves, are often relatively
ignored. Here is a selection of the most reliably slug- and
snail-proof perennials for the garden.

Bergenia 'Silberlicht'
BERGENIA
☼ ☀ 3-8   ↕ 12in (40cm) ↔ 12in (30cm)

Fleshy, shining, semievergreen leaves
form a basal mound. Upright, fleshy stems
bear loose clusters of white flowers, aging
to pink, above the foliage in spring.

Corydalis lutea
YELLOW CORYDALIS
☼ ☀ 5-8   ↕ 14in (35cm) ↔ 12in (30cm)

Slender racemes of tubular yellow flowers
are produced continually from late spring
to early autumn above mounds of fernlike, semievergreen leaves. It will reseed.

Allium 'Globemaster'
ORNAMENTAL ONION
☼ 4-8   ↕ 32in (80cm) ↔ 12in (30cm)

Magnificent for group plantings, this bulb
has arching, strap-shaped leaves and huge
heads of deep violet flowers in summer. It
is loved by both butterflies and bees.

OTHER SLUG-PROOF PERENNIALS

Achillea spp. and cvs.
Aconitum carmichaelii
Anemone vitifolia
Artemisia spp. and cvs.
Campanula persicifolia
Dicentra eximia
Epimedium spp. and cvs.
Euphorbia spp. and cvs.
Helleborus spp. and cvs.
Heuchera spp. and cvs.
Stachys byzantina, see p.51

Aster ericoides 'Esther'
HEATH ASTER
☼ 5-8   ↕ 28in (70cm) ↔ 12in (30cm)

Bushy clumps of leafy, slender-branched
stems are topped by broad heads of small
pink, yellow-eyed daisies in late summer
and autumn. Useful for its late flowering.

Galanthus 'Atkinsii'
SNOWDROP
☼ 3-9   ↕ 8in (20cm) ↔ 3in (8cm)

Ideal for naturalizing, this strong-growing
bulb has narrow, fleshy, blue-green leaves.
In late winter, erect stems carry pendent,
pure white flowers with green markings.

Geranium macrorrhizum
WILD CRANESBILL
☼ ☀ **3-8**   ↕ 20in (50cm) ↔ 24in (60cm)

An adaptable and reliable, semievergreen carpeter with lobed, aromatic leaves often coloring well in autumn. Clusters of pink to purple flowers appear in early summer.

Helleborus x *nigercors*
HELLEBORE
☼ **6-8**   ↕ 12in (30cm) ↔ 36in (90cm)

Welcome clusters of saucer-shaped, white or pink-tinted flowers open from winter to spring above the basal clump of divided, coarse-toothed, evergreen leaves.

Hosta 'Halcyon'
HOSTA
☼ ☀ **3-8**   ↕ ↔ 28in (70cm)

One of the best slug-proof hostas forming bold clumps of attractive, heart-shaped, bluish gray leaves. In summer, pendent, bell-shaped, lavender-blue flowers appear.

Iris chrysographes
IRIS
☼ **2-9**   ↕ ↔ 20in (50cm)

This iris forms handsome, erect clumps of narrow, sword-shaped, gray-green leaves. Stems of fragrant, velvety, dark purple flowers appear during summer.

Pulmonaria angustifolia subsp. *azurea*
BLUE LUNGWORT
☼ ☀ **2-8**   ↕ 10in (25cm) ↔ 18in (45cm)

An attractive lungwort developing a low clump of bristly, unmarked green leaves. In spring, it bears nodding clusters of rich gentian-blue, tubular flowers, red in bud.

Rudbeckia hirta
BLACK-EYED SUSAN
☼ ☀ **3-7**   ↕ 30in (80cm) ↔ 36in (90cm)

If kept moist during summer, this cheery biennial or short-lived perennial will bear a succession of dark-eyed yellow daisies in summer and autumn.

Sedum
spectabile 'Iceberg'
SHOWY STONECROP
☼ **3-9**   ↕ ↔ 18in (45cm)

Reliable and easy to grow, with mounds of gray-green leaves and fleshy stems topped by flattened heads of white flowers from summer to autumn. Loved by butterflies.

Rabbit-proof Perennials

Rabbits can be a massive source of plant damage and loss in the garden, especially in country areas or those close to large, open spaces. Although deer are undoubtedly the more serious pest, rabbits can eat their way through a bed or border faster than any slug or snail. Various methods are recommended for their control, but it does no harm to grow some perennials that rabbits find unpalatable or uninteresting.

Bergenia stracheyi
BERGENIA
☼ 4-8   ↕ 8in (20cm) ↔ 12in (30cm)

During early spring, the low mound of leathery, semievergreen leaves is crowned by dense clusters of fragrant, bell-shaped pink flowers. It makes a fine groundcover.

Aster ericoides 'Golden Spray'
HEATH ASTER
☼ 3-8   ↕ 36in (90cm) ↔ 12in (30cm)

From late summer into autumn, branched heads of small white, pink-tinted daisies with rich yellow centers are produced on a bushy clump of erect, leafy stems.

Agapanthus 'Blue Giant'
AFRICAN LILY
☼ 7-11   ↕ 36in (90cm) ↔ 24in (60cm)

During late summer and early autumn, stout stems bearing large, loose heads of rich blue flowers rise above the bold clump of long, strap-shaped green leaves.

Euphorbia griffithii 'Fireglow'
GRIFFITH'S SPURGE
☼ ☼ 4-8   ↕ 30in (75cm) ↔ 36in (90cm)

A vigorous, creeping perennial eventually forming large patches of leafy stems that color richly in autumn. Terminal clusters of fiery orange flowers emerge in summer.

Alchemilla mollis
LADY'S-MANTLE
☼ ☼ 3-8   ↕ ↔ 14in (35cm)

This adaptable, reliable plant has mounds of downy, scalloped and lobed, gray-green leaves topped by yellowish green flower clusters during summer. It will self-seed.

Astilbe 'Straussenfeder'
ASTILBE
☼ ☼ 3-9   ↕ 36in (90cm) ↔ 24in (60cm)

Also known as 'Ostrich Plume', which neatly describes the arching sprays of pink flowers in summer and autumn. Its young leaves are attractively bronze-tinted.

Helleborus hybridus
LENTEN ROSE
☼ 4-9   ↕ ↔ 18in (45cm)

A beautiful and sought-after group of hybrids bearing semievergeen leaves and large, nodding, saucer-shaped flowers in a range of colors from late winter to spring.

Lamium maculatum 'Beacon Silver'
SPOTTED LAMIUM
☼ ☀ **3-8**   ↕ 8in (20cm) ↔ 3ft (1m)

An excellent groundcover forming carpets of toothed, silvery, green-margined, semi-evergreen leaves. Clusters of pretty, pale pink flowers are produced during summer.

OTHER RABBIT-PROOF PERENNIALS

Aconitum spp. and cvs.
Anemone × *hybrida* and cvs.
Aquilegia × *hybrida* and cvs.
Aster novi-belgii and cvs.
Convallaria majalis
Crocosmia spp. and cvs.
Kniphofia spp. and cvs.
Nepeta × *faassenii*
Pulmonaria saccharata and cvs.
Sedum spp. and cvs.
Tradescantia × *andersoniana*

Paeonia officinalis 'Rubra Plena'
PEONY
☼ ☀ **3-8**   ↕ 30in (75cm) ↔ 36in (90cm)

The reliable, old-fashioned, double red peony of cottage gardens. It has clumps of glossy green leaves and bears red blooms with ruffled petals in early summer.

Narcissus 'Mount Hood'
DAFFODIL
☼ ☀ **3-8**   ↕ 18in (45cm) ↔ 20in (50cm)

A classic large-flowered trumpet daffodil producing gorgeous white flowers with cream-colored trumpets during spring. It is excellent for planting in groups.

Trollius × *cultorum* 'Earliest of All'
GLOBEFLOWER
☼ ☀ **3-6**   ↕ 20in (50cm) ↔ 16in (40cm)

Not the first, but still an early perennial, forming loose clumps of deeply cut leaves. Branched stems bear globular, clear yellow flowers in spring. It prefers heavy soils.

Veratrum album
FALSE HELLEBORE
☼ ☀ **5-9**   ↕ 6ft (2m) ↔ 24in (60cm)

Worth growing for its large, handsomely pleated leaves alone, this bold perennial is impressive in groups. The tall plumes of white flowers in summer are a bonus.

Deer-proof Perennials

WITHOUT A DOUBT the most destructive garden visitors of all are deer. Increasingly, deer have become a major problem for gardeners in suburban areas as well as rural and wooded areas. To find a favorite plant demolished after an evening or early morning browsing can be demoralizing. The answer, other than erecting fences or providing deterrents, is to grow at least some perennials that deer are known to find uninteresting or, better still, unpalatable.

Centranthus ruber
RED VALERIAN
☼ 4-8 ‡ 36in (90cm) ↔ 24in (60cm)

This woody-based plant has bold clumps of leafy, gray-green stems and fragrant, pink, red, or white flowers in spring and early summer. It thrives in alkaline soil.

Aconitum lycoctonum subsp. *vulparia*
WOLFSBANE
☼ ☼ 5-8 ‡ 5ft (1.5m) ↔ 36in (90cm)

This handsome perennial has finely cut, glossy green foliage and produces straw yellow flowers in summer. Its roots were once used in parts of Europe as wolf bait.

Astilbe 'Deutschland'
ASTILBE
☼ ☼ 3-9 ‡ 20in (50cm) ↔ 12in (30cm)

In summer, erect panicles of white flowers top the bright, glossy green mound of deeply divided leaves. Good for cutting, it needs some moisture in summer to excel.

Digitalis purpurea Excelsior Group
FOXGLOVE
☼ 4-8 ‡ 6ft (2m) ↔ 24in (60cm)

A bold and colorful short-lived perennial or biennial with a rosette of hairy foliage. Tall, erect spires of funnel-shaped flowers in pastel shades emerge in early summer.

Artemisia ludoviciana 'Silver Queen'
WHITE SAGE
☼ 3-9 ‡ ↔ 30in (75cm)

A clump-forming, but creeping, perennial worth growing for its lance-shaped, silver-white leaves and heads of woolly white flowers that appear from summer onward.

OTHER DEER-PROOF PERENNIALS

Achillea spp. and cvs.
Aconitum napellus
Actaea spp. and cvs.
Allium spp. and cvs.
Amsonia tabernaemontana
Anemone spp. and cvs.
Aster novi-belgii
Bergenia spp. and cvs.
Dictamnus albus, see p.114
Epimedium spp. and cvs.
Geranium sanguineum
Helleborus spp. and cvs.
Iris foetidissima
Lamium maculatum
Lavandula angustifolia
Paeonia spp. and cvs.
Rudbeckia fulgida
Santolina chamaecyparissus
Stachys byzantina, see p.51

Narcissus 'Spellbinder'
DAFFODIL
☼ ◐ **3-8**   ↕ ↔ 20in (50cm)

This strong-growing daffodil is especially impressive when planted in bold drifts. The spring flowers are sulphur yellow and have coronas that fade to white with age.

Geranium macrorrhizum 'Bevan's Variety'
☼ ◐ **3-8**   ↕ 20in (50cm) ↔ 24in (60cm)

An excellent, all-round, semievergreen plant, especially useful as groundcover. It flowers in early summer and has aromatic leaves that often color well in autumn.

Papaver orientale 'Beauty of Livermere'
☼ **2-7**   ↕ ↔ 36in (90cm)

In early summer, erect, hairy stems bear crimson-scarlet flowers with basal black marks. Clumps of deeply cut, hairy leaves disappear after the flowers fade.

Iris orientalis
IRIS
☼ **6-9**   ↕ ↔ 36in (90cm)

This robust perennial forms erect clumps or patches of strap-shaped leaves. In early summer, stiff stems carry a succession of attractive white, yellow-stained flowers.

Lysimachia clethroides
LOOSESTRIFE
☼ ◐ **3-8**   ↕ 36in (90cm) ↔ 24in (60cm)

A vigorous, fast-spreading perennial that forms a clump of erect, narrowly leafy stems. Its characteristic swan-neck spikes of white flowers are borne in summer.

x *Solidaster luteus* 'Lemore'
SOLIDASTER
☼ **5-9**   ↕ ↔ 32in (80cm)

Dense clumps of erect stems clothed in narrow leaves sport sparsely branched heads of pale lemon yellow flowers from summer to autumn. It is good for cutting.

93

FLORAL EFFECT

THE GREATEST ATTRIBUTE of many perennials, flowers can be relied upon to bring fragrance and color to any situation in the garden or home. With blooms in all shades and shapes, in some cases borne over several months, there is scope for imaginative combinations, and for flowers all year round.

△ SUMMER BLOOMS *Mixed colors and flower forms are the strength of this scree planting, which flanks an informal path.*

Anemone × hybrida 'September Charm' for autumn flowers

Whatever their other attractions, most gardeners grow perennials for their often abundant and reliably borne flowers. In all but the coldest areas, where snow or ice lie heavy on the garden during winter, there is hardly a day in the year when a perennial of some kind is not flowering. From spring to summer, and on into autumn, perennials can provide gardens with an unbroken, colorful and often fragrant display. From late winter into early spring, there is a small but reliable fraternity of perennials that will produce flowers despite the often poor light and intimidating cold.

FLOWER COLOR

With flowers ranging from white and subtle pastel shades to strident reds and golden yellows, perennials will bring a truly formidable range of colors to the garden. These colors can be used to create varied effects, depending on whether you choose to mix them in a natural arrangement, or match them as part of a more structured theme. The strong color contrasts often seen in the wild, where perennials such as goldenrod (*Solidago*) and violet-blue native asters grow together, can inspire garden plantings either using the same or similar plants. To evoke a particular mood, a selection of perennials with similarly toned blooms, whether hot, cool, or pale in color, can be grown together. For a more formal design, themed borders using only one flower color are also an option.

FORM AND STRUCTURE

Flowerheads make an important, if temporary, contribution to the form and structure of a garden landscape. Varying from the statuesque to the fragile, the spheres, plumes, sprays, tall spikes, or flattened flowerheads of perennials can be combined for eye-catching contrast and effect.

△ HOT COLORS *A fiery display of* Hemerocallis *'Stafford' and* Lilium *'Enchantment' brings warmth to a border.*

◁ STRONG CONTRAST *Striking effects can be achieved by using a few contrasting colors, here mainly blue and yellow.*

▷ INFORMAL BEAUTY *Pale Oriental poppies, foxgloves, and* Dictamnus *make a delightful study in height and color.*

Perennials with Spring Flowers

NO GARDEN PERENNIALS are more eagerly awaited than those that flower in spring. This is especially true in cold climates, where there is often little color in the garden to relieve the long, bleak winters. With the increasing warmth and daylight of spring, the garden is rejuvenated as a wealth of perennials, including many bulbs, burst into flower.

Hylomecon japonica
HYLOMECON
☼ ☼ **5-8**   ↕ ↔ 12in (30cm)

This charming poppy relative is excellent in shade, especially as a groundcover. It has deeply divided, toothed leaves and bears its simple flowers into early summer.

Bergenia 'Sunningdale'
BERGENIA
☼ ☼ **3-8**   ↕ 18in (45cm) ↔ 24in (60cm)

The clumps of leathery, semievergreen leaves turn a warm copper red in winter. Spring brings loose clusters of bell-shaped, lilac-magenta flowers on red stems.

Chionodoxa luciliae
GLORY-OF-THE-SNOW
☼ **3-9**   ↕ 6in (15cm) ↔ 4in (10cm)

One of the loveliest and most reliable of early spring bulbs, with loose clusters of starry, sky blue, white-eyed flowers. It is particularly impressive planted in drifts.

SPRING-FLOWERING EVERGREEN TO SEMIEVERGREEN PERENNIALS

Aurinia saxatilis
Epimedium pinnatum subsp. *colchicum*, see p.52
Erysimum 'Bowles' Mauve'
Fragaria vesca
Helleborus argutifolius, see p.120
Helleborus foetidus
Iberis sempervirens
Mitchella repens
Muscari armeniacum

Boykinia jamesii
BOYKINIA
☼ **4-8** **PH**   ↕ ↔ 6in (15cm)

A choice perennial bearing loose, upright sprays of frilled, bell-shaped, pinkish red, green-centered flowers above mounds of rounded or kidney-shaped leaves.

Doronicum 'Frühlingspracht'
LEOPARD'S BANE
☼ ☼ **3-8**   ↕ 16in (40cm) ↔ 36in (90cm)

This colorful plant, also sold as 'Spring Beauty', bears double, golden flowerheads above clumps of scalloped, heart-shaped leaves, which disappear during summer.

Lathyrus vernus 'Alboroseus'
SPRING VETCHLING
☼ ☼ **5-9**   ↕ 16in (40cm) ↔ 18in (45cm)

The crowded, erect stems of this clump-former produce deeply divided leaves and loose, one-sided racemes of pea-shaped, pink and white flowers. Good with bulbs.

Primula denticulata var. *alba*
DRUMSTICK PRIMROSE
☼ ☼ **3-8** ↕ ↔ 18in (45cm)

This is the white form of a popular and easily grown perennial. Its rounded heads of yellow-eyed flowers are carried on stout stems above lush, leafy rosettes.

Leucojum vernum var. *carpathicum*
SPRING SNOWFLAKE
☼ ☼ **4-9** ↕ 10in (25cm) ↔ 6in (15cm)

Charming for group plantings, this bulb has tufts of strap-shaped leaves and fleshy stems bearing nodding, bell-shaped white flowers with yellow-tipped segments.

Pulmonaria 'Mawson's Blue'
PULMONARIA
☼ ☼ **4-7** ↕ 14in (35cm) ↔ 18in (45cm)

Low clumps of softly-hairy leaves and clusters of dark blue flowers appear from late winter to spring. A pretty alternative to pulmonarias with spotted leaves.

SPRING-FLOWERING HERBACEOUS PERENNIALS

Adonis vernalis, see p.104
Bergenia ciliata
Brunnera macrophylla, see p.84
Cardamine spp.
Euphorbia polychroma, see p.85
Hacquetia epipactis, see p.43
Pachyphragma macrophyllum
Trillium spp. and cvs.
Trollius x *cultorum* 'Earliest of All', see p.91

Narcissus 'King Alfred'
DAFFODIL
☼ ☼ **4-9** ↕ 18in (45cm) ↔ 12in (30cm)

Spectacular in large groups or drifts, this classic daffodil is popular for naturalizing. Strong stems carry large, trumpet-shaped, golden yellow flowers in early spring.

Narcissus 'Thalia'
DAFFODIL
☼ ☼ **4-9** ↕ 14in (35cm) ↔ 6in (15cm)

One of a group of hybrids of *N. triandrus*, this beautiful daffodil has upright stems, each carrying a pair of nodding, milk-white flowers with yellow-tinged throats.

Perennials with Flowers from Early to Midsummer

AFTER THE INITIAL RUSH OF FLOWERS during spring, the scene is set for the wealth of perennials that flower from early to midsummer. Some even bloom intermittently into early autumn. They include many of our most popular and reliable garden and border plants, as well as others that are perhaps less well known, though equally desirable.

Buphthalmum salicifolium
BUPHTHALMUM
☼ ☀ 4-9   ↕ 24in (60cm) ↔ 18in (45cm)

Yellow daisylike flowers, good for cutting, are borne continuously in summer. The clumps of upright stems are clothed with narrow, willowlike, dark geen leaves.

Aconitum 'Ivorine'
MONKSHOOD
☼ ☀ 4-7   ↕ ↔ 36in (90cm)

A vigorous, bushy perennial with clumps of deeply lobed, jaggedly cut leaves. The branching stems carry dense racemes of hooded ivory flowers in early summer.

SMALL PERENNIALS WITH EARLY/MIDSUMMER BLOOMS

Astrantia major
Campanula carpatica
Coreopsis verticillata and cvs.
Digitalis grandiflora
Geranium spp. and cvs.
Helianthemum spp. and cvs.
Heuchera sanguinea and cvs.
Incarvillea delavayi, see p.124
Oenothera spp. and cvs.
Platycodon grandiflorus, see p.83

Baptisia australis
BLUE FALSE INDIGO
☼ 3-9   ↕ 5ft (1.5m) ↔ 36in (90cm)

Long racemes of blue, white-marked pea-shaped flowers borne in early summer are followed by inflated seed pods. The three-parted leaves are a bloomy blue-green.

Delphinium 'Fanfare'
DELPHINIUM
☼ 3-7   ↕ 7ft (2.2m) ↔ 18in (45cm)

Tall and beautiful, this impressive plant bears deeply cut, lobed leaves and dense, branched racemes of semidouble, white-eyed, silver-mauve summer flowers.

FLORAL EFFECT

Geranium 'Johnson's Blue'
CRANESBILL
☼ ☀ 4-8 ‡ 18in (45cm) ↔ 24in (60cm)

One of the best garden cranesbills, this forms a clump of long-stalked, deeply cut leaves. Lavender-blue flowers with pale blue or pink eyes open freely in summer.

Gypsophila paniculata 'Bristol Fairy'
☼ 3-9 ‡ ↔ 3½ft (1.1m)

This popular perennial produces a loose mound of slender, branched stems, narrow leaves, and clouds of small, double white summer flowers. Excellent for cut flowers.

Hemerocallis middendorffii
MIDDENDORFF DAYLILY
☼ 3-9 ‡ 36in (90cm) ↔ 18in (45cm)

Fragrant, deep orange-yellow flowers open from reddish brown buds in early summer above the bold clumps of arching, strap-shaped leaves. Reblooms during summer.

Iris 'Blue Eyed Brunette'
BEARDED IRIS
☼ ☀ 3-8 ‡ 36in (90cm) ↔ 24in (60cm)

The typical fans of sword-shaped, grayish green leaves are topped in early summer by striking, large, reddish brown flowers with lilac splashes and golden beards.

MEDIUM TO TALL PERENNIALS WITH EARLY/MIDSUMMER BLOOMS

Actaea racemosa
Aruncus dioicus, see p.24
Campanula persicifolia
Crambe cordifolia, see p.28
Dictamnus albus, see p.114
Euphorbia griffithii 'Fireglow', see p.90
Geranium psilostemon, see p.87
Heliopsis helianthoides and cvs.
Hemerocallis spp. and cvs.
Iris sibirica

Malva alcea var. *fastigiata*
MALLOW
☼ 4-8 ‡ 32in (80cm) ↔ 24in (60cm)

The continuous display of hollyhock-like, five-petaled, deep pink flowers often lasts into autumn. Finely divided leaves clothe the narrow clumps of upright stems.

Scabiosa caucasica 'Clive Greaves'
SCABIOUS
☼ 3-7 ‡ ↔ 24in (60cm)

This long-blooming perennial is always reliable in its flowering. The flattened, lavender-blue flowers, good for cutting, are borne from early summer to autumn.

Stachys macrantha
STACHYS
☼ 4-8 ‡ 24in (60cm) ↔ 12in (30cm)

From early summer onward, the handsome rosettes of wrinkled and scalloped, heart-shaped leaves are topped by spikes of long-tubed, pink-purple flowers.

FLORAL EFFECT

99

Perennials with Flowers from Mid- to Late Summer

MANY OF THE PERENNIALS that flower in the middle of summer do so over a long period, taking advantage of the available warmth and sunlight. The following selection includes some plants that begin flowering in early summer and others that continue blooming into early autumn, earning their place in the garden by extending the period of interest.

FLORAL EFFECT

Aster amellus 'Veilchenkönigin'
ITALIAN ASTER
☼ 5-8   ↕ 20in (50cm) ↔ 18in (45cm)

An excellent late summer perennial with clumps of erect, leafy stems topped by broad, flattened clusters of bright yellow-centered, violet-purple daisy flowers.

Coreopsis grandiflora 'Badengold'
LARGE-FLOWERED TICKSEED
☼ ☀ 4-9   ↕ 36in (90cm) ↔ 18in (45cm)

This bright, cheerful-looking perennial has finely divided leaves and clumps of slim, erect stems bearing orange-centered, deep yellow daisies throughout summer.

Digitalis x *mertonensis*
STRAWBERRY FOXGLOVE
☼ ☀ 3-8   ↕ 36in (90cm) ↔ 12in (30cm)

A robust, clump-forming plant bearing tall, upright spikes of tubular, strawberry pink, rose, or white summer flowers. Its veiny leaves are also attractive.

Inula ensifolia
SWORD-LEAVED INULA
☼ ☀ 4-9   ↕ 24in (60cm) ↔ 12in (30cm)

A thoroughly reliable perennial producing narrow leaves and dense, bushy clumps of erect stems. These carry golden yellow daisies over a long period in late summer.

Kniphofia 'Samuel's Sensation'
TORCH LILY
☼ ☀ 5-9   ↕ 5ft (1.5m) ↔ 30in (75cm)

From late summer to early autumn, the bold clumps of long, strap-shaped leaves are dwarfed by stiff-stemmed heads of bright scarlet flowers, aging to yellow.

OTHER PERENNIALS WITH FLOWERS IN MIDSUMMER

Allium senescens
Aster x *frikartii*
Campanula poscharskyana
Ceratostigma plumbaginoides, see p.50
Crocosmia 'Lucifer', see p.122
Hemerocallis spp. and cvs.
Tanacetum parthenium
Tricyrtis hirta
Veronica austriaca subsp. *teucrium*
  'Crater Lake Blue'

Lavatera × *clementii* 'Rosea'
MALLOW
☀ 8-10   ↕ ↔ 6ft (2m)

A popular and reliable mallow for warm-climate gardens that forms a large, woody-based, semievergreen bush covered with deep pink flowers during summer.

OTHER PERENNIALS WITH
FLOWERS IN LATE SUMMER

Aconitum × *cammarum* 'Bicolor', see p.24
Aster novae-angliae
Begonia grandis
Boltonia asteroides
Gentiana asclepiadea, see p.113
Helenium 'Septemberfuchs', see p.110

Nepeta sibirica
CATMINT
☀ ☀ 3-7   ↕ 36in (90cm) ↔ 18in (45cm)

Aromatic, toothy leaves clothe the erect clumps of four-angled stems. The long, interrupted spikes of large, deep violet to lilac-blue flowers are loved by bees.

Salvia × *sylvestris*
'Mainacht'
☀ 5-9   ↕ 24in (60cm) ↔ 12in (30cm)

In English, its name, 'May Night', aptly describes the velvety, dark indigo-blue flowers with purple bracts that are borne in long spikes on leafy, four-angled stems.

Monarda 'Prärienacht'
BEE BALM
☀ ☀ 4-8   ↕ 36in (90cm) ↔ 24in (60cm)

The dense clumps of downy, four-angled stems bear crowded heads of purple-lilac flowers with red-tinted green bracts. All parts are aromatic when bruised.

Physostegia virginiana 'Vivid'
OBEDIENT PLANT
☀ ☀ 3-9   ↕ 24in (60m) ↔ 12in (30cm)

During summer, spikes of bright purple-pink flowers, excellent for cutting, top the dense clumps of smooth, four-angled, erect stems clothed in narrow leaves.

Verbena bonariensis
VERBENA
☀ 7-9   ↕ 6ft (2m) ↔ 18in (45cm)

Bees and butterflies are both attracted to the clusters of tiny lilac-purple flowers that crown the tall, branching stems. It is often grown as an annual. Seeds freely.

Perennials with Autumn Flowers

FOR MANY GARDENERS, especially in cool temperate zones, autumn is dominated by the brilliant tints of dying leaves and the equally colorful effect of seedheads, berries, and other fruits. Comparatively few perennials choose to flower at this time, but those that do are all the more valued, as their late displays enliven the garden before the onset of winter.

Aconitum carmichaelii 'Arendsii'
MONKSHOOD
☀ ☀ 3-9   ↕ 4ft (1.2m) ↔ 24in (60cm)

A bold, clump-forming perennial valued for its stems of dense, deeply cut, dark green leaves and panicles of helmeted, purple-blue, dark-eyed flowers.

Actaea matsumurae 'Elstead'
KAMCHATKA BUGBANE
☀ ☀ 3-8   ↕ 4ft (1.2m) ↔ 24in (60cm)

The tall, arching stems of this graceful perennial bear long, cylindrical racemes of tiny white flowers above deeply divided, dark green to purple-tinted leaves.

Cyclamen hederifolium
HARDY CYCLAMEN
☀ 5-9   ↕ 4in (10cm) ↔ 6in (15cm)

Neatly lobed, beautifully marbled leaves follow the exquisite, slender-stalked, pink or white flowers. Useful as a groundcover under trees or for group plantings.

Leucanthemella serotina
MOON DAISY
☀ ☀ 4-9   ↕ 6ft (2m) ↔ 36in (90cm)

Late and lovely, this bold daisy has clumps of tall, leafy stems and sprays of big white blooms that face and follow the sun. Once known as *Chrysanthemum uliginosum*.

Anemone x hybrida 'September Charm'
JAPANESE ANEMONE
☀ ☀ 5-9   ↕ 30in (75cm) ↔ 24in (60cm)

This handsome anemone forms clumps of dark shoots with three-lobed leaflets. It produces a long succession of clear pink flowers from late summer into autumn.

Colchicum 'Waterlily'
AUTUMN CROCUS
☀ 4-9   ↕ 5in (12cm) ↔ 4in (10cm)

This is one of the most spectacular dwarf bulbs, especially in large drifts. Its double, slender-tubed, pinkish lilac blooms may need support. Leaves emerge in spring.

Nerine bowdenii 'Mark Fenwick'
NERINE
☀ 8-10   ↕ 18in (45cm) ↔ 12in (30cm)

Spectacular in autumn, this bulb's smooth stems flaunt loose umbels of lilylike pink flowers. The narrow, strap-shaped leaves follow later. It is superb in group plantings.

Schizostylis coccinea 'Major'
CRIMSON FLAG
☼ **6-9**   ↕ 24in (60cm) ↔ 12in (30cm)

This relative of gladiolus bears narrow, flattened, sword-shaped leaves and bold spikes of large, satin-textured red flowers. Plant it in groups for a striking effect.

> **OTHER PERENNIALS WITH AUTUMN FLOWERS**
>
> *Anemone* × *hybrida*
> *Aster* spp. and cvs.
> *Colchicum* spp. and cvs.
> *Crocus speciosus*
> *Eupatorium* spp. and cvs.
> *Gentiana* spp. and cvs.
> *Kniphofia triangularis*, see p.111
> *Leucojum autumnale*
> *Tricyrtis hirta* f. *alba*
> *Vernonia* spp.

Strobilanthes atropurpurea
STROBILANTHES
☼ ☀ **7-9**   ↕ 4ft (1.2m) ↔ 36in (90cm)

An excellent plant that is not commonly cultivated. The curved, hooded, indigo-blue or purple flowers are borne freely on densely branched, bushy, and leafy stems.

Sedum 'Vera Jameson'
STONECROP
☼ **3-9**   ↕ 10in (25cm) ↔ 18in (45cm)

A true gem among the autumn-flowering sedums, this has low mounds of bloomy, blue-purple leaves and crowded, rounded heads of star-shaped, rose-pink flowers.

Tricyrtis formosana
TOAD LILY
☼ ☀ **5-9**   ↕ 32in (80cm) ↔ 18in (45cm)

The curious white flowers, spotted red-purple, of this erect, clump-forming plant deserve a close look to fully appreciate their beauty. The foliage is handsome too.

Vernonia crinita
IRONWEED
☼ ☀ **4-7**   ↕ 6ft (2m) ↔ 3ft (90cm)

From late summer to autumn, flattened clusters of reddish purple flowerheads top the erect, strong-growing, narrow-leaved stems of this stately, native ironweed.

FLORAL EFFECT

Perennials with Winter Flowers

IN CLIMATES WHERE winters bring almost all growth to a standstill, the appearance of any plant in flower is always a surprise. However, certain perennials, including many bulbs, bloom during winter or very early spring despite the hostile conditions. Those suggested here will bring much-needed color at a time when other herbaceous plants have died down.

Eranthis hyemalis
WINTER ACONITE
☼ ☀ 4-9   ↕ 3in (8cm) ↔ 2in (5cm)

The cup-shaped, bright yellow flowers of winter aconite are a cheery sight above the ruffs of toothed leaves in winter and early spring. Superb planted in large drifts.

Adonis vernalis
ADONIS
☼ 5-8   ↕ 15in (38cm) ↔ 18in (45cm)

In late winter and early spring, cupped, golden yellow flowers top clumps of ferny, bright green leaves. For earliest bloom, plant in a sheltered, south-facing location.

Crocus tommasinianus
CROCUS
☼ ☀ 3-8   ↕ 4in (10cm) ↔ 3in (7.5cm)

Easily naturalized, this popular bulb bears slender-tubed, scented, pale silvery lilac to reddish purple flowers in winter and early spring above clumps of narrow leaves.

OTHER PERENNIALS WITH WINTER FLOWERS

Adonis amurensis
Bergenia × *schmidtii*, see p.84
Chionodoxa luciliae, see p.96
Crocus chrysanthus
Helleborus argutifolius, see p.120
Helleborus hybridus, see p.90
Iris reticulata
Narcissus 'February Gold'
Pulmonaria spp. and cvs.
Viola odorata

Arisarum vulgare
MONK'S COWL
☼ ☀ 8-9   ↕ 6in (15cm) ↔ 5in (13cm)

This curious *Arum* relative bears broadly arrow-shaped green leaves followed by hooded, brown- or purple-striped flowers, each with a protruding "nose".

Cyclamen coum f. *albissimum*
HARDY CYCLAMEN
☼ ☀ 5-9   ↕ 4in (10cm) ↔ 6in (15cm)

The low mounds of kidney-shaped, fleshy green or attractively marbled leaves are accompanied in winter and early spring by white flowers with carmine-red mouths.

Galanthus nivalis 'Sandersii'
SNOWDROP
☼ 3-9   ↕ ↔ 4in (10cm)

A charming and unusual variation of the familiar snowdrop, in which the flower ovaries and the tips of the inner segments are bright yellow. It is slow to increase.

Iris unguicularis 'Walter Butt'
WINTER IRIS
☼ 7-9　　　　↕12in (30cm) ↔ 16in (40cm)

Over many weeks, this beautiful winter-flowering plant produces a succession of large, fragrant, pale lavender-blue flowers from clumps of narrow, evergreen leaves.

Galanthus reginae-olgae subsp. *vernalis*
SNOWDROP
☼ 6-9　　　　↕↔4in (10cm)

Faintly scented, nodding white flowers borne in late winter and spring have inner segments tipped green. It differs from the common snowdrop in its darker leaves.

Lathraea clandestina
BLUE TOOTHWORT
☼ ☼ 5-9　　　↕2in (5cm) ↔ 12in (30cm)

This parasitic plant can grow on the roots of trees such as alder, willow, and poplar. Two-lipped mauve flowers emerge from the white, scaly clumps during late winter.

Helleborus foetidus Wester Flisk Group
STINKING HELLEBORE
☼ ☼ 6-9　　　↕32in (80cm) ↔ 18in (45cm)

The stems, fingerlike leaves, and flower-stalks of this evergreen plant are suffused with red. The pendent, bell-shaped, pale green flowers have purple mouths.

Helleborus niger 'Potter's Wheel'
CHRISTMAS ROSE
☼ 3-8　　　　↕12in (30cm) ↔ 18in (45cm)

A reliable selection of a favorite cottage-garden perennial producing bowl-shaped white flowers with green eyes above low clumps of leathery, overwintering foliage.

Narcissus 'Bowles' Early Sulphur'
DAFFODIL
☼ ☼ 3-7　　　↕8in (20cm) ↔ 5in (13cm)

Bearing mid-yellow flowers in late winter, this seedling of *N. asturiensis* is one of the earliest-flowering small daffodils. It forms clumps of narrow, strap-shaped leaves.

FLORAL EFFECT

105

Perennials with a Long Flowering Season

MOST GARDEN PERENNIALS, especially spring-blooming ones, flower only for a relatively limited period. The invaluable perennials suggested below offer unusually long flowering seasons. They either bloom throughout summer or from summer into autumn. They are especially effective for bringing an element of continuity to the garden.

Astrantia major 'Shaggy'
MASTERWORT
☼ ☼ 5-8   ↕ 36in (90cm) ↔ 18in (45cm)

Clusters of tiny flowers surrounded by large, jagged, green-tipped white bracts are borne on branching stems in summer. The deeply cut leaves form bold clumps.

Dicentra 'Stuart Boothman'
DICENTRA
☼ 3-9   ↕ 12in (30cm) ↔ 16in (40cm)

A creeping perennial forming clumps of divided, fernlike, blue-gray leaves. Sprays of locket-shaped, pendent, deep pink flowers emerge from spring to summer.

Geranium × *riversleaianum* 'Russell Prichard'
☼ ☼ 6-8   ↕ 12in (30cm) ↔ 3ft (1m)

Ideal as a groundcover, this low-grower has trailing stems clothed in neatly lobed, sharply toothed, gray-green leaves. Deep magenta flowers appear during summer.

OTHER PERENNIALS WITH A LONG FLOWERING SEASON

Aster × *frikartii* 'Mönch', see p.22
Campanula carpatica
Coreopsis verticillata 'Moonbeam', see p.114
Corydalis lutea, see p.88
Dicentra eximia and cvs.
Gaura lindheimeri, see p.114
Geranium sanguineum 'Prostratum'
Hemerocallis 'Stella de Oro', see p.22
Viola cornuta, see p.87

Dianthus deltoides
MAIDEN PINK
☼ 3-9   ↕ 8in (20cm) ↔ 12in (30cm)

This reliable pink bears dark-eyed, white, pink, or red flowers throughout summer above spreading mats of slender, narrow-leaved stems. Thrives in well-drained soil.

Epilobium glabellum
EPILOBIUM
☼ ☼ 5-8   ↕ ↔ 8in (20cm)

Clumps of arching stems densely clothed in semievergreen leaves produce creamy white or pink-tinted flowers in summer. It prefers a site in cool, damp shade.

Geum 'Red Wings'
GEUM
☼ ☼ 4-7   ↕ 24in (60cm) ↔ 16in (40cm)

Flowering freely throughout summer, this perennial produces semidouble, brilliant scarlet flowers on branched stems above clumps of softly-hairy, fresh green foliage.

Scabiosa caucasica 'Miss Willmott'
SCABIOUS

☀ 3-7 ↕ 36in (90cm) ↔ 24in (60cm)

Large, solitary white flowerheads with creamy white centers adorn the clumps of upright stems in summer. The gray-green stem leaves are deeply divided.

Oenothera macrocarpa
OZARK SUNDROPS

☀ 4-8 ↕ 6in (15cm) ↔ 20in (50cm)

Better known as *O. missouriensis*, this vigorous plant has prostrate stems, willowy leaves, and a succession of golden yellow flowers from late spring into autumn.

Tradescantia Andersoniana Group 'Isis'
SPIDERWORT

☀ ◐ 3-9 ↕ ↔ 20in (50cm)

Dense clumps of upright stems clothed in long, strap-shaped leaves carry clusters of attractive, large, three-petaled, dark blue flowers during summer and autumn.

Phygelius x *rectus* 'African Queen'
CAPE FIGWORT

☀ 8-9 ↕ 3ft (1m) ↔ 4½ft (1.4m)

A free-flowering plant with loose clumps of four-angled, woody-based stems. The pendent, tubular, pale red flowers, borne in summer, have yellow mouths.

Salvia microphylla
SAGE

☀ ◐ 10-11 ↕ ↔ 4ft (1.2m)

The softly-hairy, evergreen leaves of this woody-based perennial smell of black currants when bruised. Bright red flowers are produced from summer to autumn.

Viola 'Bowles' Black'
JOHNNY-JUMP-UP

☀ ◐ 3-8 ↕ 4in (10cm) ↔ 8in (20cm)

A charming pansy relative with evergreen tufts of leafy stems. It bears a succession of velvety black flowers with golden eyes from spring to autumn. Self-seeds freely.

FLORAL EFFECT

Perennials with Flowers in Flattened Heads or Sprays

THERE ARE MANY WAYS of creating interest in a border other than using plants of differing heights or varying foliage. One is to plant perennials that branch horizontally, or have flattened flowerheads or flowers borne along the same plane. These will provide a sharp contrast to plants that have an upright or rounded habit, or bear tall spikes of flowers.

Sedum spectabile
SHOWY STONECROP
☼ 3-8   ‡↔ 18in (45cm)

This easy-to-grow perennial is adored by butterflies and bees. During late summer, flattened heads of pink flowers cover the low mound of fleshy, grayish leaves.

Achillea 'Coronation Gold'
YARROW
☼ 3-9   ‡ 36in (90cm) ↔ 18in (45cm)

The flattened heads of tiny yellow flowers in summer and autumn are excellent for cutting and drying. Deeply divided, silver-gray leaves form a semievergreen clump.

Chaerophyllum hirsutum 'Roseum'
CHAEROPHYLLUM
☼ ☼ 5-8   ‡ 24in (60cm) ↔ 20in (50cm)

Flattened, lilac-pink flowerheads, borne in early summer, create a lacy effect above the clumps of hairy stems covered with ferny, deeply divided leaves.

Selinum wallichianum
SELINUM
☼ ☼ 7-9   ‡ 4ft (1.2m) ↔ 24in (60cm)

A lovely member of the carrot family with erect stems and divided, ferny leaves. In summer and autumn, tiny white flowers with black anthers are borne in flat heads.

Aster lateriflorus 'Horizontalis'
CALICO ASTER
☼ ☼ 3-8   ‡ 24in (60cm) ↔ 16in (40cm)

This dense, bushy aster has a distinctive horizontal branching habit, small leaves, and tiny pink-mauve flowers in autumn, when the leaves turn coppery purple.

Sambucus ebulus
DWARF ELDERBERRY
☼ ☼ 4-9   ‡ 36in (90cm) ↔ indefinite

A vigorous, suckering perennial with erect stems clothed in deeply divided leaves. The large, sweet-scented white flowers in summer are followed by black berries.

OTHER PERENNIALS WITH FLAT HEADS OR SPRAYS OF FLOWERS

Achillea filipendulina (see p.76) and cvs.
Aster amellus and cvs.
Ligularia dentata
Phlox stolonifera
Sambucus adnata
Solidago 'Crown of Rays'
Solidago rigida
Solidago 'Summer Sunshine'
Thalictrum aquilegiifolium
Verbena canadensis

Perennials with Flowers in Spikes

PERENNIALS WITH TALL, SPIKELIKE HEADS of flowers can create bold and dramatic effects, bringing structure and height to garden displays as they rise above other plants in stiff, tight spires or elegant, tapering racemes. In most flower spikes, the blooms open from the base upwards but some, like those of *Liatris* species, open from the top down.

Ligularia 'The Rocket'
LIGULARIA
☼ ☼ 4-8   ↕ 6ft (1.8m) ↔ 3ft (1m)

Tall, black-stemmed spires of tiny yellow flowers rise impressively in summer above the clumps of long-stalked, heart-shaped, toothy leaves. Best in constantly moist soil.

Delphinium 'Butterball'
DELPHINIUM
☼ 3-7   ↕ 5ft (1.5m) ↔ 30in (75cm)

In early summer, this gorgeous perennial bears dense, tapered racemes of creamy white, semidouble flowers on sturdy, erect stems clothed in deeply cut leaves.

Epilobium angustifolium var. *album*
WHITE-FLOWERED FIREWEED
☼ ☼ 3-7   ↕ 5ft (1.5m) ↔ 3ft (1m)

The erect stems of this vigorous perennial are clothed in narrow, willowlike leaves and sport long spires of white flowers with green sepals in summer. Self-seeds freely.

OTHER PERENNIALS WITH FLOWERS IN SPIKES

Actaea racemosa
Dictamnus albus, see p.114
Digitalis x *mertonensis*, see p.100
Liatris spp. and cvs.
Lobelia cardinalis
Lysimachia punctata, see p.57
Salvia x *superba*
Solidago sempervirens
Veronicastrum virginicum f. *album*, see p.35

FLORAL EFFECT

Digitalis parviflora
RUSTY FOXGLOVE
☼ 7-9   ↕ 4ft (1.2m) ↔ 18in (45cm)

Stiff, dense spikes of golden brown, red-veined flowers rise over low, leafy rosettes in summer, creating an effect quite unlike the common foxglove (*D. purpurea*).

Kniphofia 'Erecta'
TORCH LILY
☼ ☼ 6-9   ↕ 36in (90cm) ↔ 24in (60cm)

A robust, clump-forming plant with stiff stems and strap-shaped leaves. The dense pokers of coral-red flowers become erect after opening in summer.

Verbascum chaixii 'Album'
NETTLE-LEAVED MULLEIN
☼ 4-8   ↕ 36in (90cm) ↔ 18in (45cm)

Striking and reliable, this mullein bears erect, often branched stems crowded with white, mauve-centered flowers in summer over rosettes of hairy, gray-green leaves.

Perennials with Hot, Fiery-colored Flowers

FIERY-COLORED FLOWERS may not appeal to gardeners with delicate tastes, but for many others they inject life and passion into the garden. A single hot-colored perennial, reflecting the intensity and warmth of the sun, can brighten an otherwise bland border. Alternatively, combining a few of them in a mixed planting will create a riot of color.

OTHER PERENNIALS WITH ORANGE FLOWERS

Belamcanda chinensis
Euphorbia griffithii 'Fireglow', see p.90
Fritillaria imperialis
Helenium 'Brilliant'
Helianthemum 'Fire Dragon'
Kniphofia 'Pfitzeri'
Lilium 'Enchantment'
Lilium superbum
Phlox paniculata 'Orange Perfection'
Silene virginica

Asclepias tuberosa
BUTTERFLY WEED
☼ 3-9   ↕ 3ft (90cm) ↔ 24in (60cm)

Rounded, glowing orange flower clusters crown the erect stems of this sun-loving native wildflower in summer, attracting butterflies. Do not move once established.

Dahlia 'Bishop of Llandaff'
DAHLIA
☼ 7-11   ↕ 3½ft (1.1m) ↔ 18in (45cm)

In late summer, the semidouble, glowing red blooms of this popular tender plant are striking against its dusky red leaves. Overwinter the roots indoors in the north.

Geum coccineum
SCARLET AVENS
☼ ☼ 4-7   ↕ 20in (50cm) ↔ 12in (30cm)

Throughout spring and summer, slender, branching stems carry orange-red flowers with golden stamens above a loose clump of deeply divided, hairy green leaves.

Crocosmia masoniorum
CROCOSMIA
☼ ☼ 5-9   ↕ 4ft (1.2m) ↔ 24in (60cm)

A classic perennial forming bold clumps of sword-shaped, pleated leaves. Arching spikes of trumpet-shaped, rich orange-red flowers in open summer. Good for cutting.

Gaillardia x *grandiflora* 'Dazzler'
BLANKET FLOWER
☼ 4-9   ↕ 30in (75cm) ↔ 18in (45cm)

This bushy, often short-lived perennial has big, daisy flowerheads in summer and early autumn. The orange-red blooms are yellow-tipped with maroon centers.

Helenium 'Septemberfuchs'
HELENIUM
☼ 3-7   ↕ 5ft (1.5m) ↔ 24in (60cm)

In late summer and autumn, stout clumps of upright, leafy stems carry a multitude of brilliant orange-brown, yellow-suffused daisy flowers with brown hearts.

Lychnis chalcedonica 'Flore Pleno'
MALTESE CROSS
☼ 3-9 ↕ 4ft (1.2m) ↔ 18in (45cm)

During summer, erect, hairy, leafy stems carry dense clusters of double scarlet flowers. It may need support. The single-flowered form is also very attractive.

Potentilla 'Monsieur Rouillard'
POTENTILLA
☼ 5-9 ↕ 18in (45cm) ↔ 24in (60cm)

This potentilla has a loose clump of erect or spreading stems with deeply divided leaves. Its double, deep blood red flowers with yellow markings open in summer.

Hemerocallis fulva 'Flore Pleno'
DAYLILY
☼ ☼ 2-9 ↕ 30in (75cm) ↔ 4ft (1.2m)

In summer, erect stems bearing trumpet-shaped, double, orange-brown flowers with dark red centers rise above the bold clump of strap-shaped, arching leaves.

Primula 'Inverewe'
CANDELABRA PRIMROSE
☼ ☼ 6-8 ↕ ↔ 30in (75cm)

A strong-growing, semievergreen primrose for damp sites with a rosette of toothed leaves. Mealy-white stems carry whorls of striking, bright red flowers in summer.

Kniphofia triangularis
RED HOT POKER
☼ 6-9 ↕ 30in (75cm) ↔ 18in (45cm)

This species is late-flowering and reliable. It forms a clump of slender, grassy leaves and produces dramatic spikes of reddish orange flowers during autumn.

Monarda 'Squaw'
BEE BALM
☼ 4-8 ↕ 36in (90cm) ↔ 18in (45cm)

In summer and autumn, bold clumps of hairy stems carry dense clusters of bright red flowers loved by bees and humming-birds. Leaves are aromatic when bruised.

OTHER PERENNIALS WITH RED FLOWERS

Achillea 'Fanal'
Crocosmia 'Lucifer', see p.122
Hemerocallis 'Pardon Me'
Heuchera 'Mount Saint Helens'
Hibiscus moscheutos 'Lord Baltimore'
Lilium canadense
Lobelia cardinalis
Monarda didyma 'Gardenview Scarlet'
Papaver orientale 'Glowing Embers'
Potentilla 'Gibson's Scarlet', see p.81

FLORAL EFFECT

111

Perennials with Cool-colored Flowers

PINK, BLUE, AND PALE YELLOW are all colors that are cool to the eye. They bring a delicate subtlety to plantings in the garden. White too, plays a similar role. When used with care and discretion, these cool-colored flowers can achieve a soothing effect at any season, but especially if they bloom during the heat of summer.

Centaurea pulcherrima
CENTAUREA
☀ 4-8   ↕ 16in (40cm) ↔ 24in (60cm)

Slender stems rise from clumps of deeply lobed or entire, woolly-backed leaves to bear lovely rose-pink, pale-centered flowers from late spring to early summer.

Agapanthus 'Snowy Owl'
AFRICAN LILY
☀ ☀ 8-10   ↕ 4ft (1.2m) ↔ 24in (60cm)

Sturdy stems carry large, loosely rounded umbels of bell-shaped, pure white flowers in late summer above the bold clumps of narrow, strap-shaped green leaves.

Astilbe × *arendsii* 'Venus'
ASTILBE
☀ ☀ 3-9   ↕ 36in (90cm) ↔ 18in (45cm)

Large, frothy, conical plumes of tiny pink flowers rise above robust clumps of much-divided, bright green, handsome leaves in early summer. It prefers a moist soil.

OTHER PERENNIALS WITH EARLY, COOL-COLORED FLOWERS

Anemone nemorosa
Brunnera macrophylla, see p.84
Corydalis flexuosa 'China Blue', see p.71
Dicentra spectabilis 'Alba', see p.114
Epimedium grandiflorum
  'Rose Queen', see p.156
   Heuchera 'Chatter Box'
   Phlox divaricata
Polemonium caeruleum
Thalictrum aquilegiifolium

Anchusa azurea 'Loddon Royalist'
ITALIAN BUGLOSS
☀ 3-8   ↕ 36in (90cm) ↔ 24in (60cm)

The sturdy clumps of erect, leafy, roughly-hairy stems sport branched heads of pretty, deep blue flowers, each with a white eye, in early summer. It will self-sow.

Campanula persicifolia
'Telham Beauty'
☀ ☀ 3-7   ↕ 36in (90cm) ↔ 12in (30cm)

A lovely form of a popular cottage-garden perennial with racemes of large, light blue, bell-shaped flowers on tall, slender stems in summer. Easy to grow and reliable.

Chrysanthemum 'Clara Curtis'
CHRYSANTHEMUM
☀ 4-9   ↕ 30in (75cm) ↔ 24in (60cm)

Scented, long-lasting, clear pink daisylike flowers are borne freely from late summer into autumn. Finely-cut leaves cover the bushy clump of stems.

Delphinium 'Blue Bees'
DELPHINIUM
☼ 3-7 ‡ 3ft (1m) ↔ 18in (45cm)

The wiry, upright, branching stems bear
deeply cut leaves and racemes of long-
spurred, clear blue, white-eyed flowers in
early summer and again in late summer.

Iris winogradowii
IRIS
☼ 7-9 ‡ 3in (7.5cm) ↔ 4in (10cm)

In early spring, primrose yellow flowers
with green-flecked falls rise above tufts of
four-sided, slender leaves. It is excellent
for containers, troughs, or a rock garden.

Monarda 'Croftway Pink'
BEE BALM, BERGAMOT
☼ ☼ 4-8 ‡ 36in (90cm) ↔ 24in (60cm)

Popular with bees, this aromatic perennial
has erect stems clothed in paired leaves.
In summer, it freely bears clusters of clear
rose-pink flowers with dark bracts.

Penstemon heterophyllus
'Blue Gem'
☼ ☼ 6-9 ‡ ↔ 16in (40cm)

Striking in flower, this evergreen or semievergreen, woody-based perennial bears
slender, glossy leaves and dense, erect
racemes of tubular blue summer flowers.

**OTHER PERENNIALS WITH LATE,
COOL-COLORED FLOWERS**

Anemone japonica 'Pamina'
Begonia grandis
Boltonia asteroides 'Pink Beauty'
Clematis integrifolia
Geranium x *oxonianum* 'A.T. Johnson'
Liriope muscari, see p.71
Nepeta 'Six Hills Giant', see p.127
Phlox paniculata 'Fujiyama',
    see p.115
Platycodon grandiflorus f. *albus*

Gentiana asclepiadea
WILLOW GENTIAN
☼ ☼ 5-7 ‡ 36in (90cm) ↔ 12in (60cm)

Pairs of willowlike leaves clothe the bold
clumps of arching stems. Pale or deep
blue flowers emerge from the upper leaf
axils during late summer and autumn.

Paeonia lactiflora 'Sarah Bernhardt'
PEONY
☼ ☼ 3-8 ‡ ↔ 36in (90cm)

This robust perennial produces clumps of
upright, leafy stems that bear very large,
fragrant, fully double, rose-pink blooms in
early summer. Excellent for cutting.

Sidalcea 'Elsie Heugh'
CHECKERBLOOM
☼ 5-8 ‡ 36in (90cm) ↔ 18in (45cm)

A reliable plant with erect or spreading
stems that bear deeply lobed stem leaves,
and tall racemes of long-lasting, satiny,
purple-pink flowers during summer.

Perennials with Pale-colored Flowers

PALE-COLORED FLOWERS provide one of the most effective means of illuminating a dark corner or shaded border in the garden. They shine when set against a backdrop of dark foliage. At the end of the day when darkness is falling, they attract and reflect any available light, drawing attention to borders and beds.

Dictamnus albus
GAS PLANT
☼ ☼ 3-8　　↕ 36in (90cm) ↔ 24in (60cm)

A slow-growing plant forming clumps of aromatic, deeply divided foliage. In early summer, bold, erect racemes of white flowers with conspicuous stamens appear.

OTHER PERENNIALS WITH PALE-COLORED FLOWERS

Achillea 'Moonshine'
Alcea rugosa
Aquilegia canadensis 'Corbett'
Echinacea purpurea 'White Swan'
Lilium candidum
Phlox carolina 'Miss Lingard'
Platycodon grandiflorus 'Shell Pink'
Polemonium carneum
Potentilla recta var. *sulphurea*
Salvia govaniana

Coreopsis verticillata 'Moonbeam'
THREADLEAF COREOPSIS
☼ ☼ 3-9　　↕ 20in (50cm) ↔ 18in (45cm)

In summer, a profusion of lemon yellow flowerheads covers this low, bushy plant. Its slender, branched stems bear finely cut leaves. Ideal for the front of a border.

Anthemis tinctoria 'Sauce Hollandaise'
GOLDEN MARGUERITE
☼ 3-8　　↕ ↔ 24in (60cm)

Long-stalked, yellow-centered, pale cream daisy heads are borne freely over many weeks in summer above clumps of finely divided, dark green leaves.

Campanula persicifolia 'Chettle Charm'
PEACH-LEAVED BELLFLOWER
☼ ☼ 3-7　　↕ 36in (90cm) ↔ 12in (30cm)

One of the loveliest cultivars of a popular perennial with tall slender stems, narrow leaves, and sprays of pale, bell-shaped summer flowers tinged blue at the edges.

Dicentra spectabilis 'Alba'
BLEEDING HEART
☼ 2-9　　↕ 24in (30cm) ↔ 18in (45cm)

This beautiful and elegant perennial has ferny, pale green foliage and produces long stems hung with locket-shaped white flowers from late spring to early summer.

Gaura lindheimeri
WHITE GAURA
☼ ☼ 5-9　　↕ 4ft (1.2m) ↔ 36in (90cm)

Branched stems of slender leaves give this native perennial a bushy, loose habit. Pink buds open to elegant sprays of white star-shaped flowers from summer to autumn.

Phlox paniculata 'Fujiyama'
BORDER PHLOX
☼ ☼ 4-8   ↕ 36in (90cm) ↔ 24in (60cm)

Impressive large heads of snow white
flowers crown the stout clumps of upright,
leafy stems in late summer. This is one of
the best perennials for white flowers.

Phygelius aequalis 'Yellow Trumpet'
PHYGELIUS
☼ 7-9   ↕ 3ft (1m) ↔ 4ft (1.2m)

This shrubby perennial has clumps of
woody-based, leafy stems bearing loose
racemes of drooping, tubular, pale yellow
flowers from summer to early autumn.

Gillenia trifoliata
BOWMAN'S-ROOT
☼ ☼ 4-8   ↕ 3ft (1m) ↔ 24in (60cm)

Wiry, reddish stems bear divided, bronze-
green leaves and sprays of small white
flowers in spring and summer. Decorative
red calyces remain after the petals fall.

Kirengeshoma palmata
KIRENGESHOMA
☼ 5-8   ↕ 4ft (1.2m) ↔ 30in (75cm)

A handsome perennial for moist soil with
dark stems and large, boldly toothed or
lobed leaves. Sprays of waxy, pale yellow
flowers open in late summer and autumn.

Kniphofia 'Little Maid'
TORCH LILY
☼ ☼ 5-9   24in (60cm) ↔ 18in (45cm)

Erect stems rise from clumps of grassy
leaves in late summer to bear dense spikes
of tubular, buff-tinted yellow flowers that
are pale green in bud, fading to ivory.

Trollius × *cultorum* 'Alabaster'
GLOBEFLOWER
☼ ☼ 3-6   ↕ 24in (60cm) ↔ 16in (40cm)

Beautiful, rounded, pale primrose yellow
flowers rise on long stems above clumps
of long-stalked, lobed, glossy leaves from
late spring to summer. It likes moist soil.

Perennials with Fragrant Flowers

I**T IS OFTEN SURPRISING** to find that a beautiful flower does not have a scent to match. However, most highly fragrant perennials have relatively small flowers and those with large, scented blooms are frequently white or pale colored. Many fragrant flowers are at their best at the end of the day, when night-flying pollinators visit the garden.

Iris graminea
IRIS
☼ ☀ 6-9　　↕ 16in (40cm) ↔ 12in (30cm)

During late spring and early summer, the small, violet-purple flowers of this clump-forming, grassy-leaved iris give off a very distinctive, plumlike fragrance.

PERENNIALS WITH FRAGRANT SPRING FLOWERS

Convallaria majalis
Hyacinthoides non-scripta
Hyacinthus orientalis
Iris reticulata
Iris unguicularis
Muscari spp. and cvs.
Narcissus jonquilla
Narcissus × odorus
Petasites fragrans
Phlox divaricata
Viola odorata

Dianthus 'Doris'
PINK
☼ 4-8　　↕ ↔ 16in (40cm)

Double, pale pink, dark-centered flowers top the bloomy, blue-gray, narrow-leaved stems of this reliable pink during summer and early autumn. It has evergreen leaves.

Hemerocallis 'Marion Vaughn'
DAYLILY
☼ ☀ 4-9　　↕ 34in (85cm) ↔ 30in (75cm)

During summer, clusters of very fragrant, trumpet-shaped, lemon yellow flowers are borne freely on upright stems above bold clumps of narrow, strap-shaped leaves.

Erysimum cheiri 'Harpur Crewe'
ENGLISH WALLFLOWER
☼ 8-9　　↕ 12in (30cm) ↔ 14in (60cm)

The scent of wallflowers is one of the joys of spring. Although short-lived, they are available in many flower colours. This one bears cheerful, double yellow blooms.

Hosta 'Honeybells'
HOSTA
☼ ☀ 3-8　　↕ 30in (75cm) ↔ 4ft (1.2m)

This vigorous hosta develops clumps of heart-shaped, veined, and wavy-margined leaves. Fragrant, pale lavender flowers are borne on erect stems in late summer.

Lilium regale
REGAL LILY
☼ 3-8　　↕ 5ft (1.5m) ↔ 16in (40cm)

One of the best known fragrant lilies, this is a must for sunny gardens. Robust stems flaunt clusters of trumpet-shaped white, pink-striped flowers during summer.

Narcissus poeticus var. *recurvus*
POET'S NARCISSUS
☼ ☼ 4-9　　↕ 14in (35cm) ↔ 12in (30cm)

Beautiful, crisp white flowers with pale yellow, red-rimmed cups rise above the narrow, strap-shaped leaves in late spring. In time, it will form clumps.

Nicotiana sylvestris
FLOWERING TOBACCO
☼ ☼ 9-11　　↕ 5ft (1.5m) ↔ 24in (60cm)

The robust, leafy stems carry large heads of long-tubed, fragrant, pure white flowers in summer. A tender perennial generally cultivated as an annual. It will reseed.

> **PERENNIALS WITH FRAGRANT SUMMER FLOWERS**
>
> *Dianthus* spp. and cvs.
> *Dictamnus albus*, see p.114
> *Hemerocallis lilioasphodelus*
> *Hesperis matronalis*
> *Hosta plantaginea*
> *Hymenocallis narcissiflora*
> *Lilium candidum*
> *Nepeta* x *faassenii*
> *Paeonia lactiflora* 'Sarah Bernhardt', see p.113

Phlox maculata 'Alpha'
WILD SWEET WILLIAM
☼ ☼ 3-9　　↕ 36in (90cm) ↔ 24in (60cm)

This cultivar of a native phlox produces erect clumps of leafy stems bearing large heads of fragrant pink flowers in summer. It has glossy, mildew-resistant leaves.

Primula auricula var. *albocincta*
AURICULA PRIMROSE
☼ ☼ 2-8　　↕ ↔ 8in (20cm)

Umbels of fragrant yellow, white-eyed flowers rise above the small clumps of gray-green, white-edged leaves in spring. Excellent for a rock garden or container.

Tulbaghia violacea
SOCIETY GARLIC
☼ 8-11　　↕ 20in (50cm) ↔ 10in (25cm)

Erect stems carry loose umbels of fragrant lilac flowers in summer and early autumn over evergreen clumps of narrow, gray-green leaves. Prefers a warm, sunny site.

Verbena corymbosa 'Gravetye'
VERBENA
☼ 9-11　　↕ 3ft (90cm) ↔ 24in (60cm)

This tender but very attractive perennial produces dense heads of pinkish purple, white-eyed flowers throughout summer that give off a sweet perfume.

FLORAL EFFECT

117

FOLIAGE EFFECT

WHILE MOST FLOWERS bloom for a relatively brief period, foliage can provide a continuous source of drama and atmosphere in the garden. Perennials that have contrasting leaf shapes, textures, and colors will enliven beds and borders. They can also make a striking display as specimen plants.

Hosta 'Big Daddy' for bold foliage

△ DELICATE CONTRAST *A feathery-leaved* Dicentra *complements the silver-splashed, rounded foliage of a* Lamium.

Foliage provides a constant focus in the garden, acting as both a foil for flowers and a firm basis for design. The perennials in this section offer a huge range of leaf arrangements, shapes, and colors which, used thoughtfully and with flair, can be combined for spectacular effects. Large-leaved perennials, such as ornamental rhubarbs (*Rheum*), can make impressive specimen plants, or add structure and impact to beds and borders. Foliage perennials will also prove their worth in containers, providing a satisfying, long-lasting display that can be moved around the garden. Richly colored foliage is often associated with autumn, but it is worth remembering that many perennials offer leaves that are attractively variegated or colored for much of the year. Excellent for brightening a dull border, they are also useful for shady sites where other plants may struggle to flower without sufficient sun. In winter, when most other perennials lie below ground, those with evergreen or overwintering leaves, such as heucheras and hardy ferns, can also be used to bring interest and life to the garden landscape.

FOLIAGE CHARACTERISTICS

Leaf arrangements, shapes, and colors are all important elements to consider when combining foliage perennials for eye-catching contrasts and effects.

ARRANGEMENT *of leaves is a characteristic feature of every plant. Exploit this to bring structure and texture to the garden.*

SHAPE AND SIZE *can be contrasted for extra interest. Leaves with jagged, feathery, or spiny margins will all create different effects.*

COLOR *in foliage can be used to create a calm, dark backdrop, or to bring brightness and warmth to shady sites in the garden.*

◁ COLOR CONTAINER *Yellow-striped* Hakonechloa *and blue-leaved* Acaena *contrast here with upright* Imperata.

▷ DRAMATIC LEAVES *Perennials with bold foliage make good specimen plants or can be used to great effect in a border.*

Perennials with Evergreen or Overwintering Foliage

I N WINTER, when most herbaceous perennials have died down to below ground level and no longer provide a focus in the garden, it is important to have at least a scattering of plants with evergreen leaves or foliage that overwinters in an attractive state. Even when flowerless, these plants will bring continual color and interest to any garden.

FOLIAGE EFFECT

Asarum europaeum
EUROPEAN WILD GINGER
☼ ☀ 4-8   ↕ 3in (8cm) ↔ 12in (30cm)

One of the best perennial groundcovers, and attractive all year round. During late spring, the dense carpet of kidney-shaped, glossy leaves hides curious little flowers.

Helleborus argutifolius
CORSICAN HELLEBORE
☼ ☀ 7-8   ↕ ↔ 36in (90cm)

This handsome plant can be admired all year. Pale green, overwintering stems bear beautifully veined, prickle-toothed leaves and apple green flowers in late winter.

Kniphofia caulescens
RED HOT POKER
☼ ☀ 6-9   ↕ 4ft (1.2m) ↔ 36in (90cm)

An impressive perennial producing large clumps of fine-toothed, blue-green leaves topped in late summer by imposing coral red flower spikes that fade to yellow.

Bergenia cordifolia 'Purpurea'
BERGENIA
☼ ☀ 3-9   ↕ 24in (60cm) ↔ 30in (75cm)

The leathery, rounded, deep green leaves form a low patch and turn purple- or red-tinted in winter. Stems of magenta-purple flowers emerge during early spring.

Iris foetidissima 'Variegata'
STINKING IRIS
☼ ☀ 6-9   ↕ ↔ 24in (60cm)

A superb, variegated form of the species with evergreen, strap-shaped, shiny leaves boldly margined in white. Orange seedheads follow the purple summer flowers.

Phormium cookianum subsp. *hookeri* 'Tricolor'
☼ 9-11   ↕ ↔ 6ft (2m)

A colorful tender perennial eventually forming a large mound of arching, glossy green leaves with creamy yellow and red margins. It can be overwintered indoors.

Polypodium interjectum 'Cornubiense'
POLYPODY
☼ ◐ 5-8   ↕ ↔ 16in (40cm)

The deeply divided, rich green fronds of
this vigorous, creeping fern make it an
excellent groundcover. It is also suitable
for a rock garden, wall, or container.

Pulmonaria saccharata 'Leopard'
PULMONARIA
☼ ◐ 3-8   ↕ 12in (30cm) ↔ 24in (60cm)

Silvery-spotted, semievergreen foliage
makes this perennial particularly effective
groundcover. Violet-red flowers are borne
during late winter and early spring.

Tellima grandiflora
FRINGE CUPS
◐ 4-8   ↕ 32in (80cm) ↔ 12in (30cm)

Semievergreen clumps of long-stalked,
heart-shaped, hairy and scalloped leaves
are topped by handsome, loose spikes of
greenish white flowers during spring.

OTHER EVERGREEN OR OVERWINTERING PERENNIALS

Acanthus mollis
Arum italicum
Carex morrowii 'Variegata'
Chiastophyllum oppositifolium
Dryopteris intermedia
Equisetum hyemale
Helictotrichon sempervirens, see p.137
Helleborus orientalis
Iberis sempervirens
Lavandula angustifolia
Liriope muscari 'Variegata'
Phlomis russeliana
Polypodium spp. and cvs.
Polystichum acrostichoides
Polystichum munitum, see p.148
Santolina chamaecyparissus
Sasa veitchii, see p.141
Yucca filamentosa

Vinca minor 'Argenteovariegata'
COMMON PERIWINKLE
☼ ◐ 4-9   ↕ 6in (15cm) ↔ indefinite

All periwinkles are useful groundcovers,
but this also has leaves with attractive,
creamy white margins. Pale violet-blue
flowers emerge in spring and autumn.

FOLIAGE EFFECT

121

Perennials with Strap- or Sword-shaped Leaves

PERENNIALS THAT FORM CLUMPS of long, slender leaves are irresistible and always striking. Regardless of whether the leaves stand stiff and upright, or bend and arch in a more graceful manner, they are invaluable for contrasting with more conventional, broad-leaved perennials in beds or borders. They can also be used as dramatic specimen plants.

FOLIAGE EFFECT

Arundo donax 'Macrophylla'
GIANT REED
☼ 5-9   ↕ 15ft (5m) ↔ 6ft (2m)

This giant grass produces long, arching, slender, glaucous leaves and bamboolike stems that flaunt feathery plumes in summer. It prefers a warm, sheltered site.

Eryngium agavifolium
ERYNGIUM
☼ 7-9   ↕ 4ft (1.2m) ↔ 24in (60cm)

The sharply toothed, glossy, evergreen leaves form a striking, erect clump above which sturdy stems carry cylindrical heads of tiny, greenish white flowers in summer.

Iris pseudacorus 'Variegata'
YELLOW FLAG
☼ ☼ 4-9   ↕ ↔ 4ft (1.2m)

A vigorous iris for wet sites forming a large patch of tall green leaves with bold white or creamy yellow bands. Yellow flowers are borne on erect stems during summer.

EVERGREEN AND SEMIEVERGREEN PERENNIALS WITH STRAP- OR SWORD-SHAPED LEAVES

Acorus gramineus
Crocosmia paniculata
Eryngium eburneum, see p.28
Eryngium pandanifolium
Hemerocallis aurantiaca
Iris foetidissima 'Variegata', see p.120
Watsonia pillansii
Yucca filamentosa
Yucca recurvifolia

Crocosmia 'Lucifer'
CROCOSMIA
☼ ☼ 5-9   ↕ 4ft (1.2m) ↔ 18in (45cm)

A bright and cheerful perennial forming a clump of robust, sword-shaped leaves. Its arching, branched spikes of brilliant red, late-summer flowers are good for cutting.

Hemerocallis 'Gentle Shepherd'
DAYLILY
☼ ☼ 4-9   ↕ 26in (65cm) ↔ 4ft (1.2m)

Bold clumps of semievergreen, narrow, arching green leaves are topped by ivory-white, trumpet-shaped flowers with green throats during summer.

Iris sibirica 'Perry's Blue'
IRIS
☼ ☼ 2-9   ↕ 4ft (1.2m) ↔ 3ft (1m)

Erect clumps of narrow, grasslike leaves are topped by blue-violet flowers on erect, soldierlike stems in early summer. The winter seed capsules are also decorative.

Kniphofia 'Wrexham Buttercup'
TORCH LILY
☼ **5-9**   ↕ 4ft (1.2m) ↔ 24in (60cm)

The long, arching, narrow green leaves
of this perennial form a dense clump. Its
pokerlike heads of rich yellow flowers are
carried on strong, erect stems in summer.

Persicaria macrophylla
PERSICARIA
☼ ☼ **5-8**   ↕ ↔ 12in (30cm)

A semievergreen perennial with lance-
shaped, conspicuously veined leaves and
dense spikes of pink to red flowers borne
through summer into autumn.

Phormium tenax
NEW ZEALAND FLAX
☼ **9-11**   ↕ 12ft (4m) ↔ 6ft (2m)

Few perennials are as eye-catching as this
one with its sword-shaped, glaucous gray,
evergreen leaves and statuesque panicles
of waxy, dark red flowers in summer.

Sisyrinchium striatum 'Aunt May'
SISYRINCHIUM
☼ **7-8**   ↕ 20in (50cm) ↔ 12in (30cm)

This irislike perennial has striking fans of
sword-shaped, gray-green leaves boldly
striped creamy yellow. In summer, it bears
straw yellow flowers in stiff spikes.

Yucca flaccida
YUCCA
☼ **6-9**   ↕ 22in (55cm) ↔ 5ft (1.5m)

Reliable and evergreen, this yucca forms
a bold rosette of narrow, dark blue-green
leaves with wispy marginal fibers. Large
spikes of ivory flowers emerge in summer.

**HERBACEOUS PERENNIALS WITH
STRAP- OR SWORD-SHAPED LEAVES**

Belamcanda chinensis
Carex siderosticha 'Variegata', see p.144
Elymus arenarius
Eremurus stenophyllus, see p.39
Eryngium yuccifolium
Gladiolus communis subsp. *byzantinus*,
  see p. 39
Hemerocallis fulva
Iris Bearded Hybrids
Liatris spicata
Pyrrosia lingua
Tradescantia virginiana

FOLIAGE EFFECT

Perennials with Jagged or Deeply Cut Leaves

A SUBTLE, YET EFFECTIVE WAY to add contrast and texture to a planting is to combine plants with different leaf shapes. Plants with deeply cut or jaggedly cut foliage are especially effective contrasted with bold, entire leaves. Many of these plants have the added advantage of attractive flowers.

Rodgersia henrici
RODGERSIA
☼ ☀ 5-8   ↕ ↔ 3ft (1m)

All rodgersias sport handsome foliage, but this one is particularly desirable. It has large, horsechestnut-like leaves and pink or white flower plumes in summer.

Astilbe 'Bronce Elegans'
ASTILBE
☼ ☀ 5-8   ↕ 12in (30cm) ↔ 10in (25cm)

One of the smallest and daintiest astilbes forming mounds of ferny, glossy, dark green leaves. In summer, it produces neat little plumes of pinkish red flowers.

Incarvillea delavayi
HARDY GLOXINIA
☼ ☀ 6-8   ↕ 24in (60cm) ↔ 12in (30cm)

Attractive clumps of bold, deeply divided, dark green leaves are truly eye-catching in summer when topped with erect stems of trumpet-shaped, rose-pink flowers.

Sinacalia tangutica
CHINESE RAGWORT
☼ ☀ 4-7   ↕ 4ft (1.2m) ↔ indefinite

Creeping rootstocks produce stout, dark stems clothed in jaggedly cut leaves. In autumn, conical heads of yellow flowers emerge. This plant can be invasive.

Actaea simplex Atropurpurea Group
KAMCHATKA BUGBANE
☼ 3-8   ↕ 4ft (1.2m) ↔ 24in (60cm)

The loose clumps of large, much-divided, dark green to purplish leaves are topped in autumn by cylindrical, dark-stemmed racemes of tiny white flowers.

Ligularia przewalskii
LIGULARIA
☼ ☀ 3-8   ↕ 6ft (2m) ↔ 3ft (1m)

This perennial has large clumps of sharply divided, deeply cut, rounded leaves. The dark-stemmed spires of yellow flowers are borne in summer. Requires moist soil.

OTHER PERENNIALS WITH JAGGED OR DEEPLY CUT LEAVES

Acanthus spinosus, see p.126
Aconitum spp. and cvs.
Astrantia major
Eryngium amethystinum
Kirengeshoma palmata, see p.115
Geranium palmatum, see p.129
Rheum palmatum var. *tanguticum*, see p.129
Rodgersia pinnata, see p.67
Rodgersia podophylla, see p.139

FOLIAGE EFFECT

Perennials with Feathery Foliage

MANY FERNS AND SOME PERENNIALS have leaves so finely divided that they create a striking feathery effect in the garden – the perfect foil for more dramatic foliage or for hot-colored flowers, which stand out against the delicate leaves. Many will also make excellent specimen plants in containers or in a prominent garden site.

Meum athamanticum
BALDMONEY, SPIGNEL
☼ 5-8 ↕ 18in (45cm) ↔ 12in (30cm)

Like fennel, this plant is a member of the carrot family, with similar feathery, deeply divided, aromatic leaves. Dense heads of tiny white flowers are borne in summer.

Adiantum pedatum
MAIDENHAIR FERN
☼ 2-8 ↕ ↔ 16in (40cm)

Given time and a sheltered, moist site, this lovely, hardy native fern will develop a large clump of slender, glossy black stalks with delicate, much-divided fronds.

OTHER PERENNIALS WITH FEATHERY FOLIAGE

Achillea millefolium
Artemisia ludoviciana
Astilbe spp. and cvs.
Athyrium filix-femina, see p.148
Dicentra eximia
Ferula communis
Myrrhis odorata, see p.55
Paesia scaberula
Paeonia tenuifolia, see p.157
Polystichum setiferum, see p.148

Corydalis cheilanthifolia
CORYDALIS
☼ ☼ 5-7 ↕ 12in (30cm) ↔ 10in (25cm)

Each finely divided, orange-tinted leaf is like a green feather. Slender racemes of deep yellow flowers are borne in spring and summer. It will seed around if happy.

Aruncus aethusifolius
ARUNCUS
☼ ☼ 4-7 ↕ 10in (25cm) ↔ 16in (40cm)

A charming plant producing small mounds of finely divided, crisp green leaves that turn orange or yellow in autumn. Small white flower plumes are borne in summer.

Foeniculum vulgare 'Purpureum'
PURPLE FENNEL
☼ 5-9 ↕ 6ft (1.8m) ↔ 18in (45cm)

This aromatic fennel has attractive, finely divided, plumed leaves that are bronze-purple when young, aging to blue-green. Flat yellow flowerheads open in summer.

Onychium japonicum
CARROT FERN
☼ ☼ 9-11 ↕ 20in (50cm) ↔ 12in (30cm)

An elegant tender fern producing a dense clump of finely divided, bright green fronds on slender, wiry stalks. In northern zones, this fern is grown under glass.

FOLIAGE EFFECT

Perennials with Spiny Leaves

THE JAGGED EFFECT of spiny or prickly-leaved plants has a definite appeal for some gardeners. Often architectural in habit as well as ornamental, these distinctive perennials can bring structure to borders or make bold specimens. Many are particularly useful for dry sites, as their spiny leaves are specially adapted to minimize water loss.

Eryngium variifolium
SEA HOLLY
☼ 5-9   ↕ 14in (35cm) ↔ 10in (25cm)

A beautiful evergreen forming a rosette of rounded, silver-veined leaves. In summer, erect, branched stems bear small, gray-blue flowerheads with spiny white collars.

OTHER PERENNIALS WITH SPINY LEAVES
Agave havardiana
Berkheya macrocephala
Cynara cardunculus, see p.130
Dasylirion wheeleri
Echinops sphaerocephalus
Eryngium bourgatii, see p.20
Eryngium eburneum, see p.22
Sabal minor
Yucca gloriosa, see p.31
Yucca rupicola

Acanthus spinosus
SPINY BEAR'S-BREECH
☼ ☼ 7-10   ↕ 4ft (1.2m) ↔ 24in (60cm)

The large, deeply divided, green or gray-green leaves have white midribs and spiny margins. Tall racemes of purple-bracted white flowers open in spring and summer.

Aciphylla aurea
GOLDEN SPANIARD
☼ 8-10   ↕ ↔ 3ft (1m)

This slow-growing, evergreen plant forms an imposing rosette of stiff, spine-tipped, deeply divided, gray-green leaves with bold, golden yellow midribs and margins.

Eryngium maritimum
SEA HOLLY
☼ 5-8   ↕ ↔ 12in (30cm)

Found in maritime sands or gravels in the wild, this sea holly has formidably spiny, deeply lobed, leathery, bloomy, blue-gray leaves. Pale blue flowers open in summer.

Puya chilensis
PUYA
☼ 10-11   ↕ 12ft (4m) ↔ 6ft (2m)

After several years, a tall, stout stem with a head of waxy, yellow-green flowers rises from the massive rosette of rapierlike, spine-toothed, leathery, evergreen leaves.

Perennials with Aromatic Leaves

SCENTS CAN MAKE an important and evocative contribution to a garden and are most commonly associated with the fragrance of flowers. The leaves of most perennials, however, also give off at least a faint aroma, and some even have foliage with a very distinctive or strong scent. In some cases, this is released by simply brushing against the plant.

Nepeta 'Six Hills Giant'
CATMINT
☼ ☀ **3-8**   ↕ 36in (90cm) ↔ 24in (60cm)

This dense, bushy, clump-forming plant bears aromatic, light gray-green leaves and leafy spikes of lavender-blue summer flowers. Loved, but also damaged, by cats.

Helichrysum italicum
CURRY PLANT
☼ **8-9**   ↕ 24in (60cm) ↔ 36in (90cm)

Aromatic, evergreen, narrow, felted, silver-gray leaves clothe the woolly stems of this woody-based perennial or subshrub. Deep yellow flower clusters open in summer.

OTHER PERENNIALS WITH AROMATIC LEAVES

Acorus calamus
Artemisia absinthium
Dictamnus albus, see p.108
Foeniculum vulgare 'Purpureum',
  see p.119
  Lavandula angustifolia
  Mentha spp. and cvs.
Monarda didyma
  Myrrhis odorata, see p.49
  Origanum vulgare
Perovskia atriplicifolia
Thymus spp. and cvs.

Agastache foeniculum 'Alabaster'
ANISE HYSSOP
☼ **6-9**   ↕ 36in (90cm) ↔ 12in (30cm)

Downy, anise-scented leaves, paler green beneath, clothe the erect stems. Spikes of two-lipped white flowers, loved by bees, are borne from midsummer to autumn.

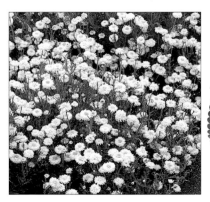

Chamaemelum nobile 'Flore Pleno'
DOUBLE CHAMOMILE
☼ **4-8**   ↕ 12in (30cm) ↔ 18in (45cm)

This small, creeping, aromatic perennial produces dense mats of finely divided, hairy leaves. Long-stalked, double white flowers are borne freely in summer.

Melissa officinalis
LEMON BALM
☼ ☀ **4-9**   ↕ 3ft (1m) ↔ 24in (60cm)

When rubbed, the leaves of this bushy perennial release a sharp lemon aroma. In summer, its four-angled stems bear spikes of pale yellow flowers that fade to white.

Salvia officinalis 'Icterina'
GARDEN SAGE
☼ **3-9**   ↕ ↔ 12in (30cm)

An ornamental variegated form of the popular kitchen-garden herb forming a low, woody-based mound of attractive, aromatic, woolly, green-and-yellow leaves.

FOLIAGE EFFECT

Perennials with Bold Leaves

OTHER HERBACEOUS PERENNIALS
WITH BOLD LEAVES

Acanthus mollis
Agave havardiana
Darmera peltata, see p.66
Gunnera manicata
Hosta sieboldiana and cvs.
Inula magnifica
Ligularia dentata 'Desdemona'
Polygonatum commutatum
Polygonatum odoratum 'Variegatum'
Rodgersia aesculifolia, see p.25

PERENNIALS WITH BOLD LEAVES, whether broad like those of hostas or deeply cut and fernlike, provide gardens with some of the most memorable show-stoppers. In sites where space is no object, they are eye-catching planted in groups or drifts. They can be just as successful, and possibly even more dramatic, as single specimens in smaller gardens.

FOLIAGE EFFECT

Aralia cachemirica
ARALIA
☼ ☼ 6-9   ↕ 10ft (3m) ↔ 6ft (2m)

Given a good site, this aralia forms a huge, suckering clump of large, arching, divided leaves. Black berries follow tall, branched heads of tiny flowers in early summer.

Dicksonia antarctica
AUSTRALIAN TREE FERN
☼ ☼ 9-11   ↕ 20ft (6m) ↔ 12ft (4m)

This majestic, evergreen fern has a single rhizome forming a false, erect trunk that is clothed in a dense, thick mass of roots and crowned on top with a huge ruff of fronds.

OTHER TENDER PERENNIALS
WITH BOLD LEAVES

Arum creticum, see p.38
Beschorneria yuccoides
Brugmansia spp. and cvs.
Canna 'Assaut', see p.70
Geranium maderense
Ligularia japonica
Pelargonium spp. and cvs.
Phormium cookianum subsp. *hookeri*
   'Tricolor', see p.120
Phormium tenax, see p.123

Astilboides tabularis
ASTILBOIDES
☼ 5-7   ↕ 5ft (1.5m) ↔ 4ft (1.2m)

In summer, slender plumes of tiny, creamy white flowers rise above the large clumps of huge, rounded, sharply lobed leaves. It enjoys a site with moist to boggy soil.

Filipendula purpurea
MEADOWSWEET
☼ ☼ 4-9   ↕ 4ft (1.2m) ↔ 24in (60cm)

Large, deeply lobed and toothed leaves cover the bold clumps of upright, crimson-purple stems. Tall, branched plumes of carmine-red flowers are borne in summer.

Geranium palmatum
CRANESBILL
☼ ☼ **8-10**   ↕↔ 3ft (1m)

Branched heads of purplish pink flowers
top the large rosettes of semievergreen,
long-stalked, deeply lobed, sharp-toothed
leaves in summer.

Telekia speciosa
TELEKIA
☼ **5-8**   ↕ 6ft (2m) ↔ 4ft (1.2m)

This strapping plant forms a large patch of
branching stems that bear heart-shaped
leaves. Rich yellow, brown-centered, daisy
heads appear in late summer and autumn.

Rheum palmatum var. *tanguticum*
ORNAMENTAL RHUBARB
☼ ☼ **5-9**   ↕ 8ft (2.5m) ↔ 6ft (1.8m)

The striking, huge, toothed and jaggedly
lobed leaves are red-suffused when young.
In summer, branched heads of white, red,
or pink flowers emerge. Superb by water.

Hosta 'Big Daddy'
HOSTA
☼ ☼ **3-9**   ↕ 24in (60cm) ↔ 3ft (1m)

Aptly named, this hosta forms mounded
clumps of large, rounded to heart-shaped,
veined and puckered, blue-gray leaves.
White flowers are borne during summer.

Rheum 'Ace of Hearts'
ORNAMENTAL RHUBARB
☼ ☼ **5-9**   ↕ 4ft (1.2m) ↔ 36in (90cm)

The impressive mounds of heart-shaped
leaves are red-veined above and purple-
red beneath. Branching stems carry sprays
of pale pinkish white flowers in summer.

Symplocarpus foetidus
SKUNK CABBAGE
☼ ☼ **3-7**   ↕↔ 24in (60cm)

Curious, hooded, purplish red flowers in
spring are followed by the clump of large,
rather leathery leaves. An excellent bog
plant, it needs plenty of moisture.

Veratrum viride
INDIAN POKE
☼ ☼ **3-7**   ↕ 6ft (2m) ↔ 24in (60cm)

The clumps of pleated, rich green leaves
that emerge in spring are more striking
than the tall, branched spikes of yellowish
green, star-shaped summer flowers.

Perennials with Yellow- or Gold-variegated Foliage

VARIEGATED PERENNIALS AND ORNAMENTAL GRASSES that have leaves blotched or spotted with yellow or gold are prized for their ability to bring warmth and light to plantings dominated by dark green foliage. Many also make impressive specimen plants on their own, grown either in containers or in small beds.

FOLIAGE EFFECT

Aquilegia vulgaris Vervaeneana Group
EUROPEAN COLUMBINE
☼ ☼ [3-9]   ↕ 36in (90cm) ↔ 18in (45cm)

The rounded, divided leaves are streaked and mottled yellow in this curious form of an old cottage-garden favorite. Spring or summer flowers are white, pink, or purple.

Carex oshimensis 'Evergold'
EVERGOLD JAPANESE SEDGE
☼ ☼ [7-9]   ↕ 12in (30cm) ↔ 14in (35cm)

This bright little evergreen sedge forms a dense, low clump of handsome, arching, grasslike foliage. Each dark green leaf has a broad, creamy yellow central stripe.

Convallaria majalis 'Hardwick Hall'
LILY-OF-THE-VALLEY
☼ [4-9]   ↕ 9in (23cm) ↔ 12in (30cm)

A choice form of a much-loved perennial that slowly forms patches of attractively veined, bright green leaves with narrow, paler margins. It has white spring flowers.

Cortaderia selloana 'Aureolineata'
PAMPAS GRASS
☼ [8-11]   ↕ 7ft (2.2m) ↔ 5ft (1.5m)

A variegated form of a familiar, evergreen grass producing huge mounds of arching, saw-toothed, yellow-margined leaves. Tall flower plumes in summer are a bonus.

Hakonechloa macra 'Aureola'
HAKONE GRASS
☼ ☼ [5-9]   ↕ 14in (35cm) ↔ 16in (40cm)

One of the most pleasing of all grasses, with low mounds of yellow, green-striped leaves. In autumn, it bears airy panicles of spikelets and the leaves flush red.

OTHER YELLOW- OR GOLD-VARIEGATED PERENNIALS

Gaura lindheimeri 'Corrie's Gold'
Hosta 'Golden Tiara', see p.153
Hosta sieboldii f. *kabitan*
Hosta montana 'Aureomarginata', see p.153
Hosta ventricosa var. *aureomaculata*
Lamium maculatum 'Golden Anniversary'
Liriope muscari 'Variegata'
Mentha × *gracilis* 'Variegata'
Yucca smalliana 'Bright Edge'

Hosta 'Gold Standard'
HOSTA
☼ [3-8]   ↕ 26in (65cm) ↔ 3ft (1m)

This singularly attractive perennial forms clumps of heart-shaped, greenish yellow leaves fading to green margins. Tall stems bear lavender-blue flowers in summer.

Hosta ventricosa 'Aureomarginata'
HOSTA
☼ 3-9   ↕ 20in (50cm) ↔ 3ft (1m)

Big, bold clumps of heart-shaped, deep-veined green leaves have irregular yellow margins aging to creamy white. Tall stems carry deep purple flowers in summer.

Iris pallida 'Variegata'
SWEET IRIS
☼ 4-8   ↕ 4ft (1.2m) ↔ 24in (60cm)

An effective variegated perennial with stout clumps of sword-shaped, gray-green or green leaves striped light-yellow. In late spring, it bears scented, soft blue flowers.

Miscanthus sinensis 'Zebrinus'
ZEBRA GRASS
☼ 5-9   ↕ ↔ 4ft (1.2m)

This ornamental grass is very popular for specimen planting. The bold clumps of slender, canelike stems bear long, narrow green leaves banded white or pale yellow.

Symphytum 'Goldsmith'
COMFREY
☼ ☀ 4-9   ↕ ↔ 12in (30cm)

A superb groundcover, this creeping plant forms large patches of hairy leaves with irregular gold or cream margins. Blue and white, pink-tinted flowers occur in spring.

Tolmiea menziesii 'Taff's Gold'
PIGGY-BACK PLANT
☼ ☀ 6-9   ↕ 20in (50cm) ↔ 24in (60cm)

Loose clumps of semievergreen, hairy, maplelike leaves are pale green, spotted and blotched cream and pale yellow. The tiny flowers are of little consequence.

Trifolium pratense 'Susan Smith'
CLOVER
☼ 7-10   ↕ 6in (15cm) ↔ 18in (45cm)

The characteristic clover leaves of this mat-forming perennial have green leaflets that are curiously but attractively netted with golden yellow veins.

Yucca flaccida 'Golden Sword'
YUCCA
☼ 4-11   ↕ 5ft (1.5m) ↔ 3ft (1m)

A bold, clump-forming evergreen bearing stiff, swordlike, blue-green leaves with central yellow bands. Panicles of white bell-shaped flowers open in late summer.

OTHER YELLOW-STRIPED GRASSES

Arundo donax 'Variegata'
Carex morrowii 'Gold Band'
x *Hibanobambusa tranquillans*
  'Shiroshima'
Miscanthus sinensis 'Goldfeder'
Miscanthus sinensis 'Variegatus'
Molinia caerulea 'Variegata'
Phalaris arundinacea var. *picta*
  'Luteopicta'
Pleioblastus auricomus

Perennials with White- or Cream-variegated Foliage

I T IS A CURIOUS FACT that there are far more perennials with white- or cream-variegated foliage than with yellow or gold variegation. Patterned with stripes, spots, blotches, marbling, or marginal lines, these leaves provide a useful contrast for plants with green or purple foliage, and can brighten up dark corners or dull combinations in the garden.

FOLIAGE EFFECT

Armoracia rusticana 'Variegata'
HORSERADISH
☼ **5-9**   ↕ 3ft (1m) ↔ 18in (45cm)

This variegated form of the well-known herb has clumps of large, coarse, wholly or partially white leaves. Branched stems of white flowers appear during summer.

Convallaria majalis 'Albostriata'
LILY-OF-THE-VALLEY
☼ **4-9**   ↕ 9in (23cm) ↔ 12in (30cm)

The leaves of this favorite garden plant are striped lengthwise with creamy white. Sprays of nodding, fragrant, bell-shaped white flowers are borne in spring.

Hemerocallis fulva 'Kwanso Variegata'
DAYLILY
☼ **2-9**   ↕ 30in (75cm) ↔ 4ft (1.2m)

Long, strap-shaped, arching leaves with white stripes form a bold clump. Double, tawny orange flowers rise above the foliage on strong, erect stems in summer.

Brunnera macrophylla 'Dawson's White'
SIBERIAN BUGLOSS
☼ **3-8**   ↕ 18in (45cm) ↔ 24in (60cm)

Low mounds of softly-hairy, heart-shaped leaves are irregularly margined in creamy white. Sprays of bright blue, forget-me-not flowers rise over the foliage in spring.

Euphorbia characias subsp. *wulfenii*
'Burrow Silver'
☼ **7-9**   ↕ ↔ 4ft (1.2m)

Bushy and woody-based, this evergreen has dense, gray-green leaves with creamy margins. Rounded heads of bright yellow-green flowers open in spring and summer.

Hosta 'Shade Fanfare'
HOSTA
☼ **3-9**   ↕ 18in (45cm) ↔ 24in (60cm)

An excellent groundcover that produces clumps of bold, heart-shaped leaves with irregular cream-white margins. Lavender-blue flowers are borne in summer.

Phlox paniculata 'Harlequin'
GARDEN PHLOX
☼ 4-8 ↕ 4ft (1.2m) ↔ 3ft (1m)

Robust clumps of erect stems bear leaves boldly margined in creamy white. Showy panicles of fragrant, red-purple flowers open in summer.

Symphytum × uplandicum 'Variegatum'
COMFREY
☼ ◐ 4-9 ↕ 36in (90cm) ↔ 24in (60cm)

A tough, deep-rooted perennial producing a spectacular clump of white-margined leaves. In summer, striking variegated stems bear blue and pink flowers.

Physostegia virginiana 'Variegata'
PHYSOSTEGIA
☼ ◐ 3-9 ↕ ↔ 18in (45cm)

The willowlike leaves of this easily grown perennial, borne on erect stems, are gray-green, variegated white. Magenta-pink flower spikes emerge in late summer.

OTHER PERENNIALS WITH WHITE- OR CREAM-VARIEGATED FOLIAGE

Ajuga reptans 'Silver Beauty'
Hosta 'White Christmas'
Iris pallida 'Argentea Variegata',
    see p.73
Mentha suaveolens 'Variegata'
Miscanthus sinensis 'Cabaret',
    see p.146
Polygonatum odoratum 'Variegatum'
Sedum erythrostictum
    'Mediovariegatum'

Myosotis scorpioides 'Maytime'
FORGET-ME-NOT
☼ 3-8 ↕ ↔ 12in (30cm)

Strikingly variegated, this waterside plant forms patches of white-margined leaves. Sprays of bright blue flowers open in early summer. Needs a constantly moist site.

Pulmonaria 'Roy Davidson'
LUNGWORT
☼ ◐ 3-9 ↕ 12in (30cm) ↔ 24in (60cm)

A good groundcover with clumps of semi-evergreen, roughly-hairy, white-spotted leaves. Clusters of tubular, blue and pink flowers appear in spring. It will self-seed.

Vinca major 'Variegata'
LARGE PERIWINKLE
☼ ◐ 7-9 ↕ 18in (45cm) ↔ 6ft (2m)

This fast-growing, scrambling evergreen forms blankets of striking, paired, creamy white-margined leaves. Pale blue flowers appear from late spring through summer.

FOLIAGE EFFECT

Perennials with Yellow or Gold Foliage

A SURPRISING NUMBER of garden perennials have produced sports with yellow or gold leaves. In some plants, the best foliage effect is achieved in spring; in others, the color is retained throughout summer. All have an important role in the garden, especially in semi-shaded or dimly lit corners, or as a contrast to greens and purples.

Hosta 'Midas Touch'
PLANTAIN LILY
☼ ☀ 3-9   ↕ 20in (50cm) ↔ 26in (65cm)

There are many golden-leaved hostas available, but this is one of the best. It has big, bold, handsomely corrugated foliage and bears lavender-blue summer flowers.

Aquilegia 'Mellow Yellow'
COLUMBINE
☼ 3-9   ↕ 24in (60cm) ↔ 18in (45cm)

An attractive form of a popular perennial with golden leaves in spring that pale to yellow-green in summer, when pretty, white to pale blue flowers are produced.

Carex elata 'Aurea'
BOWLES' GOLDEN SEDGE
☼ ☀ 5-9   ↕ 28in (70cm) ↔ 36in (90cm)

This clump-forming sedge has arching, grassy, bright golden leaves. Probably the best golden-leaved perennial for water-side sites, it is superb by streams or pools.

Lamium maculatum 'Cannon's Gold'
GOLDEN SPOTTED LAMIUM
☼ 3-8   ↕ 8in (20cm) ↔ 3ft (1m)

The coarsely toothed, semievergreen leaves of this lamium form a soft yellow carpet in spring and summer. Its mauve-pink flowers emerge in early summer.

Campanula garganica 'Dickson's Gold'
GARANGO BELLFLOWER
☼ ☀ 6-8   ↕ 2in (5cm) ↔ 12in (30cm)

This cheerful perennial forms a mound of neat little toothed, kidney-shaped leaves. These turn golden in summer at the same time as small blue flowers appear.

Centaurea montana 'Gold Bullion'
PERENNIAL CORNFLOWER
☼ 3-8   ↕ 18in (45cm) ↔ 24in (60cm)

A beautiful, golden-leaved version of an old garden favorite. The pronounced leaf color during spring and early summer is a perfect foil for the large blue flowers.

Lysimachia nummularia 'Aurea'
GOLDEN CREEPING JENNY
☼ ☀ 3-8   ↕ 2in (5cm) ↔ indefinite

One of the brightest and most reliable golden-leaved plants, its round leaves on creeping stems turn greenish yellow in shade. Yellow flowers emerge in summer.

Tradescantia Andersoniana Group
'Blue and Gold'
☼ ☼ **3-9**   ↕ ↔ 18in (45cm)

During summer, rich blue, three-petaled flowers on erect, fleshy stems contrast well with this clump-forming perennial's long, strap-shaped, yellow-green leaves.

Melissa officinalis 'All Gold'
LEMON BALM
☼ **4-9**   ↕ ↔ 24in (60cm)

This bushy, aromatic perennial produces a dense clump of lemon-scented, yellow-green stems and leaves. It is especially effective during spring and early summer.

Valeriana phu 'Aurea'
GOLDEN VALERIAN
☼ ☼ **5-8**   ↕ 5ft (1.5m) ↔ 24in (60cm)

The prime attraction of this tall, branching perennial is its gold spring foliage, which gradually fades to green in summer. Its small white flowers open in late summer.

OTHER PERENNIALS WITH GOLD FOLIAGE

Acanthus mollis 'Hollard's Gold'
Acorus gramineus 'Ogon'
Carex elata 'Bowles' Golden'
Filipendula ulmaria 'Aurea'
Hosta 'Sum and Substance', see p.71
Hosta 'Zounds', see p.66
Lamium maculatum 'Aureum'
Luzula sylvatica 'Aurea'
Milium effusum 'Aureum', see p.33
Origanum vulgare 'Aureum', see p.55
Persicaria amplexicaulis
  'Cottesbrooke Gold'
Saxifraga exarata subsp. *moschata*
  'Cloth of Gold'
Symphytum ibericum 'Gold in Spring'
Thymus × *citriodorus* 'Archer's Gold'
Tricyrtis 'Lemon Lime'
Veronica prostrata 'Trehane'

Stachys byzantina 'Primrose Heron'
LAMB'S EARS
☼ **4-8**   ↕ 18in (45cm) ↔ 24in (60cm)

A vigorous, semievergreen plant forming a dense carpet of velvety, hairy gray stems and woolly leaves that are yellow-green during spring and early summer.

Tanacetum vulgare 'Isla Gold'
GOLDEN TANSY
☼ **3-8**   ↕ ↔ 36in (90cm)

This golden form of the common tansy has bold clumps of erect stems clothed in aromatic, finely divided, yellowy leaves. It bears yellow flowerheads in summer.

FOLIAGE EFFECT

135

Perennials with Silver or Blue-gray Foliage

PERENNIALS THAT HAVE SILVER or blue-gray foliage are invaluable in the garden for separating strong-colored plants, such as those with red, purple, or even plain green leaves. They can also provide a lovely foil for pastel-colored flowers, especially those in pink, lavender-purple, pale blue, and yellow. There is a vast number of perennials to choose from for a gray or silver bed or border. They can also make a spectacular display as specimen plants or grouped together with other contrasting foliage plants in containers. Most perennials with silver leaves prefer to be grown in a warm, sunny situation.

Cynara cardunculus
CARDOON
☼ **9-10**   ↕ 5ft (1.5m) ↔ 4ft (1.2m)

The deeply divided, spiny, silver-gray leaves of this statuesque plant form big, bold clumps. During summer, stout blue flowerheads open on branched stems.

Anaphalis triplinervis 'Sommerschnee'
PEARLY EVERLASTING
☼ **3-8**   ↕ 32in (80cm) ↔ 24in (60cm)

The clumps of gray stems bear leaves that are woolly white beneath. In late summer, dense white flower clusters emerge. A German selection of a reliable perennial.

Cerastium tomentosum
SNOW-IN-SUMMER
☼ **2-7**   ↕ 3in (8cm) ↔ 5ft (1.5m)

One of the best gray groundcover plants for walls and sunny banks. During late spring and summer, white flowers pepper the carpet of evergreen, downy leaves.

Dicentra 'Langtrees'
FRINGED BLEEDING HEART
☼ **4-8**   ↕ 12in (30cm) 18in (45cm)

A charming plant with mounds of ferny, silver-blue leaves topped in late spring and early summer by nodding clusters of white flowers. It forms patches in time.

Artemisia ludoviciana var. *albula*
ARTEMISIA
☼ **3-9**   ↕ 4ft (1.2m) ↔ 24in (60cm)

Erect clumps of slender, woolly stems bear willowlike, aromatic, woolly white leaves. Dense clusters of white flowers are borne from summer into autumn.

Crambe maritima
SEA KALE
☼ **6-9**   ↕ 30in (75cm) ↔ 24in (60cm)

This bold, mound-forming plant has large, deeply lobed and twisted, bloomy, blue-green leaves. The branched heads of small white flowers are borne in early summer.

Galanthus elwesii Glaucous Forms
SNOWDROP
☀ ☀ **3-9**   ↕ 6in (15cm) ↔ 3in (8cm)

This vigorous snowdrop has broad, blue-green leaves and nodding white flowers with green-marked inner segments. It will eventually form large colonies.

Hosta 'Blue Moon'
HOSTA
☀ **3-9**   ↕ 4in (10cm) ↔ 12in (30cm)

This slow-growing hosta is worth waiting for with its attractive clump of bloomy, heart-shaped, blue-green leaves. Racemes of nearly white flowers open in summer.

EVERGREEN PERENNIALS WITH SILVER OR BLUE-GRAY FOLIAGE

Acaena saccaticupula 'Blue Haze'
Artemisia 'Powis Castle', see p.26
Festuca glauca 'Elijah Blue'
Heuchera 'Pewter Veil'
Lavandula angustifolia
Santolina chamaecyparissus
Sedum spathulifolium 'Cape Blanco'
Stachys byzantina 'Big Ears'
Tanacetum argenteum
Thymus pseudolanuginosus

HERBACEOUS PERENNIALS WITH SILVER OR BLUE-GRAY FOLIAGE

Achillea 'Moonshine'
Artemisia schmidtiana 'Nana'
Eryngium yuccifolium
Hosta 'Hadspen Blue', see p.73
Lychnis flos-jovis
Macleaya cordata
Nepeta spp. and cvs.
Perovskia atriplicifolia
Rudbeckia maxima
Thalictrum aquilegiifolium

Helictotrichon sempervirens
BLUE OAT GRASS
☀ **4-9**   ↕ 5ft (1.5m) ↔ 24in (60cm)

A striking, evergreen grass forming a bold clump of stiff, narrow, gray-blue leaves. A sheaf of erect stems bears panicles of tiny spikelets above the leaves in summer.

Lysimachia ephemerum
LOOSETRIFE
☀ ☀ **7-9**   ↕ 3ft (1m) ↔ 12in (30cm)

The erect stems of this fine perennial are densely clothed in willowy, bloomy, sea green leaves. Slender spires of small white flowers are produced in summer.

Verbascum olympicum
OLYMPIC MULLEIN
☀ **6-8**   ↕ 6ft (2m) ↔ 24in (60cm)

This stately, silvery, white-woolly biennial or perennial has a rosette of overwintering leaves. Tall, branched stems bearing dense spikes of yellow flowers appear in summer.

FOLIAGE EFFECT

Perennials with Purple, Red, or Bronze Foliage

WHEN USED SELECTIVELY in garden plantings, perennials with unusual deep purple, bronze, or red foliage can provide a striking contrast among plants with lighter green, gray, or even yellow leaves. In some perennials, like *Acataea simplex* 'Brunette', the color is long-lasting or even permanent, while in others it is mainly a spring display created by newly emerging foliage and stems. Sometimes the rich leaf color is also attractively overlaid by a lovely pale bloom, as is the case in several sedums.

*Artemisia
lactiflora* Guizhou Group
WHITE MUGWORT
☼ 4-9 ‡ 5ft (1.5m) ↔ 3ft (1m)

A vigorous perennial producing clumps of branching, dark purple-flushed stems and deeply cut leaves. Sprays of tiny white flowers open from summer into autumn.

**TENDER PERENNIALS WITH
PURPLE, RED, OR BRONZE LEAVES**

Canna 'Red King Humbert'
Coleus 'Molten Lava'
Cordyline australis 'Purpurea'
Dahlia 'Bishop of Llandaff', see p.110
Dahlia 'Ellen Houston'
Euphorbia amygdaloides 'Purpurea'
Pennisetum setaceum 'Rubrum', see p.140
Phormium tenax Purpureum Group,
  see p.77
Tradescantia pallida 'Purpurea'

Heuchera 'Rachel'
CORAL BELLS
☼ ☼ 3-8 ‡ 24in (60cm) ↔ 18in (45cm)

This striking plant forms a low clump of large, crinkled and lobed, shiny, bronze-purple leaves, purple beneath. Sprays of tiny, off-white flowers open in summer.

FOLIAGE EFFECT

Actaea simplex 'Brunette'
KAMCHATKA BUGBANE
☼ 3-8 ‡ 4ft (1.2m) ↔ 24in (60cm)

This superb perennial has clumps of large, divided, purplish brown leaves. Arching stems bear tall racemes of purple-tinted white flowers above the foliage in autumn.

Euphorbia dulcis 'Chameleon'
SPURGE
☼ ☼ 4-9 ‡ ↔ 12in (30cm)

The branching, purplish stems bear small red-purple leaves that color richly in autumn. Clouds of yellow, purple-tinted flowers appear in summer. It self-seeds.

Imperata cylindrica 'Rubra'
JAPANESE BLOOD GRASS
☼ ☼ 5-9 ‡ 16in (40cm) ↔ 12in (30cm)

An attractive grass with erect, leafy shoots and long green leaves that turn a deep blood red from the tips down. In summer, it bears sprays of silver-white spikelets.

Ranunculus ficaria 'Brazen Hussy'
LESSER CELANDINE
☀ ☀ 4-8 ‡ 2in (5cm) ↔ 6in (15cm)

The small rosettes or patches of long-stalked, heart-shaped, glossy, chocolate-brown leaves are an ideal backing for the shining, golden yellow flowers in spring.

Sedum telephium 'Matrona'
SEDUM
☀ 5-9 ‡ 24in (60cm) ↔ 12in (30cm)

From late summer into autumn, flattened heads of starry pink flowers rise on stout, fleshy, purple-red stems above the robust clumps of fleshy, bloomy purple leaves.

Ophiopogon planiscapus 'Nigrescens'
MONDO GRASS
☀ ☀ 5-9 ‡ 8in (20cm) ↔ 12in (30cm)

Low tufts of narrow, leathery, black-purple leaves form patches in time. It has slender purple-white flower sprays in summer. An excellent evergreen groundcover.

Rodgersia podophylla
RODGERSIA
☀ ☀ 5-7 ‡ 5ft (1.5m) ↔ 6ft (1.8m)

Bronze-red when young, the large clumps of long-stalked, deeply divided and lobed leaves color red again in autumn. White flower plumes are borne in summer.

Phormium 'Dazzler'
NEW ZEALAND FLAX
☀ 9-11 ‡ 3ft (1m) ↔ 4ft (1.2m)

This flax has stout clumps of evergreen, arching, strap-shaped, leathery leaves, impressively striped red, orange, and pink on a bronze-purple background.

HERBACEOUS PERENNIALS WITH PURPLE, RED, OR BRONZE LEAVES

Anthriscus sylvestris 'Ravenswing'
Clematis recta 'Purpurea'
Foeniculum vulgare 'Purpureum',
· see p.125
Heuchera micrantha var. *diversifolia*
 'Palace Purple'
Lysimachia ciliata 'Firecracker'
Penstemon digitalis 'Husker Red'
Sedum telephium 'Arthur Branch'
Tiarella cordifolia 'Brandywine'

Sedum 'Sunset Cloud'
SEDUM
☀ 5-9 ‡ 10in (25cm) ↔ 18in (45cm)

One of the best of the low-growing purple sedums, it has fleshy, trailing or lax stems, bloomy foliage, and flattened pink flower-heads in late summer and autumn.

FOLIAGE EFFECT

Perennials with Richly Tinted Autumn Foliage

OTHER PERENNIALS WITH RICHLY
TINTED AUTUMN FOLIAGE

Aruncus aethusifolius, see p.125
Athyrium filix-femina, see p.148
Ceratostigma plumbaginoides, see p.50
Euphorbia griffithii 'Fireglow', see p.90
Geranium macrorrhizum, see p.89
Hosta ventricosa
Imperata cylindrica 'Rubra', see p.138
Miscanthus sinensis 'Purpurascens'
Osmunda regalis, see p.67
Polygonatum odoratum

ALL TOO OFTEN when we think of autumn color in the garden we look to woody deciduous plants like maples or sumacs. It is worth remembering that many herbaceous perennials, like those below, also produce a burst of bright color before the onset of winter.

Geranium wlassovianum
CRANESBILL
☼ ☼ 4-8   ↕ ↔ 24in (60cm)

The clumps of long-stalked, deeply lobed, velvety leaves emerge pinkish bronze in spring. They turn red with purple-bronze in autumn. Purple summer flowers.

Calamagrostis × *acutiflora* 'Karl Foerster'
☼ ☼ 5-9   ↕ 6ft (1.8m) ↔ 24in (60cm)

This striking, clump-forming ornamental grass has stiffly erect stems and arching leaves. The pinky bronze spikelets turn a warm buff or pale brown in autumn.

Schizachyrium scoparium
LITTLE BLUESTEM
☼ 3-10   ↕ 3ft (1m) ↔ 12in (30cm)

The dense tufts of arching, grayish green leaves and stems of this native grass turn purple to orange-red in autumn. Narrow, whiskery flower spikes appear in summer.

Darmera peltata 'Nana'
UMBRELLA PLANT
☼ ☼ 5-7   ↕ 14in (35cm) ↔ 24in (60cm)

Like the full-size umbrella plant, this dwarf form has rounded leaves that turn red or orange-copper in autumn. Leafless stems bear clusters of pink spring flowers.

Pennisetum setaceum 'Rubrum'
FOUNTAIN GRASS
☼ 9-11   ↕ 3ft (1m) ↔ 24in (60cm)

Grown as an annual in the north, this spectacular grass forms a clump of erect, rich purple stems and leaves. The arching pink spikelets fade to pink-buff or white.

Sedum aizoon
AIZOON STONECROP
☼ 4-9   ↕ ↔ 18in (45cm)

In autumn, the clumps of erect, reddish stems and fleshy, coarsely toothed leaves turn red or orange-red. Flattened heads of starry yellow flowers open in summer.

FOLIAGE EFFECT

Perennials with Decorative Winter Foliage

I F PERENNIALS WITH RICHLY TINTED FOLIAGE in autumn are useful in the garden, then those with decorative foliage in winter are invaluable. When many plants have either died down or lost their leaves, these perennials will brighten up borders and beds. Several have yellow- or white-variegated leaves; others red-suffused, silver-hairy, or marbled foliage.

Epimedium x *rubrum*
RED EPIMEDIUM
☼ ☼ 4-8   ↕ ↔ 12in (30cm)

The clumps of much-divided leaves, red flushed when young, become red-tinted in autumn. Evergreen in southern zones. Spring flowers are crimson and yellow.

OTHER PERENNIALS WITH DECORATIVE WINTER FOLIAGE

Armeria maritima 'Rubrifolia'
Asplenium scolopendrium Crispum Group, see p.149
Carex morrowii 'Variegata'
Helleborus argutifolius 'Pacific Frost'
Heuchera 'Chocolate Veil'
Lunaria annua 'Variegata'
Ophiopogon japonicus 'Nanum'
Polystichum acrostichoides
Vinca minor 'Variegata'

Arum italicum 'Marmoratum'
ITALIAN ARUM
☼ 6-9   ↕ 12in (30cm) ↔ 10in (25cm)

A reliable and eye-catching winter foliage plant with shiny arrow-shaped, cream-veined leaves. It produces greenish white flowers in early spring and red fall berries.

Celmisia semicordata
NEW ZEALAND DAISY
☼ ☼ 7-9 PH   ↕ 20in (50cm) ↔ 12in (30cm)

Gray-green above and silvery beneath, the sword-shaped, silky-hairy leaves form a bold rosette. Gray-downy stems bear large daisylike flowerheads in summer.

Bergenia 'Ballawley'
BERGENIA
☼ ☼ 4-9   ↕ 24in (60cm) ↔ 18in (45cm)

The low clumps of leathery, glossy green leaves turn rich bronze-purple in winter. In spring, upright red stems carry clusters of bell-shaped crimson flowers.

Cyclamen coum Pewter Group
HARDY CYCLAMEN
☼ 5-9   ↕ 3in (8cm) ↔ 4in (10cm)

A beautiful selection of an early-spring flowering cyclamen with kidney-shaped, silvered leaves, often marked with dark green. Red-pink flowers add to its charm.

Sasa veitchii
HARDY BAMBOO
☼ ☼ ☼ 5-10   ↕ 5ft (1.5m) ↔ indefinite

This vigorous, creeping bamboo has bold, evergreen leaves that wither at the edges in autumn, giving them decorative white margins for winter. It needs lots of space.

FOLIAGE EFFECT

141

SPECIALIST PLANTS

CERTAIN PERENNIALS are now some of the most enthusiastically collected garden plants. Valued for their foliage, flowers, or form, their increasing availability is making it easier than ever to create a unique plant collection.

Polystichum munitum
for moisture
or shade

△ HELLEBORES *Excellent groundcovers,* Helleborus hybridus *seedlings are some of the most desirable perennials.*

Imagine a garden filled with 100 different hardy geraniums, or 50 assorted peonies, or even a great multitude of hardy ferns. In fact, there are many such gardens, and they are increasing in number as collecting members of a single genus or family continues to catch gardeners' imaginations. Collecting has appealed to plantsmen and women in Europe for the last 400 years at least, and for many centuries more in China and Japan. In recent years, it has become very popular in North America as well.

The perennials in this section are among the most sought-after plants. Some, such as hostas and hardy geraniums, have long been popular, with numerous cultivars already available, and many more introduced each year. Others, like ornamental grasses, which have the combined attraction of elegant habit, foliage, and seedheads, and hellebores and epimediums, have been "discovered" more recently, but are now avidly collected.

MIX AND MATCH

While the search for as many selections of a particular perennial as possible can be a mixture of fun and adventure, the entire garden does not have to be filled with just one plant and its variations. If you are selective, choosing only the best plants, or those that appeal to you, it is possible to combine a collection of a particular perennial with other garden plants to provide varied, year-round appeal.

ESTABLISHING A COLLECTION

So many different perennials are available that it is easy to establish a collection to suit the size and situation of your garden. Sedums or saxifrages, for example, can be grown in a small urban backyard using troughs or containers, and if your chosen plants are large shrubs or bush roses, groundcovers such as hardy geraniums can be grown beneath them. Given the right garden conditions, a number of collections can be established together: hardy ferns, snowdrops, pulmonarias, and epimediums will all thrive in each other's company.

△ PEONIES *Famed for their foliage and flowers, classics like* Paeonia 'Smouthii' *will make a striking show in the garden.*

◁ GERANIUMS *Justifiably popular and very easy to grow, geraniums are perfect for ground cover, or for borders and beds.*

▷ MIXED GRASSES *When planted for contrasting effect, as here, ornamental grasses can make a spectacular collection.*

Small Grasses and Sedges

LONG NEGLECTED, perennial grasses and sedges are now being rediscovered and increasingly cultivated for their ornamental value. Ideal for smaller gardens, those suggested below will make a striking addition to a border or as specimen plants, especially in containers.

Carex muskingumensis
PALM SEDGE
☼ ☼ [4-9] ↕ 24in (60cm) ↔ 18in (45cm)

With its loosely tufted habit, erect, leafy shoots, and horizontally spreading leaves, this native sedge resembles a miniature palm tree or a bamboo.

Carex siderosticha 'Variegata'
BROAD-LEAVED SEDGE
☼ ☼ [6-9] ↕ 12in (30cm) ↔ 16in (40cm)

One of the most ornamental sedges with a creeping habit excellent for ground cover. Its arching, strap-shaped, white-margined leaves form a low, dense mound.

Chionochloa conspicua
PLUMED TUSSOCK GRASS
☼ [6-9] ↕ 4ft (1.2m) ↔ 3ft (1m)

Graceful, branched heads of creamy white spikelets, maturing pale silver-brown, rise on tall shoots in summer above the clump of evergreen, reddish brown-tinted leaves.

Carex phyllocephala 'Sparkler'
TENJIKE SEDGE
☼ ☼ [5-9] ↕ ↔ 18in (45cm)

A strikingly variegated sedge with erect stems topped by dense crowns of narrow, spreading, grasslike leaves with cream margins. Prefers moist soil in a warm site.

OTHER SMALL GRASSES

Festuca glauca 'Sea Urchin'
Imperata cylindrica 'Rubra', see p.138
Miscanthus sinensis 'Yaku Jima'
Nassella tenuissima, see p.77
Pennisetum alopecuroides 'Little Bunny'

Chionochloa rubra
RED TUSSOCK GRASS
☼ [8-9] ↕ ↔ 24–36in (60–90cm)

From mountains and bogs, this tough, rugged perennial is grown for its dense mound of quill-like, copper-red leaves. Prefers moist soil. Excellent in a container.

Deschampsia cespitosa 'Goldschleier'
TUFTED HAIR GRASS
☼ ☼ 4-9 PH ⬇ ↕ ↔ 3ft (1m)

During summer, slender shoots bearing showers of tiny green spikelets that mature a bright silvery yellow rise above the clumps of narrow, evergreen leaves.

Elymus magellanicus
WILD RYE
☼ 5-9 ↕ 24in (60cm) ↔ 12in (30cm)

Both the tufts of long, slender leaves and the shoots that carry narrow flower spikes in summer are an intense, almost electric, blue. Excellent as a specimen plant.

Festuca glauca 'Blaufuchs'
BLUE FESCUE
☼ 4-9 ↕ 12in (30cm) ↔ 10in (25cm)

Good for contrast, this is one of the best small, blue-leaved grasses. Its name, 'Blue Fox', aptly describes the dense tufts of narrow, bright blue leaves and stiff shoots.

Hordeum jubatum
FOXTAIL BARLEY   ☼ 4-8
↕ 18–30in (45–75cm) ↔ 12–18in (30–45cm)

A short-lived perennial commonly grown as an annual. It is best from seed, planted in drifts to best enjoy its long-whiskered salmon-pink flower spikes in summer.

Pennisetum orientale
FOUNTAIN GRASS
☼ 7-9 ↕ 24in (60cm) ↔ 30in (75cm)

A superb specimen plant forming a dense, neat mound of narrow leaves. The arching shoots carry spikes of soft, long-bristled, pink-tinted spikelets during summer.

Stipa barbata
FEATHER GRASS
☼ 4-9 ↕ 30in (75cm) ↔ 6in (15cm)

The small clump of narrow leaves gives rise in summer to slender, arching plumes of long-whiskered spikes. Best on a well-drained or stony soil, with dwarf shrubs.

Stipa pulcherrima
FEATHER GRASS
☼ 7-9 ↕ 30in (75cm) ↔ 18–24in (45–60cm)

Named for its exquisite, slender, feathery, arching plumes in summer. They are greenish at first then age to fluffy white, when the seeds depart in the wind.

Large Ornamental Grasses

GROWN AS SPECIMENS IN A LAWN or in a bed underplanted with smaller perennials, these bold grasses can create a grand spectacle, especially in late summer or autumn when in flower. They are all easy to grow and can be planted singly or in groups for a more immediate effect.

Miscanthus sinensis 'Cabaret'
MISCANTHUS
☼ 5-9   ↕ 6ft (1.8m) ↔ 4ft (1.2m)

Conspicuous white stripes line the leaves of this attractive, clump-forming grass. In autumn, it bears feathery copper-hued flowerheads that rise above the foliage.

Calamagrostis brachytricha
REED GRASS
☼ ☼ 5-9   ↕ 4ft (1.2m) ↔ 3ft (1m)

Dense clumps of erect shoots bear narrow heads of purplish spikelets in late summer or autumn. Excellent for winter effect, the spikelets later turn a warm brown.

Miscanthus sinensis 'Malepartus'
MISCANTHUS
☼ 4-9   ↕ 7ft (2.1m) ↔ 5ft (1.5m)

An impressive grass forming a dense clump of erect stems with arching leaves that sometimes turn golden orange in autumn. Silvery flower plumes appear in autumn.

Cortaderia richardii
TOE TOE
☼ 7-9   ↕ 10ft (3m) ↔ 6ft (2m)

Tall shoots extend from the mound of arching, evergreen leaves during summer to flaunt graceful, drooping, creamy white, shaggy plumes that persist into winter.

Cortaderia selloana 'Sunningdale Silver'
☼ 8-11   ↕ 10ft (3m) ↔ 8ft (2.5m)

A big, bold, evergreen pampas grass with sturdy stems bearing large, silvery white plumes that last well into winter. This is a popular and well-proven cultivar.

Miscanthus sinensis 'Morning Light'
MISCANTHUS
☼ 4-9   ↕ ↔ 4ft (1.2m)

Considered to be the best all-around miscanthus due to its neat habit. It has a fountainlike clump of white-edged leaves and reddish flower plumes in autumn.

Molinia caerulea susbp. *arundinacea* 'Windspiel'
☼ 5-9   ↕ 7ft (2.1m) ↔ 16in (40cm)

The rounded clump of arching leaves is topped from late summer by slender, upright stems carrying large, glistening plumes that tremble in the wind.

Panicum virgatum 'Heavy Metal'
BLUE SWITCH GRASS
☼ 5-9   ↕ 5ft (1.5m) ↔ 18in (45cm)

A glaucous blue grass forming a tight clump of stiffly erect, leafy stems that never flop after rain. They are topped from mid-summer with airy heads of pinkish flowers.

Panicum virgatum 'Warrior'
BLUE SWITCH GRASS
☼ 5-9   ↕ 5ft (1.5m) ↔ 18in (45cm)

A tough, clump-forming grass with crowded, erect, leafy stems crowned from midsummer with loose plumes. In autumn, the entire plant turns golden yellow.

Pennisetum macrourum
PENNISETUM
☼ 7-9   ↕ 6ft (1.8m) ↔ 4ft (1.2m)

This evergreen, clump-forming grass bears long, pokerlike flower spikes in late summer and early autumn. They age from pale green to pale brown then purple.

OTHER LARGE GRASSES

Andropogon gerardii
Arundo donax 'Macrophylla', see p.122
Chasmanthium latifolium, see p.76
Miscanthus sacchariflorus
Miscanthus sinensis 'Silberfeder'

Stipa gigantea
GIANT OATS, GOLDEN OATS
☼ 8-10   ↕ 6–7ft (2–2.4m) ↔ 3ft (1m)

One of the loveliest large grasses, with clumps of evergreen leaves topped in summer by showers of golden, long-whiskered flowers that pale with age.

SPECIALIST PLANTS

147

Ferns for Moisture or Shade

O F ALL NON-FLOWERING PERENNIALS, ferns are easily the most garden-worthy, offering an exciting variety of shapes and heights for use as specimen plants or in bold groupings. Most of the following ferns are of medium to large size and will thrive given humus-rich soil, moisture, and shade.

Asplenium scolopendrium
HART'S TONGUE FERN
☼ ☀ 5-9   ↕ ↔ 24in (60cm)

This bold fern is easily recognized by its long, leathery, strap-shaped, evergreen fronds, marked beneath with stripes of brown spores. It is fond of alkaline soil.

OTHER FERNS FOR MOISTURE OR SHADE

Dryopteris affinis
Dryopteris dilatata
Dryopteris filix-mas
Dryopteris goldieana
Matteuccia struthiopteris, see p.71
Osmunda cinnamomea
Osmunda regalis, see p.67
Polystichum braunii

Athyrium filix-femina
EUROPEAN LADY FERN
☼ 4-8   ↕ 4ft (1.2m) ↔ 24in (60cm)

The feathery, finely divided, light green fronds form a graceful clump with a green or red-brown central stalk. It is especially good for waterside sites.

Dryopteris erythrosora
AUTUMN FERN
☼ ☀ 5-8   ↕ ↔ 24in (60cm)

One of the most colorful of hardy ferns, its coppery red young fronds in spring and summer contrast with the overwintering, shiny, dark green, mature fronds.

Dryopteris wallichiana
WALLICH'S WOOD FERN
☼ 5-8   ↕ 36in (90cm) ↔ 30in (75cm)

The erect fronds of this lovely fern form a big, semievergreen clump and have dark-scaly stalks. Its fronds will grow much taller if rich soil and shelter are provided.

Polystichum munitum
WESTERN SWORD FERN
☼ ☀ 6-9   ↕ 36in (90cm) ↔ 4ft (1.2m)

Once it is established this luxuriant fern can transform an otherwise dull corner or border. Its laddered, evergreen fronds will form a large, handsome clump.

Polystichum polyblepharum
JAPANESE TASSEL FERN
☼ ☀ 5-8   ↕ 24in (60cm) ↔ 36in (90cm)

The distinctive clump of prickle-toothed, much-divided fronds is covered at first with golden hairs. It is especially effective when planted with other ferns.

Polystichum setiferum
SOFT SHIELD FERN
☼ ☀ 5-8   ↕ 4ft (1.2m) ↔ 36in (90cm)

This graceful and beautiful fern develops a large, loose clump of semievergreen, finely divided, dark green fronds. It will thrive in a shady rock garden.

SPECIALIST PLANTS

Ferns for Walls and Crevices

FERNS THAT PREFER growing in the crevices of rocks and cliffs in the wild are mostly small to very small in size. They can be established in similar situations in the garden – in damp stone walls where space between the stones allows – or they may be used as charming container or trough plants.

Asplenium trichomanes
MAIDENHAIR SPLEENWORT
☼ ☼ ☼ 2-9 ↕ 6in (15cm) ↔ 8in (20cm)

Delicate-looking but tough, this little fern produces an evergreen rosette of slender, black-stalked fronds with neatly paired divisions. It prefers alkaline conditions.

Asplenium adiantum-nigrum
BLACK SPLEENWORT
☼ ☼ 8-9 ↕ 6in (15cm) ↔ 8in (20cm)

A tough little evergreen fern with wiry black stalks and triangular, much-divided, leathery, shiny green fronds. It thrives in alkaline soils.

Asplenium ruta-muraria
WALL RUE SPLEENWORT
☼ ☼ ☼ 4-7 ↕ 4in (10cm) ↔ 5in (12.5cm)

Often found growing with *A. trichomanes* in the wild, this fern forms dense colonies of small, much-divided, leathery, evergreen fronds. It is fond of alkaline conditions.

Polypodium cambricum
Pulcherrimum Group
☼ ☼ 8-9 ↕ 18in (45cm) ↔ 24in (60cm)

The decorative, deeply divided, triangular to lance-shaped fronds have crested tips. The fronds emerge during the summer and stay fresh and green until late winter.

Asplenium ceterach
RUSTY-BACK FERN
☼ ☼ 7-9 ↕ 5in (12.5cm) ↔ 10in (25cm)

This species forms a tuft of strap-shaped, deeply lobed, scaly-backed, evergreen fronds that curl in times of drought, and recover again after rain.

OTHER FERNS FOR WALLS
AND CREVICES

Adiantum capillus veneris
Asplenium viride
Cheilanthes tomentosa
Cystopteris fragilis
Pellaea atropurpurea
Polypodium interjectum 'Cornubiense', see p.121
Polypodium cambricum

Asplenium scolopendrium Crispum Group
HART'S TONGUE FERN
☼ ☼ 5-9 ↕ 20in (50cm) ↔ 24in (60cm)

The strap-shaped, wavy-margined, shiny, fronds of this attractive evergreen fern gradually form a bold clump. Also ideal for the front of a shady border.

Woodsia polystichoides
HOLLY FERN WOODSIA
☼ 5-8 ↕ 8in (20cm) ↔ 10in (25cm)

One of the prettiest ferns for walls or rock crevices producing small clumps of lance-shaped, deeply divided, pale green fronds. It may be damaged by late spring frosts.

Tall, Vigorous Bamboos

THE LUSH INFORMALITY and glossy, evergreen foliage of these tall-growing bamboos make them excellent for screening, especially on moist, well-drained soils in sheltered sites. All can be extremely invasive. Their growth can be curbed effectively by planting them in containers.

Semiarundinaria fastuosa
NARIHIRA BAMBOO
☼ ☀ 6-9   ↕ 15ft (5m) ↔ 12ft (4m)

This stately, erect bamboo has purple-brown-striped canes with dense sprays of foliage. Clump-forming in cool climates, it spreads extensively in warmer areas.

Chimonobambusa quadrangularis
SQUARE-STEMMED BAMBOO
☼ 8-11   ↕ 6ft (5m) ↔ indefinite

The older canes of this very fast-growing bamboo are peculiarly four-angled and mature from green to brown. They carry large sprays of arching, shiny green leaves.

Pseudosasa japonica
SLASH BAMBOO
☼ ☀ 7-11   ↕ 20ft (6m) ↔ indefinite

A handsome bamboo commonly grown for screening. The heavy mass of striking green foliage forces the dense stands of green canes to arch at the tips in maturity.

OTHER TALL, VIGOROUS BAMBOOS

Phyllostachys aurea
Phyllostachys aureosulcata
Phyllostachys aureosulcata 'Spectabilis'
Phyllostachys dulcis
Phyllostachys nigra
Phyllostachys vivax 'Aureocaulis'
Pleioblastus simonii
Semiarundinaria yashadake
Yushania maculata

Phyllostachys viridiglaucescens
PHYLLOSTACHYS
☼ ☀ 7-11   ↕ 5m (16ft) ↔ indefinite

Like all *Phyllostachys* species, it produces pairs of branches from the cane joints. Large stands of green canes arch widely under the weight of its lush, glossy foliage.

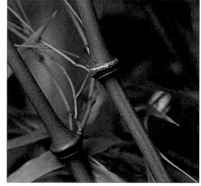

Chimonobambusa tumidissinoda
QIONGZU CANE
☼ 6-8   ↕ 15ft (5m) ↔ indefinite

Recently introduced from China, this bamboo with swollen cane joints is famous as a source of walking sticks. The sprays of narrow leaves ideally need shade.

Yushania anceps
ANCEPS BAMBOO
☼ ☀ 8-10   ↕ 12ft (4m) ↔ indefinite

An excellent bamboo for screening that forms a dense thicket of slender, glossy canes. The arching to pendent branches are thickly clothed in fresh green foliage.

Clump-forming Bamboos

OTHER CLUMP-FORMING BAMBOOS

Chusquea culeou 'Tenuis'
Fargesia denudata
Fargesia robusta
Himalayacalamus falconeri 'Damarapa'
Thamnocalamus crassinodus
  'Kew Beauty'
Thamnocalamus spathiflorus

THERE ARE FEW MORE ELEGANT and impressive evergreen perennials than those bamboos that slowly increase to form single clumps of canes. They are best displayed as specimens in a sheltered lawn, bed, or woodland glade, and are lovely by water as long as they are not planted in wet soil.

Chusquea culeou
FOXTAIL BAMBOO
☼ ☼ 6-9   ↕ 20ft (6m) ↔ 8ft (2.5m)

The densely packed, yellowish or green canes form an impressive, vase-shaped clump and look like foxtails with their clusters of branches crowded at each joint.

Fargesia nitida
FOUNTAIN BAMBOO
☼ ☼ 5-8   ↕ 15ft (5m) ↔ 10ft (3m)

This aptly named bamboo has a bold, dense clump of slender, arching, purplish canes, which mature to yellow-green and bear handsome showers of narrow leaves.

Fargesia murielae
UMBRELLA BAMBOO
☼ 5-8   ↕ 12ft (4m) ↔ 10ft (3m)

An excellent specimen plant producing a vase-shaped clump of arching, bloomy white canes aging to green then yellow-green with large plumes of slender leaves.

Semiarundinaria yamadorii
SEMIARUNDINARIA
☼ ☼ 7-9   ↕ 10ft (3m) ↔ 6ft (2m)

Well-furnished with a mass of handsome, dense green foliage, this is a bamboo of real character and value. Its tall, narrow green canes form a dense, upright clump.

Thamnocalamus tessellatus
ZULU BAMBOO
☼ ☼ 7-9   ↕ 12ft (4m) ↔ 6ft (2m)

Conspicuous, papery white sheaths clothe the tall canes of this dense, clump-forming bamboo, giving them a banded effect. It was once used to make Zulu shields.

SPECIALIST PLANTS

151

Geraniums for Collectors

HARDY GERANIUMS, or cranesbills as they are also called, are among the most popular of all perennials. This is partly because of their many uses in the garden, and partly because of their great variety of habit, foliage, and flowers. No garden should be without at least a few of the following.

OTHER GERANIUMS FOR COLLECTORS

Geranium 'Brookside', see p.33
Geranium clarkei 'Kashmir Pink'
Geranium dalmaticum
Geranium × *magnificum*
Geranium × *riversleaianum* 'Russell Prichard', see p.106
Geranium sinense
Geranium wlassovianum, see p.140

Geranium 'Salome'
CRANESBILL
☼ ☀ **6-9**   ‡ 12in (30cm) ↔ 6ft (2m)

The faintly marbled leaves of this low-grower are suffused yellow when young. Dusky violet-pink flowers with dark veins and eyes appear from summer to autumn.

Geranium himalayense 'Plenum'
LILAC CRANESBILL
☼ ☀ **4-8**   ‡ 10in (25cm) ↔ 24in (60cm)

Also known as 'Birch Double', this pretty cranesbill is ideal for the front of a border. It has neatly divided leaves and loosely double, old-fashioned blooms in summer.

Geranium 'Nimbus'
CRANESBILL
☼ ☀ **3-7**   ‡ 16in (40cm) ↔ 24in (60cm)

This low-grower spreads by underground, creeping stems to form a mound of prettily divided leaves that are yellowish when young. It has purple-pink summer flowers.

Geranium sylvaticum 'Amy Doncaster'
WOOD CRANESBILL
☼ ☀ **3-8**   ‡ 28in (70cm) ↔ 18in (50cm)

In summer, this lovely form of the wood cranesbill bears white-eyed, deep purple-blue flowers. It commemorates the plants-woman who first selected it in her garden.

Geranium kishtvariense
CRANESBILL
☼ ☀ **6-9**   ‡ 12in (30cm) ↔ 24in (60cm)

Underground, creeping stems form a low patch of wrinkled, deeply lobed leaves. The brilliant pinkish purple, finely-lined flowers appear in summer and autumn.

Geranium phaeum 'Lily Lovell'
CRANESBILL
☼ ☀ **5-8**   ‡ 32in (80cm) ↔ 18in (45cm)

A charming form of the mourning widow cranesbill producing attractively lobed, light green leaves. In summer, showers of mauve-purple, white-eyed flowers appear.

Geranium wallichianum
CRANESBILL
☼ ☀ **4-8**   ‡ 12in (30cm) ↔ 36in (90cm)

The attractively lined, lilac-purple flowers of this carpeting cranesbill are borne over a long period during summer and autumn. Its marbled leaves are shallowly lobed.

Hostas for Collectors

THE ALREADY BEWILDERING NUMBER of hostas increases each year, with new variations in leaf shape, size, texture, and color, as well as the bonus of attractive flowers. Here is a selection of favorites for planting singly or in groups or drifts. Classic plants for shade, they are also handsome in containers.

Hosta lancifolia
HOSTA
☀ ☀ 4-9　↕ 18in (45cm) ↔ 30in (75cm)

Long grown in gardens, this hosta forms a loose clump of narrow, glossy, dark green leaves. It makes a good groundcover. In summer, racemes of purple flowers appear.

Hosta gracillima
HOSTA
☀ ☀ 4-9　↕ 2in (5cm) ↔ 7in (18cm)

Charming for containers, rock gardens, or walls, this tiny hosta's spreading, narrow leaves have wavy margins. It bears slender spires of pinkish violet flowers in autumn.

Hosta 'Buckshaw Blue'
HOSTA
☀ ☀ 3-9　↕ 14in (35cm) ↔ 24in (60cm)

The heart-shaped, slightly "dished" leaves are boldly veined and beautifully bloomy, forming a striking clump. Nodding flowers open in short-stalked racemes in summer.

> **OTHER HOSTAS FOR COLLECTORS**
>
> *Hosta* 'Aphrodite'
> *Hosta fluctuans* 'Variegated'
> *Hosta* 'Great Expectations'
> *Hosta* 'Inniswood'
> *Hosta* 'Northern Halo'
> *Hosta* 'Paul's Glory'
> *Hosta* 'Summer Fragrance'
> *Hosta tokudama* f. *flavocircinalis*
> *Hosta* 'Zounds', see p.66

Hosta montana 'Aureomarginata'
HOSTA
☀ ☀ 3-9　↕ 28in (70cm) ↔ 36in (90cm)

Slow to establish but worth the wait, this superb specimen plant has long-stalked, large, shiny leaves with irregular, bright gold margins and white summer flowers.

Hosta 'Golden Tiara'
HOSTA
☀ ☀ 3-9　↕ 12in (30cm) ↔ 20in (50cm)

One of the best small hostas, this forms a compact clump of heart-shaped, yellow-margined leaves. It produces tall racemes of lavender-purple flowers in summer.

Hosta hypoleuca
HOSTA
☀ ☀ 4-9　↕ 18in (45cm) ↔ 36in (90cm)

This attractive species has large, pale green leaves with a gray bloom above and striking, mealy-white undersides. It bears pale mauve to white flowers in summer.

Hosta tokudama
HOSTA
☀ ☀ 3-9　↕ 14in (35cm) ↔ 36in (90cm)

Beautiful but slow-growing, this hosta has pale mauve to white flowers in summer and forms a compact clump of rounded to heart-shaped, corrugated, glaucous leaves.

Snowdrops for Collectors

I F YOU ARE THRILLED BY THE SIGHT of a drift of common snowdrops in the late winter garden or in woodland, then prepare for a pleasant surprise. There are dozens of lesser known varieties of snowdrop, each with its own particular charm and characteristics, and most are very easy to cultivate.

Galanthus nivalis Scharlockii Group
SNOWDROP
☼ 3-9   ↕↔4in (10cm)

This curious form of the common snow-drop has nodding, green-tipped flowers, with spathes split into two segments that stand above the blooms like rabbit's ears.

Galanthus 'Augustus'
SNOWDROP
☼ 3-9   ↕6in (15cm) ↔3in (8cm)

This robust snowdrop has relatively wide, silver-channeled leaves and distinctly rounded, large flowers with green-tipped inner segments. It forms colonies in time.

OTHER SNOWDROPS FOR COLLECTORS

Galanthus 'Benhall Beauty'
Galanthus elwesii 'Comet'
Galanthus 'Merlin'
Galanthus nivalis subsp.
  imperati 'Ginns'
Galanthus nivalis 'Lady Elphinstone'
Galanthus 'S. Arnott'
Galanthus nivalis 'Sandersii', see p.104

Galanthus 'Magnet'
SNOWDROP
☼ 3-9   ↕8in (20cm) ↔3in (6cm)

The distinguished, scented flowers sway in the slightest breeze on their unusually long and slender stalks. This is one of the best and most reliable snowdrops.

Galanthus 'Ophelia'
SNOWDROP
☼ 3-9   ↕6in (15cm) ↔8in (20cm)

A must for every collection, this very early snowdrop has fully double blooms on slender stalks. The outer segments have pinched tips, sometimes marked green.

Galanthus 'John Gray'
SNOWDROP
☼ 3-9   ↕6in (15cm) ↔3in (8cm)

Exquisite and early flowering, this is one of the most collectable snowdrops. It has pendent flowers carried on long, slender stalks, with inner segments marked green.

Galanthus 'Mighty Atom'
SNOWDROP
☼ 3-9   ↕5in (12cm) ↔3in (8cm)

An outstanding, easily grown snowdrop bearing attractive, slender-stalked flowers with inner segments that are distinctively stained green at their tips.

Galanthus reginae-olgae
SNOWDROP
☼ 6-9   ↕4in (10cm) ↔3in (8cm)

The earliest-flowering snowdrop, usually blooming in autumn before its green, silver-channeled leaves emerge. It is slow to increase, growing best in a sunny site.

Hellebores for Collectors

HELLEBORES ARE AMONG the most fashionable and collectable perennials for partially shaded sites in the garden. The range of species is not great, but despite this, an ever-increasing number of named hybrids and selected seedlings are being made available.

Helleborus × *sternii* 'Boughton Beauty'
HELLEBORE

☼ ☀ **6-9**　　↕ ↔ 20in (50cm)

In late winter, green-tinted pink flowers are borne above the mound of evergreen, beautifully veined and marbled, grayish leaves. Needs protection in cold areas.

Helleborus atrorubens
HELLEBORE

☼ **5-9**　　↕ 12in (30cm) ↔ 18in (45cm)

A choice species with circular, deeply divided, long-stalked leaves, often purple-tinted when young. Its starry, late winter flowers vary from deep purple to green.

Helleborus multifidus subsp. *hercegovinus*
HELLEBORE

☼ ☀ **6-9**　　↕ 12in (30cm) ↔ 18in (45cm)

Best known for the lacy effect of its finely dissected leaves, this hellebore also bears attractive, yellowish or pale green flowers during late winter or early spring.

Helleborus torquatus Party Dress Group
HELLEBORE

☼ ☀ **6-9**　　↕ 16in (40cm) ↔ 12in (30cm)

A delightful, if unusual, group of small hellebores that produces multi-petaled flowers in a variety of colors from winter to early spring before the leaves emerge.

Helleborus lividus
HELLEBORE

☼ **7-9**　　↕ 18in (45cm) ↔ 12in (30cm)

Silver-veined, evergreen leaves, tinted pink beneath, are accompanied by apple-green, pink-flushed flowers in winter. Best grown in an alpine house in cold areas.

Helleborus odorus
HELLEBORE

☼ ☀ **6-9**　　↕ ↔ 20in (50cm)

This showy, easy-to-grow species is free-flowering, with masses of scented, green to yellow-green flowers in late winter or early spring. A bold, clump-forming plant.

OTHER HELLEBORES FOR COLLECTORS

Helleborus argutifolius 'Pacific Frost'
Helleborus dumetorum
Helleborus niger 'Potter's Wheel', see p.105
Helleborus orientalis
Helleborus purpurascens
Helleborus torquatus
Helleborus viridis subsp. *occidentalis*

Helleborus vesicarius
HELLEBORE

☼ **6-9**　　↕ 18in (45cm) ↔ 12in (30cm)

This curious but desirable hellebore bears small, cupped, green-and-purple blooms in late winter and early spring followed by inflated pods. It is dormant in summer.

SPECIALIST PLANTS

155

Epimediums for Collectors

THE INTRODUCTION OF MANY NEW SPECIES from China has elevated epimediums to among the most collectable perennials. As woodland plants with attractive deciduous or semievergreen foliage, they make excellent groundcovers. Once established, they will thrive in a dry, shady site.

Epimedium acuminatum
EPIMEDIUM
☀ 6-9   ↕ 18in (45cm) ↔ 30in (75cm)

A magnificent, clump-forming evergreen with large, lance- or arrow-shaped leaflets and long-spurred, pale purple, or purple and white flowers in spring and summer.

Epimedium davidii
EPIMEDIUM
☀ 5-8   ↕ 12in (30cm) ↔ 18in (45cm)

The dark, shining stems of this choice epimedium species bear semievergreen, divided leaves and nodding, long-spurred yellow flowers from spring into summer.

OTHER EPIMEDIUMS TO COLLECT

Epimedium franchetii
Epimedium grandiflorum 'Lilafee'
Epimedium grandiflorum f. *violaceum*
Epimedium ogisui
Epimedium pinnatum subsp. *colchicum*, see p.52
Epimedium pubigerum
Epimedium x *versicolor* 'Sulphureum'
Epimedium x *warleyense*

Epimedium grandiflorum
'Rose Queen'
☀ 4-8   ↕ 12in (30cm) ↔ 18in (45cm)

The heart-shaped, prickle-toothed leaflets form a low mound and are prettily tinted when young. Showers of long-spurred, deep rose-pink flowers open in spring.

Epimedium leptorrhizum
EPIMEDIUM
☀ 6-9   ↕ 10in (25cm) ↔ 18in (45cm)

In time, this creeping evergreen develops patches of stems with attractively veined, prickle-toothed leaflets. Its long-spurred flowers open in spring and early summer.

Epimedium x *perralchicum*
'Frohnleiten'
☀ 5-8   ↕ 16in (40cm) ↔ 24in (60cm)

Worth growing for its foliage alone, as the prickle-toothed, glossy, dark green leaves are beautifully bronze-tinted when young. Pendent spring flowers are bright yellow.

Epimedium stellulatum 'Wudang Star'
EPIMEDIUM
☀ 5-8   ↕ 16in (40cm) ↔ 12in (30cm)

Multitudes of small, starry white flowers, with bold yellow beaks, are borne on wiry stems in spring above the heart-shaped, prickle-toothed, shiny, evergreen leaflets.

Epimedium x *versicolor* 'Versicolor'
EPIMEDIUM
☀ 4-8   ↕ ↔ 12in (30cm)

This is a real charmer with its low clump of semievergreen foliage, red-tinted when young. The loose sprays of yellow, pink-suffused flowers also open in spring.

Peonies for Collectors

WILD HERBACEOUS PEONIES, bearing their simple, usually single blooms of fragile petals and gold stamens, never fail to bring a touch of elegance to the garden. Although their flowering period is relatively brief, they often have decorative foliage that extends their value in the garden.

Paeonia 'Smouthii'
PEONY
☀ ☀ 4-8 ↕ ↔ 28in (70cm)

A little-known but reliable hybrid that forms clumps of finely divided leaves and produces fragrant, cup-shaped, bright red blooms in late spring and early summer.

Paeonia cambessedesii
MAJORCAN PEONY
☀ 7-8 ↕ 22in (55cm) ↔ 24in (60cm)

This very distinctive peony has purple- and red-flushed stems and shiny, metallic gray-green leaves that are red or purple beneath. It spring flowers are rose-pink.

OTHER PEONIES TO COLLECT

Paeonia delavayi
Paeonia japonica
Paeonia lactiflora 'White Wings'
Paeonia obovata
Paeonia obovata var. *alba*
Paeonia peregrina 'Otto Froebel'
Paeonia potaninii
Paeonia tenuifolia 'Rosea'
Paeonia veitchii var. *woodwardii*

Paeonia mascula subsp. *arietina*
PEONY
☀ ☀ 5-8 ↕ 30in (75cm) ↔ 24in (60cm)

This stout clump-former has handsome, deeply divided, grayish green leaves and bears bowl-shaped, reddish pink flowers with creamy yellow stamens during spring.

Paeonia tenuifolia
PEONY
☀ 5-8 ↕ ↔ 18in (45cm)

Quite unlike any other species, this forms bold clumps of beautiful, finely dissected leaves. The cupped, deep red flowers are borne in late spring and early summer.

Paeonia emodi
HIMALAYAN PEONY
☀ ☀ 6-8 ↕ ↔ 32in (80cm)

In late spring, slightly nodding, cupped, fragrant white flowers are carried by the handsome clump of branched stems with deeply divided leaves. Enjoys semi-shade.

Paeonia mlokosewitschii
CAUCASIAN PEONY
☀ ☀ 5-8 ↕ ↔ 28in (70cm)

This well-known peony has stout clumps of downy, gray-green leaves. Its lemon-yellow blooms in late spring and summer are followed by bright red seed capsules.

Paeonia wittmanniana
PEONY
☀ ☀ 5-8 ↕ ↔ 36in (90cm)

An outstanding species with bold clumps of glossy, dark green leaves. Bowl-shaped, pale yellow flowers, borne from late spring to summer, are followed by red seed pods.

SPECIALIST PLANTS

CLIMBERS

THE MOST COMMON climbers are woody-stemmed perennials or shrubs with scrambling or otherwise long, slender stems. Self-clinging by adhesive tendril tips or aerial roots, or in need of artificial support from wire or a trellis, they may be trained into trees and shrubs, and to cover walls or other structures.

△ IVY-CLAD SHED *This bold-leaved ivy (Hedera colchica 'Dentata Variegata') is perfect for covering an unsightly wall.*

△ *Abutilon megapotamicum*

THE BEAUTY OF CLIMBERS

- Useful as cover on tree stumps or unsightly buildings.
- Offer interest for every season.
- Versatile shrubs double as climbers.
- Provide bold or decorative foliage.
- Offer fragrant flowers.
- Give shelter or nesting sites for birds.
- Provide brilliant leaf tints in autumn.
- Offer decorative fruit or seedheads.
- Create multiseason effects if one plant is used as support for another.

All plants recommended in this section are either true climbers, or shrubs suitable for training against walls. They offer a large variety of attributes, from colorful or prolific flowers to decorative or unusual fruits. Many have attractive leaves, and some deciduous climbers are also noted for their autumn tints. Once established, both wall shrubs and climbers can support further plants, creating, when planned, a continuous, multiseason feature. All the climbers recommended on the following pages are deciduous unless specified as evergreen.

CLIMBING TO THE SUN
Numerous climbers grown for their flowering qualities thrive best in a sunny site, such as most climbing roses and honeysuckles. Two popular favorites, clematis and wisteria, prefer to have their heads in the sun and their roots shaded (place a large stone or tile over their roots). When grown against a wall, climbers benefit from the reflected heat, which helps ripen growth and initiate flower bud formation.

WOODLAND SHADE
The cooler conditions of shady walls, often combined with moist but well-drained soils, are a perfect home for many natural woodland climbers. Ivies are a good example, especially colored-leaved varieties, which flourish on shady or partially shaded walls, as do those lovely South American woodlanders, *Lapageria* and *Berberidopsis*.

△ SUPPORT IN DISGUISE *Evergreen spring-flowering ceanothus and twining honeysuckle beautifully decorate this pole.*

◁ PRETTY WINDOW *Wisteria, rose, and two clematis varieties combine to provide a delightful frame for this window.*

▷ SUMMER SENSATION *Luxuriant early summer growth of clematis, purple grapes, and golden hops clothes this wall.*

Climbers for Warm, Sunny Walls and Fences

SUNNY WALLS AND FENCES are excellent for climbers. When carefully selected and matched, several can be trained to grow into one another to give a continuous display. The surface, especially of a brick or stone wall, absorbs heat, and this helps promote growth and encourages flowering. All the climbers featured here require support from wires or netting.

Lonicera x *americana*
HONEYSUCKLE
☼ 6   ↕ ↔ 22ft (7m)

This free-flowering scrambler has clusters of fragrant, pink-tubed, creamy yellow flowers from summer into early autumn. Its leaves are purplish when young.

Actinidia kolomikta
ACTINIDIA
☼ 5   ↕ ↔ 13ft (4.5m)

This striking climber is slow to establish but it is well worth the wait. It has bold, heart-shaped leaves, often splashed cream and pink, and white flowers in summer.

Passiflora caerulea
BLUE PASSION FLOWER
☼ 8   ↕ ↔ 30ft (10m)

Fast-growing with fingered leaves, this climber bears beautiful, unusual flowers from summer into autumn. They may be followed by attractive seed pods.

Clematis 'Bill MacKenzie'
CLEMATIS
☼ 5   ↕ ↔ 22ft (7m)

Vigorous and scrambling, this clematis has beautiful, lanternlike, nodding flowers in late summer and autumn. These are followed by pretty, silky seedheads.

Clematis 'Jackmanii'
CLEMATIS
☼ 3   ↕ ↔ 10ft (3m)

A long-established garden favorite, this climbs by twining leaf stalks. Masses of large, velvety, dark purple flowers, turning violet with age, appear in summer.

Rosa 'Dublin Bay' ('Macdub')
CLIMBING ROSE
☼ 5   ↕ ↔ 7ft (2.2m)

'Dublin Bay' is a climbing floribunda rose of dense growth, with glossy, dark green leaves and clusters of double, fragrant flowers from summer to early autumn.

Rosa 'Madame Grégoire Staechelin'
CLIMBING ROSE

☼ 5   ↕ ↔ 10ft (3m)

One of the most beautiful climbing roses, this is vigorous, with shining green leaves and abundant clusters of rounded, slightly fragrant flowers in summer.

Vitis vinifera 'Purpurea'
CLARET VINE

☼ 6   ↕ ↔ 22ft (7m)

A vigorous form of the grape vine, with young leaves that mature to wine purple. These color richly in autumn, when small bunches of blue-black grapes ripen.

SELF-CLINGING CLIMBERS FOR SUNNY WALLS AND FENCES

Campsis radicans
Cissus striata
Decumaria sinensis, see p.172
Ficus pumila
Hydrangea anomala subsp. *petiolaris*,
   see p.175
Parthenocissus tricuspidata 'Lowii'
Trachelospermum asiaticum, see p.175
Trachelospermum jasminoides
   'Variegatum'

OTHER CLIMBERS FOR SUN

Aristolochia macrophylla
Campsis × *tagliabuana* 'Madame Galen'
Celastrus orbiculatus
Clematis armandii, see p.170
Jasminum officinale f. *affine*
Lonicera periclymenum
   'Graham Thomas', see p.169
Lonicera sempervirens
Parthenocissus quinquefolia
Rosa banksiae 'Lutea'
Sollya heterophylla
Trachelospermum asiaticum
Wisteria sinensis, see p.173

Rosa 'Maigold'
CLIMBING ROSE

☼ 5   ↕ ↔ 12ft (4m)

This vigorous climber has thorny stems and lush foliage. Fragrant bronze-yellow blooms, reddish in bud, appear in early summer and less profusely in autumn.

Solanum laxum 'Album'
POTATO VINE

☼ 8   ↕ ↔ 20ft (6m)

Semievergreen and slender-stemmed, this climber will grow vigorously through any support. Loose clusters of starry flowers occur from summer into autumn.

Wisteria floribunda 'Alba'
WHITE JAPANESE WISTERIA

☼ 5   ↕ ↔ 28ft (9m)

The handsome leaves of this powerful climber are compound. Long spikes of white pea flowers emerge in early summer. Thrives in neutral to slightly acid soils.

CLIMBERS

Climbers for Shady Walls and Fences

THE COOLER CONDITIONS normally found in places that do not receive the sun's glare directly suit a good number of climbers, many of which grow naturally in woodland, or similarly shaded places in the wild. Most need to be tied to a wire or trellis support, and even the self-clinging ones, such as ivy, benefit from this for a year or two after planting.

Berberidopsis corallina
CORAL PLANT
☀ ☀ 8 PH ▽   ↕ ↔ 14ft (4.5m)

Coral Plant's long, rambling stems bear heart-shaped evergreen leaves. Pendent, globular flowers are carried from summer into autumn.

Clematis montana f. *grandiflora*
CLEMATIS
☀ ☀ 6   ↕ ↔ 30ft (10m)

In time, this vigorous climber will produce blankets of leafy growth, bronze-purple when the leaves are young. Large white spring flowers are borne in abundance.

Hedera colchica 'Dentata Variegata'
PERSIAN IVY
☀ ☀ 7   ↕ ↔ 15ft (5m)

A spectacular evergreen with broad-based, leathery leaves, each irregularly margined creamy white. Shoots have aerial roots that cling to the surface of a support.

OTHER DECIDUOUS CLIMBERS FOR SHADY WALLS

Actinidia arguta
Akebia quinata, see p.168
Akebia trifoliata
Hydrangea anomala subsp. *petiolaris*, see p.175
Parthenocissus henryana, see p.175
Parthenocissus quinquefolia
Parthenocissus tricuspidata 'Lowii'
Schizophragma hydrangeoides 'Moonlight'
Schizophragma hydrangeoides 'Roseum'

Clematis x *jouiniana* 'Praecox'
CLEMATIS
☀ ☀ 6   ↕ ↔ 10ft (3m)

Vigorous and sprawling, this dense-growing climber should be trained to a support. Its coarse foliage backs masses of small, fragrant, tubular flowers in late summer.

Clematis 'Nelly Moser'
CLEMATIS
☀ 4   ↕ ↔ 11ft (3.5m)

Large, single, pale mauve flowers, with a carmine stripe on each petal, cover this popular twining clematis in early summer. Their color fades in strong sunlight.

Hedera colchica 'Sulphur Heart'
PERSIAN IVY
☀ ☀ 6   ↕ ↔ 15ft (5m)

This dramatic ivy with its boldly gold-splashed leaves is similar to *H. colchica* 'Dentata Variegata' *(above)*. They are most effective when grown together.

Hedera helix 'Eva'
ENGLISH IVY
☼ ☀ 6   ↕ ↔ 4ft (1.2m)

The evergreen leaves of this variegated English ivy cultivar are green and gray-green with broad, creamy white margins. It is self-clinging.

Hedera helix 'Green Ripple'
ENGLISH IVY
☼ ☀ 5   ↕ ↔ 4ft (1.2m)

This distinctive cultivar of English ivy has deeply lobed and pointed bright evergreen leaves with pale veins. Self-clinging, it is ideal for low walls.

Humulus lupulus 'Aureus'
GOLDEN HOP
☼ ☀ 5   ↕ ↔ 20ft (6m)

A strong-growing herbaceous climber, this has hairy, twining stems and boldly lobed yellow-green leaves. Clusters of green fruits (hops) are produced in autumn.

Lapageria rosea
CHILEAN BELLFLOWER
☼ ☀ 9 PH   ↕ ↔ 15ft (5m)

Strongly twining stems support leathery evergreen leaves and, from summer into late autumn, beautiful, pendulous, tubular flowers with fleshy petals.

OTHER EVERGREEN CLIMBERS FOR SHADY WALLS

Clematis armandii, see p.170
Euonymus fortunei 'Coloratus'
Ficus pumila
Holboellia coriacea

Lonicera japonica 'Halliana'
JAPANESE HONEYSUCKLE
☼ ☼ ☀ 5   ↕ ↔ 30ft (10m)

Evergreen or semievergreen, this prolific, twining climber produces loose clusters of fragrant flowers, emerging white and aging to yellow, from late spring into autumn.

Schizophragma integrifolium
SCHIZOPHRAGMA
☼ ☀ 6   ↕ ↔ 40ft (12m)

In time, this slow-growing, self-clinging climber will reach great heights. Flattened heads of creamy white flowers appear in summer among pointed green leaves.

Shrubs for Warm, Sunny Walls and Fences

SUNNY WALLS AND FENCES are a bonus to the gardener since they offer both the warmth and shelter necessary for less hardy plants. They are also ideal for shrubs with trailing or fragile stems that need some support. Most will greatly increase their average height when grown against a wall. Careful pruning and training onto wires or a trellis may be necessary.

Abutilon megapotamicum
FLOWERING MAPLE
☼ 8   ↕ ↔ 10ft (3m)

This free-growing shrub is of virtually pendulous habit. From late spring to autumn it produces flowers that resemble colorful Chinese lanterns.

Callistemon pallidus
BOTTLEBRUSH
☼ 9 PH   ↕ ↔ 10ft (3m)

In flower, bottlebrushes are among the most exotic of evergreen shrubs. This is certainly no exception, with its brushes of creamy yellow flowers borne in summer.

Ceanothus arboreus 'Trewithen Blue'
CATALINA CEANOTHUS
☼ 9   ↕ ↔ 20ft (6m)

This vigorous evergreen shrub is ideal for covering a large surface. It flowers for many weeks in late winter and spring. Prefers well-drained, acid soils.

OTHER DECIDUOUS SHRUBS FOR WARM, SUNNY WALLS AND FENCES

Abeliophyllum distichum
Buddleia globosa, see p.206
Caesalpinia japonica
Chimonanthus praecox 'Grandiflorus', see p.236
Clianthus puniceus
Edgeworthia chrysantha
Enkianthus campanulatus
Hamamelis mollis 'Pallida'
Indigofera heterantha, see p.194
Iochroma cyaneum
Prunus mume 'Peggy Clarke'
Punica granatum 'Rubrum Flore Pleno'
Pyracantha coccinea
Ribes speciosum
Viburnum macrocephalum
Vitex agnus-castus var. *latifolia*
Xanthoceras sorbifolium, see p.195

Buddleia crispa
BUTTERFLY BUSH
☼ 8   ↕ ↔ 8ft (2.5m)

The oval leaves of this choice shrub are all covered in a woolly pelt of soft, grayish white down. Its small, fragrant flowers are carried in dense clusters in summer.

Cytisus battandieri
MOROCCAN BROOM
☼ 8   ↕ ↔ 12ft (4m)

Worth growing for its leaves alone, which are divided into leaflets and covered in silky silvery hairs. Yellow pineapple-scented pea flowers appear in summer.

Acca sellowiana
PINEAPPLE GUAVA
☼ 8   ↕ ↔ 10ft (3m)

The summer flowers of this interesting
evergreen shrub have fleshy, edible petals
and crimson stamens. Edible, egg-shaped
fruits are produced after a hot summer.

Robinia hispida
ROSE ACACIA
☼ 5   ↕ ↔ 8ft (2.5m)

Large rose-pink pea flowers are borne in
drooping clusters in late spring. The
leaves, with numerous lush green leaflets,
are held on fragile stems.

Fremontodendron 'California Glory'
FLANNEL BUSH
☼ 9   ↕ ↔ 25ft (8m)

This fast-growing evergreen has beautiful
yellow flowers from spring into autumn.
Prune regularly if it is on a small fence or
wall. Be sure the roots are not too wet.

Rosa x *odorata* 'Mutabilis'
CHINA ROSE
☼ 7   ↕ ↔ 10ft (3m)

This vigorous China rose is popular for its
dark purple shoots, coppery young leaves,
and lovely fragrant summer flowers. It will
grow taller than usual against a wall.

**OTHER EVERGREEN SHRUBS FOR
WARM, SUNNY WALLS AND FENCES**

Abelia floribunda
Carpenteria californica, see p.228
Ceanothus 'Concha'
Viburnum awabuki

Desmodium elegans var. spicatum
DESMODIUM
☼ ❄❄   ↕ ↔ 6–10ft (2–3m)

From late summer into autumn, long
racemes of pink flowers project from soft
downy leaves. Except in cold areas, old
growth is best pruned back every spring.

Itea ilicifolia
HOLLYLEAF SWEETSPIRE
☼ 8   ↕ ↔ 15ft (5m)

On warm evenings from late summer into
autumn, long greenish catkins give off a
honeylike aroma. The dark green, glossy,
hollylike leaves are evergreen.

Solanum crispum 'Glasnevin'
BLUE POTATO VINE
☼ 8   ↕ ↔ 20ft (6m)

This vigorous and scrambling shrub is
evergreen in warmer areas. Loose clusters
of star-shaped flowers appear over a long
period in summer. Needs support.

CLIMBERS

Shrubs for Shady Walls and Fences

SOME GARDENERS may perceive a wall or fence that does not receive direct sunlight as a curse, and consider it unsightly. It need not be a problem, however, as long as it receives some light. Many shrubs (and climbers) will thrive, and some even prefer the normally cooler conditions of such a site, while others flower freely in or out of the sun.

Forsythia suspensa
WEEPING FORSYTHIA
☼ ☼ ☀ 5   ↕ ↔ 10ft (3m)

A vigorous, rambling shrub that requires regular pruning and training to prevent it from becoming overpowering. Star-shaped flowers wreathe the branches in spring.

Chaenomeles x *superba* 'Rowallane'
FLOWERING QUINCE
☼ ☼ ☀ 5   ↕ ↔ 5ft (1.5m)

Superb in spring, when the previous year's branches are hidden beneath brilliant red flower clusters. Like 'Moerloosei', best pruned and trained close to the wall.

Azara microphylla
AZARA
☼ ☀ 8   ↕ ↔ 20ft (6m)

This elegant evergreen will grow to small tree size if allowed. Arching branchlets are clothed with leaves and, in late winter or spring, with tiny vanilla-scented flowers.

Garrya elliptica (male form)
SILK-TASSEL BUSH
☼ ☼ ☀ 9   ↕ ↔ 15ft (5m)

From midwinter through to early spring the branches are draped with long tassels, which tremble in the slightest breeze. This shrub has leathery evergreen leaves.

Chaenomeles speciosa 'Moerloosei'
FLOWERING QUINCE
☼ ☼ ☀ 5   ↕ ↔ 8ft (2.5m)

A reliable, adaptable, and vigorous shrub, this carries large flower clusters in spring and early summer followed by aromatic fruits. Prune regularly, and train on wires.

Euonymus fortunei 'Silver Queen'
SILVER QUEEN EUONYMUS
☼ ☼ ☀ 5   ↕ ↔ 8ft (2.5m)

A handsome evergreen shrub, low and bushy in a bed, but rising higher against a wall if trained. Glossy dark green leaves have broad, irregular creamy margins.

Illicium anisatum
CHINESE STAR ANISE
☼ ☀ 8   ↕ ↔ 8ft (2.5m)

The aromatic leaves of this slow-growing evergreen are joined by loose clusters of yellow, star-shaped flowers in spring. The wood also has a strong, agreeable aroma.

Jasminum humile
HIMALAYAN JASMINE
☼ ☼ ☀ 8   ↕ ↔ 6ft (2m)

The numerous greenish stems of this bushy evergreen are clothed in attractive, much-divided leaves. It sports clusters of yellow flowers from spring into autumn.

Pyracantha rogersiana
FIRETHORN
☼ ☼ ☀ 7   ↕ ↔ 10ft (3m)

The spiny branches of this vigorous evergreen are clothed in narrrow, glossy leaves. Flower clusters in early summer are replaced by orange-red berries.

OTHER EVERGREEN SHRUBS FOR SHADY WALLS AND FENCES

Azara serrata
Camellia japonica 'Debutante'
Camellia sasanqua
Crinodendron hookerianum, see p.200
Euonymus fortunei 'Emerald Gaiety', see p.184
Itea ilicifolia, see p.165
Jasminum humile 'Revolutum'
Ligustrum japonicum
Pyracantha 'Orange Glow', see p.239

Kerria japonica 'Pleniflora'
DOUBLE KERRIA
☼ ☼ ☀ 5   ↕ ↔ 10ft (3m)

Popular and easy to grow, this vigorous shrub has long green shoots that need support, along with sharply toothed leaves and rich yellow spring flowers.

OTHER DECIDUOUS SHRUBS FOR SHADY WALLS AND FENCES

Chaenomeles speciosa 'Cameo'
Chaenomeles speciosa 'Texas Scarlet'
Chaenomeles speciosa 'Toyo Nishiki'
Cornus alba 'Variegata', see p.218
Cotoneaster horizontalis
Hamamelis virginiana
Lonicera x *purpusii* 'Winter Beauty', see p.237
Rhodotypos scandens, see p.203
Viburnum acerifolium

Jasminum nudiflorum
WINTER JASMINE
☼ ☼ ☀ 6   ↕ ↔ 10ft (3m)

This is a popular and reliable winter-flowering shrub, with long shoots bearing yellow flowers through winter into spring. Prune after flowering to keep plants neat.

Piptanthus nepalensis
EVERGREEN LABURNUM
☼ ☼ ☀ 9   ↕ ↔ 10ft (3m)

This strong-growing shrub has lush semi-evergreen or evergreen foliage. Its clusters of bright yellow pea flowers are produced from spring into summer.

Ribes laurifolium (male form)
BAYLEAF CURRANT
☼ ☀ 8   ↕ ↔ 6ft (2m)

A curious, slow-growing evergreen currant that needs training to gain height. Its bold leaves are joined by drooping flower clusters from late winter into early spring.

Climbers to Train into Trees and Shrubs

I F YOU LACK WALLS OR FENCES, encourage climbers to grow into trees or large shrubs, where they can create spectacular effects when in flower or leaf. It is important to match each climber to its supporting plant: grow strong climbers into large trees, and weaker ones into small trees or shrubs. Careful pruning may be necessary to control growth.

Clematis rehderiana
CLEMATIS
☼ 6   ↕↔22ft (7m)

As well as a dense growth of divided leaves, loose clusters of primrose yellow, cowslip-scented flowers cover this twining climber from late summer into autumn.

OTHER FOLIAGE CLIMBERS FOR TRAINING INTO TREES

Actinidia kolomikta, see p.160
Ampelopsis brevipedunculata
Aristolochia macrophylla
Humulus lupulus 'Aureus', see p.163
Parthenocissus quinquefolia
Vitis vinifera 'Purpurea', see p.161

Akebia quinata
CHOCOLATE VINE
☼ ☼ 4   ↕↔30ft (10m)

The clusters of vanilla-scented, brownish purple flowers in spring are followed by sausage-shaped fruits. This vigorous semi-evergreen climbs by twining.

Clematis 'Madame Julia Correvon'
CLEMATIS
☼ 5   ↕↔11ft (3.5m)

From summer to early autumn, this twining climber with slender stems freely produces magnificent, four-petaled wine-red flowers with cream-colored stamens.

Celastrus orbiculatus Hermaphrodite Group
☼ ☼ 4   ↕↔70ft (20m)

This vigorous climber is showy in autumn when the leaves turn yellow and clusters of orange seed capsules first appear; the seeds continue into winter.

Clematis montana var. *rubens*
CLEMATIS
☼ 6   ↕↔30ft (10m)

Masses of pink flowers in spring cover the dense curtains of growth produced by this vigorous, twining climber. Many good color selections exist.

Hedera colchica
PERSIAN IVY
☼ ☼ ☼ 6   ↕↔30ft (10m)

Persian Ivy is a strong-growing, evergreen, self-clinging climber, which also makes a splendid groundcover. Its shining, dark green leaves are pointed and leathery.

Rosa 'Albertine'
CLIMBING ROSE
☀ 6 ↕↔ 15ft (5m)

An old and popular vigorous rambling rose, 'Albertine' has thorny reddish stems and richly fragrant, double salmon-pink flowers, freely borne in summer.

Lonicera periclymenum 'Graham Thomas'
☀ 5 ↕↔ 22ft (7m)

Vigorous and dense-growing, this twining climber has oval leaves and, in summer, loose clusters of freely borne, fragrant flowers that are white aging to yellow.

Rosa filipes 'Kiftsgate'
CLIMBING ROSE
☀ 6-7 ↕↔ 30ft (10m)

Rampant if unpruned, this rose has fresh, glossy green foliage and branched heads of fragrant, yellow-centered white flowers in summer, followed by small red hips.

Vitis coignetiae
JAPANESE GRAPE
☀ 5 ↕↔ 70ft (20m)

This vigorous vine climbs by means of twining tendrils. It is chiefly grown for its handsome, heart-shaped leaves that turn crimson and scarlet in autumn.

OTHER FLOWERING CLIMBERS FOR TRAINING INTO TREES

Clematis 'Perle d'Azur'
Clematis virginiana
Hydrangea anomala subsp. *petiolaris*, see p.175
Jasminum officinale
Lonicera x *americana*, see p.160
Rosa 'Veilchenblau'
Schisandra rubriflora
Schizophragma hydrangeoides
Wisteria sinensis, see p.173

Fallopia baldschuanica
SILVER LACE VINE
☀ 4 ↕↔ 40ft (12m)

Well known, popular, and rampant, this twining climber has stringlike tassels of white or pink-tinged flowers in summer and early autumn. Dislikes dry soils.

Tropaeolum speciosum
FLAME CREEPER
☀ 7 ↕↔ 10ft (3m)

Brilliant, long-spurred flowers adorn this climber, with fleshy, twining stems and long-stalked leaves, from summer into autumn. Bright blue fruits follow.

Wisteria floribunda 'Multijuga'
WISTERIA
☀ 5 ↕↔ 30ft (10m)

In early summer, this vigorous, twining climber produces fragrant lilac, darker-flushed pea flowers in handsome, pendent tassels up to 4ft (1.2m) long.

Evergreen Climbers

EXCEPT FOR IVIES, the number of evergreen climbers suitable for cool, temperate regions is relatively few when compared with the abundance of deciduous climbers. This makes them all the more valuable, especially in winter, when their persistent foliage provides a welcome touch of color. They can be used to hide unsightly structures, as well as providing useful shelter for wildlife. Most evergreen climbers need support, but self-clinging plants are specified here.

Hedera helix 'Buttercup'
GOLDEN ENGLISH IVY
☼ ☀ 7   ↕↔20ft (6m)

The three-lobed leaves of this self-clinging climber form a dense cover. They become a rich yellow in summer, though excessive sun can scorch them.

Clematis armandii
CLEMATIS
☼ 8   ↕↔15ft (5m)

The leaflets of this vigorous climber are dark, glossy green. Fragrant white or pink-flushed flowers are borne in bold clusters in early spring. Best in a sheltered position.

Clematis cirrhosa
CLEMATIS
☼ 7   ↕↔10ft (3m)

Slender, twining stems and small, fernlike leaves form a dense curtain. Loose clusters of nodding, bell-shaped, creamy flowers open from late winter into early spring.

Clematis x *cartmanii* 'Avalanche'
CLEMATIS
☼ ☀ 6   ↕↔10–15ft (3–5m)

This vigorous clematis bears finely cut, ferny leaves and an abundance of large white flowers in spring. It needs a firm support and careful training.

Hedera canariensis 'Gloire de Marengo'
CANARY ISLAND IVY
☼ ☀ 6   ↕↔15ft (5m)

A long-established and well-proven ivy suitable for a wall or as groundcover. The large, lobed leaves are cream-variegated, making a striking contrast with green forms.

Hedera helix 'Cavendishii'
ENGLISH IVY
☼ ☀ 5   ↕↔24ft (8m)

Superb and reliable, the self-clinging stems are crowded with neatly lobed leaves margined creamy yellow. Also good in containers or as a groundcover.

Hedera helix 'Maple Leaf'
ENGLISH IVY
☼ ☀ 5   ↕ ↔ 6ft (2m)

An unusual form with deeply lobed and toothed leaves. It gives a dense cover and will grow as a groundcover, combining well with small-leaved, variegated ivies.

OTHER EVERGREEN CLIMBERS

Cissus striata
Clematis fasciculiflora
Ficus pumila
Hedera colchica 'Sulphur Heart', see p.162
Lapageria rosea, see p.163

Holboellia latifolia
HOLBOELLIA
☼ ☀ 9   ↕ ↔ 30ft (10m)

The evergreen, many-fingered leaves of this vigorous twiner create a dense cover punctuated by bell-shaped, fragrant, violet-tinged white flowers in spring.

Hydrangea seemannii
CLIMBING HYDRANGEA
☼ ☀ 8   ↕ ↔ 30ft (10m)

A vigorous, self-clinging climber making a dense, dark green cover. Shallowly domed, lace-cap heads of white then greenish white flowers appear in summer.

Pileostegia viburnoides
PILEOSTEGIA
☼ ☀ 7   ↕ ↔ 20ft (6m)

This slow-growing hydrangea relative is self-clinging, climbing by aerial roots. Its branched heads of tiny, creamy flowers open in late summer and early autumn.

Trachelospermum jasminoides
CONFEDERATE JASMINE
☼ 8   ↕ ↔ 20ft (6m)

Best started on supporting wires, this self-clinging climber has dark green leaves that may turn red in winter. Clusters of creamy white summer flowers are fragrant.

Climbers with Fragrant Flowers

MENTION FRAGRANT CLIMBERS, and most people instantly picture honeysuckle scrambling over a hedge or framing a cottage door. No one would deny its attraction, but there are many other climbers whose flowers produce fragrances which, once experienced, are not forgotten.

Clematis flammula
CLEMATIS
☼ ⑦   ↕ ↔ 15ft (5m)

The herbaceous stems of this vigorous climber are clothed with deeply divided green leaves and, in late summer and early autumn, almond-scented white flowers.

Clematis montana 'Mayleen'
CLEMATIS
☼ ⑥   ↕ ↔ 25–30ft (8–10m)

An extremely vigorous climber suitable for growing into a tree. The bronze-colored young foliage is an ideal backing for the masses of pink, late spring flowers.

Clematis terniflora
SWEET AUTUMN CLEMATIS
☼ ④   ↕ ↔ 15ft (5m)

This vigorous climber forms a dense tangle of growth if not pruned. Masses of small, starry white flowers appear on the current year's growth in autumn.

Decumaria sinensis
DECUMARIA
☼ ⑦   ↕ ↔ 12ft (4m)

This self-clinging evergreen climber has aerial roots, fairly narrow pointed leaves, and heads of tiny, greenish white, honey-scented flowers, borne freely in spring.

Holboellia latifolia
HOLBOELLIA
☼ ☼ ⑩   ↕ ↔ 22ft (7m)

A vigorous, evergreen, twining climber with leaves held limply when young. Flowers appear in spring, sometimes followed by sausage-shaped purple fruits.

OTHER CLIMBERS WITH FRAGRANT FLOWERS

Clematis armandii, see p.170
Gelsemium sempervirens
Jasminum x *stephanense*
Lonicera japonica 'Halliana', see p.163
Mandevilla laxa
Rosa, many
Trachelospermum jasminoides, see p.171
Wisteria floribunda

CLIMBERS

Rosa 'Wedding Day'
CLIMBING ROSE
☼ 8   ↕ ↔ 25ft (8m)

The yellow buds of this climbing rose,
with glossy green leaves and thorny stems,
open in summer to richly scented, creamy
white flowers. Blooms age to pale pink.

Lonicera periclymenum 'Serotina'
LATE DUTCH HONEYSUCKLE
☼ ☼ 5   ↕ ↔ 15ft (5m)

In summer, the young purple shoots of
this vigorous climber carry fragrant, long-
tubed, purple flowers, fading to yellow
within. Bears many red berry clusters.

Wisteria brachybotrys 'Shiro-kapitan'
JAPANESE WISTERIA
☼ ☼ 6   ↕ ↔ 30ft (10m)

One of the loveliest wisterias, bearing
drooping clusters of large, fragrant white
flowers in late spring and early summer.
Previously known as *W. venusta*.

Jasminum officinale
'Argenteo-variegatum'
☼ 7   ↕ ↔ 15ft (5m)

Strong-growing and semievergreen, this
climber has twining stems, much-divided
cream-margined leaves, and richly fragrant,
pink-budded, white summer flowers.

Lonicera periclymenum 'Sweet Sue'
HONEYSUCKLE
☼ ☼ 5   ↕ ↔ 6–10ft (2–3m)

An attractive, twining climber good for a
raised bank. During summer it is covered
with clusters of sweet-scented white
flowers; red berries follow in autumn.

Wisteria sinensis
CHINESE WISTERIA
☼ 5   ↕ ↔ 70ft (20m)

This twining climber has fresh green
leaves and crowded tassels of lilac to pale
violet flowers in late spring. Pruning is
required if it is grown against a wall.

C L I M B E R S

Climbing Annuals and Biennials

M OST OF THE CLIMBERS commonly grown from seed, and treated as annuals in cool gardens, are actually perennial in the wild, or when cultivated in warmer climates. When they are planted in containers, many of these can be overwintered under glass, and some may survive for several years outside in a warm, sheltered spot, especially where winters are mild.

Rhodochiton atrosanguineus
PURPLE-BELL VINE
☼   ↕ ↔ 15ft (5m)

Borne from spring to autumn, the curious, pendulous blooms of this tender perennial each have a rose-pink, bell-like calyx and a maroon-black tubular flower.

Cobaea scandens
CUP-AND-SAUCER VINE
☼   ↕ ↔ 20ft (6m)

Climbing by tendrils, this vigorous, leafy perennial grown as an annual has curious yellow-green, cup-shaped flowers that turn purple with age.

Ipomoea 'Heavenly Blue'
MORNING GLORY
☼   ↕ ↔ 10ft (3m)

Sporting lovely, large sky blue flowers from summer into autumn, this vigorous annual or tender perennial has twining stems and long-pointed, heart-shaped leaves.

> **OTHER CLIMBING ANNUALS**
>
> *Cardiospermum halicacabum*
> *Cucurbita pepo* var. *ovifera*
> *Ipomoea alba*
> *Ipomoea quamoclit*
> *Lablab purpureus*

Eccremocarpus scaber
CHILEAN GLORY FLOWER
☼ 9   ↕ ↔ 10ft (3m)

This vigorous, scrambling tender evergreen perennial climbs by means of tendrils. It has ferny leaves and spikes of orange, red, or yellow flowers in summer.

> **OTHER CLIMBING ANNUALS**
>
> *Lathyrus odoratus*
> *Mina lobata*
> *Phaseolus coccineus*
> *Tropaeolum majus*
> *Tropaeolum peregrinum*

Thunbergia alata
BLACK-EYED SUSAN VINE
☼   ↕ ↔ 10ft (3m)

A succession of striking, dark-eyed, orange-yellow flowers covers this vigorous, twining annual through summer and into autumn. It bears abundant, heart-shaped leaves.

Self-clinging Climbers

EW SELF-CLINGING CLIMBERS, apart from the ubiquitous ivies, are hardy enough for cool, temperate gardens, especially when compared with the large number that climb by other means. Hardy, self-clinging species, therefore, have a value of their own, not only for clothing walls and fences, but also for growing up the stems or trunks of suitable trees. This selection includes climbers that cling by means of aerial roots and those that have tendrils tipped with sucker pads.

Parthenocissus henryana
PARTHENOCISSUS
☼ ☼ ☼ 6　　　　　　　↕ ↔ 20ft (6m)

This free-growing ornamental vine clings by adhesive tendrils. Leaves are divided into silver-veined, velvety green or bronze leaflets. They color richly in autumn.

Hydrangea anomala subsp. *petiolaris*
CLIMBING HYDRANGEA
☼ ☼ ☼ 5　　　　　　　↕ ↔ 30ft (10m)

The stems of this robust shrub, which climbs by means of aerial roots, have rich brown, peeling bark. Its white flowers, in lacecap flowerheads, open in summer.

Parthenocissus tricuspidata 'Veitchii'
BOSTON IVY
☼ ☼ ☼ 5　　　　　　　↕ ↔ 50ft (15m)

This vigorous vine, which clings with disk-tipped tendrils, soon clothes walls with its ivylike green leaves. These color brilliantly in autumn.

Hedera helix 'Oro di Bogliasco'
ENGLISH IVY
☼ ☼ ☼ 6-7　　　　　　↕ ↔ 10ft (3m)

Striking and easy to recognize, this ivy has dark, glossy evergreen leaves with a gold central splash. Green-leaved reversions should be removed as soon as they appear.

OTHER SELF-CLINGING CLIMBERS

Campsis radicans
Decumaria barbara
Decumaria sinensis, see p.172
Euonymus fortunei 'Coloratus'
Euonymus fortunei 'Longwood'
Ficus pumila
Hedera canariensis 'Gloire de Marengo', see p.170
Hedera colchica, see p.168
Hedera colchica 'Sulphur Heart', see p.162
Hedera helix, many
Hedera nepalensis
Hydrangea seemannii, see p.171
Hydrangea serratifolia
Parthenocissus quinquefolia
Parthenocissus tricuspidata 'Lowii'
Pileostegia viburnoides, see p.171
Schizophragma hydrangeoides
Schizophragma integrifolium

Trachelospermum asiaticum
☼ 7　　　　　　　↕ ↔ 20ft (6m)

Self-clinging in a wind-free situation, the slender stems of this climber twine around any support. Clusters of fragrant, creamy white flowers in summer age to yellow.

SHRUBS

ORNAMENTAL SHRUBS in the garden are the bridge between trees and perennials, forming the middle layer in mixed borders or beds. Their flexibility is legendary. Many shrubs are so distinctive in habit or impressive in flower or leaf that they make excellent single specimens in a lawn or border, where they can freely develop to their fullest potential.

△ *Aucuba japonica* 'Crotonifolia'

△ INSECT PARADISE *The nectar-filled flowers of the Butterfly Bush (Buddleia davidii) attract bees and other insects, too.*

THE BEAUTY OF SHRUBS

- Flowering and fruiting shrubs attract wildlife, birds, and insects.
- Offer numerous forms and shapes.
- Provide flowers for every season of the year, including winter.
- Evergreens are attractive in winter.
- Ideal specimens for lawns or beds.
- Excellent in mixed plantings with perennials, climbers, and/or conifers.
- Useful for massed spring display.
- Provide good groundcover.

The range of shrubs stretches from small carpeting plants to the larger stalwarts. Between is a host of shrubs whose habits make a substantial contribution to garden design. Horizontally extending branches such as *Viburnum plicatum* 'Mariesii', arching or weeping growth such as the brooms *(Cytisus)*, and those of upright habit such as *Viburnum sargentii* 'Onondaga' can all play a part in creating pleasing and useful architectural effects.

SOME TOUGH, SOME TENDER
Most shrubs in this section are winter hardy, but some prefer to be planted in warmer sites. In cold areas, grow tender shrubs in pots and bring them under cover for the winter. Some shrubs flourish during summer but are cut back by winter cold. These plants are known as subshrubs, and any dead growth should be removed when regrowth commences in spring.

STABILITY OR DIVERSITY
Evergreens bring an important sense of stability and continuity to the garden, most notably when deciduous or herbaceous plants are leafless or below ground. Shrubs in this section are deciduous unless described as evergreen. Numerous deciduous shrubs are worth growing for their foliage alone, especially those having bold or otherwise dramatic leaves, perhaps variegated or colored. Some produce brilliant autumn tints, of which just one can make a real impact in the garden.

△ GROUNDCOVER *The Partridgeberry* (Gaultheria procumbens) *is an attractive groundcover for acid soil.*

◁ SPRING PAGEANT *Rhododendrons and evergreen azaleas grow together in the wild and combine well in the garden.*

▷ LATE SUMMER MAGIC *This mop-headed form of* Hydrangea macrophylla *provides a reliable show late in the season.*

Large Shrubs for Specimen Planting

MOST GARDENS have at least one situation suitable for planting something particularly special – maybe in a lawn, a courtyard, or as a border feature. A tree is frequently chosen for this role, but a refreshing alternative is to consider one of the following ultimately large and impressive shrubs instead. All have character and presence as well as flowers.

Abelia triflora
ABELIA
☼ 7   ↕ 13–15ft (4–5m) ↔ 10ft (3m)

A strong-growing shrub that spreads with age, bearing clusters of small and fragrant, rosy white flowers in early summer. Its corrugated gray stems are of winter interest.

Aesculus parviflora
BOTTLEBRUSH BUCKEYE
☼ ☼ 5   ↕ 10ft (3m) ↔ 15ft (5m)

In time this shrub forms a bold thicket or mound of leaves, bronze-red when young and yellow in autumn. Long, tapering flower spikes are produced in summer.

Azara serrata
AZARA
☼ 9   ↕ ↔ 10–13ft (3–4m)

A dense, rounded bush with bright green, serrated, evergreen foliage, joined in late spring to midsummer by fluffy yellow flowers along the upper sides of the shoots.

Buddleia colvilei 'Kewensis'
BUDDLEIA
☼ ☼ 8   ↕ ↔ 20ft (6m)

A strong-growing shrub often grown against a wall for protection. It has bold foliage and clusters of dark pink or red, bell-shaped flowers in early summer.

Chionanthus virginicus
FRINGE TREE
☼ 4   ↕ 10ft (3m) ↔ 12ft (4m)

This large, bushy shrub bears bold, deep green leaves that turn yellow in autumn. Sprays of fragrant white flowers drape the branches in summer. Dislikes dry soils.

Clerodendrum trichotomum
HARLEQUIN GLORYBOWER
☼ 6   ↕ 10ft (3m) ↔ 12ft (4m)

The leaves of this spreading shrub are aromatic. Pink or greenish buds open into clusters of fragrant white flowers from late summer. Turquoise blue berries follow.

Clethra barbinervis
JAPANESE CLETHRA
☼ 6   ↕ 10ft (3m)

This shrub has large, boldly veined leaves and clusters of white, bell-shaped, fragrant flowers from late summer. Its red and yellow autumn colors are a bonus.

Magnolia liliiflora 'Nigra'
LILY MAGNOLIA
☼ ☼ 5 PH⤵   ↕ 10ft (3m) ↔ 10ft (3m)

One of the most satisfactory and reliable magnolias, this forms a compact mound of glossy leaves. Flowers appear from spring into summer, and in early autumn.

Pieris formosa var. *forrestii* 'Wakehurst'
PIERIS
☼ 8 PH⤵   ↕ 10ft (3m) ↔ 10ft (3m)

The new leaves of this handsome, mounded evergreen emerge brilliant red in spring. These follow drooping sprays of white lily-of-the-valley flowers.

Heptacodium miconioides
SEVEN-SON FLOWER
☼ ☼ 6   ↕ 10–15ft (3–5m)

A strong-growing shrub with attractive, peeling bark and bold foliage. Large heads of fragrant white flowers appear from late summer to autumn, followed by red calyces.

OTHER LARGE SHRUBS FOR
SPECIMEN PLANTING

Exochorda racemosa
Hibiscus syriacus 'Diana'
Hydrangea macrophylla cvs.
Kolkwitzia amabilis 'Pink Cloud',
 see p.194
Loropetalum chinense
Nerium oleander
Photinia serrulata
Viburnum plicatum var. *tomentosum*
Viburnum setigerum

Ligustrum sinense
CHINESE PRIVET
☼ ☼ 7   ↕ 15ft (5m) ↔ 15ft (5m)

Upright at first, this strong-growing semi-evergreen spreads with age. Its arching, leafy branches terminate in large heads of tiny, sweet-scented white summer flowers.

Vitex agnus-castus var. *latifolia*
CHASTE TREE
☼ 6   ↕ ↔ 10–15ft (3–4m)

This vigorous shrub bears attractive, aromatic leaves and large spikes of fragrant blue flowers in autumn. Prune hard in late winter to encourage strong shoots.

S H R U B S

Medium-sized Shrubs

SOME OF THE LOVELIEST and most desirable of all shrubs are found in the medium-size range of 5–8ft (1.5–2.5m) in height. Where space is no object, many of these can be planted to glorious effect in groups, or even drifts. In smaller gardens, where space is limited, any of the shrubs featured here makes an impressive single specimen in the lawn. They may also be used in combination with smaller shrubs or groundcovers to create informal groups in beds or borders.

Hydrangea macrophylla 'Lilacina'
LACECAP HYDRANGEA
☀ 6   ↕5ft (1.5m) ↔6ft (2m)

This shrub is particularly lovely when in flower in late summer. Its lacecap flower-heads are carried above mounds of slender, pointed leaves. Dislikes dry soils.

Clerodendrum bungei
CLERODENDRUM
☀ 8   ↕6ft (2m) ↔indefinite

From late summer into autumn, fragrant, deep pink flowerheads nestle among the aromatic, heart-shaped leaves. A suckering shrub, this has erect purple shoots.

Exochorda 'The Bride'
PEARLBUSH
☀ 5   ↕5ft (1.5m) ↔8ft (2.5m)

Wider than it is tall, this mounded shrub is covered by pure white blossoms in spring and early summer. Its arching or weeping branches are densely leafy.

OTHER DECIDUOUS MEDIUM-SIZED SHRUBS

Cornus alba 'Sibirica', see p.238
Cytisus scoparius 'Moonlight'
Paeonia suffruticosa cvs.
Philadelphus 'Belle Etoile'
Spiraea x *vanhouttei*, see p.203
Syringa patula 'Miss Kim'
Viburnum dilatatum 'Erie'
Viburnum nudum
Viburnum opulus 'Compactum'
Weigela 'Mont Blanc'

Deutzia x *elegantissima* 'Rosealind'
DEUTZIA
☀ 6   ↕5ft (1.5m) ↔5ft (1.5m)

This is among the best flowering shrubs for smaller gardens. Its mound of arching, leafy branches is wreathed in clusters of pink flowers in summer.

Hydrangea aspera
HYDRANGEA
☀ 6   ↕8ft (2.5m) ↔8ft (2.5m)

The large, downy leaves of this impressive shrub are an excellent foil for the lacecap flowerheads with marginal florets in late summer and autumn. Dislikes dry soils.

Lavatera x *clementii* 'Rosea'
TREE MALLOW
☀ 8   ↕6ft (2m) ↔6ft (2m)

Tree mallow is one of the most continuous and free-flowering of all garden shrubs, with its pink blooms opening throughout summer. The lobed leaves are downy.

Syringa pubescens subsp. *microphylla*
'Superba'
☼ 5   ↕ 6ft (2m) ↔ 6ft (2m)

Slender-stemmed and spreading, with
pointed leaves, this lilac produces fragrant
pink flowerheads, darker in bud, in late
spring and again in early autumn.

OTHER EVERGREEN MEDIUM-SIZED SHRUBS
Daphne odora *Ilex crenata* *Kalmia latifolia* cvs. *Rhododendron* PJM hybrids

Philadelphus coronarius 'Variegatus'
MOCK ORANGE
☼ 4   ↕ 8ft (2.5m) ↔ 8ft (2.5m)

Striking, white-margined leaves are the
main attraction of this dense, bushy shrub.
Its richly fragrant flower clusters in late
spring and early summer are a bonus.

Viburnum plicatum 'Pink Beauty'
DOUBLEFILE VIBURNUM
☼ ☀ 5   ↕ 6ft (2m) ↔ 5ft (1.5m)

Elegant, spreading, layered branches carry
neat, pleated leaves and, in early summer,
lacecap flowerheads that are white when
they emerge and mature to pink.

Paeonia delavayi
TREE PEONY
☼ ☀ 6   ↕ 6ft (2m) ↔ 5ft (1.5m)

Cup-shaped, dark crimson flowers, each
with a leafy bract beneath it, appear in
late spring on long stalks above bold,
deeply cut bright green leaves.

Pieris japonica
JAPANESE ANDROMEDA
☼ ☀ 5 PH   ↕ 6ft (2m) ↔ 6ft (2m)

This compact evergreen shrub has narrow,
leathery leaves, which are bronze when
young. Drooping tassels of white flowers
appear in late winter and early spring.

Viburnum sargentii
'Onondaga'
☼ ☀ 4   ↕ 8ft (2.5m) ↔ 5ft (1.5m)

The maplelike foliage of this vigorous
shrub is bronze when young and colors
richly in autumn. Its beautiful spring lacecap flowers are white, but pink in bud.

SHRUBS

Small Shrubs

THE VARIETY OF ATTRACTIVE small shrubs available to gardeners is exciting, if potentially bewildering. In large gardens, many of these can be planted in groups of three to five or more, but where space is more limited, any of the following will make an attractive and satisfying feature as a single plant, either alone or used as a centerpiece in a mixed border. They include some of the best small shrubs, and most are sun-loving.

S H R U B S

Cytisus x *praecox* 'Warminster'
WARMINSTER BROOM
☼ 6   ↕ 4ft (1.2m) ↔ 5ft (1.5m)

This is one of the most reliable of all small flowering shrubs. In late spring, its slender green branches are wreathed with small, scented, creamy yellow pea flowers.

Caryopteris x *clandonensis*
'Arthur Simmonds'
☼ 6   ↕ 30in (75cm) ↔ 30in (75cm)

Numerous clusters of small lavender-blue flowers adorn this mound-forming shrub in late summer and early autumn. It has slender stems and gray-green leaves.

Cistus x *aguilarii* 'Maculatus'
SUNROSE
☼ 9   ↕ 4ft (1.2m) ↔ 4ft (1.2m)

Magnificent white flowers, each with dark red blotches and a yellow eye, appear in summer. Wavy-edged leaves, clammy to the touch, cover this bushy evergreen.

OTHER SMALL DECIDUOUS SHRUBS

Berberis thunbergii 'Aurea', see p.220
Caryopteris x *clandonensis* 'Longwood'
Daphne x *burkwoodii* 'Somerset'
Daphne mezereum
Deutzia gracilis 'Nikko'
Fothergilla gardenii, see p.227
Hydrangea macrophylla
  'All Summer Beauty'
Potentilla fruticosa 'Goldfinger'
Prunus glandulosa 'Sinensis'
Spiraea japonica

Ceratostigma willmottianum
CHINESE PLUMBAGO
☼ 7   ↕ 3ft (1m) ↔ 3ft (1m)

This loosely domed shrub carries cobalt-blue flowers from late summer through to autumn, when its neat, pointed leaves turn red. Dies down in severe winters.

Cistus x *hybridus*
SUNROSE
☼ 8   ↕ 30in (75cm) ↔ 4ft (1.2m)

A broad mound of wrinkled, wavy-edged leaves is obscured in summer by masses of white, yellow-eyed flowers, pink when in bud. Among the hardiest sun roses.

Deutzia gracilis
SLENDER DEUTZIA
☼ 5   ↕ 3ft (1m) ↔ 3ft (1m)

The bright green leaves of this elegant shrub form a most attractive backdrop for its white flower clusters that last from late spring to early summer.

Fuchsia 'Mrs. Popple'
FUCHSIA
☼ 8   ↕ 4ft (1.2m) ↔ 4ft (1.2m)

One of the hardiest fuchsias, this vigorous shrub has glossy foliage and a continuous supply of richly colored, pendent flowers from summer into autumn.

Philadelphus 'Manteau d'Hermine'
MOCK ORANGE
☼ 5   ↕ 30in (75cm) ↔ 5ft (1.5m)

Clusters of long-lasting, fragrant, double, creamy white flowers are borne in summer, covering this broad, low shrub of compact, bushy habit.

Potentilla fruticosa 'Abbotswood'
SHRUBBY POTENTILLA
☼ 6   ↕ 30in (75cm) ↔ 4ft (1.2m)

In summer and early autumn, this low-domed bush is plastered with small white flowers, resembling miniature roses. Its deeply divided leaves are gray-green.

Rhododendron yakushimanum
YAK RHODODENDRON
☼ ☼ 6 PH   ↕ 3ft (1m) ↔ 5ft (1.5m)

This small rhododendron is popular and reliable, and forms a tight evergreen dome. Its trusses of pink flowers, in late spring and early summer, fade to white.

Hebe recurva
HEBE
☼ 9   ↕ 24in (60cm) ↔ 4ft (1.2m)

This low, dome-shaped evergreen hebe produces narrow blue-gray leaves and an abundance of white flowers, carried on small, slender spikes in summer.

OTHER SMALL EVERGREEN SHRUBS
Artemisia arborescens
Aucuba japonica
Choisya 'Aztec Pearl', see p.212
Daphne tangutica Retusa Group
Erica terminalis
Hedera helix 'Conglomerata'
Paxistima canbyi
Phlomis italica, see p.199
Pieris japonica 'Pygmaea'
Sarcococca hookeriana var. *humilis*
Skimmia japonica, see p.241

Phygelius x *rectus* 'Moonraker'
PHYGELIUS
☼ 8   ↕ 5ft (1.5m) ↔ 5ft (1.5m)

Long, upright spires of pendulous, tubular, creamy yellow flowers are held by this striking evergreen or semievergreen from summer into autumn. Of suckering habit.

Salix hastata 'Wehrhahnii'
WILLOW
☼ 5   ↕ 3ft (1m) ↔ 5ft (1.5m)

This handsome, shrubby little willow is well worth growing for the silvery catkins that emerge in spring, before its leaves unfurl. Dislikes dry soils.

S H R U B S

Shrubs for Groundcover

THE NUMBER OF SHRUBS that make good groundcovers is enormous. Some have far-reaching, trailing, or creeping stems that lie close to the soil surface, while others produce short ascending or arching branches that give a low, mounded effect. Yet more are of a suckering nature. To achieve good results as quickly as possible, groundcover shrubs should be planted in groups of three or five, or even more, depending on the area to be covered. Remove weeds before planting.

S H R U B S

Euonymus fortunei 'Emerald 'n' Gold'
EVERGREEN EUONYMUS
☼ ☼ ☼ 5 ↕ 24in (60cm) ↔ 4ft (1.2m)

This adaptable, bright-foliaged evergreen forms dense hummocks of green shoots and gold-margined leaves, usually pink-tinted in winter. Climbs if supported.

OTHER EVERGREEN SHRUBS FOR GROUNDCOVER

Arctostaphylos uva-ursi 'Vancouver Jade'
Calluna vulgaris, many
Ceanothus thyrsiflorus var. *repens*
Iberis sempervirens
Leucothoe catesbaei
Mahonia repens
Paxistima canbyi
Santolina chamaecyparissus, see p.223
Sarcococca hookeriana var. *humilis*
Vaccinium vitis-idaea

Cornus canadensis
BUNCHBERRY
☼ ☼ ☼ 2 PH ↕ 5in (13cm) ↔ 12in (30cm)

In late spring and early summer, the starry, white-bracted flowerheads of this carpeting perennial are borne above ruffs of oval leaves. Red berries follow.

Cotoneaster dammeri
BEARBERRY COTONEASTER
☼ ☼ 6 ↕ 3in (8cm) ↔ 6ft (2m)

This is one of the best evergreen ground-covering shrubs. Its densely leafy, trailing stems are studded with white flowers in summer and red berries in winter.

Euonymus fortunei 'Emerald Gaiety'
EVERGREEN EUONYMUS
☼ ☼ ☼ 5 ↕ 3ft (1m) ↔ 5ft (1.5m)

Tough, adaptable, and easy to grow, this shrub forms a dense, low cover of rounded leaves, margined white and marbled gray. Leaves are often pink-tinted in winter.

x *Halimiocistus sahucii*
SUNROSE
☼ 8 ↕ 12in (30cm) ↔ 4ft (1.2m)

Crowded with narrow, dark green leaves, this dense, low, bushy evergreen is covered with small, roselike, yellow-eyed, white flowers in late spring and early summer.

Hedera helix 'Glacier'
ENGLISH IVY
☼ ☀ ☀ 6   ↕4in (10cm) ↔10ft (3m)

One of the best variegated ivies suitable
for groundcover, this will climb if given
support. The evergreen silver-gray leaves
each have an irregular white margin.

Hedera helix 'Ivalace'
ENGLISH IVY
☼ ☀ ☀ 5   ↕4in (10cm) ↔5ft (1.5m)

This attractive groundcover forms dense
hummocks or patches of glossy dark green
leaves, which are shallowly lobed and
crinkled. Will climb with support.

Hypericum calycinum
ST. JOHN'S-WORT
☼ ☀ 6   ↕12in (30cm) ↔5ft (1.5m)

The creeping roots of this evergreen form
a close green carpet of leafy shoots, topped
by golden yellow flowers with red-tipped
stamens from summer into autumn.

Leptospermum rupestre
LEPTOSPERMUM
☼ 9   ↕3in (8cm) ↔6ft (2m)

This evergreen shrub will create a packed
carpet of tiny, deep green leaves, studded
in summer with small white flowers. Its
leaves turn bronze in winter.

**OTHER DECIDUOUS SHRUBS
FOR GROUNDCOVER**

Rhus aromatica
Rosa wichuraiana
Rubus calycinoides
Xanthorhiza simplicissima

Viburnum davidii
DAVID VIBURNUM
☼ ☀ 8   ↕3ft (1m) ↔5ft (1.5m)

Broad mounds of boldly veined evergreen
leaves need space. The white flowers are
small, and pollinated female plants bear
striking blue berries in autumn.

Vinca minor
CREEPING MYRTLE
☼ ☀ 5   ↕4in (10cm) ↔5ft (1.5m)

Long, slender, prostrate stems and paired,
glossy green leaves provide reliable groundcover. Charming blue, purple, or white
flowers open from spring into summer.

S H R U B S

185

Small Shrub Roses for Limited Space

NUMEROUS SHRUB ROSES are medium to large in size and require considerable space in which to develop to their full potential. Fortunately, certain roses are of lesser stature and therefore suitable for planting where space is limited. Some of the following may need support to prevent their slender stems from flopping to the ground when in flower.

Rosa gallica var. *officinalis*
APOTHECARY'S ROSE
☼ 4   ↕ 3ft (1m) ↔ 3ft (1m)

Lush foliage and an abundant supply of scented, semidouble, deep pink flowers cover this spreading, low-branching species rose in summer. Hips are attractive.

Rosa x *centifolia* 'Cristata'
CRESTED MOSS ROSE
☼ 4   ↕ 5ft (1.5m) ↔ 4ft (1.2m)

Distinct green, mossy buds open to reveal richly scented pink blooms on nodding stalks in summer. The rather lax stems of this prickly bush may need support.

Rosa gallica 'Versicolor'
ROSA MUNDI GALLICA ROSE
☼ 4   ↕ 3ft (1m) ↔ 3ft (1m)

This well-known rose began as a mutation of *R. gallica* var. *officinalis*, and differs in its flowers, which are pale pink with crimson stripes. Prune to maintain its size.

Rosa 'Buff Beauty'
HYBRID MUSK ROSE
☼ 6   ↕ 4ft (1.2m) ↔ 4ft (1.2m)

A popular and reliable rose with shining green foliage that is coppery brown when young. Deliciously scented, fully double flowers are freely borne in summer.

Rosa x *centifolia* 'Muscosa'
COMMON MOSS ROSE
☼ 4   ↕ 5ft (1.5m) ↔ 4ft (1.2m)

Coarse foliage provides a good backdrop for the richly scented pink flowers opening from mossy buds in summer. This loose-stemmed bush may need support.

OTHER SMALL SHRUB ROSES
Rosa 'De Rescht'
Rosa 'Cécile Brünner'
Rosa x *harrisonii* 'Lutea Maxima'
Rosa 'Marchesa Boccella'
Rosa 'Madame Knorr'
Rosa 'Margo Koster'
Rosa 'Marie Pavie'
Rosa nitida
Rosa 'Perle d'Or'
Rosa 'The Fairy'
Rosa 'White Pet'

Low-growing Roses for Groundcover

IN SUNNY SITUATIONS, low-spreading roses or those with trailing stems provide a useful and charming groundcover. They are particularly suited to steep banks, wall tops, or beneath plantings of other roses, especially those whose stems become unsightly with age. In recent years, a host of new, free-flowering cultivars have become available. Where space permits, you can achieve impressive displays with generous plantings, but in small gardens a single plant can give as much pleasure.

Rosa Grouse ('Korimro')
ROSE CULTIVAR
☼ 5   ↕ 18in (45cm) ↔ 10ft (3m)

In summer, this free-growing rose, with its long, trailing stems and shining evergreen foliage, produces a succession of small, fragrant,   pale pink blooms.

Rosa x *jacksonii*
'Max Graf'
☼ 4   ↕ 18in (45cm) ↔ 10ft (3m)

Large, single flowers have an apple scent and are carried in summer. The shining, bright green foliage of this dense rose is carried on long, trailing stems.

Rosa 'Nozomi'
ROSE CULTIVAR
☼ 5   ↕ 18in (45cm) ↔ 1.2m (4ft)

This charming creeping rose has arching stems clothed with small, neat, dark green leaves, and bears single blush pink and white flowers in summer.

OTHER GROUNDCOVER ROSES

Rosa Bonica ('Meidomonac')
Rosa 'Macrantha'
Rosa Magic Carpet ('Jaclover')
Rosa nitida
Rosa 'Paulii'
Rosa Pheasant ('Kordept')
Rosa Rosy Cushion ('Interall')
Rosa 'The Fairy'
Rosa White Flower Carpet ('Noaschnee')
Rosa virginiana

Rosa Partridge ('Korweirim')
ROSE CULTIVAR
☼ 5   ↕ 18in (45cm) ↔ 10ft (3m)

The pure white flowers of this rose, borne in abundance throughout summer, are small and fragrant. It is similar in growth to *R.* Grouse, to which it is related.

MINIATURE ROSES

Rosa Black Jade ('Benblack')
Rosa 'Cupcake'
Rosa 'Dee Bennett'
Rosa Jean Kenneally ('Tineally')
Rosa 'Minnie Pearl'
Rosa 'New Beginning'
Rosa 'Pacesetter'
Rosa Pretty Polly ('Meitonje')
Rosa 'Rainbow's End'
Rosa Starina ('Megabi')
Rosa White Cloud ('Korstacha')

Rosa 'Seagull'
ROSE CULTIVAR
☼ 5   ↕ 24in (60cm) ↔ 12ft (4m)

A strong-growing climbing rose, good for groundcover where space allows. Large, branched clusters of fragrant, semidouble white flowers open in summer.

S H R U B S

Large Shrub Roses for Specimen Planting

Most shrub roses in the wild occur as single, scattered specimens, with space to expand and show their flowers to advantage. In gardens where space permits, shrub roses should be grown in the same way, either singly or in groups as highlights in mixed borders. Grow spreading kinds alone on the lawn, where their display can be admired from all sides.

Rosa 'Madame Isaac Pereire'
BOURBON ROSE

☼ 6 ↕ 7ft (2.2m) ↔ 6ft (2m)

This lovely bourbon rose has a vigorous, prickly, arching growth. Richly fragrant flowers, deep rose with magenta shading, appear from summer into autumn.

Rosa 'Complicata'
GALLICA ROSE

☼ 5 ↕ 7ft (2.2m) ↔ 8ft (2.5m)

A bold, reliable gallica rose with vigorous, thorny, arching branches. Lightly scented, single, white-centered pink flowers occur in summer. May also be trained into trees.

OTHER SHRUB ROSES WITH FRUITS
Rosa blanda
Rosa carolina
Rosa davidii
Rosa macrophylla
Rosa moyesii
Rosa roxburghii
Rosa rugosa 'Alba'
Rosa rugosa 'Frau Dagmar Hartopp'
Rosa setipoda
Rosa sweginzowii
Rosa virginiana

Rosa Alexander ('Harlex')
HYBRID TEA ROSE

☼ 7 ↕ 5½ft (1.7m) ↔ 30in (75cm)

This strong-growing hybrid tea rose with erect stems makes an excellent informal hedge. Lightly fragrant, double red flowers are carried from summer into autumn.

Rosa Iceberg ('Korbin')
FLORIBUNDA ROSE

☼ 6 ↕ 5ft (1.5m) ↔ 4ft (1.2m)

Iceberg is a popular, reliable floribunda rose with strong, upright growth, glossy foliage, and clusters of fully double, lightly scented flowers in summer and autumn.

Rosa 'Marguerite Hilling'
SHRUB ROSE

☼ 5 ↕ 7ft (2.2m) ↔ 7ft (2.2m)

This is a vigorous shrub with dense, leafy growth. In summer, and to a lesser degree autumn, it is crowded with large, fragrant, deep pink flowers with pale centers.

Rosa 'Geranium'
SPECIES ROSE
☀ 4   ↕ 10ft (3m) ↔ 7ft (2.2m)

This tall, vigorous species rose is upright.
Its branches arch widely and sport small,
saucer-shaped summer flowers that are
followed by flask-shaped red hips.

Rosa 'Roseraie de l'Haÿ'
RUGOSA ROSE
☀ 4   ↕ 7ft (2.2m) ↔ 6ft (2m)

A strong-growing rugosa rose of dense
habit, this has attractive green foliage and
richly scented, velvety, deep crimson
flowers from summer into autumn.

Rosa 'Tour de Malakoff'
PROVENCE ROSE
☀ 4   ↕ 6ft (2m) ↔ 3ft (1m)

Provence rose of vigorous, open growth,
with fragrant, loosely petaled flowers in
summer. The magenta blooms fade to a
grayish purple. May require support.

Rosa 'Nevada'
SHRUB ROSE
☀ 5   ↕ 7ft (2.2m) ↔ 7ft (2.2m)

This vigorous, leafy shrub rose produces
an abundance of scented, creamy white
flowers in summer – fewer in autumn.
The flowers turn pink in hot weather.

Rosa soulieana
SPECIES ROSE
☀ 7   ↕ 10ft (3m) ↔ 10ft (3m)

The distinct stems of this rose are prickly,
and its foliage is bluish green. Numerous
scented summer flowers are yellow in bud
and open white. May need support.

Rosa
'Pink Grootendorst'
☀ 4   ↕ 6ft (2m) ↔ 5ft (1.5m)

A rugosa hybrid of bushy, upright growth,
this has prickly stems and wrinkled leaves.
Dense clusters of carnation-like flowers
occur from summer into autumn.

**OTHER LARGE SHRUB ROSES
FOR SPECIMEN PLANTING**

Rosa 'Alba Semiplena'
Rosa 'Blanche Double de Coubert'
Rosa 'Dupontii'
Rosa rubiginosa, see p.239
Rosa 'Fritz Nobis'
Rosa 'Frühlingsgold'
Rosa glauca, see p.223
Rosa 'Madame Hardy'
Rosa 'White Grootendorst'
Rosa 'Nymphenburg'

Rosa xanthina 'Canary Bird'
SPECIES ROSE
☀ 6   ↕ 7ft (2.2m) ↔ 7ft (2.2m)

The arching branches of this vigorous
species rose carry small, fernlike foliage.
Musk-scented yellow flowers appear in
spring, with a few in autumn.

SHRUBS

Shrubs for Heavy Clay Soils

I F YOU HAVE A CLASSIC clay soil (one that is heavy and sticky when wet, shrinking and cracking when it is dry), then it is a good idea to try to improve it by careful drainage and by adding liberal and frequent amounts of very coarse sand, together with rough, especially fibrous, organic matter. Avoid working clay soil when it is wet. Despite the doom and gloom that is commonly associated with heavy clay, however, a large and diverse selection of shrubs can thrive in such soils.

Cytisus 'Killiney Red'
BROOM
☼ 6 PH ▼   ↕ 3ft (1m) ↔ 4ft (1.2m)

One of many brooms tolerant of clay soils, 'Killiney Red' is a dwarf, compact variety. Slender green shoots carry many flowers in late spring and early summer.

Berberis darwinii
DARWIN'S BARBERRY
☼ 7   ↕ 10ft (3m) ↔ 12ft (4m)

This large, mounded evergreen shrub is densely covered with small, dark green leaves. Clusters of orange-yellow flowers in spring are followed by black berries.

OTHER DECIDUOUS SHRUBS FOR HEAVY CLAY SOILS

Berberis thunbergii
Cotinus coggygria 'Royal Purple', see p.224
Cytisus x *praecox* 'Allgold', see p.196
Deutzia gracilis 'Nikko'
Forsythia x *intermedia* 'Lynwood', see p.204
Kerria japonica 'Pleniflora', see p.167
Lonicera fragrantissima
Magnolia 'Susan'
Rhododendron occidentale, see p.202
Ribes sanguineum 'White Icicle'
Sambucus nigra 'Guincho Purple', see p.225
Spiraea x *vanhouttei*, see p.203
Syringa vulgaris cvs.
Viburnum sargentii 'Onondaga' see p.181

Chaenomeles x *superba* 'Nicoline'
FLOWERING QUINCE
☼ ☼ 5   ↕ 3ft (1m) ↔ 5ft (1.5m)

The branches of this tough, reliable shrub are studded in spring with a profusion of large scarlet flowers. These are followed by small, yellow, applelike fruits.

Escallonia 'Langleyensis'
ESCALLONIA
☼ 8   ↕ 6ft (2m) ↔ 6ft (2m)

Evergreen and wind-tolerant, this tried and tested shrub has arching stems, small, glossy leaves on weeping branches, and tiny bunches of pink summer flowers.

Hydrangea arborescens 'Grandiflora'
HILLS OF SNOW HYDRANGEA
☼ ☼ 4   ↕ 5ft (1.5m) ↔ 6ft (2m)

Large heads of white flowers appear from summer through to early autumn. Broad, oval leaves clothe this tough and reliable, mounded shrub. It dislikes dry soils.

Magnolia stellata 'Waterlily'
STAR MAGNOLIA
☼ 4   ↕ 10ft (3mm) ↔ 12ft (4m)

Eventually broader than it is high, this charming shrub is slow-growing. Fragrant, multipetaled blooms cover the branches in spring. Leaves turn yellow in autumn.

Neillia thibetica
NEILLIA
☼ 6   ↕ 8ft (2.5m) ↔ 8ft (2.5m)

The flowers of this strong-growing shrub are held in lax, tail-like spikes on arching branches amid its jagged, pointed leaves from late spring into early summer.

Philadelphus 'Virginal'
MOCK ORANGE
☼ 5   ↕ 10ft (3m) ↔ 8ft (2.5m)

A strong-growing shrub, this is deservedly one of the most popular, due to its great abundance of large, richly fragrant, double or semidouble white summer flowers.

Potentilla fruticosa 'Elizabeth'
SHRUBBY POTENTILLA
☼ 2   ↕ 30in (75cm) ↔ 5ft (1.5m)

This broad, low mounding plant bears dense branches and small, deeply divided leaves. It is covered with bright yellow flowers from late spring to autumn.

Rhododendron 'Mrs G.W. Leak'
RHODODENDRON
☼ ☼ 7   ↕ 12ft (4m) ↔ 12ft (4m)

This large evergreen shrub is particularly striking in late spring, when it is covered with bold trusses of pink, funnel-shaped flowers splashed brown and crimson.

OTHER EVERGREEN SHRUBS FOR HEAVY CLAY SOILS

Aucuba japonica
Berberis verruculosa
Choisya ternata, see p.228
Cotoneaster franchetii
Escallonia rubra 'Crimson Spire'
Mahonia bealei
Osmanthus x *burkwoodii*, see p.229
Pyracantha 'Mohave'
Skimmia japonica, see p.241
Viburnum davidii, see p.185

Spiraea japonica 'Anthony Waterer'
SPIREA
☼ 4   ↕ 4ft (1.2m) ↔ 4ft (1.2m)

Erect and compact, this is an extremely popular flowering shrub. It produces dark green, jaggedly toothed leaves, and flat crimson-pink flowerheads in summer.

Spiraea nipponica 'Snowmound'
SPIREA
☼ 4   ↕ 6ft (2m) ↔ 6ft (2m)

Tufts of white flowers are carried all along the upper sides of densely leafy, arching stems, making this a spectacular shrub at its peak in late spring.

S H R U B S

Shrubs for Acid Soils

THE SHRUBS PREFERRING, if not demanding, acid soils are relatively few in number, but they encompass some of the loveliest, most popular shrubs. Rhododendrons, camellias, and heathers are well-known acid-lovers, but many other shrubs have similar requirements. Although they thrive in naturally acid soils, many of these plants will grow reasonably well in specially prepared beds, or in containers filled with acid soil mix.

Daboecia cantabrica 'Bicolor'
DABOECIA
☼ 5 PH   ‡ 18in (45cm) ↔ 24in (60cm)

This low, bushy, evergreen shrub is dense and wiry, with nodding white, purple, or purple-striped flowers, held in loose spikes, from late spring into autumn.

Camellia x *williamsii* 'Donation'
CAMELLIA
☼ 7 PH   ‡ 10ft (3m) ↔ 6ft (2m)

One of the best camellias for general cultivation, this free-growing, upright evergreen carries an abundance of large flowers from late winter into spring.

Desfontainea spinosa
DESFONTAINEA
☼ 8 PH   ‡ 6ft (2m) ↔ 5ft (1.5m)

Tubular red flowers are borne from mid-summer to autumn in the leaf axils of this slow-growing evergreen. The leaves are small and hollylike. Dislikes dry soils.

Calluna vulgaris 'Annemarie'
HEATHER, LING
☼ 5 PH   ‡ 18in (45cm) ↔ 18in (45cm)

Reliable and free-flowering, this heather forms a compact bush. Long spires of double, light pink flowers rise above dark evergreen foliage in autumn.

Camellia japonica 'Adolphe Audusson'
CAMELLIA
☼ 7 PH   ‡ 10ft (3m) ↔ 8ft (2.5m)

This reliable camellia is a dense, bushy evergreen with glossy, dark green leaves. Large, deep red, gold-stamened flowers appear from late winter into spring.

Clethra delavayi
CLETHRA
☼ 7 PH   ‡ 12ft (4m) ↔ 10ft (3m)

Dense, horizontal spikes of fragrant white flowers, pink when in bud, give this shrub a most distinguished appearance when they open in summer. Dislikes dry soil.

Enkianthus cernuus var. *rubens*
ENKIANTHUS
☼ 6 PH   ‡ 8ft (2.5m) ↔ 6ft (2m)

Bunches of fringed, bell-shaped flowers hang beneath neat clusters of leaves in late spring. The leaves color richly in autumn. Dislikes dry soils.

SHRUBS

Erica cinerea 'C.D. Eason'
BELL HEATHER
☼ 6 ⌷   ↕ 12in (30cm) ↔ 24in (60cm)

From summer to autumn, this dense, low-growing evergreen is covered by crowded spikes of carmine pink, pitcher-shaped flowers. It has needlelike leaves.

Pieris 'Forest Flame'
PIERIS
☼ 7 ⌷   ↕ 12ft (4m) ↔ 6ft (2m)

The leaves of this erect evergreen emerge crimson, and then lighten to pink and cream before turning glossy green. Its sprays of white flowers appear in spring.

Rhododendron 'May Day'
RHODODENDRON
☼ ☼ 7 ⌷   ↕ 5ft (1.5m) ↔ 5ft (1.5m)

Excellent for all but the very coldest areas, this flat-topped or domed evergreen bears dark green leaves and is covered in spring with trusses of red trumpet flowers.

OTHER EVERGREEN SHRUBS FOR ACID SOIL

Arbutus unedo
Calluna vulgaris 'Blazeaway'
Crinodendron hookerianum, see p.200
Gardenia augusta
Gaultheria shallon
Grevillea juniperina f. *sulphurea*
Kalmia latifolia 'Ostbo Red'
Leptospermum scoparium 'Red Damask'
Rhododendron PJM hybrids
Rhododendron yakushimanum, see p.183

Kalmia latifolia
MOUNTAIN LAUREL
☼ ☼ 5 ⌷   ↕ 10ft (3m) ↔ 10ft (3m)

Free-flowering and impressive, this shrub, clad in cheerful glossy evergreen leaves, bears clusters of small pink flowers, darker when in bud, in early summer.

OTHER DECIDUOUS SHRUBS FOR ACID SOIL

Clethra alnifolia
Cyrilla racemiflora
Enkianthus campanulatus
Fothergilla gardenii, see p.227
Itea virginica
Rhododendron prunifolium
Rhododendron schlippenbachii
Vaccinium corymbosum, see p.203
Viburnum nudum
Zenobia pulverulenta

Rhododendron 'Hinomayo'
EVERGREEN AZALEA
☼ ☼ 6 ⌷   ↕ 5ft (1.5m) ↔ 5ft (1.5m)

This dense, twiggy evergreen is crowded with small leaves and plastered in spring by little funnel-shaped pink flowers. It will not tolerate dry soils.

Rhododendron 'Narcissiflorum'
GHENT AZALEA
☼ 5 ⌷   ↕ 6ft (2m) ↔ 6ft (2m)

A vigorous shrub that produces masses of pale yellow, darker-flushed flowers with a sweet scent in spring and early summer. Leaves often color bronze in autumn.

SHRUBS

Shrubs for Alkaline Soils

FAR FROM BEING PROBLEMATIC, alkaline soils are suitable for a huge variety of shrubs, many of which actually thrive in the high pH and the warmer, free-draining conditions that prevail there. A number of these plants are also drought-tolerant, although this does not mean moisture is not essential. Such soils need to be given organic matter as well, in the form of a mulch. Sufficient water and enough organic matter improves the ability of most garden shrubs to grow well, and keeps leaves a healthy green.

Indigofera heterantha
INDIGO
☼ 7   ↕ 5ft (1.5m) ↔ 5½ft (1.7m)

This multistemmed shrub has arching branches clothed in fernlike leaves. Small, rich mauve-pink pea flowers are produced all through summer into autumn.

Buddleia davidii 'Dartmoor'
BUTTERFLY BUSH
☼ 6   ↕ 8ft (2.5m) ↔ 8ft (2.5m)

In late summer and autumn, distinctive flowerheads, popular with butterflies and bees, cover this vigorous shrub. Its arching branches carry long, pointed leaves.

Kolkwitzia amabilis 'Pink Cloud'
BEAUTY BUSH
☼ 5   ↕ 10ft (3m) ↔ 10ft (3m)

A vigorous shrub of mounded habit this has small, oval leaves, and masses of bell flowers in spring and early summer. Pale, bristly seed clusters follow.

Deutzia longifolia 'Veitchii'
DEUTZIA
☼ 7   ↕ 7ft (2.2m) ↔ 5½ft (1.7m)

One of the most reliable of all deutzias, this has arching branches, narrow leaves, and large clusters of star-shaped summer flowers that are rich, lilac-stained pink.

Hibiscus syriacus 'Red Heart'
ROSE OF SHARON
☼ 6   ↕ 7ft (2.2m) ↔ 7ft (2.2m)

The branches of this shrub slowly spread with age. Boldly lobed leaves unfurl late in the season. Large flowers are carried from late summer into autumn.

OTHER EVERGREEN SHRUBS
FOR ALKALINE SOIL

Berberis darwinii, see p.190
Choisya 'Aztec Pearl', see p.212
Escallonia 'Iveyi'
Itea ilicifolia, see p.165
Jasminum humile, see p.167
Mahonia x *media* 'Buckland', see p.237
Olearia macrodonta, see p.214
Osmanthus x *burkwoodii*, see p.229
Sarcococca hookeriana var. *digyna*,
   see p.237

Osmanthus delavayi
OSMANTHUS, FALSE HOLLY
☀ ☼ 8   ↕ 7ft (2.2m) ↔ 7ft (2.2m)

Mounded evergreen shrub with slender, arching stems packed with little, dark green leaves. In spring, clusters of small, sweet-smelling, tubular flowers appear.

Santolina pinnata subsp.
neapolitana 'Sulphurea'
☀ 7   ↕ 28in (70cm) ↔ 3ft (1m)

Long-stalked, button-shaped clusters of tiny flowers top narrow, feathery leaves in midsummer. This is a low, dome-shaped evergreen shrub of dense habit.

Weigela 'Looymansii Aurea'
WEIGELA
☀ 6   ↕ 5ft (1.5m) ↔ 3½ft (1.1m)

This shrub is principally grown for its golden foliage, which later becomes yellowish green. Funnel-shaped flowers open in late spring and early summer.

Philadelphus 'Boule d'Argent'
MOCK ORANGE
☀ 5   ↕ 5ft (1.5m) ↔ 5ft (1.5m)

One of several mock oranges suitable for small gardens, this has a bushy habit and arching branches. Striking clusters of lightly fragrant flowers appear in summer.

Spiraea canescens
SPIREA
☀ 7   ↕ 7ft (2.2m) ↔ 5½ft (1.7m)

The arching stems of this graceful shrub are covered for much of their length with clusters of tiny white summer flowers set above small gray-green leaves.

Prunus tenella
DWARF RUSSIAN ALMOND
☀ 2   ↕ 28in (70cm) ↔ 4ft (1.2m)

This low, bushy shrub has many slender stems, narrow, glossy green leaves, and bright pink flowers crowding the branches in spring. 'Fire Hill' is a superb selection.

Syringa x *persica*
PERSIAN LILAC
☀ 3   ↕ 7ft (2.2m) ↔ 7ft (2.2m)

A reliable and justifiably popular lilac, this forms a large bush in time. Slender branches bear spectacular conical heads of fragrant flowers in late spring.

Xanthoceras sorbifolium
YELLOWHORN
☀ 5   ↕ 10ft (3m) ↔ 7ft (2.2m)

An uncommon, unusual shrub of upright growth, with much-divided leaves and erect flower spikes from late spring. It may produce large fruits after a hot summer.

OTHER DECIDUOUS SHRUBS
FOR ALKALINE SOILS

Abelia triflora
Buddleia alternifolia 'Argentea'
Chaenomeles speciosa 'Moerloosei',
   see p.166
Cotinus coggygria
Dipelta floribunda
Forsythia x *intermedia* 'Lynwood',
   see p.204
Hydrangea paniculata
Rubus 'Benenden', see p.235

SHRUBS

195

Shrubs for Sandy Soils

NUMEROUS SHRUBS favor sandy soils because they provide well-drained soil conditions. In times of drought, however, sandy soils can turn to dust, and plants growing in them may require a great deal of irrigation. Such soils can, of course, be improved by changing their structure with the addition of liberal and regular amounts of moisture-retentive organic matter such as compost, but it is still a good idea to plant shrubs tolerant of drought and rapid drainage.

Cytisus x *praecox* 'Allgold'
BROOM
☼ 6 ↕ 6ft (2m) ↔ 6ft (2m)

The slender, arching shoots of this shrub form a compact mound. Its gray-green branchlets are crowded with small, long-lasting, yellow pea flowers in spring.

Ballota acetabulosa
BALLOTA
☼ 7 ↕ 24in (60cm) ↔ 30in (75cm)

This gray-green, woolly plant has erect stems with rounded leaves, and bears tiny, two-lipped pink flowers in summer. Prune back hard if damaged in cold winters.

Callistemon citrinus 'Splendens'
BOTTLEBRUSH
☼ 10 ↕ 6ft (2m) ↔ 6ft (2m)

Brilliant red, tightly packed, brushlike spikes adorn this evergreen in summer. It has many arching stems and branches of narrow, leathery, glossy green leaves.

OTHER SHRUBS FOR SANDY SOIL
Baccharis halimifolia
Ceanothus americanus
Hypericum prolificum
Kolkwitzia amabilis 'Pink Cloud' see p.194
Myrica pensylvanica
Nerium oleander
Prunus maritima
Rosa carolina
Robinia hispida, see p.165
Santolina chamaecyparissus, see p.223

Brachyglottis monroi
SHRUBBY SENECIO
☼ 9 ↕ 3ft (1m) ↔ 5ft (1.5m)

Low-domed and compact, this evergreen shrub is crowded with small, wavy-edged, dark green, white-backed leaves. It carries yellow daisy flowers in summer.

Cistus x *purpureus*
SUNROSE
☼ 9 ↕ 3ft (1m) ↔ 3ft (1m)

In early summer, this rounded, bushy evergreen carries single, roselike flowers. Narrow gray-green leaves are a perfect foil for its deep purplish pink blooms.

Lotus hirsutus
HAIRY CANARY CLOVER
☼ 7 ↕ 24in (60cm) ↔ 24in (60cm)

This small, mounded shrub is entirely covered with silvery gray down. Clusters of little white pea flowers in summer are followed by attractive reddish seed pods.

Grevillea 'Canberra Gem'
GREVILLEA
☀ 9 ᴾᴴ   ‡ 6ft (2m) ↔ 6ft (2m)

One of the hardiest grevilleas, 'Canberra Gem' forms an evergreen mound of green, needlelike leaves. Loose flower clusters are borne from late winter into spring.

Hibiscus syriacus 'Woodbridge'
ROSE OF SHARON
☀ 6   ‡ 8ft (2.5m) ↔ 10ft (3m)

Slow-growing and late-leafing, this shrub is upright at first, spreading as it matures. Beautiful, saucer-shaped flowers are produced in summer and autumn.

Lespedeza thunbergii
LESPEDEZA
☀ 6   ‡ 5ft (1.5m) ↔ 8ft (2.5m)

This is one of the best autumn-flowering shrubs. Its long, arching stems become weighed down with large sprays of purple pea flowers. May require support.

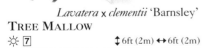

Lavatera x *clementii* 'Barnsley'
TREE MALLOW
☀ 7   ‡ 6ft (2m) ↔ 6ft (2m)

All through summer, this semievergreen carries a succession of lovely, pale blush pink, almost white, red-eyed flowers. Its lobed leaves are sage green and downy.

Potentilla fruticosa 'Manchu'
SHRUBBY POTENTILLA
☀ 2   ‡ 18in (45cm) ↔ 24in (60cm)

Twiggy branches, clothed with silver gray leaves, form a low mound. The bush is densely packed with small, single white flowers from late spring into early autumn.

Romneya coulteri
CALIFORNIA POPPY
☀ 8   ‡ 6ft (2m) ↔ 6ft (2m)

This strong-growing plant has blue-gray stems and deeply cut foliage. Large, fragrant white poppy flowers with golden stamens appear in late summer.

S H R U B S

197

Shrubs for Dry, Sunny Sites

A GREAT MANY SHRUBS thrive in situations that are sunny and relatively dry; if your winters are mild, then the choice is both immense and exciting. Where winter temperatures are not as favorable, make use of any shelter available, be it a backing wall or protection provided by more hardy plants nearby. Many of the shrubs thriving in dry, sunny situations hail from regions such as the Mediterranean, where sun, heat, and stony, well-drained soils often go hand in hand.

Euphorbia characias subsp. *wulfenii*
SHRUBBY EUPHORBIA
☼ 7 ↕ 3ft (1m) ↔ 3ft (1m)

This evergreen produces erect, biennial stems with gray-green leaves the first year, followed next spring by large heads of little yellow-green, cup-shaped flowers.

Cistus × *cyprius*
SUNROSE
☼ 7 ↕ 6ft (2m) ↔ 5ft (1.5m)

Large white flowers with yellow stamens and red blotches appear in early summer. Both the shoots and leaves of this vigorous evergreen are sticky to the touch.

OTHER SHRUBS FOR DRY SUN

Artemisia 'Powis Castle', see p.26
Caragana arborescens
Carpenteria californica, see p.228
Caryopteris incana
Fremontodendron 'California Glory', see p.165
Lavandula angustifolia 'Hidcote', see p.234
Potentilla fruticosa
Xanthoceras sorbifolium, see p.195
Zauschneria californica

Erythrina crista-galli
CORAL TREE
☼ 9 ↕ 6ft (2m) ↔ 6ft (2m)

Eye-catching spikes of waxy coral-red flowers open in late summer. The prickly shoots bear leaves, each composed of three leaflets. Dies back in cold winters.

Euryops pectinatus
EURYOPS
☼ 9 ↕ 3ft (1m) ↔ 3ft (1m)

An evergreen mound of deeply cut gray-green leaves is topped with long-stalked, bright yellow, daisylike flowers, from late winter through to early summer.

Grindelia chiloensis
GRINDELIA
☼ 9 ↕ 30in (75cm) ↔ 24in (60cm)

Reminiscent of a yellow aster, this shrub is evergreen and bears long-stalked, bright yellow daisy flowers from late winter into early summer. It is sticky to the touch.

Hibiscus syriacus 'Oiseau Blue'
ROSE OF SHARON
☼ 6 ↕ 8ft (2.5m) ↔ 6ft (2m)

Erect at first, this late-leafing shrub spreads with age and carries a wealth of large trumpet-shaped, lilac-blue flowers in late summer and autumn.

Phlomis fruticosa
JERUSALEM SAGE
☼ 7 ↕ 3ft (1m) ↔ 3ft (1m)

This low, mound-forming evergreen is worth growing exclusively for its downy, aromatic, gray-green leaves; golden flowers during summer are an added bonus.

Phlomis italica
PHLOMIS
☼ 9 ↕ 3ft (1m) ↔ 24in (60cm)

The stems and leaves of this low, upright evergreen are covered with gray-green, woolly hairs. Whorls of two-lipped summer flowers are a lovely shade of lilac-pink.

Fabiana imbricata f. *violacea*
FABIANA
☼ 9 ↕ 8ft (2.5m) ↔ 6ft (2m)

The stems of this upright to vase-shaped evergreen are clothed with tiny, heathlike leaves and crowded in early summer with pale violet flowers. Avoid shallow chalk.

Olearia x *scilloniensis*
'Darrien-Smith'
☼ 9 ↕ 5ft (1.5m) ↔ 5ft (1.5m)

During late spring, the stems and narrow, wavy-edged leaves of this dense evergreen are almost completely obscured by masses of white, daisylike flowers.

Sophora davidii
SOPHORA
☼ 6 ↕ 5ft (1.5m) ↔ 6ft (2m)

Loose-stemmed when young, this shrub becomes dense and spiny with age. Bluish white pea flowers are produced among its small, deeply divided leaves in summer.

S H R U B S

199

Shrubs Tolerant of Shade

YOU MAY BE SURPRISED at the range of shrubs suitable for growing in shade. Many are woodlanders in the wild, preferring to grow where they are not directly exposed to the sun's rays. This does not mean they can survive without any light – all green-leaved plants need light to photosynthesize. Some, however, are more tolerant of lower light levels than others, and it is these that are most successful when planted in the shade of deciduous trees, or that cast by buildings.

Euonymus fortunei 'Sunshine'
EVERGREEN EUONYMUS
☼ ☀ 5   ↕24in (60cm) ↔5ft (1.5m)

A low-growing, dense, evergreen shrub crowded with leathery, gold-margined leaves, looking bright gold from afar. Ideal as a groundcover or as a specimen shrub.

Euonymus fortunei   var. *vegetus*
EVERGREEN EUONYMUS
☼ ☀ 5   ↕12in (30cm) ↔6ft (2m)

The presence of both creeping and erect stems enable this tough, bushy evergreen to form extensive patches. Its green leaves and pinkish seed capsules are numerous.

Crinodendron hookerianum
LANTERN TREE
☼ ☀ 9 PH   ↕10ft (3m) ↔6ft (2m)

From late spring through to early summer, the branches of this handsome evergreen are strung with beautiful red flowers that resemble lanterns. Dislikes dry soils.

OTHER DECIDUOUS SHRUBS
TOLERANT OF SHADE

Berberis thunbergii, see p.226
Cornus canadensis, see p.184
Euonymus alatus, see p.227
Euonymus obovatus
Hydrangea macrophylla
Hypericum androsaemum
Kerria japonica
Rhodotypos scandens, see p.203
Rubus odoratus
Symphoricarpos x *chenaultii* 'Hancock'

Daphne laureola subsp. *philippi*
SPURGE LAUREL
☼ ☀ ☀ 7   ↕12in (30cm) ↔2ft (60cm)

A dwarf variety of a woodland evergreen, this is just as effective when grown in full sun. Crowded light green flower clusters emerge in late winter and early spring.

Hydrangea macrophylla 'Veitchii'
LACECAP HYDRANGEA
☼ ☀ 6   ↕5ft (1.5m) ↔8ft (2.5m)

Broader than it is high, this bold-foliaged bush carries heads of tiny flowers, each surrounded by a ring of larger florets, from mid- to late summer. Dislikes dry soils.

SHRUBS

Hydrangea serrata 'Bluebird'
LACECAP HYDRANGEA
☼ ☀ 6   ↕ 4ft (1.2m) ↔ 5ft (1.5m)

The pointed leaves of this dense, bushy
shrub often color well in autumn. Violet-
blue, lacecap flowers in summer have pale
marginal florets. Dislikes dry soils.

Pachysandra terminalis
JAPANESE SPURGE
☼ ☀ 4   ↕ 4in (10cm) ↔ 8in (20cm)

This evergreen, suckering shrublet likes
moist soils and makes a superb groundcover for shade. Its dark green leaves back
little white flower spikes in spring.

Skimmia japonica 'Wakehurst White'
SKIMMIA
☼ ☀ 7   ↕ 30in (75cm) ↔ 30in (75cm)

This spring-flowering cultivar will
produce an abundance of white berries if
you plant a male variety of this dense, low
evergreen nearby to effect pollination.

Lonicera pileata
SHRUBBY HONEYSUCKLE
☼ ☀ 6   ↕ 24in (60cm) ↔ 6ft (2m)

Its low and wide-spreading habit makes
this an excellent evergreen groundcover.
Tiny, inconspicuous, late spring flowers
are occasionally followed by violet berries.

Prunus laurocerasus 'Otto Luyken'
CHERRY LAUREL
☼ ☀ 6   ↕ 3ft (1m) ↔ 6ft (2m)

The branches of this low evergreen shrub
are clothed with narrow, glossy, leathery
leaves. Erect spikes of white flowers in
late spring are followed by black fruits.

Mahonia nervosa
CASCADES MAHONIA
☼ ☀ 6 PH   ↕ 24in (60cm) ↔ 3ft (1m)

This evergreen, suckering shrub produces
short, erect stems with handsome leaves
that turn red or purplish in winter. Spikes
of yellow flowers appear in early summer.

**OTHER EVERGREEN SHRUBS
TOLERANT OF SHADE**

Aucuba japonica
x *Fatshedera lizei*, see p.212
Fatsia japonica, see p.216
Ilex crenata
Osmanthus heterophyllus
Rhododendron catawbiense
Rubus tricolor
Ruscus hypoglossum
Sarcococca hookeriana var. *humilis*
Viburnum davidii, see p.185

Vinca major 'Variegata'
VARIEGATED LARGE PERIWINKLE
☼ ☀ 7   ↕ 12in (30cm) ↔ 5ft (1.5m)

Striking, variegated leaves are margined
creamy white and form a superb groundcover that is rampant if unchecked. Blue
flowers last from spring to autumn.

SHRUBS

Shrubs Tolerant of Wet Soil or Streambanks

PERMANENTLY MOIST SOILS, or sites that occasionally flood, are not ideal planting spots. This makes shrubs tolerant of wet soil valuable to gardeners faced with damp or boggy areas. Where practical and desirable, you can modify such soils by draining, but if you decide to leave them alone, the following plants can generally be relied upon to thrive.

Aronia arbutifolia
RED CHOKEBERRY
☀ ☼ 5   ↕ 10ft (3m) ↔ 6ft (2m)

This vigorous shrub forms clumps of erect stems that eventually arch widely. Small white spring flowers are followed by red berries. Its leaves turn red in autumn.

Clethra alnifolia
SWEET PEPPERBUSH
☀ ☼ 4 ᴾᴴ   ↕ 6ft (2m) ↔ 5ft (1.5m)

Spikes of small, sweetly scented white flowers are produced in late summer. The toothed leaves of this upright, frequently suckering shrub give yellow autumn tints.

Lindera benzoin
SPICEBUSH
☼ 5 ᴾᴴ   ↕ 10ft (3m) ↔ 10ft (3m)

The bright green foliage of this free-growing shrub is aromatic and turns clear yellow in autumn. Clusters of small, greenish yellow flowers appear in spring.

OTHER SHRUBS TOLERANT OF WET SOIL OR STREAMBANKS

Amelanchier canadensis
Aronia melanocarpa
Calycanthus floridus
Cephalanthus occidentalis
Cornus alba 'Elegantissima'
Cornus stolonifera 'Flaviramea', see p.238
Dirca palustris
Hamamelis vernalis
Ilex glabra
Ilex verticillata
Myrica cerifera
Photinia villosa, see p.303
Rhododendron vaseyi
Rosa carolina
Sorbaria tomentosa var. *angustifolia*
Viburnum opulus 'Xanthocarpum'
Viburnum sieboldii

Myrica gale
SWEET GALE, BOG MYRTLE
☀ 4 ᴾᴴ   ↕ 3ft (1m) ↔ 3ft (1m)

Catkins crowd this small, aromatic shrub in spring, before its blue-green leaves unfurl. Fruiting spikes, seen here, follow. Tolerant of extremely boggy conditions.

Physocarpus opulifolius 'Dart's Gold'
NINEBARK
☀ 2   ↕ 6ft (2m) ↔ 6ft (2m)

Golden yellow leaves, carried from spring and all through summer, eclipse the late spring flowers of this tough and adaptable shrub. The bark on older stems peels.

Rhododendron occidentale
WESTERN AZALEA
☀ 6 ᴾᴴ   ↕ 6ft (2m) ↔ 6ft (2m)

Bold clusters of fragrant, funnel-shaped flowers appear in early summer, and vary from white to pink or pale yellow. Glossy green leaves color richly in autumn.

Rhodotypos scandens
JETBEAD
☼ ☀ 5   ↕ 6ft (2m) ↔ 6ft (2m)

Pure white flowers, borne from late spring through summer, are followed by small, shining black fruits. This vigorous shrub has toothed, conspicuously veined leaves.

SHRUBBY WILLOWS TOLERANT OF WET SOIL OR STREAMBANKS

Salix acutifolia
Salix discolor
Salix elaeagnos
Salix exigua, see p.223
Salix gracilistyla 'Melanostachys'
Salix irrorata
Salix japonica
Salix purpurea 'Nana'
Salix triandra
Salix udensis 'Sekka'

Spiraea x *vanhouttei*
BRIDAL WREATH
☼ 4   ↕ 5ft (1.5m) ↔ 5ft (1.5m)

The arching stems of this strong-growing shrub form a dense mound. Clusters of white flowers are carried all along the upper sides of its branches in summer.

Salix daphnoides
VIOLET WILLOW
☼ 5   ↕ 20ft (6m) ↔ 20ft (6m)

This vigorous shrub is grown for its pale violet winter shoots. Male forms such as 'Aglaia' have attractive catkins in spring, silver at first, then turning to yellow.

Vaccinium corymbosum
HIGHBUSH BLUEBERRY
☼ ☀ 4 PH   ↕ 5ft (1.5m) ↔ 5ft (1.5m)

Clusters of small flowers in late spring are white or pale pink in color, and followed by edible black berries. In autumn, the leaves of this bushy shrub turn crimson.

Viburnum opulus
CRANBERRY BUSH
☼ ☀ 4   ↕ 12ft (4m) ↔ 12ft (4m)

White lacecap flowerheads opening in summer give way to clusters of glistening red berries. The leaves of this vigorous shrub are orange, purple, or red in autumn.

Shrubs Tolerant of Air Pollution

THE DAYS WHEN INDUSTRIAL AIR POLLUTION was commonplace in manufacturing towns and cities are thankfully now ended. Pollution, however, remains a problem, particularly from vehicle exhausts, hence the value of shrubs showing some degree of tolerance. The following are among the most successful.

OTHER EVERGREEN SHRUBS
TOLERANT OF AIR POLLUTION

Aucuba japonica
Camellia japonica 'Adolphe Audusson', see p.192
Cotoneaster sternianus, see p.232
Elaeagnus x *ebbingei* 'Gilt Edge', see p.219
Euonymus fortunei 'Emerald Gaiety', see p.184
Sarcococca hookeriana var. *digyna*, see p.237

Brachyglottis 'Sunshine'
SHRUBBY SENECIO
☀ 9   ↕ 3ft (1m) ↔ 5ft (1.5m)

Of all flowering shrubs, this is one of the most reliably tolerant, with its striking gray-green foliage, silvery when young, and bright yellow summer flowers.

Forsythia x *intermedia* 'Lynwood'
FORSYTHIA
☀ ☀ 5   ↕ 10ft (3m) ↔ 8ft (2.5m)

Spectacular in flower, and thus deservedly popular. The branches of this robust shrub are wreathed with masses of rich yellow bell-shaped, starlike flowers in spring.

Buddleia davidii 'Royal Red'
BUTTERFLY BUSH
☀ 6   ↕ 12ft (4m) ↔ 12ft (4m)

The arching branches of this vigorous shrub produce silvery leaves that become green in summer, when its fragrant flower spikes appear, lasting into autumn.

Hypericum 'Hidcote'
SHRUBBY HYPERICUM
☀ ☀ 6   ↕ 4ft (1.2m) ↔ 5ft (1.5m)

From summer into autumn, this vigorous evergreen or semievergreen shrub carries a long succession of large, golden yellow flowers amid neat, dark green foliage.

Mahonia aquifolium 'Smaragd'
OREGON GRAPEHOLLY
☀ ☀ 5   ↕ 30in (75cm) ↔ 5ft (1.5m)

This low-growing, spreading evergreen bears glossy green, spine-toothed leaves, bronze when young. Bright yellow flower clusters are produced in spring.

Skimmia x *confusa* 'Kew Green'
SKIMMIA
☼ ☼ ☼ 7   ↕30in (75cm) ↔4ft (1.2m)

Deep green, aromatic leaves are topped in spring by dense, conical heads of fragrant, creamy white flowers. An excellent and adaptable, mounded evergreen shrub.

Olearia x *haastii*
DAISY BUSH
☼ 8   ↕6ft (2m) ↔6ft (2m)

Crowded heads of fragrant, white, daisy-like flowers cover this tough, reliable, compact evergreen in summer. Its small oval leaves have white-felted undersides.

**OTHER DECIDUOUS SHRUBS
TOLERANT OF AIR POLLUTION**

Amelanchier lamarckii, see p.296
Buddleia, many
Colutea x *media* 'Copper Beauty'
Lonicera ledebourii
Sambucus nigra 'Guincho Purple',
   see p.225
Sorbaria tomentosa var. *angustifolia*
Spartium junceum, see p.207
Viburnum opulus, see p.203
Weigela 'Florida Variegata', see p.219

Rhododendron 'Susan'
RHODODENDRON
☼ 6 PH ▼   ↕10ft (3m) ↔10ft (3m)

Compact, bushy, and quite vigorous, this evergreen bears rounded flower trusses in spring. The flowers, with dark margins and purple spots, fade to near white.

Syringa vulgaris 'Madame Lemoine'
LILAC
☼ 4   ↕12ft (4m) ↔10ft (3m)

Spectacular, crowded heads of fragrant white flowers are produced in late spring and early summer. Upright when young, it spreads with age.

Philadelphus 'Beauclerk'
MOCK ORANGE
☼ 5   ↕8ft (2.5m) ↔6ft (2m)

This lovely shrub is well worth growing for its abundance of large, broad-petaled white flowers, carried from early to mid-summer. The blooms are fragrant.

Ribes sanguineum 'Pulborough Scarlet'
FLOWERING CURRANT
☼ 6   ↕8ft (2.5m) ↔6ft (2m)

Fairly upright when young and spreading as it matures, this vigorous shrub's aromatic leaves are preceded, or accompanied, by pendent red flower clusters in spring.

Tamarix tetrandra
TAMARISK
☼ 6   ↕12ft (4m) ↔12ft (4m)

The dark shoots of this loose-stemmed shrub are clothed with scalelike green leaves. In late spring and early summer, crowded plumes of tiny flowers appear.

SHRUBS

Shrubs Tolerant of Coastal Exposure

ᴄONTRARY TO POPULAR BELIEF, a great number of shrubs can be grown in gardens near the sea. Some are more than happy to take the full blast of coastal winds and even salt spray. Others, however, while tolerant to a degree, prefer some shelter to thrive. Those listed here are among the most reliable for seaside gardens.

Atriplex halimus
SEA ORACH
☼ 7 ⬍ 6ft (2m) ↔ 6ft (2m)

This bushy evergreen shrub, with its attractive, silvery gray foliage, is partially deciduous in cold areas. It is excellent as a specimen or as an informal hedge.

Bupleurum fruticosum
SHRUBBY HARE'S-EAR
☼ 7 ⬍ 6ft (2m) ↔ 6ft (2m)

A bushy evergreen shrub, mainly grown for its shining, dark bluish green leaves. It produces tiny yellowish flowerheads from summer into autumn.

Escallonia 'Apple Blossom'
ESCALLONIA
☼ 8 ⬍ 6ft (2m) ↔ 6ft (2m)

Shining, dark green foliage clothes this dense evergreen shrub. Clusters of pink and white flowers the color of apple blossoms adorn it in summer.

> **OTHER DECIDUOUS SHRUBS TOLERANT OF COASTAL EXPOSURE**
>
> *Baccharis halimifolia*
> *Elaeagnus angustifolia*
> *Halimodendron halimifolium*
> *Hippophae rhamnoides*, see p.284
> *Hydrangea macrophylla* 'Ayesha'
> *Lycium barbarum*
> *Myrica pensylvanica*
> *Rosa* 'Harison's Yellow'
> *Rosa rugosa*, see p.209
> *Tamarix ramosissima*

Buddleia globosa
GLOBE BUTTERFLY BUSH
☼ 7 ⬍ 10ft (3m) ↔ 10ft (3m)

When in flower in summer, the tiny, tight, globular orange-yellow heads make this shrub stand out. Robust, with bold leaves, it is semievergreen in mild areas.

Colutea arborescens
BLADDER SENNA
☼ 6 ⬍ 8ft (2.5m) ↔ 8ft (2.5m)

A vigorous shrub of open habit, this has small, much-divided leaves. The clusters of yellow pea flowers in summer are replaced by inflated seed capsules.

Fuchsia magellanica
HARDY FUCHSIA
☼ 7 ⬍ 6ft (2m) ↔ 6ft (2m)

Dense, leafy mounds make this ideal as a specimen plant or an informal hedge. Its lanternlike flowers hang freely from the shoots from midsummer into autumn.

Hebe x *franciscana* 'Blue Gem'
HEBE

☼ 9   ↕ 24in (60cm) ↔ 4ft (1.2m)

This evergreen shrub makes an excellent specimen in mild-winter areas. Its short violet flower spikes are produced from summer to early winter.

Hydrangea macrophylla
'Lanarth White'

☼ ☼ 7   ↕ 5ft (1.5m) ↔ 6ft (2m)

In summer, long-lasting, domed heads of dark blue, fertile flowers and starry white, sterile florets cover this reliable, compact, mounded shrub. Leaves are light green.

Olearia nummulariifolia
DAISY BUSH

☼ 9   ↕ 6ft (2m) ↔ 6ft (2m)

Stiff shoots crowded with tiny, leathery evergreen leaves characterize this rounded shrub. Small, fragrant flowers open near the ends of the branches in summer.

Spartium junceum
SPANISH BROOM

☼ 8   ↕ 8ft (2.5m) ↔ 8ft (2.5m)

Spanish Broom is a vigorous shrub with smooth, dark green, almost leafless shoots, and sprays of fragrant yellow pea flowers lasting from early summer into autumn.

OTHER EVERGREEN SHRUBS
TOLERANT OF COASTAL EXPOSURE

Arctostaphylos uva-ursi
Ilex glabra
Nerium oleander
Ruscus aculeatus, see p.241

Lupinus arboreus
TREE LUPINE

☼ 8   ↕ 3ft (1m) ↔ 3ft (1m)

This vigorous, mounded semievergreen, with the fingered leaves that are typical of lupines, bears numerous tapered spikes of fragrant yellow flowers in early summer.

Tamarix ramosissima
TAMARISK

☼ 3   ↕ 12ft (4m) ↔ 12ft (4m)

Openly branched and vigorous, this shrub has feathery blue-green foliage on long branches, and plumes of tiny pink flowers from late summer into early autumn.

S H R U B S

207

Shrubs for Screening or Hedges

SHRUBS SUITABLE FOR HEDGING can be pruned or clipped annually for a formal effect, or allowed to develop a more natural appearance. Those of stronger growth and ultimately large habit are useful for screening to hide intrusive views, filter noise, or lessen the effect of wind. Sizes given refer to the average ultimate size of a single plant without pruning.

OTHER SHRUBS FOR SMALL HEDGES

Berberis thunbergii 'Atropurpurea Nana', see p.224
Buxus sempervirens 'Suffruticosa', see p.240
Ilex crenata 'Convexa'
Lavandula angustifolia 'Hidcote', see p.234
Myrtus communis subsp. *tarentina*
Santolina chamaecyparissus, see p.223
Teucrium x *lucidrys*

Berberis x *stenophylla*
BARBERRY
☼ 7   ↕ 8ft (2.5m) ↔ 8ft (2.5m)

Useful as an informal hedge, this tough, adaptable evergreen has slender arching stems, narrow dark green leaves, and tiny golden yellow flowers in spring.

Cotoneaster lacteus
COTONEASTER
☼ 7   ↕ 12ft (4m) ↔ 10ft (3m)

One of the best evergreens for a formal hedge or an informal screen, this bears veined leaves, white summer flowers, and red berries from autumn into winter.

OTHER EVERGREEN SHRUBS FOR SCREENING OR HEDGES

Berberis julianae
Camellia, many
Elaeagnus pungens
Euonymus kiautschovicus
Ilex cornuta 'Burfordii'
Ilex glabra
Osmanthus heterophyllus
Pittosporum, many
Rhaphiolepis indica
Viburnum tinus 'Eve Price', see p.237

Buxus sempervirens 'Handsworthensis'
HANDSWORTH BOXWOOD
☼ ☼ 6   ↕ 10ft (3m) ↔ 10ft (3m)

This evergreen is upright, densely leafy, and strong-growing, making it reliable as a formal hedge or screen. Its leathery deep green leaves are rounded or oblong.

Cotoneaster simonsii
COTONEASTER
☼ 6   ↕ 8ft (2.5m) ↔ 6ft (2m)

Shiny deciduous or semievergreen leaves cover this vigorous shrub, ideal as a formal hedge. White flowers open in summer, and red berries ripen in autumn.

SHRUBS

Elaeagnus x *ebbingei*
ELAEAGNUS
☼ 6   ↕ 12ft (4m) ↔ 12ft (4m)

In autumn, small, fragrant, silvery white flowers crowd the branches among shining green leaves. This vigorous evergreen is suitable for formal and informal screens.

Griselinia littoralis
BROADLEAF
☼ 9   ↕ 20ft (6m) ↔ 15ft (5m)

This vigorous evergreen shrub, with bright green leaves, is excellent grown alone or mixed, as it is here, with *Prunus cerasifera* 'Nigra'. Well-suited to seaside gardens.

Prunus laurocerasus 'Rotundifolia'
CHERRY LAUREL
☼ ☼ ☼ 6   ↕ 10ft (3m) ↔ 6ft (2m)

Cherry Laurel is an excellent choice for formal hedging, with its striking, glossy green evergreen leaves and upright growth. Can also be grown informally.

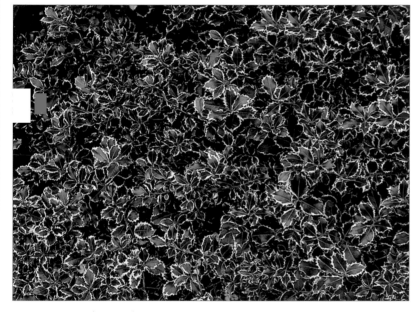

Ilex aquifolium 'Argentea-marginata'
SILVER ENGLISH HOLLY
☼ 6   ↕ 25ft (8m) ↔ 12ft (4m)

One of the best formal hedges or screens, this shrub or tree has cream-margined, prickly-toothed, evergreen leaves, and red fruits when pollinated by a male holly.

Prunus lusitanica
PORTUGAL LAUREL
☼ ☼ 8   ↕ 20ft (6m) ↔ 20ft (6m)

Particularly impressive in spring, when it produces white flower tassels, this bushy evergreen shrub carries shining, slender, pointed green leaves on red stalks.

Fuchsia 'Riccartonii'
FUCHSIA
☼ 7   ↕ 6ft (2m) ↔ 6ft (2m)

Superb as an informal hedge, particularly in coastal areas, this vigorous shrub soon forms a dense bush, strung with lanternlike flowers in late summer.

OTHER DECIDUOUS SHRUBS FOR SCREENING OR HEDGES

Berberis thunbergii f. *atropurpurea*
Chaenomeles, many
Elaeagnus angustifolia
Forsythia x *intermedia* 'Lynwood', see p.204
Hibiscus syriacus 'Oiseau Blue', see p.199
Poncirus trifoliata
Potentilla, many
Rhamnus frangula 'Columnaris'
Viburnum prunifolium

Rosa rugosa
RUGOSA ROSE
☼ 3   ↕ 5ft (1.5m) ↔ 5ft (1.5m)

This species rose is popular as an informal hedge, with its large, wrinkled leaves and magenta flowers borne from summer into autumn, followed by tomato-like hips.

S H R U B S

Shrubs for Rock Gardens, Raised Beds, and Screes

NUMEROUS SHRUBS NEAT IN HABIT, and attractive in flower, foliage, and fruit are prevented by their small size from being used in a mixed border, unless it is well away from the domination of larger, stronger-growing neighbors. Such shrubs are ideal for planting in rock gardens or raised beds where their special, smaller charms can better be appreciated.

Genista lydia
GENISTA
☼ 6   ↕ 22in (55cm) ↔ 30in (75cm)

This shrub is a superb sight in late spring and early summer, when it is covered with clusters of tiny pea flowers. Ideal for a dry wall top, where its stems can tumble.

OTHER ROCK GARDEN SHRUBS
Anthyllis hermanniae 'Minor'
Berberis x *stenophylla* 'Corallina Compacta'
Convolvulus cneorum, see p.222
Crassula sarcocaulis
Daphne sericea Collina Group
Hypericum olympicum 'Citrinum'
Ozothamnus selago
Penstemon pinifolius
Sorbus poteriifolia
Teucrium polium

Acer palmatum 'Corallinum'
JAPANESE MAPLE
☼ ☀ 6   ↕ 30in (75cm) ↔ 18in (45cm)

A striking, slow-growing, compact shrub, capable of twice the above size in moist, rich, well-drained soils. Grown mainly for its brilliant coral pink stems in spring.

Daphne tangutica Retusa Group
DAPHNE
☼ ☀ 6   ↕ 28in (70cm) ↔ 28in (70cm)

A domed shrub with leathery evergreen leaves, this bears fragrant flowers (purple when in bud) in clusters from late spring, followed by bright red berries.

Berberis empetrifolia
BARBERRY
☼ 7 PH   ↕ 12in (30cm) ↔ 18in (45cm)

The stems of this dwarf evergreen are wiry and prickly, and its branches clothed with small, narrow, spine-tipped leaves. Tiny golden flowers appear in late spring.

Euryops acraeus
EURYOPS
☼ 9   ↕ 12in (30cm) ↔ 12in (30cm)

Distinctive shrub, forming a small mound of narrow silvery leaves, above which late spring flowers rise on thin, downy stalks. Thrives in sun and well-drained soils.

Hebe cupressoides 'Boughton Dome'
HEBE
☼ 8   ↕ 12in (30cm) ↔ 18in (45cm)

This attractive evergreen mound of tiny, dark gray-green leaves resembles a dwarf juniper and produces clusters of white summer flowers. Needs good drainage.

Helianthemum 'Fire Dragon'
ROCKROSE
☼ 6   ↕ 11in (28cm) ↔ 22in (55cm)

This evergreen carpet-forming shrub has narrow gray-green leaves and is covered with brilliant orange-scarlet flowers from late spring, continuing into summer.

Penstemon serrulatus
BEARDTONGUE
☼ 5   ↕ 24in (60cm) ↔ 12in (30cm)

A loose semievergreen shrub, this forms clumps of dark green foliage, and erect stems that bear branched heads of tubular blue to purple flowers in summer.

Punica granatum var. *nana*
DWARF POMEGRANATE
☼ 8   ↕ 24in (60cm) ↔ 24in (60cm)

The glossy leaves of this charming little pomegranate turn gold in autumn. Funnel-shaped flowers appear in early autumn. Appreciates warmth and good drainage.

Linum arboreum
TREE FLAX
☼ 10   ↕ 11in (28cm) ↔ 12in (30cm)

Clusters of bright yellow flowers appear throughout summer, whenever the sun shines. This low, dome-shaped evergreen needs warmth and good drainage.

Parahebe catarractae
PARAHEBE
☼ 9   ↕ 12in (30cm) ↔ 12in (30cm)

This choice, reliable plant will form loose mounds of evergreen leaves and, in late summer and early autumn, sprays of small flowers with crimson and white centers.

OTHER CARPETING SHRUBS

Chamaecytisus purpureus 'Atropurpureus'
Cistus salviifolius 'Avalanche'
Genista sagittalis
Helianthemum apenninum
Hypericum empetrifolium subsp. *oliganthum*

Salix reticulata
NETTED WILLOW
☼ 1   ↕ 1½in (4cm) ↔ 12in (30cm)

Carpets of prostrate stems are clothed in oval leaves that are pale beneath and net-veined above. Male plants have pretty spring catkins. Best in moist soils.

SHRUBS

211

Shrubs for Containers

JUST ABOUT ANY SHRUB can be planted in a container, although some are more suitable than others. Generally, large and vigorous shrubs are best avoided unless you prune them regularly. Pots and tubs are particularly useful on patios, terraces, and in courtyards, or for growing tender shrubs that are kept under shelter in cold weather. For those who garden on a particular soil type and who wish to grow a plant unsuited to it, containers provide a practical solution to this problem.

Felicia amelloides 'Santa Anita'
BLUE DAISY
☼ 10 ↕ 12in (30cm) ↔ 12in (30cm)

Long-stalked, yellow-eyed, blue daisylike flowers rise above a bushy mound of oval evergreen leaves, from late spring through to autumn.

OTHER TENDER SHRUBS
FOR CONTAINERS

Abutilon pictum 'Thompsonii'
Brugmansia x *candida* 'Charles Grimaldi'
Cestrum nocturnum
Nerium oleander

Choisya 'Aztec Pearl'
CHOISYA
☼ ☼ 8 ↕ 4ft (1.2m) ↔ 4ft (1.2m)

The fingered leaves of this free-growing evergreen are aromatic. Its fragrant white flower clusters, pink in bud, occur in late spring, and again in late summer.

Aloysia triphylla
LEMON VERBENA
☼ 8 ↕ 6ft (2m) ↔ 6ft (2m)

Mainly grown for its deliciously lemon-scented leaves, this slender-stemmed bush produces flimsy flower spikes in summer. Prune in late winter to control size.

Cestrum elegans
CESTRUM
☼ 10 ↕ 10ft (3m) ↔ 6ft (2m)

The arching stems and leafy branches of this vigorous evergreen shrub bow beneath its freely produced clusters of tubular red flowers from spring through summer.

x *Fatshedera lizei*
FATSHEDERA
☼ ☼ 7 ↕ 6ft (2m) ↔ 6ft (2m)

This handsome evergreen shrub forms a loose mound of boldly lobed, shining, dark green leaves. Loose heads of small cream flowers are carried in autumn.

Fuchsia 'Celia Smedley'
FUCHSIA
☼ 9 ↕ 5ft (1.5m) ↔ 3ft (1m)

Vigorous and upright, this is one of the more hardy fuchsias. Pendulous, pinkish white and red flowers with greenish white tubes open throughout summer.

Fuchsia 'Thalia'
FUCHSIA
☼ 10   ↕ 3ft (1m) ↔ 3ft (1m)

Deservedly popular, this erect shrub bears
drooping clusters of long, slender flowers
carried in summer above dark reddish
green, velvety leaves.

Lantana camara
LANTANA
☼ 10   ↕ 5ft (1.5m) ↔ 5ft (1.5m)

This prickly-stemmed, summer-flowering
evergreen is rampant in hot climates, but
easily controlled by tip-pruning. Several
colors, changing with age, are available.

OTHER HARDY SHRUBS
FOR CONTAINERS

Berberis thunbergii 'Atropurpurea Nana',
  see p.224
Deutzia gracilis, see p.182
Deutzia scabra 'Variegata'
Euonymus japonicus 'Microphyllus'
Mahonia aquifolium, see p.233
Prunus laurocerasus 'Otto Luyken',
  see p.201
Skimmia japonica, see p.241
Spiraea japonica 'Goldflame', see p.221
Syringa pubescens subsp. *microphylla*
  'Superba', see p.181

Prostanthera rotundifolia
ROUND-LEAVED MINT BUSH
☼ 9   ↕ 5ft (1.5m) ↔ 5ft (1.5m)

When they are bruised, the tiny leaves of
this dense, rounded evergreen are sweetly
aromatic. Masses of bell-shaped flowers
open from spring into early summer.

Mimulus aurantiacus
SHRUBBY MIMULUS
☼ 9   ↕ 24in (60cm) ↔ 3ft (1m)

A succession of two-lipped orange-yellow
flowers are borne from late spring through
to autumn. The narrow evergreen leaves
of this low bush are sticky to the touch.

Pieris japonica 'Little Heath'
JAPANESE ANDROMEDA
☼ ☼ 5   ↕ 4ft (1.2m) ↔ 3ft (1m)

A choice, compact evergreen, this pieris is
grown mainly for its small, slender, white-
margined leaves, which are red when they
emerge in spring. Slow-growing.

Rhododendron 'Homebush'
KNAPHILL AZALEA
☼ ☼ 6   ↕ 5ft (1.5m) ↔ 6ft (2m)

This charming, relatively compact shrub
is popular on account of its tight, rounded
heads of trumpet-shaped flowers that are
produced in late spring.

S H R U B S

213

Evergreen Shrubs

WHERE WINTER TEMPERATURES are not low enough to severely inhibit their growth, shrubs having evergreen foliage provide some of the most worthwhile ornamental subjects for the garden. They come in an impressive range of shapes, sizes, textures, and colors, adding variety as well as permanence to the mixed bed or border. Most have flowers and sometimes fruit as a bonus. Some evergreen shrubs are so distinguished that they are ideal as courtyard or lawn specimens, while others with a low spreading habit make effective groundcover in sun or shade. Less hardy evergreens are usually more successful when grown in the shelter of other shrubs or a wall.

Elaeagnus pungens 'Maculata'
THORNY ELAEAGNUS
☼ 6-7   ↕ 8ft (2.5m) ↔ 10ft (3m)

Robust and dense with its brown-scaly branchlets, this shrub has gold-splashed green leaves. Clusters of tiny, scented, creamy white flowers appear in autumn.

Aucuba japonica   'Rozannie'
AUCUBA
☼ ☼ 6-7   ↕ 30in (75cm) ↔ 30in (75cm)

The tiny female flowers of this compact dwarf shrub appear in spring and produce red fruits when pollinated. This cultivar is excellent in a bed or in a container.

Olearia macrodonta
NEW ZEALAND HOLLY
☼ ☼ 9   ↕ 11ft (3.5m) ↔ 11ft (3.5m)

This sturdy shrub has attractive, pale brown, ultimately shaggy, bark and holly-like leaves. Fragrant, daisylike white flowerheads appear in early summer.

Buxus sempervirens 'Vardar Valley'
BOXWOOD
☼ ☼ 5   ↕ 30in (75cm) ↔ 4ft (1.2m)

This valuable cultivar of Boxwood has a low, wide-spreading habit. With its glossy, densely packed leathery leaves, it is superb for groundcover in most soils.

Daphne odora 'Aureomarginata'
WINTER DAPHNE
☼ 7   ↕ 3½ft (1.1m) ↔ 4ft (1.2m)

For a warm, sheltered corner, this is a most reliable evergreen. Sweetly scented flowers are borne from winter into spring, and its leaves have narrow yellow margins.

OTHER EVERGREEN SHRUBS

Berberis julianae
Camellia japonica
Choisya ternata, see p.228
Euonymus kiautschovicus
Ilex crenata
Ilex x *meserveae*
Kalmia latifolia, see p.193
Pyracantha coccinea
Rhaphiolepis umbellata
Rhododendron PJM hybrids
Skimmia japonica

S H R U B S

Ozothamnus rosmarinifolius
OZOTHAMNUS
☼ 9   ↕ 6ft (2m) ↔ 5ft (1.5m)

The erect stems of this vigorous shrub are crowded with threadlike leaves. Its tiny scented flowers are borne in early summer. Needs a warm, well-drained site.

Pittosporum tenuifolium
'Irene Paterson'
☼ 9   ↕ 8ft (2.5m) ↔ 3½ft (1.1m)

A broadly columnar shrub, this has thin black stems and small, wavy, waxy leaves, marbled white when mature, pink-tinted in winter. Excellent for containers.

Prunus lusitanica subsp. *azorica*
PORTUGAL LAUREL
☼ ☼ 8   ↕ 20ft (6m) ↔ 20ft (6m)

This vigorous form of the Portugal Laurel is densely branched with light green leaves, red at first. Shining, dark purple fruits follow fragrant summer flowers.

EVERGREEN GROUNDCOVER
SHRUBS

Arctostaphylos uva-ursi 'Vancouver Jade'
Ardisia japonica
Ceanothus gloriosus
Ceanothus thyrsiflorus var. *repens*
Gaultheria shallon
Hypericum calycinum, see p.185
Mahonia nervosa, see p.201
Rubus tricolor
Sarcococca hookeriana var. *humilis*
Viburnum davidii, see p.185

Vaccinium glaucoalbum
VACCINIUM
☼ 7 PH   ↕ 24in (60cm) ↔ 30in (75cm)

Handsome and compact, this low-growing shrub has leathery green leaves. Drooping clusters of pink-tinted white spring flowers are followed by blue-black berries.

Prunus laurocerasus 'Zabeliana'
CHERRY LAUREL
☼ ☼ 5-6   ↕ 32in (80cm) ↔ 7ft (2.2m)

A tough, wide-spreading form of the Cherry Laurel, with narrow, glossy leaves. Flower spikes in late spring are followed by red fruits, ripening to shiny black.

Rhododendron 'Dora Amateis'
RHODODENDRON
☼ ☼ 5 PH   ↕ 2ft (60cm) ↔ 2ft (60cm)

This free-flowering dwarf rhododendron of compact habit has glossy foliage, and terminal trusses of funnel-shaped, pink-tinged white flowers in late spring.

Viburnum x *pragense*
VIBURNUM
☼ 6   ↕ 8ft (2.5m) ↔ 8ft (2.5m)

The narrow green leaves of this vigorous shrub are boldly veined on top. Creamy white flowers, pink-tinged when in bud, are produced in domed heads in spring.

SHRUBS

215

Shrubs with Bold Leaves

EXPERIENCED GARDENERS sensibly choose plants as much for their foliage effect as for their attractive flowers. This is particularly important with larger plants, such as shrubs, that occupy a greater area than the average perennial. Where a shrub has both flowers and leaves worthy of attention, then give serious consideration to its inclusion; these dual-purpose plants certainly earn their place in the garden. The following is but a small selection; there are many more.

Hydrangea aspera 'Macrophylla'
HYDRANGEA
☼ 6   ↕ ↔ 8ft (2.5m)

The large, rugged leaves of this bold shrub are roughly hairy. From late summer, the branches are capped with broad, domed, blue and white, lace-cap flowerheads.

Aralia elata 'Aureovariegata'
ANGELICA TREE
☼ 4   ↕ ↔ 15ft (5m)

This broad bush has thick branches with large, handsome, yellow-margined leaves. Large white flowerheads appear in autumn. Remove green suckers if they appear.

Decaisnea fargesii
DECAISNEA
☼ ☼ 7   ↕ ↔ 10–20ft (3–6m)

A lanky-stemmed shrub that suckers to form colonies. The large, ashlike leaves turn yellow in autumn. Plant in groups to encourage blue autumn seed pods to form.

Hydrangea quercifolia
OAKLEAF HYDRANGEA
☼ 6   ↕ 5ft (1.5m) ↔ 8ft (2.5m)

Boldly lobed leaves that color richly in autumn cover this bushy shrub, forming a broad mound. Dense white flowerheads occur from summer into autumn.

Eriobotrya japonica
LOQUAT
☼ 8   ↕ 12ft (4m) ↔ 12ft (4m)

Leathery, prominently veined, dark green leaves distinguish this evergreen shrub or small tree. Fragrant white autumn flowers are followed by orange-yellow fruits.

Fatsia japonica
FATSIA
☼ ☼ 7   ↕ 10ft (3m) ↔ 10ft (3m)

This domed evergreen bears handsome, long-stalked, deeply lobed, shining green leaves. Branched clusters of white flowers in autumn precede black berries.

OTHER SHRUBS WITH BOLD LEAVES
Aralia spinosa
Hibiscus, many
Hydrangea aspera subsp. *sargentiana*
Mahonia lomariifolia
Melianthus major, see p.47

SHRUBS

Nandina domestica
SACRED BAMBOO
☼ ☼ 6   ↕ ↔ 6ft (2m)

A clump-forming, erect evergreen with
ruffs of large, much-divided leaves, purplish
when young. White flowers appear in
midsummer, followed by red berries.

Paeonia delavayi var. *ludlowii*
TREE PEONY
☼ ☼ 5   ↕ 8ft (2.5m) ↔ 8ft (2.5m)

Loose-stemmed, with boldly cut, bright
green leaves, this shrub has yellow flowers
in late spring and early summer. *P. delavayi*,
with deep red flowers, is similar in leaf.

Rhus glabra
SMOOTH SUMAC
☼ 2   ↕ 8ft (2.5m) ↔ 8ft (2.5m)

Smooth shoots support regularly divided,
deep blue-green leaves that color richly in
autumn. Summer flowers are followed by
red-brown fruits on female plants.

Salix fargesii
FARGE'S WILLOW
☼ ☼ 5   ↕ ↔ 10ft (3m)

Noted for its spreading or vase-shaped
habit, polished mahogany-red young
shoots, and its handsome, saw-toothed,
glossy leaves. A fine specimen shrub.

Variegated-leaved Shrubs

VARIEGATION COMES in a number of forms. Generally a green leaf has a white or yellow margin; occasionally, a white or yellow leaf has a green margin. There are, however, a host of shrubs with green, gray, or purple leaves that are spotted, blotched, or streaked a lighter shade. Two-color variegation may be joined by paler or darker shades of the dominant colors. The bolder the variegation, the more dramatic the effect when planted with foliage of one color.

Buxus sempervirens 'Elegantissima'
VARIEGATED BOXWOOD
☼ 6   ↕ 5½ft (1.7m) ↔ 3½ft (1.1m)

Neat and slow-growing, this is arguably the best variegated form of Boxwood. The bush is dome-shaped, with small evergreen, white-margined leaves.

Cornus alba 'Variegata'
SILVER-VARIEGATED DOGWOOD
☼ 2   ↕ 7ft (2.2m) ↔ 7ft (2.2m)

A reliable variegated dogwood that bears white-margined gray-green leaves on reddish shoots. Prune hard in late winter for brighter stems and larger leaves.

Buddleia davidii 'Harlequin'
BUTTERFLY BUSH
☼ 6   ↕ 8ft (2.5m) ↔ 8ft (2.5m)

A vigorous and attractive shrub, this has arching stems and creamy white-margined leaves. Large, dense spikes of red-purple flowers occur from summer into autumn.

OTHER DECIDUOUS VARIEGATED SHRUBS

Berberis thunbergii 'Rose Glow'
Daphne x *burkwoodii* 'Carol Mackie'
Fuchsia magellanica 'Sharpitor'
Hypericum x *moserianum* 'Tricolor'
Ligustrum sinense 'Variegatum'
Lonicera nitida 'Silver Beauty'
Philadelphus coronarius 'Variegatus'
Sambucus nigra 'Pulverulenta'
Stachyurus chinensis 'Magpie'
Weigela 'Praecox Variegata'

Cornus mas 'Variegata'
VARIEGATED CORNELIAN CHERRY
☼ ☼ 5   ↕ 12ft (4m) ↔ 12ft (4m)

This dense, bushy shrub has leaves with bold white margins. Small clusters of tiny yellow flowers stud the twigs in late winter, before the leaves unfurl.

Aucuba japonica 'Crotonifolia'
SPOTTED AUCUBA
☼ ☼ 6-7   ↕ 6ft (2m) ↔ 5½ft (1.7m)

The jade green shoots of this spectacular, dense, bushy shrub develop into shiny, leathery green leaves, blotched yellow. This is a most reliable evergreen.

Cotoneaster horizontalis 'Variegatus'
VARIEGATED COTONEASTER
☼ 6   ↕ 18in (45cm) ↔ 4ft (1.2m)

Also known as *C. atropurpureus* 'Variegata', the low, wide-spreading stems are densely clothed with tiny, cream-margined leaves. These are tinted red in autumn.

Ilex aquifolium 'Ferox Argentea'
SILVER HEDGEHOG HOLLY
☼ ☼ 6-7   ↕ 12ft (4m) ↔ 5ft (1.5m)

An attractive, bushy evergreen holly, with small, prickly leaves that have creamy white margins. This is a male form, useful as a pollinator for berrying hollies.

Rhamnus alaternus 'Argenteovariegata'
VARIEGATED BUCKTHORN
☼ 7   ↕ 8ft (2.5m) ↔ 5½ft (1.7m)

A handsome, bushy evergreen, this has small, glossy gray-green leaves, margined creamy white. Discreet yellow flowers will produce red summer berries.

Viburnum tinus 'Variegatum'
VARIEGATED LAURUSTINUS
☼ ☼ 7   ↕ 8ft (2.5m) ↔ 6ft (2m)

The leaves of this mounded or conical evergreen shrub are boldly and irregularly margined. Red-budded, fragrant white flowers occur from autumn through winter.

Elaeagnus x *ebbingei* 'Gilt Edge'
ELAEAGNUS
☼ 7   ↕ 8ft (2.5m) ↔ 8ft (2.5m)

This robust evergreen has brown, scaly stems and shining green leaves with golden yellow margins. Its small, sweetly fragrant flowers appear in autumn.

OTHER EVERGREEN VARIEGATED SHRUBS

Camellia x *williamsii* 'Golden Spangles'
Coronilla valentina subsp. *glauca* 'Variegata'
Euonymus fortunei 'Silver Queen', see p.166
Euonymus japonicus 'Chollipo'
Pieris japonica 'Little Heath', see p.213
Pittosporum 'Garnettii'
Prunus laurocerasus 'Castlewellan', see p.233

Osmanthus heterophyllus 'Variegatus'
VARIEGATED FALSE HOLLY
☼ ☼ 7   ↕ 7ft (2.2m) ↔ 4ft (1.2m)

This evergreen bush of relatively slow growth has small, white-margined, holly-like leaves. Clusters of little, sweetly scented white flowers occur in autumn.

Weigela 'Florida Variegata'
VARIEGATED WEIGELA
☼ 6   ↕ 5ft (1.5m) ↔ 5ft (1.5m)

One of the most popular and easily grown variegated shrubs, with distinctly edged leaves that provide a perfect foil for pink flowers in late spring and early summer.

SHRUBS

Shrubs with Golden or Yellow Leaves

There is nothing like a bright splash of yellow or gold foliage to bring a most welcome touch of warmth to the garden, especially in the depths of winter. An abundance of shrubs, both evergreen and deciduous, have leaves in varying shades of yellow. Careful use of these can create striking contrasts with green- or purple-leaved plants.

Berberis thunbergii 'Aurea'
GOLDEN JAPANESE BARBERRY
☼ 5   ↕ 30in (75cm) ↔ 30in (75cm)

Dense, compact mounding plants with small, rounded, vivid yellow leaves that turn yellow-green. May scorch in full sun except in cool summers.

Calluna vulgaris 'Gold Haze'
HEATHER, LING
☼ 5   ↕ 20in (50cm) ↔ 18in (45cm)

One of many similar heathers 'Gold Haze' has tightly arranged foliage of a golden hue, brighter in winter. White flowers are produced in late summer.

Choisya ternata 'Sundance'
MEXICAN ORANGE-BLOSSOM
☼ ☼ 8   ↕ 5ft (1.5m) ↔ 6ft (2m)

The bright yellow, aromatic leaves of this evergreen, mounded shrub fade with age. Fragrant white flowers are produced in late spring. Dislikes cold winds.

Cornus alba 'Aurea'
GOLDEN-LEAVED DOGWOOD
☼ ☼ 2   ↕ 10ft (3m) ↔ 10ft (3m)

This vigorous dogwood forms a sizeable mound of dark red branches, clothed all through summer and into autumn with broad leaves of a lovely soft yellow color.

Erica arborea 'Albert's Gold'
TREE HEATH
☼ 4   ↕ 6ft (2m) ↔ 6ft (2m)

Tiny, crowded golden leaves cover twiggy branches, creating plumes of golden yellow throughout the year. Masses of honey-scented white flowers appear in spring.

Fuchsia 'Genii'
FUCHSIA
☼ ☼ 9   ↕ 4½ft (1.4m) ↔ 30in (75cm)

This small, colorful, upright shrub has red shoots and bright lime yellow foliage. It carries small, pendulous violet and red flowers from summer into autumn.

Ligustrum 'Vicaryi'
GOLDEN PRIVET
☼ ☼ **5**   ↕ 10ft (3m) ↔ 10ft (3m)

This is a vigorous semievergreen shrub of dense, bushy habit. The dusty-scented white flowers and bright yellow leaves are carried throughout the summer.

OTHER DECIDUOUS SHRUBS WITH GOLDEN OR YELLOW LEAVES

Acer palmatum 'Aureum', see p.292
Acer shirasawanum 'Aureum'
Caryopteris x *clandonensis* 'Worcester Gold'
Cornus mas 'Aurea'
Fuchsia 'Golden Marinka'
Physocarpus opulifolius 'Dart's Gold', see p.202
Ptelea trifoliata 'Aurea', see p.293
Ribes alpinum 'Aureum'
Rubus cockburnianus 'Goldenvale'
Rubus parviflorus 'Sunshine Spreader'
Sambucus nigra 'Aurea', see p.241
Sambucus racemosa 'Plumosa Aurea'
Spiraea japonica 'Limemound'
Viburnum lantana 'Aureum'
Weigela 'Looymansii Aurea', see p.195
Weigela 'Rubidor'

Sambucus racemosa 'Sutherland Gold'
☼ **4**   ↕ 10ft (3m) ↔ 10ft (3m)

The large, deeply divided yellow leaves of this vigorous golden elder do not readily scorch. Clusters of yellow flowers, borne in spring, are followed by red berries.

Lonicera nitida 'Baggesen's Gold'
BAGGESEN'S GOLD HONEYSUCKLE
☼ **7**   ↕ 15ft (5m) ↔ 15ft (5m)

Attractive, tiny yellow leaves crowd the slender, arching shoots of this dense, bushy evergreen. Capable of greater height when trained against   a wall.

Ribes sanguineum 'Brocklebankii'
GOLDEN FLOWERING CURRANT
☼ **6**   ↕ 3ft (1m) ↔ 4ft (1.2m)

Although clusters of pink flowers decorate this bushy shrub in spring, the aromatic golden yellow leaves, liable to scorch in full sun, are its main attraction.

OTHER EVERGREEN SHRUBS WITH GOLDEN OR YELLOW LEAVES

Aucuba japonica 'Sulphurea'
Calluna vulgaris 'Beoley Gold'
Erica erigena 'Golden Lady'
Erica vagans 'Valerie Proudley'
Escallonia laevis 'Gold Brian'
Escallonia laevis 'Gold Ellen'
Euonymus japonicus 'Ovatus Aureus'
Ilex x *attenuata* 'Sunny Foster'
Ilex crenata 'Golden Gem'
Ligustrum ovalifolium 'Aureum'

Spiraea japonica 'Goldflame'
GOLDFLAME SPIREA
☼ **4**   ↕ 30in (75cm) ↔ 3ft (1m)

Leaves on a low, dense mound of twiggy branches emerge orange-red, then turn to golden yellow, and finally to green. Small summer flowerheads are rose pink.

Philadelphus coronarius 'Aureus'
GOLDEN MOCK ORANGE
☼ **5**   ↕ 8ft (2.5m) ↔ 5ft (1.5m)

The yellow spring leaves of this shrub fade to greenish in late summer, and can scorch in full sun. Creamy white, fragrant flowers are produced in late spring.

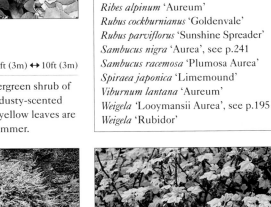

Viburnum opulus 'Aureum'
GOLDEN SNOWBALL BUSH
☼ **4**   ↕ 8ft (2.5m) ↔ 6ft (2m)

Bright yellow, maplelike leaves are red-bronze when young. Its white flowerheads appear in summer, followed by red berries in autumn. Leaves scorch in hot sun.

S H R U B S

221

Shrubs with Blue-gray or Silver Leaves

THE SILVERY FLASH of sunlight catching blue-gray leaves shifting in a breeze is a pleasing sight in any garden. Silver-foliaged shrubs can also be grown for their softening effect near leaves of a darker or brighter hue. The blue-gray or silvery color may be due to a silky or woolly coating of hairs, silvery scales, or a white, powdery bloom.

Convolvulus cneorum
CONVOLVULUS
☼ 8 ↕ 30in (75cm) ↔ 3ft (1m)

Silky, silvery leaves and stems make this one of the loveliest dwarf evergreen shrubs. White, yellow-throated flowers cover it from late spring to late summer.

Berberis dictyophylla
BARBERRY
☼ 6 ↕ 6ft (2m) ↔ 6ft (2m)

This graceful shrub has striking stems and leaves with a whitish bloom. Light yellow summer flowers give way to berries that, with the leaves, turn scarlet in autumn.

Calluna vulgaris 'Silver Queen'
HEATHER, LING
☼ 5 PH ↕ 16in (40cm) ↔ 18in (45cm)

Although it produces mauve-pink flower spikes in late summer and early autumn, this dwarf evergreen is popular mainly for its silver-gray, downy foliage.

Hebe pimeleoides 'Quicksilver'
HEBE
☼ 9 ↕ 10in (25cm) ↔ 24in (60cm)

The dark, wiry stems and branches of this low, spreading evergreen shrub bear small silver-blue leaves, and short spikes of pale lilac flowers in summer.

OTHER EVERGREEN SHRUBS WITH BLUE-GRAY OR SILVER LEAVES

Acacia baileyana
Andromeda polifolia
Artemisia 'Huntington'
Artemisia 'Powis Castle', see p.26
Ballota pseudodictamnus
Brachyglottis 'Sunshine', see p.204
Dendromecon rigida
Elaeagnus macrophylla
Euryops acraeus, see p.210
Hebe pinguifolia 'Pagei'
Lavandula angustifolia 'Hidcote', see p.234
Rhododendron campanulatum subsp. *aeruginosum*
Rhododendron cinnabarinum Concatenans Group
Teucrium fruticans
Yucca glauca

Cistus x *argenteus* 'Peggy Sammons'
SUNROSE
☼ 8 ↕ 3ft (1m) ↔ 3ft (1m)

The pale pink flowers of this lovely, bushy evergreen are freely produced in summer, and resemble small, single roses. Gray-green leaves and stems are downy.

OTHER DECIDUOUS SHRUBS WITH BLUE-GRAY OR SILVER LEAVES

Buddleia alternifolia 'Argentea'
Buddleia 'Lochinch'
Lotus hirsutus, see p.196
Elaeagnus angustifolia
Hippophae rhamnoides, see p.284
Romneya coulteri, see p.197
Rosa fedtschenkoana
Salix elaeagnos
Salvia officinalis, see p.235
Shepherdia argentea

Helichrysum italicum
CURRY PLANT
☼ 9   ↕ 24in (60cm) ↔ 3ft (1m)

Threadlike leaves crowd the erect stems
of this low, aromatic evergreen subshrub.
Its leaves and stems are silvery gray and
downy, and summer flowers are yellow.

Leptospermum lanigerum
LEPTOSPERMUM
☼ 9 PH   ↕ 10ft (3m) ↔ 6ft (2m)

The reddish shoots of this evergreen bush
are clothed in narrow gray or silvery gray
leaves. Its small white flowers are freely
produced in early summer.

Perovskia 'Blue Spire'
RUSSIAN SAGE
☼ 5   ↕ 4ft (1.2m) ↔ 4ft (1.2m)

Spires of small violet-blue flowers open in
late summer and autumn, from gray-white
upright stems. These are all clothed with
deeply cut gray-green leaves.

Rosa glauca
REDLEAF ROSE
☼ 3   ↕ 6ft (2m) ↔ 6ft (2m)

Borne on reddish violet stems, the leaves
of this rose are glaucous purple in sun and
mauve-tinted gray-green in shade. Late
spring flowers are a bonus.

Salix exigua
COYOTE WILLOW
☼ 4   ↕ 12ft (4m) ↔ 5ft (1.5m)

This tall, upright shrub has long, flexuous
stems, each clothed with beautiful leaves,
narrow, silvery, and silky, ever shifting and
shimmering in the slightest breeze.

Santolina chamaecyparissus
LAVENDER COTTON
☼ 6   ↕ 30in (75cm) ↔ 3ft (1m)

Narrow, aromatic, woolly whitish leaves
crowd this evergreen shrub, forming a low,
dense dome. Long-stalked, buttonlike
yellow flowerheads occur in summer.

223

Shrubs with Purple, Red, or Bronze Leaves

PURPLE OR REDDISH foliage in spring or summer can be extremely useful in the garden, providing that it is not overused. These relatively somber colors are particularly effective when contrasted with silver or gray foliage; even more dramatic effects can be achieved when they are placed alongside plants with yellow or gold foliage.

Berberis thunbergii 'Red Chief'
JAPANESE BARBERRY
☀ 5   ↕ 1.2m (4ft) ↔ 1.2m (4ft)

'Red Chief' is a vigorous, upright or vase-shaped shrub, spreading as it matures. It has bright red, arching shoots and narrow, glossy-topped, red-purple leaves.

Acer palmatum 'Garnet'
JAPANESE MAPLE
☀ 5   ↕ 12ft (4m) ↔ 12ft (4m)

This strong-growing shrub, with an open, spreading habit, has slender, dark shoots clothed in large, deep garnet red leaves with finely cut lobes. Dislikes dry soils.

Corylus maxima 'Purpurea'
PURPLE-LEAF FILBERT
☀ 5   ↕ 20ft (6m) ↔ 20ft (6m)

Vase-shaped at first, spreading later, this popular form of filbert is planted for its large, deep purple leaves. Purplish catkins drape branches in late winter.

Acer palmatum 'Red Pygmy'
JAPANESE MAPLE
☀ 5   ↕ 5ft (1.5m) ↔ 4ft (1.2m)

The dark purple leaves of this densely branched, slow-growing shrub turn green with age. Leaves on mature plants differ from the juvenile leaves shown here.

Berberis thunbergii 'Atropurpurea Nana'
JAPANESE BARBERRY
☀ 5   ↕ 24in (60cm) ↔ 24in (60cm)

This dwarf, dome-shaped shrub of dense, twiggy habit has small, rounded, reddish purple leaves and is particularly suitable for growing in a rock garden.

Cotinus coggygria 'Royal Purple'
SMOKE TREE
☀ 5   ↕↔ 4m (12ft)

One of the most striking shrubs for foliage, this will form a dense mound of rounded, deep red-purple leaves. Plumes of tiny, smoky pink flowers appear in summer.

Hebe 'Amy'
HEBE
☼ 9   ↕ 3ft (1m) ↔ 3ft (1m)

The glossy, dark coppery purple leaves of this small, rounded evergreen shrub turn green in time. Rich violet-purple flowers are borne in short spikes in summer.

OTHER EVERGREEN SHRUBS WITH PURPLE, RED, OR BRONZE LEAVES

Leucothoe 'Scarletta'
Nandina domestica 'Nana Purpurea'
Photinia serrulata
Pieris formosa var. *forrestii*

Pittosporum tenuifolium 'Tom Thumb'
PITTOSPORUM
☼ 9   ↕ 24in (60cm) ↔ 24in (60cm)

The dark shoots of this dome-shaped dwarf evergreen shrub are crowded with shining, crinkly-edged leaves of a deep reddish purple, which emerge green.

Prunus x *cistena*
PURPLE-LEAF SAND CHERRY
☼ 2   ↕ 5ft (1.5m) ↔ 5ft (1.5m)

Purple-leaf Sand Cherry is a small, erect shrub with glossy leaves, red at first, maturing to deep reddish purple. Small blush white flowers appear in spring.

Prunus spinosa 'Purpurea'
PURPLE-LEAF SLOE
☼ 5   ↕ 12ft (4m) ↔ 12ft (4m)

This is a dense, bushy shrub or small tree, with spiny branches and bright red leaves that change to a deep reddish purple. Small, pale pink flowers open in spring.

OTHER DECIDUOUS SHRUBS WITH PURPLE, RED, OR BRONZE LEAVES

Acer palmatum 'Bloodgood'
Hibiscus acetosella 'Red Shield'
Itea virginica 'Henry's Garnet'
Weigela florida 'Minuet'

Prunus cerasifera 'Hessei'
PURPLE-LEAF PLUM
☼ 5   ↕ 12ft (4m) ↔ 12ft (4m)

In spring, snow white blossoms precede the leaves, which emerge green and then turn bronze-purple with cream or pink variegation. Bushy form of the cherry plum.

Sambucus nigra 'Guincho Purple'
PURPLE-LEAF ELDER
☼ 6   ↕ 12ft (4m) ↔ 12ft (4m)

The deeply divided leaves of this vigorous shrub are green at first, maturing to dark purple, then red in autumn. Its pink-budded summer flowers open white.

225

Shrubs with Colorful Foliage in Autumn

GIVEN FAVORABLE CONDITIONS, many deciduous shrubs will produce colorful tints before their leaves are shed in autumn; those here have been chosen for their quality and reliability. The impact of a group of shrubs in autumn color is spectacular, but even a single well-selected and sited shrub can provide eye-catching effects in a small garden.

Cotinus coggygria 'Flame'
SMOKE BUSH
☼ 5   ↕12ft (4m) ↔12ft (4m)

Strong-growing and bushy, this shrub has clouds of purplish pink summer flowers. Its bold leaves turn fiery orange and red in autumn. The sap may cause a rash.

OTHER SHRUBS WITH COLORFUL
FOLIAGE IN AUTUMN

Aronia arbutifolia, see p.202
Chionanthus virginicus, see p.178
Enkianthus perulatus
Itea virginica
Lindera benzoin
Rhododendron schlippenbachii
Rhus copallina
Spiraea prunifolia
Vaccinium corymbosum, see p.203
Viburnum dentatum

Berberis thunbergii
JAPANESE BARBERRY
☼ 5   ↕5ft (1.4m) ↔5ft (1.4m)

Arching, thorny branches are clothed with small leaves, orange and red in autumn. Small yellow flowers are produced in spring, and scarlet berries follow in autumn.

Acer palmatum var. *heptalobum*
JAPANESE MAPLE
☼ ☼ 5   ↕20ft (6m) ↔20ft (6m)

Most Japanese maples are worth growing for their impressive autumn tints. The large, seven-lobed green leaves of this one turn red or orange-red. Dislikes dry soils.

Callicarpa japonica
BEAUTYBERRY
☼ 5   ↕4½ft (1.4m) ↔4½ft (1.4m)

The leaves of this shrub turn yellowish to purplish or pinkish lavender in autumn. When planted in groups, violet berries are usually produced at the same time.

Disanthus cercidifolius
DISANTHUS
☼ 6 ᴾᴴ   ↕10ft (3m) ↔10ft (3m)

This spreading shrub is grown principally for its rounded blue-green leaves. During autumn, they turn a rich wine purple, then crimson and orange. Dislikes dry soils.

Ribes odoratum
CLOVE CURRANT
☼ ☀ 5   ↕ 6ft (2m) ↔ 5ft (1.5m)

This open-habited shrub has upright stems
loosely clothed with lobed and rounded
leaves that turn red and purple in autumn.
Golden spring flowers are clove-scented.

Euonymus alatus
BURNING BUSH
☼ ☀ 4   ↕ 6ft (2m) ↔ 10ft (3m)

This spectacular shrub turns brilliant
shades of pink and crimson in autumn.
The green twigs have curious corky-
winged projections along their length.

Fothergilla gardenii
FOTHERGILLA
☼ ☀ 5 PH ⤓   ↕ 3ft (1m) ↔ 3ft (1m)

Although the small white flowerheads in
spring are pretty enough, autumn leaves in
brilliant orange, red, and purple are surely
this plant's most impressive feature.

Hamamelis vernalis 'Sandra'
VERNAL WITCH HAZEL
☼ ☀ 5 PH ⤓   ↕ 10ft (3m) ↔ 10ft (3m)

Young purple leaves mature green, then
become yellow, orange, red, and purple in
autumn. Tiny, crowded, spidery, scented
yellow flowers follow in late winter.

**EVERGREEN SHRUBS WITH
COLORFUL FOLIAGE IN WINTER**

Calluna vulgaris 'Blazeaway'
Eurya japonica 'Winter Wine'
Mahonia aquifolium, see p.233
Nandina domestica 'Fire Power'

S H R U B S

Shrubs with Fragrant Flowers

W̶HEN PRESENTED with a lovely flower, most people will instinctively take a sniff, assuming that a pleasing scent accompanies a beautiful blossom. Sadly, this is not always the case. Numerous shrubs do have fragrant flowers, though, and these include some whose fragrance is far more noticeable or appealing than the appearance of the flower itself.

Coronilla valentina subsp. *glauca*
CORONILLA
☼ 8   ↕ 4½ft (1.4m) ↔ 4½ft (1.4m)

The leaves of this bushy evergreen are blue-green and fleshy. Clusters of small yellow pea flowers continue from winter into early summer.

Acacia dealbata
MIMOSA, SILVER WATTLE
☼ 10 PH   ↕ 20ft (6m) ↔ 20ft (6m)

Popular with florists, this fast-growing evergreen has feathery blue-green leaves and plumes of bright yellow flower-heads from winter into spring.

Carpenteria californica
CARPENTERIA
☼ 8   ↕ 6ft (2m) ↔ 6ft (2m)

The evergreen leaves of this bushy shrub are leathery and dark green, and the bark is papery and peeling. Its summer flowers are white with yellow centers.

Daphne x *burkwoodii* 'Somerset'
DAPHNE
☼ 5   ↕ 4ft (1.2m) ↔ 4ft (1.2m)

This narrow-leaved, bushy shrub is one of the best daphnes for general cultivation. In late spring, it is plastered with clusters of small, starry pink and white flowers.

Buddleia 'West Hill'
BUTTERFLY BUSH
☼ 6-7   ↕ 10ft (3m) ↔ 10ft (3m)

This vigorous shrub, with softly hairy, pointed, gray-green leaves, bears tapered plumes of tubular, orange-eyed, lilac-blue flowers from summer into autumn.

Choisya ternata
MEXICAN ORANGE-BLOSSOM
☼ ☀ 8   ↕ 6ft (2m) ↔ 6ft (2m)

This good-looking evergreen forms a dense mound of glossy, aromatic leaves. White flowers are freely borne in late spring and again, less abundantly, in autumn.

OTHER HARDY SHRUBS WITH FRAGRANT FLOWERS

Buxus microphylla
Calycanthus floridus
Chimonanthus praecox
Chionanthus virginicus, see p.178
Clethra alnifolia, see p.202
Daphne cneorum
Elaeagnus multiflora
Fothergilla gardenii, see p.227
Hamamelis, many
Lavandula, many
Lonicera fragrantissima
Philadelphus, many
Rhododendron arborescens
Rhododendron 'Narcissiflorum', see p.193
Ribes odoratum, see p.227
Rosa, many
Sarcococca hookeriana var. *humilis*
Viburnum carlesii

Erica arborea var. *alpina*
TREE HEATH
☼ 7 PH ⏚   ↕ 6ft (2m) ↔ 6ft (2m)

Bright green, needlelike evergreen leaves
crowd this dense, compact, upright shrub.
Plumes of tiny, honey-scented flowers are
produced in spring.

Osmanthus x *burkwoodii*
OSMANTHUS
☼ 7   ↕ 10ft (3m) ↔ 10ft (3m)

This strong-growing, compact evergreen
shrub is densely packed with small, dark
green, leathery leaves, and carries masses
of small white flowers in spring.

**OTHER LESS-HARDY SHRUBS
WITH FRAGRANT FLOWERS**

Brunfelsia pauciflora
Buddleia asiatica
Citrus, many
Clerodendrum trichotomum, see p.178
Cytisus battandieri, see p.164
Daphne odora 'Aureomarginata',
   see p.214
Edgeworthia chrysantha
Elaeagnus pungens 'Maculata',
   see p.214
Euphorbia mellifera
Gardenia augusta
Hoheria lyalii
Itea ilicifolia, see p.165
Michelia figo
Myrtus communis
Osmanthus fragrans
Pittosporum tobira

Syringa vulgaris
'Madame Antoine Buchner'
☼ 4   ↕ 12ft (4m) ↔ 12ft (4m)

Upright at first, this bushy shrub spreads
with maturity. Pink-mauve flowers, in
magnificent crowded heads, are purple-
red in bud and open in midspring.

Rhododendron luteum
YELLOW AZALEA
☼ 6 PH ⏚   ↕ 8ft (2.5m) ↔ 8ft (2.5m)

Rounded trusses of funnel-shaped flowers
in spring are a lovely yellow color. Rich
green leaves turn to shades of crimson,
purple, and orange in autumn.

Viburnum x *carlcephalum*
VIBURNUM
☼ 5   ↕ 10ft (3m) ↔ 10ft (3m)

This vigorous, bushy shrub bears white
flowers, pink in bud, in rounded and
crowded heads in spring. Its dark green
leaves sometimes color richly in autumn.

SHRUBS

229

Shrubs with Aromatic Leaves

GARDENERS ARE NORMALLY aware of fragrance in flowers, but the aroma of foliage is all too often neglected. The leaves of many shrubs are aromatic, but for most the scent is subtle and detectable only when leaves are bruised. Some, such as the gummy leaves of cistus, are more obvious when it is hot and sunny.

Rosmarinus officinalis 'Roseus'
ROSEMARY

☼ 8   ↕ 5ft (1.5m) ↔ 5ft (1.5m)

Of dense habit when pruned, this is a pink-flowered version of a popular evergreen. Narrow leaves crowd its stems, as do the flowers in late spring and early summer.

Cistus ladanifer
GUM CISTUS

☼ 8   ↕ 4ft (1.2m) ↔ 4ft (1.2m)

The narrow, willowlike, dark green leaves of this evergreen shrub are coated, like the branches, in a sticky, aromatic gum. Large white flowers appear in summer.

Elsholtzia stauntonii
MINT BUSH

☼ 5   ↕ 5ft (1.5m) ↔ 5ft (1.5m)

This bushy subshrub has sharply toothed leaves that smell of mint when bruised. Dense spikes of mauve flowers are carried in late summer and early autumn.

Salvia microphylla 'Kew Red'
LITTLELEAF SAGE

☼ 7   ↕ 4ft (1.2m) ↔ 3ft (1m)

The slender, upright stems of this bushy shrub are clothed with apple green leaves. Spikes of brilliant scarlet flowers are borne from summer into early autumn.

OTHER DECIDUOUS SHRUBS WITH AROMATIC LEAVES

Aloysia triphylla, see p.212
Artemisia abrotanum
Comptonia peregrina
Myrica pensylvanica

Prostanthera cuneata
PROSTANTHERA

☼ 9   ↕ 3ft (1m) ↔ 4½ft (1.4m)

The branches of this shrub are crowded with tiny, glossy, dark green leaves that smell of wintergreen. It produces masses of white flowers in spring.

OTHER EVERGREEN SHRUBS WITH AROMATIC LEAVES

Buxus sempervirens
Choisya ternata, see p.228
Eucalyptus, several
Helichrysum italicum, see p.223
Illicium anisatum, see p.166
Laurus nobilis
Lavandula angustifolia 'Imperial Gem'
Myrtus communis
Santolina chamaecyparissus, see p.223
Thymus vulgaris, see p.235

Shrubs with Ornamental Fruit

Most shrubs with ornamental fruit, especially the many kinds that bear edible berries, bring a welcome touch of color to the garden and provide birds and small animals with a useful source of food. Many fruit freely, but some need to be planted in groups to ensure pollination, while others require a male to pollinate a group of berry-bearing females.

Ilex x *meserveae* 'Blue Princess'
BLUE HOLLY
☼ ◑ 5   ↕10ft (3m) ↔4ft (1.2m)

This is a dense, upright evergreen with spiny, purple-tinged leaves. Red berries are freely borne if its spring flowers are pollinated by those of a male form.

OTHER SHRUBS WITH ORNAMENTAL FRUIT

Ilex verticillata
Pyracantha coccinea
Symplocos paniculata
Viburnum dilatatum
Viburnum opulus 'Xanthocarpum'

Callicarpa bodinieri var. *giraldii*
BEAUTYBERRY
☼ 7   ↕7ft (2.2m) ↔6ft (2m)

Clusters of small, bright mauve or pale violet berries are borne in autumn, when the leaves are mauve-tinted. Plant several together for good pollination.

Euonymus hamiltonianus 'Red Elf'
SPINDLE
☼ ◑ 5   ↕ ↔10ft (3m)

Upright at first, this strong-growing shrub spreads with age. It is grown mainly for the clusters of deep pink capsules that split to reveal orange seeds in autumn.

Cotoneaster frigidus 'Fructu Luteo'
TREE COTONEASTER
☼ ◑ 7   ↕20ft (6m) ↔20ft (6m)

This large, strong-growing shrub or small, multistemmed tree has bold foliage, white flowers in summer, and bunches of long-lasting yellow berries in autumn.

Gaultheria mucronata 'Wintertime'
PERNETTYA
☼ 7 PH   ↕3ft (1m) ↔4ft (1.2m)

If you include a male plant in a group for good pollination, this suckering evergreen will bear white berries from autumn into winter. Forms dense clumps in time.

Viburnum wrightii var. *hessei*
VIBURNUM
☼ ◑ 5   ↕3ft (1m) ↔3ft (1m)

Heads of small white flowers are produced in early summer, and form bunches of red berries in autumn. The broad, veined leaves often color richly in autumn.

Shrubs that Provide Berries for Birds

ANY WOULD SAY A GARDEN is incomplete without the presence of birds, be they residents or just regular visitors. Songbirds are particularly desirable. In spring and summer there is plenty of food to attract them, but in autumn and winter it can be scarce. Entice birds to visit by planting some shrubs that produce reliable crops of berries.

Cotoneaster frigidus 'Cornubia'
COTONEASTER
☀ ☀ 7   ↕ 20ft (6m) ↔ 20ft (6m)

This strong-growing semievergreen shrub has clusters of tiny white flowers in early summer, and ample bunches of large red berries from autumn into early winter.

Cotoneaster sternianus
COTONEASTER
☀ ☀ 6   ↕ 10ft (3m) ↔ 10ft (3m)

The branches of this evergreen or semi-evergreen shrub are clothed with small gray-green leaves, and covered in autumn with clusters of orange-red berries.

Crataegus schraderiana
HAWTHORN
☀ ☀ 6   ↕ 15ft (5m) ↔ 15ft (5m)

Masses of white flowers cover this large shrub or small tree in late spring or early summer. The blooms are followed by drooping clusters of dark purple-red berries.

Ilex aquifolium 'J.C. van Tol'
VAN TOL'S ENGLISH HOLLY
☀ ☀ 6   ↕ 20ft (6m) ↔ 12ft (4m)

This extremely useful holly carries few-spined leaves and red berries that crowd the purple shoots in winter. It will fruit even when no male plant is present.

OTHER LARGE SHRUBS THAT PROVIDE BERRIES FOR BIRDS

Amelanchier x *grandiflora*
Aralia spinosa
Aronia arbutifolia
Berberis koreana
Cornus mas, see p.236
Cornus racemosa
Cotoneaster multiflorus
Elaeagnus multiflora
Photinia villosa, see p.303
Rosa, many
Rubus spectabilis
Sambucus canadensis
Sambucus racemosa
Viburnum opulus, see p.203

Leycesteria formosa
HIMALAYAN HONEYSUCKLE
☀ ☀ 7   ↕ 6ft (2m) ↔ 5ft (1.5m)

An upright shrub (or subshrub in colder climates), this carries drooping clusters of white flowers with claret-colored bracts in summer. Reddish purple berries follow.

Lonicera xylosteum
EUROPEAN FLY HONEYSUCKLE
☀ ☀ 4   ↕ 10ft (3m) ↔ 10ft (3m)

Strong-growing and bushy, this shrub has spreading or arching branches and bears creamy white flowers in spring or early summer, followed by red berries.

Mahonia aquifolium
OREGON GRAPE
☀ ☀ ☀ 5   ↕ 3ft (1m) ↔ 5ft (1.5m)

The glossy green leaves of this dense, low evergreen shrub are prickly. Its bloomy blue-black berries are preceded in spring by crowded yellow flower clusters.

Sambucus nigra
ELDERBERRY
☀ ☀ 6   ↕ 20ft (6m) ↔ 20ft (6m)

This European elderberry produces flattened heads of fragrant, creamy white flowers in early summer, followed by its heavy bunches of tiny black berries.

Prunus laurocerasus 'Castlewellan'
VARIEGATED CHERRY LAUREL
☀ ☀ 6-7   ↕ 15ft (5m) ↔ 15ft (5m)

Dense and compact, this bright-foliaged evergreen has green- and cream-marbled leaves. White flower spikes in late spring are followed by shining black fruits.

OTHER SMALL SHRUBS THAT PROVIDE BERRIES FOR BIRDS

Aronia melanocarpa
Berberis thunbergii
Cotoneaster apiculatus
Cotoneaster horizontalis
Daphne mezereum
Gaultheria mucronata
Gaultheria shallon
Hedera helix 'Arborescens', see p.234
Mahonia nervosa, see p.201
Malus sargentii 'Tina'
Myrica pensylvanica
Ribes odoratum, see p.237
Rosa nitida
Vaccinium corymbosum, see p.203
Vaccinium parvifolium
Vaccinium vitis-idaea Koralle Group
Viburnum acerifolium
Viburnum nudum

Viburnum opulus 'Compactum'
COMPACT SNOWBALL BUSH
☀ ☀ 4   ↕ 5ft (1.5m) ↔ 5ft (1.5m)

The maplelike leaves of this dense shrub color richly in autumn, when its bunches of bright red berries appear. Lacecap heads of white flowers open in spring.

S H R U B S

233

Shrubs Attractive to Butterflies

FLOWERING SHRUBS that appeal to butterflies offer a bonus that few gardeners would wish to ignore. Many are also sweetly scented. The nectar of their flowers is attractive to butterflies, as well as to a host of other beneficial insects, including hoverflies and bees. All these industrious creatures help make the garden a more interesting and lively place.

Buddleia davidii 'Peace'
BUTTERFLY BUSH
☼ 6   ↕ 12ft (4m) ↔ 12ft (4m)

Buddleias come in many colors and are among the most popular plants with bees and butterflies. 'Peace' has fragrant white flower spikes from summer into autumn.

Calluna vulgaris 'Anthony Davis'
HEATHER, LING
☼ 5 PH   ↕ 18in (45cm) ↔ 20in (50cm)

This fine, bushy heather is crowded with gray-green evergreen foliage. Long sprays of white flowers are produced from late summer into early autumn.

Escallonia 'Donard Seedling'
ESCALLONIA
☼ 8   ↕ 3m (10ft) ↔ 3m (10ft)

A favorite in milder climates, this shrub has arching stems, each densely clothed in glossy evergreen leaves. Masses of pale pink buds open white or blush in summer.

Hebe albicans
HEBE
☼ 9   ↕ 24in (60cm) ↔ 3ft (1m)

In summer, spikes crowded with white flowers grow from the upper leaf axils of this dwarf, mounded, compact hebe. Its evergreen leaves are blue-green.

Hedera helix 'Arborescens'
TREE IVY
☼ ☼ ☀ 6   ↕ 4½ft (1.4m) ↔ 6ft (2m)

This ivy forms a dense evergreen mound of glossy leaves. Heads of brownish green flowers in autumn are a veritable honey pot for late-flying insects.

Lavandula angustifolia 'Hidcote'
LAVENDER
☼ 6   ↕ 24in (60cm) ↔ 30in (75cm)

In summer, long-stalked spikes with small, fragrant violet flowers rise above the narrow gray-green leaves of this aromatic evergreen. A deservedly popular plant.

Pyracantha 'Watereri'
FIRETHORN
☼ ☼ 7   ↕ 8ft (2.5m) ↔ 8ft (2.5m)

The spreading branches of this vigorous evergreen bear narrow, glossy, dark green leaves. White flower clusters occur in early summer, and red berries in autumn.

Rubus 'Benenden'
FLOWERING RASPBERRY
☼ 5   ↕ 10ft (3m) ↔ 10ft (3m)

The strong, upright stems of this shrub are arching and eventually wide-spreading. Lovely flowers, like small white roses, are borne in late spring and early summer.

Syringa x *hyacinthiflora* 'Esther Staley'
EARLY LILAC
☼ 3   ↕ 12ft (4m) ↔ 10ft (3m)

Upright at first, and spreading later, this is a strong-growing, bushy shrub. Striking, dense heads of fragrant lilac-pink flowers appear in spring.

OTHER SMALL SHRUBS ATTRACTIVE TO BUTTERFLIES

Caryopteris x *clandonensis*
  'Arthur Simmonds', see p.182
Lavandula stoechas
Salvia greggii

OTHER LARGE SHRUBS ATTRACTIVE TO BUTTERFLIES

Abelia x *grandiflora*
Amorpha canescens
Aralia spinosa
Buddleia 'West Hill', see p.228
Ceanothus americanus
Clerodendrum bungei, see p.180
Clethra alnifolia, see p.202
Ligustrum sinense, see p.179
Syringa pubescens subsp. *microphylla*
  'Superba', see p.181

Ligustrum quihoui
PRIVET
☼ ☼ 6   ↕ 8ft (2.5m) ↔ 8ft (2.5m)

A most elegant privet, this has slender, arching branches, glossy evergreen leaves, and branched, conical heads of tiny white flowers from late summer into autumn.

Salvia officinalis
COMMON SAGE
☼ 6   ↕ 24in (60cm) ↔ 3ft (1m)

Sage is a popular culinary herb. It forms a mound of semievergreen, aromatic gray-green leaves, and produces spikes of two-lipped purple-blue flowers in late spring.

Thymus vulgaris
COMMON THYME
☼ 6   ↕ 12in (30cm) ↔ 10in (25cm)

Most often used in the herb garden, this dwarf subshrub has narrow, aromatic, gray-green leaves with slender spikes of pale purplish pink flowers all through summer.

SHRUBS

235

Late-winter-flowering Shrubs

FLOWERING SHRUBS are at no time more welcome and more valued than during the late winter months. This is partly due to their being few in number and, having fewer rivals, they command our full attention, particularly when planted where their flowers are easily seen against a darker background such as a wall or an evergreen hedge.

Daphne bholua 'Jacqueline Postill'
DAPHNE
☼ ☀ 9   ↕ 6ft (2m) ↔ 5ft (1.5m)

Best in a sheltered position, this vigorous, upright evergreen bears clusters of richly fragrant flowers that bloom over a long period. Dislikes dry soils.

Erica carnea 'Springwood White'
WINTER HEATH
☼ ☀ 3   ↕ 6in (15cm) ↔ 18in (45cm)

This reliable, scented evergreen shrublet forms a good, low groundcover with its dense, needlelike foliage. Spikes of small white bellflowers continue into spring.

Chimonanthus praecox 'Grandiflorus'
WINTERSWEET
☼ 6   ↕ 8ft (2.5m) ↔ 10ft (3m)

This large, slow-growing, spreading shrub is justly famous for its deliciously fragrant, small, cup-shaped flowers. These are pale yellow with a purple heart.

Cornus mas
CORNELIAN CHERRY
☼ ☀ 5   ↕ 15ft (5m) ↔ 15ft (5m)

The twigs of this broad, rounded shrub or small tree are studded with little clusters of tiny yellow flowers. These twigs are also useful for cutting to display inside.

OTHER LATE-WINTER-FLOWERING SHRUBS

Abeliophyllum distichum
Daphne odora 'Aureomarginata', see p.214
Garrya elliptica, see p.166
Hamamelis x *intermedia* 'Pallida'
Lonicera fragrantissima
Rhododendron dauricum
Skimmia japonica, see p.241
Stachyurus praecox
Viburnum farreri

Hamamelis x *intermedia* 'Jelena'
WITCH HAZEL
☼ ☀ 5 PH   ↕ 12ft (4m) ↔ 12ft (4m)

In autumn, the large, softly hairy leaves turn orange-red and scarlet, and in winter, spidery orange flowers densely crowd the bare twigs. Dislikes dry soils.

Sycopsis sinensis
SYCOPSIS
☼ ☀ [8]　　　↕ 15ft (5m) ↔ 12ft (4m)

This uncommon, erect evergreen shrub
carries glossy, dark green, pointed leaves
and produces compact clusters of tiny
flowers. Grows best in a sheltered site.

Viburnum x *bodnantense* 'Dawn'
WINTER-FLOWERING VIBURNUM
☼ ☀ [6]　　　↕ 10ft (3m) ↔ 8ft (2.5m)

From autumn all through to spring, the
leafless twigs of this reliable shrub are
studded with clusters of strongly fragrant
pink flowers, darker in bud.

Mahonia x *media* 'Buckland'
MAHONIA
☼ ☀ [8]　　　↕ 10ft (3m) ↔ 10ft (3m)

Erect at first, this big and bold evergreen
spreads with age. Long, cylindrical spikes
of tiny, fragrant yellow flowers are borne
above divided, prickle-toothed leaves.

Lonicera x *purpusii* 'Winter Beauty'
WINTER HONEYSUCKLE
☼ ☀ [5]　　　↕ 6ft (2m) ↔ 12ft (4m)

Vigorous, and with a spreading habit, this
honeysuckle is mainly grown for its small,
sweetly fragrant white flowers. These are
carried over a very long period.

Sarcococca hookeriana var. *digyna*
CHRISTMAS BOX, SWEET BOX
☼ ☀ ☀ [6]　　　↕ 4ft (1.2m) ↔ 3ft (1m)

This suckering evergreen in time forms
dense clumps of upright shoots. Clusters
of tiny, sweetly scented white flowers are
carried in the axils of its narrow leaves.

Viburnum tinus 'Eve Price'
LAURUSTINUS
☼ ☀ [9]　　　↕ 8ft (2.5m) ↔ 8ft (2.5m)

Heads of reddish buds open into many
white flowers with a subtle fragrance from
autumn onward. Neat and rounded, this
shrub has glossy, dark evergreen leaves.

SHRUBS

237

Shrubs with Ornamental Twigs in Winter

ORNAMENTAL FEATURES that enliven a garden in winter are most welcome. In addition to the indisputable attraction of winter flowers and evergreen foliage, the stems and twigs of many plants offer surprisingly decorative colors and forms. The dramatic effect of some, such as dogwood and willow, can be improved by hard pruning.

Cornus stolonifera 'Flaviramea'
GOLDEN-TWIGGED DOGWOOD
☼ ☀ 2   ↕ 6ft (2m) ↔ 10ft (3m)

The greenish yellow winter shoots of this vigorous suckering and layering shrub are brighter if regularly pruned and if in full sun. Leaves turn yellow in autumn.

Cornus alba 'Sibirica'
TATARIAN DOGWOOD
☼ ☀ 2   ↕ 6ft (2m) ↔ 6ft (2m)

This is among the best in cultivation for colored stems. It produces red winter shoots, and large summer leaves when pruned. These give rich autumn tints.

SHRUBS WITH ORNAMENTAL BARK FOR WINTER EFFECT

Abelia triflora
Clethra barbinervis
Deutzia scabra
Dipelta floribunda
Euonymus alatus, see p.227
Heptacodium miconioides
Physocarpus opulifolius
Prunus tomentosa
Rhododendron barbatum
Stephanandra tanakae

Cornus sanguinea 'Winter Beauty'
REDTWIG DOGWOOD
☼ ☀ 4   ↕ 5ft (1.5m) ↔ 6ft (2m)

With regular pruning, this shrub produces winter stems that are a fiery orange-yellow at the base, shading to pink and red at the tips. Leaves turn golden yellow in autumn.

Corylus avellana 'Contorta'
HARRY LAUDER'S WALKING STICK
☼ ☀ 5   ↕ 15ft (5m) ↔ 15ft (5m)

In late winter, charming lamb's-tail catkins enliven the coiled and twisted shoots of this strong-growing shrub.

OTHER COLORED-STEMMED SHRUBS FOR WINTER EFFECT

Cornus alba 'Kesselringii'
Cornus sericea 'Silver and Gold'
Hydrangea macrophylla 'Nigra'
Kerria japonica 'Pleniflora', see p.167
Leycesteria formosa, see p.232
Rosa sericea f. *pteracantha*
Rubus biflorus
Rubus thibetanus, see p.239
Salix alba subsp. *vitellina* 'Britzensis'
Salix irrorata

Shrubs with Spines or Thorny Branches

FOR MANY GARDENERS, shrubs whose stems or branches are spiny or thorny have a positive security value because they can deter prowlers and uninvited guests. Others find they are at best a nuisance, and at worst a danger. Whatever your attitude to plants that happen to be hostile to the touch, they undeniably include some very fine ornamental shrubs.

Rubus thibetanus
WHITE-STEMMED BRAMBLE
☼ ☼ 7   ↕ 8ft (2.5m) ↔ 10ft (3m)

Clumps of thorny, bloomy white, purple-barked winter stems become clothed with prettily divided, fernlike, silvery-hairy leaves. Small summer flowers are pink.

OTHER SHRUBS WITH SPINES OR THORNY BRANCHES
Berberis koreana
Chaenomeles, most
Poncirus trifoliata
Paliurus spina-christi
Pyracantha 'Mohave'
Robinia hispida
Rosa roxburghii
Rubus cockburnianus
Rubus ulmifolius 'Bellidiflorus'
Ulex europaeus 'Flore Pleno'

Berberis 'Goldilocks'
BARBERRY
☼ ☼ 8   ↕ 12ft (4m) ↔ 12ft (4m)

The stems and arching branches of this bushy evergreen are viciously spiny. It has shiny, dark green, prickle-toothed leaves, and golden yellow flowers in spring.

Pyracantha 'Orange Glow'
FIRETHORN
☼ ☼ 6 ❄   ↕ 12ft (4m) ↔ 12ft (4m)

This vigorous evergreen shrub has spiny branches, glossy green oblong leaves, clusters of white flowers in summer, and orange berries in autumn and winter.

Rosa rubiginosa
SWEET BRIAR, EGLANTINE
☼ 4   ↕ 8ft (2.5m) ↔ 8ft (2.5m)

The arching, thorny stems of this vigorous shrub are clothed in apple-scented leaves. It produces single pink flowers in summer, and small red hips in autumn.

Zanthoxylum piperitum
JAPAN PEPPER
☼ ☼ 6   ↕ 8ft (2.5m) ↔ 8ft (2.5m)

The erect, ascending, spiny stems of this bushy shrub bear aromatic, glossy green leaves that become yellow in autumn. Red fruits in autumn contain peppery seeds.

Rabbit-proof Shrubs

SHRUBS THAT RABBITS IGNORE are surely all worthy of consideration, particularly by gardeners in rural areas. It may be the taste of the leaves and shoots, or their texture, that is unpalatable to rabbits, but whatever it is, such plants are extremely valuable where these creatures are a problem. It may be assumed that most other forms of the shrubs featured here, as well as their immediate relatives, are also rabbitproof.

Hypericum kouytchense
SHRUBBY HYPERICUM
☼ 7   ↕ 30in (75cm) ↔ 4ft (1.2m)

From summer into autumn, the arching stems of this mounded semievergreen carry numerous yellow flowers. These are followed by bronze-red seed capsules.

Aucuba japonica
AUCUBA
☼ ☼ ☼ 7   ↕ 8ft (2.5m) ↔ 6ft (2m)

Long, pointed, glossy, dark green leaves cover this dense evergreen. Female plants produce red berries when pollinated by a male. Several forms exist, some variegated.

Fuchsia 'Tom Thumb'
FUCHSIA
☼ 8   ↕ 20in (50cm) ↔ 20in (50cm)

Dwarf and upright, this neat fuchsia has small, glossy green leaves and showers of charming, pendent red and purple flowers, through summer and into early autumn.

Kalmia angustifolia 'Rubra'
RED SHEEP LAUREL
☼ 2 PH ↕ 18in (45cm) ↔ 3ft (1m)

Red Sheep Laurel forms a low, bushy mound of narrow evergreen leaves. Clusters of small, deep red flowers are produced in early summer. Dislikes dry soils.

Buxus sempervirens 'Suffruticosa'
EDGING BOXWOOD
☼ 6   ↕ 30in (75cm) ↔ 30in (75cm)

All forms of boxwood are unpalatable to rabbits. This dense and compact cultivar has long been used as a low, evergreen edging to borders, as well as in parterres.

Gaultheria mucronata 'Mulberry Wine'
PERNETTYA
☼ 7 PH ↕ 3ft (1m) ↔ 3ft (1m)

This low evergreen with pointed, leathery leaves on wiry branches spreads in time. When pollinated by a male, large berries are borne from autumn through winter.

Rhododendron 'Strawberry Ice'
EXBURY AZALEA
☼ 6 PH ↕ 8ft (2.5m) ↔ 8ft (2.5m)

Showy clusters of yellow-throated, pale pink trumpet flowers are carried in spring. The leaves of this bushy azalea may color attractively before they fall in autumn.

Sambucus nigra   'Aurea'
GOLDEN ELDER
☼ 6   ↕ 12ft (4m) ↔ 4m (12ft)

This large, bushy shrub has golden yellow leaves, and bears flattened heads of tiny, fragrant white flowers in summer. Shining black berries follow in autumn.

Rosa Rosy Cushion ('Interall')
SHRUB ROSE
☼ 5-6   ↕ 3ft (1m) ↔ 4ft (1.2m)

Glossy green foliage offsets clusters of scented pink flowers with white centers throughout summer. A strong-growing rose, this is low, dense, and spreading.

DEERPROOF SHRUBS

Berberis thunbergii, see p.226
Buddleia davidii
Buxus sempervirens
Cornus alba
Euonymus alatus, see p.227
Lindera benzoin, see p.202
Pieris japonica, see p.181
Poncirus trifoliata
Robinia hispida, see p.165
Viburnum sargentii
Weigela florida

Skimmia japonica
SKIMMIA
☼ ◐ 7   ↕ 4ft (1.2m) ↔ 4ft (1.2m)

This bushy mound of aromatic evergreen leaves is dotted with white flower clusters in spring and, if both sexes are present, female plants then produce red berries.

OTHER RABBITPROOF SHRUBS

Ceanothus thyrsiflorus var. *repens*
Cornus sanguinea
Cotoneaster horizontalis
Daphne tangutica
Euonymus alatus
Poncirus trifoliata
Prunus laurocerasus 'Otto Luyken', see p.201
Spiraea japonica 'Anthony Waterer', see p.191
Vinca minor

Rosmarinus officinalis
ROSEMARY
☼ 7   ↕ 5ft (1.5m) ↔ 5ft (1.5m)

Rosemary is a popular, aromatic evergreen bush. Small, purplish blue flowers clothe the branches all through summer, along with its narrow gray-green leaves.

Ruscus aculeatus
BUTCHER'S BROOM
☼ ◐ 7   ↕ 30in (75cm) ↔ 3ft (1m)

Tough and adaptable, this evergreen shrub forms clumps of erect stems, crowded with spine-tipped leaves. If pollinated, the female plants produce long-lasting fruits.

SHRUBS

CONIFERS

ALL CONIFERS ARE EITHER trees or shrubs but, as is usual, I have chosen to treat them separately. They comprise a distinct and primitive group of woody plants and add an individual element to the garden. All but a few are evergreen. The deciduous kinds, specified in the descriptions, offer the interesting feature of autumn color.

△ Tsuga heterophylla

△ DOMED SPECIMEN Chamaecyparis pisifera *'Filifera Aurea' makes an ideal golden yellow specimen for a larger lawn.*

Conifers are extremely versatile due to their great variety in size, form, color, and texture. You can use them for countless effects and situations. Many are of such noble proportions and elegance of form that they can make magnificent specimens for important positions.

THE BEAUTY OF CONIFERS

- Large conifers are linchpins, giving a feeling of permanence to a garden.
- Offer a wonderfully wide selection of shapes, colors, and textures.
- Contribute evergreen foliage effects, especially valuable in winter.
- Deciduous foliage changes seasonally.
- Dwarf and slow-growing conifers are ideal for rock gardens, patios, screes.
- Provide shelter in the garden when used as screens, hedges, windbreaks.

DECORATIVE FOLIAGE

Conifer foliage tends to be either small and scalelike, as in cypress and *Thuja*, or long and needlelike, as in pine, spruce, and cedar. Junipers have needlelike or scale-like leaves and, in some cases, both. Yew has narrow, strap-shaped leaves, and many conifer cultivars have lovely mossy or soft, feathery juvenile foliage. Add to this all the shades of blue, green, and yellow,

as well as the interesting variegations, and it is obvious why conifers occupy such a special place among garden plants. Deciduous conifers, such as larch, *Metasequoia*, and *Ginkgo*, brighten autumn with a final flash of gold or yellow before their leaves fall.

TOO BIG, TOO SOON

As with broad-leaved trees, consider the vigor, ultimate height and shape, and intended purpose of your chosen conifer. Some species used as hedging, for instance, grow rapidly and require regular pruning to achieve the best results. Do not plant fast-growing hedges if you cannot maintain them – there are numerous small- to medium-sized conifers for limited space.

△ WINTER APPEAL *The rich reddish brown bark of deciduous* Metasequoia glyptostroboides *is impressive.*

◁ CONIFERS AND HEATHERS *This is an excellent example of the use of conifers with late-winter-flowering ericas.*

▷ COLOR AND TEXTURE *Just a few well-chosen conifers combine to create a colorful and extremely showy feature.*

Large Conifers

SOME OF THE MOST SPECTACULAR large trees in the world are conifers. Given the evergreen nature of all but a small minority, they bring a sense of permanence and continuity to the large garden or estate. Most conifers are comparatively long-lived. They generally thrive best on deep, moist, but well-drained soils, although they are remarkably adaptable to most sites. A handful are tolerant of wet sites, but few will survive in completely waterlogged conditions.

Cryptomeria japonica
JAPANESE RED CEDAR
☼ ☀ 6   ↕ 70ft (20m) ↔ 22ft (7m)

The narrow leaves of this columnar to conical tree are arranged spirally on the shoots. Fibrous bark is reddish brown, and its small green cones mature to brown.

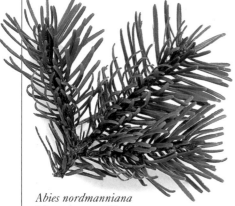

Abies nordmanniana
NORDMANN FIR
☼ ☀ 5   ↕ 80ft (25m) ↔ 28ft (9m)

The spreading branches of this columnar to conical fir are packed with slender green leaves. Erect, greenish brown cones appear in summer on the upper branches.

Cedrus libani
CEDAR OF LEBANON
☼ 6   ↕ 78ft (24m) ↔ 50ft (15m)

This conifer is a familiar sight in parks. Conical when young, it later assumes the typical flat-topped and tiered cedar habit. Sharp leaves are green to blue-green.

OTHER LARGE COLUMNAR OR
CONICAL CONIFERS

Abies concolor
Abies grandis
Abies magnifica
Araucaria heterophylla
Calocedrus decurrens
Cedrus atlantica 'Fastigiata'
Chamaecyparis lawsoniana 'Wisselii', see p.248
x *Cupressocyparis leylandii* 'Naylor's Blue'
Cupressus sempervirens
Juniperus virginiana 'Canaertii'
Metasequoia glyptostroboides, see p.252
Picea omorika
Picea orientalis
Pinus strobus 'Fastigiata'
Taxodium distichum var. *imbricatum* 'Nutans', see p.251

Araucaria araucana
MONKEY PUZZLE, CHILE PINE
☼ 7   ↕ 60ft (18m) ↔ 40ft (12m)

When young, this tree is conical, and has whorled branches to ground level. Finally, it is mop headed with a tall stem. Broad, sharp leaves densely clothe the branches.

Ginkgo biloba
GINKGO, MAIDENHAIR TREE
☼ ☀ 4   ↕ 70ft (20m) ↔ 22ft (7m)

This distinctive deciduous conifer has an ancient pedigree. Conical when young with rising branches, it later spreads. Fan-shaped leaves turn yellow in autumn.

Sequoia sempervirens
REDWOOD, COAST REDWOOD
☼ ☀ 8   ↕ 100ft (30m) ↔ 25ft (8m)

Conical when it is young, this distinctive conifer becomes columnar later. It has rich red, fibrous, spongy bark, and its branches are clothed with lush, yewlike foliage.

Picea abies
NORWAY SPRUCE
☼ ☀ 2   ↕ 80ft (25m) ↔ 22ft (7m)

Norway Spruce, a traditional Christmas tree, is conical at first, but broadens and spreads with age. Its layered branches are closely packed with dark green needles.

OTHER LARGE CONIFERS OF ULTIMATELY SPREADING HABIT

Cedrus atlantica f. *glauca*, see p.263
Cupressus macrocarpa, see p.254
Larix decidua
Larix x *marschlinsii*
Larix kaempferi
Larix x *pendula*
Picea sitchensis
Pinus ayacahuite
Pinus x *holfordiana*
Pinus muricata, see p.255
Pinus nigra, see p.257
Pinus radiata, see p.257
Pinus strobus, see p.252
Pinus sylvestris
Pinus wallichiana
Pseudotsuga menziesii
Tsuga canadensis, see p.251
Tsuga heterophylla, see p.253

Pinus jeffreyi
JEFFREY PINE
☼ 5   ↕ 70ft (20m) ↔ 28ft (9m)

This robust, distinguished pine is conical or rounded at first, then broad-columnar later. Its fissured bark is dark gray-brown, and its long needles are blue-green.

Sequoiadendron giganteum
GIANT SEQUOIA, GIANT REDWOOD
☼ 6   ↕ 100ft (30m) ↔ 35ft (11m)

Renowned worldwide for its longevity, this species will form a tall column of down-curved branches clothed with blue-green foliage. Bark is reddish brown.

Wide-spreading and Vase-shaped Conifers

CONIFERS WITH ASCENDING or wide-spreading branches, ultimately wider than they are high, are numerous. They make excellent single specimens where a severe or formal line, such as the straight edge of a long border, needs to be broken or softened. Alternatively, consider them as a feature in a lawn, where their full spread can be admired.

Cupressus macrocarpa 'Gold Spread'
MONTEREY CYPRESS
☼ 7   ↕ 3ft (1m) ↔ 8ft (2.5m)

This ornamental form of the Monterey Cypress is low and compact. Horizontal or slightly ascending branches are densely crowded with bright yellow foliage.

Juniperus x *pfitzeriana* 'Blue and Gold'
JUNIPER
☼ 4   ↕ 5ft (1.5m) ↔ 5ft (1.5m)

The stems crowding the base of this choice juniper are packed with intense blue-gray foliage, scattered with sprays of creamy yellow. Whole shoots can be creamy yellow.

Juniperus x *pfitzeriana*
'Pfitzeriana Glauca'
☼ 4   ↕ 6ft (2m) ↔ 12ft (4m)

'Pfitzeriana Glauca' is a strong-growing juniper of dense habit, whose ascending and spreading stems are densely crowded with prickly blue-gray foliage.

Juniperus chinensis
'Expansa Variegata'
☼ 5   ↕ 30in (75cm) ↔ 6ft (2m)

Low and wide-spreading, this vigorous juniper has virtually horizontal branches crowded with prickly, bluish green foliage, interspersed with creamy white sprays.

Juniperus x *pfitzeriana*
'Pfitzeriana Aurea'
☼ 4   ↕ 6ft (2m) ↔ 12ft (4m)

The terminal shoots and closely packed foliage of this strong-growing juniper are suffused golden yellow in summer, and become yellowish green in winter.

Juniperus x *chinensis* 'Plumosa Aurea'
JUNIPER
☼ 4   ↕ 5ft (1.5m) ↔ 6ft (2m)

The many stems of this compact juniper are crowded with plumelike sprays, each crammed with yellow, scalelike foliage that turns bronze-gold in winter.

C O N I F E R S

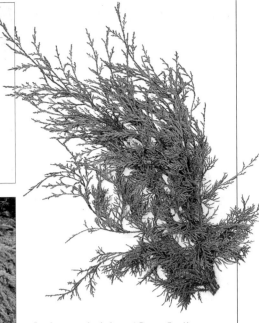

OTHER WIDE-SPREADING
CONIFERS

Cephalotaxus harringtonia
 'Duke Gardens'
Cephalotaxus harringtonia 'Prostrata'
Chamaecyparis lawsoniana
 'Tamariscifolia'
Picea abies 'Tabuliformis'
Picea bicolor 'Howell's Dwarf'
Pinus strobus 'Prostrata'
Taxus baccata 'Repandens'
Torreya californica 'Spreadeagle'

Juniperus squamata 'Blue Carpet'
SINGLESEED JUNIPER

☼ 5 ↕ 12in (30cm) ↔ 6ft (2m)

The wide-spreading stems of this vigorous
juniper form a large, low carpet of prickly
glaucous blue foliage. It is one of the most
effective plants of its kind.

Juniperus virginiana 'Grey Owl'
EASTERN RED CEDAR

☼ 3 ↕ 8ft (2.5m) ↔ 12ft (4m)

A handsome and strong-growing juniper,
this has ascending branches densely
clothed with soft, silvery gray foliage. A
most effective, and ultimately large, shrub.

OTHER WIDE-SPREADING JUNIPERS

Juniperus chinensis 'Blaauw'
Juniperus chinensis 'Kaizuka'
Juniperus chinensis 'Maney'
Juniperus chinensis 'Mint Julep'
Juniperus x *pfitzeriana* 'Gold Coast'
Juniperus x *pfitzeriana* 'Old Gold'
Juniperus x *pfitzeriana* 'Sulphur Spray'
Juniperus x *pfitzeriana* 'Wilhelm Pfitzer'
Juniperus virginiana 'Blue Cloud'
Juniperus virginiana 'Hetzii'

Juniperus sabina 'Tamariscifolia'
SAVIN JUNIPER

☼ 4 ↕ 3ft (1m) ↔ 6ft (2m)

This effective and low-growing form of
the Savin Juniper produces close-packed
layers of spreading branches, each densely
clothed in bright green, prickly leaves.

OTHER WEEPING, WIDE-
SPREADING CONIFERS

Cedrus deodara 'Pendula'
Cedrus atlantica 'Glauca Pendula'
Larix kaempferi 'Pendula'
Microbiota decussata, see p.260

Taxus baccata 'Dovastonii Aurea'
ENGLISH YEW

☼ ☼ 6 ↕ 15ft (5m) ↔ 20ft (6m)

This elegant shrub or small tree has tiers
of horizontal branches and long, sweeping
branchlets. Leaves on golden shoots have
bright yellow margins. Non-fruiting.

CONIFERS

247

Columnar or Narrowly Conical Conifers

SLENDER OR NARROW CROWNS are great assets in conifers, because they can be planted in restricted spaces. Their generally compact nature means that they very rarely, if ever, need to be pruned. Their strong, vertical lines make them ideal for breaking or lifting otherwise low plantings. They also provide a striking focal point.

Austrocedrus chilensis
CHILEAN CEDAR
☀ 9   ↕ 40ft (12m) ↔ 10ft (3m)

The short, ascending branches of this uncommon, dense conifer are clothed in feathery sprays of green or blue-green, scalelike foliage. Small terminal cones.

OTHER COLUMNAR CONIFERS

Calocedrus decurrens
Cupressus sempervirens
 'Swane's Gold', see p.262
Juniperus chinensis 'Aurea'
Juniperus communis 'Compressa'
Juniperus virginiana 'Glauca'
Sequoiadendron giganteum 'Glaucum'
Taxus baccata 'Standishii'
Taxus × media 'Flushing'
Thuja occidentalis 'Holmstrup'
Thuja occidentalis 'Spiralis'

OTHER COLUMNAR CYPRESSES

Chamaecyparis lawsoniana
 'Alumii Magnificent'
C. lawsoniana 'Blom'
C. lawsoniana 'Columnaris'
C. lawsoniana 'Fraseri'
C. lawsoniana 'Grayswood Pillar'
C. lawsoniana 'Green Pillar', see p.256
C. lawsoniana 'Hillieri'
C. lawsoniana 'Kilmacurragh'
C. lawsoniana 'Pottenii'
C. lawsoniana 'Winston Churchill'

Chamaecyparis lawsoniana 'Wisselii'
LAWSON CYPRESS
☀ 6   ↕ 50ft (15m) ↔ 10ft (3m)

A distinctive form of Lawson cypress, this has erect, close-packed branches and blue-green foliage in three-dimensional sprays. Tiny cones in spring are brick red.

Cupressus sempervirens Stricta Group
ITALIAN CYPRESS
☀ 8   ↕ 50ft (15m) ↔ 10ft (3m)

The gray-green, scalelike leaves that form this characteristic narrow column are held in erect sprays. Fairly large, shiny gray-brown cones ripen in their second year.

Juniperus chinensis 'Keteleeri'
CHINESE JUNIPER
☀ 4   ↕ 50ft (15m) ↔ 15ft (5m)

This columnar to narrowly conical tree of dense, compact habit has closely packed sprays of gray-green, scalelike foliage. Excellent and reliable for formal planting.

Juniperus communis 'Hibernica'
IRISH JUNIPER
☼ 4　　　‡ 12ft (4m) ↔ 20in (50cm)

This juniper forms a dense, slender column composed of crowded, needlelike leaves. Each of these has a fine silver line on its inside face.

Pinus omorika
SERBIAN SPRUCE
☼ ☀ 4　　　‡ 60ft (18m) ↔ 15ft (5m)

The downswept branches of this spirelike spruce arch at their tips and are crowded with narrow, dark green leaves. Clusters of long purple cones mature to brown.

Taxus baccata 'Fastigiata Robusta'
ENGLISH YEW
☼ ☀ 6　　　‡ 30ft (10m) ↔ 5ft (1.5m)

In habit, this yew is erect, columnar, and eventually cigar-shaped, with ascending, close-packed branches. Narrow, dark green leaves are arranged all around the shoots.

Juniperus scopulorum 'Skyrocket'
ROCKY MOUNTAIN JUNIPER
☼ 4　　　‡ 25ft (8m) ↔ 30in (75cm)

One of the narrowest of all conifers, this is a tall, slender, columnar juniper with a compact habit. Crowded sprays of blue-gray, scalelike foliage pack the branches.

Pinus sylvestris Fastigiata Group
SCOTS PINE
☼ 2　　　‡ 20ft (6m) ↔ 3ft (1m)

This is a columnar form of the Scots pine. The bark is reddish brown and its erect, close-packed branches are clothed with blue-green needles. Dislikes exposed sites.

Thuja occidentalis 'Smaragd'
AMERICAN ARBORVITAE
☼ ☀ 2　　　‡ 8ft (2.5m) ↔ 30in (75cm)

The branches of this dense, narrowly conical conifer are clothed with flattened sprays of rich green foliage, which has a pleasant "fruity" scent when bruised.

CONIFERS

Medium-sized Conifers

A WIDE SELECTION of conifers exists in the height range of 20–50ft (6–15m), including many wild species that have both botanical interest and ornamental merit. Even more abundant are the numerous cultivars of conifers such as the Lawson Cypress, Hinoki Cypress, and Arborvitae (*Thuja* species). Any of these is worth considering in all but very small gardens. Most are rather hardy, but those that are less so will grow happily in milder areas or in a sheltered site.

Cupressus cashmeriana
KASHMIR CYPRESS
☼ ☀ 9   ↕ 40ft (12m) ↔ 18ft (5.5m)

This beautiful conical tree, which spreads with age, is perfect for a sheltered site. Its bloomy blue-green foliage is carried in elegant, drooping sprays. Dislikes dry soils.

Abies koreana
KOREAN FIR
☼ ☀ 5   ↕ 30ft (10m) ↔ 15ft (5m)

The ascending or spreading branches of this broad, conical tree are densely clothed with dark green, silvery-backed needles. Even small plants bear violet-blue cones.

Chamaecyparis obtusa
'Tetragona Aurea'
☼ 5   ↕ 30ft (10m) ↔ 15ft (5m)

Easily recognized and popular, this Hinoki cypress is bushy when young but becomes loosely conical. Mosslike sprays of yellow foliage clothe its angular branches.

OTHER MEDIUM-SIZED CONIFERS
Chamaecyparis nootkatensis 'Pendula'
Cupressus arizonica 'Pyramidalis'
Juniperus chinensis 'Aurea'
Picea glauca
Pinus bungeana
Pinus parviflora
Pinus sylvestris Aurea Group, see p.262
Pseudolarix amabilis
Sciadopitys verticillata
Thuja occidentalis 'Spiralis'
Tsuga mertensiana

Chamaecyparis obtusa 'Crippsii'
HINOKI CYPRESS
☼ 5   ↕ 30ft (10m) ↔ 15ft (5m)

This popular, colorful, loosely conical conifer has bright golden, aromatic foliage borne in large, flattened sprays. Rounded cones are brown. Dislikes dry soils.

Cunninghamia lanceolata
CHINA FIR
☼ ☀ 6   ↕ 43ft (13m) ↔ 15ft (5m)

The branches of this columnar tree are all lined with two rows of narrow, glossy green leaves that are silvery beneath, and sharp. Does not like exposed sites or dry soils.

Fitzroya cupressoides
ALERCE
☼ 7   ↕ 30ft (10m) ↔ 15ft (5m)

Columnar when young, this bushy, juniper-like tree becomes more lax in habit with age. It has peeling, reddish brown bark and sprays of white-banded, scalelike leaves.

CONIFERS

Taxodium distichum var. *imbricatum* 'Nutans'
☼ **5**   ↕ 50ft (15m) ↔ 15ft (5m)

Pond Cypress is a deciduous, columnar tree. Its ascending branches are crowded above with slender sprays of bright green foliage. Ideal in deep or moist soils.

Pinus aristata
BRISTLECONE PINE
☼ **4**   ↕ 25ft (8m) ↔ 15ft (5m)

Suitable for any but the smallest gardens, this slow-growing, dense, bushy pine has branches crowded with dark blue-green, white-flecked needles. Cones are whiskery.

Picea breweriana
BREWER SPRUCE
☼ ☼ **5**   ↕ 40ft (12m) ↔ 20ft (6m)

This is one of the most distinctive of the spruces. Its spreading branches support long, pendulous branchlets clothed with narrow leaves. Cylindrical brown cones.

Podocarpus salignus
PODOCARPUS
☼ **9**   ↕ 30ft (10m) ↔ 20ft (6m)

A most attractive columnar tree (broadly conical later), this podocarpus has stringy, reddish brown bark and narrow, shiny, willowlike leaves. Dislikes dry soils.

Tsuga canadensis
EASTERN HEMLOCK
☼ ☼ **3**   ↕ 50ft (15m) ↔ 30ft (10m)

This multistemmed tree has pendent or arching sprays of small, dark green, silver-backed leaves. Cones are freely borne and ripen to brown. Dislikes dry soils.

C O N I F E R S

251

Conifers for Heavy Clay Soil

MANY CONIFERS will grow in heavy clay soil, providing that it is not permanently waterlogged. They encompass an extremely wide selection of sizes and shapes, and have foliage of great variety, both in color and texture. These are easy to grow and are evergreen unless specified deciduous.

Cryptomeria japonica
'Elegans Compacta'
☼ 6   ↕ 10ft (3m) ↔ 6ft (2m)

This is a dense, billowy, bushy form of Japanese Red Cedar. The fresh green foliage is soft to touch and turns a rich reddish bronze color in winter.

Pinus heldreichii
BOSNIAN PINE
☼ 5   ↕ 60ft (18m) ↔ 28ft (9m)

A handsome tree of dense, conical habit, this pine broadens as it ages. Its special features include rich green needles, white hairy buds, and cobalt blue cones.

Pinus peuce
MACEDONIAN PINE
☼ 5   ↕ 60ft (18m) ↔ 20ft (6m)

Worth growing where space is available, this impressive pine has densely crowded gray-green needles and pendent, curved and cylindrical, resin-flecked cones.

OTHER EVERGREEN CONIFERS FOR HEAVY CLAY SOIL

Abies koreana, see p.250
Chamaecyparis nootkatensis 'Pendula'
Chamaecyparis obtusa
Picea abies, see p.245
Picea glauca var. *albertiana* 'Conica', see p.259
Pinus coulteri
Pinus ponderosa
Saxegothaea conspicua
Thuja plicata, see p.257

Metasequoia glyptostroboides
DAWN REDWOOD
☼ ☼ 5   ↕ 70ft (20m) ↔ 15ft (5m)

The feathery leaves of this magnificent deciduous conifer turn tawny pink in autumn. An ancient and vigorous tree, it is narrowly conical to almost columnar.

Pinus mugo 'Mops'
MOUNTAIN PINE
☼ 2   ↕ 3ft (1m) ↔ 4ft (1.2m)

This dwarf mountain pine in time forms a compact mound of dark green needles. Slow-growing, it is ideal for a large rock garden or a big pot.

Pinus strobus
WHITE PINE
☼ 3   ↕ 70ft (20m) ↔ 28ft (9m)

A well-known conical pine, this broadens with age. Open branches bear slender gray-green needles and pendulous cones. Will not tolerate air pollution.

Pinus thunbergii
JAPANESE BLACK PINE
☼ 5   ↕ 43ft (13m) ↔ 25ft (8m)

Its dark green needles and hairy silvery buds distinguish this easy-to-grow pine. Conical when young and broadening with age, this makes an excellent coastal tree.

Taxodium distichum
BALDCYPRESS
☼ 4   ↕ 70ft (20m) ↔ 28ft (9m)

This attractive deciduous, conical conifer is excellent for a damp site. It has fibrous, reddish brown bark and feathery green leaves that turn gold in autumn.

Thuja koraiensis
KOREAN ARBORVITAE
☼ 6   ↕ 22ft (7m) ↔ 10ft (3m)

Loose and slow-growing, this columnar conifer has broad sprays of bright green, scaly foliage, silver-white beneath. When bruised, the foliage smells of almonds.

OTHER DECIDUOUS CONIFERS FOR HEAVY CLAY SOILS

Ginkgo biloba, see p.244
Larix decidua
Larix kaempferi
Taxodium distichum var. *imbricatum*

Taxus baccata Aurea Group
GOLDEN ENGLISH YEW
☼ ☼ 6   ↕ 15ft (5m) ↔ 10ft (3m)

The leaves of this striking golden form of the English Yew become green in their second year. Trim it annually to obtain a neat, conical habit, as seen here.

Tsuga heterophylla
WESTERN HEMLOCK
☼ ☼ 6   ↕ 70ft (20m) ↔ 30ft (10m)

Slender branches, crowded with green, silver-backed needles and drooping at the tips, form graceful layers. This fast-growing conical conifer has small cones.

Conifers for Dry, Sunny Sites

MANY CONIFERS ARE NATIVE to warm, dry regions of the world, and a good number of these are readily available for planting in gardens where warm, dry summers are a regular feature. Some are vigorous, and soon create shade; others are slow-growing. All are evergreen, and best planted when small to give them the best chance of establishing.

Pinus cembroides
MEXICAN PINYON
☼ 4   ↕ 20ft (6m) ↔ 15ft (5m)

This unusual and attractive, slow-growing pine is bushy and conical when young, becoming rounded with age. Stout, stiff gray-green needles crowd its branches.

Cedrus deodara
DEODAR CEDAR
☼ 7   ↕ 80ft (25m) ↔ 40ft (12m)

A handsome, vigorous conifer, this has long, drooping branches when young, and ultimately assumes a typical flat-topped cedar shape with layered branches.

Juniperus drupacea
SYRIAN JUNIPER
☼ 7   ↕ 40ft (12m) ↔ 5ft (1.5m)

Distinctive and easily recognized, this juniper of close columnar habit is superb as a specimen in the lawn or in a border. It has bright green, needlelike leaves.

OTHER PINES FOR DRY, SUNNY SITES
Pinus aristata, see p.251
Pinus armandii
Pinus bungeana
Pinus contorta
Pinus coulteri
Pinus edulis
Pinus monophylla
Pinus pinaster
Pinus sylvestris
Pinus yunnanensis

Cupressus macrocarpa
MONTEREY CYPRESS
☼ 8   ↕ 70ft (20m) ↔ 76ft (22m)

This popular, fast-growing conifer, with its sprays of feathery green foliage, is often grown in coastal areas as a screen. When young it is columnar, but spreads with age.

Juniperus rigida
TEMPLE JUNIPER
☼ 5   ↕ 25ft (8m) ↔ 15ft (5m)

Loosely branched and often sprawling, this tree or large bush has drooping sprays of needlelike green leaves that become bronze in winter, and peeling bark.

Pinus halepensis
ALEPPO PINE
☼ 9   ↕ 46ft (14m) ↔ 20ft (6m)

Excellent on sandy soils, this pine rounds with age. Needles on juvenile trees are blue-green; they are bright green on older trees. Egg-shaped cones are glossy orange.

CONIFERS

Pinus muricata
BISHOP PINE
☼ 7 PH ▼   ↕60ft (18m) ↔ 28ft (9m)

This tough and adaptable, fast-growing
pine is columnar at first, broadening and
often becoming flat-topped later. It is very
good on poor, or acid, sandy soils.

Pinus pinea
STONE PINE, UMBRELLA PINE
☼ 8   ↕40ft (12m) ↔ 30ft (10m)

Conical when young, Stone Pine gradually
develops its characteristic head of packed,
radiating branches. Mature trees have dark
green foliage; juveniles have blue-green.

Pinus virginiana
SCRUB PINE, VIRGINIA PINE
☼ 5 PH ▼   ↕46ft (14m) ↔ 28ft (9m)

Loose and often untidy, this is a pine with
densely crowded gray to yellow-gray
needles on pinkish white shoots. It bears
small, prickly orange-brown winter cones.

Taxus cuspidata
JAPANESE YEW
☼ ☼ ☀ 4   ↕15ft (5m) ↔ 15ft (5m)

This multibranched shrub opens out and
spreads with age. Yellowish green leaves,
sometimes red-brown in winter, clothe its
branches. Female plants bear red fruits.

Torreya californica
CALIFORNIA NUTMEG
☼ 6   ↕60ft (18m) ↔ 25ft (8m)

An impressive, upright conifer, this has
whorled branches and long, narrow, spine-
tipped leaves. If pollinated, female trees
produce pendent, olivelike fruits.

**OTHER CONIFERS FOR DRY,
SUNNY SITES**

Abies concolor
Cedrus atlantica f. *glauca*, see p.263
x *Cupressocyparis leylandii*, see p.256
Cupressus arizonica 'Pyramidalis'
Cupressus sempervirens, see p.248
Juniperus chinensis 'Mountbatten'
Juniperus communis 'Berkshire'
Juniperus conferta 'Blue Pacific'
Juniperus horizontalis 'Blue Chip'
Juniperus x *pfitzeriana*
   'Pfitzeriana Compacta'
Juniperus squamata 'Blue Star',
   see p.259
Juniperus virginiana 'Canaertii'
Picea glauca var. *albertiana* 'Conica',
   see p.259
Picea pungens 'Koster', see p.263
Tsuga heterophylla, see p.253

CONIFERS

255

Conifers for Hedges, Windbreaks, or Screening

CONIFERS ARE SUPERB subjects for hedging and screens – most are evergreen and provide an attractive permanent effect once established. The filtering effect on winds, and subsequent benefit to plants they are sheltering, has also long been recognized. Most conifers used for formal hedges or screening are ultimately big and need regular trimming.

OTHER CONIFERS FOR HEDGES AND SCREENING

Chamaecyparis lawsoniana cvs.
Chamaecyparis obtusa 'Crippsii', see p.250
x *Cupressocyparis leylandii* 'Naylor's Blue'
Juniperus chinensis 'Mountbatten'
Juniperus chinensis 'Spartan'
Thuja occidentalis 'Techny'
Thuja plicata 'Atrovirens'
Tsuga canadensis, see p.251

Chamaecyparis lawsoniana 'Green Hedger'
☼ 6   ↕ 50ft (15m) ↔ 20ft (6m)

Well clothed down to its base with sprays of rich green foliage, this is one of the best cypresses for screening. It is conical as a single specimen. Dislikes dry soils.

x *Cupressocyparis leylandii* 'Castlewellan'
☼ 6   ↕ 80ft (25m) ↔ 18ft (5.5m)

Commonly planted as a hedge or screen, this evergreen grows rapidly but can be cut back hard. Densely packed bronze-yellow foliage is golden on young plants.

Chamaecyparis lawsoniana 'Green Pillar'
☼ 6   ↕ 50ft (15m) ↔ 10ft (3m)

Good for screens or hedges, this columnar cypress is moderately sized and requires little clipping. Its vertical sprays of green foliage are gold-tinged in early spring.

x *Cupressocyparis leylandii* LEYLAND CYPRESS
☼ 6   ↕ 78ft (24m) ↔ 18ft (5.5m)

One of the fastest growing of all conifers – too fast for many gardens – this is ideal as a temporary screen or tall hedge. Its foliage is dark green or gray-green.

Picea asperata CHINESE SPRUCE
☼ 5   ↕ 50ft (15m) ↔ 30ft (10m)

The yellow-brown shoots of this tough, conical spruce are all crowded with blue-gray, needlelike foliage. Adaptable to most soils, it makes a useful windbreak.

CONIFERS

Pinus nigra
AUSTRIAN PINE
☼ 4   ↕ 80ft (25m) ↔ 70ft (20m)

This tough, rugged, ultimately large tree is excellent as a windbreak for exposed sites. It has a domed crown and spreading branches. Dislikes dry soils.

Taxus baccata
ENGLISH YEW
☼ ☼ ☀ 6   ↕ 40ft (12m) ↔ 30ft (10m)

Yews, with their narrow, blackish green leaves, are popular for hedging. Regular clipping will encourage a dense habit, which is particularly effective in topiary.

Taxus x *media* 'Hicksii'
HICK'S YEW
☼ ☼ ☀ 5   ↕ 20ft (6m) ↔ 6ft (2m)

Tough, adaptable, and slow-growing, this yew is very good for screening or hedging. Columnar when young, it matures to vase-shaped. Bears red fruit if pollinated.

OTHER CONIFERS FOR WINDBREAKS

Abies concolor
Cupressus macrocarpa, see p.254
Juniperus virginiana
Picea abies
Picea nordmanniana
Picea sitchensis
Pinus cembra
Pinus heldreichii, see p.252
Pinus strobus
Pinus sylvestris
Pseudotsuga menziesii

Pinus radiata
MONTEREY PINE
☼ 7 PH⤵   ↕ 80ft (25m) ↔ 70ft (20m)

An impressive large pine for shelter on exposed sites (except in cold inland areas), this has bold bunches of green needles, and attractive male cones in spring.

CONIFERS FOR SMALL HEDGES

Cryptomeria japonica 'Elegans Nana'
Juniperus communis 'Berkshire'
Thuja occidentalis 'Globosa'
Thuja orientalis 'Conspicua'
Thujopsis dolabrata 'Nana'

Thuja plicata
WESTERN RED CEDAR
☼ ☼ 5   ↕ 80ft (25m) ↔ 25ft (8m)

This handsome conical conifer makes a first-rate hedge or screen, with its close-packed sprays of glossy, scalelike foliage that smells of pineapple when bruised.

CONIFERS

Slow-growing or Dwarf Conifers

SLOW-GROWING CONIFERS, or those with a naturally dwarf habit, are ideal for small gardens, rock gardens, raised beds, or containers. Most are mutations of a normal-sized tree and are propagated by grafting onto seedling stock. Few other hardy woody plants offer such a wide range of shape, form, and color throughout the year.

Chamaecyparis lawsoniana 'Gnome'
LAWSON CYPRESS
☼ 6-7 ↕ 12in (30cm) ↔ 12in (30cm)

Dense, slow-growing form of the Lawson Cypress, this has flat sprays of scalelike foliage. Occasional tufts of coarse growth should be cut away to maintain shape.

OTHER DWARF CONIFERS OF ROUNDED OR DOMED HABIT

Chamaecyparis obtusa 'Caespitosa'
Picea abies 'Gregoryana'
Pinus mugo 'Gnome'
Pinus strobus 'Minima'
Pinus sylvestris 'Beuvronensis'
Platycladus orientalis 'Meldensis'
Thuja occidentalis 'Sunkist'
Thuja occidentalis 'Tiny Tim'
Thujopsis dolobrata 'Nana'
Tsuga canadensis 'Jeddeloh'

Abies balsamea 'Nana'
BALSAM FIR
☼ 3 ↕ 20in (50cm) ↔ 30in (75cm)

This low, domed form of the Balsam Fir is dense and compact. The short, spreading, glossy green leaves have two grayish bands beneath and crowd the branchlets.

Abies nordmanniana
'Golden Spreader'
☼ 5 ↕ 18in (45cm) ↔ 4ft (1.2m)

This form of the Caucasian Fir is low-spreading and flat-topped. The crowded leaves are yellow above, yellowish white beneath, and golden yellow in winter.

Abies concolor 'Compacta'
WHITE FIR
☼ 4 ↕ 3½ft (1.1m) ↔ 4½ft (1.3m)

Ideal for larger rock gardens, this is a handsome, compact form of the White Fir. Its habit is irregular, with branches of narrow, spreading, grayish blue leaves.

Cedrus libani 'Sargentii'
CEDAR OF LEBANON
☼ 6 ↕ 30in (75cm) ↔ 8ft (2.5m)

A splendid, low-domed cedar. The long, weeping branches are covered with needle-like blue-green leaves. Tie the main stem upright to a stake to give height.

Chamaecyparis obtusa 'Nana Aurea'
HINOKI CYPRESS
☼ 5 ↕ 4½ft (1.3m) ↔ 26in (65cm)

An excellent golden dwarf conifer for general cultivation, this slow-growing, conical form of the Hinoki Cypress has fan-shaped sprays of scalelike foliage.

Juniperus squamata 'Blue Star'
DWARF JUNIPER

☼ **5**   ↕ 18in (45cm) ↔ 20in (50cm)

The branches of this slow-growing juniper of squat habit are densely crowded with needlelike, silvery blue leaves. A most satisfactory blue-gray dwarf conifer.

Picea pungens 'Montgomery'
BLUE COLORADO SPRUCE

☼ **2**   ↕ 3½ft (1.1m) ↔ 3½ft (1.1m)

This reliable, dome-shaped form of the Colorado Spruce is ideal for larger rock gardens or as a specimen. Sharp-pointed grayish needles crowd its branches.

Pinus heldreichii 'Schmidtii'
BOSNIAN PINE

☼ **5**   ↕ 3ft (1m) ↔ 30in (75cm)

A slow-growing form of the Bosnian Pine that forms a globular or conical bush, this is compact in habit. Its short branches are crowded with needlelike green leaves.

> **OTHER DWARF CONIFERS OF COLUMNAR OR CONICAL HABIT**
>
> *Abies lasiocarpa* 'Compacta'
> *Chamaecyparis lawsoniana* 'Ellwood's Gold'
> x *Cupressocyparis leylandii* 'Hyde Hall'
> *Juniperus communis* 'Compressa'
> *Juniperus communis* 'Sentinel'
> *Picea abies* 'Remontii'
> *Picea glauca* var. *albertiana* 'Laurin'
> *Pinus parviflora* 'Negishi'
> *Thuja plicata* 'Rogersii'

Picea glauca var. *albertiana* 'Conica'
DWARF ALBERTA SPRUCE

☼ **2**   ↕ 6ft (2m) ↔ 36in (90cm)

This popular form of the White Spruce retains its tight, conical habit if stray side shoots are removed. Needlelike green leaves crowd the branchlets.

> **OTHER SLOW OR DWARF CONIFERS**
>
> *Chamaecyparis obtusa* 'Rigid Dwarf'
> *Cryptomeria japonica* 'Vilmoriniana'
> *Pinus densiflora* 'Umbraculifera'
> *Platycladus orientalis* 'Elegantissima'
> *Tsuga canadensis* 'Horstmann'

Thuja plicata 'Stoneham Gold'
WESTERN RED CEDAR

☼ **6**   ↕ 5½ft (1.7m) ↔ 30in (75cm)

A choice form of the Western Red Cedar, developing a conical habit. The aromatic, scalelike leaves are borne in flat sprays and become darker as they mature.

CONIFERS

Conifers for Groundcover

LOW-GROWING conifers are among the most effective groundcovers for the garden. Their evergreen leaves form a dense, carpetlike cover, and come in a variety of shades, including bright green, blue-green, and gray-green. Many were developed from mutations found on taller-growing conifers and are grafted or grown from cuttings.

Picea abies 'Reflexa'
NORWAY SPRUCE
☀ 2 ↕ 18in (45cm) ↔ 15ft (5m)

The branches of this unusual, irregular, low-growing form of the Norway Spruce are long, prostrate, and crowded with needlelike leaves that form a dense mat.

OTHER CONIFERS FOR GROUNDCOVER

Cephalotaxus harringtonia 'Prostrata'
Juniperus conferta 'Blue Pacific'
Juniperus conferta 'Emerald Sea'
Juniperus horizontalis 'Blue Chip'
Juniperus horizontalis 'Wiltonii'
Juniperus squamata 'Blue Carpet'
   see p.247
Picea pungens 'Procumbens'
Taxus baccata
   'Repandens'

Juniperus communis 'Green Carpet'
COMMON JUNIPER
☀ 3 ↕ 5in (12cm) ↔ 4ft (1.2m)

This prostrate juniper makes an excellent groundcover and blends well with others of its kind. Its branches are crowded with prickly, needlelike, bright green leaves.

Juniperus procumbens 'Nana'
CREEPING JUNIPER
☀ 5 ↕ 12in (30cm) ↔ 6ft (2m)

Slightly raised mats or carpets are formed by the tightly packed, prostrate branches of this dwarf juniper. Bristly blue-green leaves crowd its shoots.

Juniperus horizontalis 'Plumosa'
CREEPING JUNIPER
☀ 4 ↕ 6in (15cm) ↔ 6ft (2m)

Seen here next to *J. horizontalis* 'Glauca', with which it combines well, this reliable groundcover has sprays of gray-green foliage that turn bronze-purple in winter.

Microbiota decussata
MICROBIOTA
☀ ☀ ☀ 3 ↕ 12in (30cm) ↔ 6ft (2m)

The arching, spraylike branches of this low-growing, wide-spreading conifer are densely clothed with bright green, scale-like leaves, which turn bronze in winter.

Taxus baccata
'Repens Aurea'
☀ ☀ 6 ↕ 18in (45cm) ↔ 6ft (2m)

Short, overlapping branchlets, crowded with yellow-margined leaves, dark green in shade, fill the long branches of this low-spreading form of the English Yew.

CONIFERS

Variegated Conifers

THE VARIEGATION IN CONIFERS usually takes the form of white or yellow sprays scattered in otherwise green foliage. Occasionally, however, the additional color is banded, such as in *Thuja plicata* 'Zebrina' (*see right*), or the overall effect may appear speckled. These variegations may not appeal to all gardeners, but they can provide a pleasing contrast to greens, especially in winter. Such conifers also make interesting single specimens for the lawn.

Thuja plicata 'Zebrina'
WESTERN RED CEDAR
☼ 5   ↕ 70ft (20m) ↔ 40ft (12m)

A striking conical conifer, this is easily recognized by the dark green sprays of pineapple-scented foliage, boldly banded cream-yellow, and its reddish, fibrous bark.

OTHER VARIEGATED CONIFERS

Chamaecyparis lawsoniana 'Fletcher's White'
Chamaecyparis obtusa 'Mariesii'
Chamaecyparis pisifera 'Snow'
x *Cupressocyparis leylandii* 'Silver Dust'
Juniperus chinensis 'Gold Star'
Pinus densiflora 'Oculus-draconis'
Pinus thunbergii 'Oculus-draconis'
Taxus baccata 'Fastigiata Aurea'
Thuja occidentalis 'Elegantissima'
Tsuga canadensis 'Gentsch White Tip'

Calocedrus decurrens 'Aureovariegata'
INCENSE CEDAR
☼ 6   ↕ 40ft (12m) ↔ 10ft (3m)

The short, spreading branches of this slow-growing cedar are covered by sprays of aromatic green foliage, interspersed with yellow sprigs.

x *Cupressocyparis leylandii* 'Harlequin'
VARIEGATED LEYLAND CYPRESS
☼ 6   ↕ 70ft (20m) ↔ 20ft (6m)

This variegated cultivar is just as easy and vigorous as the species, but its packed, plumelike, gray-green foliage is relieved by scattered, creamy white sprays.

Chamaecyparis nootkatensis 'Variegata'
VARIEGATED NOOTKA CYPRESS
☼ 5   ↕ 50ft (15m) ↔ 20ft (6m)

Pendulous sprays of pungent green foliage are coarse to the touch and interspersed with creamy white sprays. Nootka Cypress is loosely conical and dislikes dry soils.

Juniperus chinensis 'Variegated Kaizuka'
☼ 4   ↕ 10ft (3m) ↔ 6ft (2m)

The protruding branches of this distinctly angular, slow-growing juniper are crowded with bright green, almost mossy foliage, marked with patches of creamy white.

Thujopsis dolabrata 'Variegata'
VARIEGATED HIBA
☼ 6   ↕ 30ft (10m) ↔ 20ft (6m)

Broad, flattened sprays of aromatic green foliage have silvery marks beneath, and random sprays are splashed creamy white. It is slow-growing, and dislikes dry soils.

CONIFERS

Conifers with Golden or Yellow Foliage

A WIDE VARIETY of conifers with golden or yellow foliage is available for both the large or small garden. In some cases, only the growing tips show yellow; in others, the entire foliage retains this cheerful color throughout the year, adding a warm glow to the garden during the drab winter months. All those illustrated here are reliable.

OTHER MEDIUM-SIZED TO LARGE CONIFERS WITH GOLDEN FOLIAGE

Cedrus deodara 'Aurea'
Chamaecyparis lawsoniana 'Lutea'
Chamaecyparis obtusa 'Crippsii', see p.250
Juniperus chinensis 'Aurea'
Picea abies 'Aurea'
Picea orientalis 'Skylands'
Thuja occidentalis 'Europa Gold'
Thuja plicata 'Aurea'
Thuja plicata 'Irish Gold'

Chamaecyparis pisifera 'Filifera Aurea'
SAWARA CYPRESS
☼ 5 ↕ 40ft (12m) ↔ 15ft (5m)

This dense, conical or mounded conifer produces numerous long, threadlike branches clothed with tiny, bright yellow leaves. It only slowly increases in size.

Cupressus macrocarpa 'Goldcrest'
MONTEREY CYPRESS
☼ 7 ↕ 30ft (10m) ↔ 10ft (3m)

One of the best of its color, this is a vigorous, columnar or slender, conical tree. It is dense and compact, with crowded, plumelike foliage. Avoid clipping.

Cupressus sempervirens 'Swane's Gold'
☼ 8 ↕ 30ft (10m) ↔ 24in (60cm)

For very small gardens, this is probably the best conifer of its shape and color. It forms a tall, slender column of golden-tinged foliage in dense, crowded sprays.

OTHER SMALL OR SLOW-GROWING CONIFERS WITH GOLDEN FOLIAGE

Cedrus deodara 'Golden Horizon'
Cryptomeria japonica 'Cristata'
Cupressus macrocarpa 'Gold Spread', see p.246
Juniperus communis 'Gold Cone'
Pinus sylvestris 'Moseri'
Thuja occidentalis 'Golden Globe'
Thuja occidentalis 'Rheingold'
Thuja orientalis 'Aureus Nanus'
Thuja plicata 'Stoneham Gold', see p.259

Pinus sylvestris Aurea Group
GOLDEN SCOTS PINE
☼ 2 ↕ 40ft (12m) ↔ 15ft (5m)

The normally blue-green needles of this slow-growing, broad, columnar tree turn a rich yellow from winter into spring. The colder the winter, the richer the color.

Thuja plicata 'Collyer's Gold'
WESTERN RED CEDAR
☼ 6 ↕ 6ft (2m) ↔ 3ft (1m)

This is a slow-growing conifer of compact, dense, dome-shaped or conical habit. Its crowded sprays of foliage emerge a rich golden yellow, then turn light green.

CONIFERS

Conifers with Blue-gray or Silver foliage

WHEN SEEN AGAINST a darker background, blue-gray or silvery conifers have a striking effect in the garden. The Blue Atlas Cedar and the Blue Colorado Spruce are perhaps the two most well known in general cultivation but, happily, there are many others of similar effect and equal merit, some suitable for small gardens. All shown here are evergreen.

Picea glauca 'Coerulea'
WHITE SPRUCE
☼ 2   ↕ 43ft (13m) ↔ 20ft (6m)

This vigorous, conical spruce has branches that are ascending at first, and spread with age. They are crowded with short blue-gray to silver needles. Dislikes dry soils.

Abies concolor 'Candicans'
WHITE FIR
☼ 3   ↕ 70ft (20m) ↔ 22ft (7m)

The branches of this handsome conical conifer are clothed with spreading, needle-like leaves, colored a striking silver-white or blue-gray. Dislikes dry soils.

Chamaecyparis lawsoniana 'Pembury Blue'
☼ 6   ↕ 50ft (15m) ↔ 20ft (6m)

An excellent blue-gray cypress, 'Pembury Blue' is a conical tree, bearing numerous sprays of scalelike foliage on its loosely arching branches. Dislikes dry soils.

OTHER CONIFERS WITH BLUE-GRAY OR SILVER FOLIAGE

Abies pinsapo 'Glauca'
Chamaecyparis lawsoniana 'Pelt's Blue'
Cupressus arizonica 'Pyramidalis'
Juniperus chinensis 'Ames'
Juniperus scopulorum 'Blue Heaven'
Picea pungens 'Fat Albert'
Pinus koraiensis
Pinus parviflora 'Glauca'
Pinus wallichiana 'Nana'
Pseudotsuga menziesii 'Glauca'

Cedrus atlantica f. *glauca*
BLUE ATLAS CEDAR
☼ 6   ↕ 78ft (24m) ↔ 50ft (15m)

This spectacular conifer is recognizable by its fast growth when young, its wide-spreading habit, barrel-shaped cones, and silver-blue needles. Dislikes dry soils.

Juniperus sabina 'Blaue Donau'
SAVIN JUNIPER
☼ 5   ↕ 10in (25cm) ↔ 5ft (1.5m)

Its low, wide-spreading habit makes this a most effective conifer for the rock garden or scree. Branches have ascending tips and are crowded with light blue-gray foliage.

Picea pungens 'Koster'
BLUE COLORADO SPRUCE
☼ 2   ↕ 43ft (13m) ↔ 15ft (5m)

A striking spruce, this is one of several similar selections. It has scaly gray bark, whorled branches, and prickly, needle-like, silver-blue leaves fading to green.

TREES

I BELIEVE THAT ALL PLANTS, no matter how small, are important, but, I confess, trees are to me the most inspirational. This is partly due to their size, but more significant is the sense of continuity and permanence that they bring to the garden. To plant a tree, particularly a potentially large or long-lived one, is to express a belief in the future.

△ *Quercus canariensis*

△ CRABAPPLE CHEER *The cherrylike crabapples of* Malus x robusta *'Red Sentinel' last well into winter.*

Trees are the anchors in many gardens, holding together diverse design elements. They can offer a seasonal display of flowers, fruit, or foliage, or an attractive habit, as well as provide a useful focal point for one's neighbors. The mountain ash (*Sorbus*), hawthorn (*Crataegus*), and ornamental crabapple (*Malus*) are examples that boast several of these attractive features.

ANNUAL ANTICIPATION

In cooler temperate climates, the number and variety of deciduous trees far exceeds their evergreen counterparts. Evergreen trees do, however, provide an excellent foil, often being used as background trees, screens, or windbreaks, though they should be considered for prime sites where conditions suit. The miracle of renewal – bud flush, flowering, fruiting, and leaf fall – that deciduous trees annually enact is something we never tire of. All the trees in this section are deciduous unless otherwise stated.

BIG IS NOT ALWAYS BETTER

Trees vary in height and shape, providing plenty of candidates for every type and size of garden. Small trees need not be confined to small gardens, while a single large tree in place of several small ones can provide a welcome focus for all nearby. Whatever your priorities, available space should always be paramount. Large trees need space to develop; it is foolhardy to plant one where space is limited.

△ GLORIOUS GOLD *Striking and very reliable, golden* Robinia pseudoacacia *'Frisia' brightens dull corners in summer.*

◁ DUAL DELIGHT Amelanchier lamarckii*'s lovely snow white spring blossoms are matched by its autumn tints.*

▷ NOBLE AUTUMN SPECIMEN *This Tulip Tree* (Liriodendron tulipifera *'Fastigiatum'*) *is ideal for a large lawn.*

Bold Specimens for Large Gardens

TREES THAT ultimately grow to a large size – many native to forests – form an impressive sight in gardens big enough to accommodate them. Where conditions suit, some live to a great age, and may be enjoyed for years to come by future generations.

Catalpa speciosa
WESTERN CATALPA
☼ 4
Vigorous growth
‡ 70ft (20m) ↔ 50ft (15m)

The glossy, dark green leaves of this imposing tree are broad at the base, and each has a narrow point. Bell-shaped white flowers, spotted lightly inside, are carried in large heads in summer, followed by slender, pendulous pods.

Acer saccharinum
SILVER MAPLE
☼ 4
Vigorous growth
‡ 80ft (25m) ↔ 50ft (15m)

This handsome tree weeps and spreads with age. Its slender branchlets carry jagged leaves with silvery undersides that flash when disturbed by the wind. These turn yellow in autumn. Pendulous selections with more finely cut leaves are available.

Fagus sylvatica var. *heterophylla* 'Aspleniifolia'
FERN-LEAVED BEECH
☼ 5
Vigorous growth
‡ 80ft (25m) ↔ 80ft (25m)

A tree that combines impressive stature and grace, this beech is often broader than it is tall and eventually forms a large, dome-shaped crown. The slender, spreading branchlets are clothed in narrow, toothed leaves that turn gold, then brown, in autumn.

Castanea sativa
SWEET, OR SPANISH, CHESTNUT
☼ ☀ 5
Vigorous growth
‡ 80ft (25m) ↔ 50ft (15m)

A magnificent tree that develops reddish brown, ridged bark in time. Clusters of slender summer flower spikes precede prickly capsules that contain the familiar edible chestnuts, and the leaves turn yellow in autumn. Best in rich acid soils.

Liriodendron tulipifera
TULIP TREE, TULIP POPLAR
☼ 5
Vigorous growth
‡ 80ft (25m) ↔ 50ft (15m)

This is one of the noblest ornamental trees, its impressive conical habit spreading with age. Tuliplike flowers appear in early summer, and its distinctively shaped leaves turn yellow in autumn. Seed-grown trees rarely flower until they are 15–20 years old.

Nothofagus obliqua
ROBLÉ BEECH
☼ 7 PH ▼
Vigorous growth
‡ 70ft (20m) ↔ 60ft (18m)

This elegant relative of the beech comes from the Southern Hemisphere and it develops a domed crown of slightly drooping branches. The deep green leaves turn red and orange in autumn. Happiest in moist but well-drained soils, in a sheltered site.

Quercus frainetto
HUNGARIAN OAK
☼ 6
Vigorous growth
‡ 70ft (20m) ↔ 60ft (18m)

One of the most handsome and distinct of all oaks in leaf, this species has large, glossy green leaves that are boldly and regularly lobed, and borne on stout shoots. Its habit is spreading, and the bark is darkly and deeply fissured. Tolerates most sites and soils.

OTHER BOLD SPECIMEN TREES
Acer saccharum
Aesculus hippocastanum
Ailanthus altissima
Carya ovata, see p.296
Cercidiphyllum japonicum, see p.296
Cladrastis kentukea, see p.278
Corylus colurna, see p.302
Eucalyptus gunnii, see p.286
Fraxinus americana
Gymnocladus dioica
Liquidambar styraciflua
Magnolia acuminata
Nyssa sylvatica
Quercus macrocarpa
Quercus virginiana
Tilia tomentosa
Zelkova serrata

Quercus palustris
PIN OAK
☼ 5 PH ▼
Vigorous growth
‡ 70ft (20m) ↔ 40ft (12m)

Good-looking and dome-shaped, Pin Oak is a superb tree for a large lawn. Spreading branches, the lowest of which are pendent, bear beautiful, sharply lobed leaves. Shining green in summer, they turn spectacular bronze, russet, or red in autumn.

Pterocarya x *rehderiana*
HYBRID WINGNUT
☼ 6
Vigorous growth
‡ 70ft (20m) ↔ 70ft (20m)

In summer, the branchlets of this walnut relative are draped with long catkins that are replaced by even longer strings of green, winged fruits. Its leaves turn a clear yellow in autumn. Thrives in deep soils, or in a moist situation. An imposing tree at all times.

Zelkova carpinifolia
CAUCASIAN ELM
☼ 6
Slow growth
‡ 100ft (30m) ↔ 80ft (25m)

This slow-growing tree is one to plant for your grandchildren to enjoy. Mature specimens develop a characteristic dense, broad-topped crown with strongly upswept branches and a short, stout stem. Its green leaves often turn orange-brown in autumn.

TREES

Medium-sized Trees

SOME OF THE LOVELIEST trees are found in the medium size range of 20–50ft (6–15m); they are suitable for many average-sized gardens. This selection encompasses the full variety of ornamental effects, from spring flowers, through attractive autumn foliage and berries, to attractive winter bark. All make fine shade or specimen trees.

Magnolia x *loebneri* 'Leonard Messel'
MAGNOLIA
☼ 5   Moderate growth
↕ 30ft (10m) ↔ 20ft (6m)

One of the loveliest of its kind, this magnolia is upright to vase-shaped in habit, becoming conical to rounded in maturity. The leafless branches are flooded during spring with fragrant, multi-petaled, pale lilac-pink flowers, a deeper color when in bud.

Aesculus x *neglecta* 'Erythroblastos'
SUNRISE HORSE CHESTNUT
☼ ☀ 5   Moderate growth
↕ 30ft (10m) ↔ 20ft (6m)

Grown principally for its spring foliage, this is a choice tree of upright habit, spreading later. The leaves are bright pink when they emerge, changing to yellow and then to green. In autumn the leaves turn orange and yellow. Not suitable for exposed sites.

Magnolia x *kewensis* 'Wada's Memory'
MAGNOLIA
☼ 5   Moderate growth
↕ 30ft (10m) ↔ 22ft (7m)

This tree has a conical or oval crown. The fragrant white flowers that crowd its dense branches in spring are large, lax, and multi-petaled. Its leaves, aromatic when bruised, are dark green above and paler beneath. Spectacular when in full bloom.

Cornus macrophylla
BIGLEAF DOGWOOD
☼ ☀ 5   Moderate growth
↕ 40ft (12m) ↔ 30ft (10m)

The branches of this uncommon spreading tree grow in glossy, leafy layers. Flattened clusters of small, creamy white flowers are held above the foliage during summer, and are followed by blue-black berries in autumn. An attractive tree of loosely tiered habit.

> **OTHER MEDIUM-SIZED TREES GROWN FOR FLOWERS**
>
> *Cladrastis kentukea*, see p.278
> *Cornus kousa* var. *chinensis*
> *Davidia involucrata*, see p.302
> *Koelreuteria paniculata*, see p.277
> *Magnolia* x *loebneri* 'Merrill'
> *Oxydendrum arboreum*, see p.275
> *Pterostyrax hispida*
> *Sorbus alnifolia*, see p.273
> *Stewartia pseudocamellia*, see p.275
> *Styrax obassia*

Malus hupehensis
TEA CRAB
☼ 5
Vigorous growth
↕ 25ft (8m) ↔ 25ft (8m)

The spreading branches of this dense, round-headed tree are crowded in spring with large, fragrant white flowers, pink in bud. Small, dark red fruits held on slender stalks follow and remain after the leaves have fallen, eventually to be eaten by birds.

Prunus avium 'Plena'
DOUBLE SWEET CHERRY
☼ 4
Vigorous growth
↕ 40ft (12m) ↔ 40ft (12m)

In spring, the rounded to spreading crown of this popular, strong-growing flowering cherry is heavily laden with drooping clusters of clear white, double flowers. The leaves turn an attractive red and yellow in autumn. Makes an excellent specimen tree.

OTHER MEDIUM-SIZED TREES GROWN FOR FOLIAGE

Acer triflorum, see p.270
Alnus glutinosa 'Imperialis'
Betula maximowicziana
Eucommia ulmoides
Gleditsia triacanthos cvs.
Parrotia persica, see p.297
Phellodendron amurense
Robinia pseudoacacia 'Frisia', see p.264
Sassafras albidum, see p.275
Tilia mongolica

Prunus jamasakura
HILL CHERRY
☼ 6
Moderate growth
↕ 40ft (12m) ↔ 40ft (12m)

This beautiful cherry has a vase-shaped, later spreading, crown. In spring, the branches are crowded with white or pink blossoms. The leaves are bronze at first, and color richly in autumn. When in full bloom, this tree is visible from a considerable distance.

Styrax japonicus
JAPANESE SNOWBELL
☼ 5
Moderate growth
↕ 30ft (10m) ↔ 30ft (10m)

Neat, bright green leaves pack the spreading branches of this dense-headed tree. The undersides of its branches are crowded in early summer with drooping white, star-shaped flowers, each with a yellow beak of stamens.

T R E E S

Small Trees for Limited Space

SELECTING a single tree for a small space is a pleasant but difficult task because there are so many attractive candidates. Plant any of the suggestions here, alone as a specimen, or perhaps along your property line, where it can be enjoyed by neighbors or passersby.

Aesculus pavia 'Atrosanguinea'
DARK RED BUCKEYE
☀ 4   Slow growth   ↕ 15ft (5m) ↔ 12ft (4m)

Because of its slow growth and compact, dome-shaped habit, this tree makes an ideal lawn specimen. The dark green leaves form an excellent backdrop for its red, tubular summer flowers. These are followed by smooth-skinned, pale brown fruits.

Acer palmatum var. *coreanum*
JAPANESE MAPLE
☀ ☀ 5   Vigorous growth   ↕ 15ft (5m) ↔ 15ft (5m)

The slender branches of this reliable and easily grown tree are clothed with attractive green leaves that become a spectacular red-orange in autumn. Tiny, reddish purple flower clusters emerge with the leaves in spring. Dislikes dry soils.

Acer triflorum
THREEFLOWER MAPLE
☀ 5   Slow growth   ↕ 25ft (8m) ↔ 22ft (7m)

The rugged, peeling gray-brown bark of this handsome maple is especially noticeable in winter. Its leaves, consisting of three hairy leaflets, give brilliant gold, orange, and red autumn tints. The small, greenish yellow flowers appear in clusters in late spring.

Cornus alternifolia   'Argentea'
VARIEGATED PAGODA DOGWOOD
☀ 4   Moderate growth   ↕ 10ft (3m) ↔ 6ft (2m)

In time, distinct layers of slender branches with narrow leaves create a pagoda effect, making this a perfect specimen tree. You can prune and train it to a single stem or leave it with branches to the base. Its small clusters of white flowers appear in spring.

T R E E S

Cornus florida 'White Cloud'
FLOWERING DOGWOOD   Moderate growth
☼ 5   ↕ 15ft (5m) ↔ 20ft (6m)

This low, bushy tree with a spreading crown needs space to expand. It has two main seasons of interest – the first in spring, when distinctive white flowerheads appear, and the second in autumn, when dark green leaves become suffused red and purple.

Eucalyptus pauciflora subsp. *niphophila*
SNOW GUM   Moderate growth
☼ 7   ↕ 30ft (10m) ↔ 25ft (8m)

One of the most popular of all eucalypts, this is worth growing for its evergreen gray-green leaves and its fluffy clusters of white summer flowers. It is best known, however, for its beautiful bark – green, gray, cream, and silver create a marbled effect.

Eucryphia glutinosa
EUCRYPHIA   Moderate growth
☼ 8 PH   ↕ 20ft (6m) ↔ 15ft (5m)

This much-branched, rather bushy tree has shining, dark green leaflets that turn orange and red in autumn. Clusters of fragrant, roselike flowers occur from mid- to late summer. It prefers a moist but well-drained soil with its roots shaded from the sun.

Rhus trichocarpa
SUMAC   Moderate growth
☼ 7   ↕ 22ft (7m) ↔ 22ft (7m)

In autumn, the large, deeply divided, ashlike green leaves of this spreading tree provide purplish, then orange and red tints, alongside the drooping clusters of bristly yellow fruits. The sap of this sumac is poisonous and may cause an allergic reaction.

OTHER SMALL TREES

Acer griseum, see p.300
Acer japonicum 'Aureum'
Amelanchier x *grandiflora*
Aralia elata
Carpinus caroliniana
Magnolia virginiana
Malus 'Red Jewel'
Ostrya virginiana
Prunus 'Okame'
Prunus 'Spire'
Viburnum prunifolium

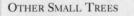

△ *Sorbus vilmorinii*
'Pearly King'

Sorbus vilmorinii
CHINESE MOUNTAIN ASH   Moderate growth
☼ 6   ↕ 12ft (4m) ↔ 15ft (5m)

The arching branches of this elegant tree are clothed in neat sprays of fernlike leaves that color orange or red in autumn. It bears white flowers in late spring, and loose clusters of small pink berries from autumn into early winter. 'Pearly King' is similar.

T R E E S

271

Trees Tolerant of Heavy Clay Soils

CLAY SOILS are frequently among the most fertile in gardens, although their physical characteristics do cause problems. Gardeners can take heart from the following selection of trees, all of which will grow happily in heavy clay, as long as it is not waterlogged.

Alnus incana
GRAY ALDER
☼ 2   Moderate growth
↕ 60ft (18m) ↔ 30ft (10m)

This is a tough and adaptable tree with a loosely conical habit. Its dark green leaves are strongly veined, and each has a downy gray underside. Drooping yellow catkins drape the branches in late winter or early spring. Gray Alder dislikes dry soils.

Catalpa bignonioides
CATALPA, INDIAN BEAN TREE
☼ 5   Moderate growth
↕ 40ft (12m) ↔ 50ft (15m)

Often broader than it is high, this is a bold, spreading tree. It has light green, heart-shaped leaves, purple-tinged when young, and bears large, loose heads of bell flowers with purple and yellow spots in summer. These are followed by long, thin seed pods.

Aesculus hippocastanum 'Baumannii'
DOUBLE HORSE CHESTNUT
☼ 4   Vigorous growth
↕ 100ft (30m) ↔ 50ft (15m)

A large tree with a spreading crown, Double Horse Chestnut has bold leaves, each divided into broad, fingerlike leaflets. It produces erect, conical spires of double white flowers in spring, which have red or yellow markings. Nonfruiting.

Cotoneaster frigidus
TREE COTONEASTER
☼ ☼ 7   Vigorous growth
↕ 30ft (10m) ↔ 30ft (10m)

Although it is most often multistemmed with a spreading crown, this cotoneaster can be trained to a single stem. It carries large leaves, and white flowerheads in early summer, to be followed in autumn and early winter by bold bunches of red fruit.

+ *Laburnocytisus* 'Adamii'
ADAM'S LABURNUM
☼ 5
Moderate growth
↕ 25ft (8m) ↔ 22ft (7m)

This tree resembles a laburnum in habit and leaf, but the tassels of both yellow and pink flowers that are produced in late spring or early summer are accompanied by the occasional fuzzy clump of purple-flowered blooms.

Quercus robur
ENGLISH OAK
☼ 5
Slow growth
↕ 80ft (25m) ↔ 80ft (25m)

A famous tree, and one that is very popular in English folk culture, the English Oak fully justifies its position as a symbol of toughness and longevity. Its rugged bark, wavy-lobed green leaves, and long-stalked acorns are among its credentials.

Magnolia x
soulangiana ▷

Magnolia x *soulangiana*
SAUCER MAGNOLIA
☼ 4
Moderate growth
↕ 20ft (6m) ↔ 22ft (7m)

Fragrant, goblet-shaped white, pink, or purple-flushed blooms grace this magnolia in spring and often sporadically throughout summer. It has a spreading, low-branched crown and bold foliage. There are many excellent cultivars.

OTHER TREES TOLERANT OF HEAVY CLAY SOILS

Betula utilis var. *jacquemontii* 'Doorenbos', see p.300
Carpinus betulus 'Fastigiata'
Crataegus viridis 'Winter King'
Eucalyptus glaucescens
Ilex opaca
Malus hupehensis, see p.269
Platanus x *hispanica*, see p.283
Prunus 'Okame'
Quercus palustris, see p.267
Salix pentandra
Sorbus aucuparia, see p.284
Tilia mongolica

Populus maximowiczii
POPLAR
☼ 4
Vigorous growth
↕ 70ft (20m) ↔ 30ft (10m)

This poplar is a tall tree with ascending, then shortly spreading, branches. Its bold, heart-shaped, bright green leaves turn yellow in autumn. The spring catkins produced by female trees ripen to fluffy white in summer. Dislikes dry soils.

Sorbus alnifolia
KOREAN MOUNTAIN ASH
☼ ☼ 4
Moderate growth
↕ 35ft (11m) ↔ 25ft (8m)

The crown of this tough and adaptable tree is conical or oval, and spreads later. Its bright green leaves become orange and red in autumn. White flower clusters are produced in late spring, and these are followed by bright red fruits in autumn.

T R E E S

Trees for Acid Soils

EW TREES WILL ACTUALLY FAIL to grow in alkaline soils, but quite a few perform poorly in such places, preferring to grow in soils of an acid or neutral reaction. The trees shown here grow best in acid soils, especially where they are reasonably fertile and sufficient moisture is available during the growing season, usually summer.

Eucryphia x *nymansensis* 'Nymansay'
EUCRYPHIA
☼ ☼ 8 ᴾᴴ ⌄
Moderate growth
↕ 43ft (13m) ↔ 20ft (6m)

From late summer into early autumn, the shoots of this compact, columnar evergreen tree are crowded with clusters of white rose-like flowers. Its leaves are typically divided into glossy green leaflets. Enjoys moist, well-drained soils, with its roots shaded.

Cornus nuttallii
PACIFIC DOGWOOD
☼ ☼ 7 ᴾᴴ ⌄
Vigorous growth
↕ 43ft (13m) ↔ 25ft (8m)

The dark green leaves of this beautiful tree become yellow or red in autumn. Tiny spring flowers borne in tight clusters are surrounded by large white bracts and are followed by showy red fruit clusters. Thrives in moist but well-drained soils.

TREES TOLERANT OF BOTH HIGH ACIDITY AND HIGH ALKALINITY
Betula pendula
Crataegus monogyna
Fagus sylvatica, see p.281
Ilex aquifolium
Populus alba, see p.284
Populus x *canescens*
Quercus cerris
Quercus robur, see p.273
Sorbus x *hybrida*
Sorbus intermedia

Embothrium coccineum Lanceolatum Group
CHILEAN FIRE TREE
☼ ☼ 8
Vigorous growth
↕ 30ft (10m) ↔ 15ft (5m)

Easily one of the most spectacular and eye-catching of all trees when in flower. It is erect in habit when young, broadening later. The long, willowlike leaves are joined in early summer by crowded, firecracker red flowers. Best in moist, free-draining soil.

Magnolia fraseri
FRASER'S MAGNOLIA
☼ 5 ᴾᴴ ⌄
Moderate growth
↕ 30ft (10m) ↔ 25ft (8m)

Uncommon in general cultivation, this attractive, loose-spreading magnolia is easily distinguished by its enormous green leaves. The large, fragrant flowers are carried from late spring into early summer, and may be followed by cylindrical red fruit clusters.

Nothofagus nervosa
RAULI
☼ ☀ 7 PH ▼
Vigorous growth
↕ 70ft (20m) ↔ 40ft (12m)

A straight-stemmed, good-looking tree with its shoots clothed in large, conspicuously veined leaves. These emerge bronze, then become green in summer, giving attractive orange and red tints in autumn. Rauli is not suitable for exposed sites.

Sassafras albidum
SASSAFRAS
☼ ☀ 5 PH ▼
Moderate growth
↕ 70ft (20m) ↔ 25ft (8m)

Famous for a medicinal tea brewed from its aromatic root bark, this handsome tree is clothed with variously lobed leaves that turn yellow, orange, or purple in autumn. Its rugged bark and pale branches are a winter attraction.

> ### OTHER TREES FOR ACID SOILS
>
> *Acer japonicum* 'Aconitifolium'
>   *Acer rubrum*
>   *Eucryphia glutinosa*, see p.271
>   *Franklinia alatamaha*
>   *Ilex opaca*
>   *Liquidambar styraciflua*
>   *Michelia doltsopa*
>   *Nothofagus dombeyi*
>   *Nyssa sylvatica*
>   *Quercus rubra*
>   *Styrax japonicus*, see p.269
>   *Styrax obassia*

Oxydendrum arboreum
SOURWOOD
☼ ☀ 6 PH ▼
Moderate growth
↕ 40ft (12m) ↔ 25ft (8m)

This conical, later spreading, tree produces handsome, glossy green leaves that turn brilliant red or purple in autumn. Tiny, scented flowers appear in late summer and last into autumn. Thrives in moist, well-drained soils with its roots shaded.

Stewartia pseudocamellia
JAPANESE STEWARTIA
☼ ☀ 5 PH ▼
Moderate growth
↕ 40ft (12m) ↔ 20ft (6m)

This superb decorative tree has many garden qualities. Spreading in habit, its reddish brown bark flakes with age to form patches that are attractive in winter. White flowers open from midsummer, and the leaves turn a striking orange or red in autumn.

T R E E S

275

Trees for Alkaline Soils

HAVING AN ALKALINE SOIL in all or part of your garden does not mean your planting choices are limited. Free-draining, and warming faster than most other soils in spring, alkaline soils suit a range of ornamental trees. Many of the trees here will perform quite well in a range of soils, from slightly acid to alkaline.

Albizia julibrissin
MIMOSA, SILK TREE
☼ 6
Vigorous growth
↕ 30ft (10m) ↔ 30ft (10m)

For most of its relatively short life, the Silk Tree is broader than tall, with spreading branches and finely divided, fernlike leaves. Its clusters of fluffy, pink-stamened flowers are produced in late summer and autumn. *A. julibrissin* 'Rosea' is a hardier selection.

Cercis siliquastrum
JUDAS TREE
☼ 6
Moderate growth
↕ 30ft (10m) ↔ 30ft (10m)

Occasionally multistemmed, this more often single-stemmed, spreading tree has heart-shaped blue-green leaves. Rosy lilac pea flowers emerge in spring and are followed by flattened red seed pods. 'Bodnant' is a form with deep purple flowers.

OTHER TREES FOR ALKALINE SOILS

Acer campestre
Acer negundo 'Flamingo', see p.290
Acer platanoides, see p.281
Aesculus californica
Aesculus hippocastanum
Arbutus x andrachnoides, see p.302
Fagus sylvatica, see p.281
Ligustrum lucidum, see p.286
Malus x moerlandsii 'Profusion'
Malus x robusta 'Red Sentinel', see p.298
Morus nigra
Paulownia tomentosa
Prunus 'Shirotae'
Prunus 'Shôgetsu'
Prunus 'Ukon'
Quercus macrocarpa
Sophora japonica
Tilia tomentosa

△ *Crataegus laciniata*

Crataegus laciniata
ORIENTAL HAWTHORN
☼ 6
Slow growth
↕ 18ft (5.5m) ↔ 18ft (5.5m)

This slow-growing ornamental hawthorn will eventually develop a dense, rounded crown clothed in deeply lobed, dark green leaves. Clusters of pretty white blossoms emerge in late spring, and its large, downy red fruits are produced in autumn.

TREES

Fraxinus ornus
MANNA ASH
☼ 6   Moderate growth
                       ↕ 50ft (15m) ↔ 43ft (13m)

Typically round-headed, this attractive tree has much-divided, pale green leaves and produces large, branched heads of scented, creamy white flowers from late spring into early summer. Bronze-tinted fruits follow. A reliable tree of dense habit.

Malus floribunda
JAPANESE CRABAPPLE
☼ 5   Moderate growth
                       ↕ 25ft (8m) ↔ 30ft (10m)

This is one of the most popular and reliable of all the flowering crabapples. Its dense, rounded crown is flooded in spring with pale pink flowers. Masses of pea-sized yellow, red-cheeked fruits are borne in autumn. Among the first crabapples to flower.

Koelreuteria paniculata
GOLDEN-RAIN TREE   Moderate growth
☼ 5   ↕ 30ft (10m) ↔ 30ft (10m)

The leaves of this domed tree, which is sometimes broader than it is tall, are regularly divided into numerous toothed leaflets and turn yellow in autumn. Large, branched, yellow flowerheads in summer are followed by conspicuous, inflated seed pods.

Prunus x *yedoensis*
YOSHINO CHERRY
☼ 6   Moderate growth
                       ↕ 25ft (8m) ↔ 30ft (10m)

Eventually broad-domed, this cherry has wide-spreading, arching branches. In early spring, these are profusely hung with drooping clusters of almond-scented, white or pale blush blossoms, pink in bud. One of the most reliable of all flowering cherries.

Laburnum alpinum
SCOTCH LABURNUM
☼ 5   Moderate growth
                       ↕ 22ft (7m) ↔ 22ft (7m)

Scotch Laburnum is broad-headed, with a short, stocky stem and lush, deep green, three-parted leaves. Long, pendent chains of bright yellow pea flowers appear in late spring or early summer and are deliciously fragrant. All parts are poisonous if eaten.

Sorbus aria 'Lutescens'
WHITEBEAM
☼ 5   Moderate growth
                       ↕ 35ft (11m) ↔ 25ft (8m)

This is an attractive ornamental tree with an erect to oval crown at first, later spreading. Its leaves are creamy white when they first emerge in spring and become gray-green as they mature. White flowers are produced from late spring into early summer.

TREES

Trees for Dry, Sunny Sites

THOSE WITH gardens in dry, sunny places will be all too familiar with the problems that a summer drought can bring to trees. A fast-draining sandy or gravelly soil can be an added difficulty. Fortunately, some trees tolerate, if not relish, such conditions.

Eucalyptus dalrympleana
MOUNTAIN GUM
☼ 8   Vigorous growth
                                      ↕ 70ft (20m) ↔ 28ft (9m)

Columnar when young, the handsome Mountain Gum broadens later. Its evergreen leaves are rounded on younger trees, and elongated and drooping later. Leaves are joined by white flower clusters in late summer. Young creamy white bark is attractive.

Celtis australis
SOUTHERN NETTLE TREE
☼ 6   Moderate growth
                                      ↕ 60ft (18m) ↔ 50ft (15m)

Uncommon but easy to grow, this ornamental tree has smooth, pale gray bark. It is broadly columnar with a dome-shaped crown, although the branches on older trees are often pendulous. The surfaces of its slender, pointed leaves are rough to the touch.

Cladrastis kentukea
YELLOWWOOD
☼ 4   Moderate growth
                                      ↕ 40ft (12m) ↔ 40ft (12m)

This excellent ornamental tree has numerous attractive features: a rounded or dome-shaped crown, ashlike leaves that become clear yellow in autumn, and large, branched, drooping heads of fragrant white pea flowers that are produced in summer.

Gleditsia triacanthos 'Sunburst'
SUNBURST HONEYLOCUST
☼ 3   Moderate growth
                                      ↕ 30ft (10m) ↔ 25ft (8m)

The stem and branches of this specimen tree are gray-brown. Its pretty, much-divided, glossy leaves are golden yellow when they emerge, darken to green later, then turn pale yellow in autumn. Honeylocusts are tolerant of extreme air pollution.

Maackia amurensis
MAACKIA
☼ 3   Slow growth   ↕ 22ft (7m) ↔ 22ft (7m)

This wide-spreading tree with grayish brown bark has ashlike, deep green leaves, silver-blue when young. Dense, stubby spikes of flowers, white, tinged the palest slate blue, are produced in summer and held in clusters above the branches.

Sophora japonica 'Violacea'
PAGODA TREE
☼ 5   Vigorous growth   ↕ 60ft (18m) ↔ 60ft (18m)

The gray-brown bark of this round-headed tree is prominently ridged. Its ashlike leaves emerge late in the season, and the loose heads of small white, lilac-tinged pea flowers are borne from late summer into early autumn. Drooping seed pods follow.

Pittosporum crassifolium 'Variegatum'
VARIEGATED KARO
☼ 9   Moderate growth   ↕ 15ft (5m) ↔ 10ft (3m)

Unless trained to a single stem, this evergreen tree with its dense, bushy crown will remain shrubby. The leathery leaves are gray-green with a white margin. Small, scented, reddish purple flowers appear in spring. Karo is excellent for mild coastal areas.

> **OTHER TREES FOR DRY, SUNNY SITES**
>
> *Arbutus* x *andrachnoides*, see p.302
> *Cercis siliquastrum*, see p.276
> *Evodia daniellii*
> *Fraxinus velutina*
> *Genista aetnensis*
> *Koelreuteria paniculata*, see p.277
> *Ligustrum lucidum*, see p.286
> *Phellodendron amurense*
> *Quercus alba*
> *Quercus macrocarpa*

Quercus canariensis
ALGERIAN OAK
☼ 8   Moderate growth   ↕ 70ft (20m) ↔ 40ft (12m)

The habit of this distinct and handsome oak is broadly columnar when young, becoming more rounded with age. Its upswept branches are densely covered with large, regularly lobed leaves, which are usually retained into late winter.

Umbellularia californica
CALIFORNIA BAY, HEADACHE TREE
☼ 8   Moderate growth   ↕ 40ft (12m) ↔ 30ft (10m)

A relative of sweet bay *(Laurus nobilis)*, this dense, bushy-headed evergreen tree produces clusters of delicate yellowish flowers in spring. Its bright green, leathery leaves are pungent if crushed, and the vapor may cause nausea if inhaled.

T R E E S

Trees for Watersides

Few sights, to me, are more appealing than a weeping willow growing on a river bank. Not many of us are fortunate enough to have a river running through our garden, but there is no reason why a suitable tree should not be planted next to a pool or stretch of water. As long as you maintain a sense of scale, the possibilities are endless.

Pterocarya fraxinifolia
CAUCASIAN WINGNUT
☼ 6
Moderate growth
↕ 80ft (25m) ↔ 70ft (20m)

Eventually a large, broad-spreading tree, this has much-divided, ashlike leaves and long, drooping tassels of green flowers. Its green winged fruits follow. Suckers that appear should always be removed, unless you want to encourage a grove.

OTHER TREES FOR WATERSIDES

Acer rubrum
Alnus glutinosa
Nyssa sylvatica
Populus maximowiczii, see p.273
Quercus bicolor
Salix babylonica var. *pekinensis* 'Tortuosa', see p.301
Salix pentandra

Alnus rubra
RED ALDER
☼ 6
Vigorous growth
↕ 50ft (15m) ↔ 30ft (10m)

This is a fast-growing tree of conical habit. In early spring, before the leaves unfurl, its branches are draped with yellowish orange male catkins that can be up to 6in (15cm) long. Its toothed leaves are boldy veined. Older trees have pale gray bark.

△ *Salix* x *sepulcralis* var. *chrysocoma*

Betula nigra
RIVER BIRCH
☼ 4
Moderate growth
↕ 50ft (15m) ↔ 50ft (15m)

River birch is distinctive, quite unlike the more usual white-stemmed kinds. The bark of the stem and main branches is peeling and shaggy, pinkish gray in color, maturing to dark brown. Its leaves are diamond-shaped and pale beneath.

Salix x *sepulcralis* var. *chrysocoma*
GOLDEN WEEPING WILLOW
☼ 3
Vigorous growth
↕ 20m (70ft) ↔ 25m (80ft)

This is a popular subject for the waterside, but it is too large for the small gardens in which it is often planted. It has long curtains of weeping, golden yellow branches in winter. These are covered with slender, bright green leaves in spring and summer.

T R E E S

Trees for Screening or Windbreaks

I N ADDITION TO CONIFERS, various medium-sized to large broad-leaved trees make a good line of defense against persistent winds, and can screen unattractive views or unsightly objects. Many also have ornamental features.

Fagus sylvatica
EUROPEAN BEECH
☼ 5
Moderate growth
↕ 120ft (35m) ↔ 50ft (15m)

One of the temperate world's most beautiful trees, this matures to form a dome-shaped crown. Smooth gray bark in winter and pale green leaves in spring, turning shiny midgreen in summer and golden yellow in autumn, make this a tree for all seasons.

Acer platanoides
NORWAY MAPLE
☼ 3
Vigorous growth
↕ 80ft (25m) ↔ 50ft (15m)

One of the most adaptable and reliable of all trees, Norway Maple develops a rounded crown. Yellow-green flower clusters emerge in midspring, before the leaves appear, followed by green winged fruits. The leaves may turn yellow in autumn.

OTHER TREES FOR SCREENING OR WINDBREAKS

Acer pseudoplatanus
Fraxinus americana
Maclura pomifera
Populus x *canadensis* 'Robusta'
Quercus imbricaria
Quercus phellos

△ *Prunus serotina*

Alnus cordata
ITALIAN ALDER
☼ 6
Vigorous growth
↕ 80ft (25m) ↔ 35ft (11m)

This handsome columnar tree becomes conical later. Bunches of long yellow male catkins drape the branches in late winter or early spring. In summer, its conelike fruits develop among the large, rounded leaves with shining, dark green upper surfaces.

Prunus serotina
BLACK CHERRY
☼ ☼ 3
Moderate growth
↕ 50ft (15m) ↔ 43ft (13m)

This free-growing tree has an oval crown of pendulous or arching branches. Its deep green, glossy leaves are deciduous, becoming yellow or red in autumn. Small white spring flowers are carried in drooping tassels, and give way to shining black fruits.

T R E E S

281

Trees Tolerant of Air Pollution

ITES SUBJECT to air pollution would not seem to be ideal areas for growing trees. Given adequate soil preparation and after-care, however, a good variety of trees, both large and small, will perform just as well as they would in places enjoying clean air.

Fraxinus angustifolia
NARROW-LEAVED ASH
☼ 6

Vigorous growth
↕ 70ft (20m) ↔ 40ft (12m)

More elegant in habit than the European Ash *(Fraxinus excelsior),* this large tree has spreading branches that form an attractive oval to rounded crown. Its leaves are regularly divided into narrow, smooth, glossy green leaflets that become yellow in autumn.

Amelanchier laevis
ALLEGHENY SERVICEBERRY
☼ ☼ 5

Moderate growth
↕ 20ft (6m) ↔ 20ft (6m)

Clusters of white flowers flood the branches of this small, often multistemmed tree or large shrub in spring. It has a dense, spreading habit, and leaves which are bronze in spring, changing to green in summer, and then red or orange in autumn.

Ilex x *altaclerensis* 'Belgica Aurea'
HIGHCLERE HOLLY
☼ ☼ 6

Moderate growth
↕ 25ft (8m) ↔ 10ft (3m)

The bold leaves of this evergreen holly are lance-shaped with occasional spines. They are a mottled gray-green in color, and irregularly edged pale or creamy yellow. From autumn onward, this dense, compact columnar tree also bears red berries.

Crataegus laevigata 'Paul's Scarlet'
PAUL'S SCARLET HAWTHORN
☼ 5

Moderate growth
↕ 20ft (6m) ↔ 25ft (8m)

This is an attractive tree, with a dense, rounded or spreading crown. In late spring and early summer, the branches are covered in numerous clusters of double red flowers. The toothed leaves are glossy dark green. 'Punicea' is similar, with single crimson flowers.

OTHER TREES TOLERANT OF AIR POLLUTION

Acer pseudoplatanus
Aesculus x *carnea* 'Briotii'
Ailanthus altissima
Alnus cordata, see p.281
Carpinus betulus
Catalpa bignonioides, see p.292
Celtis occidentalis
Fraxinus americana
Ginkgo biloba, see p.244
Koelreuteria paniculata, see p.277
Magnolia x *soulangiana,* see p.273
Malus cvs.
Phellodendron amurense
Platanus occidentalis
Populus alba
Quercus rubra
Sophora japonica
Tilia cordata

△ *Crataegus laevigata* 'Paul's Scarlet'

Prunus dulcis 'Roseoplena'
DOUBLE ALMOND
☼ 7   Moderate growth
↕ 25ft (8m) ↔ 25ft (8m)

In late winter and early spring, the spreading branches of this tree are studded with double, pale pink flowers. These emerge ahead of the dark green, lance-shaped, long, and pointed leaves, brightening the dullest of late winter days.

Laburnum x *waterei* 'Vossii'
VOSS'S LABURNUM
☼ 5   Moderate growth
↕ 22ft (7m) ↔ 22ft (7m)

The crown of this tree, the most commonly planted laburnum, is spreading and crowded with leaves composed of three leaflets. Long, tapering chains of pea flowers hang from its branches in late spring or early summer. All parts are poisonous if eaten.

Pyrus calleryana 'Chanticleer'
ORNAMENTAL PEAR
☼ 6   Moderate growth
↕ 40ft (12m) ↔ 20ft (6m)

Tough and hardy, this compact, conical tree has rounded, glossy green leaves that turn reddish purple in autumn. The branches are hidden by beautiful white blossoms in spring, at which time the tree is clearly visible from afar.

Platanus x *hispanica*
LONDON PLANE
☼ 5   Moderate growth
↕ 100ft (30m) ↔ 70ft (20m)

This enormous tree develops a massive splotchy stem and a large spreading crown. Broad, maplelike leaves with five big, toothed lobes are carried in summer. From summer onward, strings of bristly, spherical fruits hang on stalks, like baubles.

Robinia pseudoacacia
BLACK LOCUST
☼ 3   Vigorous growth
↕ 70ft (20m) ↔ 40ft (12m)

The shoots of this tough and adaptable tree are prickly, and its leaves ashlike with oval leaflets. Drooping clusters of white pea flowers are fragrant and occur from late spring into early summer. Develops rugged bark in time, and will sucker if pruned hard.

T R E E S

283

Trees Tolerant of Coastal Exposure

ONLY THE TOUGHEST TREES will survive the twin problems of strong winds and salt spray in seaside gardens. The following are among the most tolerant, and are well worth considering if only as an outer planting to provide shelter for shrubs and perennials.

Populus alba
WHITE POPLAR, ABELE
☼ 4
Vigorous growth
↕ 70ft (20m) ↔ 43ft (13m)

This well-known, spreading tree has imposing, gray-fissured bark. The leaves, which vary in shape from rounded and toothed to lobed and maplelike, are dark green above and covered below with a white felt, making a striking contrast when blown by wind.

Hippophae rhamnoides
SEA BUCKTHORN
☼ 3
Moderate growth
↕ 20ft (6m) ↔ 20ft (6m)

Due to its bushy nature, careful pruning and training are needed to make a single- or few-stemmed tree. Narrow, silver-gray leaves crowd the thorny branches. Plant both male and female plants to produce brilliant orange berries that may last all winter.

OTHER TREES TOLERANT OF COASTAL EXPOSURE

Alnus rubra, see p.280
Populus x canadensis 'Robusta'
Quercus ilex
Tilia cordata

Salix alba
WHITE WILLOW
☼ 2
Vigorous growth
↕ 70ft (20m) ↔ 43ft (13m)

A handsome willow of conical habit at first, this soon spreads to be as broad as it is tall. Its narrow silvery leaves shimmer in the sun. Suited to damp places, but do not plant near underground drains, water systems, or buildings because of its invasive roots.

Phillyrea latifolia
PHILLYREA
☼ 8
Slow growth
↕ 25ft (8m) ↔ 25ft (8m)

This little-known, but valuable, evergreen tree is rather like a small version of the Holly Oak *(Quercus ilex)*. The narrow, glossy, dark green leaves are leathery and toothed. Its tiny cream-yellow flowers are borne in dense clusters from late spring into summer.

Sorbus aucuparia
EUROPEAN MOUNTAIN ASH
☼ ☼ 3
Moderate growth
↕ 30ft (10m) ↔ 22ft (7m)

The leaves of this gray-barked tree of spreading habit resemble those of an ash, often turning red or yellow in autumn. Clusters of white spring flowers are followed by drooping bunches of orange-red berries, maturing to bright red. Better in cooler areas.

Trees with Bold Leaves

Y OU CAN TRANSFORM your garden by growing a tree with bold foliage. A single specimen with leaves of impressive size is worth planting in its own right, creating a tropical effect in the most mundane planting. Bold foliage can also be effective when contrasted with smaller-leaved subjects. Many bold-foliaged trees have the further bonus of attractive flowers and fruits.

Toona sinensis
CHINESE TOON TREE
☼ 6
Vigorous growth
‡ 50ft (15m) ↔ 30ft (10m)

This fast-growing tree has large, much-divided leaves that can grow up to 24in (60cm) long. These are bronze-red when young and turn yellow in autumn. In summer, mature trees carry large, drooping heads of small, fragrant white flowers.

> ### OTHER TREES WITH BOLD LEAVES
> *Aralia elata* 'Variegata'
> *Catalpa bignonioides*, see p.272
> *Firmiana simplex*
> *Liriodendron tulipifera*, see p.291
> *Paulownia tomentosa*

Kalopanax septemlobus
CASTOR ARALIA
☼ 5
Moderate growth
‡ 40ft (12m) ↔ 30ft (10m)

A handsome tree, this has prickly stems and trunk, and maple-like leaves that turn yellow in autumn. Rounded clusters of tiny whitish flowers in late summer are followed by blue-black berries. Thrives in moist, well-drained soils.

Magnolia obovata
JAPANESE BIG-LEAF MAGNOLIA
☼ 5 PH
Vigorous growth
‡ 70ft (20m) ↔ 30ft (10m)

The large, firm leaves of this magnificent conical tree, broadest in their upper halves, are carried in impressive whorls at the ends of the branches. Strongly fragrant, bowl-shaped flowers are borne in summer and followed by cylindrical red fruit clusters.

Trachycarpus fortunei
CHUSAN PALM, WINDMILL PALM
☼ 8
Slow growth
‡ 25ft (8m) ↔ 8ft (2.5m)

This is probably the hardiest palm suitable for cool, temperate regions, especially in coastal areas. It is a familiar sight, with its shaggy, fibrous bark, rounded head of fan-shaped, many-fingered leaves, and sprays of fragrant creamy flowers in early summer.

Evergreen Trees

APART FROM CONIFERS, evergreen trees are greatly outnumbered by deciduous trees in temperate climates. This makes evergreens all the more desirable in the garden, especially in winter when their rich green, colored, or variegated foliage offers a striking contrast to bare twigs or winter-flowering shrubs. They also provide effective year-round screening.

Ligistrum lucidum
CHINESE PRIVET
☼ ☼ 8   Moderate growth
‡ 30–40ft (10–12m) ↔ 30ft (10m)

At all times a handsome tree with its fluted trunk and dense crown of large, glossy, dark green foliage. In early autumn the canopy is smothered with richly scented cream flowerheads. An ideal specimen tree for a large lawn, but avoid exposed sites.

Eucalyptus gunnii
CIDER GUM
☼ 8   Vigorous growth
‡ 60–80ft (18–25m) ↔ 30–50ft (9–15m)

The most commonly planted eucalypt in cool-temperate gardens, although it is too vigorous for all but the largest gardens. It has decorative cream and gray exfoliating bark; leathery blue, gray, or gray-green leaves; and fluffy white flowerheads in summer.

Ilex x *koehneana* 'Chestnut Leaf'
HYBRID HOLLY
☼ ☼ 7   Moderate growth
‡ 40ft (12m) ↔ 8–12ft (2.5–3.5m)

A bold and noble holly with a compact, well-branched habit, notable for its striking, polished, chestnutlike leaves, which are leathery and spine-toothed. Abundant red berries appear from autumn to winter if pollinated by a male tree.

Magnolia grandiflora
BULL BAY, SOUTHERN MAGNOLIA
☼ 7   Moderate growth
‡ 20–60ft (6–18m) ↔ 15–50ft (4.5–15m)

Easily recognized by its dense, conical, or sometimes bushy habit and its large, leathery, polished leaves. Few trees are so long-flowering, with big, bowl-shaped, fragrant, cream flowers from summer into autumn. Thrives and flowers best in a warm site.

Maytenus boaria
MAITEN
☼ ☀ 9   Moderate growth
↕ 30ft (10m) ↔ 25ft (8m)

This unusual and elegant tree has an effect not unlike a weeping willow. Erect when young, it gradually broadens into a round-headed tree, its branches well clothed with narrow, glossy green, toothed leaves. Tiny spring flowers are of little ornamental merit.

Pittosporum tenuifolium
KOHUHU
☼ 9   Moderate growth
↕ 20ft (6m) ↔ 15ft (5m)

Columnar when young, Kohuhu is later dome-shaped and compact. Slender branchlets bear glossy leaves and small, honey-scented, bell-shaped purple flowers appear in late spring. It is excellent as a screen or single specimen, especially in coastal areas.

OTHER EVERGREEN TREES

Arbutus unedo
Drimys winteri
Eucalyptus coccifera
Eucryphia x *intermedia* 'Rostrevor'
Ilex opaca
Ilex pedunculosa
Laurus nobilis
Prunus lusitanica, see p.209
Quercus agrifolia
Quercus virginiana
Trachycarpus fortunei, see p.285

Luma apiculata
LUMA
☼ ☀ 9   Vigorous growth
↕ 22ft (7m) ↔ 15ft (5m)

Luma is a splendid year-round performer. From midsummer into autumn the glossy, dark green leaves of this dense-habited tree are interspersed with masses of small white flowers. Golden brown bark peels with age to reveal patches of creamy new bark.

Quercus ilex
HOLM OAK, EVERGREEN OAK
☼ ☀ 7   Moderate growth
↕ 60–80ft (18–24m) ↔ 60–70ft (18–21m)

An ultimately large tree for screening and as a specimen in large gardens. The rounded canopy is crowded with leathery, glossy, dark green leaves that are variable in shape when young. Clusters of yellow catkins cover the canopy in June.

Rhododendron arboreum
TREE RHODODENDRON
☼ 7   Slow growth
↕ 40ft (12m) ↔ 10ft (3m)

This magnificent, slow-growing rhododendron broadens as it ages. The leaves are leathery and dark green on top, silver or brownish beneath. Red, pink, or occasionally white bell-shaped flowers are carried in dense, globular heads in spring.

TREES

287

Weeping Trees

NOT EVERY GARDENER likes weeping trees. Some find them too messy or sad, but a well-sited weeping tree on a lawn, or by water or a border edge, can add both interest and dramatic effect. To attain a good height, such trees generally require further training to a stake for a few years, especially when bought as young, grafted plants.

Fagus sylvatica 'Pendula'
WEEPING EUROPEAN BEECH
☼ ⑤   Vigorous growth
                                    ↕ 60ft (18m) ↔ 70ft (20m)

The Weeping European Beech is a magnificent tree for a large lawn. Its arching or spreading branches are all draped with long, hanging branchlets, and it remains attractive throughout the year. Several other forms are also in cultivation.

Betula pendula 'Youngii'
YOUNG'S WEEPING BIRCH
☼ ☼ ②   Vigorous growth
                                    ↕ ↔ 25ft (8m)

A popular weeping tree, especially as a lawn feature. It eventually develops a flat-topped or low-domed crown with a curtain of long, slender branches and branchlets clothed with small, glossy green, diamond-shaped leaves that turn yellow in autumn.

Fraxinus excelsior 'Pendula'
WEEPING EUROPEAN ASH
☼ ☼ ⑤   Vigorous growth
                                    ↕ 50ft (15m) ↔ 30ft (10m)

Tough and adaptable, this weeping form of the European Ash has thick, arching branches and pendulous shoots forming a domed crown, broadening with age. As with all weeping trees, train the leader to a tall stake when young.

Cercidiphyllum japonicum f. *pendulum*
WEEPING KATSURA
☼ ☼ ④   Vigorous growth
                                    ↕ 40ft (12m) ↔ 20ft (6m)

Few hardy trees are more graceful or more pleasing to the eye than the Katsura, especially in autumn, when the leaves turn to pale yellow. This gracefully weeping form makes the perfect lawn specimen. It dislikes dry soils.

Ilex aquifolium 'Pendula'
WEEPING HOLLY
☼ ☼ ⑦   Moderate growth
                                    ↕ ↔ 15–18ft (4.5–5m)

An excellent evergreen weeping tree for year-round effect. It develops a dome-shaped crown of densely packed, pendulous, purple-barked branches and glossy dark green, prickly leaves. Red berries appear from autumn to winter if a male tree is nearby.

Prunus 'Cheal's Weeping'
CHEAL'S WEEPING CHERRY
☼ 6
Moderate growth
↕ 8ft (2.5m) ↔ 10ft (3m)

Normally low-domed, this small, weeping Japanese cherry tree is very popular in gardens where space is at a premium. In spring, the arching and pendent branches are crowded with bright pink, double flowers. It looks particularly effective by a small pool.

Salix caprea 'Kilmarnock'
KILMARNOCK WILLOW
☼ 5
Vigorous growth
↕ 6ft (2m) ↔ 4½ft (1.4m)

This dense-crowned cultivar of the goat willow is suitable for even the smallest garden. It has numerous weeping branches that, in spring, are studded with silver-gray male catkins that turn yellow as they mature.

OTHER WEEPING TREES

Morus alba 'Pendula'
Pyrus salicifolia 'Pendula', see p.294
Salix x *sepulcralis* var. *chrysocoma*, see p.280
Sophora japonica 'Pendula'

Salix caprea
'Kilmarnock' ▷

Prunus pendula 'Pendula Rubra'
WEEPING SPRING CHERRY
☼ 5
Moderate growth
↕ 15ft (5m) ↔ 20ft (6m)

The dome-shaped crown of this beautiful, elegant cherry can be trained to a greater height than 15ft (5m) if desired. Masses of small, deep rose pink, single blossoms, carmine in bud, crowd its slender, weeping branches in spring.

Tilia 'Petiolaris'
WEEPING SILVER LINDEN
☼ 5
Vigorous growth
↕ 100ft (30m) ↔ 70ft (20m)

A most notable tree, suitable for large gardens only, and a superb specimen for a spacious lawn. The domed crown tops a broad column of weeping branches clothed with glossy dark green, white-backed leaves. Scented flowers appear in late summer.

T R E E S

Trees with Variegated Leaves

BESIDES the novelty appeal they afford, trees with variegated leaves are valuable when used as a contrast against plain green or darker-leaved subjects. This is particularly true of foliage whose variegation consists of a strong white or yellow margin against green.

Gymnocladus dioica 'Variegata'
KENTUCKY COFFEE TREE
☼ 5
Slow growth
↕ 50ft (15m) ↔ 40ft (12m)

Presently a rare tree in cultivation, but well worth searching for. The large, twice-divided leaves are comparatively late in appearing, pink at first, later margined and marbled white, creating a striking effect. A splendid specimen tree for a large lawn or border.

Acer negundo 'Flamingo'
BOX ELDER
☼ 5
Vigorous growth
↕ ↔ 30ft (10m)

One of the easiest and most decorative of all variegated maples. Its bloomy young shoots and young, pink-suffused leaves age to green with bold white margins. Prune hard in late winter; the resulting strong shoots give larger and more colorful foliage.

OTHER VARIEGATED TREES
Acer crataegifolium 'Veitchii'
Cornus alternifolia 'Argentea'
Fagus sylvatica 'Purpurea Tricolor'
Fraxinus pennsylvanica 'Variegata'
Zelkova serrata 'Variegata'

Cornus controversa 'Variegata'
JAPENESE PAGODA DOGWOOD
☼ 5
Slow growth
↕ 30ft (10m) ↔ 30ft (10m)

As a lawn specimen, this beautiful tree is unmatched. Frequently broader than it is high, it develops a tabulated, or tiered, crown of spreading branches, ideally to ground level. These are clothed with slender-pointed leaves, broadly margined creamy white.

Ilex x *altaclerensis* 'Camelliifolia Variegata'
HIGHCLERE HOLLY
☼ ☼ 6
Slow growth
↕ 25ft (8m) ↔ 10ft (3m)

This broadly columnar evergreen is densely packed with short-spreading branches that reach all the way down to the base. Its oblong leaves are glossy dark green, and each has a broad yellow margin. Bears red berries when pollinated.

Ligustrum lucidum 'Excelsum Superbum'
CHINESE PRIVET
☼ 8   Moderate growth
$\updownarrow$ ↔ 30ft (10m)

A striking form of the Chinese Privet with large, glossy evergreen leaves edged with yellow or greenish yellow. It has a dense crown, a compact habit, and fragrant white flowers in autumn. Suitable for a lawn, but avoid exposed sites.

Liriodendron tulipifera 'Aureomarginatum'
VARIEGATED TULIP TREE
☼ 5   Vigorous growth
$\updownarrow$ 60ft (18m) ↔ 35ft (11m)

Strong-growing and erect, this tree spreads with age. Its peculiarly shaped leaves are dark green with yellow margins in full sun, and pale to light green in shade. They turn a golden color in autumn. Established trees produce cup-shaped, greenish white flowers.

Platanus x *hispanica* 'Suttneri'
LONDON PLANE
☼ 5   Vigorous growth
$\updownarrow$ 70ft (20m) ↔ 60ft (18m)

This tree has all the qualities of the London Plane but differs in its bold and conspicuous, creamy white-variegated foliage. It is most suitable as a specimen tree on a large lawn, especially when grown against a dark background.

Liquidambar styraciflua 'Variegata'
SWEET GUM
☼ 6   Moderate growth
$\updownarrow$ 50ft (15m) ↔ 30ft (10m)

Sometimes listed as 'Aurea', this attractive tree develops a conical habit well-clothed with boldly lobed, glossy green leaves blotched and striped yellow; they become pink-tinted then purple-suffused in autumn. Not suited to shallow, chalky soils.

Quercus cerris 'Argenteovariegata'
VARIEGATED TURKEY OAK
☼ 6   Moderate growth
$\updownarrow$ 30ft (10m) ↔ 40ft (12m)

This broad-spreading oak needs to be given plenty of space to develop and is one of the most effective hardy, variegated trees. Its branches are crowded with bristle-toothed, deeply lobed, dark green, glossy leaves, each with an irregular, creamy white margin.

T R E E S

Trees with Golden or Yellow Leaves

FLOWERING DISPLAYS ASIDE, no trees bring a brighter effect to the garden than those with golden or yellow foliage. A single tree of this kind, especially in a lawn, immediately attracts attention, as well as providing a bold contrast to a plain or dark background.

Acer shirasawanum 'Aureum'
GOLDEN FULLMOON MAPLE
☼ ☼ 5   Slow growth
                                        ↕ 18ft (5.5m) ↔ 15ft (5m)

This beautiful maple is upright to begin with, and spreads later. Its rounded, many-lobed leaves are golden yellow, often with a thin scarlet edge. It is one of the best golden-leaved trees but may be susceptible to sun scorch, particularly in hot, dry sites.

Acer cappadocicum 'Aureum'
GOLDEN CAPPADOCIAN MAPLE
☼ ☼ 6   Vigorous growth
                              ↕ ↔ 50–60ft (15–18m)

One of the most satisfactory of large trees with yellow foliage, best planted as a specimen on a large lawn. The sharply five-lobed leaves emerge crimson-purple, soon turning yellow, then paling to green-yellow in late summer. Suitable for most soils.

OTHER GOLD OR YELLOW TREES
Alnus incana 'Aurea'
Betula pendula 'Golden Cloud'
Gleditsia triacanthos 'Sunburst', see p.278
Populus alba 'Richardii'
Populus x *canadensis* 'Aurea'
Tilia x *europaea* 'Wratislaviensis'

Acer palmatum 'Aureum'
GOLDEN JAPANESE MAPLE
☼ 6   Vigorous growth
                          ↕ 25ft (8m) ↔ 15ft (5m)

A lovely maple of upright growth initially, later more spreading. The small, neatly five-lobed leaves are an attractive yellow with a touch of scarlet on the margins. New summer growth is even better, and in autumn the leaves turn golden yellow.

Catalpa bignonioides 'Aurea'
GOLDEN CATALPA
☼ 5   Moderate growth
                              ↕ 30ft (10m) ↔ 30ft (10m)

Eventually, Golden Catalpa grows to be domed or round-headed. The large, heart-shaped leaves are bronze-purple when young and mature to bright yellow. Its bell-shaped white flowers with purple and yellow spots are produced in summer.

T R E E S

Fagus sylvatica 'Zlatia'
GOLDEN BEECH
☼ ☀ 5
Moderate growth
↕ 70ft (20m) ↔ 50ft (15m)

Slower growing than more common green-leaved beeches, this tree has leaves of a soft yellow at first, becoming green by late summer. In autumn, the foliage ages to the typically golden yellow so familiar to tree lovers.

Laurus nobilis 'Aurea'
GOLDEN BAY
☼ 8
Moderate growth
↕ 40ft (12m) ↔ 15–20ft (5–6m)

This handsome golden form of the Bay Laurel or Sweet Bay develops a broad columnar or conical habit. The closely packed branches are densely clothed with aromatic, evergreen, golden yellow foliage. It is particularly effective in winter.

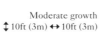

Ptelea trifoliata 'Aurea'
GOLDEN HOP TREE
☼ ☀ 4
Moderate growth
↕ 10ft (3m) ↔ 10ft (3m)

The aromatic, three-parted leaves of this small, round-headed or bushy tree are soft yellow when young, maturing through yellow-green to green. It is less harsh on the eye than most other golden trees. Greenish summer flowers are followed by winged fruits.

Quercus rubra 'Aurea'
GOLDEN RED OAK
☼ ☀ 5 PH
Slow growth
↕ 50ft (15m) ↔ 30ft (10m)

Although it is seldom planted, Golden Red Oak is a lovely tree, with a spreading crown of large, boldly lobed leaves. These are a clear, soft yellow when they emerge, becoming green later. It prefers a site that is sheltered from cold winds.

Quercus robur 'Concordia'
GOLDEN OAK
☼ ☀ 5
Slow growth
↕ ↔ 30ft (10m)

Patience is required with this tree, because it is painfully slow to develop. The leaves are a lovely color, suffused golden yellow from spring through summer, paling to green eventually. The ultimate specimen tree for a lawn.

Robinia pseudoacacia 'Frisia'
GOLDEN BLACK LOCUST
☼ ☀ 4
Moderate growth
↕ 50ft (15m) ↔ 25ft (8m)

This is one of the most popular and commonly planted golden-leaved trees. Its much-divided, ashlike leaves are a rich golden color when young, maturing through yellow to greenish yellow. They then become orange-yellow in autumn.

TREES

Trees with Blue-gray or Silver Leaves

COMPARED with the abundance of shrubs, there are very few trees with blue-gray or silver leaves suitable for gardens in cool, temperate climates. Fortunately, the few that are encompass a wide range of sizes. Their presence can contribute much to the garden.

Elaeagnus 'Quicksilver'
OLEASTER
☼ ⁴   Moderate growth
                                       ↕ 15ft (5m) ↔ 15ft (5m)

Although it has a bushy habit, this oleaster can be trained on a single stem to form a small tree (as can many large shrubs), with a loose, spreading crown of narrow silver-gray leaves. Fragrant, star-shaped, creamy yellow flowers open in late spring or summer.

Eucalyptus perriniana
SPINNING GUM
☼ ⁸   Vigorous growth
                                       ↕ 20ft (6m) ↔ 12ft (4m)

The stems of this small evergreen tree are darkly blotched and they have a white sheen. The leaves on juvenile trees are round and a shimmering silver-blue, but as the tree matures, its leaves are larger and longer, and their color more blue-green.

Pyrus salicifolia 'Pendula'
WEEPING WILLOW-LEAVED PEAR
☼ ⁵   Vigorous growth
                                       ↕ 25ft (8m) ↔ 20ft (6m)

This is a popular small tree that will form a domed or mushroom-shaped crown of arching and weeping branches, each clothed in narrow gray, downy leaves. The white flowers produced in spring are followed by small green fruits. Easy and reliable.

OTHER TREES WITH BLUE-GRAY OR SILVER LEAVES
Elaeagnus angustifolia
Eucalyptus coccifera
Eucalyptus glaucescens
Eucalyptus globulus
Eucalyptus gunnii, see p.286
Populus alba, see p.284
Pyrus nivalis
Salix alba var. *sericea*
Salix exigua, see p.223
Tilia 'Petiolaris', see p.289

△ *Sorbus thibetica* 'John Mitchell'

Sorbus thibetica 'John Mitchell'
HIMALAYAN WHITEBEAM
☼ ◑ ⁶   Vigorous growth
                                       ↕ 40ft (12m) ↔ 30ft (10m)

This broad, eventually round-headed, tree produces large leaves that are gray-green above when young and white-felted beneath. Leaves of young, vigorous trees can be more than 6in (15cm) long. Clusters of white flowers appear in late spring.

Trees with Purple, Red, or Bronze Leaves

PURPLE- OR BRONZE-LEAVED trees in a garden do not appeal to all gardeners, and there is no doubt that such a strong color can be an eyesore in the wrong place. Used with discretion, however, purple foliage can be very effective, especially when contrasted with shades of silver or blue-gray.

Acer platanoides 'Crimson King'
NORWAY MAPLE
☼ 3

Vigorous growth
↕ 60ft (18m) ↔ 50ft (15m)

One of the most commonly planted trees of this color, 'Crimson King' is a large tree with sharply-toothed, deep crimson-purple leaves. Even the clusters of small, deep yellow flowers that occur in spring have a reddish tinge. Displays rich autumn color.

Fagus sylvatica Atropurpurea Group
PURPLE BEECH, COPPER BEECH
☼ 5

Vigorous growth
↕ 100ft (30m) ↔ 75ft (22.5m)

This striking, round-headed beech is the largest tree of its color. The oval, wavy-margined leaves are shiny purple, turning a rich coppery color in autumn. 'Riversii' is also an excellent selection, with rich autumn tints, and is one of the most commonly planted.

OTHER TREES WITH PURPLE, RED, OR BRONZE LEAVES

Acer palmatum, many cvs.
Gleditsia triacanthos 'Rubylace'
Malus x *moerlandsii* 'Liset'
Prunus virginiana 'Schubert'

△ *Prunus cerasifera* 'Nigra'

Cercis canadensis 'Forest Pansy'
REDBUD
☼ 6

Moderate growth
↕ 25ft (8m) ↔ 25ft (8m)

This is a small, often multistemmed, tree with a broad, rounded crown. It has relatively large, heart-shaped leaves that are a rich reddish purple. The small pink pea flowers, which are borne in spring, are not always freely produced.

Prunus cerasifera 'Nigra'
PURPLE-LEAF PLUM
☼ 5

Moderate growth
↕ 30ft (10m) ↔ 30ft (10m)

In spring, the branches of this commonly planted, dense-headed tree are flooded with pink flowers. These are followed by its red leaves that turn to blackish purple. 'Pissardii' is a very similar and an equally popular cultivar with white, pink-budded blooms.

T R E E S

Trees for Autumn Color

FEW SIGHTS warm the heart more than a Japanese maple in autumn, its canopy a blaze of color. The foliage of many other trees, however, offers equally rich tints, and also more subtle shades of yellow, pink, and purple. These are some of the most reliable.

Amelanchier lamarckii
SNOWY SERVICEBERRY
☼ ☼ 4
Moderate growth
↕ 70ft (20m) ↔ 50ft (15m)

A superb tree, Snowy Serviceberry has two main seasons of interest: spring, when the bushy crown is a cloud of white blossoms, and autumn, when it is ablaze with red and orange foliage. Dislikes dry soils. A most reliable tree for autumn color.

Acer palmatum 'Osakazuki'
JAPANESE MAPLE
☼ ☼ 5
Moderate growth
↕ 20ft (6m) ↔ 20ft (6m)

This beautiful tree is commonly acknowledged to be one of the most impressive and reliable of its kind. It is rounded and bushy, with seven-lobed leaves that turn a brilliant scarlet in autumn. All the Japanese maples dislike exposed sites and dry soils.

Carya ovata
SHAGBARK HICKORY
☼ ☼ 4
Moderate growth
↕ 70ft (20m) ↔ 50ft (15m)

The bold, divided, ashlike leaves of this robust tree, which has an ultimately spreading crown, turn a rich golden yellow in autumn. Its grayish brown bark peels in vertical plates. This is the most reliable member of a colorful group of hickories.

Acer rubrum 'Schlesingeri'
RED MAPLE
☼ 4
Moderate growth
↕ 50ft (15m) ↔ 40ft (12m)

'Schlesingeri' is an old selection, but still one of the earliest and best of its color. The three- to five-lobed leaves turn wine-red and have contrasting pale undersurfaces, which are eye-catching even when shed and lying on the ground.

Cercidiphyllum japonicum
KATSURA TREE
☼ ☼ 5
Vigorous growth
↕ 60ft (18m) ↔ 50ft (15m)

This is a lovely tree of graceful, spreading habit, with slender branches. Its rounded, paired leaves are bronze when they first unfurl, changing through blue-green in summer to yellow, pink, or purple in autumn, with a sweet fragrance. Dislikes dry soils.

T R E E S

296

Nyssa sinensis
CHINESE TUPELO
☼ ☀ 7   Moderate growth
‡ 40ft (12m) ↔ 30ft (10m)

Erect or conical when young, this tree spreads with maturity. Its long, narrow leaves emerge purplish, turn green, and become a brilliant scarlet in autumn, perhaps equal to the American tupelo *(N. sylvatica)* in autumn effect. Dislikes dry soils.

Cotinus 'Grace'
SMOKE TREE
☼ ☀ 5   Vigorous growth
‡ 15ft (5m) ↔ 15ft (5m)

This can be a small, bushy, round-headed tree or a large, multi-stemmed shrub. The striking leaves are wine purple in summer, coloring to a brilliant orange-red later. Large plumes of purplish pink flowers are produced in summer.

OTHERS FOR AUTUMN COLOR
Acer saccharum
Fraxinus americana
Nyssa sylvatica
Oxydendrum arboreum, see p.275
Phellodendron amurense
Prunus sargentii, see p.303
Quercus coccinea

Parrotia persica
PERSIAN IRONWOOD
☼ ☀ 5   Moderate growth
‡ 22ft (7m) ↔ 40ft (12m)

Persian Ironwood will eventually become a broad, spreading tree with mottled bark. It produces small red flower clusters in late winter or early spring, and its glossy green leaves turn yellow, orange, and red-purple in autumn. Dislikes dry soils.

Liquidambar styraciflua 'Lane Roberts'
SWEET GUM
☼ ☀ 5   Moderate growth
‡ 70ft (20m) ↔ 35ft (11m)

One of the darkest and most reliable of all the autumn-coloring trees, this handsome specimen of conical, later spreading, habit has shining green maplelike leaves that turn through a range of colors from pale orange to deep red-purple. Dislikes dry soils.

Rhus typhina 'Dissecta'
CUTLEAF STAGHORN SUMAC
☼ 4   Vigorous growth
‡ 10ft (3m) ↔ 15ft (5m)

Generally wider than it is tall, this low-crowned tree has deeply divided, fernlike leaves that are large and downy. They turn orange-red in autumn, when dense, conical clusters of red fruits are borne. Sensitive skin may react to the sap of this sumac.

T R E E S

Trees with Autumn-to-winter Fruit

Many trees produce attractive fruits during autumn, but few carry them into winter, when they are of most ornamental value to gardeners, frequently hanging from or clinging to the often leafless branches. Birds, too, appreciate these during the winter months.

Malus 'John Downie'
CRABAPPLE
☼ 5   Moderate growth
↕ 25ft (8m) ↔ 15ft (5m)

This ornamental crabapple is erect at first, and spreads with maturity. White blossoms are carried in spring. The slightly elongated, red-flushed orange crabapples that crowd the branches from autumn onward are edible.

Malus x *zumi* 'Professor Sprenger'
CRABAPPLE
☼ 5   Moderate growth
↕ 18ft (5.5m) ↔ 18ft (5.5m)

From autumn onward, this free-fruiting crabapple with a dense, dome-shaped crown bears little, rounded orange-red fruit. Its pink-budded white flowers open in spring, and the glossy green leaves become yellow in autumn.

Ilex x *altaclerensis* 'Lawsoniana'
HIGHCLERE HOLLY
☼ ☼ 6   Moderate growth
↕ 30ft (10m) ↔ 15ft (5m)

This is a dense evergreen holly with a wide, columnar habit that broadens further with age. It has large, yellow-splashed leaves and a heavy crop of red berries from autumn onward. Plant a male form nearby for pollination.

OTHER TREES WITH AUTUMN-TO-WINTER FRUIT

Arbutus unedo
Crataegus phaenopyrum
Crataegus viridis 'Winter King'
Idesia polycarpa
Ilex aquifolium, many cvs.
Ilex opaca
Malus 'Donald Wyman'
Malus 'Winter Gold'
Melia azedarach
Phellodendron amurense

Malus x *robusta* 'Red Sentinel'
CRABAPPLE
☼ 5   Moderate growth
↕ 18ft (5.5m)) ↔ 18ft (5.5m)

One of the best fruiting crabapples for the smaller garden, this develops a compact, rounded crown. White flowers are borne in spring, and the autumn clusters of glossy-skinned, cherrylike fruits mature to bright red, lasting well into winter.

Photinia davidiana
STRANVAESIA
☼ ☀ 6
Moderate growth
↕ 15ft (5m) ↔ 15ft (5m)

Although it is often grown as a large evergreen shrub, this can be trained on a single stem to form a small tree. White flowers are produced in early summer, and the clusters of bright red berries that appear in autumn last through the winter months.

Sorbus forrestii
MOUNTAIN ASH
☼ ☀ 7
Moderate growth
↕ 20ft (6m) ↔ 20ft (6m)

Each leaf of this small, rounded tree is composed of numerous blue-green leaflets. Flattened heads of white flowers are carried in late spring, and the large bunches of small white berries that emerge in the autumn persist all through winter.

Sorbus cashmiriana
KASHMIR MOUNTAIN ASH
☼ ☀ 5
Moderate growth
↕ 25ft (8m) ↔ 25ft (8m)

Erect when young, this openly branched tree has divided leaves that become gold or russet in autumn. Blush pink flowers open in early summer, and the clusters of marble-sized white berries decorate the branches from autumn onward.

Sorbus 'Joseph Rock'
MOUNTAIN ASH
☼ ☀ 7
Vigorous growth
↕ 30ft (10m) ↔ 18ft (5.5m)

One of the showiest of all mountain ashes, 'Joseph Rock' has the characteristic vase-shaped crown that spreads with age. Its rich green, regularly divided leaves color brilliantly in autumn, when the yellow berries, carried in drooping bunches, ripen.

Sorbus commixta
JAPANESE MOUNTAIN ASH
☼ ☀ 6
Vigorous growth
↕ 30ft (10m) ↔ 18ft (5.5m)

This is a handsome tree with ascending, eventually spreading, branches. It has white flowers in spring, and regularly divided leaves that color richly in autumn. Large bunches of red berries are borne from autumn onward.

Sorbus scalaris
MOUNTAIN ASH
☼ ☀ 5
Moderate growth
↕ 30ft (10m) ↔ 30ft (10m)

The glossy green leaves of this wide-spreading tree grow in neat rosettes, turning red and purple in autumn. Flattened white flowerheads appear in late spring, and its large, densely packed bunches of red berries persist from autumn into winter.

TREES

Ornamental Bark or Shoots in Winter

THE BARK of many trees is attractive or interesting when examined closely, but some trees have colored or peeling bark that is especially ornamental. Others boast colored or unusually twisted shoots that have visual appeal, particularly in winter.

Arbutus menziesii
MADRONE
☼ 7   Moderate growth   ↕ 50ft (15m) ↔ 40ft (12m)

Madrone is a handsome evergreen tree with a spreading crown of dark green leaves. The smooth reddish bark peels away to reveal its pea green, new bark. White urn-shaped flowers are produced in early summer; these are followed by orange-red fruits.

Acer griseum
PAPERBARK MAPLE
☼ ☼ 5   Moderate growth   ↕ 30ft (10m) ↔ 25ft (8m)

Famous for its peeling, papery orange-brown bark, this maple has the characteristic three-parted leaves that turn orange and red in autumn. The branches are ascending at first, spreading later. It is excellent for growing in a border or a large lawn.

△ *Betula utilis* var. *jacquemontii*

Acer palmatum 'Sango-kaku'
CORALBARK MAPLE
☼ ☼ 6   Moderate growth   ↕ 20ft (6m) ↔ 20ft (6m)

In their first year, the winter shoots of this stunning Japanese maple, borne on ascending branches, are an attractive coral-pink, darkening later. The neatly lobed leaves are orange-yellow in spring, mature to green, and then turn yellow in autumn.

Betula utilis var. *jacquemontii* 'Doorenbos'
WEST HIMALAYAN BIRCH
☼ ☼ 6   Vigorous growth   ↕ 50ft (15m) ↔ 25ft (8m)

This strong-growing birch is popular for the white bark of its stem and branches. Its leaves turn yellow in autumn. 'Silver Shadow' and 'Grayswood Ghost' are selections with similarly white bark, as is 'Jermyns', whose catkins drape the branches in spring.

△ *Eucalyptus
pauciflora* subsp.
niphophila

△ *Prunus serrula*

Eucalyptus pauciflora subsp. *niphophila*
SNOW GUM
☼ 8   Moderate growth
                                         ↕ 30ft (10m) ↔ 25ft (8m)

The leathery gray-green leaves of this evergreen grow on glossy
shoots, bloomy white when young. The bark of its main branches
and stem flakes to form a patchwork of gray, cream, and green.
Fluffy summer flowerheads are white. Plant when small.

Prunus serrula
PAPERBARK CHERRY
☼ 6   Moderate growth
                                         ↕ 30ft (10m) ↔ 30ft (10m)

Its mahogany red, polished and peeling bark makes this one of
the most popular of all cherry trees. Small, inconspicuous white
flowers are produced in spring. Its slender, lance-shaped, pointed
green leaves become yellow in autumn.

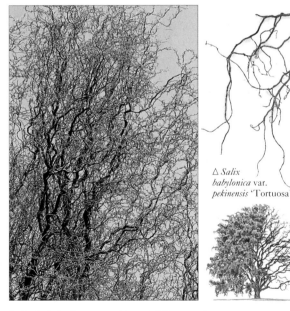

△ *Salix
babylonica* var.
pekinensis 'Tortuosa'

Prunus maackii
MANCHURIAN BIRD CHERRY
☼ ☀ 2   Moderate growth
                                         ↕ 40ft (12m) ↔ 30ft (10m)

Conical at first, this tree eventually spreads. Its smooth, glossy,
yellowish brown or amber bark peels in bands like that of a birch.
Small white flower spikes are produced in spring, and its leaves
turn yellow in autumn. 'Amber Beauty' also has attractive bark.

Salix babylonica var. *pekinensis* 'Tortuosa'
DRAGON'S CLAW WILLOW
☼ 6   Vigorous growth
                                         ↕ 50ft (15m) ↔ 30ft (10m)

Erect when young, and spreading later, this willow is easy to
recognize. Its long, twisted branches and shoots are clothed with
narrow, contorted leaves. When the branches are bare in winter,
the dramatic outline of this tree is very striking.

T R E E S

Multipurpose Trees

When choosing a suitable tree for your garden, it makes sense to consider those offering more than one attraction. This is particularly important in small gardens, where space is limited. Fortunately, many trees offer a combination of ornamental features such as attractive flowers, fruit, and foliage, or impressive autumn color and winter bark.

Cornus 'Porlock'
Dogwood
DOGWOOD ☼ ◐ 5 — Moderate growth ↕ ↔ 25ft (8m)

Worth growing alone for its star-shaped, creamy white flowerheads that cover the spreading branches in early summer. These become rose-tinted with age and are replaced in autumn by pendulous, strawberry-like fruits. The leaves may persist into winter.

△ *Acer capillipes*

Acer capillipes
SNAKEBARK MAPLE
☼ 5 — Moderate growth ↕ 30ft (10m) ↔ 25ft (8m)

Bark and autumn color are the principal attributes of this most attractive maple with spreading branches, and three-lobed leaves that color richly. The bark on its stems and main branches is a dark green color, with silvery or pale green striations.

Corylus colurna
TURKISH HAZEL
☼ 5 — Moderate growth ↕ 60ft (20m) ↔ 20–30ft (6–10m)

A splendid tree easily recognized by its conical crown – even in old age – and its rugged gray bark in winter. Pendent catkins are borne in late winter, followed by large, heart-shaped leaves that turn yellow in autumn.

Arbutus × *andrachnoides*
HYBRID STRAWBERRY TREE
☼ 8 — Moderate growth ↕ 25ft (8m) ↔ 25–30ft (8–10m)

Commonly a multistemmed tree, this handsome evergreen is notable for its oxblood red old bark, peeling to pea green new bark. Glossy green, toothed leaves are joined from autumn to spring by drooping clusters of white flowers and red fruits.

Davidia involucrata
DOVE TREE, HANDKERCHIEF TREE
☼ ◐ 6 — Moderate growth ↕ 50ft (15m) ↔ 30–50ft (10–15m)

This impressive and seductively beautiful tree has rugged bark in winter, rich autumn color, and striking, pendulous, white-bracted flowers in late spring. Its only drawback is that it takes 15 years or so to flower!

OTHER MULTIPURPOSE TREES

Acer griseum, see p.300
Arbutus unedo
Betula nigra, see p.280
Cornus kousa
Lagerstroemia indica
Magnolia grandiflora, see p.286
Salix x *sepulcralis* var. *chrysocoma*,
  see p.280
Ulmus parvifolia

△ *Malus baccata* var. *mandschurica*

Malus baccata var. *mandschurica*
MANCHURIAN CRAB
☼ 3   Vigorous growth
‡ 40ft (12m) ↔ 40ft (12m)

The slender branches of this round-headed tree are covered with scented white blossoms in spring. Its small, rounded red fruits are carried from autumn into winter, and the mottled, flaking bark provides yet another attraction. Reliable and tough.

Prunus sargentii
SARGENT CHERRY
☼ ☼ 5   Vigorous growth
‡ 30–40ft (10–12m) ↔ 20–30ft (6–10m)

One of the most reliable and strongest-growing of the Japanese cherries. Abundant, single, pink blossoms appear with the bronze-red young foliage in early spring. In early autumn, the foliage produces glorious red and orange tints.

Malus florentina
FLORENTINE CRAB
☼ ☼ 6   Moderate growth
‡ 30ft (10m) ↔ 15–18ft (5–5.5m)

Dome-shaped at first, then becoming more rounded in habit, this little-known crabapple has gray and orange-brown, flaking winter bark. Prettily lobed leaves color purple or red in autumn, and showers of small, pink-budded white flowers appear in late spring.

Photinia villosa
ORIENTAL PHOTINIA
☼ ☼ 5 PH ▽   Moderate growth
‡ 15ft (5m) ↔ 15ft (5m)

This versatile, wide-spreading shrub or small tree has dark green leaves that are bronze-tinted when young, turning a magnificent fiery orange-red in autumn. Clusters of white flowers open in spring, and small red fruits are carried from late summer onward.

Stewartia monadelpha
TALL STEWARTIA
☼ 7 PH ▽   Moderate growth
‡ 30ft (10m) ↔ 25ft (8m)

Upright and conical when it is young, this stewartia spreads with age. Small white flowers are carried among the green leaves in summer. The foliage becomes orange and red in autumn, and its bark peels, giving a splotchy effect. Dislikes dry soils.

T R E E S

303

Columnar Trees

TREES OF COLUMNAR habit are uniquely useful. They are easily accommodated where space is at a premium, such as in small gardens or those that are long and narrow. They are also effective architecturally for breaking up otherwise low or horizontal plantings, as well as for providing a focal point. Most offer other ornamental features.

Fagus sylvatica 'Dawyck Purple'
PURPLE DAWYCK BEECH
Vigorous growth
☼ ☼ 5   ↕ 70ft (20m) ↔ 15ft (5m)

Described by some as flame-shaped, this deep-purple version of the green-leaved Dawyck Beech is a striking feature in the garden, especially when associated with trees of a lesser size and a more rounded or spreading habit.

Acer rubrum 'Columnare'
COLUMNAR RED MAPLE
Moderate growth
☼ 4   ↕ 50ft (15m) ↔ 15ft (5m)

This cultivar is slender and columnar at first, and its long, upright branches are loosely packed to the stem. These branches broaden later, covered in leaves that turn yellow, orange, and red in autumn. *A. rubrum* 'Bowhall' is another excellent cultivar.

Hoheria sexstylosa 'Stardust'
RIBBONWOOD
Vigorous growth
☼ ☼ 9   ↕ 25ft (8m) ↔ 6–12ft (2–4m)

A nice tree suitable for a smaller property in warmer areas. When young it is broadly columnar and compact, broadening into old age. It has small, glossy green, toothed leaves, and masses of star-shaped white flowers from midsummer.

Acer saccharum subsp. *nigrum* 'Temple's Upright'
SUGAR MAPLE
Slow growth
☼ 3   ↕ 40ft (12m) ↔ 15ft (5m)

The ascending branches of this broad, columnar tree are densely clothed with large, five-lobed leaves that turn yellow and orange in autumn. Performs best where summers are warm and winters are cold, such as in northern Europe and the Midwest.

Liriodendron tulipifera 'Fagistiatum'
TULIP TREE

☼ ☀ 5   Moderate growth
                                         ↕ 70ft (20m) ↔ 25ft (8m)

The Tulip Tree is one of the most handsome and distinguished trees for large gardens. This fastigiate form is just as impressive, columnar when young, becoming narrowly conical with age. The curiously shaped leaves turn yellow in autumn.

OTHER COLUMNAR TREES

Carpinus betulus 'Fastigiata'
Malus baccata 'Columnaris'
Populus alba 'Raket'
Populus nigra 'Italica'

△ *Prunus* 'Amanogawa'

Prunus 'Amanogawa'
JAPANESE CHERRY

☼ 6   Moderate growth
                                         ↕ 30ft (10m) ↔ 12ft (4m)

The branches of this cherry are closely held at first, but they spread out with maturity. Large, fragrant, semidouble pale pink flowers crowd its branches in spring. The leaves often give rich autumn tints. One of the most striking of all flowering cherries.

Quercus petraea 'Columna'
SESSILE OAK

☼ ☀ 5   Moderate growth
                                         ↕ 70ft (20m) ↔ 20ft (6m)

A distinguished form of the European Sessile Oak of columnar to broadly columnar habit, with closely packed, ascending branches and dark green foliage. Like *Q. robur* f. *fastigiata* (*below*), it is well suited to avenue planting and formal designs.

Quercus robur f. *fastigiata*
CYPRESS OAK

☼ 5   Slow growth
                                         ↕ 60ft (18m) ↔ 20ft (6m)

Cypress Oak is a broad, columsnar form of English Oak. Its ascending branches are thickly clothed with the bright green foliage. *Q. robur* 'Fastigiata Koster' is a very attractive compact selection. Both are long-lived.

T R E E S

305

INDOOR PLANTS

However attractive and comfortably furnished your home, it can be improved by plants. Even small rooms can accommodate at least one, and there is a wealth of choice, colorful flowers and foliage to bring the natural world indoors.

△ AN UNOBTRUSIVE GUEST Isolepis cernua *is small enough to be accommodated in the tightest space, as long as light is available.*

◁ INDOOR GARDEN *A greenhouse or conservatory allows you to grow your favorite exotic plants, assuming enough heat is provided in winter.*

Where do Houseplants Come From?

IF WE WERE TO REPRODUCE at home the environments in which many houseplants grow in the wild, we would need to move out – the conditions in which most of them grow would be very oppressive to us. But knowledge of a plant's native habitat can help you understand and meet at least some of its needs, giving it the best opportunity to flourish in your home. The majority of plants commonly grown indoors come from one of three main climate types: tropical, semi-desert, and Mediterranean.

TROPICAL RAINFOREST
Tropical rainforests are found mainly in southeast Asia, northeast Australia, equatorial Africa, and Central and South America. Here, constant warmth, high humidity,

◁ RAINFOREST CLIMBER *Canopy dwellers such as this* Philodendron erubescens *require medium light and high humidity to thrive – conditions similar to those in their rainforest homes.*

and plentiful rainfall combine to encourage lush, continuous, varied plant growth. Vines and creepers such as *Epipremnum*, *Monstera*, and *Philodendron* climb into the canopy of tall trees, so at home they need plenty of space and the support of a moist moss pole or frame. The trees' often moss-clad branches are home to many epiphytes – non-parasitic plants that are adapted to live above the competition on the forest floor. Epiphytes commonly grown as houseplants include many ferns and orchids and most bromeliads, including *Aechmea*, *Billbergia*, *Tillandsia*, and *Vriesea*. You can grow epiphytes on bark or in hanging baskets made for indoor use. The tropical rainforest's dim, decaying floor, protected from the sun's glare by the canopy, is the natural habitat of many foliage plants such as *Aglaonema*, *Calathea*, *Dieffenbachia*, and *Syngonium*. In the home, they need a warm humid atmosphere away from direct sun.

ARID OR SEMIDESERT
Semidesert habitats are found in parts of southern Africa, the south-west United States, Mexico, and South America. These dry, sunny regions, which can be scorching by day and freezing cold at night, are home to a surprising number of plants, including *Aloe*, *Crassula*, *Euphorbia*, *Haworthia*, *Kalanchoe*, and cacti such as *Echinocactus*, *Ferocactus*, *Mammillaria*, *Opuntia*, *Oreocereus*, and *Rebutia*. Many cacti and succulents that enjoy hot, dry conditions are best suited to sunny windowsills or similar spots in the house. However, epiphytic cacti, such as *Rhipsalis* and *Schlumbergera* from Brazil and *Epiphyllum* from Mexico and Central America to the

◁ PUERTO RICAN RAINFOREST *The lush vegetation covers every inch of space as plants compete for light and moisture. The trees host epiphytic bromeliads.*

◁ SEMIDESERT CLIMATE *Arid regions, like this Arizona canyon, are home to a surprising array of species.* Oreocereus trollii, *left, is a typical dry heat lover.*

NATURAL LIGHT

For the majority of flowering plants, from seasonal plants such as *Cyclamen* to exotics such as *Bougainvillea*, good light is the most crucial factor, whatever their origin or heat and humidity requirements. There are also many flowering plants from cool temperate areas, such as crocuses and primroses, that are hardy and can be planted in the garden after flowering.

ADAPTABLE SURVIVORS

Remember, plants are extremely adaptable, hence their survival in many challenging habitats. Don't be put off from trying to grow them; they can tolerate seemingly adverse conditions so long as these are not severe or permanent.

West Indies, are forest dwellers and therefore cannot tolerate exposure to the hottest summer sun.

TEMPERATE MEDITERRANEAN

In between these two extremes are regions that enjoy a Mediterranean climate of warm, usually dry summers and mild, often wet winters. The Mediterranean basin, South Africa, southeast Australia, parts of the southwest United States, and central Chile are such areas. Many houseplants, including *Boronia*, Cape heaths, *Euryops*, *Myrtus*, *Pelargonium*, *Prostanthera*, *Strelitzia*, and many palms, originate in this type of climate. Indoors, a warm, sunny spot and regular watering are ideal conditions for most of them.

▷ MEDITERRANEAN PALMS *The Canary Island date palm (*Phoenix canariensis*), right, and the Chilean wine palm (*Jubaea chilensis*), far right, can both be grown indoors when young.*

Choosing the Right Plants for your Home

THE RIGHT PLANT in the right location will be healthy, full of vitality, and will flourish for years; an unsuitable plant in the wrong place will never perform well and may even die. So take time to match a houseplant to the conditions in the spot you wish to fill, and consider other factors, such as tolerance of neglect, that may also affect where you place it.

BENEFICIAL HOUSEPLANTS

Research indicates that many plants, as well as absorbing carbon dioxide and releasing oxygen, filter out chemical toxins and other pollutants from the air, creating a healthier indoor environment wherever they grow.

AIR-FRESHENING SPIDER PLANT

△ BEDROOMS *In your own room, let personal taste dominate – here, bold foliage makes a statement. Temperatures are usually moderate and rarely fluctuate, which is ideal for many plants.*

Foliage begonias for the living room

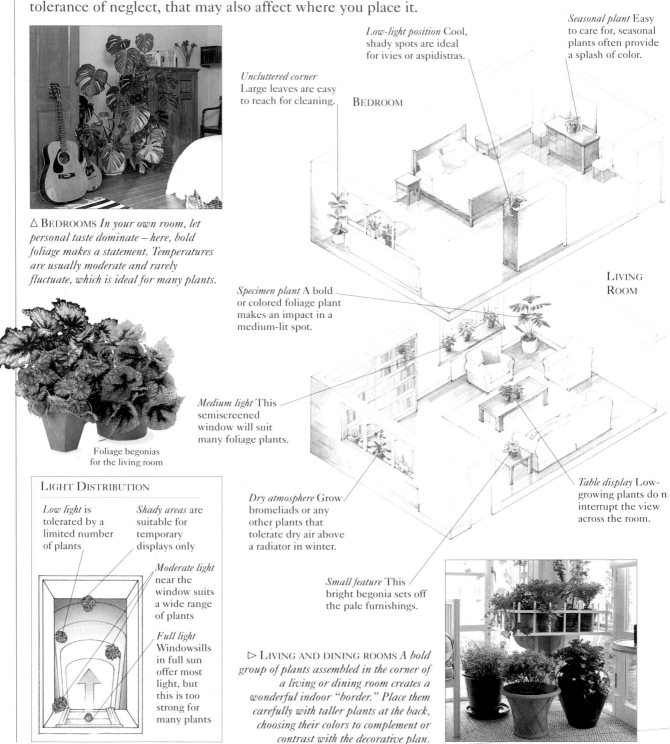

Low-light position Cool, shady spots are ideal for ivies or aspidistras.

Uncluttered corner Large leaves are easy to reach for cleaning.

BEDROOM

Seasonal plant Easy to care for, seasonal plants often provide a splash of color.

LIVING ROOM

Specimen plant A bold or colored foliage plant makes an impact in a medium-lit spot.

Medium light This semiscreened window will suit many foliage plants.

Dry atmosphere Grow bromeliads or any other plants that tolerate dry air above a radiator in winter.

Table display Low-growing plants do n[ot] interrupt the view across the room.

Small feature This bright begonia sets off the pale furnishings.

LIGHT DISTRIBUTION

Low light is tolerated by a limited number of plants

Shady areas are suitable for temporary displays only

Moderate light near the window suits a wide range of plants

Full light Windowsills in full sun offer most light, but this is too strong for many plants

▷ LIVING AND DINING ROOMS *A bold group of plants assembled in the corner of a living or dining room creates a wonderful indoor "border." Place them carefully with taller plants at the back, choosing their colors to complement or contrast with the decorative plan.*

COMMON HAZARDS

Handle poisonous plants with care, and teach children not to eat any plant material or soil mix. Site poisonous or spiny plants out of reach, and leave walkways clear of hanging baskets or large, floor-standing plants. Attach hanging baskets and brackets securely.

▷ BATHROOMS *A light, warm bathroom, the ideal home for exotic houseplants, is a good place in which to create your own miniature "jungle." Regular showers create humidity, but beware of open windows letting in chilly drafts.*

High humidity Ferns thrive in warm, humid, medium-lit spots such as the bathtub area.

Exotic specimen This stromanthe, like other exotics, can flourish in a warm bathroom.

Neglected corner Plants tucked away in corners may be overlooked; yuccas tolerate neglect.

BATHROOM

LANDING

PROBLEM CORNERS

All plants need some light; few will be happy in dark corners. Use temporary houseplants here, or permanent ones for a few weeks only. Reflect light into the area with mirrors, or paint the surrounding walls white. An aspidistra is one of the few plants that tolerates drafty corners opposite doors.

Clean air Use beneficial plants to help counteract emissions from office equipment.

HOME OFFICE

Drafty hallway The front door brings in cold drafts that may kill plants.

HALL

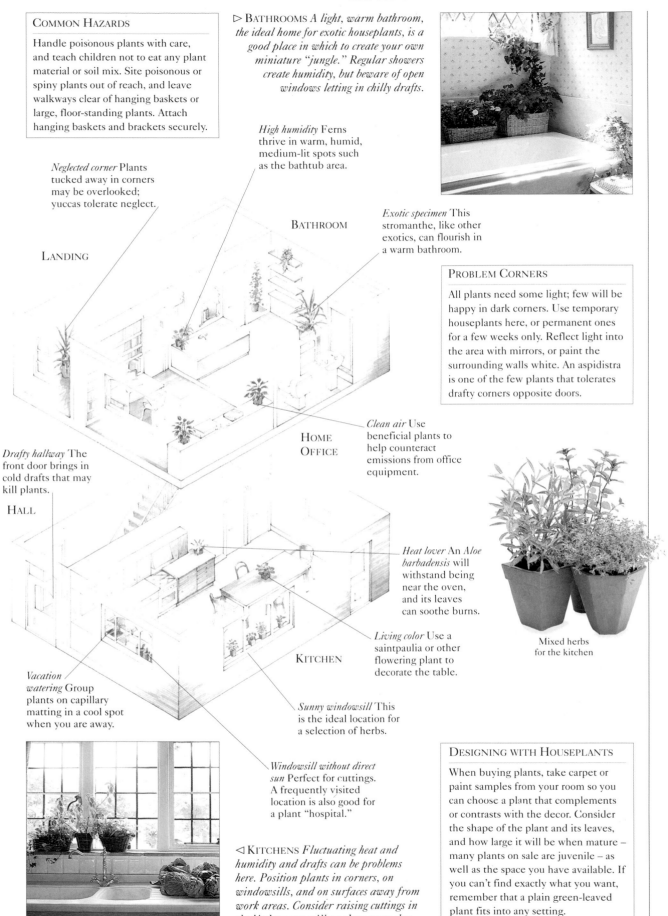

Heat lover An *Aloe barbadensis* will withstand being near the oven, and its leaves can soothe burns.

Living color Use a saintpaulia or other flowering plant to decorate the table.

KITCHEN

Mixed herbs for the kitchen

Vacation watering Group plants on capillary matting in a cool spot when you are away.

Sunny windowsill This is the ideal location for a selection of herbs.

DESIGNING WITH HOUSEPLANTS

When buying plants, take carpet or paint samples from your room so you can choose a plant that complements or contrasts with the decor. Consider the shape of the plant and its leaves, and how large it will be when mature – many plants on sale are juvenile – as well as the space you have available. If you can't find exactly what you want, remember that a plain green-leaved plant fits into any setting.

Windowsill without direct sun Perfect for cuttings. A frequently visited location is also good for a plant "hospital."

◁ KITCHENS *Fluctuating heat and humidity and drafts can be problems here. Position plants in corners, on windowsills, and on surfaces away from work areas. Consider raising cuttings in the kitchen: you will see them every day.*

Everyday Care

GOOD HUSBANDRY is necessary if you want to grow quality houseplants that are noticed for the right reasons. Having chosen a healthy plant and found a position that satisfies its needs for light and heat, a regular feeding and watering routine is essential. It may take a little time each day, but the effort will be handsomely rewarded.

SELECTING A HEALTHY SPECIMEN

Buy plants from reputable outlets such as florists or garden centers, rather than from grocery stores or roadside stands where they may be an afterthought. Look around to find a good-quality supplier. Avoid buying tender plants, such as poinsettias, if they have been displayed on a cold pavement or in a drafty store. Before you buy, give the plant a quick health check. It should be undamaged and have a good shape, and its leaves should show no signs of wilting. Check for signs of pests or diseases (see left). Flowering plants should have many buds, a few open flowers, and no dead blooms. Bulbs should be plump and undamaged. A plant's roots are also a good indicator of its health – don't be afraid to remove a plant from the pot for a closer look. Ignore any plant with a poor-looking root system, or one whose pot is congested with roots – a sure sign is if roots are growing through the drainage holes. Ensure the soil mix is moist, neither bone dry nor waterlogged. Finally, avoid plants with "display fatigue" – tired-looking, lackluster specimens.

CHECK FOR PESTS
Look for pests under the leaves and on any flower buds and growing tips.

CHECK FOR STEM ROT
Inspect the center for any slimy or rotting leaves.

LIGHT

Most houseplants thrive in moderate to bright light, and the nearer you can get to satisfying each plant's individual needs, the better it will grow. Note that plants with variegated or colored leaves usually need higher light levels than green-leaved plants.

Only a few plant groups, for example cacti and succulents, can tolerate hot sun, which can be particularly fierce when it is magnified by the glass of a window. Always provide protection or relief from the hottest summer sun, even for sun-loving plants. Shade-tolerant plants, particularly those with brightly colored leaves, can be used for temporary display in very dark corners, but remember to move them into a brighter position every two or three weeks to recover. You can also use "grow lights" or fluorescent tubes to provide light in these conditions and where winter light levels are extremely low.

Since plants naturally grow toward the nearest light source, turn their pots regularly to encourage balanced growth. The exceptions are some flowering plants, such as *Schlumbergera*; turning causes their buds to drop.

SUN-SEEKER
This plant has grown bent over in the direction of a light source.

TEMPERATURE

If the temperature is too low for a plant, its growth slows or stops; too high and its growth is spindly, particularly at low light levels. However, plants will often tolerate lower temperatures (for example in winter) if watering is reduced. Equally, with notable exceptions such as cacti and succulents, most plants will tolerate higher temperatures provided humidity is increased and ventilation improved. However, most houseplants prefer a constant temperature; beware of drafts, radiators being switched off at night, or the use of ovens and other household equipment, which can cause heat levels to fluctuate. In addition, when overnight temperatures are low, move plants from windowsills before closing the curtains, since even central heating will not protect plants from the sharp drop in temperature. Otherwise, leave curtains open.

HUMIDITY

As a general rule, the higher the temperature, the higher the humidity plants will need. One easy way of increasing humidity is to mist your plants with an atomizer several times a day. Use tepid soft water; in hard-water areas, use cooled boiled water or fresh rainwater, or you may find chalky deposits on the

MOIST PEBBLE TRAY
Stand pots on a layer of pebbles. Add water to just below the base of the pots, refilling when necessary.

leaves. Do not spray delicate blooms (particularly in bright light) or hairy-leaved plants, and avoid spraying the surrounding furnishings. Alternatively, group plants with similar requirements together, preferably on a pebble tray (see above). Each plant will transpire moisture, increasing humidity. You can also stand a plant inside a larger pot or container, fill the space between the two with moist peat, and water as needed. Enthusiasts might buy a humidifier.

FEEDING

Regular feeding is essential for good results. Use flowering houseplant (or tomato) fertilizer to promote flowering, and foliage houseplant fertilizer (high in nitrogen) for leaf growth. Otherwise, use general fertilizer, which contains balanced nutrients for healthy growth. Where fertilizer for acid-loving plants is recommended, that plant will also benefit from soft water and acidic soil mix. Feed only during active growth; unless stated in the individual entry, do not feed a resting plant. Never feed a plant if its soil mix is dry or waterlogged. Under-feeding makes plants weak and lackluster; overfeeding causes the roots to scorch and produces symptoms similar to those of overwatering.

FOLIAR FEEDING
Misting with dilute liquid fertilizer boosts flagging plants.

Slow-release fertilizers, in the form of spikes or pills (see below), are added to the soil mix and are ideal if you are likely to forget to feed your plants; liquid fertilizer or soluble powder types are rapidly absorbed. Special fertilizers are produced for specific plant groups such as African violets, cacti, acid-loving plants, and orchids.

FERTILIZER TYPES

| SPIKES | SOLUBLE POWDER | LIQUID | PILLS |

WATERING

Water with care – overwatering kills more houseplants than anything else, but give too little water and the roots at the bottom of the pot will desiccate. To judge if a plant needs watering, push your finger into the soil mix; if soil adheres, it is still moist. Alternatively, squeeze some soil between your fingers to check how moist it is or use water indicator sticks that change color when water is needed.

WATER FROM BELOW
Fill the saucer with water; discard any not absorbed.

Always use tepid water. Tap water is fine for most plants, except in hard-water areas, where cooled boiled tap water, or fresh rainwater, should be used. Acid-loving plants such as azaleas always need soft water. Plants in small pots, those with hairy leaves, and cyclamen should be watered from below (see left). Otherwise, topwatering (see below), using a watering

TOPWATERING
Water the soil mix, avoiding the leaves.

can with a narrow spout, suits most plants. After watering, drain any excess away; do not allow the pot to stand in a saucer of water. Plants that have been allowed to dry out should be immersed in water (see below). Remove water-logged plants from the pot and allow soil mix to dry before repotting.

REVIVING A PARCHED PLANT
Break up dry soil, then stand the pot in a bowl of tepid water until moist; spray the leaves. Drain, and allow to recover.

CLEANING HOUSEPLANTS

Wipe glossy leaves (right) with a soft, slightly damp cloth or a cotton ball. If they are very dusty, use a soft brush first. Do not dust or wipe new leaves, since they are easily damaged. "Leaf shine" can be used occasionally

on smooth leaves but not on young or hairy leaves. Dust hairy leaves with a makeup brush (left). To wash plants, stand them out in a light, warm rain or under a tepid, soft-water shower at low pressure. Invert small plants into a bowl of tepid water. Wrap the pot in a plastic bag, or use your fingers, to prevent the soil mix from falling out.

Longer-term Maintenance

ALONGSIDE THE daily routine of house-plant care, other tasks are necessary to ensure that your plants remain in excellent condition. Regular potting on and pruning increases their life span and encourages flowers, foliage, and fruit. Training is essential for climbing plants, providing support and making an eye-catching feature.

WINTER COLOR

POTTING ON AND REPOTTING

Most plants need potting on (moving to a larger pot) every 2–3 years. Pot on if a plant is too tall for the size of its pot, if roots appear through the drainage holes, if growth is stunted and yellow (even when the plant is fed often), if frequent watering is needed, or if the rootball is congested. Plants such as *Clivia*, and all orchids, should be potted on only if they are "climbing" out of the pot.

Check all plants annually, potting them on before they begin to grow. New purchases may need immediate potting on. Make sure you are using a suitable soil mix for each plant (see box left).

To remove most plants, soak the rootball by watering heavily, allow the excess to drain, then pull the plant out of its pot. You may need to slide an old kitchen knife between the pot and the soil mix or even break the pot to do this. An assistant might be useful to hold a large plant while you slide its pot off. If the roots are a solid mass, tease them outward to encourage them to grow into the new mix. Use a sleeve of paper to remove a prickly plant from its pot.

SOIL MIX TYPES

HOUSEPLANT
Peat-based mix; soil-based is good for many plants.

COIR BULB FIBER
Peat-free mixture that provides good drainage.

CACTUS
Contains slow-release nutrients; use for succulent plants.

CHOOSING A POT

Terracotta pots are porous, so plants in them are unlikely to be overwatered, while plastic pots retain more water, so plants do not need watering as often. Unglazed pots are not waterproof. Heavy clay pots are more stable for tall plants. Stand pots in a saucer to catch drips and avoid damage to furniture. For pots that do not have a hole in the base, use a deeper layer of drainage material, water carefully, and take care that they do not become waterlogged.

THE RIGHT POT

When it is time to pot on, pick a clean pot 1–2in (2.5–5cm) larger than the old one. Soak new terracotta pots overnight before use. Cover the drainage hole with a piece of window screen to keep soil mix in and let water drain out. Place the plant in the center of the pot so that the rootball is about 2in (5cm) below the rim. Fill between the pot and the rootball with soil mix, firming it in as you build up layers. When the mix is just above the rootball, water with tepid water and allow to drain. Stand the plant in moderate light for two weeks then move into its permanent position. Do not water again until the soil surface begins to dry out. Repot plants in their old pots (see above) to restrict their growth.

REPOTTING
Loosen the soil mix, replace the top 2in (5cm), fertilize, then replace plant in its pot.

HOW TO POT ON

TIME TO POT ON
Protruding roots indicate this plant needs a new pot.

REMOVE FROM THE POT
Scrape off the top layer of soil mix from the rootball.

PREPARE THE NEW POT
Add drainage material. Cover with moist soil mix.

FIRM IN
Place plant in new pot and firm in with soil mix.

PRUNING

Keep plants under control with light pruning. This is ideally done in spring. Always cut back to an outward-facing bud or pair of buds. Cutting back hard to within a few buds of the base will encourage bushy growth and can regenerate plants that have become old and straggly. Trailing plants such as *Tradescantia* respond well to this treatment.

GETTING INTO SHAPE
Pruning improves a plant's shape, thins tangled growth, and controls plant size.

After hard pruning, reduce watering until new growth appears, and then increase as the stems lengthen again. Feeding plants with a general houseplant fertilizer will also help recovery. However, do not prune vigorous plants hard, unless you want to encourage masses of regrowth.

Soft, young growth can be nipped off with a finger and thumb or florists' scissors. This process, known as "pinching out," encourages a bushy growth habit. The material removed is a useful source of cuttings. Harder, mature wood should be cut off with sharp pruners.

PRUNING TOOLS

SCISSORS PRUNERS

Remove fading flowerheads immediately, or detach from the flower cluster. There are exceptions, such as plants with ornamental fruit, or *Hoya*, which should not be deadheaded because the spurs on which the flowers form bear buds for the next flower cluster.

Finally, encourage well-shaped, healthy specimens by removing any signs of weak, diseased, dying, and dead growth, and any stems spoiling the shape by growing into the center of the plant as soon as they appear.

PINCHING OUT
Nip off soft growing tips to promote bushiness and prevent straggly growth.

WHEN YOU ARE ON VACATION

Stand plants on capillary matting or a substitute such as an old towel, and trail one end in a tray of water (left). Alternatively, make a wick from a cotton shoelace or string; dip one end in water and bury the other in the soil mix. Or simply group plants away from extreme heat or light and ask a friend to water them.

TRAINING

The right method of training a climber will vary according to the plant's growth habit. Natural or colored stakes, used singly or in tripods, are popular supports. Secure the plant's flexible growths to the support with clips or soft string or raffia (trim the ends neatly). Avoid tying tightly around the stems. Thin stems of plants such as jasmine can be twisted around wire hoops. At the end of the hoop turn the stem back on itself or carry on around. Prune annually and tie in new growth (see right). Plants can also be trained up a trellis that is firmed into the soil mix or attached to a wall. *Cissus* and other plants with tendrils or twining stems will eventually cover the frame and support themselves.

REGULAR TRAINING
Unwind straggling stems, prune, and resecure. Cut out old stems at the base. New growth will develop rapidly.

Moss poles are good supports for climbing or twining plants, especially those with aerial roots and humidity-lovers. Make your own using a tube of chicken wire with crossed bamboo stakes at the base. Fill the tube with moss and insert into the pot, surrounding it with soil mix. Always keep the moss moist. Pin aerial roots to the pole using hairpins or bent wire. As an alternative, wrap a thick layer of sphagnum moss around some narrow plastic piping, then tie it with nylon fishing line. Leave the base of the pipe free of moss so it can be inserted into the soil mix.

To display air plants, attach them to a piece of dead wood, pack sphagnum moss at the roots, and tie the moss in firmly with nylon line.

GROWING UP A MOSS POLE
Permanently moist moss poles are the best climbing supports.

SUPPORTS FOR TRAINED PLANTS

BAMBOO TRIPOD
Twine tendrils around the stakes, tying in the stems.

SINGLE STAKE
Insert stake with care to avoid damaging roots.

SIMPLE WIRE HOOPS
Two hoops are used here; add more if the plant outgrows them.

Propagation

PROPAGATING HOUSEPLANTS is a simple, cheap, and enjoyable way to add to your collection. Spring is the usual time for this, but many plants can be propagated at any time of year. The most popular methods are briefly outlined here; for individual plants, use the method suggested in each entry.

TIP AND SEMIRIPE CUTTINGS

Tip cuttings are taken from soft shoot tips, while semiripe cuttings have a firm base, yielding under pressure. Take cuttings from spring to late summer from non-flowering shoots. Cut with a sharp knife below a leaf joint, 3–4in (7.5–10cm) from the tip of a healthy shoot. Remove bottom leaves, then dip the stem into hormone rooting powder. Make a hole in a pot of cuttings medium and insert the stem, lightly firming the medium around it. You can plant several cuttings in one pot. Water well and allow to drain, then label with the date and name and put the pot into a propagating case, or use a loosely tied clear plastic bag. Do not cover cacti, succulents, or geraniums; they will rot. Place in bright light, away from direct sun, at around 64°F (18°C). Once there are signs of growth, remove the cuttings and allow them to acclimatize for two weeks before moving to the plant's final position.

CHOOSE A SHOOT
Select a healthy shoot that has not yet flowered. Cut straight across with a sharp knife.

INSERT THE CUTTING
Make a hole using a dibble, a pencil, or your finger, then insert. Firm the medium.

STEM CUTTINGS

These are taken from the firm part of the stem, well below the soft growth tip. Using a sharp knife, make one cut just above a leaf joint, and another just under the leaf joint below it. Remove the basal leaves, then follow the procedure for tip cuttings.

LEAF CUTTINGS

This method is often used to increase *Saintpaulia* and *Streptocarpus*. Cut a mature leaf from the center of the plant, using a sharp knife. Leave 1–1½in (2.5–4cm) of stalk. Insert into the medium at an angle, until the leaf blade just sits on the surface. Treat as tip cuttings.

STEM SECTIONS

Cut mature stem sections, at least 2in (5cm) long, with at least two leaf joints or leaf scars; even if buds are not visible, they will be stimulated into growth. Remove the leaves and press the sections horizontally into the medium until only the top half is exposed. Alternatively, insert them vertically into the medium, burying the end that was nearest to the base of the plant. Then treat as tip cuttings.

DIVISION

This involves separating the existing plant into sections, each with a growth point, leaves, and a vigorous root system; the divisions are then potted up (see right and below). Many plants form obvious divisions. If not, take the youngest sections from the outer part of the plant. A saw or sharp knife may be needed to divide old, woody plants. Divide in spring or early summer.

UNPOT THE PLANT
Water the plant well, leave it for an hour, then ease it from the pot onto newspaper. Support the crown with your fingers.

DIVIDE THE ROOTBALL
Tease loose soil mix from the roots and divide the plant carefully at natural breaks.

PLANT UP DIVISIONS
Place divisions in pots, then water. Give medium light and a little water until established.

ROOTING A CUTTING IN WATER

Many plants will root easily in water. Prepare as tip cuttings, removing leaves below water level, and prop the cutting inside the container. Place in bright light, away from sun. If you use a glass jar, change the water regularly. When a good root system has formed, pot up and treat as tip cuttings. Handle fragile roots with care.

STORAGE ORGANS

Storage organs such as rhizomes (right) and tubers can be separated. Detach new growths such as bulbils, cormlets, and tubercles from the main storage organ.

LAYERING AND AIR LAYERING

Layering (see below) is used for many plants, such as climbers and trailers, that have long, flexible stems that root at the leaf joints. Detach from the parent plant when new roots have formed. Air layering is for more experienced propagators. Make an incision in the plant's stem and tightly enclose it in a plastic sleeve packed with moist sphagnum moss. Keep the moss moist. After about eight weeks, when roots show through the moss, sever the stem below the sleeve, discard the plastic, and pot up the plant.

LAYERING A PHILODENDRON
Peg a mature healthy shoot into a pot of moist soil mix using a hairpin. Detach from the parent plant when roots have formed.

OFFSETS AND ROSETTES

Offsets are small plants that form around the base of the parent plant; many bromeliads and cacti produce them. Detach the offsets with a sharp knife, retaining as much root as possible, and dust the cuts with fungicide. Transplant them, then protect from direct sunlight until they are established. Some plants produce leaf rosettes that can be detached from the parent in the same way and grown on.

REMOVING AN OFFSET
Look for a well-established offset, clear away the soil mix around it, and cut it off using a sharp knife.

PLANTLETS

Plantlets are small plants, produced on leaves or fronds, that often root in the soil mix around the parent plant. Detach or lift them with care and pot into moist mix. Some plantlets, borne on runners, can be put into a separate pot while still attached to the parent plant (right).

PROPAGATING BY RUNNERS
Detach the new plant only when it is well rooted in its new pot.

SEED

Sow seed in spring or summer. Use a 3½–5in (9–12cm) pot, filled with firmed seed medium. Water well, or stand the pot in a tray of tepid water to two-thirds its height for about an hour. Allow to drain. Scatter small seeds over the surface and cover thinly with medium or vermiculite, or press larger seeds in gently so they are covered to their own depth in medium, then treat as tip cuttings. If you germinate seeds in an enclosed space, remove them as soon as growth appears.

HOW TO GROW FROM SEED

SOW THE SEEDS
Scatter a thin layer of seeds and cover finely with medium. Firm larger seeds in gently.

ALLOW TO GERMINATE
Cover pot with plastic wrap. Remove when most of the seeds have germinated.

REMOVE SEEDLINGS
Place seedlings in bright light. Turn regularly. Remove when second set of leaves appears.

PLANT THE SEEDLINGS
Plant in small pots, holding seedlings by the leaves so stem and roots are not damaged.

SUCCULENT LEAVES

Succulents can be propagated from single leaves. Detach several healthy leaves from a plant, dust the cuts with fungicide, and leave in a bright position for two to three days for protective tissue to form. Insert the cut end of the leaf into a pot filled with one-third cutting medium and two-thirds coarse sand. Stand in moderate light, keep the medium slightly moist, and transplant the new plants as they form.

FERN SPORES

Remove a mature frond with brown, dustlike spores on the underside. Place it on a sheet of paper to shed its spores. Scatter the spores over watered peat in a clean pot, cover with plastic, and stand in a saucer of water. Leave in a warm position and refill the saucer as necessary. After several months, small fronds will appear, each of which can be potted up.

Houseplant Problems

HEALTHY HOUSEPLANTS that are well fed, carefully watered, and growing in suitable conditions are less likely to have problems with pests and diseases than those that are weakened through neglect or stress. Check new plants daily for the first few weeks for signs of pests or diseases, isolating them if problems arise. Once established, examine them regularly and deal with problems promptly.

Discolored yellow leaves

OVERWATERING

Overwatering may be the cause if your plant wilts, the stems and leaves rot, growth is poor, or moss grows on the soil mix surface. It is certainly a problem for most plants left standing in water. To correct waterlogging, stop watering and take the plant out of the pot. Replace it when the excess moisture has dried out, then water as necessary.

Moss on soil mix surface

Excess water left in saucer

Rotten leaves

YELLOW LEAVES

Yellow leaves may signal overfeeding, waterlogging, or drafts. If yellow appears between leaf veins, it shows a lack of iron or magnesium; feed the plant (give an acid-loving plant fertilizer). If an acid-loving plant's leaves are pale yellow, you may be watering with hard water or using a soil mix containing lime.

LIGHT PROBLEMS

Excessive light can make leaves pale yellow, scorched, or even bleached. If so, move the plant to a suitable position with lower light levels, away from direct light or sun. Too little light causes loss of variegation, spindly or arrested growth, leaf drop, and small, pale leaves. Stems may bend toward the light, and flowers may not form. Move to a brighter spot, remove damaged leaves, and cut out or shorten spindly growth.

Brown marks indicate scorching

UNDERWATERING

If your plant wilts and has falling leaves and flowers that fade and drop rapidly, under-watering is probably the cause. It is definitely the case if the soil mix shrinks from the sides of the pot. To revive a parched plant, soak it thoroughly, breaking up the soil mix first to allow water to penetrate (see p.15). Then follow the correct watering regime.

Limp, wilted stems and leaves

OVER- AND UNDERFEEDING

Overfeeding can be the cause of excessive soft, weak growth that is vulnerable to sap-sucking pests such as aphids and whitefly. It can also cause root damage, stunted growth, and scorched leaves. To correct these problems, return the plant to a suitable feeding regime. On the other hand, it is possible to starve your plants. Underfeeding makes growth slow or stunted, and leaves pale and lackluster. Fertilizer may not be absorbed efficiently if plants are potbound. To avoid this, feed plants regularly when they are in active growth, and repot them as soon as they become congested with roots.

Scorched leaves caused by overfeeding

ROUTINE MAINTENANCE

Inspect your plants as often as possible. Look out for any sign of pests or diseases, and deal with them as soon as possible if they occur. Remove any damaged leaves entirely; if they remain, they may attract fungal diseases. Once any flowers have finished, remove them and their stalks, or the stalks may rot in the center of the plant.

PLANT MAINTENANCE
Remove dead leaves since they spoil the general appearance of a plant and may also invite disease.

AIR AND VENTILATION

Browning leaf tips and shriveling leaves and buds are usually caused by a too-dry atmosphere. Raise the humidity by misting or using a pebble tray (see p.313), or move the plant to a more humid location. However, dry, shriveled leaves can also be caused by overwatering, underwatering, or drafts. In addition, brown leaf tips can be a sign of over-watering, underwatering, too-low temperatures, watering with cold water (always use tepid water), or potbound plants, so make sure you identify the correct cause before treatment.

Suitable ventilation is also important. Drafts can cause leaves to become yellow, shrivel, or drop, and

Shriveled leaves

Brown leaf tips caused by dry air

leaf tips to become brown. If any of these becomes a problem, move the plant to a more suitable position, avoiding drafts and fluctuating temperatures.

FLOWERING PROBLEMS

If flowers die very quickly, it could be due to overdry air or temperatures that are too high. Correct these as necessary. If flowers do not appear, it is usually due to insufficient light or incorrect feeding with too much nitrogen. If lack of light is to blame, give high-potassium fertilizer as well as more light. Moving a plant in bud, or keeping it at too low a temperature, can cause buds to drop. Prevent this by finding the plant a permanent home at the correct temperature.

ARRESTED GROWTH

If plant growth stops altogether, light levels may be too low, or the plant may be starving or potbound. Nurse your plant by moving it to a brighter position, feeding it regularly with a high-nitrogen or general houseplant fertilizer. Repot if necessary.

COMMON HOUSEPLANT PESTS AND DISEASES

The table below offers advice on identifying and dealing with the most common houseplant pests and diseases. Treatment with chemical sprays may be the most effective remedy for these problems. Some may need several treatments before they are under control, so don't give up. When you use chemical sprays, always follow the manufacturer's instructions, and use an atomizer kept especially for chemicals. It is best to spray plants outside on a warm, still day, but remember not to leave them standing in hot sun.

PLANT PEST OR DISEASE	APPEARANCE AND SYMPTOMS	CONTROLS
WHITEFLY	Small white insects, found on leaf under-sides; brush the leaf and clouds fly up. They weaken plants by sucking sap and secrete honeydew, causing sooty mold.	Spray the plant with insecticidal soap.
APHIDS	Small sap-sucking insects, seen on soft growth and buds, that also shed white skins on leaves. They distort tissue, secrete honeydew, and transmit viruses.	Spray with an environmentally friendly insecticide such as derris, soft soap, or pyrethrum.
SPIDER MITES	Minute, pale orange mites. They cause mottling, becoming yellowish white, on leaf surfaces. Heavy infestations give the appearance of fine webbing on leaves.	Increase humidity – spider mites flourish in hot, dry conditions. Spray the plant with insecticidal soap.
SCALE INSECTS	Flat, yellowish brown, shieldlike scale insects are found on stems and leaves, particularly along main veins. They suck sap, secreting honeydew.	Remove insects with a soft, damp cloth. In spring, the mobile young can be seen through a magnifying glass; spray them thoroughly with insecticidal soap.

PLANT PEST OR DISEASE	APPEARANCE AND SYMPTOMS	CONTROLS
MEALYBUGS	Gray-white or pink insects, to 1/6in (4mm), covered in white "meal," often found in awkward parts of the plant. They suck sap, secreting honeydew.	Spray the plant with insecticidal soap.
DOWNY MILDEW	Infection causes yellow spots on leaf surfaces, with corresponding gray fuzzy mold below. Mainly a problem on soft-leaved houseplants.	Raise temperature and avoid cool, damp conditions. Remove any infected parts immediately, then spray the plant with a fungicide.
POWDERY MILDEW	Powdery mildew appears as gray powder covering the surface of buds, leaves, and flowers. Leaves become distorted and eventually drop.	Improve ventilation, avoid dryness at the roots, and remove infected parts at once. Spray or dust with a fungicide.
SOOTY MOLD	A black fungus that grows on the sticky, sugary secretions left by sap-sucking insects. Sooty mold causes weak growth and spoiled flowers and fruit.	Carefully wipe off the mold using a soft, damp cloth. Control sap-sucking insects such as whitefly, scale insects, mealybugs, and aphids as above.

FLORAL EFFECT

HOUSEPLANTS ARE desired for their flowers more than for any other reason, and the sometimes short-lived appearance of the blooms makes them all the more desirable. Always colorful, flowers invariably draw the eye, so choose them with care – a bowl of bulbs can enliven a plain windowsill, while a single bold flower can transform a dull room.

Ixora 'Jacqueline' for summer flowers

△ WINTER AND SPRING FLOWERS *Daffodils, hyacinths, and primroses, grouped in shallow bowls, provide bright color and delicious spring fragrance.*

Flowering plants have many points of interest: flower shape, color, and scent can all turn a houseplant into an eye-catching feature. Bold-colored flowers bring a cheerful note to a formal room, while those in paler shades can enhance a brighter background or subtly lighten a darker color scheme. Some flowers offer the bonus of a delicious scent. It is worth thinking carefully before you decide where to place these plants, making sure they are accessible enough for the fragrance to be fully savored.

Among the most varied attributes of flowering plants are the shapes and sizes of their flowerheads. These range from large, flattened heads of daisy flowers, long, tubular bells, wide trumpets, and tiny stars to tall spikes, showers, and variously branched clusters.

SEASONAL PERFORMANCE

If you have room for only a few flowering plants, then choose those that bloom continuously or over a long season, or those whose flowers are long-lasting. Remember that you can encourage some plants to flower more than once by careful pruning or deadheading. However, don't forget those hardy house-plants and bulbs that can be planted outside in the garden after they have flowered, where they may give many years of pleasure.

Flowering houseplants are now available all year round and are often forced to flower outside their natural season. Some are sold solely for one season's flowering display, after which they are thrown away; this may seem wasteful to many avid indoor gardeners. Some, such as poinsettias and Cape heaths, can be kept to flower again – it is tricky to accomplish, but with patience and care it can be done.

△ BRIGHT COLOR *This begonia and calceolaria group makes a strong focal point, complemented by the tiny foliage of a compact baby's tears.*

◁ WINDOWSILL COLLECTION *Most flowering houseplants love light, and these popular African violets are no exception.*

▷ STRIKING SPECIMENS *Beautifully shaped and colored flowers, interesting foliage, and an elegant form make these calla lilies perfect feature plants.*

Houseplants with Fragrant Flowers

MOST OF US APPRECIATE fragrance in flowers, and there are many fragrant-flowered house-plants. Ideally, they should be sited so that their perfume can be relished close up. To enjoy them fully, place them alone as specimens, rather than mixing different kinds of fragrance in the same room, and remember that their perfume may be overpowering in a small, warm room.

△ *Boronia megastigma*
BROWN BORONIA
↕ 3ft (1m) or more ↔ 2ft (60cm) or more

An erect, densely twiggy Australian bush clothed in narrow, aromatic leaves and, in spring, nodding, bell-shaped, scented, reddish brown flowers, yellow within.

☼ Bright, but avoid summer sun ⧗ Moderate to warm. Moderate humidity ◐ Every three weeks, using acidic fertilizer ◊ When dry. Water sparingly in winter ⬚ Semiripe cuttings

△ *Exacum affine*
PERSIAN VIOLET
↕ ↔ 8in (20cm)

From Yemen, this member of the gentian family is compact and bushy, with shiny leaves and blue, pink, or white, scented summer flowers. Grow as an annual.

☼ Bright, but avoid summer sun ⧗ Warm. Moderate to high humidity ◐ Biweekly ◊ Water when soil surface just dry. Reduce watering in winter ⬚ Seed

Freesia hybrids ▷
FLORISTS' FREESIA
↕ 16in (40cm) ↔ 10in (25cm)

These South African perennials, grown from corms, have flat, pointed leaves and produce sprays of richly fragrant flowers from late winter to early spring.

☼ Bright, but avoid summer sun ⧗ Warm, but cool in dormancy. Moderate humidity ◐ Biweekly as buds form, using flowering houseplant fertilizer ◊ Sparingly, increase when in growth, then reduce ⬚ Cormlets

OTHER HOUSEPLANTS WITH FRAGRANT FLOWERS

Citrus, many
Cytisus canariensis
Eucharis amazonica
Hoya carnosa
Mitriostigma axillare
Murraya paniculata, see p.371
Nerium oleander
Osmanthus fragrans
Pittosporum tobira, see p.379
Trachelospermum asiaticum

◁ *Gardenia augusta* cultivars
GARDENIA
↕ ↔ 3ft (1m)

Few plants have a more exotic fragrance than these. Large, fully double, white to cream flowers appear from spring to autumn on a bushy, evergreen shrub.

☼ Bright, but avoid summer sun ⧗ Warm. Moderate to high humidity ◐ Half-strength fertilizer for flowering acid-loving plants, when watering. Rarely in winter ◊ When dry ⬚ Semiripe cuttings

△ *Hyacinthus orientalis* hybrids
HYACINTH
↕ 8in (20cm) ↔ 4in (10cm)

Hyacinths' unrivaled rich fragrance makes them superb for a late winter or spring display. Hybrids are available in various colors; plant out after flowering.

☼ Bright to moderate, with some sun ≣ Cool to moderate. Moderate humidity ◉ Every three weeks ◌ Sparingly, increase as growth appears, keep moist in full growth, and reduce as leaves die 🖾 Offsets

△ *Lilium longiflorum*
EASTER LILY
↕ 3ft (90cm) ↔ 20in (50cm)

Large, trumpet-shaped, white summer flowers are richly fragrant. Widely grown for cut flowers, but an ideal winter pot plant if removed to a garden room.

☼ Bright to moderate. Avoid sun ≣ Moderate to warm. Moderate humidity ◉ Biweekly as buds appear ◌ Sparingly, keep moist in growth, and reduce as leaves die 🖾 Seed, scales, bulbils

△ *Narcissus tazetta* cultivars
TAZETTA NARCISSUS
↕ 20in (50cm) ↔ 6in (15cm)

Many scented cultivars flower from late autumn to spring. Force them for early flowering; afterward, discard them or plant them outside if hardy.

☼ Bright to moderate. Likes some sun ≣ Cool to moderate. Moderate humidity ◉ Biweekly ◌ Sparingly, increase as growth appears, keep moist in full growth, and reduce as leaves die 🖾 Offsets

OTHER TEMPORARY HOUSEPLANTS WITH FRAGRANT FLOWERS

Convallaria majalis
Iris reticulata, see p.400
Matthiola incana (Brompton Stock)
Narcissus 'Soleil d'Or'
Nemesia 'Fragrant Cloud'
Viola odorata

Jasminum polyanthum ▷
PINK JASMINE
↕ 6ft (2m) or more
↔ 3ft (1m) or more

This vigorous, twining shrub, with attractive, dark evergreen leaves, is easily trained to a frame. Richly fragrant, pink-budded white flowers appear from late winter to spring.

☼ Bright to moderate. Likes some sun ≣ Moderate, avoiding fluctuating temperatures and cold drafts. Moderate humidity ◉ Biweekly ◌ Keep moist, but avoid waterlogging. In winter, water when dry 🖾 Semiripe cuttings

◁ *Stephanotis floribunda*
STEPHANOTIS
↕ 6ft (2m) or more
↔ 12in (30cm) or more

A strong-growing, evergreen, twining shrub best kept small by pruning and training. Waxy, very fragrant white flowers appear from spring to autumn.

☼ Bright, but avoid summer sun ≣ Warm. Dislikes drafts and fluctuating temperatures. Moderate to high humidity ◉ Biweekly. Occasionally in winter ◌ When soil surface dry 🖾 Tip cuttings, seed

Houseplants with Long-lasting Flowers

Plants whose flowers are long-lasting, or whose flowering is continuous or recurrent, are well worth considering. They are good value and particularly useful if you have room for only one flowering houseplant, or if you wish to add a reliable spot of color to a drab, colorless location. Such plants perform best with regular deadheading, and in a position that offers cooler temperatures but that also benefits from good light.

◁ *Achimenes* hybrids
HOT-WATER PLANT
↕ ↔ 12in (30cm)

Although the individual flowers are short-lived, with regular deadheading these attractive plants will bloom for weeks from summer into autumn. They are available in many colors.

☼ Bright, but avoid summer sun ▤ Warm. Moderate humidity ◖ Biweekly, using flowering houseplant fertilizer ◌ Water freely in summer, reduce in autumn, keep dry during winter rest, and increase in spring ▦ Tubercles

OTHER CONTINUOUS OR REPEAT-FLOWERING HOUSEPLANTS

Begonia semperflorens cvs.
Brunfelsia pauciflora 'Macrantha'
Catharanthus roseus, see p.374
Cyclamen persicum hybrids, see p.330
Euphorbia milii var. *tulearensis*, see p.386
Fuchsia 'Swingtime'
Hibiscus rosa-sinensis cvs.
Impatiens walleriana hybrids, see p.385
Spathiphyllum wallisii 'Clevelandii', see p.381
Streptocarpus 'Kim', see p.361

◁ *Aechmea fasciata*
URN PLANT
↕ ↔ 20in (50cm)

This splendid bromeliad from Brazil is well worth growing for its beautiful, strap-shaped, silvery gray leaves alone. The long-lasting, dense head of sugar pink bracts and mauve-blue flowers is produced in summer.

☼ Bright, but avoid summer sun ▤ Warm. Low to moderate humidity ◖ Biweekly, using flowering houseplant fertilizer ◌ When dry. Water sparingly in winter. Keep "urn" filled in summer ▦ Offsets

△ *Anthurium andraeanum* 'Acropolis'
FLAMINGO FLOWER
↕ ↔ 2ft (60cm)

Breathtaking white spathes complement the polished, heart-shaped green leaves. The exotic flowers are produced through much of the year and seem to last forever.

☼ Bright, but avoid direct sun ▤ Warm, avoiding fluctuation. Moderate to high humidity ◖ Flowering houseplant fertilizer biweekly ◌ Water when dry. Avoid waterlogging ▦ Division, offsets

△ *Begonia scharffii*
SPECIES BEGONIA
↕ 4ft (1.2m) ↔ 2ft (60cm)

Previously known as *Begonia haageana*, this hairy plant has bronze-green leaves, reddish beneath, and clusters of pinkish white flowers through winter and spring.

☼ Bright to moderate ▤ Moderate to warm. Moderate humidity ◖ Biweekly, using flowering houseplant fertilizer. Monthly in winter ◌ Water when dry, unless dormant ▦ Division, leaf cuttings

Pink-flushed
cream flowers

△ *Kalanchoe blossfeldiana* 'Debbie'
KALANCHOE
↕ ↔ 16in (40cm)

A compact, shrublike houseplant
with large, succulent, red-margined
green leaves. For many weeks,
from winter to summer, this
kalanchoe is topped with dense
heads of small, deep coral-pink flowers.

☼ Bright, with some direct sun 🌡 Moderate to
warm. Low humidity 💧 Feed every three weeks
💧 Water when soil surface dry 🌱 Leaf cuttings

△ *Cymbidium* Showgirl
CYMBIDIUM
↕ 18in (45cm) ↔ 2ft (60cm)

Relatively easy to grow, this
terrestrial orchid produces
long-lasting flowers over a
lengthy period in winter and spring.
Showgirl is a deservedly popular variety
because of its many flower spikes.

☼ Bright. Needs some winter sun 🌡 Moderate to
warm. Moderate humidity 💧 Biweekly, using half-
strength flowering houseplant fertilizer. Monthly in
winter 💧 Keep moist. Reduce in winter 🌱 Division

△ *Impatiens niamniamensis* 'Congo
Cockatoo'
IMPATIENS
↕ 2ft (60cm) ↔ 12in (30cm)

Curiously shaped, red-and-yellow flowers
appear at any time of the year on this
succulent plant from tropical Africa. A
short-lived houseplant with novelty value.

☼ Bright 🌡 Warm. Moderate to high humidity
💧 Biweekly. Occasionally in winter 💧 Water when
soil surface becomes dry 🌱 Tip cuttings, seed.
Roots easily in water

△ *Saintpaulia* 'Bright Eyes'
AFRICAN VIOLET
↕ ↔ 6in (15cm)

African violets are among the most
popular of all flowering houseplants. This
neat, deep purple variety will produce
flowers virtually all year.

☼ Bright to moderate. Avoid sun 🌡 Moderate to
warm. Avoid fluctuation. Moderate to high humidity
💧 Biweekly, using African violet fertilizer. Monthly
in winter 💧 When just dry 🌱 Division, leaf cuttings

◁ x *Doritaenopsis* Andrew
HYBRID MOTH ORCHID
↕ 2ft (60cm) ↔ 12in (30cm)

A fine orchid, with a basal
rosette of fleshy leaves that is
topped, throughout most of the
year, by a sparsely branched
spike of beautifully formed,
pale pink and
rose-pink,
long-lived flowers.

☼ Bright, but avoid
scorching sun
🌡 Moderate to warm,
avoiding drafts. High humidity
💧 Biweekly, using half-strength
orchid fertilizer 💧 Keep moist,
but avoid waterlogging 🌱 Plantlets

**OTHER HOUSEPLANTS WITH
LONG-LASTING FLOWERS**

Anthurium scherzerianum 'Sunshine',
   see p.332
Aphelandra squarrosa 'Dania', see p.368
Celosia argentea Olympia Series
Cymbidium hybrids, see p.410
Cymbidium mini hybrids
Gerbera jamesonii cvs.
Phalaenopsis hybrids, see p.411

Houseplants with Bold-colored Flowers

BOLD-COLORED FLOWERS always attract attention, so they need to be placed with extra care and thought. They should be eye-catching but not distracting, and welcoming but not overwhelming. The bright colors of the plants featured here can be used to transform a sparsely furnished or uninspiring room, or effectively displayed as bold specimen houseplants.

Begonia 'Batik' ▷
WINTER-FLOWERING BEGONIA
↕ 9in (23cm) ↔ 8in (20cm)

Crowded, roselike, double apricot-pink flowers top the glossy leaves of this neat and compact begonia from late autumn to early spring. Show it off on a windowsill.

☼ Bright to moderate, avoiding summer sun ∄ Moderate to warm. Moderate humidity ◗ Biweekly, using flowering houseplant fertilizer. Monthly in winter ◊ When dry. Stop if dormant in winter ▦ Division, tip cuttings

△ *Clivia miniata*
CLIVIA, KAFFIR LILY
↕ ↔ 20in (50cm) or more

This robust South African perennial is available in orange and yellow shades; the flowers appear in spring, especially if the plant is potbound. Needs a winter rest.

☼ Bright. Avoid summer sun ∄ Moderate to warm. Moderate humidity ◗ Biweekly, using flowering houseplant fertilizer. Occasionally in winter ◊ When just dry. Water sparingly in winter ▦ Division, seed

---

OTHER HOUSEPLANTS WITH BOLD-COLORED FLOWERS

Begonia 'Illumination Orange'
Cyrtanthus elatus
Gerbera Sunburst Series
Hippeastrum 'Red Lion'
Nopalxochia ackermannii
Pericallis x *hybrida* 'Spring Glory'
Schlumbergera truncata, see p.363
Sinningia 'Waterloo'

Intense magenta bracts

Bougainvillea 'Alexandra' ▷
BOUGAINVILLEA, PAPER FLOWER
↕ ↔ 3ft (1m) or more

Few houseplants evoke the Mediterranean and the tropics better than this thorny scrambler, whose bracts last from summer to autumn. A situation in plenty of light will give best results.

☼ Bright, with some sun ∄ Moderate to warm. Low to moderate humidity ◗ Biweekly, using flowering houseplant fertilizer ◊ When just dry. Water sparingly in winter ▦ Tip cuttings

Calceolaria Herbeohybrida Group ▷
POUCH FLOWER
↕ 9in (23cm) ↔ 6in (16cm)

Spring is the time when these curious, blotched, pouched flowers appear in a range of rich, bright colors. A Victorian favorite, it is best grown on a pebble tray.

☼ Bright, but avoid summer sun ∄ Moderate. Moderate to high humidity ◗ Biweekly, using half-strength general houseplant fertilizer ◊ Keep moist. Do not let the soil mix dry out ▦ Seed

Euphorbia pulcherrima 'Lilo' ▷
POINSETTIA

↕ ↔ 20in (50cm)

These popular shrubs with their
flamboyant winter bracts are
commonly grown as
temporary plants, but
with patience they can be
encouraged to flower for a
second year or more.

☀ Bright 🌡 Warm, avoiding drafts
and fluctuation. Moderate to high
humidity 💧 Monthly 💧 Water when
soil surface just dry. Avoid
waterlogging ✂ Tip cuttings

**OTHER SHRUBBY HOUSEPLANTS
WITH BOLD-COLORED FLOWERS**

Bougainvillea 'Miss Manila'
Bougainvillea 'Scarlett O'Hara'
Euphorbia pulcherrima 'Menorca'
Hibiscus rosa-sinensis 'Scarlet Giant',
    see p.359
Hydrangea macrophylla 'Hobella'
Nerium oleander 'Mrs. George Roeding'

FLORAL EFFECT

Hippeastrum hybrids ▷
AMARYLLIS

↕ 20in (50cm) ↔ 12in (30cm)

A popular bulbous plant with stunning,
trumpet-shaped flowers. It is sold dry in autumn for
winter or spring flowering. With care can be grown for
years; it needs a few months' rest after the leaves die.

☀ Bright 🌡 Moderate to warm. Moderate humidity 💧 Biweekly
during leaf growth, using flowering houseplant fertilizer 💧 Water
sparingly as growth starts, keep moist in growth, reduce watering in
late summer, and keep dry when dormant ✂ Offsets

Gerbera
'Freya' ▷
**GERBERA,
TRANSVAAL
DAISY**

↕ 26in (65cm) ↔ 14in (35cm)

Big, bold, long-lasting daisy flowers, borne
on strong stems, are the trademark of this
South African houseplant. It will flower
from late spring to late summer.

☀ Bright, with some sun 🌡 Moderate. Low
humidity 💧 Biweekly, using flowering houseplant
fertilizer. Occasionally in winter 💧 Water when
soil surface dry. Avoid waterlogging
✂ Division, seed

△ *Kalanchoe blossfeldiana* 'Gold Strike'
KALANCHOE

↕ ↔ 16in (40cm)

Golden yellow flowerheads rise above a
mound of fleshy, toothed leaves from
winter into spring. Cultivars of this easily
grown succulent are sold in many colors.

☀ Bright, with some direct sun 🌡 Moderate to
warm. Low humidity 💧 Feed every three weeks
💧 Water when soil surface becomes dry
✂ Division, leaf cuttings

Hibiscus 'Royal Yellow' ▷
ROSE OF CHINA

↕ ↔ 3ft (1m) or more

Sun-loving and a popular choice
for windowsills, this plant will flower from
spring until autumn in the right place.
Numerous cultivars, in many colors and
with single or double flowers, are available.

☀ Bright 🌡 Warm, avoiding fluctuation. Moderate to high
humidity 💧 Biweekly. Stop feeding at lower temperatures
💧 When soil surface just dry. Water sparingly in winter. Avoid
waterlogging ✂ Semiripe cuttings

Houseplants for Flowers and Foliage

Plants grown specifically for either their flowers or their foliage have a part to play in any decorative plan in the home, but just as important are those that offer more than one attraction. Many houseplants are worth growing for both foliage and flowers; with beautiful leaves on display when the flowering season is over, they give you the best of both worlds.

Anthurium andraeanum 'Carre' ▷
FLAMINGO FLOWER
↕ ↔ 2ft (60cm)

Large, long-stalked, heart-shaped, glossy dark green leaves are joined at intervals throughout the year by exotic-looking flowers with shiny red spathes. A striking specimen plant.

☼ Bright, but avoid direct sun 🌡 Warm, avoiding fluctuation. Moderate to high humidity 💧 Biweekly, using flowering houseplant fertilizer 💧 Water when dry. Avoid waterlogging 🔲 Division

Cyclamen persicum 'Sylvia' △
FLORISTS' CYCLAMEN
↕ ↔ 9in (23cm)

Just one of a range of cyclamen offering a stunning combination of beautiful flowers, freely borne in winter, and mounds of striking, silver- and green-zoned foliage.

☼ Bright 🌡 Moderate. Moderate to high humidity 💧 Flowering houseplant fertilizer monthly in winter. Biweekly in spring 💧 Keep moist in growth, stop when dormant, then water for regrowth 🔲 Seed

◁ *Calathea crocata*
CALATHEA
↕ ↔ 12in (30cm)

Handsome for its combination of striking, dusky dark green foliage with purple undersides and erect, long-stalked flowerheads with bright orange bracts. The flowerheads are borne in summer.

☼ Bright to moderate. Avoid direct sun 🌡 Warm, avoiding fluctuation. High humidity 💧 Biweekly, using foliage houseplant fertilizer. Monthly in winter 💧 Keep moist. Water when dry if cool 🔲 Division.

△ *Eucomis comosa*
PINEAPPLE LILY
↕ 2ft (60cm) ↔ 12in (30cm)

This is an attractive bulbous plant with a rosette of fleshy, pale green leaves and erect, cylindrical, dense racemes of late summer flowers. It is dormant in winter.

☼ Bright, with some sun 🌡 Cool to moderate. Moderate humidity 💧 Biweekly, using flowering houseplant fertilizer 💧 When dry, then reduce as leaves die. Keep dry in dormancy 🔲 Offsets, seed

Kalanchoe pumila ▷
KALANCHOE
↕ 8in (20cm) ↔ 18in (45cm)

This small, succulent subshrub produces white, bloomy foliage, perfectly matched in spring by lilac flowers. An ideal plant for a windowsill or a hanging basket.

☼ Bright, with some sun ▯ Moderate to warm, but cool in winter. Low humidity 💧 Every three weeks 💧 When soil surface dry. Water sparingly in winter 🔲 Tip or stem cuttings

OTHER HOUSEPLANTS FOR FLOWERS AND FOLIAGE

Aechmea chantinii, see p.366
Clivia miniata, see p.326
   Episcia cupreata, see p.398
   Eucharis grandiflora
   Musa velutina
   Pelargonium 'Mr. Henry Cox'
Strelitzia reginae, see p.379
Veltheimia capensis

△ *Senecio grandifolius*
SENECIO
↕ ↔ 3ft (1m) or more

Big, bold leaves on purple-downy stems are crowned in winter by equally large, crowded heads of tiny yellow flowers. Allocate plenty of room for it to grow.

☼ Bright, with some direct sun ▯ Moderate to warm. Low to moderate humidity 💧 Every three weeks 💧 When soil surface dry. Water sparingly in winter 🔲 Tip cuttings, seed

△ *Ledebouria socialis*
LEDEBOURIA
↕ 5in (13cm) ↔ 3in (8cm)

Sociable is the word for this popular little bulbous plant with purple-backed leaves, which soon fills a pot with its offsets. The flowers are borne in spring and summer.

☼ Bright, but avoid direct sun ▯ Cool to moderate. Moderate humidity 💧 Monthly 💧 When soil surface dry. Water sparingly during winter 🔲 Division, offsets

Fully open flowerhead of Medinilla magnifica

Medinilla magnifica ▷
ROSE GRAPE
↕ ↔ 3ft (90cm)

A truly magnificent plant, producing big, glossy, boldly veined leaves, and show-stopping, pendent flowers in spring and summer. Warmth and humidity are vital.

☼ Bright, but avoid direct sun ▯ Warm, avoiding drafts and fluctuation. High humidity 💧 Monthly 💧 Water when soil surface dry 🔲 Semiripe cuttings, air layering

Zantedeschia elliottiana △
GOLDEN CALLA
↕ 2ft (60cm) ↔ 10in (25cm)

An elegant, tuberous perennial with lush, heart-shaped leaves topped in summer by slim, golden yellow flowers. Hybrids are sold in pink, red, bronze, and orange.

☼ Bright, but avoid summer sun ▯ Moderate to warm. Moderate to high humidity 💧 Biweekly 💧 Keep soil mix moist. Reduce watering during the resting period 🔲 Division, offsets

Houseplants with Winter or Spring Flowers

WINTER NEED NOT deprive you of the pleasure of flowers. Although it can be a dull season in the garden, many houseplants will bloom at this time, including some of the most spectacular plants for the home and some trusted favorites. Mass-produced plants forced into flower need special care if they are to have a long life.

△ *Hyacinthus* 'Pink Pearl'
HYACINTH
‡ 12in (30cm) ↔ 3in (8cm)

Use several in a pot or bowl to display the dense heads of richly fragrant pink flowers. Other hybrids are available. After flowering, plant out in a warm spot.

☼ Bright to moderate. Likes some sun 🌡 Cool to moderate. Moderate humidity 💧 Every three weeks ◊ Sparingly, increase as growth appears, keep moist in full growth, and reduce as leaves die 🏺 Offsets

Cyclamen persicum hybrids ▷
FLORISTS' CYCLAMEN
‡ 12in (30cm) ↔ 10in (25cm)

The gracefully swept back flowers of these hybrids rise above firm, beautifully marbled, silver and green leaves. Hybrids come in many colors and enjoy cool conditions.

☼ Bright 🌡 Cool to moderate. Moderate to high humidity 💧 Biweekly in spring, using flowering houseplant fertilizer. Monthly in winter ◊ Keep moist in growth. Keep dry in dormancy 🏺 Seed

△ *Erica gracilis*
CAPE HEATH
‡ ↔ 12in (30cm) or more

A dwarf shrub from South Africa with tiny, rich cerise flowers. Repot after it has flowered. It will not survive the winter if planted outside in cooler climates.

☼ Bright, but avoid direct sun 🌡 Cool. Moderate humidity 💧 Biweekly, using acidic houseplant fertilizer ◊ Keep moist, but avoid waterlogging 🏺 Semiripe cuttings

Euphorbia pulcherrima 'Regina' △
POINSETTIA
‡ 12in (30cm) ↔ 16in (40cm)

Strongly associated with winter, these Mexican plants are always popular. Red-bracted varieties are commonly seen; this compact white form is a welcome change.

☼ Bright 🌡 Warm, avoiding drafts and fluctuating temperatures. Moderate to high humidity 💧 Monthly ◊ When soil surface just dry. Avoid waterlogging 🏺 Tip cuttings

OTHER FORCED BULBS WITH WINTER OR SPRING FLOWERS

Crocus vernus cvs., see p.377
Hippeastrum 'Apple Blossom'
Hyacinthus orientalis 'Blue Jacket'
Iris reticulata cvs.
Narcissus papyraceus
Tulipa 'Oranje Nassau'

OTHER HOUSEPLANTS WITH WINTER OR SPRING FLOWERS

Begonia 'Gloire de Lorraine'
Cyclamen persicum Puppet Series
Justicia brandegeeana, see p.361
Kalanchoe 'Wendy'
Phalaenopsis hybrids, see
  p.411
Schlumbergera truncata, see p.363
Veltheimia capensis

△ *Justicia rizzinii*
JUSTICIA
↕ ↔ 18in (45cm)

Charming and reliable, this small shrub has many small, nodding, red-and-yellow tubular flowers in autumn and winter. Also known as *Jacobinia pauciflora*.

☼ Bright to moderate, avoiding direct sun 🌡 Warm, avoiding drafts. Moderate to high humidity 🍃 Monthly ◊ Keep moist, but avoid waterlogging 🎴 Semiripe cuttings, seed

△ *Lachenalia aloides* 'Nelsonii'
CAPE COWSLIP
↕ 11in (28cm) ↔ 2in (5cm)

This bulbous perennial from South Africa makes a pretty late winter and early spring display when several are planted together. Flourishes in a cool room.

☼ Bright, with some sun 🌡 Moderate. Moderate humidity 🍃 Biweekly in full leaf ◊ Keep dry in dormancy, increase as foliage appears, and after flowering, water when dry 🎴 Seed, bulbils

△ *Primula obconica*
POISON PRIMROSE
↕ 12in (30cm) ↔ 10in (25cm)

This primrose is a winner for a winter or spring display, but note that the roughly hairy leaves can cause a rash on sensitive skin. It is available in a range of colors.

☼ Bright 🌡 Cool to moderate. Moderate to high humidity 🍃 Biweekly. Monthly in winter ◊ Water when soil surface just dry. Avoid waterlogging 🎴 Seed

△ *Kalanchoe* 'Tessa'
KALANCHOE
↕ 12in (30cm) ↔ 2ft (60cm)

Arching, then drooping stems, with succulent, red-margined leaves, carry clusters of pendent, tubular flowers from late winter into spring. One of the best of its kind for indoor cultivation.

☼ Bright, with sun 🌡 Moderate to warm, but cool in winter. Low humidity 🍃 Every three weeks. Monthly in winter ◊ When soil surface dry. Water sparingly in winter 🎴 Tip or stem cuttings

Rhododendron 'Inga' △
FLORISTS' AZALEA
↕ 16in (40cm) ↔ 20in (50cm)

Azalea cultivars, very popular for winter flowers, come in many colors; this one has pale pink-bordered, darker pink flowers. It likes cool conditions and needs lots of light to do its best.

☼ Bright to moderate, with some sun 🌡 Cool to moderate. Moderate to high humidity 🍃 Biweekly, using acidic houseplant fertilizer ◊ Keep moist, but avoid waterlogging 🎴 Semiripe cuttings

Houseplants with Summer Flowers

S UMMER IS A TIME when the garden is bursting with color, so it is easy to forget about using flowering plants indoors. Of course, color can be provided by cut flowers, but these are often short-lived, and there is a wealth of houseplants that flower in summer which, if chosen and placed with care, will provide a long-lasting feature in any room. Remember that houseplants should not be exposed to the intense heat of the midday summer sun, although bright indirect light will do no harm.

△ *Begonia* Non-Stop Series
TUBEROUS BEGONIA
↕ ↔ 12in (30cm)

Winter-dormant, tuberous-rooted plants grown for their compact bushy habit, bold leaves, and large double flowers in a range of colors. They are long flowering.

☼ Bright to moderate ▮▮ Moderate to warm. Moderate humidity ◉ Biweekly in summer, using flowering houseplant fertilizer ◉ Water when dry. Stop when dormant ▦ Division

Achimenes hybrids ▷
HOT-WATER PLANT
↕ ↔ 12in (30cm)

These bushy, sometimes trailing perennials are dormant in winter but produce a mass of leafy stems, with flowers of many colors from summer into autumn.

☼ Bright, but avoid summer sun ▮▮ Warm. Moderate humidity ◉ Biweekly, using flowering houseplant fertilizer ◉ Water freely in summer, reduce in autumn, keep dry in winter, and increase in spring ▦ Tubercles

OTHER SUMMER-FLOWERING HOUSEPLANTS IN BOLD COLORS

Abutilon 'Nabob'
Celosia argentea 'Cristata'
Cyrtanthus elatus
Fuchsia 'Mary'
Hibiscus rosa-sinensis 'Scarlet Giant', see p.359
Pelargonium 'Caligula'
Sinningia 'Waterloo'

◁ *Anthurium scherzerianum* 'Sunshine'
FLAMINGO FLOWER
↕ 2ft (60cm) ↔ 18in (45cm)

One of the most impressive of all flowering evergreens, especially when the brilliant, waxy red spathes appear above the bold leaves in summer. Deserves special attention.

☼ Bright, but avoid direct sun ▮▮ Warm, avoiding fluctuation. Moderate to high humidity ◉ Biweekly, using flowering houseplant fertilizer ◉ Water when soil surface dry. Avoid waterlogging ▦ Division

△ *Campanula isophylla*
FALLING STARS
↕ 8in (20cm) ↔ 12in (30cm)

A superb plant for a hanging basket where the leafy, trailing stems of blue or white flowers can be seen. With deadheading, it will continue blooming in autumn.

☼ Bright, but avoid direct sun ▮▮ Moderate. Moderate humidity ◉ Biweekly ◉ When soil surface just dry. Reduce watering in winter ▦ Tip cuttings, seed

△ *Eustoma grandiflorum*
PRAIRIE GENTIAN
↕ 20in (50cm) ↔ 12in (30cm)

Also known as *Lisianthus*, this gentian relative is generally short-lived but gives a rich display of large, erect, satiny, bell-shaped flowers above gray-green foliage.

Bright. Likes some sun · Moderate. Moderate humidity · Biweekly, using flowering houseplant fertilizer · Water when soil surface dry. Avoid waterlogging · Seed

△ *Gerbera* 'Kozak'
GERBERA, TRANSVAAL DAISY
↕ 26in (65cm) ↔ 14in (35cm)

Large, long-lasting yellow daisies are carried above a rosette of bold foliage. This taprooted plant hates disturbance, so repot with care. Other colors available.

Bright, with some sun · Moderate. Moderate humidity · Biweekly, using flowering houseplant fertilizer. Occasionally in winter · When soil surface dry. Avoid waterlogging · Division, seed

Ixora 'Jacqueline' ▷
IXORA, JUNGLE FLAME
↕↔ 3ft (1m) or more

This plant is especially beautiful when the orange-red flower clusters appear, shining above the dark green foliage. It is tricky for beginners to grow, since it hates cold air, drafts, and being moved, so once placed, let it be. Pinch out the tips to encourage bushiness.

Bright, avoiding direct summer sun · Moderate. Moderate to high humidity · Biweekly, using acidic houseplant fertilizer · When soil surface dry. Reduce in winter · Semiripe cuttings

Saintpaulia 'Mina' ▷
AFRICAN VIOLET
↕ 4in (10cm)
↔ 8in (20cm)

These shocking pink flowers are well worth cultivating. A popular summer houseplant, it will in fact flower almost continuously through the year. African violets produce single, semidouble, or double flowers.

Bright to moderate. No direct sun · Moderate to warm. Moderate to high humidity · Biweekly, using flowering houseplant fertilizer. Monthly in winter · When just dry · Division, leaf cuttings

OTHER SUMMER-FLOWERING HOUSEPLANTS IN COOL COLORS

- x *Doritaenopsis* Andrew, see p.325
- *Hedychium coronarium*
- *Pachypodium lamerei*, see p.409
- *Plumbago auriculata*
- *Streptocarpus* 'Chorus Line'
- *Streptocarpus* 'Falling Stars'

Streptocarpus 'Paula' ▷
CAPE PRIMROSE
↕ 6in (15cm) ↔ 8in (20cm)

Cape primroses are from the same family as *Saintpaulia* and may become as popular. 'Paula' has purple flowers with distinct dark purple veins and yellow throats.

Bright to moderate. Avoid direct sun · Warm. Moderate to high humidity · Biweekly, using flowering houseplant fertilizer. Monthly in winter, if not dormant · When dry · Division, leaf cuttings

FOLIAGE EFFECT

ATTRACTIVE FOLIAGE has great long-term value. Plants grown for their decorative leaves will give satisfaction all year round – an excellent reason to cultivate as wide a range as possible. Different houseplants produce leaves in a fascinating variety of shapes, sizes, colors, textures, and even scents.

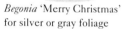

△ TEXTURE AND FORM *Contrasting growth habits and leaf shapes combine to make this foliage group a pleasing whole.*

giant-sized, deeply lobed or divided foliage. Plants with strap- or sword-shaped leaves are very versatile since they can fit into narrow or awkward spaces, and their strong vertical or arching shapes provide excellent contrast to mound-forming or spreading plants, or those with broad or rounded leaves. Rough-, hairy-, or smooth-textured and aromatic leaves offer further variety.

Foliage plants are also effective for adding detail above eye level. Site trailing plants in indoor hanging baskets or in containers on tall pedestals or high shelves.

Begonia 'Merry Christmas' for silver or gray foliage

Leaves range in size from the selaginella's tiny scalelike foliage to the great leathery blades of a Swiss cheese plant. They also vary enormously in shape, from elegant, frondlike or plumed leaves to

A SPLASH OF COLOR

Almost every color exists in the world of plant foliage. Yellow, silver, red, or purple leaves provide

an attractive foil or background for green-leaved plants. Colorful variegated plants also make superb single specimens. As a general rule, pale or brightly colored foliage "lifts" dark areas, while dark leaves appear best against a pale background. Remember that green, the color of most foliage, comes in an astonishing range of shades. Dramatic effects can be achieved with the different textures, sizes, growth habits, and shades of color found on green-leaved plants alone.

△ SIMPLE STYLE *The small leaves of this delicate-looking pilea are eye-catching and add detail to the trailing stems.*

◁ COLORFUL VARIETY *A red croton and bright-bordered coleus are set off by varied shapes and shades of green foliage, displayed at different levels.*

▷ DRAMATIC EFFECT *The narrow foliage of this gold-variegated croton makes a bold statement, providing a good focal point for a living room or bedroom.*

Houseplants with Small Foliage

SMALL-LEAVED HOUSEPLANTS lend themselves to restricted spaces, particularly where they can be examined in detail, and can be a foil to larger-leaved plants. Those with a trailing habit will fill narrow gaps as hanging baskets or on high surfaces, while slow-growing varieties are effective in bottle gardens and terraria. Group plants of contrasting leaf shapes together in a large bowl, trough, or container.

Begonia
Brazil (new
species) ▷
BEGONIA
↕ 8in (20cm)
↔ 12in (30cm)

Small, rounded, fuzzy-textured, dark green leaves, marked with paler green veins, and with dark red undersides, form into the crowded mound of this intriguing, and as yet unclassified, begonia from Brazil.

☼ Bright to moderate, avoiding summer sun ◫ Moderate to warm. Moderate humidity ◐ Biweekly in summer, monthly in winter ◊ When dry, unless dormant in winter ▭ Division, tip cuttings

Callisia repens ▷
CALLISIA
↕ 4in (10cm) ↔ 3ft (1m)

A versatile creeping perennial with small green leaves, and neat white flowers in autumn. It forms a compact carpet among other plants since it will take root from its leaf joints; it is also a good choice for a hanging basket.

☼ Bright. Likes some sun ◫ Moderate to warm. Moderate to high humidity ◐ Biweekly. Occasionally in winter ◊ Water when soil surface dry ▭ Tip cuttings, layering. Roots easily in water

△ *Euonymus japonicus* 'Microphyllus Variegatus'
JAPANESE EUONYMUS
↕ 3ft (1m) ↔ 18in (45cm)

This hardy evergreen shrub, with bright, white-margined leaves, can be kept trim by pruning or pinching out. Slow-growing, it is suitable for use with creeping plants.

☼ Bright. Likes some sun ◫ Cool to moderate. Moderate humidity ◐ Every three weeks. Occasionally in winter ◊ When soil surface dry. Water sparingly in winter ▭ Semiripe cuttings

△ *Ficus pumila*
CREEPING FIG
↕ ↔ 32in (80cm) or more

The juvenile form of this evergreen is a useful houseplant, either clipped into a mound or trained on a frame. Grown against a wall it reaches a good height.

☼ Bright, but avoid summer sun ◫ Moderate to warm. Moderate to high humidity ◐ Biweekly. Occasionally in winter ◊ When soil surface dry. Reduce at lower temperatures ▭ Tip cuttings

△ *Peperomia rotundifolia*
CREEPING BUTTONS
↕ 6in (15cm) ↔ 12in (30cm)

Best grown in a small hanging basket or in a pot on a high surface where the delicate trailing stems, studded with small, round, fleshy leaves, can be seen to advantage.

☼ Bright to moderate, with some sun ▐ Warm. Moderate to high humidity ◌ Every three weeks. Occasionally in winter ◌ Water when soil surface dry. Avoid waterlogging ▦ Tip cuttings

◁ *Streptocarpus saxorum*
CAPE PRIMROSE
↕ 6in (15cm) ↔ 2ft (60cm)

Fascinatingly different from other Cape primroses, this east African species is prostrate in habit and branched, with small, thick leaves. It bears charming flowers in spring and summer.

☼ Bright to moderate, avoiding direct sun ▐ Warm. Moderate to high humidity ◌ Biweekly, using flowering houseplant fertilizer. Monthly in winter, unless dormant ◌ When dry ▦ Tip cuttings

△ *Pilea depressa*
PILEA
↕ 4in (10cm) ↔ 12in (30cm)

A creeping evergreen, with trailing stems bearing small, fleshy, bright green leaves. Display as *Peperomia rotundifolia* (above) in a small hanging basket or raised pot.

☼ Bright to moderate, with some sun ▐ Warm. Moderate to high humidity ◌ Every three weeks. Occasionally in winter ◌ Water when soil surface just dry. Avoid waterlogging ▦ Tip cuttings

---

OTHER TRAILING HOUSEPLANTS WITH SMALL FOLIAGE

Aptenia cordifolia 'Variegata'
Ceropegia linearis subsp. *woodii*, see p.390
Dichondra micrantha
Ficus pumila 'Minima'
Hedera helix 'Spetchley'
Peperomia prostrata
Senecio rowleyanus, see p.391

OTHER HOUSEPLANTS WITH SMALL FOLIAGE

Aichryson × *domesticum* 'Variegatum'
Begonia 'Queen Olympus'
Cuphea hyssopifolia, see p.378
Peperomia campylotropa
Punica granatum var. *nana*
Saintpaulia 'Midget Valentine'

Saintpaulia 'Pip Squeek' △
AFRICAN VIOLET
↕ ↔ 4in (10cm)

This neat, compact African violet forms a tuffet of small, dusky green, dark-stalked leaves. Miniature, bell-shaped, pale pink flowers are borne throughout the year.

☼ Bright to moderate, avoiding direct sun ▐ Moderate to warm. Moderate to high humidity ◌ Biweekly, using African violet fertilizer. Monthly in winter ◌ When just dry ▦ Division, leaf cuttings

△ *Tripogandra multiflora*
TRIPOGANDRA
↕ 8in (20cm) ↔ 3ft (1m)

A loose mass of trailing stems with small, narrow leaves is set off by white flowers, freely produced from autumn to spring. Best suited to a hanging basket.

☼ Bright, but avoid direct sun ▐ Moderate. Moderate to high humidity ◌ Biweekly. Rarely in winter ◌ Keep moist. When soil surface dry in winter ▦ Tip cuttings. Roots easily in water

Houseplants with Large Foliage

HOUSEPLANTS WITH LARGE FOLIAGE always make excellent specimen plants, particularly in larger rooms. Young, small plants can first be displayed as table center-pieces then moved as they grow. Large-leaved houseplants make superb focal points, especially when displayed against a plain background to accentuate their striking foliage and bold outlines. They can also be used effectively in a group of different plants, all with similar cultivation requirements but with contrasting shapes and sizes.

△ *Cordyline fruticosa* 'Red Edge'
CORDYLINE
↕ 3ft (1m) ↔ 2ft (60cm)

This compact plant with broad green, red-margined leaves is best displayed in a group. Use the bold leaves to contrast with the surrounding furnishings.

☼ Bright, but avoid direct sun 🌡 Moderate to warm, avoiding drafts. Moderate to high humidity 💧 Biweekly. Monthly in winter 💧 Let soil mix dry before watering, particularly in cool conditions 🪴 Division; tip or stem cuttings

△ *Anthurium crystallinum*
CRYSTAL ANTHURIUM
↕ ↔ 2ft (60cm)

A stunning foliage plant producing large, velvety, dark green, white-veined leaves that are pink-bronze when young. It needs growing conditions similar to those in its native Colombian rainforest home.

☼ Bright, but avoid direct summer sun. Tolerates some shade 🌡 Warm, avoiding drafts. High humidity 💧 Biweekly in summer. Monthly in winter 💧 Keep moist 🪴 Division

---

OTHER HOUSEPLANTS WITH LARGE FOLIAGE

Codiaeum variegatum var. *pictum*, see p.368
Epipremnum aureum, see p.390
Ficus lyrata, see p.395
Philodendron bipinnatifidum, see p.364
Platycerium bifurcatum, see p.407
Spathiphyllum 'Euro Gigant', see p.371
Yucca elephantipes, see p.385

△ *Cordyline fruticosa* 'Lord Robertson'
CORDYLINE
↕ 10ft (3m) ↔ 2ft (60cm)

Green and cream leaves gradually turn red-purple with rose margins. Perfect for a richly decorated room, this elegant plant lives up to its aristocratic cultivar name.

☼ Bright, but avoid summer sun 🌡 Moderate to warm. Moderate to high humidity 💧 Biweekly. Monthly in winter 💧 Water only when dry. Reduce in cool conditions 🪴 Division; tip or stem cuttings

△ *Dieffenbachia* 'Compacta'
DUMB CANE
↕ 3ft (1m) ↔ 2ft (60cm)

Dumb canes have beautifully mottled leaves, here with elegant cream markings. They have poisonous sap: wear gloves to handle them, and wash hands afterward.

☼ Bright, but avoid direct sun 🌡 Moderate to warm. Moderate to high humidity 💧 Biweekly. Monthly in winter 💧 Water when soil surface has dried out 🪴 Tip cuttings, stem sections

Fatsia japonica ▷
JAPANESE ARALIA
↕ ↔ 6ft (2m)

Ideal for a cooler room, this bold, glossy-leaved aralia can be kept within bounds by pruning and can be planted outside in warm areas if it outgrows its allotted position.

☼ Moderate ❄ Cool to moderate. Moderate humidity 💧 Biweekly, using foliage houseplant fertilizer. Once in winter 💧 When dry. Reduce if cool 🌱 Tip cuttings, air layering

△ *Monstera deliciosa*
SWISS CHEESE PLANT
↕ 10ft (3m) or more ↔ 4ft (1.2m) or more

South American rainforests are home to this giant, popular for its vigorous growth and large, beautifully sculpted leaves. An impressive climber, it is best grown up a moss pole or trellis.

☼ Bright to moderate ❄ Moderate to warm. Moderate to high humidity 💧 Biweekly. Twice during winter 💧 Let soil surface dry before watering 🌱 Stem cuttings, air layering

△ *Ficus elastica*
RUBBER PLANT
↕ 10ft (3m) or more ↔ 3ft (1m) or more

The bold form of their leathery, paddle-shaped, glossy dark green leaves make rubber plants highly desirable specimens. Will eventually outgrow an average room.

☼ Bright to moderate ❄ Moderate to warm. Moderate to high humidity 💧 Foliage houseplant fertilizer biweekly; monthly in winter 💧 When dry; reduce watering if cool 🌱 Tip cuttings, air layering

△ *Grevillea robusta*
SILKY OAK
↕ 10ft (3m) or more ↔ 5ft (1.5m) or more

Silk oaks' large leaves are composed of leaflets that create a delicate filigree. In their native Australia they become huge trees. Grow in acidic soil mix.

☼ Bright to shady, avoiding direct sun ❄ Cool to warm. Moderate humidity 💧 Biweekly, spring to autumn, using foliage houseplant fertilizer 💧 When soil surface dry 🌱 Semiripe cuttings, seed

△ *Philodendron erubescens* 'Imperial Red'
BLUSHING PHILODENDRON
↕ 10ft (3m) or more ◀▶ 3ft (1m) or more

The young leaves of this philodendron are deep claret, maturing to dark green, deeply veined and glossy. Bushy when young, it will climb when established.

☼ Bright to moderate ❄ Warm. Moderate to high humidity 💧 Biweekly, using foliage houseplant fertilizer. Monthly in winter 💧 Water when soil surface dry 🌱 Tip cuttings

Houseplants with Narrow or Sword-shaped Foliage

NARROW-LEAVED PLANTS can be very effective, especially when contrasted with broad-leaved subjects. Used with flair, many houseplants with sword-shaped foliage can contribute height to a group and break up hard horizontal lines in the display. As specimen plants, tall varieties can provide a strong focal point as well as being useful "fillers" in narrow spaces and awkward corners.

△ *Acorus gramineus* 'Ogon'
JAPANESE SWEET FLAG
↕ 10in (25cm) ↔ 18in (45cm)

Erect when young, this small, clump-forming perennial forms a broad mound of arching, aromatic, green- and gold-striped, narrow leaves. Color fades in poor light.

☼ Bright to moderate, with some sun
🌡 Cool to moderate. Moderate humidity
💧 Every three weeks. Occasionally in winter 💧 Keep moist ▦ Division

Codiaeum 'Goldfinger' ▷
CROTON
↕ ↔ 3ft (1m) or more

The long, narrow, gold-variegated leaves of this shrub, one of the colorful croton family, bring an exotic flavor to any room. It loves generous amounts of light, heat, and humidity.

☼ Bright, with some sun
🌡 Warm, avoiding drafts and fluctuation. Moderate to high humidity 💧 Biweekly, using foliage houseplant fertilizer. Occasionally in winter
💧 Keep moist. In winter, water when soil surface dry ▦ Tip cuttings

Leaves arch with age

Carex conica 'Snowline' ▷
ORNAMENTAL SEDGE
↕ 6in (15cm) ↔ 10in (25cm)

Quite hardy and suitable for an unheated room, this small, densely tufted evergreen is a useful houseplant with narrow, dark green leaves, margined creamy white and arching outward.

☼ Bright to shady, with some sun 🌡 Cool to moderate. Moderate humidity 💧 Every three weeks. Occasionally in winter 💧 When soil surface dry. Reduce watering in winter ▦ Division

Cordyline australis 'Red Star' △
NEW ZEALAND CABBAGE TREE
↕ 10ft (3m) ↔ 3ft (1m)

When young this plant produces a glorious, leafy rosette, but it soon forms a woody stem with leaves only on the summit. An excellent window plant when young.

☼ Bright to moderate 🌡 Moderate to warm. Moderate to high humidity
💧 Biweekly 💧 Water when soil surface just dry. Reduce watering in winter
▦ Stem sections

FOLIAGE EFFECT

Cordyline australis 'Sundance' ▷
NEW ZEALAND CABBAGE TREE
↕ 10ft (3m) ↔ 3ft (1m)

This striking plant from New Zealand has long, narrow, leathery leaves that form a wide arch from the base. Young specimens are ideal for a sunny window position.

☀ Bright to moderate ≣ Moderate to warm. Moderate to high humidity ◊ Biweekly ◊ Water when soil surface just dry. Reduce watering in winter ⊡ Stem sections

△ *Isolepis cernua*
SLENDER CLUB-RUSH
↕ 6in (15cm) ↔ 18in (45cm)

A charming, tufted little rushlike plant with threadlike, arching or drooping leaves and equally slender shoots bearing tiny brown spikes. Useful with small bulbs or ferns.

☀ Bright to shady, with some sun ≣ Cool to moderate. Moderate humidity ◊ Every three weeks. Occasionally in winter ◊ When soil surface dry. Reduce watering in winter ⊡ Division

△ *Pandanus veitchii*
SCREW PINE
↕ ↔ 4ft (1.2m) or more

Like a pineapple in habit, except that the white-margined, dark green leaves droop at the tips. A dramatic houseplant, but it has vicious spiny teeth, so place with care.

☀ Bright to moderate, avoiding summer sun ≣ Warm. High humidity ◊ Biweekly. Occasionally in winter ◊ Keep moist. Reduce watering in winter ⊡ Division, stem sections

Magenta-edged evergreen leaves

Dracaena cincta 'Magenta' ▷
DRACAENA
↕ 10ft (3m) ↔ 4ft (1.2m)

Slow-growing and with slender stems, this evergreen will branch with age, displaying its crowded rosettes of long, narrow, arching leaves. Good light gives the best color.

☀ Bright to moderate, avoiding summer sun ≣ Warm. Moderate to high humidity ◊ Biweekly. Occasionally in winter ◊ Water when soil surface dry. Water sparingly in winter ⊡ Tip cuttings, stem sections

OTHER HOUSEPLANTS WITH NARROW FOLIAGE

Ananas bracteatus 'Tricolor', see p.358
Billbergia x *windii*, see p.414
Cordyline australis 'Albertii'
Dracaena fragrans 'Janet Craig', see p.388
Nolina recurvata, see p.394
Ophiopogon jaburan 'Vittatus'
Phormium 'Cream Delight'
Phormium 'Crimson Devil'
Tradescantia spathacea
Yucca elephantipes, see p.385

△ *Phormium* 'Sundowner'
NEW ZEALAND FLAX
↕ ↔ 5ft (1.5m)

Bold in habit and in leaf, this has tall, erect, leathery, sword-shaped leaves, with a dull purple center and broad edges of pink, fading to cream. A fine focal point.

☀ Bright to moderate, with some sun ≣ Cool to moderate. Moderate humidity ◊ Biweekly. Occasionally in winter ◊ When soil surface dry. Reduce watering in winter ⊡ Division

Houseplants with Textured Foliage

THE HUGE VARIETY of leaf surfaces that plants present to the touch provide a seemingly unending source of pleasure. Some leaves are rough, with distinctive ridges or wrinkles, while others have a smooth or velvety patina that begs to be stroked. Try using several of these in a feature group. People with sensitive skin should take care with bristly-leaved plants, which can cause skin irritation or a rash.

Begonia 'Beatrice Haddrell' ▷
RHIZOMATOUS BEGONIA
↕ 6in (15cm) ↔ 10in (25cm)

Worth growing just for its sharply angled, almost star-shaped, velvety, dark brownish leaves, which have light green veins and centers and deep red undersides. Sprays of pale pink or white flowers appear from winter into early spring.

☼ Bright to moderate, avoiding summer sun ▤ Moderate to warm. Moderate humidity ◖ Biweekly. Monthly in winter ◊ When soil surface dry. Stop watering if winter dormant ▥ Division

△ *Begonia masoniana*
IRON CROSS BEGONIA
↕ ↔ 20in (50cm)

An old favorite from New Guinea, the iron cross begonia takes its name from the distinctive dark mark in the center of each bright green, puckered, hairy leaf. A stunning foliage plant.

☼ Bright to moderate, avoiding summer sun ▤ Moderate to warm. Moderate humidity ◖ Biweekly. Monthly in winter ◊ When dry. Stop watering if dormant in winter ▥ Division, leaf cuttings

---

OTHER HOUSEPLANTS WITH SMOOTH-TEXTURED FOLIAGE

Anthurium andraeanum
Aspidistra elatior, see p.386
Asplenium nidus, see p.406
Begonia 'Thurstonii'
Codiaeum variegatum var. *pictum,* see p.368
Dracaena fragrans 'Massangeana', see p.375
Ficus elastica, see p.339
Veltheimia capensis

△ *Begonia bowerae*
EYELASH BEGONIA
↕ 10in (25cm) ↔ 7in (18cm)

Easy to grow and very popular, eyelash begonias have crinkly-margined, dark-spotted, whiskery leaves. Grow them on a windowsill where they can be easily seen.

☼ Bright to moderate, avoiding summer sun ▤ Moderate to warm. Moderate humidity ◖ Biweekly. Monthly in winter ◊ When soil surface dry. Water sparingly in winter ▥ Division

◁ *Gynura aurantiaca*
'Purple Passion'
PURPLE VELVET PLANT
↕ 10ft (3m) ↔ 2ft (60cm)

Purple velvet is exactly what the leaves of this scrambling plant from Java look and feel like. To maintain a compact habit, train stems to a support and pinch out the tips. Nip off buds of the evil-smelling flowers when they appear.

☼ Bright, but avoid summer sun ▤ Warm. Moderate to high humidity ◖ Biweekly. Occasionally in winter ◊ Water when soil surface dry. Avoid overwatering ▥ Tip cuttings

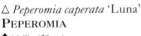

△ *Kalanchoe tomentosa*
PANDA PLANT
↕ 3ft (1m) ↔ 8in (20cm)

Everyone will enjoy stroking the soft, white, felted leaves of this Madagascan shrub; its stems have the same texture. Avoid wetting leaves when watering.

☼ Bright, with some sun ◫ Moderate to warm, but cool in winter. Low humidity ◑ Every three weeks. Monthly in winter ◌ When dry. Water sparingly in winter ▱ Tip or stem cuttings

△ *Peperomia caperata* 'Luna'
PEPEROMIA
↕ ↔ 8in (20cm)

The corrugated surfaces of these neatly heart-shaped, deep red leaves are not easily forgotten. The foliage is set off by slender spikes of white summer flowers.

☼ Bright to moderate, with some sun ◫ Warm. Moderate to high humidity ◑ Every three weeks. Occasionally in winter ◌ When soil surface dry. Avoid waterlogging ▱ Tip or leaf cuttings

△ *Pilea* 'Silver Tree'
PAN-AMERICAN FRIENDSHIP PLANT
↕ 8in (20cm) ↔ 12in (30cm)

Puckered, quilted, sharply toothed, pointed leaves, strikingly marked with silver on a bronze-green ground, form the low mound of this eye-catching plant.

☼ Bright to moderate, with some sun ◫ Warm. Moderate to high humidity ◑ Every three weeks. Occasionally in winter ◌ Water when soil surface just dry. Avoid waterlogging ▱ Tip cuttings

OTHER HOUSEPLANTS WITH ROUGH-TEXTURED FOLIAGE

Begonia gehrtii
Bertolonia marmorata
Fittonia verschaffeltii var. *argyroneura*
Geogenanthus undatus
Hemigraphis 'Exotica'
Nautilocalyx bullatus
    Pelargonium tomentosum, see p.345
        Peperomia caperata 'Emerald Ripple'
 Pilea involucrata
Pilea 'Norfolk'
Saxifraga stolonifera, see p.391

△ *Pelargonium* 'Mabel Grey'
SCENTED-LEAVED GERANIUM
↕ 14in (35cm) ↔ 8in (20cm)

Deeply cut and roughly textured, the leaves of this geranium are just waiting to be rubbed, which releases their rich lemon aroma. Small mauve flowers are borne in spring and summer. Easy to grow and propagate.

☼ Bright. Likes sun ◫ Moderate to warm, but cool in winter. Low humidity ◑ Biweekly, using high-potassium fertilizer ◌ When soil surface dry. Water sparingly in winter ▱ Tip cuttings

◁ *Sinningia* 'Mont Blanc'
GLOXINIA
↕ 12in (30cm)
↔ 18in (45cm)

This warmth-loving plant bears large, fleshy green leaves with a smooth, velvety texture. The foliage is a perfect foil for the big, trumpet-shaped white flowers that are produced in summer. Gloxinias are available in many other colors.

☼ Bright to moderate, avoiding sun ◫ Warm, but moderate when dormant. High humidity ◑ Bi-weekly, using flowering houseplant fertilizer ◌ Keep moist, but keep dry when dormant ▱ Division

Houseplants with Aromatic Foliage

JUST AS FRAGRANT flowers are a bonus, so too are aromatic leaves; their scent gives a plant added interest and can freshen stale air. Place these plants where they can be easily touched, since some leaves release their aroma only when rubbed between the fingers. There is a wide range of geraniums with aromatic foliage, but the different scents they offer are best not mixed.

△ *Pelargonium* 'Fragrans'
NUTMEG GERANIUM
↕ 10in (25cm) ↔ 8in (20cm)

When rubbed, the sage green, velvety foliage of this small, bushy plant releases a distinct fragrance. Small white flowers are produced in clusters in spring and summer. A reliable plant for cultivating on a windowsill.

☼ Bright, with sun 🌡 Moderate to warm, but cool in winter. Low humidity
💧 Biweekly, using high-potassium fertilizer
💧 When soil surface dry. Water sparingly in winter 🔲 Tip cuttings

Myrtus communis ▷
COMMON MYRTLE
↕ ↔ 3ft (1m) or more

Famed since antiquity for its fragrant foliage, this plant also produces scented flowers from summer to autumn, followed by black berries. Easily trained and maintained as a treelike standard. Keep small by pruning.

☼ Bright, with sun 🌡 Moderate to warm. Low to moderate humidity 💧 Every three weeks 💧 When soil surface dry. Water sparingly in winter 🔲 Semiripe cuttings

---

OTHER HOUSEPLANTS WITH AROMATIC FOLIAGE

Acorus gramineus 'Ogon', see p.340
Aloysia triphylla
Laurus nobilis, see p.402
Lavandula dentata
Plectranthus amboinicus
Plectranthus madagascariensis
Rosmarinus officinalis

Pelargonium crispum 'Variegatum' ▷
LEMON-SCENTED GERANIUM
↕ 18in (45cm) ↔ 6in (15cm)

A trusted favorite since 1774, with a stiffly upright habit and small, green and cream, crinkly-margined, lemon-scented leaves. Pale mauve flowers are borne in spring and summer.

☼ Bright, with some direct sun 🌡 Moderate to warm, but cool in winter. Low humidity
💧 Biweekly, using high-potassium fertilizer
💧 When soil surface dry. Water sparingly in winter 🔲 Tip cuttings

△ *Pelargonium* 'Graveolens'
ROSE GERANIUM
↕ 2ft (60cm) ↔ 16in (40cm)

Oil of geranium is extracted from the deeply cut, lemon-rose-scented foliage of this hybrid. It is bushy, but its strong scent makes it an ideal plant for a windowsill.

☼ Bright, with sun 🌡 Moderate to warm, but cool in winter. Low humidity 💧 Biweekly, using high-potassium fertilizer 💧 When soil surface dry. Water sparingly in winter 🔲 Tip cuttings

Branched flower clusters

Attractive, heavily-veined leaves

△ *Pelargonium* 'Lady Plymouth'
SCENTED-LEAVED GERANIUM
↕ 16in (40cm) ↔ 8in (20cm)

Known in cultivation for 200 years, this geranium has deeply cut, bright green leaves, margined with silver, which are eucalyptus scented when rubbed.

☼ Bright, with sun ‖ Moderate to warm, but cool in winter. Low humidity ♦ Biweekly, using high-potassium fertilizer ◊ When soil surface dry. Water sparingly in winter ▧ Tip cuttings

**OTHER GERANIUMS
WITH AROMATIC FOLIAGE**

Pelargonium abrotanifolium
Pelargonium 'Attar of Roses'
Pelargonium 'Dr. Livingston'
Pelargonium 'Fair Ellen'
Pelargonium grossularioides
Pelargonium 'Mabel Grey', see p.343
Pelargonium 'Prince of Orange'
Pelargonium 'Rober's Lemon Rose'

◁ *Plectranthus oertendahlii*
CANDLE PLANT
↕ 8in (20cm) ↔ 3ft (1m)

A charming plant of trailing habit, with fleshy, rounded and scalloped, pale green aromatic leaves with white veins. White or pale blue flowers are produced intermittently throughout the year.

☼ Bright to moderate, with sun ‖ Warm, avoiding fluctuation. Low humidity ♦ Biweekly. Monthly in winter ◊ When dry. Reduce watering in winter. Avoid waterlogging ▧ Tip cuttings

△ *Pelargonium* 'Old Spice'
SCENTED-LEAVED GERANIUM
↕ 12in (30cm) ↔ 6in (15cm)

Attractive pale green leaves impart a pleasant spicy aroma to this erect plant, which also bears clusters of white summer flowers. Fairly bushy when in growth.

☼ Bright, with sun ‖ Moderate to warm, but cool in winter. Low humidity ♦ Biweekly, using high-potassium fertilizer ◊ When soil surface dry. Water sparingly in winter ▧ Tip cuttings

△ *Pelargonium tomentosum*
PEPPERMINT-SCENTED GERANIUM
↕ 3ft (90cm) ↔ 30in (75cm)

White or pale pink flowers, borne from spring to summer, complement the softly gray-woolly, peppermint-scented foliage. This robust spreader may need pruning.

☼ Bright, with sun ‖ Moderate to warm, but cool in winter. Low humidity ♦ Biweekly, using high-potassium fertilizer ◊ When soil surface dry. Water sparingly in winter ▧ Tip cuttings

△ *Prostanthera rotundifolia*
MINT BUSH
↕ ↔ 3ft (1m)

Brush against this bush and smell the minty aroma of its tiny leaves. Also grown for its masses of small purple flowers in spring and early summer.

☼ Bright, with some sun ‖ Moderate to warm. Low humidity ♦ Biweekly ◊ Water when soil surface becomes dry. Water sparingly in winter ▧ Stem cuttings

Houseplants with Red, Pink, or Purple Foliage

P URPLE OR SIMILARLY bright-colored foliage houseplants can be used to provide a bold, dramatic effect, especially when set against a pale background or placed in combination with green, yellow, white, or variegated plants. Good light levels are usually needed to bring out the rich colors, so bear each plant's light requirements in mind when placing it.

△ *Hypoestes phyllostachya* 'Splash'
POLKA-DOT PLANT
↕ ↔ 26in (65cm)

Named for the pale pink splashes on its thin and otherwise dark green leaves, this plant's color is most vivid in good light and may revert to green in low light.

☼ Bright, but avoid summer sun ▮ Warm. Moderate to high humidity ◊ Biweekly. Occasionally in winter ◊ When soil surface just dry ▭ Tip cuttings. Roots easily in water

Begonia rex hybrids ▷
REX BEGONIA
↕ 10in (25cm) ↔ 12in (30cm)

The cultivars and hybrids of this Himalayan begonia, grown principally for their ornamental foliage, exhibit a spectacular range of colors including many in purple and silver shades.

☼ Bright to moderate. Avoid hot sun ▮ Moderate to warm. Moderate humidity ◊ Biweekly in summer. Monthly in winter ◊ When dry. Stop if dormant in winter ▭ Division, leaf cuttings

OTHER BEGONIAS WITH RED, PINK, OR PURPLE FOLIAGE

Begonia 'Enech'
Begonia 'Helen Lewis'
Begonia 'Merry Christmas', see p.352
Begonia 'Mini Merry'
Begonia 'Rajah'
Begonia 'Tiny Bright'

△ *Calathea sanderiana*
PEACOCK PLANT
↕ ↔ 2ft (60cm)

Found wild on Peruvian rainforest floors, this plant forms a bold clump of deep olive green leaves, purple beneath and with rose-red parallel stripes aging to silver above. Short conical spikes of violet and white flowers appear among the leaves in summer.

☼ Bright to moderate, avoiding direct sun ▮ Warm, avoiding fluctuation. High humidity ◊ Biweekly, using foliage houseplant fertilizer. Monthly in winter ◊ Keep moist. When dry in cool conditions ▭ Division

△ *Leea coccinea* 'Burgundy'
WEST INDIAN HOLLY
↕ 32in (80cm) ↔ 2ft (60cm)

This Burmese shrub, commonly grown in gardens in the West Indies, produces handsome sprays of deeply divided, deep red leaves. A very elegant houseplant.

☼ Bright, but avoid summer sun ▮ Warm, avoiding fluctuation. Moderate to high humidity ◊ Biweekly. Occasionally in winter ◊ When dry. Avoid waterlogging ▭ Semiripe cuttings, air layering

FOLIAGE EFFECT

*Flowers may be
pinched out for
compact habit*

△ *Solenostemon* 'Volcano'
COLEUS
↕ ↔ 2ft (60cm)

Coleus leaves come in many different
color combinations, including this green-
edged deep red. Pinching out the growing
tips will give the plant a compact habit.

☼ Bright ☰ Moderate to warm. Moderate humidity
◊ Weekly. Occasionally in winter ◊ Keep moist,
but avoid waterlogging. At lower temperatures,
water as soil surface dries ▦ Tip cuttings.
Roots easily in water

△ *Strobilanthes dyerianus*
PERSIAN SHIELD
↕ ↔ 2ft (60cm)

Beautifully veined bronze-green leaves
with silvery purple markings above and
purple undersides distinguish this plant.
Flourishes in high heat and humidity.

☼ Bright, but avoid summer sun ☰ Warm. High
humidity ◊ Every three weeks ◊ Water when soil
surface dry. Reduce watering in winter ▦ Tip or
stem cuttings

△ *Oxalis
purpurata*
OXALIS
↕ ↔ 6in (15cm)

The cloverlike, purple-tinted leaves of
this southern African plant are rich purple
beneath. Cream, white, pink, or purple
flowers appear in autumn and winter.

☼ Bright, with some direct sun ☰ Moderate to
warm. Moderate humidity ◊ Biweekly ◊ Water
when soil surface dry. Water sparingly in winter
▦ Division

△ *Peperomia obtusifolia* 'Columbiana'
BABY RUBBER PLANT
↕ ↔ 25cm (10in)

The rich purple, fleshy leaves of this
peperomia are a striking contrast to the
popular, and more typical, green form.
This is an excellent plant for a terrarium.

☼ Bright to moderate, with some sun ☰ Warm.
Moderate to high humidity ◊ Every three weeks.
Occasionally in winter ◊ Water when soil surface
dry. Avoid waterlogging ▦ Tip cuttings

**OTHER HOUSEPLANTS WITH
RED, PINK, OR PURPLE FOLIAGE**

Acalypha wilkesiana 'Musaica'
Codiaeum 'Flamingo'
Cordyline fruticosa 'Atom'
Cryptanthus 'Pink Starlight'
X *Cryptbergia* 'Rubra'
Gynura aurantiaca 'Purple Passion',
   see p.342
Hemigraphis alternata
Hypoestes phyllostachya 'Vinrod',
   see p.398
Iresene herbstii
Mikania dentata
Tradescantia pallida 'Purpurea'

△ *Tradescantia zebrina* 'Quadricolor'
INCH PLANT, WANDERING JEW
↕ 10in (25cm) ↔ 2ft (60cm)

Vigorous, fleshy-stemmed, and easy to
grow, this is ideal for a hanging basket or
raised surface. The leaves are dark green,
striped silver, and flushed pink and red.

☼ Bright, but avoid direct sun ☰ Moderate.
Moderate to high humidity ◊ Biweekly. Rarely in
winter ◊ Keep moist. In winter, water when dry
▦ Tip cuttings. Roots easily in water

FOLIAGE EFFECT

Houseplants with Gold- or Yellow-variegated Foliage

GOLD AND YELLOW are bright, cheerful colors for houseplants, especially effective displayed against dark, plain backgrounds. Leaves with regular, marginal, or central markings are usually the most distinctive and dramatic, but spotted, blotched, or streaked variegation is also attractive; try combining several different leaf effects. Beware of placing these plants in low light conditions; with very few exceptions, this will cause the gold or yellow to fade.

Dieffenbachia 'Vesuvius' △
DUMB CANE
↕ ↔ 3ft (90cm)

Boldly spotted, sword-shaped leaves make this tropical South American native a distinctive houseplant. Poisonous when chewed, so keep out of children's reach.

☼ Bright to moderate, avoiding summer sun ☐ Moderate. Moderate to high humidity ◗ Biweekly, using foliage houseplant fertilizer. Monthly in winter ◊ Water when dry ▱ Tip or stem cuttings

Aucuba japonica 'Variegata' ▷
SPOTTED LAUREL
↕ 6ft (2m) ↔ 5ft (1.5m)

This tough, evergreen shrub with well-marked yellow variegation is an invaluable pot plant, suitable for cool or low-light areas. Maintain a compact size by regular pruning.

☼ Bright to shady, avoiding direct sun ☐ Cool to moderate. Moderate to high humidity ◗ Monthly. Occasionally in winter ◊ When soil surface just dry. Sparingly in winter ▱ Semiripe cuttings

OTHER GOLD- OR YELLOW-VARIEGATED HOUSEPLANTS

Abutilon pictum 'Thompsonii'
Calathea lubbersiana
Dracaena fragrans 'Yellow Stripe'
Hedera helix 'Gold Child'
Impatiens 'Fanfare'
Tolmiea menziesii 'Taff's Gold', see p.377

Codiaeum 'Gold Star' ▷
CROTON
↕ ↔ 3ft (1m) or more

Colorful, glossy, leathery foliage makes this plant a striking focal point wherever it is used, but it is worth taking a detailed look, too. Needs warmth and bright light.

☼ Bright ☐ Warm. Avoid drafts and fluctuation. Moderate to high humidity ◗ Biweekly, using foliage houseplant fertilizer. Occasionally in winter ◊ Keep moist. When dry in winter ▱ Tip cuttings

△ *Pelargonium* 'Mrs. Quilter'
ZONAL GERANIUM
↕ 16in (40cm) ↔ 6in (15cm)

One of many bright foliage geraniums, reliable and easy to grow. Eye-catching, golden yellow leaves have a distinct bronze zone that deepens in full sun.

☼ Bright, with some sun ☐ Moderate to warm, but cool in winter. Low humidity ◗ Biweekly, using high-potassium fertilizer ◊ Water when soil surface dry. Sparingly in winter ▱ Tip cuttings

Yellow-splashed leaflets

FOLIAGE EFFECT

Peperomia obtusifolia 'USA' ▷
PEPEROMIA

↕ ↔ 10in (25cm)

This upright, brightly colored evergreen plant, with large, fleshy, gold-variegated green leaves, is particularly suitable for a warm and humid spot such as a bathroom shelf. An attractive, versatile houseplant.

☼ Bright to moderate, with some sun ⊞ Warm. Moderate to high humidity ◊ Every three weeks. Occasionally in winter ◊ Water when soil surface just dry. Avoid waterlogging ⊡ Tip cuttings

△ Sansevieria trifasciata 'Golden Hahnii'
GOLDEN BIRD'S NEST

↕ 5in (12cm) ↔ 18in (45cm)

Quite unlike the familiar, erect *Sansevieria trifasciata* 'Laurentii' (see p.385), this bears dwarf rosettes of broad, fleshy green leaves with wide stripes of golden yellow.

☼ Bright to moderate ⊞ Moderate to warm. Low humidity ◊ Biweekly ◊ When soil surface dry. Water sparingly in winter. Avoid waterlogging ⊡ Division

△ Schefflera arboricola 'Yvonette'
SCHEFFLERA

↕ 6ft (1.8m) ↔ 3ft (90cm)

Use this tall schefflera as a specimen plant in a well-lit corner, or let it liven up a group of smaller, evergreen varieties. Prune it if a bushier habit is required.

☼ Bright to moderate ⊞ Warm. Avoid fluctuation. Moderate to high humidity ◊ Biweekly. Monthly in winter ◊ Water when soil surface dry ⊡ Tip cuttings, air layering

△ Pseudopanax lessonii 'Gold Splash'
GOLDEN HOUPARA

↕ ↔ 6ft (2m) or more

Normally grown in its juvenile stage, when its long-stalked, five-fingered leaves are splashed with gold, this variegated pseudopanax makes a striking and individual houseplant. As the plant ages, the variegation on the foliage becomes less marked. Prune it to maintain a more compact habit.

☼ Bright, but avoid direct sun ⊞ Moderate to warm. Moderate humidity ◊ Monthly. Occasionally in winter ◊ When soil surface dry. Reduce watering in winter ⊡ Semiripe cuttings

Boat-shaped flower cluster

◁ Tradescantia spathacea 'Variegata'
MOSES-IN-THE-CRADLE

↕ ↔ 12in (30cm)

The handsome, yellow-striped leaf rosettes of this robust, clump-forming plant have contrasting rich purple leaf undersides. Unusual boat-shaped flower clusters are produced throughout the year.

☼ Bright to moderate, avoiding direct sun ⊞ Warm. High humidity ◊ Biweekly. Occasionally in winter ◊ Keep soil mix moist. Reduce watering in winter ⊡ Offsets

Houseplants with White- or Cream-variegated Foliage

VARIEGATED LEAVES add character to a plant; house-plants with foliage in cream and white, both neutral and versatile colors, can be used to great decorative effect. Variegation is often found along leaf margins, but it is worth looking for bold stripes or unusual mottling. To emphasize the cream and white markings, display your plants against a plain, dark background.

FOLIAGE EFFECT

Acorus gramineus
'Variegatus' ▷
SWEET FLAG
↕ 12in (30cm) ↔ 18in (45cm)

The variegated leaves of this sweet flag, arching with age, have a delicate fragrance when crushed. An excellent plant for a cool room; likes damp soil mix.

☼ Bright to moderate ❄ Cool to moderate. Moderate humidity 💧 Every three weeks in summer 💧 Keep moist in summer. In winter, let the soil surface dry before watering 🔲 Division

△ *Aglaonema commutatum*
'Pseudobracteatum'
CHINESE EVERGREEN
↕ ↔ 2ft (60cm)

Attractive variegation makes this elegant plant from the Philippine rainforests a useful specimen for a table display. It is slow-growing but well worth the wait.

☼ Bright to moderate ❄ Moderate to warm, avoiding fluctuation. Moderate humidity 💧 Weekly, using foliage houseplant fertilizer. Monthly in winter 💧 When dry 🔲 Division, tip cuttings, stem sections

△ *Dracaena fragrans* 'Warneckei'
DRACAENA
↕ 2ft (60cm) or more ↔ 2ft (60cm)

Lush and leafy when young, this plant slowly develops a strong stem. Popular with interior designers, it is an efficient remover of pollutants from the air.

☼ Bright, but avoid summer sun ❄ Moderate to warm. Moderate to high humidity 💧 Biweekly. Twice during winter 💧 Allow soil surface to dry before watering 🔲 Tip cuttings, stem sections

△ *Ficus elastica* 'Tineke'
RUBBER PLANT
↕ 10ft (3m) ↔ 3ft (1m)

This rubber plant has many handsome features: dark gray-green variegation on the large leaves, cream leaf margins, and burgundy leaf stems and midribs.

☼ Bright to moderate ❄ Cool to warm. Moderate to high humidity 💧 Biweekly, using foliage house-plant fertilizer. Monthly in winter 💧 Water when soil surface dry 🔲 Tip cuttings, air layering

---

OTHER SMALL-LEAVED WHITE- OR CREAM-VARIEGATED HOUSEPLANTS

Aichryson x *domesticum* 'Variegatum'
Ficus benjamina 'Variegata'
Ficus pumila 'White Sonny', see p.363
Glechoma hederacea 'Variegata'
Hedera helix 'White Knight'
Impatiens walleriana 'Variegata'

△ *Hedera helix* 'Eva'
ENGLISH IVY
↕ 4½ft (1.4m) ↔ 12in (30cm)

This attractive ivy with purple shoots and white-margined leaves will trail or climb; display it in a hanging basket, on a raised shelf, or even in a large terrarium.

☼ Bright to moderate ▮▮ Cool to moderate. Moderate to high humidity ◊ Biweekly. Once in mid- and once in late winter ◊ When dry. Water sparingly in winter ▦ Tip cuttings, layering

OTHER LARGE-LEAVED WHITE- OR CREAM-VARIEGATED HOUSEPLANTS

Ananas comosus 'Variegatus', see p.414
X *Fatshedera lizei* 'Variegata'
Fatsia japonica 'Variegata', see p.370
Monstera deliciosa 'Variegata', see p.371
Phormium 'Cream Delight'

◁ *Syngonium* 'Arrow'
GOOSEFOOT
↕ 6ft (2m) ↔ 2ft (60cm)

Compact and pointed green leaves, suffused with creamy variegation, change shape as they mature. Initially bushy, these plants become climbers with age.

☼ Bright to moderate, avoiding direct sun ▮▮ Warm, avoiding fluctuation. Moderate to high humidity ◊ Biweekly. Monthly in winter ◊ When dry. Reduce watering in winter ▦ Tip cuttings

△ *Hypoestes phyllostachya* 'Wit'
POLKA-DOT PLANT
↕ 12in (30cm) ↔ 9in (23cm)

A striking plant, grown for its marbled leaves. Good light will produce the best foliage. The flowers are insignificant, so pinch out the tips to encourage bushiness.

☼ Bright, but avoid summer sun ▮▮ Moderate to warm. Moderate to high humidity ◊ Biweekly. Monthly in winter ◊ When dry. Reduce watering in winter ▦ Tip or stem cuttings. Roots in water

△ *Plectranthus forsteri* 'Marginatus'
CANDLE PLANT
↕ 12in (30cm) ↔ 3ft (90cm)

Display candle plants in a hanging basket or on an accessible shelf to enjoy their masses of fleshy, aromatic foliage. Pinch out the shoots to promote bushy growth.

☼ Bright, with some direct sun ▮▮ Moderate to warm. Low to moderate humidity ◊ Biweekly. Every six weeks in winter ◊ Let soil surface dry before watering ▦ Tip cuttings

△ *Tradescantia fluminensis* 'Variegata'
INCH PLANT, WANDERING JEW
↕ 6in (15cm) ↔ 2ft (60cm)

Show off this delicate, pale green, white-striped foliage by trailing it over the edge of a container. Easy to grow; pinch out the growing tips to encourage branching.

☼ Bright, but avoid direct sun. Variegation fades in shade ▮▮ Moderate to warm. Moderate to high humidity ◊ Biweekly. Once in winter ◊ Keep moist. When dry in winter ▦ Tip or stem cuttings

Houseplants with Silver or Gray Foliage

MANY OF THE MOST distinctive houseplants have silver or gray foliage. Some leaves take their color from bands or stripes, while others gain their silvery appearance from a patina of pale hairs or a dense spotting or marbled effect. All the plants shown here will provide dramatic contrast when grouped with purple- or dark green-leaved varieties.

△ *Begonia* 'Silver'
BEGONIA
↕ 8in (20cm) ↔ 10in (25cm)

Curious but very attractive, this begonia has distinctive, long, pointed leaves covered with tiny pale hairs that give the upper surfaces a silvery, satinlike sheen.

☼ Bright to moderate, avoiding summer sun
⊪ Moderate to warm. Moderate humidity
💧 Biweekly. Monthly in winter ◊ When dry. Stop if dormant in winter 🖾 Division, tip cuttings

Aglaonema 'Silver Queen' ▷
CHINESE EVERGREEN
↕ ↔ 18in (45cm)

One of the most striking and dramatic aglaonemas, bearing large, pointed, long-stalked, almost wholly silver leaves patterned with pale and dark green markings.

☼ Moderate, avoiding summer sun ⊪ Moderate to warm. Moderate humidity 💧 Every week, using foliage houseplant fertilizer. Monthly in winter ◊ When dry 🖾 Division, tip cuttings, stem sections

OTHER HOUSEPLANTS WITH SILVER OR GRAY FOLIAGE

Aechmea fasciata, see p.324
Aglaonema 'Silver King'
Astelia chathamica
Begonia 'Salamander'
Begonia 'Silver Queen'
Begonia venosa, see p.354
Cotyledon orbiculata
Echeveria secunda var. *glauca* 'Gigantea', see p.384

◁ *Begonia* 'Merry Christmas'
PAINTED-LEAF BEGONIA
↕ 10in (25cm) ↔ 12in (30cm)

The large, jaggedly toothed leaves of this *Begonia rex* hybrid are strikingly marked with silver and dark red and are pink-flushed. Pale rose-pink flowers are a bonus in autumn and early winter.

☼ Bright to moderate, avoiding summer sun
⊪ Moderate to warm. Moderate humidity
💧 Biweekly. Monthly in winter ◊ When dry. Stop if dormant in winter 🖾 Division, leaf cuttings

△ *Ctenanthe amabilis*
CTENANTHE
↕ ↔ 16in (40cm)

This beautifully variegated foliage plant from the rainforests of South America has impressive green and silver zebra marks on its large, paddle-shaped leaves.

☼ Bright to moderate, avoiding direct sun ⊪ Warm, avoiding fluctuation. High humidity 💧 Biweekly, using foliage houseplant fertilizer. Rarely in winter ◊ Water when top half of soil mix dry 🖾 Division

OTHER HOUSEPLANTS WITH FOLIAGE STRIPED, SPLASHED, OR VEINED SILVER OR GRAY

Begonia maculata
Calathea makoyana, see p.368
Fittonia verschaffeltii var. *argyroneura*
Peperomia argyreia
Piper crocatum
Pteris cretica 'Albolineata', see p.407
Sonerila margaritacea
Strobilanthes dyerianus, see p.347

Ctenanthe
'Greystar' ▷
CTENANTHE
↕ 4ft (1.2m) ↔ 3ft (1m)

A splendid houseplant with impressive foliage. The silver upper leaf surfaces are set off by contrasting dark green veins and stalks, while the leaf undersides are dark purple.

☼ Bright to moderate, avoiding direct sun ≣ Warm, avoiding fluctuation. High humidity ◊ Biweekly, using foliage houseplant fertilizer. Occasionally in winter ◊ Water when top half of soil mix dry ☷ Division

△ *Pteris ensiformis* 'Evergemiensis'
SLENDER BRAKE
↕ ↔ 12in (30cm)

This silver-striped cultivar makes a good contrast to other varieties of fern; it is even more attractive than the green form of this plant, a Victorian favorite.

☼ Bright to moderate, avoiding direct sun ≣ Moderate to warm. Moderate to high humidity ◊ Biweekly. Monthly in winter ◊ Keep moist, but avoid waterlogging ☷ Division, spores

△ *Peperomia caperata* 'Teresa'
PEPEROMIA
↕ ↔ 8in (20cm)

A charming plant that is perfect for using in a special display, bottle garden, or terrarium. The bronze-purple, puckered, rounded leaves are silvery-sheened above.

☼ Bright to moderate, with some sun ≣ Warm. Moderate to high humidity ◊ Every three weeks. Occasionally in winter ◊ When soil surface dry. Avoid waterlogging ☷ Tip cuttings

△ *Pilea cadierei*
ALUMINUM PLANT
↕ 12in (30cm) ↔ 8in (20cm)

Eye-catching, silver-splashed green leaves make this perennial from the Vietnamese rainforests a popular houseplant. Pinch out tips to maintain a compact habit.

☼ Bright to moderate, with some sun ≣ Warm. Moderate to high humidity ◊ Every three weeks. Occasionally in winter ◊ Water when soil surface just dry. Avoid waterlogging ☷ Tip cuttings

△ *Soleirolia soleirolii* 'Variegata'
BABY'S TEARS
↕ 2in (5cm) ↔ 12in (30cm) or more

A useful small plant with tiny silvered leaves densely crowding the branching stems and, in time, forming a creeping carpet. Good cover under large plants.

☼ Bright to shady, avoiding direct sun ≣ Cool to moderate. Moderate to high humidity ◊ Every three weeks. Rarely in winter ◊ Keep moist, but avoid waterlogging. Sparingly in winter ☷ Division

Houseplants with Unusual Foliage

THE ATTRACTION OF the weird and wonderful is universal. Many of us who collect plants become fascinated by the search for curious varieties, particularly among foliage plants, which offer leaves in a range of different textures, colors, shapes, and sizes. Such plants make good conversation pieces, so display them where they can be easily seen.

Begonia venosa ▷
SHRUB BEGONIA
↕ 3ft (90cm) ↔ 2ft (60cm)

Large, kidney-shaped, fleshy leaves are covered with short white hairs, giving them a frosted appearance. The fragrant white flowers, produced from late summer onward, are a bonus.

☼ Bright, but avoid summer sun ☰ Moderate to warm. Low to moderate humidity 💧 Biweekly. Monthly in winter ◊ Water sparingly. Avoid waterlogging 🌱 Division, tip cuttings

Begonia listada ▷
SHRUB BEGONIA
↕ ↔ 2ft (60cm)

A striking plant with large, dark green leaves, barred with pale green, pointed at both ends and shaped like out-stretched wings, one longer than the other. Bears white flowers in autumn and winter.

☼ Bright to moderate. Avoid summer sun ☰ Moderate to warm. Moderate humidity 💧 Biweekly. Monthly in winter ◊ When soil surface dry. Reduce watering in winter 🌱 Division, tip cuttings

△ *Begonia serratipetala*
SHRUB BEGONIA
↕ ↔ 18in (45cm)

Distinctive for its long-pointed, wavy-margined leaves, bronze-green marked with red veins above and red beneath, this shrub begonia produces pink-white flowers from winter to spring.

☼ Bright to moderate, avoiding summer sun ☰ Moderate to warm. Moderate humidity 💧 Biweekly. Monthly in winter ◊ When soil surface dry. Reduce watering in winter 🌱 Tip cuttings

△ *Codiaeum* 'Red Curl'
CROTON
↕ ↔ 3ft (1m)

Even if you have seen many variations of the croton, this one will amuse you with its long, narrow, corkscrewlike, colorful leaves. It looks well on its own or with green-leaved companions.

☼ Bright, with some sun ☰ Warm, avoiding drafts and fluctuation. Moderate to high humidity 💧 Biweekly, using foliage houseplant fertilizer. Occasionally in winter ◊ Keep moist. In winter, water when soil surface dry 🌱 Tip cuttings

△ *Cotyledon orbiculata* var. *oblonga*
SILVER CROWN
↕ 2ft (60cm) ↔ 20in (50cm)

This interesting shrubby succulent plant is dominated, especially when small, by its rounded, crinkly-edged, fleshy leaves, covered in a white, waxy bloom. Good for a sunny windowsill.

☼ Bright, with sun 🌡 Warm, but cool to moderate in winter. Low humidity 💧 Monthly, using fertilizer for cacti and succulents 💧 When dry. Water sparingly in winter ✄ Tip or leaf cuttings

---

OTHER HOUSEPLANTS WITH UNUSUAL FOLIAGE

Asplenium bulbiferum
Begonia lubbersii
Cryptanthus zonatus
Cycas revoluta, see p.394
Dionaea muscipula, see p.416
Fascicularia bicolor
Nolina recurvata, see p.394
Passiflora coriacea
Pseudopanax ferox
Tolmiea menziesii, see p.365

△ *Faucaria tigrina*
TIGER JAWS
↕ 4in (10cm) ↔ 8in (20cm)

Most small children will be fascinated by this plant – the leaves resemble those of a succulent Venus fly trap, but with sharp teeth. The yellow flowers, borne in autumn, are a pleasant surprise.

☼ Bright, with some sun 🌡 Warm, but cool to moderate in winter. Low humidity 💧 Monthly, using fertilizer for cacti and succulents 💧 When dry. Water sparingly in winter ✄ Stem or leaf cuttings

---

OTHER SUCCULENT HOUSE-PLANTS WITH UNUSUAL FOLIAGE

Haworthia attenuata f. *clariperla*
Pachyphytum ovatum
Sedum pachyphyllum
Senecio rowleyanus, see p.391
Titanopsis calcarea

△ *Crassula perforata*
STRING OF BUTTONS
↕ ↔ 12in (30cm)

A curiosity for a sunny spot. Erect stems pass through the middle of the paired, green, succulent leaves. Scented, starry, white to pink flowers appear in summer.

☼ Bright, with some sun 🌡 Warm, but cool to moderate in winter. Low humidity 💧 Monthly, using fertilizer for cacti and succulents 💧 When dry. Water sparingly in winter ✄ Tip or leaf cuttings

---

△ *Euphorbia trigona* 'Purpurea'
AFRICAN MILK TREE
↕ 5ft (1.5m) ↔ 3ft (1m)

This purple-tinted form of a succulent spurge is from Namibia. Sitting bolt upright, it has three-angled stems lined with leaves that fall at the end of summer.

☼ Bright 🌡 Warm, but cool to moderate in winter. Low humidity 💧 Monthly, using fertilizer for cacti and succulents 💧 When soil surface dry. Water sparingly in winter ✄ Stem cuttings

---

△ *Tillandsia caput-medusae*
AIR PLANT
↕ 16in (40cm) ↔ 10in (24cm)

Curved and twisted, hornlike leaves grow from a bulbous base that can be attached to a piece of hanging cork or driftwood. Blue and red flower spikes show in spring.

☼ Bright, but avoid direct sun 🌡 Warm. Low to moderate humidity 💧 Every eight weeks 💧 Mist daily. Mist four times a week in low light and at low temperatures ✄ Offsets

LOCATIONS

TEMPERATURE, HUMIDITY, and light determine the environment in any location and in turn which plants will grow well there. Before choosing a houseplant to suit a particular spot, you should also consider the size of the room, how often it is used, and for what type of activity.

Celosia argentea 'Plumosa' for sunny windowsills

Remember that indoor "climates" are affected by seasonal changes outside. Increased central heating can make the air very dry in winter, and light levels will generally be greater in summer. You may need to move your plants as the seasons change to keep them healthy.

LIGHT AND HEAT
The number and size of windows in any location will determine the level of natural light. Full light through glass, but not hot summer sun, is appreciated by the majority of plants, particularly those that flower. Poorly lit corners, where nothing seems to flourish, are more challenging but can be enlivened by a range of shade-tolerant plants.

Plants that enjoy high heat and humidity, such as tropical species, may not seem to have a place in the home, but many are extremely adaptable and will accept lower temperatures or a drier atmosphere for limited periods. You can also use a pebble tray to raise humidity. Equally adaptable are houseplants that tolerate low light, cool temperatures, or dry air; they will often grow where no others survive.

△ SUNNY LIVING ROOM *Glass doors, white walls, and a mirror make the most of all the natural light available, encouraging flowering plants to bloom.*

CHANGING ROOMS
There are few rooms in any home that cannot be improved by a plant. The principal rooms – living and dining rooms, bedrooms, studies, bathrooms, and kitchens – can be decorated with a great variety of species. Garden rooms and conservatories suit the widest range of plants, depending on their heat and humidity levels, but don't give up on small areas such as halls, landings, or washrooms – they can often support at least one plant.

△ OFFICE WINNER *Compact, easy, and tolerant of neglect,* Pilea peperomioides *is a good choice for a busy home office.*

◁ LOW-LIGHT KITCHEN *An impressive Boston fern thrives in this warm kitchen, where light levels are usually low.*

▷ HUMID BATHROOM *Many ferns will appreciate the often damp atmosphere of a warm bathroom, if it is not too bright.*

Houseplants for Sunny Windowsills

A WINDOWSILL in full sun, its heat magnified by the glass, can be the hottest spot in the house, where only a few plants other than cacti and succulents will survive for long without scorching. However, many plants enjoy such a position if they are protected from the excessive heat of midday in summer; move them back from the glass or draw blinds or curtains.

Ananas bracteatus 'Tricolor' ▷
VARIEGATED PINEAPPLE
↕ 28in (70cm) ↔ 20in (50cm)

Striking in foliage and flower, but beware of the viciously spine-toothed leaves. The impressive pineapple flowerhead appears in summer. Needs regular watering.

☼ Bright, with some sun ᴴ Warm. Moderate to high humidity ◍ Biweekly, using flowering houseplant fertilizer ◊ When soil surface just dry ▥ Offsets, rosettes

△ *Celosia argentea* 'Plumosa'
PLUME COCKSCOMB
↕ ↔ 18in (45cm)

This striking perennial, normally grown as an annual, needs plenty of light. Protect it from midday sun to prolong the richly colored, plumed summer flowerhead.

☼ Bright, but avoid hot summer sun
ᴴ Moderate to warm. Moderate humidity
◍ Biweekly ◊ Water when soil surface just dry
▥ Seed. Germinates very freely

OTHER HOUSEPLANTS FOR
SUNNY WINDOWSILLS

Cyrtanthus elatus
Nerium oleander cvs.
Pelargonium 'Graveolens', see p.344
Pentas lanceolata
Plumeria rubra
Punica granatum var. *nana*

Bougainvillea 'Dania' ▷
BOUGAINVILLEA, PAPER FLOWER
↕ ↔ 3ft (1m) or more

Brilliant, bright pink bracts are borne from summer to autumn. This exotic-looking plant can be bought young, trained to a framework, and pruned to control its size, but it will grow larger if given the space.

☼ Bright, with sun ᴴ Moderate to warm. Low humidity ◍ Biweekly, using flowering houseplant fertilizer ◊ When soil surface just dry. Water sparingly in winter ▥ Tip cuttings

Browallia speciosa 'White Troll' ▷
SAPPHIRE FLOWER
↕ ↔ 10in (25cm)

Perennial but usually grown as an annual, the sapphire flower has pointed leaves that are slightly clammy to the touch and produces abundant summer flowers. Pinch out the tips to encourage a bushy habit.

☼ Bright to moderate, avoiding hot summer sun
ᴴ Cool to moderate. Moderate humidity
◍ Biweekly ◊ Water when the soil surface becomes dry ▥ Seed

L O C A T I O N S

△ *Crassula socialis*
CRASSULA
↕ 3in (7cm) ↔ 12in (30cm)

Small, dense rosettes of horny-margined leaves soon form colonies, with heads of miniature, star-shaped white flowers produced in spring. A reliable houseplant.

☼ Bright, with some sun 🌡 Warm, but cool to moderate in winter. Low humidity 💧 Monthly, using fertilizer for cacti and succulents 💧 When dry. Water sparingly in winter 🔲 Tip or leaf cuttings

△ *Hibiscus rosa-sinensis* 'Scarlet Giant'
**CHINESE HIBISCUS,
ROSE OF CHINA**
↕ 6ft (2m) or more ↔ 5ft (1.5m) or more

A large plant, but careful pruning controls its size. It loves sun, which encourages free flowering from spring to autumn; the red blooms can be up to 7in (17cm) across.

☼ Bright, with sun 🌡 Warm, avoiding fluctuation. Moderate to high humidity 💧 Biweekly. Stop in cool conditions 💧 When just dry. Water sparingly in winter. Avoid waterlogging 🔲 Semiripe cuttings

**OTHER SUCCULENT HOUSE-
PLANTS FOR SUNNY WINDOWSILLS**

Anacampseros alstonii
Crassula perfoliata var. *minor*
Euphorbia caput-medusae
Lampranthus purpureus
Lithops leslei
Portulacaria afra 'Foliis-variegatus'

△ *Huernia thuretii* var. *primulina*
CARRION FLOWER, HUERNIA
↕ ↔ 3in (8cm)

A clump-forming succulent with sharp-angled, gray-green stems, bearing curious, creamy yellow, red-freckled flowers in summer and autumn. Do not overwater.

☼ Bright, with sun 🌡 Warm, but cool to moderate in winter. Low humidity 💧 Monthly, using fertilizer for cacti and succulents 💧 When soil surface dry. Water sparingly in winter 🔲 Tip cuttings

△ *Parodia leninghausii*
GOLDEN BALL CACTUS
↕ 2ft (60cm) ↔ 3in (8cm)

Initially ball-shaped or rounded, this cactus later develops into a fat, golden-spined column. Pale yellow flowers are produced from the tips in summer.

☼ Bright, with sun 🌡 Warm, but cool to moderate in winter. Low humidity 💧 Monthly, using fertilizer for cacti and succulents 💧 When soil surface dry. Water sparingly in winter 🔲 Seed

Richly colored leaves

◁ *Solenostemon*
'Defiance'
COLEUS
↕ ↔ 12in (30cm)

Bright green and claret foliage distinguishes this coleus. Many selections are available. Although perennial, these soft-stemmed plants are generally treated as annuals; pinch out the growing tips for bushiness.

☼ Bright, with sun 🌡 Warm. Low humidity 💧 Weekly. Occasionally in winter 💧 Keep moist, but avoid waterlogging. In winter, water when just dry 🔲 Tip cuttings. Roots easily in water

Houseplants for Full Light

A SITUATION IN FULL LIGHT, as long as there is no risk of scorching or overheating, is ideal for many houseplants. The best-lit spots in any house are usually on or near windowsills that receive plenty of daylight; this could even be early morning or late evening sun. However, all the plants featured here will need protection from strong midday sun in summer.

Capsicum annuum 'Carnival Red' ▷
ORNAMENTAL PEPPER
‡ ↔ 2ft (60cm)

A familiar plant, usually treated as an annual, but longer-lasting given cool conditions. In winter, the freely borne, brilliant orange-red fruits stud the leafy branches.

☼ Bright ‡ Cool to moderate. Moderate humidity ◑ Biweekly, alternating general fertilizer with flowering houseplant fertilizer ◊ When just dry 🗭 Tip cuttings, seed

△ *Chrysanthemum indicum*
FLORISTS' CHRYSANTHEMUM
‡ ↔ 12in (30cm)

A dwarf form with a compact habit and pale yellow flowers, borne from autumn to winter. A valuable temporary plant and one of many popular chrysanthemums.

☼ Bright, but avoid direct sun ‡ Cool to moderate. Moderate humidity ◑ Every three weeks ◊ Keep soil mix moist, but avoid waterlogging 🗭 Tip cuttings

△ *Cordyline fruticosa* 'Kiwi'
CORDYLINE
‡ ↔ 6ft (2m)

This suckering plant forms a clump of erect stems clothed in bold foliage that is striped dark green, pale green, and cream, and has subtly pink-tinted margins.

☼ Bright, but avoid summer sun ‡ Warm. High humidity ◑ Biweekly. Monthly in winter ◊ When soil surface dry. Reduce watering at lower temperatures 🗭 Tip cuttings, stem sections

---

OTHER HOUSEPLANTS FOR FULL LIGHT WITH SOME SUMMER SUN

Capsicum annuum, see p.396
Correa 'Dusky Bells'
Crassula coccinea
Cyrtanthus elatus
Fuchsia 'Ballet Girl'
Gloriosa superba 'Rothschildiana'
Heterocentron elegans
Impatiens walleriana hybrids, see p.385
Kalanchoe 'Wendy'

◁ *Crassula arborescens*
SILVER JADE PLANT
‡ 6ft (2m) ↔ 4ft (1.2m)

Slow-growing but eventually substantial, this succulent shrub bears striking, red-margined, gray-green leaves, and white starry flowers from autumn to winter.

☼ Bright, with some sun ‡ Warm, but cool to moderate in winter. Low humidity ◑ Monthly, using fertilizer for cacti and succulents ◊ When dry. Water sparingly in winter 🗭 Stem or leaf cuttings

△ *Dudleya pulverulenta*
DUDLEYA
↕ ↔ 12in (30cm) or more

Red or yellow starry flowers, produced in spring or early summer, complement this succulent's rosette of fleshy, pointed, silvery gray leaves, borne on a short stem.

☼ Bright, with sun 🌡 Warm, but cool to moderate in winter. Low humidity ◖ Monthly, using cactus and succulent fertilizer ◊ When soil surface dry. Water sparingly in winter ▭ Stem or leaf cuttings

---

OTHER HOUSEPLANTS FOR FULL LIGHT AWAY FROM SUMMER SUN

Achimenes hybrids
Aeschynanthus lobbianus
Aphelandra squarrosa
  'Dania', see p.368
Justicia rizzinii,
  see p.331
Mandevilla rosea
Pachystachys lutea
Schlumbergera
  truncata, see p.363
Thunbergia alata, see p.393

Hoya carnosa 'Variegata' ▷
WAX PLANT
↕ ↔ 6ft (2m)

Capable of great vigor, this handsome, creamy-variegated form of the twining wax plant can be trained on a frame to keep it neat and manageable. The fragrant, waxy flowers appear in summer.

☼ Bright, but avoid direct sun 🌡 Moderate to warm. Moderate to high humidity ◖ Every three weeks, using flowering houseplant fertilizer ◊ Water when soil surface dry. Avoid overwatering ▭ Tip cuttings

---

Justicia brandegeeana ▷
SHRIMP PLANT
↕ ↔ 3ft (90cm)

Free- and long-flowering, this popular plant has colorful bracts and pendent white flowers, borne throughout the year. It likes some sun. Previously called *Beloperone guttata*.

☼ Bright to moderate, avoiding hottest sun 🌡 Warm, avoiding drafts. Moderate to high humidity ◖ Monthly ◊ Keep soil mix moist, but avoid waterlogging ▭ Tip cuttings

◁ *Smithiantha* 'Orange King'
TEMPLE BELLS
↕ ↔ 12in (30cm)

Beautifully mottled, densely hairy leaves appear in spring after a winter dormancy, topped from summer to autumn by loose heads of pendulous orange flowers.

☼ Bright to moderate. Avoid hot sun 🌡 Warm, but moderate in dormancy. High humidity ◖ Biweekly, using flowering houseplant fertilizer ◊ Keep moist, increasing in growth. Stop in dormancy ▭ Division

△ *Streptocarpus* 'Kim'
CAPE PRIMROSE
↕ 8in (20cm) ↔ 14in (35cm)

This Cape primrose produces rosettes of downy leaves, and branching sprays of dark purple, white-eyed summer flowers. A classic plant for a cool, well-lit spot.

☼ Bright. Avoid direct sun 🌡 Moderate. Moderate to high humidity ◖ Biweekly, using flowering houseplant fertilizer. Monthly in winter, unless dormant ◊ When dry ▭ Division, leaf cuttings

Houseplants for Medium Light

Most rooms have an area of medium light, out of direct sunlight but not in shade. It is usually a few feet from a window, or closer if you have sheer curtains or blinds. All the plants here tolerate medium light, but will benefit from a short spell in full light.

LOCATIONS

Aglaonema 'Marie' ▷
Chinese Evergreen

↕ 4ft (1.2m) ↔ 2ft (60cm)

Aglaonemas, noted for their subtle leaf patterns, include this bushy form with large, dark green foliage splashed gray-green. A fine specimen houseplant.

☼ Bright to moderate ▮ Moderate to warm, avoiding fluctuation. Moderate humidity ◑ Foliage houseplant fertilizer weekly. Monthly in winter ◊ When dry ▦ Division, tip cuttings, stem sections

△ *Begonia* 'Tiger Paws'
Eyelash Begonia

↕ 8in (20cm) ↔ 10in (25cm)

An eye-catching houseplant that forms a compact mound of shieldlike, lime green leaves, marked and edged bronze, each with a curious fringe of "eyelash" hairs.

☼ Bright to moderate ▮ Cool to warm. Moderate humidity ◑ Biweekly. Monthly in winter ◊ Leave until soil surface just dry before watering ▦ Division, leaf cuttings

△ *Dracaena cincta* 'Bicolor'
Dracaena

↕ 12ft (4m) ↔ 3ft (1m)

This is one of several variegated forms of *Dracaena cincta*, with cream-edged leaves. Perfect for a semishady corner or hallway, or as an architectural feature plant.

☼ Bright to moderate ▮ Moderate to warm. Moderate to high humidity ◑ Biweekly. Occasionally during winter ◊ Water when soil surface dry ▦ Tip cuttings, stem sections

△ *Dracaena fragrans* 'Compacta'
Dracaena

↕ 6ft (2m) ↔ 3ft (1m)

Masses of dark green leaves top the stems of these robust plants, making them look like shaving brushes. Cut mature plants back hard in spring to promote regrowth.

☼ Bright to moderate. Growth stops in low light ▮ Moderate to warm. Moderate to high humidity ◑ Biweekly. Occasionally in winter ◊ When soil surface dry ▦ Tip cuttings, stem sections

Other Large Houseplants for Medium Light

△ *Ficus pumila* 'White Sonny'
CREEPING FIG

↕ ↔ 12in (30cm) or more

The tiny leaves of this creeping fig are edged with a bold cream line. In humid conditions, it produces climbing roots and will grow happily up a suitable support.

☼ Bright to moderate 🌡 Moderate to warm. Moderate to high humidity 💧 Biweekly, using foliage houseplant fertilizer. Occasionally in winter 💧 When dry, especially if cool 🏺 Tip cuttings

OTHER SMALL HOUSEPLANTS FOR MEDIUM LIGHT

Adiantum raddianum 'Fritz Luth', see p.380
Aglaonema 'Lilian', see p.374
Cyrtomium falcatum
Hedera helix 'Très Coupé'
Plectranthus verticillatus
Saxifraga stolonifera, see p.391
Schlumbergera × buckleyi
Tolmiea menziesii 'Taff's Gold', see p.377

△ *Hedera helix* 'California'
ENGLISH IVY

↕ 3ft (1m) ↔ 12in (30cm)

The attractive mid-green leaves of this ivy vary from triangular to broadly heart-shaped. It is ideal for growing in a hanging basket or for climbing up a support.

☼ Bright to moderate. Poor growth in low light 🌡 Cool to moderate. Moderate to high humidity 💧 Biweekly. Twice in winter 💧 When dry. Water sparingly in winter 🏺 Tip cuttings, layering

Schlumbergera truncata △
CRAB CACTUS

↕ 12in (30cm) ↔ 2ft (60cm)

From late autumn to winter, pendent, deep pink flowers cover this bold cactus, which then has a rest period. Succulent, flattened, segmented stems add interest.

☼ Moderate 🌡 Moderate to warm, but cool when resting. Moderate humidity 💧 High-potassium fertilizer biweekly in growth 💧 Keep moist in growth. Water sparingly during rest period 🏺 Stem sections

△ *Fittonia verschaffeltii* 'Janita'
NERVE PLANT

↕ 6in (15cm) ↔ 12in (30cm) or more

Display this small, dense, creeping nerve plant on a low surface to appreciate its beautiful pink-netted green leaves. Ideal for terraria or warm, humid bathrooms.

☼ Moderate 🌡 Moderate to warm. High humidity 💧 Biweekly. Feed occasionally in winter 💧 Water when soil surface just dry. Avoid waterlogging 🏺 Tip cuttings

Philodendron erubescens 'Red Emerald' ▷
BLUSHING PHILODENDRON

↕ 15ft (5m) ↔ 6ft (2m) or more

This stunning form of a vigorous rainforest climber has glossy, emerald green leaves and dark red main stems and leaf stalks. Best trained up a moss pole.

☼ Bright to shady 🌡 Moderate to warm. Moderate to high humidity 💧 Biweekly, using foliage houseplant fertilizer. Monthly in winter 💧 Water when soil surface dry 🏺 Tip cuttings

363

Houseplants for Low Light

HOUSEPLANTS THAT THRIVE in low light are a small but resilient group; of course, those featured here will all benefit from a little extra attention to help them look their best. Low-lit areas are typically those farthest from a window or other source of light; however, they do not include dark, dingy corners, where any plant will face a struggle to survive.

△ *Fittonia* 'Bianco Verde'
SILVER NET LEAF
‡ 6in (15cm) ↔ 12in (30cm)

Small, variegated leaves and a creeping habit make this fittonia an excellent terrarium plant. It thrives in low light, provided that conditions are suitably warm and moist; group several on a pebble tray to raise humidity.

☼ Moderate to shady, avoiding direct sun ☷ Warm. High humidity ♠ Biweekly. Occasionally in winter ◊ Keep moist, but avoid waterlogging ▣ Tip cuttings

Aspidistra elatior 'Milky Way' ▷
ASPIDISTRA, CAST-IRON PLANT
‡ ↔ 2ft (60cm)

Few plants tolerate poor light levels better than the cast-iron plant. It is almost impervious to neglect, but naturally responds well to generous treatment. This spotted form is particularly ornamental; a fine specimen plant.

☼ Moderate to shady. Direct sun will scorch leaves ☷ Moderate to warm. Moderate humidity ♠ Every three weeks ◊ When soil surface dry. Dislikes waterlogging ▣ Division, offsets

Deeply lobed mature leaf

△ *Duchesnea indica*
MOCK STRAWBERRY
‡ 4in (10cm) ↔ 4ft (1.2m)

A fast-creeping perennial that forms a carpet of runners covered with strawberry-like leaves. Yellow flowers are produced in summer, but to obtain the red fruits, move it to a brighter position.

☼ Moderate to shady ☷ Cool to moderate. Moderate to high humidity ♠ Every three weeks ◊ Keep moist. Reduce watering during winter ▣ Plantlets

◁ *Philodendron bipinnatifidum*
TREE PHILODENDRON
‡ 10ft (3m) ↔ 6ft (2m) or more

One of the most spectacular foliage plants, with its strong stems and large, deeply lobed, long-stalked mature leaves (see inset). Grow this Brazilian shrub on a sturdy moss pole or frame.

☼ Bright to shady ☷ Warm. Moderate to high humidity ♠ Biweekly, using foliage houseplant fertilizer ◊ Water when soil surface slightly dry ▣ Division, tip cuttings

Philodendron scandens ▷
HEART LEAF, SWEETHEART PLANT
↕ ↔ 10ft (3m)

Vigorous and, given the space, high climbing, this superb plant has deep glossy green, heart-shaped, slender-pointed leaves that can reach up to 12in (30cm) long. It makes an unusual and impressive sight in a hanging basket, or grow it on a moss pole or frame.

☼ Bright to shady ≣ Moderate to warm. Moderate to high humidity ♦ Biweekly, using foliage houseplant fertilizer. Monthly in winter ◊ Let the soil surface dry slightly before watering ▭ Tip cuttings

△ *Soleirolia soleirolii*
BABY'S TEARS
↕ 2in (5cm) ↔ 12in (30cm) or more

Resembling a moss because of its low, carpeting growth and tiny leaves, this plant makes a close groundcover for pots or baskets. Not suitable for terraria.

☼ Bright to shady, avoiding direct sun ≣ Cool to moderate. Moderate to high humidity ♦ Every three weeks. Rarely in winter ◊ Keep moist, but avoid waterlogging. Sparingly in winter ▭ Division

△ *Schefflera arboricola* 'Luciana'
SCHEFFLERA
↕ 6ft (1.8m) ↔ 3ft (90cm)

Fingered leaves are the hallmark of these evergreen shrubs from Taiwan, which all make excellent houseplants. They branch from the base, so prune to keep small.

☼ Bright to shady ≣ Warm, avoiding fluctuation. Moderate to high humidity ♦ Biweekly. Monthly in winter ◊ Water when soil surface dry ▭ Tip cuttings, air layering

△ *Selaginella martensii*
SELAGINELLA
↕ 6in (15cm) ↔ 12in (30cm)

A curious, tufted fern relative with flattened, frondlike stems, crowded with small, scalelike, glossy green leaves that give the plant a pleasantly soft texture. Makes good cover beneath other plants.

☼ Shady ≣ Warm. High humidity ♦ Every five weeks, using half-strength general houseplant fertilizer ◊ Water when soil surface just dry ▭ Stem cuttings

OTHER HOUSEPLANTS FOR LOW LIGHT

Adiantum raddianum, see p.398
Aucuba japonica 'Crotonifolia'
Chamaedorea elegans, see p.412
Ficus pumila 'White Sonny', see p.363
Hedera canariensis 'Gloire de Marengo'
Howea forsteriana
Spathiphyllum 'Euro Gigant', see p.371
Tolmiea menziesii 'Taff's Gold', see p.377

△ *Tolmiea menziesii*
PIGGY-BACK PLANT
↕ 12in (30cm) ↔ 16in (40cm)

This perennial produces young plantlets where the leaf blades join their stalks. Suitable for a cool room, it looks good in a pot or hanging basket.

☼ Moderate to shady ≣ Cool to moderate. Moderate humidity ♦ Biweekly. Occasionally in winter ◊ When soil surface dry. Reduce watering in winter ▭ Division, plantlets

Houseplants for Dry Atmospheres

CENTRAL HEATING has both benefits and drawbacks for houseplants. It keeps a room warm, which suits most exotics, but it also causes moisture in the air to evaporate, leaving the room very dry. Regular misting counteracts this, or choose from the range of plants that are tolerant of, if not comfortable in, a dry atmosphere.

LOCATIONS

Adenium obesum ▷
DESERT ROSE
↕ 5ft (1.5m) ↔ 3ft (1m)

A slow-growing succulent bush that develops a swollen base. Red, pink, or white flowers appear from midwinter to spring, usually before the leaves; the early flowers are often a surprise.

☼ Bright, with sun ❄ Warm, but moderate to cool winter rest. Low humidity 💧 Every three weeks, using cactus and succulent or high-potassium fertilizer 💧 When top 1in (2.5cm) soil dry. Water sparingly in winter ✂ Tip cuttings

△ *Aloe aristata*
LACE ALOE
↕ 5in (12cm) ↔ 12in (30cm)

Crowded rosettes of spine-tipped leaves are minutely white-toothed and spotted; the orange-red flowers appear in autumn. Easy to grow and very tolerant of neglect.

☼ Bright, with sun ❄ Warm, but moderate to cool in winter. Low humidity 💧 Every three weeks, using fertilizer for cacti and succulents 💧 When top 1in (2.5cm) soil dry. Sparingly in winter ✂ Offsets

---

OTHER HOUSEPLANTS FOR DRY ATMOSPHERES

Azorina vidalii
Bowiea volubilis
Haemanthus albiflos
Nolina recurvata, see p.394
Pelargonium 'Graveolens',
   see p.344
Sedum sieboldii
   'Mediovariegatum'

Aechmea chantinii ▷
QUEEN OF THE AECHMEAS
↕ 3ft (1m) ↔ 32in (80cm)

As long as the urnlike rosette is kept filled, this impressive, red- and yellow-bracted bromeliad tolerates a reasonably dry atmosphere, although it appreciates misting.

☼ Bright, but avoid summer sun ❄ Warm. Low to moderate humidity 💧 Biweekly 💧 When soil surface dry. Water sparingly in winter. Keep "urn" topped up with water ✂ Offsets

△ *Astrophytum myriostigma*
BISHOP'S CAP
↕ 9in (23cm) ↔ 10in (25cm)

Spiny when young, and later smooth, this squat, plump-ribbed cactus is covered in minute, white-downy scales. Pale yellow summer flowers grow from the crown.

☼ Bright, with sun ❄ Warm, but cool to moderate in winter. Low humidity 💧 Monthly, using fertilizer for cacti and succulents 💧 When soil surface dry. Water sparingly in winter ✂ Seed

△ *Euphorbia obesa*
LIVING BASEBALL
↕ ↔ 6in (15cm)

This is an attractive, variably patterned succulent spurge, with typically milky caustic sap. The small yellow flower clusters appear in spring and summer.

☼ Bright, with sun ❄ Warm, but cool to moderate in winter. Low humidity 💧 Monthly, using fertilizer for cacti and succulents 💧 When soil surface dry. Water sparingly in winter 🌱 Seed

Vibrant orange flowerhead

△ *Opuntia microdasys* var. *albispina*
BUNNY EARS
↕ ↔ 2ft (60cm)

A very decorative cactus producing bright yellow flowers in spring and summer. Handle with care; minute white spines stick into skin at the slightest touch.

☼ Bright, with sun ❄ Warm, but cool to moderate in winter. Low humidity 💧 Monthly, using cactus and succulent fertilizer 💧 When soil surface dry. Sparingly in winter 🌱 Offsets

△ *Tillandsia deiriana*
AIR PLANT
↕ ↔ 12in (30cm)

This vibrantly colored air plant is best grown on a piece of driftwood or cork and suspended from a high point that is reachable for misting. It can also be pot grown.

☼ Bright, but avoid direct sun ❄ Warm. Low humidity 💧 Every eight weeks 💧 Mist daily. Mist four times weekly in low light and cool conditions. Water sparingly 🌱 Offsets

△ *Jatropha podagrica*
BOTTLE PLANT
↕ 20in (50cm) or more ↔ 10in (25cm) or more

Swollen stems bear large, tough, long-stalked leaves, whitish beneath. Clusters of red flowers appear at the ends of long stalks in summer. It has caustic sap.

☼ Bright, with sun ❄ Warm, but cool to moderate in winter. Low humidity 💧 Monthly, using fertilizer for cacti and succulents 💧 When soil surface dry. Water sparingly in winter 🌱 Seed

Gray, curled foliage

OTHER CACTI AND SUCCULENTS FOR DRY ATMOSPHERES

Agave victoriae-reginae
Aloe variegata, see p.386
Kalanchoe daigremontiana
Mammillaria hahniana
Opuntia tunicata
Oreocereus celsianus
Pedilanthus tithymaloides 'Variegatus'

◁ *Tillandsia streptophylla*
AIR PLANT
↕ ↔ 18in (45cm)

Striking, curled and arching foliage is joined in late spring or autumn by green bracts and blue and red flowers. Grow in a pot or display on a piece of driftwood.

☼ Bright, but avoid direct sun ❄ Warm. Low humidity 💧 Every eight weeks 💧 Mist daily. Mist four times weekly in low light and cool conditions. Water sparingly 🌱 Offsets

367

Houseplants for Warm, Humid Rooms

A WARM, HUMID ENVIRONMENT is perfect for growing many tropical plants, but remember that some need constant moderate to high humidity to flourish, disliking drafts and changes in temperature. Warm bathrooms are a good choice, but beware of open windows letting in unwelcome cold air and the drying effect of heating. Garden rooms (with controlled temperature and humidity) are ideal, and enable you to nurture exotics or a miniature rainforest.

LOCATIONS

Aphelandra squarrosa 'Dania' ▷
ZEBRA PLANT
↕ ↔ 12in (30cm)

Grow this compact plant for its dark green glossy leaves with their creamy veins and midribs, and its eye-catching flowers with their bright yellow, orange-tipped bracts.

☼ Bright to moderate, avoiding hot sun ☷ Warm, avoiding fluctuation. High humidity ◐ Biweekly, spring to autumn ◊ Keep moist, but do not over-water. When dry in winter ⊟ Tip cuttings

△ *Calathea roseopicta*
PEACOCK PLANT
↕ 10in (24cm) ↔ 6in (15cm)

A distinctive plant bearing beautifully patterned, large foliage, marked with deep green; the midrib and leaf margins are a delicate rose-pink. A stunning houseplant.

☼ Moderate ☷ Moderate to warm, avoiding fluctuation. High humidity ◐ Biweekly. Monthly in winter ◊ Keep moist. At cooler temperatures, water when soil surface just dry ⊟ Division

△ *Caladium bicolor* 'Frieda Hemple'
ANGEL WINGS
↕ 12in (30cm) ↔ 18in (45cm)

Gloriously colored, paper-thin leaves emerge in spring and die down in autumn, when the tubers should be lifted and stored for replanting the following spring.

☼ Bright to moderate, avoiding direct sun ☷ Warm, but moderate in dormancy. High humidity ◐ Weekly ◊ Keep moist, reduce in autumn, and keep slightly moist in winter ⊟ Division, tubers

△ *Calathea makoyana*
PEACOCK PLANT
↕ 18in (45cm) ↔ 12in (30cm)

Also known as cathedral windows, this elegant plant has large, oval, mid-green leaves, beautifully traced with darker green and flushed purple beneath.

☼ Moderate ☷ Moderate to warm, avoiding fluctuation. High humidity ◐ Biweekly. Monthly in winter ◊ Keep moist. At cooler temperatures, water when soil surface just dry ⊟ Division

△ *Codiaeum variegatum* var. *pictum*
CROTON, JOSEPH'S COAT
↕ 6ft (2m) ↔ 4ft (1.2m)

This woody-based plant is famous for the colorful variegation along the veins of its glossy leaves. Green and yellow, or red, orange, and purple are predominant.

☼ Bright, but avoid summer sun ☷ Moderate to warm, avoiding fluctuation. High humidity ◐ Biweekly in summer, using foliage houseplant fertilizer ◊ Keep moist. When dry if cool ⊟ Tip cuttings

Maranta leuconeura
var. *kerchoveana* ▷
PRAYER PLANT
↕ ↔ 30cm (12in)

Pale green, satin-sheened leaves, each marked with dark green "footprints," distinguish this tropical American species and give it its alternative name, rabbit's foot.

△ *Cyperus albostriatus*
UMBRELLA PLANT
↕ 2ft (60cm) ↔ 12in (30cm)

Densely tufted and with strap-shaped, pale green leaves radiating from the ends of the stems, this plant also produces green flower clusters from summer to autumn.

☼ Bright to moderate. Avoid summer sun ▮▮ Cool to warm. Moderate to high humidity 💧 Biweekly, using foliage houseplant fertilizer. Twice in winter 💧 Keep moist. Likes to stand in water ✂ Division

OTHER HOUSEPLANTS FOR WARM, HUMID ROOMS

Adiantum raddianum 'Gracillimum'
Anthurium crystallinum, see p.338
Calathea crocata, see p.328
Codiaeum 'Petra'
Hypoestes phyllostachya 'Wit', see p.351
Maranta leuconeura var. *erythroneura*, see p.399
Peperomia caperata 'Little Fantasy'
Philodendron melanochrysum
Sinningia 'Mont Blanc', see p.343

☼ Moderate, avoiding direct sun ▮▮ Moderate to warm. High humidity 💧 Biweekly. Occasionally in winter 💧 Keep moist. When dry at lower temperatures ✂ Division, tip cuttings

LOCATIONS

△ *Fittonia verschaffeltii* var. *pearcei*
'Superba Red'
NERVE PLANT
↕ 6in (15cm) ↔ 12in (30cm) or more

A compact plant with dark green leaves and bright red leaf veins. It makes a neat display when grouped with several others in a shallow pot, or is ideal for a terrarium.

☼ Moderate ▮▮ Moderate to warm. High humidity 💧 Biweekly. Occasionally in winter 💧 Allow soil surface to dry slightly before watering. Dislikes being waterlogged ✂ Tip cuttings

Stromanthe 'Stripestar' ▷
PEACOCK PLANT
↕ 5ft (1.5m) ↔ 3ft (1m)

Each glossy dark green leaf has a pale green midrib and veins, with a dark purple underside that is prominent as new leaves unfurl. Not easy to grow but worth the effort.

☼ Bright to moderate, avoiding summer sun ▮▮ Moderate to warm, avoiding drafts. High humidity 💧 Biweekly. Monthly in winter 💧 Keep moist. When dry at lower temperatures ✂ Division

Houseplants for Large Rooms

OTHER HOUSEPLANTS FOR LARGE ROOMS

Begonia luxurians
Chamaedorea elegans, see p.412
Cissus rhombifolia 'Ellen Danica', see p.376
Ficus elastica 'Robusta', see p.389
Ficus lyrata, see p.395
Musa acuminata 'Dwarf Cavendish'
Sparrmannia africana, see p.387
Yucca elephantipes, see p.385

GENEROUSLY PROPORTIONED rooms call for dramatic plants to fill the space without dominating it or making it hard for people to move around. Bold-leaved specimens are often a good choice, although large plants with smaller leaves are equally effective when well placed. Some of the suggestions here need careful pruning to restrict their size.

Fatsia japonica 'Variegata' ▷
JAPANESE ARALIA
↕ ↔ 5ft (1.5m) or more

A popular variegated foliage shrub, with large, long-stalked, evergreen leaves, their lobes splashed creamy white. Tolerates relatively cool conditions, but it needs plenty of elbow room.

☼ Bright to moderate ▐ Cool to moderate. Moderate humidity ◖ Biweekly, using foliage houseplant fertilizer. Once in winter ◊ When soil surface dry. Reduce watering at low temperatures ▩ Tip cuttings, air layering

△ *Codiaeum* 'Juliet'
CROTON
↕ ↔ 3ft (1m) or more

This handsome evergreen shrub has deeply lobed, leathery, glossy green leaves, their veins picked out in bright yellow. Plant several in a container, or encourage one to branch out.

☼ Bright, with some sun ▐ Warm, avoiding drafts and fluctuation. Moderate to high humidity ◖ Biweekly, using foliage houseplant fertilizer. Occasionally in winter ◊ Keep moist. In winter, water when soil surface dry ▩ Tip cuttings

Dracaena fragrans 'Lemon Lime' ▷
DRACAENA
↕ 10ft (3m) or more ↔ 4ft (1.2m) or more

One of the most colorful of a group famed for variegated foliage. The long, tapered leaves are lime green with a wide, cream-edged, dark green central stripe.

☼ Bright to moderate, avoiding summer sun ▐ Warm. Moderate to high humidity ◖ Biweekly. Occasionally in winter ◊ When dry. Water sparingly in winter ▩ Tip cuttings, stem sections

Lime green variegated foliage

Ficus bennendijkii 'Alii' ▷
FICUS
↕ 6ft (2m) or more
↔ 30in (75cm) or more

Looking like an evergreen weeping willow, this graceful houseplant has slender stems clothed in long, narrow leaves. Its fairly narrow habit makes it suitable for a variety of spaces.

☼ Bright, but avoid summer sun ▐ Warm. Moderate to high humidity ◖ Biweekly. Occasionally in winter ◊ When soil surface dry. Reduce watering at lower temperatures ▩ Tip cuttings, air layering

Monstera deliciosa
'Variegata' ▷
SWISS CHEESE PLANT
‡ ↔ 12ft (4m) or more

Grown on a moss pole, this striking climber, with outstanding, deeply lobed green and white leaves, will prove an accent wherever it is placed. If neglected or allowed to dry out, it will become an eyesore.

☼ Bright to moderate ◫ Warm. Moderate to high humidity ◦ Biweekly. Occasionally in winter ◦ Water when soil surface just dry ▭ Stem cuttings, air layering

Ravenea rivularis ▷
MAJESTY PALM
‡ 10ft (3m) or more
↔ 5ft (1.5m) or more

A beautiful, quite fast-growing palm from Madagascar, with elegant, featherlike leaves. A newcomer to indoor cultivation, it tolerates low light and cool conditions.

☼ Bright to moderate, avoiding summer sun ◫ Moderate to warm. Moderate to high humidity ◦ Biweekly, using foliage houseplant feed. Monthly in winter ◦ When dry. Avoid waterlogging ▭ Seed

Murraya paniculata ▷
ORANGE JESSAMINE
‡ 10ft (3m)
↔ 4ft (1.2m)

An attractive shrub with dark green, divided, glossy, evergreen leaves, strongly scented if bruised, and clusters of scented, citruslike flowers from spring to summer.

☼ Bright to moderate, with sun ◫ Moderate to warm. Moderate to high humidity ◦ Biweekly. Occasionally in winter ◦ When soil surface dry. Water sparingly in winter ▭ Semiripe cuttings

△ *Philodendron erubescens* 'Burgundy'
BLUSHING PHILODENDRON
‡ ↔ 10ft (3m) or more

Large, shining, red-flushed, red-veined leaves are borne on dark purple-red stems. Best trained on a moss pole, it is an impressive plant when grown well.

☼ Bright to shady ◫ Warm. Moderate to high humidity ◦ Biweekly, using foliage houseplant fertilizer. Monthly in winter ◦ Let soil surface dry slightly before watering ▭ Tip cuttings

△ *Spathiphyllum* 'Euro Gigant'
PEACE LILY
‡ ↔ 3ft (1m)

Magnificent at its best, and an excellent specimen. Large, boldly veined, paddle-like green leaves are joined in spring and summer by tall-stemmed white flowers.

☼ Bright, but avoid direct sun ◫ Moderate to warm. Moderate to high humidity ◦ Biweekly. Monthly in winter ◦ Water when soil surface dry. Avoid overwatering ▭ Division

Houseplants for Living and Dining Rooms

IN MOST HOMES the living and dining rooms are the largest in the house. They are rooms to feel comfortable in, so all the more reason to include plants. Given their floor spaces, corners, and flat surfaces, they offer great potential for using plants to soften hard lines or edges, complement decor, and promote a relaxing atmosphere.

LOCATIONS

Chlorophytum comosum 'Variegatum' ▷
SPIDER PLANT
↕ 3ft (90cm) ↔ 2ft (60cm)

Easy and adaptable, this spider plant tolerates poor light and neglect but thrives in good conditions. It differs from the equally common *Chlorophytum comosum* 'Vittatum' in having white, rather than green, leaf margins.

☼ Bright to moderate, avoiding summer sun
🌡 Moderate to warm. Moderate to high humidity
💧 Biweekly. None at low winter temperatures
◊ Keep moist, but avoid waterlogging. In winter, water when soil surface dry 🝙 Plantlets

△ *Asparagus densiflorus* 'Myersii'
FOXTAIL FERN
↕ ↔ 18in (45cm)

This striking, tuberous-rooted foliage perennial has foxtail-like plumes of tiny, green, needlelike branchlets. Contrast with broad-leaved plants in a group.

☼ Bright to moderate. Avoid hot sun 🌡 Moderate to warm. Moderate humidity 💧 Foliage houseplant fertilizer weekly. Monthly in winter ◊ Keep moist. Water when dry in winter 🝙 Division

---

OTHER FOLIAGE HOUSEPLANTS FOR LIVING AND DINING ROOMS

Aspidistra elatior 'Milky Way', see p.364
Dracaena fragrans 'Massangeana', see p.375
Monstera deliciosa, see p.339
Radermachera sinica

Asparagus falcatus ▷
SICKLETHORN
↕ 10ft (3m) or more ↔ 3ft (1m)

An erect, strong-growing, bright green plant that in the wild clambers into trees by means of tiny spines. Grown indoors, it is more compact and easily controllable.

☼ Bright to moderate. Avoid hot sun 🌡 Moderate to warm. Moderate humidity 💧 Foliage houseplant fertilizer weekly. Monthly in winter ◊ Keep moist. Water when dry in winter 🝙 Division, seed

△ *Corynocarpus laevigatus*
KARAKA
↕ 10ft (3m) or more ↔ 5ft (1.5m) or more

In its native New Zealand the karaka is a woodland tree, but it is slower growing and easily controlled as a houseplant. It has handsome, shining, deep green leaves.

☼ Bright, with some direct sun 🌡 Moderate to warm. Moderate humidity 💧 Monthly. Occasionally in winter ◊ When soil surface dry 🝙 Semiripe cuttings, seed

OTHER FLOWERING HOUSEPLANTS FOR LIVING AND DINING ROOMS

Heliotropium arborescens
Impatiens walleriana hybrids, see p.385
Pelargonium 'Sefton'
Primula obconica, see p.331
Sinningia speciosa cvs.

△ *Dracaena cincta* 'Tricolor'
DRACAENA
↕ 10ft (3m) ↔ 4ft (1.2m)

A slow-growing shrub or small tree with slender stems and loose ruffs of long, narrow, shining green leaves, striped cream and stained pink along the margins.

☼ Bright to moderate, avoiding direct summer sun ⊞ Warm. Moderate to high humidity ◊ Biweekly. Occasionally in winter ◊ When soil surface dry. Water sparingly in winter ⊞ Tip or stem cuttings

△ *Justicia carnea*
KING'S CROWN
↕ 4ft (1.2m) ↔ 32in (80cm)

This evergreen shrub produces large, boldly veined leaves and dense spikes of two-lipped, pink to rose-pink flowers in summer or later. Keep bushy by pruning.

☼ Bright to moderate, avoiding direct sun ⊞ Warm, avoiding drafts. Moderate to high humidity ◊ Monthly ◊ Keep moist, but avoid waterlogging ⊞ Semiripe cuttings, seed

Peperomia caperata 'Lilian' ▷
PEPEROMIA
↕ 8in (20cm) ↔ 6in (15cm)

The neat tuft of corrugated, deep green leaves is topped by white flower spikes in late summer. An ideal plant for growing in a small space, bottle garden, or terrarium.

☼ Bright to moderate, with some sun ⊞ Warm. Moderate to high humidity ◊ Every three weeks. Occasionally in winter ◊ When soil surface dry. Avoid waterlogging ⊞ Leaf or tip cuttings

Hibiscus rosa-sinensis 'Lateritia' ▷
CHINESE HIBISCUS
↕ 8ft (2.5m) ↔ 5ft (1.5m)

Chinese hibiscus are capable of reaching a large size but can be pruned in winter to encourage a more bushy, compact habit. Large, yellow, deep-throated flowers appear from spring to autumn.

☼ Bright ⊞ Warm, avoiding fluctuation. Moderate to high humidity ◊ Biweekly. Stop feeding at lower temperatures ◊ When soil surface just dry. Water sparingly in winter ⊞ Tip cuttings

△ *Pericallis* x *hybrida* cultivars
FLORISTS' CINERARIA
↕ 12in (30cm) ↔ 10in (25cm)

Spectacular winter- to spring-flowering plants, these have a rosette of bold foliage crowned by usually long-lasting, large, daisylike flowers in a variety of colors.

☼ Bright, but avoid direct sun ⊞ Cool to moderate or warm. Moderate to high humidity ◊ Biweekly ◊ Keep moist, but avoid waterlogging ⊞ Seed

LOCATIONS

Houseplants for Bedrooms

IT WAS ONCE commonly believed that plants in a bedroom or hospital ward, certainly at night, were injurious to health. This misconception may have stemmed from the fact that the leaves of most plants absorb oxygen during the hours of darkness. Nowadays we know that plants in an airy bedroom will provide benefits including increased humidity, a reduction in noise, and the suppression of airborne microbes. Carefully placed, the houseplants shown here can bring a healthy, relaxing feel to any bedroom.

Achimenes hybrids ▷
HOT-WATER PLANT
↕ ↔ 12in (30cm)

Blooming profusely from summer into autumn, few houseplants are more free-flowering. Support the floppy stems or grow in a hanging basket or on a pedestal.

☼ Bright. Avoid summer sun ≣ Warm. Moderate humidity ♦ Biweekly, using flowering houseplant fertilizer ◊ Freely in summer; reduce in autumn; keep dry in winter; increase in spring ▦ Tubercles

Asparagus umbellatus ▷
ASPARAGUS FERN
↕ 4ft (1.2m) ↔ 2ft (60cm)

The asparagus fern makes a cheerful informal houseplant with its clusters of bristlelike, bright green leaves. In its native Canary Islands it is a scrambling perennial, so if pot-grown the stems may need support.

☼ Bright to moderate, avoiding summer sun ≣ Moderate to warm. Moderate humidity ♦ Foliage houseplant fertilizer weekly. Monthly in winter ◊ Keep moist. In winter, water when dry ▦ Division, seed

Aglaonema 'Lilian' ▷
CHINESE EVERGREEN
↕ ↔ 2ft (60cm)

This Chinese evergreen produces small, arumlike flowers in summer but is valued most for its beautifully marked, slender-pointed leaves, borne in a bold clump. Slow-growing but well worth it.

☼ Moderate, avoiding sun ≣ Moderate to warm. Moderate to high humidity ♦ Foliage houseplant fertilizer weekly. Monthly in winter ◊ When dry ▦ Division, tip cuttings

Catharanthus roseus ▷
MADAGASCAR PERIWINKLE
↕ ↔ 12in (30cm)

This easy-to-grow plant forms a low, rounded bush of shiny foliage and sports large pink, lavender, white, or red flowers from late spring to autumn.

☼ Bright, but avoid summer sun ≣ Warm. Moderate humidity ♦ Monthly. Biweekly in summer ◊ Water regularly; keep moist but avoid waterlogging ▦ Tip cuttings. Roots easily in water

Pilea microphylla ▷
ARTILLERY PLANT
↕ ↔ 12in (30cm)

This compact pilea forms a small hummock of foliage. It derives its common name from the pollen, which silently and harmlessly "explodes" when ripe. Suitable for a sunless position and best regarded as a temporary plant.

☼ Moderate ▐ Moderate to warm. Moderate to high humidity ◖ Biweekly. Monthly in winter ◊ Water when soil surface just dry. Avoid waterlogging ▧ Tip cuttings

OTHER FOLIAGE HOUSEPLANTS FOR BEDROOMS

Adiantum raddianum, see p.398
Aspidistra elatior, see p.386
Chlorophytum comosum 'Vittatum', see p.384
Dracaena fragrans 'White Edge'
Nephrolepis exaltata 'Bostoniensis', see p.407

△ *Solenostemon* 'Wizard'
COLEUS
↕ ↔ 8in (20cm)

Brilliantly colored leaves are the trademark of coleus; this wide-margined form is excellent for a sunny window or well-lit spot. Pinch out tips for compact growth.

☼ Bright ▐ Warm. Moderate humidity ◖ Weekly. Occasionally in winter ◊ Keep moist, but avoid waterlogging. In winter, water when soil mix just dry ▧ Tip cuttings, seed. Roots easily in water

△ *Dracaena fragrans* 'Massangeana'
CORN PALM
↕ 10ft (3m) ↔ 4ft (1.2m)

The stout stems form a miniature tree crowded with glossy green leaves with a greenish yellow central band. One of the most popular of all dracaenas.

☼ Bright to moderate, avoiding summer sun ▐ Warm. Moderate to high humidity ◖ Biweekly. Occasionally in winter ◊ When soil surface dry. Water sparingly in winter ▧ Tip cuttings, stem sections

OTHER FLOWERING HOUSEPLANTS FOR BEDROOMS

Begonia tuberosa hybrids
Cyclamen persicum hybrids, see p.330
Impatiens walleriana hybrids, see p.385
Oxalis purpurata, see p.347
Spathiphyllum 'Euro Gigant', see p.371

Dracaena reflexa 'Song of India' ▷
DRACAENA
↕ 10ft (3m) ↔ 4ft (1.2m)

Many-branched and woody-stemmed, this plant eventually grows into a small tree. Its yellow-margined leaves are usually crowded toward the branch ends.

☼ Bright to moderate, avoiding summer sun ▐ Warm. Moderate to high humidity ◖ Biweekly; occasionally in winter ◊ When soil mix dry. Water sparingly in winter ▧ Tip cuttings, stem sections

△ *Syngonium podophyllum* 'Pixie'
GOOSEFOOT
↕ ↔ 12in (30cm)

White-marbled, arrow-shaped leaves divide as this attractive, initially clump-forming perennial matures and begins to climb. Best grown on a moss pole.

☼ Bright to moderate, avoiding summer sun ▐ Warm, avoiding fluctuation. Moderate to high humidity ◖ Biweekly; monthly in winter ◊ When soil mix dry ▧ Tip cuttings

LOCATIONS

375

Houseplants for Narrow Spaces

EVERY HOME contains awkward narrow spaces, perhaps with restricted access, which call for small or upright plants rather than large or bushy specimens. They are just the spots to take most climbers, trailers, or compact, well-mannered plants that respond well to occasional pruning. Such situations can be poorly lit, so choose plants that will tolerate degrees of shade.

Handsome, glossy leaves

Asparagus setaceus 'Nanus' ▷
ASPARAGUS FERN
↕ ↔ 18in (45cm)

The delicate, feathery, frondlike foliage of this plant is commonly used in boutonnieres. Unlike the parent species, this compact form will not climb and is ideal for small spaces.

☼ Bright to moderate, avoiding summer sun ∦ Cool to warm. Moderate humidity ◐ Weekly, using foliage houseplant fertilizer. Monthly in winter ◊ Keep moist. Allow to dry out at lower temperatures ▦ Division, seed

OTHER SMALL HOUSE-
PLANTS FOR NARROW SPACES

Achimenes hybrids
Ardisia crispa
Cyperus involucratus 'Nanus'
Ficus pumila 'White Sonny', see p.363
Spathiphyllum 'Petite'

Cissus antarctica ▷
KANGAROO VINE
↕ 10ft (3m) ↔ 2ft (60cm)

This vigorous Australian plant produces attractive, glossy, dark green, leathery leaves with scalloped edges. Provide support, and pinch out the growing tips to control its height and spread.

☼ Bright to moderate, avoiding summer sun ∦ Cool to warm. Moderate to high humidity ◐ Biweekly. Monthly in winter, at higher temperatures ◊ When soil surface dry. Avoid underwatering ▦ Tip cuttings

△ *Cissus rhombifolia* 'Ellen Danica'
GRAPE IVY
↕ 6ft (2m) ↔ 18in (45cm)

Since it climbs by tendrils, train this popular form of grape ivy on a trellis or stakes to display its large, glossy, deeply lobed leaves. Young plants are best grown as trailers. Full of character.

☼ Bright to moderate, avoiding summer sun ∦ Cool to warm. Moderate to high humidity ◐ Biweekly. Monthly in winter, at higher temperatures ◊ Allow to dry out before watering. Avoid underwatering ▦ Tip cuttings

△ *Crocus* hybrids
DUTCH CROCUS
↕ 5in (12cm) ↔ 2in (5cm)

Giving a cheerful late winter or spring temporary display, this old favorite, with goblet-shaped flowers, will brighten any narrow space in a cool part of the house.

☼ Bright ⋕ Cool to moderate. Moderate humidity ♦ Unnecessary ◊ Keep moist, but avoid waterlogging ⊡ Cormlets. In temperate climates, crocuses can be planted outdoors after flowering

---

OTHER TALL HOUSEPLANTS OR
CLIMBERS FOR NARROW SPACES

Dieffenbachia 'Compacta', see p.338
Dracaena fragrans 'Compacta', see p.362
Ficus bennendijkii 'Alii', see p.370
Hedera helix 'Ivalace'
Schefflera arboricola 'Compacta',
    see p.389
Yucca elephantipes, see p.385

△ x *Fatshedera lizei* 'Pia'
FATSHEDERA
↕ 6ft (2m) ↔ 18in (45cm)

An excellent foliage shrub with glossy, five-lobed, wavy-edged leaves. Grow several together against a pale background to emphasize their leaf shape and form.

☼ Moderate. Tolerates some shade ⋕ Cool to warm. Moderate humidity ♦ Foliage houseplant fertilizer biweekly. Monthly in winter ◊ Water when dry ⊡ Tip cuttings, stem sections

△ *Hedera helix* 'Ovata'
ENGLISH IVY
↕ 6ft (2m) ↔ 12in (30cm)

This ivy has leathery, un-lobed, deep green, triangular leaves, sometimes with wedge-shaped tips. Grow it in a hanging basket or train it up a pole or frame. May be sold as 'Mein Hertz'.

☼ Bright to moderate ⋕ Cool to warm. Moderate to high humidity ♦ Biweekly. Twice in winter ◊ Let soil surface dry out before watering. Water sparingly in winter ⊡ Tip cuttings, layering

△ *Euonymus japonicus* 'Aureus'
JAPANESE SPINDLE TREE
↕ 5ft (1.5m) ↔ 2ft (60cm)

Ideal for a cool room or hallway, this delightful, slow-growing, compact plant has gold-splashed, dark green leaves. Can be planted outside if it grows too large.

☼ Bright, with some direct sun ⋕ Cool to warm. Moderate humidity ♦ Monthly, from spring to autumn ◊ When soil surface dry. Water sparingly in winter ⊡ Tip cuttings

△ *Hedera canariensis* 'Montgomery'
CANARY ISLAND IVY
↕ 12ft (4m) ↔ 3ft (1m)

Decorative bronze-purple stems produce large, sharply lobed, mid-green leaves that become a dark glossy green with maturity. May need restrictive pruning with age.

☼ Bright to moderate ⋕ Cool to warm. Moderate to high humidity ♦ Biweekly. Twice in winter ◊ When soil surface dry. Water sparingly in winter ⊡ Tip cuttings, layering

△ *Tolmiea menziesii* 'Taff's Gold'
PIGGY-BACK PLANT
↕ ↔ 12in (30cm)

Small plantlets occur where each leaf and stalk join, hence the common name of this plant with hairy, gold-mottled green leaves. A good choice for a cool spot.

☼ Bright, but avoid direct sun ⋕ Cool to moderate. Moderate humidity ♦ Biweekly. Twice in winter, if temperature raised ◊ When soil surface dry. Water sparingly in winter ⊡ Plantlets

LOCATIONS

Houseplants for Garden Rooms

GARDEN ROOMS, offering protection from unfavorable weather yet benefiting from unrestricted light, are often the ideal way to provide houseplants with optimum growing conditions, particularly in cool temperate climates. Artificial, consistent heat and humidity levels allow tropical species to grow, but a wide range of plants will thrive even in a cool garden room.

△ *Euryops chrysanthemoides*
EURYOPS
↕ 3ft (1m) ↔ 4ft (1.2m) or more

Worth growing for the cheerful, bright yellow daisy flowers alone. These are borne intermittently throughout the year over a dense, dome-shaped bush of rich green foliage. It can be pruned to maintain the required shape.

☼ Bright, with sun ❙❘ Moderate to warm. Moderate humidity ◖ Every three weeks ◔ When soil surface dry. Water sparingly in winter ⊡ Semiripe cuttings, seed

Anigozanthos flavidus ▷
KANGAROO PAW
↕ 4ft (1.2m) ↔ 18in (45cm)

Curiously shaped flowers, in either pink or yellow, are produced in clusters in late spring or summer and give this plant its common name. A plant that is suitable for a cooler garden room.

☼ Bright to moderate, avoiding summer sun ❙❘ Moderate to warm. Moderate humidity ◖ Biweekly, using fertilizer for acid-loving plants. Occasionally in winter ◔ Keep moist. Reduce watering in winter ⊡ Division, seed

OTHER HOUSEPLANTS FOR GARDEN ROOMS

Coronilla valentina subsp. *glauca*
Eupatorium sordidum
Leonotis ocymifolia
Lithodora rosmarinifolia
Metrosideros kermadecensis 'Variegatus'
Prostanthera rotundifolia, see p.345

△ *Argyranthemum* 'Vancouver'
MARGUERITE
↕ ↔ 3ft (90cm)

Abundant, anemone-centered pink flowers, from spring to autumn, give this perennial a long season of interest. Dead-head regularly to encourage more blooms.

☼ Bright, but avoid direct sun ❙❘ Cool to moderate. Moderate humidity ◖ Every three weeks ◔ Keep soil mix moist, but avoid waterlogging ⊡ Tip cuttings

Tiny flowers with spreading petals

Cuphea hyssopifolia ▷
FALSE HEATHER
↕ 2ft (60cm) ↔ 32in (80cm)

Bushy and compact, narrow-leaved false heathers are sometimes used as summer bedding plants in cool climates. Masses of small pink, purple, or white flowers are freely produced from summer through to autumn.

☼ Bright, avoiding direct sun ❙❘ Cool to moderate. Moderate humidity ◖ Every three weeks. Occasionally in winter ◔ When soil surface dry. Water sparingly in winter ⊡ Tip cuttings

△ *Pelargonium* 'Carisbrooke'
REGAL GERANIUM

↕ 18in (45cm) ↔ 12in (30cm)

Broad clusters of pale rose-pink flowers, their upper petals blazed with claret, are produced in a flowering season of short duration, from spring to midsummer.

☼ Bright, with sun ◫ Moderate to warm, but cool in winter. Moderate humidity ◑ Biweekly, using high-potassium fertilizer ◐ When soil surface just dry. Water sparingly in winter ▨ Tip cuttings

△ *Rehmannia elata*
CHINESE FOXGLOVE

↕ 30in (75cm) or more ↔ 18in (45cm)

Loose-stemmed and downy all over, this perennial member of the foxglove family produces gorgeous, pendulous, pinkish purple flowers from summer into autumn.

☼ Bright ◫ Moderate to warm. Moderate humidity ◑ Monthly. Occasionally in winter ◐ When soil surface dry. Water sparingly in winter ▨ Seed

△ *Strelitzia reginae*
BIRD OF PARADISE

↕ 5ft (1.5m) ↔ 3ft (1m)

Instantly recognizable when in flower, this spectacular South African exotic also has a bold clump of handsome paddle-shaped leaves. Plants take several years to flower; the distinctive blooms can last several weeks.

☼ Bright, with sun ◫ Moderate to warm. Moderate humidity ◑ Biweekly. Occasionally in winter ◐ When soil surface dry. Water sparingly in winter ▨ Division, seed

△ *Pittosporum tobira*
JAPANESE MOCK ORANGE

↕ ↔ 6ft (2m) or more

Creamy flower clusters, appearing in late spring and summer, are deliciously scented of orange blossoms. Attractive, glossy evergreen foliage sets off the flowers. Can be pruned into shape.

☼ Bright, with some sun ◫ Moderate to warm, but cool in winter. Moderate humidity ◑ Biweekly. Occasionally in winter ◐ When dry. Water sparingly in winter ▨ Semiripe cuttings, seed

OTHER CLIMBING HOUSEPLANTS FOR GARDEN ROOMS

Bomarea caldasii
Jasminum polyanthum, see p.323
Passiflora 'Amethyst', see p.392
Plumbago auriculata
Streptosolen jameson;i

Spectacular creamy pink flowers

◁ *Zantedeschia* 'Little Suzie'
CALLA LILY

↕ ↔ 2ft (60cm)

Given sufficient moisture during the growing season, this plant will produce a lush clump of foliage, through which the creamy pink flowers emerge in summer. It is dormant in winter.

☼ Bright, but avoid intense summer sun ◫ Moderate to warm. Moderate humidity ◑ Biweekly ◐ Keep moist. Reduce watering during resting period ▨ Division, offsets

LOCATIONS

Houseplants for the Home Office

NOWADAYS, MANY PEOPLE work from home. Growing plants in a home office (or any workplace) will improve air quality, adding moisture and helping to disperse pollutants including computer emissions; they may even help you think more clearly. Stand plants away from your equipment to prevent watering accidents.

△ *Crassula ovata*
JADE PLANT
‡ ↔ 3ft (1m) or more

One of the easiest houseplants, this slowly forms a small- to medium-sized succulent bush with red-tinted green foliage. White or pink flowers appear in autumn.

☼ Bright, sunny ≣ Warm, but moderate in winter. Low humidity ◖ Monthly, using fertilizer for cacti and succulents ◊ When soil surface dry. Water sparingly in winter ▥ Tip or leaf cuttings

△ *Aglaonema* 'Maria Christina'
CHINESE EVERGREEN
‡ ↔ 20in (50cm)

A suckering, clump-forming perennial producing handsome, large, upright, green leaves, liberally splashed and striped creamy white and pale green.

☼ Moderate, avoiding summer sun ≣ Moderate to warm. Moderate to high humidity ◖ Weekly, using foliage houseplant fertilizer. Monthly in winter ◊ When dry ▥ Division; tip or stem cuttings

---

OTHER FLOWERING HOUSE-PLANTS FOR THE HOME OFFICE

Anthurium 'Lady Jane'
Gerbera jamesonii
Impatiens walleriana hybrids, see p.385
Kalanchoe blossfeldiana
Pelargonium 'Stellar Apricot'
Schlumbergera x *buckleyi*
Schlumbergera truncata, see p.363

△ *Adiantum raddianum* 'Fritz Luth'
MAIDENHAIR FERN
‡ ↔ 2ft (60cm)

One of the best maidenhair ferns when mature, with beautifully segmented, emerald green fronds on wiry, shining black stalks. Protect from cold drafts.

☼ Moderate, avoiding direct sun ≣ Moderate to warm. Moderate to high humidity ◖ Biweekly. Monthly in winter ◊ Keep moist, but avoid waterlogging ▥ Division, spores

Aechmea fasciata
'Morgana' ▷
URN PLANT
‡ 2ft (60cm) ↔ 30in (75cm)

The big, funnel-shaped rosette of lilac-gray leaves is topped in summer by a spectacular, rose-pink, bracted flower-head. A splendid exotic for a pot or hanging basket in the right spot.

☼ Bright, but avoid summer sun ≣ Warm. Moderate to high humidity ◖ Biweekly ◊ When soil surface dry. Water sparingly in winter. Keep "urn" filled with water ▥ Offsets

△ *Cryptanthus bivittatus*
EARTH STAR
‡ 4in (10cm) ↔ 10in (25cm)

A curious-looking plant bearing flattened, star-shaped rosettes of sharply pointed, wavy-margined, green and white-striped leaves; the white may turn pink in sun.

☼ Bright to shady, avoiding direct sun ≣ Warm. High humidity. Mist regularly or stand on pebble tray ◖ Monthly, using flowering houseplant fertilizer. Twice during winter ◊ When top 2in (5cm) of soil mix dries out ▥ Offsets

Pale green and yellow variegation

△ *Pilea peperomioides*
PILEA
↕ ↔ 12in (30cm)

This easy-to-grow plant from southwest China tolerates neglect, but treat it well to fully enjoy its glossy, dark green, shield-like succulent leaves borne on long stalks.

☀ Bright to moderate, with some sun 🌡 Warm. Moderate to high humidity 💧 Every three weeks. Occasionally in winter 💧 When soil surface just dry. Avoid waterlogging ✂ Tip cuttings

Ctenanthe 'Golden Mosaic' ▷
CTENANTHE
↕ ↔ 3ft (1m)

This handsome foliage plant from Brazil forms clumps of canelike stems that bear deep green leaves, marked with paler green and creamy yellow streaks and patches. Grow ctenanthes on a pebble tray for best results.

☀ Bright to moderate, avoiding direct sun 🌡 Warm, avoiding fluctuation. High humidity 💧 Biweekly, using foliage houseplant fertilizer. Rarely in winter 💧 Keep soil mix moist. In cool winter temperatures, water when dry ✂ Division

OTHER FOLIAGE HOUSEPLANTS FOR THE HOME OFFICE

Cissus rhombifolia 'Ellen Danica', see p.376
Dracaena marginata, see p.395
Ficus benjamina, see p.384
Hedera helix 'Ivalace'
Nephrolepis exaltata 'Bostoniensis', see p.407
Pelargonium 'Graveolens', see p.344
Philodendron tuxtlanum 'Tuxtla'
Sansevieria trifasciata, see p.387
Yucca elephantipes, see p.385

LOCATIONS

◁ *Dieffenbachia seguine* 'Tropic Snow'
DUMB CANE
↕ ↔ 3ft (1m)

Grow this plant for its bold green foliage marked with pale green and cream variegation; the large leaves give out plenty of water, counteracting dry air. Thrives best on a pebble tray. It is poisonous if chewed, so keep out of the reach of small children.

☀ Bright to moderate. Avoid hot sun 🌡 Moderate to warm. Moderate to high humidity 💧 Biweekly, using foliage houseplant fertilizer. Monthly in winter 💧 When dry ✂ Tip or stem cuttings

△ *Spathiphyllum wallisii* 'Clevelandii'
PEACE LILY
↕ 26in (65cm) ↔ 20in (50cm)

Peace lilies provide humidity and can tolerate low light, so they are a boon for an office corner. Display their showy foliage and white flowers to advantage.

☀ Bright to moderate, avoiding direct sun 🌡 Moderate to warm. Moderate to high humidity 💧 Biweekly. Monthly in winter 💧 When soil surface dry. Avoid overwatering ✂ Division

SPECIFIC USES

HOUSEPLANTS ARE without doubt one of the most versatile of all plant groups, with a huge choice for every specific decorative or cultural requirement. Whether you need an architectural form, a selection for a terrarium, or an easy-to-grow houseplant, in the following pages you will find a plant that fits the bill.

△ WINTER ORNAMENT *This collection of solanums and capsicums makes the most of the brightly colored, decorative fruits and provides winter color.*

Homalomena wallisii to improve air quality

There are still many people who are convinced that all houseplants are difficult to grow. Beginners can take heart and try some of the many houseplants that are easy and totally reliable. Some will even tolerate neglect and survive in adverse conditions, although this should never be a reason to forget them. Some flowering plants are hardy and can be planted outside after blooming, giving you two uses for the price of one. All plants produce oxygen as well as absorb impurities from the air, so growing plants indoors is one of the easiest ways of maintaining a healthy home environment.

APPEALING HABITS
The growth habit of some plants, such as climbers and slender-stemmed or trailing plants, is their most interesting and useful feature. Grow trailers in hanging baskets designed for indoor use or in pots placed on raised surfaces such as shelves and cupboards. Such plants can even be used to create a living "curtain" of growth. Equally, many climbers can be trained onto moss poles or frames, providing interest for narrow spaces and awkward corners. Architectural plants that offer impressive forms make fine specimen plants if you have room.

OTHER USES
Many plants from tropical rain-forests demand heat and humidity in order to thrive. Such plants, especially slow-growing or dwarf varieties, can be housed in terraria, glass-paneled tanks, or bell jars, which can become very impressive features. Ornamental fruits or seedheads, such as the bright cherry-sized fruits of solanums, are particularly eye-catching in the home, often providing much-needed winter interest. Or why not grow culinary herbs in pots on a sunny kitchen windowsill – a fresh supply is a bonus to any cook.

△ EASY TO GROW *This* Aloe variegata *can withstand neglect and so can be used where it might be temporarily forgotten.*

◁ HERBS FOR THE KITCHEN *Herbs for cooking can be grown on a sunny, warm windowsill or ledge; in the kitchen, they will be close at hand for harvesting.*

▷ ARCHITECTURAL VALUE Nolina recurvata, *with its curved trunk and curious topknot of leaves, looks most striking when displayed as specimens.*

Houseplants for Beginners

NOTHING ENCOURAGES more than success, which breeds both confidence and the desire to know more. This is certainly true of growing houseplants, and there is a wide range of reliable plants that are particularly suitable for first-time growers. They include plants with a variety of leaf and flower forms, and habits that range from small to architectural. Most are relatively easy to propagate; after you succeed in caring for these plants, grow some for your friends.

Echeveria secunda var. *glauca* 'Gigantea' ▷
ECHEVERIA
↕ 3in (8cm) ↔ 6in (15cm)

Grow this striking succulent for its large rosettes of blue-gray fleshy leaves with red-bristled tips. Clusters of red and yellow flowers appear in early summer.

☼ Bright ⋻ Warm, but cool in winter. Low humidity ◐ Every three weeks, using cactus or high-potassium fertilizer ◊ When top 1in (2.5cm) dry. Sparingly in winter, if shriveling ▧ Leaf cuttings, offsets

△ *Chlorophytum comosum* 'Vittatum'
SPIDER PLANT
↕ 3ft (90cm) ↔ 2ft (60cm)

One of the most popular houseplants, with boldly striped leaves and pale, arching stems bearing starry white summer flowers that are followed by little plantlets. Good in a hanging basket.

☼ Bright to moderate, avoiding summer sun ⋻ Moderate to warm. Moderate to high humidity ◐ Biweekly. Stop feeding at low winter temperatures ◊ Keep moist, but avoid water-logging. Water when dry at low winter temperatures ▧ Plantlets

Pendent branches with small leaves

Cyperus involucratus 'Gracilis' ▷
UMBRELLA PLANT
↕ 18in (45cm) ↔ 12in (30cm) or more

A curious, clump-forming sedge with narrow, leafy green bracts crowded at the ends of the erect shoots. The umbrella plant provides a good contrast to ferns or broad-leaved plants.

☼ Bright to shady, avoiding direct sun ⋻ Warm. Moderate to high humidity ◐ Biweekly, using foliage houseplant fertilizer. Occasionally in winter ◊ Likes to be waterlogged. It is impossible to overwater this plant ▧ Division

Ficus benjamina ▷
WEEPING FIG
↕ 7ft (2.2m) ↔ 30in (75cm)

This is an excellent houseplant, well worth growing for its treelike habit, weeping branches, and small, neatly pointed leaves. It will occupy plenty of space when mature.

☼ Bright, but avoid summer sun ⋻ Moderate to warm, avoiding fluctuation. Moderate to high humidity ◐ Biweekly. Occasionally in winter ◊ When soil surface dry. Reduce watering at lower temperatures ▧ Tip cuttings

△ *Impatiens walleriana* hybrids
IMPATIENS
‡ 12in (30cm) ↔ 14in (35cm)

This very well-known flowering plant has fleshy stems and colorful, slender-spurred blooms throughout summer. The hybrids come in a dazzling array of shades.

☼ Bright ❄ Warm. Moderate to high humidity ◐ Biweekly. Occasionally in winter ◊ When soil surface dry ✂ Tip cuttings, seed. Roots easily in water

△ *Saxifraga stolonifera* 'Tricolor'
MOTHER OF THOUSANDS
‡ ↔ 12in (30cm)

Display this plant in a hanging basket or pot on a raised surface where its slender red runners, ending in little plantlets, can hang free. The richly variegated leaves are eye-catching.

☼ Bright, with some direct sun ❄ Cool to moderate, but cooler in winter. Moderate humidity ◐ Biweekly ◊ When dry. Sparingly in cool conditions ✂ Division, plantlets

OTHER SUCCULENT HOUSEPLANTS FOR BEGINNERS

Faucaria tigrina, see p.355
Kalanchoe pumila, see p.329
Oscularia caulescens
Pachyphytum oviferum, see p.409
Portulaca socialis
Sedum morganianum, see p.409

△ *Sansevieria trifasciata* 'Laurentii'
MOTHER-IN-LAW'S TONGUE
‡ 4ft (1.2m) ↔ 30in (75cm)

Shown here is the most popular form of this well-known plant. The upright, thick, succulent, dark green, gold-edged leaves are borne from an underground stem.

☼ Bright to moderate ❄ Moderate to warm. Low humidity ◐ Biweekly ◊ When soil surface dry. Water sparingly in winter. Avoid overwatering ✂ Division

△ *Tradescantia zebrina*
INCH PLANT, WANDERING JEW
‡ ↔ 18in (45cm) or more

Fast-growing and fleshy-stemmed, this popular perennial is a splendid trailing plant for a hanging basket. The leaf surfaces are fascinating in detail.

☼ Bright to moderate ❄ Warm. Moderate to high humidity ◐ Biweekly. Rarely in winter ◊ Water when soil surface dry ✂ Division, tip cuttings

OTHER HOUSEPLANTS FOR BEGINNERS

Asparagus setaceus
Aspidistra elatior, see p.386
Euphorbia milii var. *tulearensis*, see p.386
Haworthia attenuata, see p.387
Hedera helix 'Eva', see p.351
Plectranthus verticillatus
Schlumbergera truncata, see p.363
Tolmiea menziesii 'Taff's Gold', see p.377

△ *Yucca elephantipes*
SPINELESS YUCCA
‡ 8ft (2.5m) ↔ 6ft (2m)

Presented for sale with its sawed-off stems, this plant looks like an oddity. It soon grows into a bold exotic specimen, with long, sword-shaped, leathery leaves.

☼ Bright, with some direct sun ❄ Moderate to warm, but cooler in winter. Low humidity ◐ Biweekly ◊ Keep moist. Water sparingly at lower temperatures ✂ Stem cuttings

SPECIFIC USES

Houseplants Tolerant of Neglect

SOME PLANTS can survive the toughest conditions – high, low, or fluctuating temperatures and light levels, waterlogging, drought, or starvation. This resilience makes them perfect for students, workaholics, or nongardeners who want living color and interest at home. These plants all tolerate neglect, but with care, they'll flourish.

Aloe variegata ▷
PARTRIDGE BREAST
↕ 10in (26cm) ↔ 7in (17cm)

This compact succulent has overlapping, triangular, white-marked leaves. Salmon-pink flowers are borne from late winter to early spring, after a winter rest.

☼ Bright to moderate ≣ Warm. Moderate to cool winter rest. Low humidity ◖ Every three weeks, using fertilizer for cacti and succulents ◊ When top 2in (5cm) dry; sparingly in winter ▨ Offsets

△ *Euphorbia milii* var. *tularensis*
CROWN OF THORNS
↕ ↔ 3ft (1m)

One of the toughest of all houseplants, and one of the spiniest, too, so position it with care. Clusters of showy, pink-bracted flowers appear in spring and summer.

☼ Bright, with sun ≣ Moderate to warm. Low humidity ◖ Every three weeks, using fertilizer for cacti and succulents ◊ When dry. Reduce in winter. Overwatering causes leaf loss ▨ Stem cuttings

△ *Asparagus densiflorus* 'Sprengeri'
EMERALD FERN
↕ ↔ 32in (80cm)

The fine, ferny "leaves" of this South African plant are actually flattened stems. A graceful habit and cheerful bright green foliage make this an invaluable plant.

☼ Bright to moderate, avoiding sun ≣ Moderate to warm. Moderate humidity ◖ Weekly, using foliage houseplant fertilizer. Monthly in winter ◊ Keep moist. Reduce in winter ▨ Division

△ *Aspidistra elatior*
CAST-IRON PLANT
↕ ↔ 2ft (60cm)

A "must" for every home, this almost indestructible Victorian favorite tolerates low light, drafts, and fluctuating temperatures, as its name suggests.

☼ Moderate to shady. Direct sun scorches leaves ≣ Moderate to warm. Moderate to high humidity ◖ Every three weeks ◊ Water when soil surface dry. Dislikes waterlogging ▨ Division

△ *Ferocactus latispinus*
FISHHOOK CACTUS
↕ 10in (25cm) ↔ 15in (38cm)

Spiny and ferocious-looking, this cactus from the Mexican desert can survive heat, cold, and long periods of drought. With care, it may bear violet flowers in summer.

☼ Bright ≣ Warm, but moderate to cool winter rest. Low humidity ◖ Every three weeks, using fertilizer for cacti and succulents ◊ When top 2in (5cm) dry. Sparingly in winter if shriveling ▨ Offsets

△ *Haworthia attenuata*
ZEBRA HAWORTHIA
↕ ↔ 5in (13cm)

Neat and compact, this succulent has leaves covered with white speckles and bears long-lasting, creamy white flowers in summer. Ideal for a narrow windowsill.

☼ Bright ‖ Warm, with moderate to cool winter rest. Low humidity ◑ Every three weeks, using fertilizer for cacti and succulents ◊ When top 2in (5cm) soil mix dry. Sparingly in winter ▥ Offsets

---

OTHER HOUSEPLANTS TOLERANT OF NEGLECT

Aloe barbadensis
Asparagus setaceus
Chlorophytum comosum 'Vittatum', see p.384
Cissus antarctica, see p.376
Crassula arborescens, see p.360
Crassula ovata, see p.380
Echeveria 'Black Prince'
Euphorbia obesa, see p.367
Kalanchoe daigremontiana
Kalanchoe pumila, see p.329
Kalanchoe tomentosa, see p.343
Orbea variegata, see p.408
Pachypodium lamerei, see p.409
Plectranthus verticillatus
Tolmiea menziesii, see p.365

Sansevieria trifasciata ▷
SNAKE PLANT
↕ 4ft (1.2m) ↔ 30in (75cm)

Grow the snake plant for its elegant, variegated, sword-shaped leaves. Underground rhizomes store water for times of drought. This plant will survive anything but waterlogging or constant repotting; repot only if it is too congested.

☼ Bright to moderate ‖ Moderate to warm. Low humidity ◑ Monthly ◊ When soil surface dry. Water sparingly in winter. Avoid overwatering ▥ Division; leaf cuttings or sections

---

Sparrmannia africana ▷
AFRICAN HEMP
↕ ↔ 6ft (2m) or more

A large, vigorous South African shrub with bold, downy foliage and, in late summer, clusters of white, yellow-stamened flowers. Prune after flowering to encourage more blooms.

☼ Bright, but avoid direct sun ‖ Moderate to warm. Moderate humidity ◑ Biweekly, using high-potassium fertilizer ◊ When soil surface dry. Reduce in winter. Avoid waterlogging ▥ Tip cuttings

---

Yucca elephantipes 'Variegata' ▷
VARIEGATED SPINELESS YUCCA
↕ 8ft (2.5m) ↔ 6ft (2m)

This popular and dramatic plant is also robust and ideal as a corner specimen. With age, the narrow, sword-shaped, cream-margined leaves will drop, revealing the yucca's characteristic bare stem.

☼ Bright, with some sun ‖ Moderate to warm, but cool in winter. Low humidity ◑ Biweekly ◊ Keep moist. Water sparingly at low temperatures ▥ Stem sections

SPECIFIC USES

Beneficial Houseplants

Recent NASA research into the beneficial effects of plants has shown that they can significantly improve the indoor environment. Houseplants absorb carbon dioxide and give out oxygen, adding moisture to the air. They also alleviate "sick-building syndrome" by removing airborne pollutants released by building materials, cleaners, and new furnishings. They really do promote a healthy, stress-free environment.

△ *Chlorophytum comosum* 'Mandaianum'
Spider Plant
↕ ↔ 2ft (60cm) or more

One of the most popular and easily grown houseplants, and an active remover of indoor pollution. Display it where its trailing habit can be seen.

☼ Bright to moderate, avoiding summer sun ≡ Moderate to warm. Moderate to high humidity ◖ Biweekly. Stop if cool ◌ Keep moist. When dry if cool ▥ Plantlets

△ *Dieffenbachia seguine* 'Exotica'
Dumb Cane
↕ ↔ 3ft (90cm)

This air-pollutant-removing plant has spectacular, creamy white variegated leaves. Their large size increases their absorbent capacity. Poisonous if chewed.

☼ Bright to moderate. Avoid hot sun ≡ Moderate to warm. Moderate to high humidity ◖ Biweekly, using foliage houseplant fertilizer. Monthly in winter ◌ Water when dry ▥ Tip cuttings, stem sections

△ *Dracaena fragrans* 'Janet Craig'
Dracaena
↕ 10ft (3m) ↔ 4ft (1.2m)

A striking plant with erect stems and lush, glossy, dark green, strap-shaped leaves. The most effective dracaena for absorbing chemical toxins from the air.

☼ Bright to moderate, avoiding hot sun ≡ Warm. Moderate to high humidity ◖ Biweekly. Occasionally in winter ◌ Water when dry. Reduce at lower temperatures ▥ Tip cuttings, stem sections

△ *Ficus benjamina* 'Reginald'
Weeping Fig
↕ 10ft (3m) or more ↔ 3ft (1m) or more

Very effective at removing airborne chemicals, especially formaldehyde, the most common indoor pollutant. Its glossy green leaves are lime green when young.

☼ Bright, but avoid summer sun ≡ Warm, avoiding fluctuation. Moderate to high humidity ◖ Biweekly. Occasionally in winter ◌ When dry. Reduce watering in cool conditions ▥ Tip cuttings

Other Beneficial Houseplants for Foliage Effect

Chamaedorea elegans, see p.412
Chlorophytum comosum 'Vittatum', see p.384
Chrysalidocarpus lutescens, see p.412
Dracaena marginata, see p.395
Epipremnum aureum, see p.391
Nephrolepis exaltata 'Bostoniensis', see p.407
Philodendron scandens subsp. *oxycardium*
Rhapis excelsa, see p.413
Syngonium podophyllum

Specific Uses

△ *Ficus elastica* 'Robusta'
RUBBER PLANT
↕ 10ft (3m) or more ↔ 6ft (1.8m)

'Robusta', with its bold, glossy, leathery leaves, is one of the most handsome of the popular evergreen rubber plants. It is very effective at absorbing formaldehyde.

☼ Bright, but avoid summer sun ▮▯ Warm. Moderate to high humidity ▮◉ Biweekly. Occasionally in winter ◊ When dry. Reduce at lower temperatures ▭ Tip cuttings, air layering

△ *Hedera helix* 'Green Ripple'
ENGLISH IVY
↕ 3ft (1m) or more ↔ 12in (30cm) or more

All ivies are efficient at removing air pollutants, but English ivy is particularly good at absorbing the formaldehyde that is found in tobacco smoke and adhesives.

☼ Bright to moderate. Poor growth in low light ▮▯ Cool to moderate. Moderate to high humidity ▮◉ Biweekly. Occasionally in winter ◊ When dry. Water sparingly in winter ▭ Tip cuttings, layering

Homalomena wallisii ▷
QUEEN OF HEARTS
↕ ↔ 3ft (90cm)

The glossy, long-stalked, abruptly pointed foliage is particularly effective at removing ammonia, as well as other pollutants, from the air. A challenging plant to grow well.

☼ Moderate ▮▯ Warm, but moderate in dormancy. Dislikes drafts. High humidity ▮◉ Biweekly ◊ When soil surface just dry. Water sparingly in winter ▭ Division

OTHER BENEFICIAL HOUSE-PLANTS FOR FLORAL EFFECT

Begonia spp. and hybrids
Chrysanthemum hybrids
Clivia miniata, see p.326
Gerbera jamesonii cvs.
Schlumbergera truncata, see p.363
Tulipa hybrids, see p.401

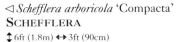

◁ *Schefflera arboricola* 'Compacta'
SCHEFFLERA
↕ 6ft (1.8m) ↔ 3ft (90cm)

Compact in habit and erect-stemmed, this easy-to-grow evergreen produces masses of shining, deep green, fingered leaves. These will absorb chemical pollutants from the air.

☼ Bright to moderate ▮▯ Moderate to warm, avoiding fluctuation. Moderate to high humidity ▮◉ Biweekly. Monthly in winter ◊ Water when dry ▭ Division, tip cuttings, air layering

△ *Spathiphyllum wallisii*
PEACE LILY
↕ ↔ 2ft (60cm)

An excellent capacity for absorbing acetone, benzene, and formaldehyde, and tolerance of low light, make this plant a winner. White spring and summer flowers.

☼ Bright, but avoid direct sun ▮▯ Moderate to warm. Moderate to high humidity ▮◉ Biweekly. Monthly in winter ◊ Water when soil mix dry. Avoid overwatering ▭ Division

SPECIFIC USES

Trailing Houseplants

TRAILING PLANTS with lax stems are excellent subjects for hanging baskets, plinths, or high shelves. Some trail naturally, while others are young specimens of plants that are really climbers. Site trailers carefully so they have plenty of room to grow without being damaged and are easily accessible for watering.

Aporocactus flagelliformis f. *flagriformis* △
RAT'S TAIL CACTUS
↕ ↔ 2ft (60cm)

In its native Mexico, this species hangs from trees, rock ledges, and crevices. It is excellent for a hanging basket but should be sited away from walkways.

☼ Bright, but avoid direct sun 🌡 Cool to warm. Moderate humidity ◦ Cactus and succulent fertilizer every three weeks, spring to autumn ◦ When dry. Rarely in winter 🝙 Division, stem cuttings, seed

OTHER TRAILING HOUSEPLANTS

Campanula isophylla, see p.332
Fuchsia 'Golden Marinka'
Glechoma hederacea 'Variegata'
Lotus maculatus
Oplismenus africanus 'Variegatus'
Rhipsalidopsis gaertneri
Sedum morganianum, see p.409

Ceropegia linearis subsp. *woodii* △
ROSARY VINE
↕ 3ft (90cm) ↔ 4in (10cm)

This apparently delicate plant is surprisingly tough and can tolerate periods of drought. Pairs of marbled, heart-shaped, succulent leaves hang from the threadlike stems, often accompanied by fascinating slender, mauve-pink vase-shaped flowers.

☼ Bright to moderate 🌡 Cool to warm. Low humidity ◦ Biweekly in summer, using high-potassium or cactus fertilizer ◦ When dry. Water sparingly in winter 🝙 Stem cuttings, tubers

△ *Epipremnum aureum*
DEVIL'S IVY
↕ 6ft (2m) ↔ 3ft (1m)

The young foliage of this handsome rainforest plant is bright green splashed with gold. Treat older plants as climbers. Easily controlled and propagated.

☼ Bright, but avoid direct sun. Variegation fades in shade 🌡 Moderate to warm. Moderate to high humidity ◦ Biweekly. Twice in winter ◦ Water when soil surface dry 🝙 Tip or stem cuttings

△ *Epipremnum* 'Neon'
DEVIL'S IVY
↕ 6ft (2m) ↔ 3ft (1m)

Unusual lime green leaves distinguish this devil's ivy, shown here when young. Initially a trailing plant, it produces climbing shoots after a year or two.

☼ Bright, but avoid direct sun. Color fades in shade 🌡 Moderate to warm. Moderate to high humidity ◦ Biweekly. Twice in winter ◦ Water when soil surface dry 🝙 Tip or stem cuttings

Saxifraga stolonifera ▷
STRAWBERRY GERANIUM
↕ ↔ 12in (30cm)

Numerous plantlets on red runners trail
from a mound of striking leaves marked
with radiating gray-green veins. It is ideal
for a cool room or minimally heated porch.

☼ Bright to moderate 🌡 Cool to warm. Moderate
humidity 💧 Biweekly. Stop feeding in winter
💧 Water when soil surface starts to dry out
✄ Division, plantlets

△ *Hedera helix* 'Midas Touch'
ENGLISH IVY
↕ 3ft (1m) or more ↔ 18in (45cm)

This vigorous ivy is worth growing for its
brightly colored, green- and yellow-
variegated leaves. One of the most
popular ivies grown as a houseplant.

☼ Bright to moderate 🌡 Cool to moderate.
Moderate to high humidity 💧 Biweekly. Twice in
winter 💧 Allow to dry before watering. Water
sparingly in winter ✄ Tip cuttings, layering

△ *Hoya lanceolata* subsp. *bella*
MINIATURE WAX PLANT
↕ ↔ 18in (45cm)

When the deliciously fragrant, waxy
flowers appear in summer, leave their
stalks on, as buds will form on them for
the next display. Also grown as a climber.

☼ Bright. Avoid direct sun 🌡 Moderate to warm.
Moderate to high humidity 💧 Every three weeks,
using flowering houseplant fertilizer. Stop in winter
💧 When dry. Rarely in winter ✄ Tip cuttings

△ *Senecio rowleyanus*
STRING OF BEADS
↕ 3ft (1m) ↔ 3in (8cm)

A strange, succulent member of the daisy
family that produces a curtain of trailing
stems with pealike leaves. Sweetly
scented white flowers appear in autumn.

☼ Bright to moderate. Avoid summer sun 🌡 Cool
to warm. Low humidity 💧 Every three weeks, using
high-potassium or cactus fertilizer. Stop in winter
💧 Water when dry. Rarely in winter ✄ Tip cuttings

△ *Tradescantia*
fluminensis 'Albovittata'
INCH PLANT, WANDERING JEW
↕ 3ft (1m) ↔ 6in (15cm)

Pure white flowers borne in summer add
interest to this fast-growing plant. Its lax
stems are clothed in fleshy, soft green
leaves, boldly marked with white stripes.

☼ Bright, but avoid summer sun. Variegation fades
in shade 🌡 Moderate to warm. Moderate to high
humidity 💧 Biweekly. Once in winter 💧 Keep
moist. When dry if cool ✄ Tip or stem cuttings

SPECIFIC USES

Climbing Houseplants

MANY CLIMBERS are native to tropical rainforests, where they clamber up tree trunks and branches in order to reach the light. Large-leaved climbers need plenty of room in which to develop, but more slender varieties are ideal for tight corners or recesses. Climbers should be trained on a moss-clad frame or pole and pruned to size.

Bougainvillea 'Mrs. Butt' ▷
BOUGAINVILLEA, PAPER FLOWER
↕ ↔ 6ft (2m) or more

Deservedly popular in tropical gardens, this plant offers stunning, crimson-shaded magenta, papery bracts. Prune back the previous year's stems hard in midwinter.

☼ Bright, sunny ⧗ Cool to warm. Moderate humidity ♦ Biweekly, using flowering houseplant fertilizer. Stop feeding in winter ♦ Water when dry. Reduce in cool conditions ▱ Tip cuttings

Monstera obliqua ▷
MONSTERA
↕ 10ft (3m) or more ↔ 4ft (1.2m)

Highly perforated leaves give this bold climber an unusual shredded look. It is worth growing for novelty value alone; train up a moss pole or similar support.

☼ Bright to moderate ⧗ Moderate to warm. Moderate to high humidity ♦ Biweekly. Once in late autumn and once in midwinter ♦ Water when soil mix just dry ▱ Stem cuttings, air layering

△ *Cissus rhombifolia*
GRAPE IVY
↕ 10ft (3m) ↔ 2ft (60cm)

Boldly toothed, glossy green leaflets cover this vigorous, tendriled plant. Trained up stakes or a trellis, it will create an attractive living screen or room divider.

☼ Bright, but avoid hot sun ⧗ Moderate to warm. Moderate to high humidity ♦ Biweekly, using foliage houseplant fertilizer. Monthly in winter ♦ Allow to dry before watering ▱ Tip cuttings

△ *Epipremnum aureum* 'Marble Queen'
DEVIL'S IVY
↕ 10ft (3m) ↔ 3ft (1m)

An outstanding climber with white-marbled foliage and white leaf stalks. The mass of eye-catching leaves is particularly distinctive when covering a moss pole.

☼ Bright, but avoid direct sun. Variegation fades in shade ⧗ Moderate to warm. Moderate to high humidity ♦ Biweekly. Twice in winter ♦ Water when soil surface dry ▱ Tip or stem cuttings

△ *Passiflora* 'Amethyst'
PASSION FLOWER
↕ ↔ 10ft (3m) or more

Vigorous even in cool climates, this plant has exotic flowers. If trained to a frame, prune long shoots to ½in (1.5cm) in spring and reattach as they grow. Leave old wood.

☼ Bright, with some sun ⧗ Moderate to warm. Moderate to high humidity ♦ Flowering houseplant fertilizer biweekly. None in winter ♦ Water when dry. Keep just moist in winter ▱ Stem cuttings

Philodendron 'Medisa' ▷
PHILODENDRON
↕ 10ft (3m) ↔ 3ft (1m)

Red shoots and leaf stalks and
large leaves, golden yellow when
young, make this a very eye-catching
plant. A forest tree-climber in the wild, in
the home it thrives best on a moss pole.

☼ Bright to moderate, avoiding direct sun
🌡 Moderate to warm. Moderate to high humidity
💧 Biweekly. Monthly in winter 💧 Water when soil
surface just dry ✄ Tip cuttings

OTHER CLIMBING HOUSEPLANTS

Cissus rhombifolia 'Ellen Danica',
    see p.376
Gelsemium sempervirens
Gloriosa superba 'Rothschildiana'
Hoya carnosa 'Tricolor'
Jasminum polyanthum, see p.323
Piper crocatum
Senecio mikanioides
Stephanotis floribunda 'Alpine'
Syngonium 'Jenny'
Tetrastigma voinierianum

Senecio macroglossus 'Variegatus' ▷
CAPE IVY, NATAL IVY
↕ 3m (10ft) ↔ 1m (3ft)

Looking like an ivy with yellow summer
and winter flowers, this daisy relative
climbs by twining stems that can be
trained up poles or thin stakes.

☼ Bright, with some sun 🌡 Cool to warm.
Moderate humidity 💧 Biweekly, from spring to
autumn 💧 When soil surface dry. Water sparingly at
low temperatures ✄ Tip cuttings

△ *Syngonium podophyllum* 'Imperial
White'
GOOSEFOOT
↕ 6ft (2m) or more ↔ 2ft (60cm)

Grow where the beautifully marked
leaves, which change shape as the plant
matures, can be appreciated. Climbing
stems may be pruned to retain bushiness.

☼ Bright to moderate, avoiding direct sun
🌡 Warm. Moderate to high humidity 💧 Biweekly,
using foliage houseplant fertilizer. Monthly in winter
💧 When dry. Reduce in winter ✄ Tip cuttings

△ *Thunbergia alata*
BLACK-EYED SUSAN VINE
↕ 6ft (2m) ↔ 12in (30cm)

This twining plant produces a display of
rich orange flowers with dark centers from
late spring to autumn, if deadheaded
regularly. Usually grown as an annual.

☼ Bright, with some sun 🌡 Moderate to warm.
Moderate humidity 💧 Biweekly once established,
using flowering houseplant fertilizer 💧 Allow soil
mix to dry out before watering ✄ Seed

393

Houseplants for Architectural Effect

NO PLANTS CONTRIBUTE more drama to the look of a room than those with large or deeply divided leaves or a striking habit. Careful siting is important if a plant's architectural qualities are to become a focal point. As a general rule, the bigger the plant and the space around it, the more effective its scale and form will appear.

Araucaria heterophylla ▷
NORFOLK ISLAND PINE
‡ 8ft (2.5m) or more ↔ 4ft (1.2m) or more

Like so many houseplants, this reaches a large size in its natural environment. Best grown indoors on a single stem, it is then less vigorous but still impressive.

☼ Bright, but avoid summer sun ▮ Moderate. Moderate humidity ◑ Biweekly. Occasionally in winter ◊ When soil surface dry. Water sparingly in winter ▦ Seed

△ *Nolina recurvata*
PONYTAIL PALM
‡ 6ft (1.8m) or more ↔ 3ft (1m) or more

An extraordinary-looking plant from Mexico that develops a bulbous base and a great topknot of slender, arching or pendulous leaves. Easy to grow.

☼ Bright, with sun ▮ Moderate to warm. Low humidity ◑ Monthly, using fertilizer for cacti and succulents ◊ When soil surface dry. Water sparingly in winter ▦ Tip cuttings, offsets, seed

△ *Cycas revoluta*
SAGO PALM
‡ ↔ 5ft (1.5m)

This primitive evergreen, not a true palm, develops its short trunk very slowly, but the stiff, leathery, deeply divided leaves are spectacular even on a young plant.

☼ Bright, but avoid direct summer sun ▮ Warm. Moderate to high humidity ◑ Monthly ◊ Water when soil surface dry ▦ Seed, buds from old or dormant plants

△ *Dracaena fragrans* 'White Stripe'
DRACAENA
‡ 6ft (2m) or more ↔ 3ft (1m)

A striking foliage plant producing stiffly erect stems and generous clusters of long, pointed green leaves with white-striped margins. This is a bold specimen plant.

☼ Bright to moderate, avoiding summer sun ▮ Warm. Moderate to high humidity ◑ Biweekly. Occasionally in winter ◊ When dry. Water sparingly in winter ▦ Tip cuttings, stem sections

OTHER NARROW-LEAVED ARCHITECTURAL HOUSEPLANTS

Cordyline australis
Dracaena draco
Pandanus veitchii, see p.341
Phormium tenax
Sansevieria trifasciata, see p.387
Yucca elephantipes, see p.385

OTHER BROAD-LEAVED
ARCHITECTURAL HOUSEPLANTS

Chamaedorea elegans, see p.412
Howea belmoreana, see p.413
Monstera deliciosa, see p.339
Pisonia umbellifera
  'Variegata'
Polyscias fruticosa
Radermachera sinica
Rhapis excelsa, see p.413

Dracaena marginata ▷
MADAGASCAR DRAGON TREE
↕ 10ft (3m) ↔ 4ft (1.2m)

Bold tufts of shining, grassy, red-edged green leaves bring a touch of the exotic to any room. This native of Madagascar is one of the most popular dracaenas for indoor cultivation.

☼ Bright to moderate, avoiding summer sun ☃ Warm, Moderate to high humidity ◐ Biweekly. Occasionally in winter ◊ When dry. Sparingly in winter ▭ Tip cuttings, stem sections

Schefflera arboricola 'Gold Capella' ▷
SCHEFFLERA
↕ 6ft (1.8m) ↔ 3ft (1m)

The umbrella tree is grown as a house-plant for its long-stalked juvenile foliage, which is divided into rich green, gold-splashed leaflets. A dark background or group setting is effective.

☼ Bright to moderate ☃ Warm, avoiding fluctuation. Moderate to high humidity ◐ Biweekly. Monthly in winter ◊ Water when soil surface dry ▭ Tip cuttings, air layering

△ *Ficus lyrata*
FIDDLE-LEAF FIG
↕ 10ft (3m) or more ↔ 6ft (1.8m) or more

Give this plant plenty of elbow room to accommodate its likely spread and show off its spectacular large, waisted leaves. This fig originates in African forests.

☼ Bright. Avoid summer sun ☃ Warm. Moderate to high humidity ◐ Biweekly. Occasionally in winter ◊ When soil surface dry. Reduce at lower temperatures ▭ Tip cuttings, air layering

Large, feather-shaped fronds

△ *Lytocaryum weddellianum*
DWARF COCONUT PALM
↕ 6ft (2m) ↔ 5ft (1.5m)

One of the most beautiful palms for the home and tolerant of low light. Handle the fragile roots with care when repotting. Formerly sold as *Microcoelum* or *Cocos*.

☼ Moderate to shady ☃ Warm. Moderate to high humidity ◐ Every three weeks ◊ When soil surface dry. Water sparingly in winter. Avoid waterlogging ▭ Seed

△ *Schefflera elegantissima* 'Castor'
FALSE ARALIA, FINGER ARALIA
↕ 6ft (2m) ↔ 3ft (90cm)

This plant produces an elegant, lacy outline. The dark coppery green leaves have long, narrow leaflets that widen with age. Also known as *Aralia* or *Dizygotheca*.

☼ Bright, avoiding direct sun ☃ Warm, avoiding fluctuation. Moderate humidity ◐ Biweekly. Monthly at low winter temperatures ◊ Water when dry. Avoid overwatering ▭ Tip cuttings, seed

SPECIFIC USES

Houseplants with Ornamental Fruit

HOUSEPLANTS WORTH growing for their fruits alone are in the minority, yet they include some very reliable and colorful varieties. Some of these are seasonal plants, useful for adding winter interest. They include capsicums, winter cherries, and shrubs such as *Aucuba* and *Skimmia*. The fruits shown here are mostly inedible, but they are not poisonous unless stated.

Capsicum annuum
'Festival Orange' △
ORNAMENTAL PEPPER
↕ ↔ 2ft (60cm)

In winter, this colorful houseplant produces conical, bright orange, long-lasting fruits, strikingly set among the dark green foliage. It will enjoy a position on a sunny windowsill.

☼ Bright, but avoid direct sun 🌡 Cool to moderate. Moderate humidity ◐ Biweekly, alternating general fertilizer with flowering houseplant fertilizer ◊ Water when soil surface just dry 🗺 Tip cuttings

Ardisia crenata ▷
CORAL BERRY
↕ 3ft (1m) ↔ 12in (30cm) or more

Grown chiefly for its colorful red berries, freely borne especially in winter, this evergreen has glossy, toothed leaves. Prune in early spring after berries finish.

☼ Bright, but avoid direct sun 🌡 Moderate. Moderate to high humidity ◐ Monthly. Occasionally in winter ◊ When soil surface dry. Reduce watering in winter 🗺 Semiripe cuttings, seed

OTHER HOUSEPLANTS WITH ORNAMENTAL FRUIT

Aechmea fulgens var. *discolor*
Ananas bracteatus 'Tricolor', see p.358
Ardisia crispa
Capsicum annuum 'Masquerade'
  Fuchsia procumbens
    Nertera balfouriana
      Punica granatum var. *nana*

Capsicum annuum ▷
CHRISTMAS PEPPER
↕ 12in (30cm)
↔ 12in (30cm) or more

Commonly available in winter, this well-known houseplant is popular for its usually conical, sometimes rounded, red or yellow, long-lasting fruits. It is usually treated as an annual pot plant.

☼ Bright 🌡 Cool to moderate. Moderate humidity ◐ Every week, alternating general fertilizer with flowering houseplant fertilizer ◊ Water when soil surface just dry 🗺 Seed

× *Citrofortunella microcarpa* ▷
CALAMONDIN ORANGE
↕ ↔ 4ft (1.2m)

Miniature oranges, 1¼–1½in (3–4cm) across, make this shrub an attractive houseplant; they are produced at almost any time, even by young plants, but are bitter to the taste.

☼ Bright, but avoid summer sun 🌡 Moderate to warm. Moderate to high humidity ◐ Biweekly, using fertilizer for acid-loving plants. Monthly in winter ◊ Water when dry 🗺 Semiripe cuttings

Rhipsalis floccosa ▷
MISTLETOE CACTUS
↕ 18in (45cm) ↔ 10in (24cm)

In spring, mistletoe-like white, sometimes pink-tinted berries are produced on the long, slender stems of this curious weeping cactus. Good for a hanging pot.

☼ Bright 🌡 Moderate to warm, with cool winter rest. Moderate to high humidity 🌢 Monthly, using flowering houseplant fertilizer. Occasionally in winter 🌢 When dry. Sparingly in winter 🌱 Stem sections

△ *Fortunella japonica*
KUMQUAT
↕ 10ft (3m) or more ↔ 5ft (1.5m) or more

Edible, golden orange fruits, lasting throughout autumn, are produced by this thorny shrub; fragrant white flowers appear in spring. Closely related to *Citrus*.

☼ Bright, but avoid summer sun 🌡 Moderate to warm. Moderate to high humidity 🌢 Biweekly, using fertilizer for acid-loving plants. Monthly in winter 🌢 Keep moist 🌱 Semiripe cuttings

Long-lasting fruits

Skimmia japonica 'Robert Fortune' ▷
SKIMMIA
↕ 2ft (60cm) ↔ 3ft (1m)

Slow-growing, and usually low-growing when cultivated as a houseplant, this evergreen shrub is a popular choice for its dense clusters of long-lasting, dark red fruits, borne from summer through to winter.

☼ Moderate to shady 🌡 Cool to moderate. Moderate humidity 🌢 Biweekly 🌢 When soil surface just dry. Reduce watering in winter 🌱 Semiripe cuttings

△ *Nertera granadensis*
BEAD PLANT, CORAL MOSS
↕ ¾in (2cm) ↔ 8in (20cm)

The mosslike, emerald green cushion or mat of slender, prostrate, interlacing stems is studded with orange berries in autumn. An irresistible plant for a windowsill.

☼ Bright. Avoid summer sun 🌡 Cool to moderate. Moderate to high humidity 🌢 Monthly. Occasionally in winter 🌢 When soil surface dry. Water sparingly in winter 🌱 Division, tip cuttings, seed

OTHER HOUSEPLANTS WITH ORNAMENTAL FRUIT

Arbutus unedo 'Elfin King'
Aucuba japonica 'Rozannie'
Duchesnea indica, see p.364
Gaultheria procumbens
Pyracantha coccinea 'Red Column'
Vaccinium vitis-idaea Koralle Group

◁ *Solanum pseudocapsicum*
JERUSALEM CHERRY
↕ ↔ 2ft (60cm)

The large, spherical, winter fruits of this plant are orange-red, bright red when ripe, and decorative but poisonous. Generally grown as an annual in the winter season.

☼ Bright, but avoid direct sun 🌡 Cool to moderate. Moderate humidity 🌢 Biweekly, alternating general fertilizer with flowering houseplant fertilizer 🌢 Water when just dry 🌱 Seed

Houseplants for Terraria

THESE CLOSED GLASS containers can be home to miniature gardens or jungles. They are draft-free and provide constant humidity and warmth, which allows a good range of interesting and ornamental plants, even "difficult" varieties, to flourish. Reasonably easy to look after, they make a distinctive focal point.

△ *Hypoestes phyllostachya*
POLKA-DOT PLANT
‡ 12in (30cm) ↔ 9in (23cm)

Pinch out the slender spikes of small flowers to preserve the effect of the pale pink-spotted leaves. For a compact habit, also pinch out the growing tips.

☼ Bright, but avoid summer sun ‡ Warm. Moderate to high humidity ◖ Biweekly. Occasionally in winter ◊ Water when soil surface just dry ⬚ Tip cuttings. Roots easily in water

Adiantum raddianum ▷
DELTA MAIDENHAIR FERN
‡ 2ft (60cm) ↔ 32in (80cm)

A mound of loosely arching, delicately divided fronds, borne on slender, wiry, shining black stalks is produced by this elegant fern from tropical South America.

☼ Moderate, avoiding direct sun ‡ Moderate to warm. Moderate to high humidity ◖ Biweekly. Monthly in winter ◊ Keep moist, but avoid waterlogging ⬚ Division, spores

△ *Hypoestes phyllostachya*
'Vinrod'
POLKA-DOT PLANT
‡ 12in (30cm) ↔ 9in (23cm)

The rich wine red leaves, marked with contrasting pink splashes, are a showy alternative to the typical polka-dot plant. Keep it compact by pinching out the growing tips and flower spikes.

☼ Bright, but avoid summer sun ‡ Warm. Moderate to high humidity ◖ Biweekly. Occasionally in winter ◊ Water when soil surface just dry ⬚ Tip cuttings. Roots easily in water

△ *Episcia cupreata*
FLAME VIOLET
‡ 6in (15cm) ↔ 12in (30cm)

A creeping, mat-forming perennial from the Amazon with attractive leaves, purple beneath and pale-veined above. The red flowers appear throughout summer.

☼ Bright to moderate, avoiding direct sun ‡ Warm. High humidity ◖ Biweekly. Occasionally in winter ◊ When soil surface just dry. Avoid waterlogging ⬚ Division, tip cuttings

△ *Fittonia verschaffeltii* var. *argyroneura*
'Mini White'
SILVER NET LEAF
‡ 4in (10cm) ↔ 12in (30cm)

This choice creeping and carpeting perennial from the rainforests of Peru has exquisitely silver-veined green leaves. A "must" for any terrarium or bottle garden.

☼ Moderate to shady, avoiding direct sun ‡ Warm. High humidity ◖ Biweekly. Occasionally in winter ◊ Keep moist, but avoid waterlogging ⬚ Tip cuttings

---

OTHER FLOWERING HOUSEPLANTS FOR TERRARIA

Episcia 'Cleopatra'
Episcia lilacina
Episcia 'Pink Panther'
Peperomia fraseri
Saintpaulia 'Blue Imp'
Saintpaulia 'Pip Squeek', see p.337
Streptocarpus saxorum, see p.337

△ *Maranta leuconeura* var. *erythroneura*
RED HERRINGBONE PLANT
↕ 10in (25cm) ↔ 12in (30cm) or more

One of the most beautiful and striking foliage plants from the rainforests of Brazil. Red herringbone plants form mats of large, pale green leaves, with darker zones and red veins.

☼ Moderate, avoiding direct sun ‖ Warm. Moderate to high humidity ◊ Biweekly. Occasionally in winter ◊ Keep moist, but avoid waterlogging. In winter, water when soil surface just dry ▥ Division, tip cuttings

△ *Pilea involucrata* 'Moon Valley'
FRIENDSHIP PLANT, PILEA
↕↔ 12in (30cm)

This trailing or creeping plant must be seen to be believed. The pale green leaves are remarkably puckered and have a network of sunken red veins. Well worth growing in a small terrarium or bell jar.

☼ Bright to moderate, with some sun ‖ Warm. Moderate to high humidity ◊ Every three weeks. Occasionally in winter ◊ Water when soil surface just dry. Avoid waterlogging ▥ Tip cuttings

△ *Pilea cadierei* 'Minima'
ALUMINUM PLANT
↕↔ 6in (15cm)

A compact form of *P. cadierei* (see p.353), with similar silver and green puckered leaves. It makes a striking specimen in a small terrarium or bell jar; in larger terraria it mixes well with green-leaved companions.

☼ Bright to moderate, with some sun ‖ Warm. Moderate to high humidity ◊ Every three weeks. Occasionally in winter ◊ Water when soil surface just dry. Avoid waterlogging ▥ Tip cuttings

△ *Peperomia obtusifolia* 'Greengold'
RADIATOR PLANT
↕↔ 10in (25cm)

Erect stems and big, fleshy, creamy yellow leaves variegated with irregular dark and pale green centers make this bushy plant spectacular when well grown.

☼ Bright to moderate, with some sun ‖ Warm. Moderate to high humidity ◊ Every three weeks. Occasionally in winter ◊ When soil surface just dry. Avoid waterlogging ▥ Tip cuttings

OTHER FOLIAGE HOUSEPLANTS FOR TERRARIA

Bertolonia marmorata
Ficus pumila 'White Sonny', see p.363
Peperomia caperata 'Little Fantasy'
Peperomia marmorata
Pilea involucrata 'Norfolk'
Pilea repens
Selaginella martensii, see p.365
Selaginella uncinata
Sonerila margaritacea 'Hendersonii'

△ *Selaginella kraussiana* 'Aurea'
SPREADING CLUBMOSS
↕ 1in (2.5cm) ↔ indefinite

This easy-to-grow fern relative produces rapidly forking, slender stems, densely crowded with tiny, yellow-green, scale-like leaves. May need reducing in size.

☼ Shady ‖ Warm. High humidity ◊ Every five weeks, using half-strength general houseplant fertilizer ◊ Water when soil surface just dry. Avoid waterlogging ▥ Stem cuttings

Dual-purpose Houseplants

An increasing number of outdoor plants are grown indoors; they include foliage plants for rooms with low heat but more commonly are flowering and bulbous plants for temporary display. So often these "one-off" plants are thrown away after their flowering season is over, when in fact they may be planted in the garden and left to flower and be enjoyed in future years.

△ *Iris reticulata*
NETTED IRIS
↕ 6in (15cm) ↔ 3in (8cm)

Planted in early autumn, this bulb bears fragrant flowers in late winter. Charming for a well-lit windowsill; plant out in a bed or rock garden in the autumn.

☼ Bright to moderate, with some sun ▮ Cool to moderate. Moderate humidity ◗ Biweekly ◌ Water sparingly, increase as growth appears, keep moist, and reduce as leaves die 🗖 Division

Aster 'Speedy Ruby Red' ▷
NEW YORK ASTER
↕ 12in (30cm) ↔ 18in (45cm)

One of several excellent dwarf New York asters, with a compact habit and reddish flowers. This plant will give a reliable early autumn display in a cool room, and is easy to divide in spring.

☼ Bright, but avoid direct sun ▮ Moderate. Moderate humidity ◗ Every three weeks ◌ Keep moist, but avoid waterlogging 🗖 Division, tip cuttings

◁ *Astilbe* 'Deutschland'
ASTILBE
↕ 20in (50cm) ↔ 12in (30cm)

Like many astilbes, this one is commonly forced to flower in early spring. It offers a lovely combination of ferny foliage and splendid, erect, plumed white flowers.

☼ Bright, with some sun ▮ Cool to moderate, with a cool winter rest. Moderate humidity ◗ Biweekly feed ◌ Keep moist 🗖 Division

Dark green ferny foliage

OTHER DUAL-PURPOSE HOUSEPLANTS

Convallaria majalis 'Fortin's Giant'
Erica carnea 'Winter Beauty'
Helleborus niger Blackthorn Group
Passiflora caerulea
Primula Polyanthus Group
Tolmiea menziesii 'Taff's Gold', see p.377

△ *Muscari armeniacum*
GRAPE HYACINTH
↕ 8in (20cm) ↔ 2in (5cm)

In autumn, plant in a pot to enjoy the sight of this cheerful-looking, blue-flowered bulb in spring. Planted outside in sun, it will quickly naturalize.

☼ Bright to moderate, with some sun ▮ Cool to moderate. Moderate humidity ◗ Biweekly ◌ Water sparingly; increase as growth appears, keep moist; reduce as leaves die 🗖 Division

Narcissus hybrids ▷
DAFFODIL
↕ 18in (45cm) ↔ 4in (10cm)

Most, if not all, daffodils make splendid flowering pot plants. Planted in autumn and forced, they can be flowering indoors as early as late winter. Plant them outside the following autumn.

☼ Bright to moderate, with some sun ◷ Cool to moderate. Moderate humidity ◊ Biweekly ◊ Water sparingly; increase as growth appears; keep moist; reduce as leaves die ⊟ Division

△ *Oxalis tetraphylla* 'Iron Cross'
GOOD LUCK PLANT, LUCKY CLOVER
↕ 10in (25cm) ↔ 6in (15cm)

Easily recognizable by its dark purple leaf markings; the flowers appear in summer. Plant it out in a sunny, well-drained spot in summer; bring back inside in autumn.

☼ Bright, with some sun ◷ Moderate to warm, but cool in winter. Moderate humidity ◊ Biweekly ◊ When soil surface dry. Water sparingly in winter ⊟ Division

△ *Puschkinia scilloides*
PUSCHKINIA
↕ 6in (15cm) ↔ 2in (5cm)

An excellent subject for a windowsill in a cool room, it should be planted in a pot in autumn for spring flowering. Afterward, dry off, store, and plant out in autumn.

☼ Bright to moderate, with some sun ◷ Cool to moderate. Moderate humidity ◊ Biweekly ◊ Water sparingly, increase as growth appears, keep moist in full growth, and reduce as leaves die ⊟ Division

◁ *Tulipa* hybrids
TULIP
↕ 2ft (60cm) ↔ 20in (50cm)

An enormous array of tulips is available for indoor use; they enjoy cool rather than heated rooms. After they flower in winter and spring, dry off, store, and plant them outside in the autumn.

☼ Bright to moderate, with some sun ◷ Cool to moderate. Moderate humidity ◊ Biweekly ◊ Water sparingly, increase as growth appears, keep moist in growth, and reduce as leaves die ⊟ Division

Bold flowers available in many colors

◁ *Primula vulgaris*
PRIMROSE
↕ 6in (15cm)
↔ 8in (20cm)

A neat habit and large, velvety flowers, produced in winter and spring, mark out this familiar perennial. Cultivars and hybrids are sold in many colors. After it has finished flowering, plant outside in a border or bed.

☼ Bright to moderate, avoiding direct sun ◷ Cool to moderate. Moderate humidity ◊ Biweekly. Monthly in winter ◊ Water when soil surface just dry ⊟ Seed

OTHER BULBOUS DUAL-PURPOSE HOUSEPLANTS

Crocus chrysanthus
Cyclamen coum
Galanthus 'Atkinsii'
Hyacinthus orientalis hybrids, see p.323
Scilla siberica

SPECIFIC USES

401

Herbs for the Kitchen

WHERE BETTER TO GROW the herbs you need for cooking than in your kitchen, giving you a constant fresh supply that is immediately at hand? There is a wide range of easy-to-grow herbs suitable for cultivating indoors. Grow them in pots on a windowledge and snip regularly to keep them compact. Replace any exhausted plants when necessary.

S P E C I F I C   U S E S

Allium schoenoprasum ▷
CHIVES
↕ ↔ 6in (15cm) or more

A favorite perennial herb for use in salads, this slender bulbous plant will soon form a clump but should not be allowed to flower. Snip off the decorative flower-heads (see inset) as they appear.

☼ Moderate ▮ Moderate, but cool in winter. Moderate humidity ◑ Biweekly ◊ When soil surface dry. Water sparingly in winter ▥ Division, seed (let flower if seed desired)

Laurus nobilis ▷
BAY
↕ 2ft (60cm) or more ↔ 12in (30cm) or more

This well-known evergreen grows into a large bush or small tree in the garden but can easily be kept at a convenient size by regular pinching of the growing tips.

☼ Bright, with some sun ▮ Moderate. Moderate humidity ◑ Feed occasionally ◊ Water when soil surface dry. Water sparingly in winter ▥ Semiripe cuttings

△ *Mentha × piperita*
BLACK PEPPERMINT
↕ ↔ 6in (15cm) or more

Hardy, fast-creeping, and clump-forming, with dark stems and fragrant green leaves, this perennial is easily controlled by pinching. Use in teas to aid digestion.

☼ Bright, with some direct sun ▮ Moderate to warm. Moderate humidity ◑ Occasional feed ◊ Keep moist. Water sparingly in winter ▥ Division, cuttings

△ *Mentha spicata* 'Crispa'
CURLY SPEARMINT
↕ ↔ 6in (15cm) or more

Crinkly leaves mark this form of the most popular and commonly cultivated garden mint. It is very vigorous but can be kept to a manageable size by regular snipping.

☼ Bright, with some direct sun ▮ Moderate to warm. Moderate humidity ◑ Occasional feed ◊ Keep consistently moist. Water sparingly in winter ▥ Division, cuttings

△ *Ocimum basilicum*
SWEET BASIL
↕ ↔ 6in (15cm) or more

Strongly scented leaves from this annual or short-lived perennial give a spicy flavor to salads and other foods. Pinch out the flowers as they appear.

☼ Bright, with some direct sun ▮ Warm. Moderate humidity ◑ Biweekly, using foliage houseplant fertilizer ◊ Water when soil surface dry ▥ Seed, cuttings

△ *Origanum vulgare*
OREGANO, WILD MARJORAM

↕ ↔ 6in (15cm) or more

The pungent, peppery-flavored leaves of this bushy, woody-based perennial are used in bouquet garni. Chew the leaves to gain temporary relief from toothache.

☀ Bright ▌ Moderate to warm. Moderate humidity
♦ Feed occasionally ◊ When soil surface dry.
Water sparingly in winter ▣ Division, semiripe cuttings, seed

△ *Petroselinum crispum*
CURLED PARSLEY

↕ ↔ 6in (15cm)

Commonly grown, this bushy biennial herb has congested clusters of emerald green curly foliage and is popular as a flavoring or garnish. Treat as an annual.

☀ Bright to moderate, avoiding direct sun ▌ Low to moderate. Moderate humidity ♦ Biweekly
◊ Keep consistently moist. Reduce watering in winter ▣ Seed

OTHER HERBS FOR THE KITCHEN

Anethum graveolens (dill)
Anthriscus cerefolium (chervil)
Artemisia dracunculus (French tarragon)
Coriandrum sativum (cilantro)
Cymbopogon citratus (lemon grass)
Origanum majorana (sweet marjoram)
Rumex scutatus (French sorrel)
Sanguisorba minor (salad burnet)

△ *Rosmarinus officinalis* Prostratus Group
PROSTRATE ROSEMARY

↕ 6in (15cm) ↔ 12in (30cm) or more

A low-growing, spreading form of the popular rosemary, whose aromatic leaves flavor shellfish, pork, and lamb. Blue flowers appear in spring and summer.

☀ Bright ▌ Moderate to warm. Moderate humidity
♦ Feed occasionally ◊ Water when soil surface dry. In winter, water sparingly ▣ Semiripe cuttings, layering

△ *Salvia officinalis*
COMMON SAGE

↕ ↔ 12in (30cm) or more

Pinch out the tips of this evergreen subshrub regularly to maintain a compact habit. Its pungent leaves are used for stuffing poultry and flavoring meat.

☀ Bright ▌ Moderate to warm. Moderate humidity
♦ Occasional feed ◊ Water when soil surface dry. Water sparingly in winter ▣ Tip or semiripe cuttings, layering, seed

---

△ *Thymus* x *citriodorus* 'Aureus'
LEMON-SCENTED THYME

↕ 6in (15cm) ↔ 8in (20cm)

A pretty, bushy, evergreen shrublet densely clothed in tiny, gold-dappled, lemon-scented leaves. This excellent herb is both useful and ornamental.

☀ Bright ▌ Moderate to warm. Moderate humidity
♦ Feed only if growth poor and leaves yellow
◊ Water when soil surface dry ▣ Division; tip or semiripe cuttings

△ *Thymus vulgaris*
COMMON THYME

↕ 6in (15cm) ↔ 10in (25cm)

Thyme is commonly used in bouquet garni and as a flavoring for soups and stews. A dense evergreen shrublet of spreading habit, it has tiny green leaves.

☀ Bright ▌ Moderate to warm. Moderate humidity
♦ Feed only if growth poor and leaves yellow
◊ Water when soil surface dry ▣ Division, semiripe cuttings, seed

SPECIFIC USES

SPECIALIST PLANTS

COLLECTING MEMBERS of a particular plant family or group is a satisfying and challenging way of growing houseplants. Although members of a family may be botanically related, they often differ greatly in appearance as well as in their individual cultivation requirements.

Succulent *Aeonium* 'Zwartkop' for special interest

The popularity of some specialist plant collections may lie in the challenge of growing "difficult" plants. However, as well as those that demand skill and experience, there are houseplant groups that are fairly easy to grow, offering gardeners – especially beginners – the encouragement they need.

△ LONG-LASTING ORCHID *The long life of these large heads of delicately colored orchid blooms adds to their appeal.*

SELECTING A PLANT GROUP

There are several factors to bear in mind when choosing a family or group of plants to collect. Beyond personal preference, there are the questions of facilities and space. Not every home can provide the different levels of temperature, light, and humidity required by, say, humidity-loving bromeliads and shade-loving ferns. Some groups require large amounts of space: palms, for example, are not suitable for a small room. It is little wonder that cacti and succulents, with their abundance of dwarf or compact, easy-to-grow species have proved such favorites: they can be comfortably contained on a sunny windowsill or similar position.

Some groups, such as the huge orchid family, offer a wide variety of flower form, color, or both. For successful orchid cultivation, bear in mind that some are epiphytes, growing on trees and rocks in the wild, while some are terrestrial, rooting in the ground. There is also an extensive range of plants with curious or even abnormal growth habits or foliage, which can make an interesting and unusual collection.

◁ FERN COLLECTION *Making the most of a cool, shady wall, this magnificent group of adiantum, asplenium, and nephrolepis displays the variety of leaf textures and growth habits to great effect.*

▷ BRIGHT BROMELIAD *The bold-colored flowerheads of most bromeliads make them eminently collectable. A warm kitchen provides the perfect opportunity to grow an assortment of these plants.*

Ferns of Special Interest

A GROUP OF FERNS is one of the most fascinating and satisfying of plant collections because of their great variety, lush foliage, and their acceptance of less than perfect growing conditions. Few plants are more tolerant of low light, and while those of rainforest or tropical origin require warmth and high humidity if they are to thrive, there are many varieties that enjoy cooler conditions or even a barely heated room.

△ *Didymochlaena truncatula*
CLOAK FERN
↕ 4ft (1.2m) ↔ 3ft (90cm)

A large but graceful plant when mature, the cloak fern is prized for its shining green, deeply divided fronds, tinted rosy pink when young. Develops a short stem.

☼ Moderate to shady, avoiding summer sun
❄ Moderate to warm. High humidity ◊ Biweekly. Occasionally in winter ◊ Keep moist, but avoid waterlogging. Reduce in winter ▦ Division, spores

Adiantum 'Bicolor' ▷
MAIDENHAIR FERN
↕ ↔ 12in (30cm)

One of many lovely maidenhairs, with the elegant characteristics of its relatives including prettily divided, emerald green fronds. Ideal for a bathroom window.

☼ Moderate to shady, avoiding direct sun
❄ Moderate to warm, avoiding drafts. Moderate to high humidity ◊ Biweekly. Monthly in winter
◊ Keep moist ▦ Division, spores

△ *Asplenium nidus*
BIRD'S NEST FERN
↕ ↔ 3ft (90cm)

Named for its large shuttlecocks or clumps of bold, glossy green fronds, this tropical fern can be very tolerant of home conditions. Excellent for bathrooms.

☼ Moderate. Avoid direct sun ❄ Warm, avoiding fluctuation and drafts. Moderate to high humidity
◊ Biweekly, using foliage houseplant fertilizer. Occasionally in winter ◊ Keep moist ▦ Spores

Blechnum gibbum ▷
DWARF TREE FERN
↕ 30in (75cm) ↔ 2ft (60cm)

This handsome fern from Fiji and New Caledonia develops a fine crown of deeply and regularly divided, leathery fronds. In time, the dwarf tree fern forms a short, densely scaly false stem.

☼ Bright to shady, avoiding direct sun ❄ Moderate to warm. High humidity ◊ Biweekly. Occasionally in winter ◊ Water when soil surface dry ▦ Spores

△ *Nephrolepis exaltata* 'Bostoniensis'
BOSTON FERN

↕ ↔ 3ft (90cm) or more

One of the most popular parlor ferns
ever, especially in North
America. It can grow to a
substantial size, so is suitable for large
containers or a strong hanging basket.

☼ Bright to moderate, avoiding direct sun
🌡 Moderate to warm. Moderate to high humidity
💧 Biweekly. Monthly in winter △ Keep consistently
moist 🗒 Division, spores

OTHER FERNS OF SPECIAL INTEREST

Adiantum raddianum 'Gracillimum'
Asplenium bulbiferum
Dicksonia antarctica
Microlepia speluncae
Onychium japonicum
Pteris multifida

△ *Platycerium bifurcatum*
STAGHORN FERN

↕ 3ft (90cm) ↔ 4ft (1.2m)

This handsome if curious
fern, a tree-dweller from
the tropics, will in time
develop into a magnificent feature
plant. The staghorn fern is especially effective when
displayed in a large hanging basket.

☼ Bright, but avoid summer sun 🌡 Moderate to warm.
Moderate to high humidity 💧 Monthly △ When
soil surface almost dry 🗒 Spores

△ *Polypodium aureum* 'Mandaianum'
HARE'S-FOOT FERN

↕ 30in (75cm) ↔ 5ft (1.5m)

Also known as *Phlebodium*, this striking
fern has a creeping rootstock and large,
arching, deeply divided gray-green fronds.
It is ideal for a hanging basket.

☼ Bright to moderate, avoiding direct sun
🌡 Moderate to warm. Moderate to high humidity
💧 Monthly △ Keep moist, but avoid waterlogging
🗒 Rhizomes, spores

△ *Pellaea rotundifolia*
BUTTON FERN

↕ 8in (20cm) ↔ 12in (30cm)

Tolerant of brighter light than most ferns,
this New Zealand plant forms a loose
hummock of hairy, deeply divided fronds.
It is ideal for growing in a small pot.

☼ Moderate, avoiding direct sun 🌡 Moderate.
High humidity 💧 Biweekly. Monthly feed in winter
△ Keep soil mix moist, but avoid waterlogging
🗒 Division, spores

OTHER FERNS FOR HANGING BASKETS

Adiantum diaphanum
Blechnum penna-marina
Davallia canariensis
Davallia mariesii
Goniophlebium biauriculatum

△ *Pteris cretica* 'Albolineata'
VARIEGATED TABLE FERN

↕ 18in (45cm) ↔ 2ft (60cm)

An impressive fern with loose clumps of
erect then arching, deeply divided fronds,
whose narrow-fingered lobes have a bold
stripe along the midrib. Easy to grow.

☼ Bright, but avoid direct sun 🌡 Warm. Moderate
to high humidity 💧 Biweekly. Monthly in winter
△ Keep soil mix moist, but avoid waterlogging
🗒 Division, spores

407

Cacti and Succulents of Special Interest

RELATIVELY EASY to grow, cacti and succulents introduce many people, especially children, to the world of plants. Most enjoy or will tolerate dry air, although this is no reason to neglect them. Curious growth forms and colorful flowers are among their specialties.

Aeonium 'Zwartkop' ▷
BLACK AEONIUM
↕ ↔ 3ft (90cm)

A dramatic plant that slowly grows into a succulent "tree" with bold rosettes of shining, blackish purple leaves. Large heads of yellow flowers appear in spring or early summer.

☼ Bright, with direct sun ≡ Warm, but cool to moderate in winter. Low humidity ◑ Monthly, using fertilizer for cacti and succulents ◊ When soil surface dry. Water sparingly in winter ▭ Leaf cuttings, leaves, rosettes

△ *Orbea variegata*
STARFISH CACTUS
↕ 4in (10cm) ↔ 12in (30cm)

Easy to grow and tolerant of neglect, this succulent forms clusters of toothed stems. The strong-smelling, star-shaped summer flowers have an exquisite mosaic pattern.

☼ Bright, with sun ≡ Warm, but cool to moderate in winter. Low humidity ◑ Monthly, using fertilizer for cacti and succulents ◊ When soil surface dry. Water sparingly in winter ▭ Stem sections

△ *Lithops salicola*
LIVING STONE
↕ 2in (5cm) ↔ 9in (23cm)

One of a large group that mimics the pebbles among which they grow in the semidesert regions of southern Africa. It flowers from summer to midautumn.

☼ Bright, with sun ≡ Warm, but cool to moderate in winter. Low humidity ◑ Monthly, using fertilizer for cacti and succulents ◊ When soil surface dry. Water sparingly in winter ▭ Offsets

△ *Mammillaria zeilmanniana* 'Ubinkii'
ROSE PINCUSHION
↕ 6in (15cm) ↔ 12in (30cm)

Excellent for beginners because it is free-flowering, even when young. Compact at first, then slowly dividing to form a broad cluster, it bears rose-pink spring flowers.

☼ Bright, with sun ≡ Warm, but cool to moderate in winter. Low humidity ◑ Monthly, using fertilizer for cacti and succulents ◊ When soil surface dry. Water sparingly in winter ▭ Offsets

△ *Oreocereus trollii*
OLD MAN OF THE ANDES
↕ 3ft (90cm) ↔ 2ft (60cm)

This cactus, multibranched when mature, forms erect, ribbed stems, clothed in long white hairs and lined with clusters of spines. Bears pink flowers in summer.

☼ Bright, with sun ≡ Warm, but cool to moderate in winter. Low humidity ◑ Monthly, using fertilizer for cacti and succulents ◊ When soil surface dry. Water sparingly in winter ▭ Offsets

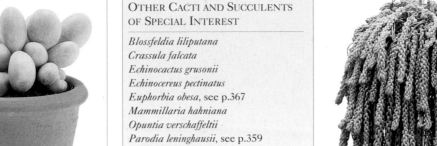

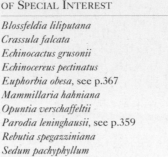

OTHER CACTI AND SUCCULENTS OF SPECIAL INTEREST

Blossfeldia liliputana
Crassula falcata
Echinocactus grusonii
Echinocereus pectinatus
Euphorbia obesa, see p.367
Mammillaria hahniana
Opuntia verschaffeltii
Parodia leninghausii, see p.359
Rebutia spegazziniana
Sedum pachyphyllum

△ *Pachyphytum oviferum*
MOONSTONES

↕ 6in (15cm) ↔ 12in (30cm)

Clusters of smooth, egg-shaped, light green, white-bloomy leaves are flushed lavender-blue. Spikes of orange-red flowers are borne from winter to spring.

☼ Bright, with sun 🌡 Warm, but cool to moderate in winter. Low humidity 💧 Monthly, using fertilizer for cacti and succulents 💧 When soil surface dry. Water sparingly in winter 🎬 Leaf cuttings

Sedum morganianum ▷
BURRO'S TAIL, DONKEY'S TAIL

↕ 3ft (90cm) ↔ 12in (30cm)

This popular succulent, native to Mexico, has a prostrate habit in the wild but is usually grown in a hanging basket to show off its long, blue-green, leafy stems.

☼ Bright, with sun 🌡 Warm, but cool to moderate in winter. Low humidity 💧 Monthly, using fertilizer for cacti and succulents 💧 When soil surface dry. Water sparingly in winter 🎬 Stem cuttings, leaves

Ribbed, spiny stem

Pachypodium lamerei ▷
MADAGASCAR PALM

↕ 6ft (2m) or more
↔ 5ft (1.5m) or more

The spiny stems of this small, treelike, eventually branching succulent bear long, narrow leaves in terminal clusters. White, yellow-throated flowers appear in summer.

☼ Bright, with sun 🌡 Warm, but cool to moderate in winter. Low humidity 💧 Monthly, using fertilizer for cacti and succulents 💧 When soil surface dry. Water sparingly in winter 🎬 Tip cuttings, seed

△ *Selenicereus grandiflorus*
QUEEN OF THE NIGHT

↕ 10ft (3m) or more ↔ 3ft (1m) or more

A plant to enjoy at night – its 12in (30cm) long, richly fragrant, creamy white flowers, borne in summer, open only after dark. The long stems need supporting.

☼ Bright, with sun 🌡 Warm, but moderate in winter. Low humidity 💧 Monthly, using fertilizer for cacti and succulents 💧 When soil surface dry. Water sparingly in winter 🎬 Stem sections

SPECIALIST PLANTS

Orchids of Special Interest

CONTRARY TO popular belief, orchids are not the preserve of specialist growers; many orchids are relatively easy to grow and are now usually available at garden centers. Follow the cultivation notes given here, use specialized orchid mixes (often bark and peat mixes), and these plants will give great satisfaction.

Cattleya hybrids ▷
CATTLEYA
↕ 8in (20cm) ↔ 18in (45cm)

These sumptuous blooms, 5in (12cm) across, are available in a range of colors and bloom seasons. Grow in epiphytic orchid mix in a pot or orchid basket.

☼ Bright to moderate, avoiding direct sun ≣ Moderate to warm. High humidity ◗ Feed with every third watering ◊ When mix surface just moist. Water sparingly in winter ▦ Division

△ *Miltoniopsis* hybrids
PANSY ORCHID
↕ ↔ 9in (23cm)

These beautiful orchids produce large, fragrant, velvet-textured, pansylike blooms in autumn. Grow in epiphytic orchid mix in a pot or orchid basket.

☼ Moderate to shady ≣ Moderate. High humidity ◗ Feed with every third watering ◊ Water when mix just dry. Reduce watering at lower temperatures ▦ Division

Cymbidium hybrids ▷
CYMBIDIUM
↕ 30in (75cm) ↔ 36in (90cm)

Among the most popular and reliable orchids for the home, with long-lasting flowers appearing from winter into spring. Available in a wide range of colors. Grow in any orchid mix.

☼ Bright, with some winter sun ≣ Moderate to warm. Moderate humidity ◗ Biweekly, using half-strength flowering houseplant fertilizer. Monthly in winter ◊ Keep moist, but avoid waterlogging. Reduce watering in winter ▦ Division

△ *Paphiopedilum insigne* hybrids
SLIPPER ORCHID
↕ 6in (15cm) ↔ 10in (25cm)

From autumn until spring, leathery basal leaves are complemented by leafless shoots, each bearing one or more large flowers with pouched lips. Grow in a pot, using terrestrial orchid mix.

☼ Bright to moderate, avoiding direct sun ≣ Moderate to warm. High humidity ◗ Feed with every third watering. Occasionally in winter ◊ Keep moist. In winter, water when barely moist ▦ Division

Widely arching, strap-shaped leaves

OTHER ORCHIDS OF SPECIAL INTEREST

x *Brassolaeliocattleya* hybrids
Cattleya mini hybrids
x *Doritaenopsis* hybrids
x *Laeliocattleya* hybrids
Ludisia discolor
Phalaenopsis equestris hybrids

Phalaenopsis hybrids ▷
MOTH ORCHID
↕ 3ft (1m) ↔ 18in (45cm)

Named the moth orchid after the winglike shape of its blooms, which are borne in arching sprays throughout the year. Grow in epiphytic orchid mix in a basket or on a piece of bark.

☼ Bright, but avoid scorching sun
☷ Warm, avoiding drafts. High humidity
💧 Biweekly, using half-strength orchid fertilizer. Monthly in winter
💧 Keep moist, but avoid waterlogging
✂ Division

△ *Pleione bulbocodioides*
PLEIONE
↕ 6in (15cm) ↔ 2in (5cm)

A dwarf, spring-flowering orchid that likes cooler conditions than most and is suited to a sunless windowsill. Grow in epiphytic orchid mix and allow a winter rest.

☼ Bright to moderate, avoiding direct sun ☷ Cool to moderate. Moderate humidity 💧 Biweekly when in leaf, using high-potassium fertilizer 💧 Keep moist after flowering. Keep dry when dormant ✂ Division

△ *Psychopsis papilio*
BUTTERFLY ORCHID
↕ 2ft (60cm) ↔ 12in (30cm)

This epiphytic orchid is a parent of several hybrids; its racemes of exquisite flowers are borne throughout the year. Grow in a basket or on bark.

☼ Moderate to shady, avoiding direct sun
☷ Warm, avoiding fluctuation. High humidity
💧 Every three weeks 💧 Keep moist, but avoid waterlogging ✂ Division

---

OTHER ORCHIDS OF SPECIAL INTEREST

Colmanara hybrids
Cymbidium mini hybrids
Dendrodium nobile (Yamamoto type) hybrids
Dendrobium x *Phalaenopsis* hybrids
x *Odontioda* hybrids
Odontoglossum hybrids
Oncidium hybrids
Paphiopedilum primulinum hybrids

Ruffled flowers with marbled color

△ *Phragmipedium* hybrids
SLIPPER ORCHID
↕ ↔ 2ft (60cm)

These terrestrial orchids produce racemes of pouched flowers at intervals throughout the year. Best grown in epiphytic orchid mix in a pot that restricts the roots.

☼ Bright to moderate, avoiding direct sun
☷ Moderate to warm. High humidity 💧 Feed with every third watering. Occasionally in winter 💧 Keep moist. In winter, water when just moist ✂ Division

◁ x *Vuylstekeara*
Cambria 'Plush'
VUYLSTEKEARA
↕ 9in (23cm) ↔ 18in (45cm)

Ruffled, marbled flowers of many colors appear from spring to autumn on this popular plant, a hybrid of *Cochlioda*, *Miltonia*, and *Odontoglossum*. Grow it in epiphytic orchid mix.

☼ Bright to moderate, avoiding direct sun
☷ Moderate to warm, but cool in winter. High humidity 💧 Monthly. Occasionally in winter
💧 Keep moist. Water sparingly in winter ✂ Division

Palms of Special Interest

FEW PLANTS bring a touch of the exotic to the home more readily than palms. Their often large, fan- or feather-shaped evergreen leaves provide any room with a focal point and a sense of visual drama. Palms grow in some of the world's wildest terrains, but many thrive indoors, where they will tolerate less than perfect conditions.

Caryota mitis ▷
BURMESE FISHTAIL PALM
‡ 10ft (3m) or more ↔ 6ft (2m) or more

This plant is easily recognized by the characteristic fishtail segments of its large, frondlike, arching leaves. A fairly easy palm to grow indoors, but it will need plenty of room in which to develop.

☼ Bright to moderate, avoiding summer sun ☷ Moderate to warm. High humidity ◊ Biweekly, using foliage houseplant fertilizer. Monthly in winter ◊ Water when dry. Avoid waterlogging ▦ Seed

Chrysalidocarpus lutescens ▷
ARECA PALM
‡ 6ft (2m) or more ↔ 4ft (1.2m) or more

Naturally clump-forming, this popular palm from Madagascar has numerous erect, slender stems, initially clothed with yellow leaf bases. These later develop into arching, feathery, rich green leaves.

☼ Bright to moderate, avoiding hot sun ☷ Moderate to warm. Moderate to high humidity ◊ Biweekly, using foliage houseplant fertilizer. Monthly in winter ◊ Water when dry. Avoid waterlogging ▦ Seed

Chamaedorea elegans ▷
PARLOR PALM
‡ ↔ 6ft (2m)

Easily the most popular palm for the home, this plant is fast-growing, elegant, and tolerant of neglect and unfavorable conditions. It is found in Mexican rainforests.

☼ Bright to moderate. Avoid hot sun ☷ Moderate to warm. Moderate to high humidity ◊ Biweekly, using foliage houseplant fertilizer. Monthly in winter ◊ Water when dry. Avoid waterlogging ▦ Seed

Cyrtostachys lakka ▷
LIPSTICK PALM
‡ 10ft (3m) or more ↔ 5ft (1.5m) or more

One of the most beautiful and colorful palms, this native of southeast Asia has slender, brilliant scarlet stems supporting erect clusters of feathery leaves.

☼ Bright to moderate, avoiding summer sun ☷ Warm. High humidity ◊ Biweekly, using foliage houseplant fertilizer. Monthly in winter ◊ When soil surface dry. Avoid waterlogging ▦ Seed

Howea belmoreana ▷
SENTRY PALM

↕ 10ft (3m) or more

↔ 6ft (2m) or more

A relative of the popular kentia palm, *Howea forsteriana*, and just as tolerant of low light levels and neglect. With maturity, the leaves of the sentry palm develop their large, curved, wide green leaflets.

☀ Bright to moderate, avoiding summer sun 🌡 Warm. Moderate to high humidity 💧 Biweekly, using foliage houseplant fertilizer. Monthly in winter 💧 Water when dry. Avoid waterlogging 🌱 Seed

Phoenix roebelenii ▷
PYGMY DATE PALM

↕ 10ft (3m) ↔ 6ft (2m) or more

With its spreading head of feathery leaves on a slender stem rough with old leaf bases, this is the perfect miniature indoor palm tree. Tolerant of low light levels and neglect, it will thrive if given care.

☀ Bright to moderate, avoiding summer sun 🌡 Moderate to warm. Moderate to high humidity 💧 Biweekly, using foliage houseplant fertilizer. Monthly in winter 💧 Water when dry. Avoid waterlogging 🌱 Seed

OTHER PALMS OF SPECIAL INTEREST

Caryota urens
Chamaedorea erumpens
Chamaedorea metallica
Chamaedorea stolonifera
Euterpe edulis
Hedyscepe canterburyana
Howea forsteriana
   Laccospadix australasica
     Lytocaryum weddellianum, see p.395
     Ravenea rivularis, see p.371
     Reinhardtia gracilis

△ *Phoenix canariensis*
CANARY ISLAND DATE PALM

↕ 15ft (5m) or more ↔ 6ft (2m) or more

Large, pinnate leaves give this date palm architectural interest. It is one of the most common garden palms in warm regions of the world, and it is a superb houseplant.

☀ Bright to moderate. Avoid hot sun 🌡 Moderate to warm. Moderate humidity 💧 Biweekly, using foliage houseplant fertilizer. Monthly in winter 💧 Water when dry. Avoid waterlogging 🌱 Seed

Rhapis excelsa △
LADY PALM

↕ 10ft (3m) ↔ 4ft (1.2m)

A fine indoor palm with its dense clump of erect, leafy, bamboolike stems, the leaf blades fan-shaped with long, fingered segments. It is tolerant of neglect.

☀ Bright to moderate. Avoid hot sun 🌡 Moderate to warm. Moderate humidity 💧 Biweekly, using foliage houseplant fertilizer. Monthly in winter 💧 Water when dry. Avoid waterlogging 🌱 Seed

△ *Washingtonia robusta*
THREAD PALM

↕ 10ft (3m) or more ↔ 6ft (2m)

Native to northwest Mexico, this fast-growing palm enjoys good light and is best suited to the garden room. Develops a single stem with fan-shaped leaves.

☀ Bright to moderate. Avoid hot sun 🌡 Moderate to warm. Moderate humidity 💧 Biweekly, using foliage houseplant fertilizer. Monthly in winter 💧 Water when dry. Avoid waterlogging 🌱 Seed

SPECIALIST PLANTS

Bromeliads of Special Interest

ALMOST ALL BROMELIADS originate in tropical or sub-tropical America. There is a multitude of species, varying remarkably in shape and color, although most grown indoors are rosette-forming plants popular for foliage, flowers, or both. Many look equally good in pots or hanging baskets.

△ *Billbergia* x *windii*
BILLBERGIA
↕ ↔ 2ft (60cm)

A handsome, clump-forming hybrid with long, arching, strap-shaped green leaves. It bears pendulous heads of green flowers from rose-pink bracts in summer.

☼ Bright, with some sun ▮ Moderate to warm. Moderate to high humidity ◉ Biweekly, using flowering houseplant fertilizer ◊ Water when soil surface just dry ▭ Offsets

---

△ *Aechmea morganii*
URN PLANT
↕ 2ft (60cm) ↔ 30in (75cm)

Striking for foliage and flowers, this big, bold bromeliad bears a rosette of glossy, dark green, strap-shaped, loosely arching leaves and branched spikes of pink bracts and blue summer flowers.

☼ Bright, but avoid summer sun ▮ Warm. Low to moderate humidity ◉ Biweekly, using flowering houseplant fertilizer ◊ Water when soil surface dry. Water sparingly in winter ▭ Offsets

---

OTHER BROMELIADS FOR FOLIAGE INTEREST

Ananas bracteatus 'Tricolor', see p.358
Billbergia Fantasia Group
Cryptanthus 'Pink Starlight'
Neoregelia carolinae 'Tricolor Perfecta'
Vriesea carinata
Vriesea 'Tiffany'

◁ *Ananas comosus* 'Variegatus'
IVORY PINEAPPLE
↕ 3ft (90cm) ↔ 2ft (60cm)

Creamy white-margined, dark green leaves, flushed red when young, make this pineapple special; the summer flowers, followed by the fruit, are a bonus. Place with care; the leaves are spiny.

☼ Bright ▮ Warm. Moderate to high humidity ◉ Biweekly, using flowering houseplant fertilizer ◊ Water when soil surface begins to dry out ▭ Offsets, rosettes

---

△ *Cryptanthus zonatus* 'Zebrinus'
EARTH STAR
↕ 5in (12cm) ↔ 16in (40cm)

A striking, star-shaped rosette plant with leathery, wavy-margined leaves, banded zebra fashion with dark gray-green and silver. Grows among rocks in east Brazil.

☼ Bright to shady, avoiding direct sun ▮ Warm. Moderate to high humidity ◉ Monthly, using flowering houseplant fertilizer. Rarely in winter ◊ Water when soil surface dry ▭ Offsets

SPECIALIST PLANTS

△ *Neoregelia carolinae* f. *tricolor*
BLUSHING BROMELIAD
↕ 12in (30cm) ↔ 2ft (60cm)

This spectacular Brazilian rainforest plant has a dense, bold rosette of spine-toothed, shiny green leaves, striped yellowish white and red. In the summer flowering season, it has a red heart, hence its common name.

☼ Bright, but avoid summer sun 🌡 Warm. High humidity
💧 Biweekly, using flowering houseplant fertilizer 💧 Water when soil surface dry 🔲 Offsets

△ *Vriesea hieroglyphica*
KING OF BROMELIADS
↕ 3ft (90cm) ↔ 39in (1m)

An impressive plant with purple-backed leaves that are yellowish green with darker bands above. Yellow and green flowerheads are borne in summer on erect stems.

☼ Moderate 🌡 Warm. Moderate to high humidity 💧 Every three weeks 💧 Water when soil surface dry 🔲 Offsets, seed

Tillandsia cyanea ▷
BLUE-FLOWERED TORCH
↕ 12in (30cm)
↔ 8in (20cm)

This striking epiphyte from Ecuador bears tufted rosettes of slender, curved, and channeled leaves, topped in late spring or autumn by a paddle-shaped head of rose bracts and violet-blue flowers.

☼ Bright, but avoid direct sun 🌡 Warm. Low to moderate humidity 💧 Every two months, using flowering houseplant fertilizer 💧 Water when soil surface dry 🔲 Offsets

OTHER BROMELIADS FOR FLOWER AND BRACT INTEREST

Aechmea chantinii, see p.366
Aechmea fasciata, see p.324
Aechmea Foster's Favorite Group
Billbergia nutans
Billbergia pyramidalis
Guzmania lingulata var. *minor*
Guzmania sanguinea
Tillandsia lindenii

◁ *Tillandsia wagneriana*
AIR PLANT
↕ ↔ 18in (45cm)

Unusual flower spikes with bracts of lavender adorn this epiphyte from the Peruvian Amazon in late spring or autumn, topping a bold, urn-shaped rosette of wavy-margined, crisp green or reddish leaves.

☼ Bright, but avoid direct sun 🌡 Warm. Moderate to high humidity 💧 Every two months, using flowering houseplant fertilizer 💧 Water when soil surface dry 🔲 Offsets

△ *Vriesea splendens*
FLAMING SWORD
↕ 3ft (90cm) ↔ 12in (30cm)

Worth growing for its rosettes of pale green leaves banded darker green, purple, or reddish brown. Red-scaled flowerheads on erect stems add summer interest.

☼ Moderate, avoiding direct sun 🌡 Moderate to warm. Moderate to high humidity 💧 Every three weeks, using flowering houseplant fertilizer 💧 Water when soil surface just dry 🔲 Offsets

SPECIALIST PLANTS

Novelty Houseplants

Plants that serve as conversation pieces are welcome in any home. Spectacular flowers and impressive foliage always catch the eye, but so too do plants with an amusing growth habit or with some peculiarity of leaf or flower. Plants not usually grown indoors, or those with a fascinating history, also make good subjects. Novelty plants engage children's imaginations and with luck will inspire a desire to know more about plants.

△ *Dionaea muscipula*
VENUS FLYTRAP
↕ 18in (45cm) ↔ 6in (15cm)

A fascinating, insectivorous, short-lived perennial of fierce appearance that you can feed with flies or tiny fragments of raw meat. Prefers rainwater to any other.

☼ Bright, with sun ▮ Moderate to warm. High humidity ◊ Feed if desired, but do not overfeed. Plant will also catch its own food ◊ Stand pot in a tray and keep waterlogged ▦ Division, leaf cuttings

---

OTHER SUCCULENT NOVELTY HOUSEPLANTS

Conophytum bilobum
Dorstenia foetida
Faucaria tigrina, see p.355
Fenestraria aurantiaca
Haworthia truncata
Kalanchoe daigremontiana
Lithops optica
Orbea variegata, see p.408

Ananas comosus
'Porteanus' △
PINEAPPLE
↕ 3ft (1m) ↔ 20in (50cm)

This plant has a handsome green rosette with spiny teeth. You can root a pineapple from the severed leafy top of a pineapple fruit, or try growing one from an offset.

☼ Bright, with sun ▮ Warm. Moderate to high humidity ◊ Biweekly, using flowering houseplant fertilizer ◊ When just dry ▦ Offsets, rosettes

Capsicum annuum
'Festival' ▷
ORNAMENTAL PEPPER
↕ ↔ 2ft (60cm)

Extremely ornamental and unusual, this small, bushy evergreen produces an eye-catching variety of different colored fruits on one plant. It is normally treated as an annual and sold as an ornamental winter plant.

☼ Bright, but avoid direct sun ▮ Cool to moderate. Moderate humidity ◊ Biweekly, alternating general fertilizer with flowering houseplant fertilizer ◊ When soil surface just dry ▦ Seed

△ *Epiphyllum laui*
NIGHT-FLOWERING CACTUS
↕ 12in (30cm) ↔ 2ft (60cm) or more

A night-flowering Mexican cactus whose fragrant, exotic-looking white flowers are produced in early summer (they may sometimes also open in daylight).

☼ Bright. Avoid direct sun ▮ Moderate to warm. Moderate to high humidity ◊ Biweekly, from bud formation until flowering ends ◊ When just dry. Water sparingly in winter ▦ Stem cuttings, seed

Euphorbia pulcherrima 'Silver Star' ▷
POINSETTIA
↕ ↔ 20in (50cm)

Poinsettias seem to be everywhere in winter, but this variety, with its strange mixture of leaf and bract colors, is uncommon. It would make an interesting addition to a group of red-bracted poinsettias.

☼ Bright ❄️ Warm, avoiding drafts and fluctuating temperatures. Moderate to high humidity 🌢 Monthly 🌢 Water when soil surface just dry. Avoid waterlogging ✂️ Tip cuttings

◁ Mimosa pudica
SENSITIVE PLANT
↕ 2ft (60cm) ↔ 16in (40cm)

Usually treated as an annual or short-lived perennial, this plant has ferny leaves that quickly fold and droop when touched; be careful not to overdo it since the plant takes up to an hour to recover.

☼ Bright to moderate, avoiding direct sun ❄️ Warm. High humidity 🌢 Monthly 🌢 When soil surface just dry. Reduce watering in winter ✂️ Seed

Selaginella lepidophylla ▷
RESURRECTION PLANT
↕ 3in (8cm) ↔ 6in (15cm)

Normally bought as a dried ball (see inset), this plant will uncurl into a rosette of rich green ferny fronds when placed in a dish of water or pot of damp soil mix.

☼ Shady ❄️ Warm. High humidity 🌢 Every five weeks, using half-strength general houseplant fertilizer 🌢 Water when soil surface just dry ✂️ Stem cuttings

OTHER NOVELTY HOUSEPLANTS

Arachis hypogaea
Darlingtonia californica
Davallia mariesii
Dracunculus vulgaris
Musa coccinea
Pinguicula grandiflora
Sarracenia flava
Tillandsia caput-medusae, see p.355
Tolmiea menziesii, see p.365

Olea europaea ▷
OLIVE
↕ ↔ 10ft (3m) or more

A gray-leaved evergreen tree or bush, easily kept small by pruning or training in spring. Older plants produce tiny, fragrant summer flowers that may bear fruit.

☼ Bright, with sun ❄️ Moderate to warm, but cool in winter. Low humidity 🌢 Monthly 🌢 When soil surface dry. Water sparingly in winter ✂️ Semiripe cuttings, seed

△ Streptocarpus wendlandii
CAPE PRIMROSE
↕ 12in (30cm) ↔ 30in (75cm)

Very different from the usual Cape primrose, this has a single, enormous, dark purple-green basal leaf, red-purple beneath, and blue flowers in summer.

☼ Bright to moderate, avoiding direct sun ❄️ Warm. Moderate to high humidity 🌢 Biweekly, using flowering houseplant fertilizer 🌢 When soil surface just dry ✂️ Seed

SPECIALIST PLANTS

417

Index

Plants that are illustrated in the book are indicated by this symbol ▣

A

Abele ▣ 284
Abelia floribunda 165
   A. × *grandiflora* 235
   A. triflora ▣ 178, 195, 238
Abeliophyllum distichum 164, 236
Abies balsamea 'Nana' ▣ 258
   A. concolor 244, 255, 257
   A. concolor 'Candicans' ▣ 263
   A. concolor 'Compacta' ▣ 258
   A. grandis 244
   A. koreana ▣ 250, 252
   A. lasiocarpa 'Compacta' 259
   A. magnifica 244
   A. nordmanniana ▣ 244
   A. nordmanniana 'Golden Spreader'
     ▣ 258
   A. pinsapo 'Glauca' 263
Abutilon × *hybridum* 47
   A. megapotamicum ▣ 158, ▣ 164
   A. 'Nabob' 332
   A. pictum 'Thompsonii' 212, 348
Acacia baileyana 222
   A. dealbata ▣ 228
Acacia
   False ▣ 283
   Rose ▣ 165
Acaena ▣ 118
   A. saccaticupula 'Blue Haze' 137
Acalypha wilkesiana 'Musaica' 347
Acanthus dioscoridis 27, ▣ 32
   A. hirsutus ▣ 26, 36
   A. mollis 121, 128
   A. mollis 'Hollard's Gold' 135
   A. mollis Latifolius Group 28
   A. spinosus 124, ▣ 126
Acataea simplex 'Brunette' ▣ 138
Acca sellowiana ▣ 165
Acer campestre 276
   A. capillipes ▣ 302
   A. cappadocicum 'Aureum' ▣ 292
   A. crataegifolium 'Veitchii' 290
   A. griseum 271, ▣ 300, 303
   A. japonicum 'Aconitifolium' 275
   A. japonicum 'Aureum' 271
   A. negundo 'Flamingo' 276, ▣ 290
   A. palmatum 'Aureum' 221, ▣ 292
   A. palmatum 'Bloodgood' 225
   A. palmatum var. *coreanum* ▣ 270
   A. palmatum cvs. 295
   A. palmatum 'Corallinum' ▣ 210
   A. palmatum 'Garnet' ▣ 224
   A. palmatum var. *heptalobum* ▣ 226
   A. palmatum 'Osakazuki' ▣ 296
   A. palmatum 'Red Pygmy' ▣ 224
   A. palmatum 'Sango-kaku' ▣ 300
   A. pensylvanicum 'Erythrocladum' 301
   A. platanoides 276, ▣ 281
   A. platanoides 'Crimson King' ▣ 295
   A. platanoides 'Drummondii' 290
   A. pseudoplatanus 281, 282
   A. rubrum 275, 280
   A. rubrum 'Columnare' ▣ 304
   A. rubrum 'Schlesingeri' ▣ 296

A. saccharinum ▣ 266
A. saccharum 267, 297
A. saccharum subsp. *nigrum* 'Temple's
   Upright' ▣ 304
A. shirasawanum 'Aureum' 221, ▣ 292
A. triflorum 269, ▣ 270
Achillea 19
   A. 'Coronation Gold' ▣ 108
   A. 'Fanal' 111
   A. filipendulina 29, ▣ 76
   A. filipendulina and cvs. 108
   A. millefolium 125
   A. 'Moonshine' 114, 137
   A. ptarmica 84
   A. ptarmica 'Boule de Neige' ▣ 54
   A. ptarmica The Pearl Group ▣ 80
   A. spp. and cvs. 36, 75, 78, 88, 92
   A. tomentosa 27, 83
Achimenes hybrids ▣ 324, ▣ 332. 361,
   ▣ 374, 376
acid (lime-free) soil 14
   perennials for 30–1
   shrubs for 192–3
   trees for 274–5
Aciphylla aurea ▣ 126
Aconite, Winter ▣ 104
Aconitum × *cammarum* 'Bicolor' ▣ 24,
   101
   A. carmichaelii 88
   A. carmichaelii 'Arendsii' ▣ 102
   A. hemsleyanum 72
   A. 'Ivorine' ▣ 98
   A. lycotonum subsp. *vulparia* ▣ 92
   A. napellus 92
   A. spp. and cvs. 91, 124
Acorus calamus 69, 127
   A. calamus 'Variegatus' 66
   A. gramineus 69, 122
   A. gramineus 'Ogon' 135, ▣ 340, 344
   A. gramineus 'Variegatus' ▣ 350
Actaea matsumarae 'Elstead' ▣ 102
   A. racemosa 99, 109
   A. rubra ▣ 42
   A. simplex 76
   A. simplex 'Scimitar' ▣ 24
   A. simplex Atropurpurea Group ▣ 124
   A. spp. and cvs. 92
Actinidia arguta 162
   A. kolomikta 160, 168
Adenium obesum ▣ 366
Adiantum 'Bicolor' ▣ 406
   A. capillus-veneris 149
   A. diaphanum 407
   A. pedatum ▣ 125
   A. raddianum 365, 375, ▣ 398
   A. raddianum 'Fritz Luth' 363, ▣ 380
   A. raddianum 'Gracillimum' 369, 407
Adonis amurensis 104
   A. vernalis 97, ▣ 104
Aechmea 308
   A. chantinii 329, ▣ 366, 415
   A. fasciata ▣ 324, 352, 415
   A. fasciata 'Morgana' ▣ 380
   A. Foster's Favourite Group 415
   A. fulgens var. *discolor* 396
   A. morganii ▣ 414
Aechmeas, Queen of the ▣ 366
Aegopodium podagraria 'Variegatum' 53
Aeonium 'Zwartkop' ▣ 404, ▣ 408
Aeonium, Black ▣ 408

Aeschynanthus lobbianus 361
Aesculus californica 276
   A. × *carnea* 'Briotii' 282
   A. hippocastanum 267, 276
   A. hippocastanum 'Baumannii' ▣ 272
   A. × *neglecta* 'Erythroblastos' ▣ 268
   A. parviflora ▣ 178
   A. pavia 'Atrosanguinea' ▣ 270
Aethionema iberideum 64
   A. 'Warley Rose' ▣ 60
African Lily ▣ 26, ▣ 70, ▣ 90, ▣ 112
African Milk Tree ▣ 355
African Violet ▣ 325, ▣ 333, ▣ 337
Agapanthus 'Blue Giant' ▣ 90
   A. 'Loch Hope' ▣ 70
   A. 'Midnight Blue' ▣ 26
   A. 'Snowy Owl' ▣ 112
   A. spp. and cvs. 47, 70
Agastache foeniculum ▣ 54
   A. foeniculum 'Alabaster' ▣ 127
Agave havardiana 126, 128
   A. victoriae-reginae 367
Aglaonema 308
   A. commutatum 'Pseudobracteatum'
     ▣ 350
   A. 'Lilian' 363, ▣ 374
   A. 'Maria Christina' ▣ 380
   A. 'Marie' ▣ 362
   A. 'Silver King' ▣ 352
   A. 'Silver Queen' ▣ 352
Aichryson × *domesticum* 'Variegatum' 337,
   350
Ailanthus altissima 267, 282
air layering, houseplants 317
Air Plant ▣ 355, ▣ 367, ▣ 415
air pollution
   perennials tolerant of 80–1
   shrubs tolerant of 204–5
   trees tolerant of 282–3
Ajuga reptans 'Catlin's Giant' ▣ 86
   A. reptans 'Jungle Beauty' ▣ 52
   A. reptans 'Multicolor' ▣ 22, 66
   A. reptans 'Silver Beauty' 133
Akebia quinata 162, ▣ 168
Akebia trifoliata 162
Albizia julibrissin ▣ 276
Alcea rugosa 114
Alchemilla conjuncta ▣ 84
   A. mollis ▣ 90
Alder
   Gray ▣ 272
   Italian ▣ 281
   Red ▣ 280
Alerce ▣ 250
Alisma plantago-aquatica 69
alkaline (limy) soil 14
   perennials for 32–5
   shrubs for 194–5
   trees for 274, 276–7
Alkanet, Green ▣ 81
Allegheny Serviceberry ▣ 282
Allium beesianum 62
   A. cristophii ▣ 32, 38
   A. flavum 59
   A. giganteum ▣ 82
   A. 'Globemaster' ▣ 88
   A. hollandicum 'Purple Sensation'
     ▣ 78
   A. insubricum ▣ 62
   A. mairei 63

◼

Acknowledgments

AUTHORS' ACKNOWLEDGMENTS
A number of people have either directly or indirectly influenced the preparation of this book, none more so than my wife, Sue, whose unfailing support, including the typing of my scribbled notes and lists, helped bring it to fruition.

I wish to say a special thank you to my friend Matthew Biggs who was joint author with me of *What Houseplant Where*, most of which has been incorporated into the present book.

Sarah Drew, Jacqueline Postill, Martin Puddle, and James Wickham all made helpful comments based on their considerable collective experience dealing with customers' problems and queries in plant centres.

My thanks also to David Barker, Joyce Cama, Cliff Dad, Dilys Davies, Pat Jackson, Danae Johnston, Chris Mortimer, Bob Mousley, and Ray Wilson of the Hardy Plant Society, who kindly helped with suggestions, as did Jean Fletcher, Hala Humphries, Sabine Liebherr, and George Smith. Beyond these few are the many who have encouraged my interest in perennials over the years. To all of you, my heartfelt thanks.

If we have learned anything in our pursuit of plant knowledge it is that who you know is often the basis of what you know, and this has certainly proved the case in the preparation of this book. Thus the ever-reliable Sarah Drew of the Hillier Plant Centre generously gave us the benefit of her "point of sales" experience, while Jim Gardiner, Curator of the RHS Garden, Wisley, and botanist Adrian Whiteley helped in their different ways. The following also gave us the benefit of their expertise: David Cooke, Royal Botanic Gardens, Kew; Dibleys Nurseries, Ruthin, North Wales; Maggie Garford, African Violet Centre, King's Lynn; John Gibson, Colegraves Seeds, Banbury; Alan Moon, Eric Young Orchid Foundation, Jersey; Stanley Mossop, Boonwood Garden Centre, Cumbria; Dr. Henry Oakeley; and David Rhodes, Rhodes & Rockliffe, Essex.

Five years of travelling the length and breadth of Britain with Channel Four Television's *Garden Club* has taken me to a multitude of gardens large and small, while also introducing me to some helpful and resourceful gardeners. In acknowledging their contribution I should also like to thank the present and former members of the *Garden Club* team, who have helped me in so many ways.

They include John Bennett, Matthew Biggs, Adrian Brennard, Karen Brown, Derek Clarke, Penny Cotter, Mary Foxall, Tony Griggs, Margaret Haworth, Elaine Hinderer, Sylvia Hines, Paddy McMullin, Ken Price, Rebecca Pow, Rebecca Ransome, Jo Redman, Sue Shepherd, Richard Stevens, and Steve Stunt.

Finally, I thank my publishers, especially Mary-Clare Jerram for asking me to compile this book, and Lesley Malkin and Colin Walton, whose enthusiasm and professionalism greatly impressed and encouraged me. I could not have asked for better. My thanks also to Anna Cheifetz, Clare Double and Helen Robson, who must have sweated at times over my schedule but remained calm and focused throughout. Thanks for your patience, guidance, and gentle prodding. I would also like to thank Gill Biggs for her help, and Jessica Biggs for not interrupting.

DORLING KINDERSLEY would like to thank: Lyn Saville and Ian Whitelaw for additional editorial assistance; Gloria Horsfall, and Sue Caffyn for design assistance; Ann Kay and Antonia Johnson for proof reading; Dr. Alan Hemsley for his assistance in finding and identifying plants to photograph; the A–Z team, particularly Ina Stradins, Helen Robson, and Susila Baybars, for their patience with our shared resources, and to Rebecca Davies for all her trips to the post office; Howard Rice for all his additional help; Lesley Malkin and Colin Walton for their support and initial work on this project; Simon Maughan for image scanning; Martin-Panter at Arnott and Mason, New Covent Garden, London, for plant supply and assistance with photography facilities; Matthew Ward for all his extra help; Lesley Riley for editorial assistance; Charlotte Oster, Christine Rista, Julia Pashley, and Sarah Duncan for picture research; Mustafa Sami for artwork research and commission

ILLUSTRATION CREDITS
Aspect illustration by Karen Cockrane 15
Tree illustrations by Laura Andrew, Marion Appleton, David Ashby, Bob Bampton, Anne Child, Karen Gavin, Tim Hayward, Janos Marffy, David More, Sue Oldfield, Liz Pepperell, Michelle Ross, Gill Tomlin, Barbara Walker
Illustrations on pages 310–1 by Richard Lee.

PHOTOGRAPHY CREDITS
Key: l=left, r=right, t=top, c=center, b=bottom
Commissioned photographs: Howard Rice, Colin Walton, and Andrew Henley; main photography in Indoor Plants section by Matthew Ward.

Additional pictures: Peter Anderson 313tl, 315br, 317cl, 317bl, 318br, 390tl, 409tr, 409cr; Deni Bown 345tl, 345bl, 387tc; Jonathan Buckley 331tl; Eric Crichton 410c, 411tc, 411bl; C. Andrew Henley 359bl, 379tc; Neil Fletcher 341br, 379tl; Dave King 314bl, 315cr, 320tr, 321, 335, 357, 383, 402tc, 405; Tom Dobbie 322bl, 323tl, 323b, 324b, 325tr, 332br, 336br, 339t, 339bl, 339bc, 341tr, 342br, 344bl, 346c, 348tl, 349br, 350bc, 362bl, 364t, 365tr, 365c, 368br, 371bc, 373tl, 373br, 376b, 377tl, 380tr, 380br, 381br, 384b, 385tl, 385c, 385b, 386b, 388bl, 390c, 390tr, 391bl, 391tr, 392tl, 392bl, 393tr, 393br, 395bc, 396bl, 398tl, 399tl, 400tr, 400br, 401tc, 401br, 406bl, 407tl, 407c, 407b, 412bl, 413tl, 413br; John Fielding 379cl; Andrew Lawson 358br; Andrew de Lory 349br; Howard Rice 325c, 344tr, 361br, 364bl, 385tr, 398bl, 401tl; Bob Rundle 392br; Juliette Wade 329tr; Steven Wooster 331tc, 401tr.
Other Dorling Kindersley photographs by Peter Anderson, Clive Boursnell, Deni Bown, Jonathan Buckley, Andrew Butler, Eric Crichton, Andrew de Lory, Christine Douglas, John Fielding, Neil Fletcher, John Glover, Derek Hall, Jerry Harpur, Sunniva Harte, C. Andrew Henley, Neil Holmes, Jacqui Hurst, Andrew Lawson, Howard Rice, Robert Rundle, Juliette Wade, Colin Walton, Matthew Ward, David Watts, and Steven Wooster.

Dorling Kindersley is grateful to the following for permission to reproduce photographs
Gillian Beckett: 329tl, 372t
Matthew Biggs: 366tl
Bruce Coleman Collection: Jules Cowan 309tl
Dibleys Nurseries, Ruthin, North Wales: 333br
Garden Picture Library: Mark Bolton

147tr; Lynne Brotchie 158bl; Brian Carter 159; Robert Estall 264br; John Glover 15tr, 16bl, 18br, 94tr, 142bl, 176br, 264bl; Neil Holmes 178c; M Lamontagne 265; John Miller 306–7; Jerry Pavia 146br; Howard Rice 334tr; Gary Rogers 15br; JS Sira 172tr, 216tr; Friedrich Strauss 320cr, 382br, 404tr; Ron Sutherland 292bl; Brigitte Thomas 242bl, 243; Michel Viard 404b; Steven Wooster 15bl, 20br, 48bl, 119, 158bl, 356bl
John Glover: 244tc, 257tc, 283bl
Derek Gould: 235bl
Harpur Garden Library: 320bl, 334bl
Houses and Interiors: Simon Butcher 310tl; Fotodienst Fehn 382bl
International Interiors: Paul Ryan 311tr, 311bl
Roy Lancaster: 6bl, 6br, 14bl, 28tl, 28bl, 30bl, 36bl, 36tc, 37tr, 42tr, 44tr, 46br, 47bc, 70tl, 77bc, 82tr, 89bc, 104bl, 108tc, 117bc, 124tr, 129tc, 129bc, 133tr, 134cr, 139c, 140bl, 140bc, 141tr, 142tr, 144bl, 144–5, 145br, 146tr, 150bc, 151tl, 155bc, 156cl, 156tc, 156cc, 162tr, 165bl, 168bl, 170tc, 170tr, 170bl, 171bl, 172bc, 172bl, 173tr, 173bc, 174tl, 174bl, 175tl, 175tr, 175cr, 179tl, 179cr, 189cr, 183cr, 196bl, 196tc, 197tl, 197tr, 200tr, 201cl, 203bc, 206tl, 208tl, 209tc, 216cl, 216br, 217bc, 221cr, 226tl, 226bc, 226tr, 227tl, 227br, 231br, 232bc, 233tl, 233bl, 234tr, 239tl, 239bl, 242tr, 242br, 244bl, 246tl, 249br, 251tr, 254tl, 255cl, 257tl, 260bl, 260bc, 261tl, 261br, 262tc, 262tr, 264tr, 270bl, 274bl, 286bl, 286br, 288bl, 290tr, 291cr, 292cl, 293tl, 293cl, 293cr, 309br, 328br, 329tc, 340tl, 378br, 378tr
Andrew Lawson: 20bl (designer: Wendy Lauderdale), 147tl, 293tr
Clive Nichols: Chenies Manor Garden, Buckinghamshire: 177; Dartington Hall Garden, Devon: 16br; Longacre, Kent: 16cl
Nature Photographers Ltd: Brinsley Burbage: 257tr
Photos Horticultural: 145cr, 170br, 209cr, 235bc, 247tc, 248tr, 256cr, 257br, 261bc, 263bc, 277bl, 282bl, 283 tr, 305bl; 349tc
Picturesmiths Limited: 146cr, 305tl
Planet Earth Pictures: Robert Jureit 308b
Howard Rice: 19tl, 19tr, 19br, 21, 33bm, 33tr, 45br, 48br, 49, 76tl, 76bl, 76bc, 76b, 77bc, 77tr, 94bl, 94br, 95, 103bc, 118bl, 118tr, 140bl, 143
Harry Smith Collection: 147tc, 171tl, 288br
Harry Smith Collection/Polunin: 280cl, 281br
Matthew Ward: 18cl (container by Malcolm Hillier)
Elizabeth Whiting Associates: Graham Henderson 310br; Spike Powell 356t.

PHOTOGRAPHERS' ACKNOWLEDGMENTS
In England: Alan Shipp, Beth Chatto Gardens, Bressingham Gardens, Broadlands Gardens, Cambridge Alpines, Cambridge Bulbs, Cambridge Garden Plants, Cambridge University Botanic Gardens, David Austin Roses Ltd., Fulbrooke Nursery, Goldbrooke Plants, Hadlow College, Hopleys Plants Ltd., John Morley, Langthorns Plantery, Monksilver Nursery, Paradise Centre, Peter Lewis, Potterton and Martin, Rickard's Hardy Ferns, Mrs. Sally Edwards, West Acre Gardens.
In Australia: Birchfield Herbs (Marcia Voce), Buskers End (Joan Arnold), Elizabeth Town Nursery (John and Corrie Dudley), Essie Huxley, Garden of St. Erth, Island Bulbs (Kevin Fagan, Viv Hale), Lambley Nursery (David Glenn), Moidart Wholesale Nursery (Graham Warwick), Otto Fauser, Penny Dunn, Rosevears Nursery (Rachael Howell) Sally Johansohn, Suz Price, Theresa Watts, Woodbank Nursery (Ken Gallander), Yates.